MORAL PUZZLES AND LEGAL PERPLEXITIES

Drawing inspiration from the profoundly influential work of legal theorist Larry Alexander, this volume tackles central questions in criminal law, constitutional law, jurisprudence, and moral philosophy. What are the legitimate conditions of blame and punishment? What values are at the heart of constitutional protections against discrimination or infringements of free speech? Must judges interpret statutes and constitutional provisions in ways that comport with the intentions of those who wrote them? Can the law obligate us to violate the demands of morality, and when can the law allow the rights of the few to be violated for the good of the many? This collection of essays by world-renowned legal theorists is for anyone interested in foundational questions about the law's authority, the conditions of its fair application to citizens, and the moral justifications of the rights, duties, and permissions that it protects.

Heidi M. Hurd is the Ross and Helen Workman Chair in Law and Professor of Philosophy at the University of Illinois. She has published articles in leading law and philosophy journals on topics in criminal law, tort law, jurisprudence, environmental ethics, and moral and political philosophy, and is the author of *Moral Combat* (Cambridge, 1999).

Moral Puzzles and Legal Perplexities

Essays on the Influence of Larry Alexander

Edited by

HEIDI M. HURD

University of Illinois

CAMBRIDGE
UNIVERSITY PRESS

CAMBRIDGE
UNIVERSITY PRESS

University Printing House, Cambridge CB2 8BS, United Kingdom

One Liberty Plaza, 20th Floor, New York, NY 10006, USA

477 Williamstown Road, Port Melbourne, VIC 3207, Australia

314–321, 3rd Floor, Plot 3, Splendor Forum, Jasola District Centre, New Delhi – 110025, India

79 Anson Road, #06-04/06, Singapore 079906

Cambridge University Press is part of the University of Cambridge.

It furthers the University's mission by disseminating knowledge in the pursuit of education, learning, and research at the highest international levels of excellence.

www.cambridge.org
Information on this title: www.cambridge.org/9781316510452
DOI: 10.1017/9781108227025

First published 2019

Printed and bound in Great Britain by Clays Ltd, Elcograf S.p.A.

A catalogue record for this publication is available from the British Library.

Library of Congress Cataloging-in-Publication Data
Names: Hurd, Heidi M. (Heidi Margaret), 1960– editor.
Title: Moral puzzles and legal perplexities : essays on the influence of Larry Alexander / edited by Heidi M. Hurd, University of Illinois.
Description: New York: Cambridge University Press, 2018. |
Includes bibliography of works by Larry Alexander.
Identifiers: LCCN 2018029896 | ISBN 9781316510452 (hardback)
Subjects: LCSH: Alexander, Larry, 1943 – Influence. | Constitutional law – United States. | Criminal law – United States – Philosophy.
Classification: LCC KF373.A383 M67 2018 | DDC 340/.112–dc23
LC record available at https://lccn.loc.gov/2018029896

ISBN 978-1-316-51045-2 Hardback

For Larry's children,
Jenny, David, and Jonathan,

and for Larry's grandchildren,
Tej, Simran, Sejal, Kai, and Luka.

Contents

List of Figures — *page* x

List of Contributors — xi

Acknowledgments — xxv

1 **Introduction: Larry Alexander** — 1
Heidi M. Hurd

PART I PUZZLES IN CRIMINAL LAW — 21

2 **Kinds of Punishment** — 23
Douglas Husak

3 **Partial Responsibility and Excuse** — 39
David O. Brink

4 **"Thank God I Failed"** — 60
R.A. Duff

5 **Does Duress Justify or Excuse? The Significance of Larry Alexander's Ambivalence** — 76
Peter Westen

6 **Alternative Lesser Evils** — 98
Gideon Yaffe

PART II PROBLEMS IN CONSTITUTIONAL LAW 111

7 Justifying Academic Freedom: Mill and Marcuse Revisited 113
Brian Leiter

8 Vindicating Judicial Supremacy 134
Laurence Claus

9 Alexander's "Simple-Minded Originalism" 153
Connie S. Rosati

10 Subjective versus Objective Intentionalism in Legal Interpretation 170
Jeffrey Goldsworthy

11 Simple-Minded Originalism? Simply Wrong! 189
Lawrence B. Solum

12 Intentions in Tension 206
Frederick Schauer

13 Alexander's Constitutionalism: A Qualified Defense 221
Alon Harel

PART III PERPLEXITIES IN JURISPRUDENCE 239

14 For Legal Principles 241
Mitchell N. Berman

15 The Court, or the Constitution? 260
William Baude

16 Alexander as Anarchist 271
Steven D. Smith

17 Exclusionary Rules 286
Emily Sherwin

18 Larry Alexander and "the Gap" 303
Leo Katz and Alvaro Sandroni

PART IV PARADOXES IN MORAL PHILOSOPHY 315

19 **Respect and Discrimination** 317
Kasper Lippert-Rasmussen

20 **The Means Principle and Optimific Wrongs** 333
Kimberly Kessler Ferzan

21 **Deontology's Travails** 350
Richard Arneson

22 **The Rationality of Threshold Deontology** 371
Michael S. Moore

23 **Real-World Criminal Law and the Norm Against Punishing the Innocent: Two Cheers for Threshold Deontology** 388
Kevin Cole

24 **Conclusion: Appreciation and Responses** 407
Larry Alexander

Bibliography of Works by Larry Alexander 441

Index 453

Figures

3.1 The Fair Opportunity Conception of Responsibility *page* 45
3.2 Proportional Justice 47
3.3 Bipartite Criminal Trials 48
3.4 Bivalent Justice 49
3.5 Proportional Justice Meets Bivalence 50
3.6 Tripartite Criminal Trials 52
3.7 Trivalent Justice 55
3.8 Trivalent Justice with Blackstone's Asymmetry 57
3.9 Tetravalent Justice with Blackstone's Asymmetry 58

Contributors

Larry Alexander
University Professor and Warren Distinguished Professor of Law
Co-Executive Director of the Institute for Law and Religion, and Co-Executive Director of the Institute for Law and Philosophy
University of San Diego School of Law

Larry Alexander writes and teaches in the areas of criminal law, constitutional law and theory, jurisprudence and legal theory, and law and religion. He joined the USD law faculty in 1970 and has been a Visiting Professor of Law at the University of Pennsylvania and the University of Texas, and a Visiting Professor of Philosophy at the University of California–San Diego. A founder and Editor of the international quarterly *Legal Theory*, Professor Alexander also serves on the editorial boards of the journals *Law and Philosophy*, *Ethics*, *Criminal Law and Philosophy*, and the *Ohio State Journal of Criminal Law*. He has lectured extensively around the globe and published more than 235 major articles and book chapters in prominent law reviews, peer-edited philosophy journals, and anthologies. He is also the author, coauthor, or editor of nine books, including *Crime and Culpability: A Theory of Criminal Law* (Cambridge University Press, 2009) (with Kimberly Kessler Ferzan and Stephen J. Morse); *Demystifying Legal Reasoning* (Cambridge University Press, 2008) (with Emily Sherwin); *Is There a Right of Freedom of Expression?* (Cambridge University Press, 2005); *The Rule of Rules: Rules, Principles, and the Dilemmas of Law* (Duke University Press, 2001) (with Emily Sherwin); and *Constitutionalism: Philosophical Foundations* (Cambridge University Press, 1998). Professor Alexander received his BA from Williams College (1965) and his LLB from Yale University (1968).

Richard Arneson
Valtz Family Chair in Philosophy
University of California–San Diego Department of Philosophy
Co-Director of the Institute for Law and Philosophy
University of San Diego School of Law

Richard Arneson works on topics in moral and political philosophy, with a focus on theories of social justice and a special focus on distributive justice. He also writes on the prospects of consequentialist moral theories in the light of deontological criticisms of this approach. He has been a member of the UC San Diego Philosophy Department since 1973, and he has visited at the University of California, Davis (1990), the Program in Ethics, Politics, and Economics at Yale University (1996), the Research School of Social Sciences, Australian National University (1999), and the Centre for Applied Philosophy and Public Ethics, Australian National University (2007). Professor Arneson has published more than 120 articles in philosophical journals, anthologies, and volumes of collected essays. He received a BA in history from Brown University in 1967 and a PhD in philosophy from the University of California at Berkeley (1975).

William Baude
Professor of Law and Aaron Director Research Scholar
University of Chicago Law School

William Baude's scholarship is concentrated in federal courts and constitutional law. He is a coauthor of *The Constitution of the United* States (3rd ed., Foundation Press, 2016), and he has authored numerous articles on topics such as the official immunity from suit, legal interpretation, and the Fourth Amendment. He has been a Visiting Professor at Stanford Law School, and he is also an Affiliated Scholar at the Center for the Study of Constitutional Originalism at the University of San Diego School of Law, a member of the American Law Institute, and an occasional blogger at the Volokh Conspiracy. Before joining the faculty of the University of Chicago Law School, Professor Baude clerked for then-Judge Michael McConnell on the United States Court of Appeals and Chief Justice John Roberts on the United States Supreme Court. He also served as a Fellow at the Stanford Constitutional Law Center and a lawyer at Robbins Russell, LLP in Washington, DC. Professor Baude received his BS in mathematics from the University of Chicago (2004) and his JD from Yale Law School (2007).

Mitchell N. Berman
Leon Meltzer Professor of Law
University of Pennsylvania Law School
Professor of Philosophy
University of Pennsylvania

Mitchell Berman writes and teaches on American constitutional law, constitutional theory, philosophy of criminal law, and general jurisprudence. Prior to joining the University of Pennsylvania School of Law, he was the Richard Dale Endowed Chair in Law at the University of Texas at Austin School of Law (2008–14), the Bernard J. Ward Centennial Professor at the University of Texas at Austin School of Law (2002–8), and an Assistant Professor at the University of Texas at Austin School of Law (1998–July 2002). He was also a Professor in the Department of Philosophy at the University of Texas (2009–14), where he codirected the Law and Philosophy Program. He has visited at the University of Chicago Law School (2003) and the University of Michigan Law School (1997–8), as well as at Hebrew University–Jerusalem (June 2012) and at the Institute of Global Law, University College London (May–June 2002). Professor Berman's major scholarly works have appeared in leading law reviews and peer-edited journals around the globe, as well as in numerous anthologies and collections of essays. Professor Berman received his AB from Harvard University (1988) and his JD (1993) and his MA in political science (1994) from the University of Michigan.

David O. Brink
Distinguished Professor of Philosophy
University of California–San Diego Department of Philosophy

David Brink's research interests are in ethical theory, history of ethics, moral psychology, and analytical, constitutional, and criminal jurisprudence. He has published over fifty articles on these topics and he is the author of three books: *Moral Realism and The Foundations of Ethics* (Cambridge University Press, 1989); *Perfectionism and the Common Good* (Clarendon Press, 2003); and *Mill's Progressive Principles* (Clarendon Press, 2013). After serving briefly as an Assistant Professor of Philosophy at Case Western Reserve University, he taught for seven years as an Assistant and then Associate Professor of Philosophy at the Massachusetts Institute of Technology, before moving to UCSD as an Associate Professor in 1994. He gave the 2013 Lindley Lecture and in 2016 he received the UCSD Faculty Senate Research Lecturer Award for the Arts, Humanities, and Social Sciences and the Chancellor's Associates Award for Excellence in Research in the Humanities and Social Sciences. In 2018 he was a Visiting Fellow at Magdalen College, Oxford, and Tang Chun-i Visiting Professor at the Chinese University of Hong Kong. He received his BA.in philosophy and political science from the University of Minnesota (1980) and his PhD in philosophy from Cornell University (1984).

Laurence Claus
Professor of Law
University of San Diego School of Law

Laurence Claus's scholarship focuses on comparative public law and legal theory. He is the author of *Law's Evolution and Human Understanding* (Oxford University Press, 2012). Among recent advisory roles in comparative constitutional law, he has been retained as a consultant by the American Bar Association Rule of Law Initiative for constitutional reform projects in Jordan and Libya. He has taught as a Visiting Professor of Law at Paris 1 University (Panthéon-Sorbonne). Before pursuing his graduate studies at Oxford University, he clerked for the Chief Justice of Queensland, Hon. John Macrossan. He also clerked for Hon. Sir Ronald Wilson on a commission of inquiry into government misconduct, and then worked at the Australian High Court on the Court's landmark early implied freedom of speech cases. He served for three years in the Office of Foreign Litigation, United States Department of Justice, based at the American Embassy in London, where he helped supervise civil litigation in European domestic courts to which the United States was party. He clerked for Hon. Frank Easterbrook of the United States Court of Appeals for the Seventh Circuit before joining the faculty at the University of San Diego School of Law in 2001. He received his BEcon (1987) and LLB (1991) from the University of Queensland and a DPhil in law from Oxford University (1998).

Kevin Cole
Professor of Law
University of San Diego School of Law

Kevin Cole writes primarily in the areas of criminal law, criminal procedure, and professional responsibility. He joined the USD School of Law faculty in 1987 and served as Dean of the school from 2005 to 2011. Prior to entering the legal academy, Professor Cole clerked on the US Court of Appeals for the Sixth Circuit and practiced law in Philadelphia. He has been a Visiting Professor at Georgetown University's Law Center and he has served as a Reporter for the Committee on Forfeiture in Drug Offense Cases at the National Conference of Commissioners on Uniform State Laws. In addition to authoring numerous articles in leading law reviews, Professor Cole is the coauthor of previous editions of the *Federal Sentencing Guidelines Handbook* (Shepard's/McGraw-Hill) and the *Federal Sentencing and Forfeiture Guide* (Del Mar Legal Publishers), and the author of *The Little White Book of Baseball Law* (ABA,2009). He is also the Editor of *CrimProfBlog*. Professor Cole received his BA from New College (1979) and his JD from the University of Pennsylvania (1983).

R.A. Duff
Emeritus Professor of Philosophy
University of Stirling Department of Philosophy

Antony Duff works on the philosophy of criminal law. His publications include *The Realm of Criminal Law* (2018); *Answering for Crime* (2007); *Punishment, Communication and Community* (2001); *Criminal Attempts* (1996); *Intention, Agency, and Criminal Liability* (1990); and *Trials and Punishments* (1986). He has led funded interdisciplinary projects on *The Trial on Trial* and on *Criminalization*. He was a cofounder and Editor of *Criminal Law and Philosophy*, an Associate Member of the Scottish Consortium on Crime and Criminal Justice, and Chair of the British Academy Working Group on Crime, Punishment and Prisons, which produced A *Presumption Against Imprisonment* (2014). He was an adviser to the Action for Children inquiry into the Scottish children's hearing system, an adviser to the Scottish Council Foundation project on public interest in criminal and youth justice, and lectured on sentencing theory for the Scottish Judicial Studies Committee. He chaired the philosophy subpanel of the 2008 Research Assessment Exercise in the UK. He is a Fellow of the British Academy and of the Royal Society of Edinburgh. He taught philosophy at the University of Stirling from 1970 until 2009. From 2010 to 2015 he held a half-time chair at the University of Minnesota Law School, where he was a founding Co-Director of the Robina Institute of Criminal Law and Criminal Justice. He took his undergraduate degree in *Literae Humaniores* at Oxford University, where he also pursued graduate studies in philosophy. He holds honorary degrees from the Universities of Edinburgh and Oslo.

Kimberly Kessler Ferzan
Harrison Robertson Professor of Law
University of Virginia School of Law
Affiliate Faculty Member
University of Virginia Department of Philosophy

Kimberly Kessler Ferzan works in the areas of criminal law and criminal theory. Prior to joining the faculty of the University of Virginia School of Law in 2014, Kimberly Kessler Ferzan was a Distinguished Professor of Law at Rutgers University School of Law and an affiliate member of the Rutgers–New Brunswick Philosophy Department. She has been a Visiting Professor at the London School of Economics Law School, Harvard Law School, the University of Chicago Law School, the University of Pennsylvania Law School, and the University of Illinois College of Law, and she was a Laurance S. Rockefeller Visiting Faculty Fellow at Princeton's

University Center for Human Values (2012–13). She is an Editor-in-Chief of *Law and Philosophy*, and she is also on the editorial boards of *Legal Theory* and *Criminal Law and Philosophy*. In addition to having authored numerous often-cited articles, she is the coauthor of *Crime and Culpability: A Theory of Criminal Law* (Cambridge University Press, 2009) with Larry Alexander and Stephen Morse. Her paper "Beyond Crime and Commitment" was selected for the 2013 American Philosophical Association's Berger Memorial Prize for the best paper written in law and philosophy for the prior two years, and her paper "Beyond Intention" was selected for the 2006 Stanford/Yale Junior Faculty Forum in the category of criminal law. She received her BA from the University of North Carolina–Chapel Hill (1991) and her JD from the University of Pennsylvania Law School (1995).

Jeffrey Goldsworthy
Professorial Fellow
The University of Melbourne Law School
Adjunct Professor of Law
The University of Adelaide Law School
Emeritus Professor of Law
Monash University Law School

Jeffrey Goldsworthy specializes in constitutional law, theory, and history, and legal philosophy. He is best known for his defense of the doctrine of parliamentary sovereignty, and of a moderate version of originalism in constitutional interpretation. His many publications include his books *The Sovereignty of Parliament: History and Philosophy* (Clarendon Press, 1999); *Parliamentary Sovereignty, Contemporary Debates* (Cambridge University Press, 2010); and *Interpreting Constitutions, A Comparative Study* (Oxford University Press, 2006). He has been a Visiting Professor or Fellow at Cambridge University, the University of Adelaide, the University of Illinois at Urbana-Champaign, the University of California, Berkeley, and the University of Nottingham. He served as President of the Australian Society of Legal Philosophy from 2007 to 2014, and he is a Fellow of the Academy of Social Sciences in Australia. He holds the degrees of LLB (Hons) and LLD from the University of Adelaide, LLM from the University of Illinois at Urbana-Champaign, and MA and PhD from the University of California–Berkeley.

Alon Harel
Phillip and Estelle Mizock Chair in Administrative and Criminal Law
Hebrew University Faculty of Law, Institute of Criminology, and Center for the Study of Rationality

Alon Harel's areas of expertise include moral and political philosophy, legal theory, law and economics, constitutional law and criminal law. Professor Harel has been a Visiting Professor at the University of Chicago Law School (2015), Columbia University Law School (1998–9), the University of Texas Law School (2008), the University of Toronto Law School (2000), and Boston University Law School, and he was a Fellow at the Ethics Center at the University of Toronto (2006–7) and at Harvard University (2002–3). He is the author of *Why Law Matters* (Oxford University Press, 2014), as well as numerous articles in major law and philosophy journals. He received his LLB from Hebrew University (1983) (with distinction), his LLM from Hebrew University (1985) (with distinction), and his DPhil in philosophy of law from Oxford University (1988).

Heidi M. Hurd
Ross and Helen Workman Chair in Law and Professor of Philosophy
Co-Director of the Illinois Program in Law and Philosophy
University of Illinois College of Law

A scholar in the areas of criminal law, torts, environmental ethics, moral philosophy, and legal theory, Heidi Hurd joined the faculty at the University of Illinois as the Dean of the College of Law (2002–7). Before her move to Illinois, she was the Herzog Faculty Scholar and Co-Director of the Institute for Law and Philosophy at the University of San Diego School of Law, and prior to that she was a Professor of Law and Philosophy at the University of Pennsylvania Law School, where she served as Associate Dean for Academic Affairs and Co-Director of the Penn Institute for Law and Philosophy. She has visited at the University of Virginia Law School, the Georgetown University School of Business, the University of Alabama School of Law, the University of Iowa Philosophy Department, the Australian National University, the University of Erlangen, the University of Tel Aviv School of Law, the Uganda Christian University School of Law, and Brazil's FGV Escola de Direito de São Paulo. In addition to authoring numerous articles and book chapters, Professor Hurd is the author of *Moral Combat* (Cambridge University Press, 1999). She received a BA from Queen's University (1982), an MA in philosophy from Dalhousie University (1984), a JD (1988) and a PhD in philosophy (1992) from the University of Southern California, a recent MEM in forestry and environmental studies from Yale University (2017), and she was awarded an honorary doctorate in humanities by Monmouth University (2007).

Douglas Husak
Distinguished Professor of Philosophy
Rutgers University–New Brunswick Department of Philosophy

Douglas Husak is a leading theorist about the connections between moral philosophy and the substantive criminal law, particularly about decisions concerning the scope of criminalization and the moral limits of criminal sanctions. He has become a prominent voice on the issue of drug prohibition as an illustration of overcriminalization. Professor Husak is Editor-in-Chief of *Criminal Law and Philosophy*, and he has written numerous books, including *The Philosophy of Criminal Law: Selected Essays* (Oxford University Press, 2010); *Overcriminalization: The Limits of the Criminal Law* (Oxford University Press, 2008); *The Legalization of Drugs* (coauthored with Peter de Marneffe) (Cambridge University Press, 2005); *Legalize This! The Case for Decriminalizing Drugs* (Verso Press, 2002); *Drugs and Rights* (Cambridge University Press, 1992); *The Philosophy of Criminal Law* (Rowman & Littlefield, 1987). He joined the philosophy faculty at Rutgers–New Brunswick in 1977, but he has visited or been a member of the faculty of eight other philosophy departments and law schools: University College London (2018), New York University (2017 and 2012), Fordham University (2013), University of Michigan (2007), Cambridge University (2001), Rutgers Law–Newark and Camden (numerous times), Barnard College (1982), and the University of Pittsburgh (1980). He received his BA from Denison University (1970) and his JD and PhD from Ohio State University (1976).

Leo Katz
Frank Carano Professor of Law
University of Pennsylvania Law School

Leo Katz's work focuses on criminal law and legal theory. By connecting criminal law, moral philosophy, and the theory of social choice, he tries to shed light on some of the most basic building blocks of the law – coercion, deception, consent, and the use and abuse of legal stratagems, among others. Professor Katz is the author of numerous articles and several books: *Bad Acts and Guilty Minds: Conundrums of the Criminal Law* (University of Chicago Press, 1987); *Ill-Gotten Gains: Evasion, Blackmail, Fraud and Kindred Puzzles of the Law* (University of Chicago Press, 1996); and, most recently, *Why the Law Is So Perverse* (University of Chicago Press, 2011), which he researched with the support of a Guggenheim Fellowship. Together with Stephen Morse and Michael Moore, he edited *Foundations of Criminal Law* (Oxford University Press, 1999). Professor Katz received his BA (1979), his MA in economics (1982), and his JD (1982) from the University of Chicago.

Brian Leiter
Karl N. Llewellyn Professor of Jurisprudence
Director of the Center for Law, Philosophy, and Human Values
University of Chicago Law School

Prior to joining the University of Chicago School of Law faculty in 2008, Brian Leiter taught for thirteen years at the University of Texas School of Law and for two years at the University of San Diego School of Law. He has also been a Visiting Professor of Law at Yale University and the University of Paris X-Nanterre, and a Visiting Professor of Philosophy at Oxford University and University College London. His teaching and research interests are in moral, political, and legal philosophy, in both the anglophone and Continental European traditions, and the law of evidence. His books include *Objectivity in Law and Morals* (Cambridge University Press, 2001) (Editor); *The Future for Philosophy* (Editor) (Oxford University Press, 2004); *Naturalizing Jurisprudence* (Oxford University Press, 2007); *Why Tolerate Religion?* (Princeton University Press, 2013); and *Nietzsche on Morality* (2nd ed., Routledge, 2015). Professor Leiter has given an extensive list of named lectures at universities around the world, and he was Editor of the journal *Legal Theory* from 2000 to 2008. He is the founder and Editor of the *Routledge Philosophers* book series and of *Oxford Studies in Philosophy of Law* (with Leslie Green). He also serves on the editorial boards of multiple journals and is the founder and author of the widely read blog, *The Leiter Reports: A Philosophy Blog*. Professor Leiter received his AB from Princeton University (1984) and his JD (1987) and PhD in philosophy (1995) from the University of Michigan.

Kasper Lippert-Rasmussen
Professor
Aarhus University Department of Political Science and Government
Professor II
University of Tromsø – The Arctic University of Norway Department of Philosophy

Kasper Lippert-Rasmussen is a political philosopher. His work ranges across topics that concern equality and discrimination, voting ethics, moral philosophy (particularly deontology), equality, healthcare theory and bioethics. Before joining the faculty at Aarhus, he was a Lecturer in philosophy at Copenhagen University (1997–2008). Professor Lippert-Rasmussen was a Visiting Scholar at Oxford University in 2017, and he is an Associate Editor of *Ethics* (2009–present). He is the author of *Born Free and Equal: A Philosophical Inquiry into the Nature of Discrimination* (Oxford University Press, 2013) and *Relational Egalitarianism: Living as Equals* (Cambridge University Press, 2018), as well as numerous articles published in leading journals around the globe. He received his MA in history and philosophy of social science from Essex University (1989), his MA in political science from Aarhus University (1990), his DPhil in philosophy from Oxford University, his *Habilitationsschrift* in philosophy from Copenhagen University (2005), and a second *Habilitationsschrift* in politics at University of Aarhus (2015).

Michael S. Moore
Charles R. Walgreen, Jr., University Chair, Professor of Law, and Professor in the Illinois Center for Advanced Studies
Co-Director of the Illinois Program in Law and Philosophy
University of Illinois College of Law

Michael Moore holds the Walgreen Chair, the only university-level chair at the University of Illinois, and he is a Professor in the Center for Advanced Studies, a campus-wide honorary appointment. Earlier, Professor Moore held distinguished chairs at University of San Diego, University of Pennsylvania, and University of Southern California, and professorships at University of California–Berkeley and University of Kansas. He has held visiting chairs at Yale Law School, University of Virginia, and University of Iowa, regular visiting professorships at Northwestern University, Stanford University, University of California–Berkeley, Tel Aviv University, Universidad Torcuato di Tella, and Universität Erlangen, and visiting fellowships at Harvard University, University of California–Irvine, and the Australian National University. Professor Moore has published over 150 articles in the disciplines of law, philosophy, psychiatry, and political science. He is the author of eight books, six published by Oxford University Press (*Mechanical Choices: The Responsibility of the Human Machine*, 2018; *Causation and Responsibility: An Essay in Law, Morals, and Metaphysics*, 2009; *Educating Oneself in Public: Critical Essays in Jurisprudence*, 2000; *Foundations of Criminal Law*, coedited with Leo Katz and Stephen Morse, 1999; *Placing Blame: A General Theory of the Criminal Law*, 1997; *Act and Crime: The Philosophy of Action and Its Implications for Criminal Law*, 1993); one by Cambridge University Press (*Law and Psychiatry: Rethinking the Relationship*, 1984); and one by Dartmouth Press (*Objectivity in Ethics and Law*, 2004). Professor Moore was Editor-in-Chief of *Law and Philosophy* from 1998 to 2010. He received his AB from the University of Oregon Honors College (1964) and his JD (1967) and SJD (1978) from Harvard University.

Connie S. Rosati
Professor of Philosophy
University of Arizona Department of Philosophy

Connie Rosati's research interests lie principally in the foundations of ethics and in jurisprudential questions about constitutional interpretation and the objectivity of law. Before joining the faculty of the University of Arizona's Philosophy Department in 2006, Professor Rosati held permanent positions in the philosophy departments of the University of California–Davis, Northwestern University, and Rutgers University. Over the years, she has visited in both law schools and philosophy departments, including the University of Pennsylvania Law School, the University of San Diego Law School, and the Arizona State Law School, as well as the University of Michigan Philosophy Department and Tufts University's Philosophy Department. Her numerous articles, published in leading law reviews and peer-reviewed philosophy journals, engage such issues as the nature of normativity, internalism v. externalism, the nature of personal good, constructivism in ethics, the objectivity of law, the moral reading of constitutions, and the nature of constitutional facts. Professor Rosati received her BA from Michigan State University (1979), her AM (1985) and PhD in philosophy (1989) from the University of Michigan, and her JD from Harvard Law School (1988).

Alvaro Sandroni
E.D. Howard Professor of Political Economy
Northwestern University Kellogg School of Management Department of Managerial Economics and Decision Sciences

Alvaro Sandroni's research is in the areas of behavioral sciences, strategic forecasting, economic theory, game theory, political science, general equilibrium theory, and philosophy and law. He has published several journal articles in economics, political science, statistics, philosophy, game theory and law journals, as well as in the Proceedings of the National Academy of Sciences. He is the recipient of several grants from the National Science Foundation and is a coauthor of the textbook *Managerial Statistics: A Case-Based Approach* (2005). He serves on the editorial boards of *Economic Theory* and the *International Journal of Game Theory* and is a Fellow of the Economic Theory Society. Professor Sandroni received his BSc in mathematics from the Pontífica Universidade Católica (Brazil) (1986), his PhD in mathematics from the Instituto de Matemática Pura e Aplicada (Brazil) (1994), and his PhD in economics from the University of Pennsylvania (1996).

Frederick Schauer
David and Mary Harrison Distinguished Professor of Law
University of Virginia School of Law

Frederick Schauer writes about legal authority, rules, legal reasoning, the theory of rights, and freedom of expression. Before joining the Virginia faculty, he was Frank Stanton Professor of the First Amendment at Harvard University and, earlier, Professor of Law at the University of Michigan. A fellow of the American Academy of Arts and Sciences and former holder of a Guggenheim Fellowship, Professor Schauer is the author of *The Law of Obscenity* (BNA, 1976); *Free Speech: A Philosophical Enquiry* (Cambridge University Press, 1982); *Playing By the Rules: A Philosophical Examination of Rule-Based Decision-Making in Law and in Life* (Oxford University Press, 1991); *Profiles, Probabilities, and Stereotypes* (Harvard University Press, 2003); *Thinking Like a Lawyer: A New Introduction to Legal Reasoning* (Harvard University Press, 2009), and *The Force of Law* (Harvard University Press, 2015); Editor of Karl Llewellyn's, *The Theory of Rules* (University of Chicago Press, 2011); and a cofounder and Editor of *Legal Theory*. Professor Schauer's writings are the subject of two books, *Rules* and *Reasoning: Essays in Honour of Fred Schauer* (Hart, 1999) and *The Force of Law Reaffirmed: Frederick Schauer Meets the Critics* (Springer, 2016); special issues of the Notre Dame, Connecticut, and Quinnipiac law reviews, *Politeia*, the *Harvard Journal of Law & Public Policy*, and *Materiali per una Storia della Cultura Giuridica*; and symposia on the force of law in *Law & Social Inquiry*, *Ratio Juris*, and *Jurisprudence*. Professor Schauer received his AB (1967) and MBA (1968) from Dartmouth College (1967) and his JD from Harvard Law School (1972).

Emily Sherwin
Frank B. Ingersoll Professor of Law
Cornell University Law School

Emily Sherwin specializes in jurisprudence, property, and remedies. She joined the Cornell University faculty in 2003 after serving as a member of the faculties of law at the University of San Diego and the University of Kentucky. She has also visited at the University of Pennsylvania Law School and the Boston University School of Law. She is the coauthor of three books: *Ames, Chafee, and Re on Remedies* (Foundation Press, 2012), with Theodore Eisenberg; *Demystifying Legal Reasoning* (Cambridge University Press, 2008); and *The Rule of Rules: Morality, Rules, and the Dilemmas of Law* (Duke University Press, 2001), the latter two with Larry Alexander. In addition, she has published numerous articles, book chapters, and reviews in her subjects of specialty, and has served as a member of the advisory committee for the ALI's Restatement (Third) of Restitution and Unjust Enrichment. Professor Sherwin received her BA from Lake Forest College (1977), her JD from Boston University School of Law (1981), and her PhD in philosophy from Cornell (2017).

Steven D. Smith
Warren Distinguished Professor of Law
Co-Executive Director of the Institute for Law and Religion, and Co-Executive Director of the Institute for Law and Philosophy
University of San Diego School of Law

Steven Smith writes in the areas of law and religion, constitutional law, torts, and jurisprudence. Before joining the USD law faculty in 2002, he was the Robert and Marion Short Professor of Law at the University of Notre Dame Law School, and before that, the Byron R. White Professor of Law at the University of Colorado School of Law. He has also been a Visiting Professor of Law at the University of Michigan and the University of Virginia. In addition to his numerous articles on constitutional law and law and religion in scholarly legal journals, Professor Smith is the author of *The Rise and Decline of American Religious Freedom* (Harvard University Press, 2014); *The Disenchantment of Secular Discourse* (Harvard University Press, 2010); *Law's Quandary* (Harvard University Press, 2004); *The Constitution and the Pride of Reason* (Oxford University Press, 1998); and *Foreordained Failure: The Quest for a Constitutional Principle of Religious Freedom* (Oxford University Press, 1995). He received his BA from Brigham Young University (1976) and his JD from Yale University (1979).

Lawrence B. Solum
Carmack Waterhouse Professor of Law
Georgetown University Law Center

Lawrence Solum works in constitutional theory, procedure, and the philosophy of law and is well known for his work on the philosophy of language and constitutional interpretation. He was a pioneer in the development of "virtue jurisprudence," now the subject of numerous articles, monographs, and scholarly conferences. Before joining the Georgetown faculty in 2011, Professor Solum was the John E. Cribbet Professor of Law and Professor of Philosophy at the University of Illinois. He was also a member of the law faculties at the University of San Diego and Loyola Marymount University, and he has been a Visiting Professor of Law at Boston University and the University of Southern California. Professor Solum's volume on prior adjudication and related doctrines in *Moore's Federal Practice* has been cited by the United States Supreme Court and every circuit court of appeal. He has lectured at dozens of universities throughout the world, authored numerous scholarly articles in leading Anglo-American journals, and is the Editor of *Legal Theory Blog*, an influential weblog that focuses on developments in contemporary normative and positive legal theory. Professor Solum earned his BA from the University of California–Los Angeles (1981) and his JD from Harvard Law School (1984).

Peter Westen
Frank G. Millard Professor of Law Emeritus
University of Michigan Law School

Peter Westen's principal scholarly interests are in the fields of criminal law and legal theory. He has authored a lengthy list of articles and book chapters that have appeared in prominent journals and volumes of collected essays, and he is the author of *The Logic of Consent: The Diversity and Deceptiveness of Consent as a Defense to Criminal Conduct* (Routledge, 2004) and *Speaking of Equality: The Rhetoric of "Equality" in Moral and Legal Discourse* (Princeton University Press, 1990). Prior to joining the faculty of the University of Michigan Law School in 1973, Professor Westen served as law clerk to Justice William O. Douglas of the Supreme Court of the United States. He was a Fellow of the International Legal Center in Bogota, Colombia, where he advised the Colombian Ministry of Economic Development on commercial code reform. When he returned to the United States, he became an Associate in the Washington, DC office of Paul, Weiss, Rifkind, Wharton & Garrison and appeared as counsel in several cases before the US Supreme Court. Professor Westen was also a Guggenheim Fellow in 1981. He earned his BA from Harvard College (1964). He spent the following year in Vienna on an Austrian state scholarship studying contemporary Austrian political history, and he then earned his JD from the University of California–Berkeley (1968).

Gideon Yaffe
Professor of Law, Professor of Philosophy and Professor of Psychology
Yale University Law School

Gideon Yaffe's research interests include the philosophy of law, particularly criminal law; metaphysics, including causation, free will and personal identity; the philosophy of mind and action; and the history of early modern philosophy. Prior to joining the Yale faculty in 2011, Professor Yaffe was a Professor of Philosophy and Law at the University of Southern California. He was a member of the MacArthur Foundation's Law and Neuroscience Project and he continues to collaborate with several neuroscientists to devise experiments that aim to be of legal and philosophical significance. In 2015 he was named a Guggenheim Fellow. Professor Yaffe has written four books: *The Age of Culpability: Children and the Nature of Criminal Responsibility* (Oxford University Press, 2018); *Attempts: In the Philosophy of Action and the Criminal Law* (Oxford University Press, 2010); *Manifest Activity: Thomas Reid's Theory of Action* (Oxford University Press, 2004); and *Liberty Worth the Name: Locke on Free Agency* (Princeton University Press, 2000). He has also written articles that have appeared in leading law and philosophical journals. Professor Yaffe holds an AB from Harvard University (1992) and a PhD in philosophy from Stanford University (1998).

Acknowledgments

This collection reflects the work of a great many people who share deep respect and abiding affection for Larry Alexander. I thank the twenty-two internationally renowned contributors who crafted challenging critiques of Larry's signature positions that are worthy of their prominent stature in the academy. Thanks also go to Yale Law School's Center for Law and Philosophy for cohosting with the University of Illinois' Program in Law and Philosophy a May 2017 conference at Larry's alma mater, the Yale Law School, that allowed many of these authors to test the mettle of Larry's provocative theses through the presentation and defense of their chapters. I am also much obliged to the University of Illinois College of Law, its David C. Baum Professorship, and Georgetown University's Institute for the Study of Markets and Ethics in the McDonough School of Business (where I wrote the proposal for this volume) for their generous financial support of my work on this Festschrift.

Jessica Lietz (University of Illinois College of Law, Class of 2019) is owed an enormous debt for her dedicated research and meticulous initial editing of each of the chapters contained in this collection. This volume represents hundreds of hours of her law school career and it simply could not have been produced without this very substantial sacrifice on her part. I am also grateful to Donald Zheng (University of Illinois College of Law, Class of 2019), who lent invaluable support to the final phases of production. Professor Heather Simmons, the University of Illinois College of Law's brilliant Reference Librarian, lent her formidable skills to this project, for which I am very appreciative. I owe sincere thanks to my University of Illinois College of Law assistant, Jackie Hadler, for adding to her already breathless work on my behalf the formidable tasks involved in assembling and polishing the collective effort of twenty-four scholars from five different countries. Readers will be grateful for the detailed index carefully compiled by Geoff Bailey, which provides a comprehensive survey of the topics addressed in this volume. Finally, I and my co-contributors to this volume benefitted very considerably from the meticulous corrections and helpful suggestions of freelance copy-editor Virginia Hamilton, to whom we are all very grateful.

It is a fitting compliment to Larry's goodness as a person that his family so loves and respects him, and I have been the grateful beneficiary of that affection at numerous points during the production of this volume. I thank my family as well, and particularly my husband, Michael Moore, whose lifelong philosophical companionship and generous willingness to invest in each of my scholarly projects have been at the root of my happiness within the academy.

And finally, my sincere thanks to Larry himself. In an early biographical letter to me, Larry was willing to give me a rare glimpse into the childhood that shaped his ambitious adult life and, as his coauthors could predict, his responses to my pleas for help, my requests for information, and my iterative edits of his contributions were superhumanly instantaneous. I will live the rest of my life in awe of Larry's insatiable appetite for the life of the mind, and I am grateful that his energy for scholarship reaches to the mind-numbing minutiae that require attention during the editing and production of a volume like this. It has been my very great honor and privilege to know, learn from, and through this volume, pay my deepest respects to Larry.

1

Introduction

Larry Alexander

Heidi M. Hurd

Larry Alexander is one of the most profound and influential legal scholars in the last century. His voluminous portfolio of work spans numerous areas of law and both grapples with, and creatively invents, illuminating puzzles of extraordinary interest, difficulty, and importance for those who work at the intersections of law and philosophy. Larry's typically ingenious solutions to these puzzles have served as invitations to other scholars to explore whole new areas of legal inquiry and previously undiscovered philosophical terrain. Anyone who now sets out to write in the areas of criminal law, constitutional law, jurisprudence and legal reasoning, or moral philosophy cannot help but engage with the tantalizing difficulties that Larry has identified and the beguiling and contrarian positions that he has staked out. It is the distinctive signature of great scholars that one cannot enter their fields without being forced to engage with their work while doing one's own, and by that measure Larry enjoys formidable scholarly prowess, for scholars within numerous disciplines and over numerous decades have had to shape their work to fit the contours of topics molded by Larry's path-breaking contributions.

Larry's legacy within the legal and philosophical academies, however, is not confined to the ways in which he has seismically altered intellectual landscapes through his scholarship. It is also defined by the impacts he has had as a colleague and mentor on those within his fields of inquiry. Simply put, Larry is widely beloved. He has invested extraordinary energy in the work of his academic colleagues, writing warm but philosophically rigorous critiques of their work and hosting them to intellectual gatherings that have united them with others in common pursuit of solutions to problems that haunt branches of scholarly inquiry. It is hard to find anyone who works on topics within criminal law, constitutional law, legal theory, or moral philosophy who does not feel beholden to Larry and who does not bear tremendous respect for the energy that he brings not just to academic inquiry, but to the cultivation of others' work and to the collaborative pursuit of knowledge.

This collection of essays reflects the shared desire on the part of prominent figures within the legal academy to honor Larry's intellectual legacy by engaging with some of his most important scholarly contributions. Yet this volume is far more than a tribute to Larry's towering reputation within the academy. More importantly, it is a very helpful "reader's guide" for anyone who seeks to master the positions that Larry has defended across the array of disciplines to which he has contributed, as well as the systematic philosophical connections between those positions that might be lost on one who only reads disparate essays. Because Larry's work is sure to have a very long half-life, scholars for years to come will be forced to grapple with the puzzles, paradoxes, and perplexities that he has teased out of core legal doctrines. They shall thus find the essays in this volume fertile sources of insight and innovation as they seek their own means of surmounting the philosophical obstacles that Larry has famously devised to thwart complacency about the defensibility of the law's most central tenets.

1.1 THE MAKING OF THE MAN

Larry Alexander grew up in Corpus Christi, Texas, the city in which his father's family had settled when it was a small frontier town a fraction of the size it is today. As he describes it, his family was "bookish."[1] That rather understates it, for academic ambition and accomplishment characterized generations reaching back on both sides of his family. His paternal grandmother was one of eleven children born to "a sort of patrician Jewish family,"[2] who went on to college and thereafter became one of the original members of the American Association of University Women. Larry's paternal grandfather was a University of Texas graduate whose brother became an editor of *Collier's* magazine.

Before World War II broke out, Larry's father, Simon Ray Alexander, had been pursuing a PhD in chemistry at the University of Texas, but by the time the war was over he faced the challenge of supporting a wife and two children – Larry and his sister Candy – and so he never returned to the academy. Instead, he became the owner of a record and phonograph store, which guaranteed Larry the enviable status of owning the best record collection of anyone in his school.

Larry's mother, Helen Rosenwasser Alexander, hailed from the small West Texas town of Stamford, where she was the salutatorian of her high school class and the 1938 Queen of the Texas Cowboy Reunion, the largest amateur rodeo in the world. The Rosenwasser family was one of only two Jewish families in Stamford at that time, and they owned a small department store. Its competition was a similar store owned

1 Larry Alexander, letter to author, July 7, 2017 (on file with author).
2 Ibid.

by the other Jewish family in town – Helen's aunt and uncle. One of their sons, Helen's first cousin, was Robert Strauss, who went on to marry Helen's roommate at the University of Texas and to become, inter alia, the head of the Democratic National Committee and a Washington power broker.

As Larry describes it, while Corpus Christi was a ranching community, it was surprisingly "democratic" for its time and location.[3] Upon settling in the town, his grandparents became "very Texan,"[4] and as merchants they acquired considerable ranch land in payment for goods. Jews were well accepted in the area; indeed, as Larry recalls, the mayor was Jewish and his great uncles and grandfather founded the Corpus Christi Country Club together with their non-Jewish friends.

Larry and his sister, Candy, attended public schools in Corpus Christi where both acquired obvious analytic talents. Candy went on to major in mathematics at the University of Texas and became a high school math teacher, teaching everything from calculus to remedial algebra. Larry went on to study philosophy at Williams College where he had the highest GPA among the eighteen philosophy majors in his class. He was elected to Phi Beta Kappa in his junior year and graduated *magna cum laude* with Highest Honors in Philosophy. Having also captained the varsity golf team at Williams, he aspired to apply for a Rhodes Scholarship[5] with which to complete a DPhil at Oxford University. But several of his teachers who knew of his interest in public policy persuaded him to change course and to apply to the Yale Law School. Knowing of its reputation for adopting a philosophical approach to legal education, they assured him that it would afford him the American equivalent of the DPhil. Larry was disappointed to discover that, in his words, "the school's philosophical credentials were largely hype."[6] Most of the instruction was, in fact, like that of most other law schools, "its focus far more doctrinal than philosophical."[7]

Yet, as Larry has always insisted, he never regretted his choice to attend Yale Law School. He had some of the most celebrated teachers of the day – Alexander Bickel, Boris Bittker, Guido Calabresi, and Ronald Dworkin. Far more importantly, it was at Yale that he met his wife, Elaine, who was also in the Class of 1968. They were married after their first year of law school, having never revealed their 1L grades to one another (a point of pride to this day, though it makes one wonder what other secrets they will take to their graves). They were happily relieved when they both graduated within the top 10 percent (during years when Yale had real grades and real GPAs) and shared the honor of being named to the Order of the Coif.

3 Ibid.

4 Ibid.

5 At the time, those who applied for Rhodes scholarships were required to have played a varsity sport in college in addition to accumulating a superb academic record.

6 Larry Alexander, letter to author, July 7, 2017 (on file with author).

7 Ibid.

Larry and Elaine both developed a lifelong interest in criminal law while at Yale because their respective criminal law teachers both used the casebook then edited by Sanford Kadish and Monrad Paulsen[8] – a text that Larry describes as "much more interesting than our classes."[9] Indeed, to Sandy Kadish's delight, Elaine credited him with her career choice. In their final year, Larry and Elaine wrote a joint senior thesis under the supervision of Steven Duke in which they (rather immodestly!) presented a full-blown theory of the criminal law. Upon his retirement from Yale a few years ago, Professor Duke found their thesis among his papers and sent it to Larry. Larry was amazed at how similar their views in 1968 were to his views today (prompting his closest colleagues to conclude that he either peaked or calcified at a very young age).

1.2 ELAINE ALEXANDER: LARRY'S PARTNER IN LIFE, LOVE, AND INTELLECTUAL INQUIRY

In 1970, after law school and clerkships, Larry was appointed to the faculty at the University of San Diego School of Law, while Elaine went into the practice of criminal law, founding Appellate Defenders, Inc., in 1973 and becoming its Executive Director in 1979. ADI is a non-profit law firm that administers the appointed counsel system for the California Court of Appeal, Fourth Appellate District. Elaine pioneered ADI to improve the quality of indigent appellate representation in criminal and juvenile delinquency cases, and today ADI has a large staff of attorneys who operate under contract with the California Administrative Office of the Courts. Elaine has been showered with local, state, and national awards for the work she has done on behalf of indigent people unjustly convicted or unjustly treated by our imperfect system of criminal justice. These moments of recognition for Elaine have evoked rare expressions of exuberant pride from Larry, who is characteristically modest about his own achievements. But it has been words like those of Harvey Davis, for whom ADI finally won parole after 27 years and numerous procedural setbacks, that best capture Larry's sense that Elaine and the organization to which she has devoted her life's blood practices what he preaches, and by so doing completes his life's work. Harvey Davis wrote to Elaine: "There really aren't enough words to properly voice the good that you have done in the hearts of many men!!!"[10]

[8] That casebook has metamorphosized over the years a good deal, but it remains the most philosophically rich book in the field. See the most recent edition by Sanford H. Kadish, Stephen J. Schulhofer, and Rachel E. Barkow, *Criminal Law and Its Processes: Cases and Materials*, 10th ed. (New York: Wolters Kluwer, 2017).

[9] Larry Alexander, letter to author, July 7, 2017 (on file with author).

[10] Cheryl Geyerman, "Richard Pfeiffer's Chain Victories in Parole Cases," Appellate Defenders, Inc., www.adi-sandiego.com/news_alerts/pdfs/2009/029-Pfeiffer-parole-article-for-newsletter.pdf.

Larry's first two law review articles were coauthored with Elaine and he credits her, to this day, with being his most valued discussant. In the first of their coauthored articles, they criticized the turn away from color blindness and the legal entrenchment of various forms of "color consciousness." Here is Larry's description of the metamorphosis of his thinking about this issue:

> During college, I had been a campaigner in both the North and the South for passage of the 1964 Civil Rights Act, which made color blindness the law of employment and public accommodations. It embodied Martin Luther King, Jr.'s ideal of focusing on the content of character, not the color of skin. Elaine and I decried, on grounds of principle, the turn away from that ideal in affirmative action programs. I later came to the view that we were wrong to claim that color consciousness was a violation of moral principle, but I still think that we were nonetheless right to oppose it. The correct basis for opposition was (and is) pragmatic. Color consciousness, and identity politics more generally, has proved to be highly divisive, and on campuses it has led to balkanization, the creation of departments of grievance polemics, and a rhetoric of postmodern gibberish. I have written several articles since that first one making such points – though obviously, if my voice has been heard at all, it has thus far failed in its mission.[11]

The other article that Larry and Elaine coauthored represented Larry's only foray into the field of evidence law. In it, they attacked what came to be known several years later as "conditional relevance." As far as I can glean, theirs was the first article to attack the notion. And it explains why, when I interviewed at the University of San Diego Law School as an entry-level candidate, Larry proved to be a formidable debate opponent when I illustrated my thesis that evidence law is a rich source of philosophical conundrums by outlining a puzzle that turned on the concept of conditional relevance. That was not the first – nor will it be the last – time that I stuck my foot in my mouth during an intensive grilling, but I remember it vividly because Larry figuratively grabbed my foot and gleefully shoved it down my throat.

1.3 MAPPING LARRY'S SCHOLARLY PORTFOLIO AND THE MAJOR POINTS OF CONTENTION WITH CRITICS

Larry matured into one of the legal academy's most creative contributors by developing an approach to identifying fruitful topics of inquiry that aspiring scholars would be well advised to emulate. First, Larry reads the legal and philosophical literatures voraciously to locate the specific issues about which leading scholars are persistently disagreeing. He then considers whether there is a deep reason for their

[11] Larry Alexander, letter to author, July 7, 2017 (on file with author).

persistent disagreement. He asks: Are the premises from which the arguments begin ill-formed, or is there a basic incoherence or paradox at the heart of the controversy? As he has chortled, "Occasionally, I even find incoherence embedded within matters of broad agreement – such as when the Supreme Court unanimously affirms what I take to be an illusory distinction between the President's acting illegally under federal law and his acting unconstitutionally." Larry's general strategy of first uncovering and then proffering solutions to conceptual puzzles at the core of persistent disputes (and sometimes at the core of smug agreements) is emblematic of most of Larry's scholarship.

Although he has written on an extraordinary number of other topics, Larry's scholarship is largely concentrated in four somewhat overlapping areas: the philosophical underpinnings of criminal law; the theoretical foundations of constitutional law; the core disputes in general jurisprudence, including the authority of law and the rationality of rule following; and the central debates in moral philosophy, including the structure and content of deontological ethics. This volume of essays tracks this organization.

Within the arena of criminal law, to which Part I of this volume is dedicated, one of Larry's earliest and most-cited pieces has as its centerpiece an imagined doomsday machine and deals with the question of why punishment should be proportional to the offender's desert when the defendant has noticed that disproportionate punishment will be levied for violations.[12] Larry concludes in this early work that penalties imposed to deter have more in common with safes, moats, and electric fences than with desert-based punishment of the sort recommended by a principled retributive theory. After this early foray into punishment theory, Larry went on to write further ground-breaking articles on the justification of inflicting suffering on wrongdoers, reprising the doomsday machine thesis,[13] exploring the implications of inadvertently punishing the innocent,[14] analyzing how underserved suffering affects retributive desert,[15] and tracing the ways in which retributive desert interacts with distributive justice.[16]

In their contributions to this volume, both Doug Husak and David Brink explore aspects of Larry's retributivism, arguing that its defense remains incomplete. In Doug Husak's view, while Larry has morally motivated a retributive theory of punishment, he has glossed over the central question of how to match kinds or modes of

[12] Larry Alexander, "The Doomsday Machine: Proportionality, Prevention and Punishment," *The Monist* 69, no. 2 (1980): 199.

[13] Larry Alexander, "Consent, Punishment, and Proportionality," *Philosophy and Public Affairs* 15, no. 2 (1986): 178.

[14] Larry Alexander, "Retributivism and the Inadvertent Killing of the Innocent," *Law and Philosophy* 2, no. 2 (1983): 233.

[15] Larry Alexander, "You Got What You Deserved," *Criminal Law and Philosophy* 7, no. 2(2013): 309.

[16] Larry Alexander, "Retributive Justice," in *Oxford Handbook of Distributive Justice*, ed. Serena Olsaretti (Oxford: Oxford University Press, 2018), 177–94.

punishment with claims of desert.[17] Husak worries that, absent a principled basis for matching a given offense with a given penalty, Larry's retributivism cannot vindicate our use of imprisonment as a legitimate form of punishment (nor could it vindicate any other form of punishment, such as corporal punishment or the death penalty). David Brink, in turn, fears that because moral responsibility is scalar, any system that calls upon juries to find defendants either guilty or innocent (as ours largely does) is destined to offend against a retributive theory of punishment.[18] As he argues, retributivists like Larry ought to urge the abandonment of a bivalent system that fails to conceive of guilt as a scalar property, and that thus falls well shy of imposing punishments that approximate defendants' just deserts.

Larry's decades of work on legal responsibility ultimately reached beyond the justification for punishing wrongdoers to examine every doctrinal nook and theoretical cranny in the edifice of Anglo-American criminal law. For example, he has defended the counterintuitive claim that incomplete attempts – namely, attempts that fall shy of constituting the last acts defendants intend to do – are not culpable.[19] But he has simultaneously elevated *mens rea* elements above *actus reus* elements in the analysis of prima facie liability by arguing that genuine but failed attempts are every bit as blameworthy as successfully completed crimes. In short, results don't matter.[20] This thesis is the target of Antony Duff's contribution to this volume.[21] As Duff suggests, the best explanation of why we have different psychological reactions to those who fail at their attempts and to those who succeed – such as the relief felt by someone who fails to perpetrate a harm ("Thank God I failed!") – is that these possess very different moral pedigrees.

Larry has further explored in depth the structure of omission liability.[22] He has mapped the relations between both inculpatory and exculpatory mistakes of fact and

17 Douglas Husak, "Kinds of Punishment," this volume.

18 David O. Brink, "Partial Responsibility and Excuse," this volume.

19 Larry Alexander and Kimberly Kessler Ferzan, "Risk and Inchoate Crimes: Retribution or Prevention?" in *Seeking Security: Pre-Empting the Commission of Criminal Harms*, ed. G.R. Sullivan and Ian Davis (Oxford: Hart, 2012), 103–20; Larry Alexander and Kimberly Kessler Ferzan, "Danger: The Ethics of Preemptive Action," *Ohio State Journal of Criminal Law* 9, no. 2 (2012): 637.

20 Larry Alexander, "Crime and Culpability," *Journal of Contemporary Legal Issues* 5, no. 1 (1994): 1; Larry Alexander and Kimberly Kessler Ferzan, "Results Don't Matter," in *Criminal Law Conversations*, ed. Paul H. Robinson, Kimberly Kessler Ferzan, and Stephen P. Garvey (Oxford: Oxford University Press, 2009), 147–53; Larry Alexander, "Michael Moore and the Mysteries of Causation in the Law," *Rutgers Law Journal* 42, no. 2 (2011): 301; Larry Alexander and Kimberly Kessler Ferzan, "'Moore or Less' Causation and Responsibility," *Criminal Law and Philosophy* 6, no. 1 (2012): 81; Larry Alexander and Kimberly Kessler Ferzan, "Ferzander's Surrebuttal," *Criminal Law and Philosophy* 6, no. 3 (2012): 463.

21 Antony Duff, "'Thank God I Failed,'" this volume.

22 Larry Alexander, "Criminal Liability for Omissions: An Inventory of Issues," in *Criminal Law Theory: Doctrines of the General Part*, ed. Stephen Shute and Andrew Simester (Oxford: Oxford University Press, 2002), 121–42.

mistakes of law.[23] And he has examined the conditions that justify the commission of prima facie criminal offenses and compared these to conditions that function to excuse such offenses. In his contribution to this volume, Peter Westen vindicates Larry's ongoing ambivalence concerning the conventional categorization of the defense of duress as an excuse.[24] Westen argues that duress lacks any family resemblance to the cognitive and volitional deficits that are paradigmatically exonerating (e.g., infancy, insanity), and demonstrates that, in its important moral respects, duress most resembles the conditions that Larry and others take to be manifestly justifying.

Larry's explorations of the classic justifications recognized by the criminal law have been profoundly influential. He has advanced a nuanced theory of self-defense that seeks to answer concerns about pre-emptive proportionality[25] and he has identified previously unexplored moral conundrums raised by the lesser evils defense.[26] It is to one of these latter conundrums that Gideon Yaffe dedicates his contribution to this volume.[27] In his view, Larry cannot explain without the aid of consequentialism (which he takes to be an illegitimate crutch) why the law should give the lesser evils defense to an offender whose prima facie criminal deed prevented a great evil but failed to constitute the least evil means available. Yaffe argues that, contrary to Larry's assumption, the lesser evils defense is not a means of entrenching in law a substantive safety valve made available in morality, but rather constitutes a procedural mechanism essential to preserving not just the state's power, but its legitimate political authority. Were the criminal justice system to punish a defendant who chose a lesser evil, but not the least evil, it would be inconsistently committed to both preventing the greater evil and preventing the greater evil's prevention.

23 Larry Alexander, "Inculpatory and Exculpatory Mistakes and the Fact/Law Distinction: An Essay in Memory of Myke Bayles," *Law and Philosophy* 12, no. 1 (1993): 33; Larry Alexander, "Facts, Law, Exculpation, and Inculpation: Comments on Simons," *Criminal Law and Philosophy* 3, no. 3 (2009): 241; Larry Alexander, "What's Inside and Outside the Law," *Law and Philosophy* 31, no. 2 (2012): sec. 2.

24 Peter Westen, "Does Duress Justify or Excuse? The Significance of Larry Alexander's Ambivalence," this volume.

25 Larry Alexander, "Justification and Innocent Aggressors," *Wayne Law Review* 33, no. 4 (1987): 1177; Larry Alexander, "Self-Defense, Justification, and Excuse," *Philosophy and Public Affairs* 22, no. 1 (1993): 53; Larry Alexander, "A Unified Defense of Preemptive Self-Protection," *Notre Dame Law Review* 74, no. 5 (1999): 1475; Larry Alexander, "Self-Defense," in *The Routledge Companion to Philosophy of Law*, ed. Andrei Marmor (Abingdon: Routledge, 2012), sec. 3.1.6; Larry Alexander, "Recipe for a Theory of Self-Defense: The Ingredients and Some Cooking Suggestions," in *The Ethics of Self-Defense*, ed. Christian Coons and Michael Weber (Oxford: Oxford University Press, 2016), 20–50.

26 Larry Alexander, "Lesser Evils: A Closer Look at the Paradigmatic Justification," *Law and Philosophy* 24, no. 6 (2005): 611.

27 Gideon Yaffe, "Alternative Lesser Evils," this volume.

Perhaps the most fertile source of Larry's signature challenges to common assumptions and conventional theses about criminal responsibility is his 2009 book, *Crime and Culpability: A Theory of Criminal Law*, coauthored with Kim Ferzan (with contributions by Stephen Morse),[28] the publication of which constituted an intellectual watershed within the criminal law academy. Consider just three of the profound, and profoundly surprising, claims that Larry and his coauthors defend in this detailed analysis of the conditions of criminal responsibility. First, in keeping with their conviction, explored by Antony Duff, that results don't matter, they reject the claim that culpably causing harm is more blameworthy than culpably risking it – making the driver who recklessly speeds home without incident as deserving of a manslaughter conviction as one whose recklessness causes a deadly accident. Second, they take an actor to be culpable if, and only if, she subjectively believes that she is imposing a risk on another's protected interests that is, by the law's measure (not hers), an unjustifiable one. This position prompts them to reject the criminal law's assumption that there is special moral and legal significance to be attached to acts that are done with the purpose or with knowledge that they will harm, and to thus collapse purposeful harms and harms knowingly caused into the singular category of recklessness.[29] Third, their theory of culpability implies their rejection of the deeply held intuition that negligence is culpable, and they thus argue that those who risk or cause harm through inadvertence should be exempted from any blame or punishment.[30] The mother who forgets that her child is in the car on a sweltering summer day, the driver who dozes off at the wheel while traveling along the interstate, the mechanic who forgets to check the brakes on a customer's car – all of these are free from moral blame, and when the predictable harms ensue, all of these are to be exonerated from legal liability for the losses of life they cause.

Larry has explored and defended conclusions as surprising, and as surprisingly hard to circumvent, in the arena of constitutional law, to which Part II of this volume is dedicated. In early articles Larry waded into the doctrinal morass of the "state action" issue, arguing, first, that what people thought was the state action issue was, in fact, easily resolvable, but then pointing to a different, very real, and very difficult

28 Larry Alexander and Kimberly Kessler Ferzan, with Stephen Morse, *Crime and Culpability: A Theory of Criminal Law* (Cambridge: Cambridge University Press, 2009).

29 Larry first articulated and defended this unitary conception of culpability in Larry Alexander, "Insufficient Concern: A Unified Conception of Criminal Culpability," *California Law Review* 88, no. 3 (2000): 931.

30 This thesis emerged in a number of earlier pieces. See, for example, Larry Alexander and Kimberly Kessler Ferzan, "Against Negligence Liability," in *Criminal Law Conversations*, ed. Paul Robinson, Kimberly Kessler Ferzan, and Stephen Garvey (Oxford: Oxford University Press, 2009), 273–81; Larry Alexander, "Insufficient Concern," 931; Larry Alexander, "Negligence, Crime and Tort: Comments on Hurd and Simons," *Boston University Law Review* 76, no. 1/2 (1996): 301.

state action issue that had been lurking in the shadows ever since the Supreme Court had glimpsed it over a century before.[31] He then dove into unconstitutional conditions theory, developing the important notions of constitutionally optional benefits and burdens and tracing their theoretical presuppositions and implications for equal protection, the equal protection modes of free speech and free exercise, and the relation between substantive rights and procedural due process.[32]

Among Larry's many fruitful intellectual partnerships over the years is one with former San Diego colleague, Sai Prakash. After writing two solo articles in which Larry employed Arrow's impossibility theorem to demonstrate the incoherence of the claim that gerrymanders dilute votes,[33] he and Sai teamed up to launch a final concerted attack on the academic orthodoxy regarding the unconstitutionality of gerrymanders.[34] They then crossed the aisle in a pair of articles to defend the majority position regarding the constitutionality of legislative delegations of power against the contrarian view advanced by Eric Posner and Adrian Vermeule, arguing that the Posner-Vermeule position logically generates a set of outlandish conclusions. And they then tacked back in characteristically heterodox form to argue that Congress's statutes defining terms in future statutes violated the principle that Congress cannot entrench its laws.[35]

Larry also deservedly enjoys a very considerable reputation within the field of constitutional law for his work on free speech theory. Early in his years of teaching constitutional law he concluded that the judicial invalidation of regulations that affect, but are not aimed at, the content of speech – Laurence Tribe's so-called Track Two regulations – cannot be based on any principle that is content free.

[31] Larry Alexander, "The Public/Private Distinction(s)," *Constitutional Commentary* 10, no. 2 (1993): 361; Larry Alexander, "State Action," in *The Philosophy of Law: An Encyclopedia*, ed. Christopher Berry Grey (New York: Garland, 1999); Larry Alexander, "What's Inside and Outside the Law," *Law and Philosophy* 31, no. 2 (2012): 213.

[32] Larry Alexander, *Is There a Right of Freedom of Expression?* (Cambridge: Cambridge University Press, 2005), chap. 3; Larry Alexander, "Rules, Rights, Options and Time," *Legal Theory* 6, no. 4 (2000): 391; Larry Alexander, "Constitutional Theory and Constitutionally Optional Benefits and Burdens," *Constitutional Commentary* 11, no. 2 (1994): 287; Larry Alexander, "Modern Equal Protection Theories: A Metatheoretical Taxonomy and Critique," *Ohio State Law Journal* 42, no. 1 (1981): 3. See also Larry Alexander "Understanding Constitutional Rights in a World of Optional Baselines," *San Diego Law Review* 26, no. 2 (1989): 175.

[33] Larry Alexander, "Lost in the Political Thicket," *Florida Law Review* 41, no. 3 (1989): 563; Larry Alexander, "Still Lost in the Political Thicket (or Why I Don't Understand the Concept of Vote Dilution)," *Vanderbilt Law Review* 50, no. 2 (1997): 327. See also Larry Alexander, "Constitutional Rules, Constitutional Standards, and Constitutional Settlement: *Marbury v. Madison* and the Case for Judicial Supremacy," *Constitutional Commentary* 20, no. 2 (2003): 369.

[34] Larry Alexander and Saikrishna Prakash, "Tempest in an Empty Teapot: Why the Constitution Does Not Regulate Gerrymandering," *William and Marry Law Review* 50, no. 1 (2008): 1.

[35] Larry Alexander and Saikrishna Prakash, "Mother May I? Imposing Mandatory Prospective Rules of Statutory Interpretation," *Constitutional Commentary* 20, no. 1 (2003): 97.

Rather, such judicial interventions must inevitably rely upon judicial preferences concerning the messages affected.[36] After a few more years Larry concluded that the critique he had leveled at Track Two decisions applied with equal force to decisions about Track One regulations aimed at the substantive messages within speech, as well as to Track Three regulations concerning government speech.[37] This intellectual journey led Larry to his now well-known and persistently controversial view, consolidated and developed in his 2005 book, *Is There a Right of Freedom of Expression?*,[38] that a right of free speech lacks grounding in any deep principle, but must rest, at best, on pragmatic time and place considerations.

The protection of academic freedom, about which Larry has also written important articles,[39] is not, on his account, best thought of as a special case of the protection of free speech. While academic freedom often translates into rights to research, write, and teach without threat of censorship, in his view its rationale varies substantially from the best rationale for the protection of speech. While freedom of expression is a right best understood as a reflection of the government's inability to fairly regulate the content of speech, academic freedom is best understood as a discipline-relative employment right accorded to those who are appointed to contribute to the marketplace of ideas through research and teaching. In his contribution to this volume, Brian Leiter makes the case for thinking of academic freedom as a species of freedom of expression, at least when background conditions exist that make academic freedom more likely than not to maximize the discovery of truth.[40]

36 Larry Alexander, "Trouble on Track Two: Incidental Regulations of Speech and Free Speech Theory," *Hastings Law Journal* 44, no. 4 (1993): 921. See also Larry Alexander and Paul Horton, "The Impossibility of a Free Speech Principle," *Northwestern University Law Review* 78, no. 5 (1983): 1319.

37 Larry Alexander, "Compelled Speech," *Constitutional Commentary* 23, no. 2 (2006): 147; Larry Alexander, "Freedom of Expression as a Human Right," in *Protecting Human Rights*, ed. Thomas Campbell, Jeffrey Goldsworthy, and Adrienne Stone (Oxford: Oxford University Press, 2003), 39–73; Larry Alexander, "Banning Hate Speech and the Sticks and Stones Defense," *Constitutional Commentary* 13, no. 1 (1996): 71; Larry Alexander, "Free Speech and Speaker's Intent," *Constitutional Commentary* 12, no. 1 (1995): 21; Larry Alexander, "Low Value Speech," *Northwestern University Law Review* 83, no. 3 (1989): 547; Larry Alexander, "Is There an Overbreadth Doctrine?" *San Diego Law Review* 22, no. 2/3 (1985): 541.

38 For the extension of his work on freedom of expression into more recent times, see Larry Alexander, "The Misconceived Search for the Meaning of 'Speech' in Freedom of Speech," *Open Journal of Philosophy* 5, no. 1 (2015): 39–42; Larry Alexander "Is Freedom of Expression a Universal Right?" *San Diego Law Review* 50, no. 3 (2013): 707; Larry Alexander, "Freedom of Expression," in *Encyclopedia of Modern Political Thought*, ed. Gregory Claeys, Michael S. Cummings, and Lyman Tower Sargent (Washington, DC: CQ Press, 2013), 304–6; Larry Alexander, "Freedom of Expression," in *Encyclopedia of Applied Ethics*, 2nd ed., vol. 2, ed. Ruth Chadwick (Cambridge: Academic Press, 2012), 339–44.

39 Larry Alexander, "Academic Freedom," *University of Colorado Review* 77, no. 4 (2006): 883; Larry Alexander, "Fish on Academic Freedom: A Merited Assault on Nonsense, But Perhaps a Bridge Too Far," *Florida International Law Review* 9, no. 1 (2013): 1.

40 Brian Leiter, "Justifying Academic Freedom: Mill and Marcuse Revisited," this volume.

Through reflections on both Mill's libertarian account of freedom of expression and Marcuse's Marxist account of the background conditions required to ensure that freedom of expression is truth- and utility-maximizing, Leiter constructs a theory of academic freedom that harmonizes its rationale with that of free speech, and thus offers Larry an account that integrates the value of these theoretical cousins.

While I think of a theory of legal interpretation as a component of a theory of adjudication generally best classified under the rubric of general jurisprudence, there is no question that those who work in the arena of constitutional law have been the most engaged in recent years in debates about how best to interpret the meaning of constitutional provisions, and derivatively, how best to interpret the meaning of statutory enactments. For this reason, I have incorporated this aspect of Larry's theory of adjudication within Part II of this volume so as to combine debates over his substantive views on constitutionally protected rights with those that target his views on constitutional and statutory interpretation.

Larry has braved strong winds to plant his flag at the loneliest pole in the literature on legal interpretation,[41] uncompromisingly defending the thesis that interpretation in law, as in life, must be a search for speakers' meaning. As he has insisted in one article after another,[42] as well as in his provocative 2008 book on adjudication with Emily Sherwin, *Demystifying Legal Reasoning*, "If one is interpreting, one is seeking the author's intended meaning. When one is constructing a meaning that may not be the meaning intended by the author … one is not interpreting but establishing a rule."[43] At the core of his rejection of alternative nonintentionalist theories of interpretation is Larry's conviction that the method of interpretation available to judges

41 About his only frequently cited company in this inhospitable camp is that of his coauthor Emily Sherwin and Richard Kay. See, e.g., Richard S. Kay, "Construction, Originalist Interpretation and the Complete Constitution," *University of Pennsylvania Journal of Constitutional Law Online* 19, no. 1 (2017): 1, www.pennjournalconlaw.com/uploads/4/7/7/5/47752841/kay_final.pdf; Richard S. Kay, "Original Intention and Public Meaning in Constitutional Interpretation," *Northwestern University Law Review* 103, no. 2 (2009): 703.

42 Larry Alexander, "All or Nothing at All? The Intentions of Authorities and the Authority of Intentions," in *Law and Interpretation*, ed. Andrei Marmor (Oxford: Oxford University Press, 1995), 357–404; Larry Alexander and Emily Sherwin, "Interpreting Rules: The Nature and Limits of Inchoate Intentions," in *Legal Interpretation in Democratic States*, ed. Jeffrey Goldsworthy and Tom Campbell (Farnham: Ashgate, 2002), 3–28; Larry Alexander, "Originalism, or Who is Fred?," *Harvard Journal of Law & Public Policy* 19, no. 2 (1995): 321; Larry Alexander, "Fancy Theories of Interpretation Aren't," *Washington University Law Quarterly* 73, no. 3 (1995): 1081; Larry Alexander, "Of Living Trees and Dead Hands: The Interpretation of Constitutions and Constitutional Rights," *Canadian Journal of Law and Jurisprudence* 22, no. 2 (2009): 227; Larry Alexander, "Telepathic Law," *Constitutional Commentary* 27, no. 1 (2010): 139; Larry Alexander, "Originalism: The Why and the What," *Fordham Law Review* 82, no. 2 (2013): 539.

43 Larry Alexander and Emily L. Sherwin, *Demystifying Legal Reasoning* (Cambridge: Cambridge University Press, 2008), 139. See also Larry Alexander and Emily Sherwin, *The Rule of Rules: Rules, Principles, and the Dilemmas of Law* (Durham, NC: Duke University Press, 2001), chap. 5.

follows from the law's authority. In his view, we select lawmakers in large part based on our assessment of their moral expertise – that is, their ability to craft rules that represent moral improvements over the status quo ante. If it is the moral expertise of lawmakers that justifies our obedience to the rules they craft, then it must be that we should resolve interpretive questions by seeking their intentions, for only by seeking their intentions do we access their expertise.

In his contribution to this volume, Laurence Claus finds historical support for the theory of judicial supremacy that Larry constructs on conceptual, ahistorical grounds (discussed in Part III below). But he then challenges Larry's insistence on intentionalism in constitutional interpretation by arguing that this history licenses judicial lawmaking unconstrained by constitutional text and indifferent to the intentions of its original authors.[44] Connie Rosati,[45] Jeff Goldsworthy,[46] Larry Solum,[47] and Fred Schauer[48] all take issue in their contributions with Larry's self-described "simple-minded originalism."[49] In distinctively different ways, they all seek to demonstrate that Larry's subjective intentionalism begs the question against those who defend a conventional meaning theory of interpretation (such as Schauer), as well as those who defend what Goldsworthy describes as the "objective" or "weak intentionalism" of public meaning originalists (who, like Goldsworthy and Solum, believe that the meaning of texts is given not by their speaker's subjective intentions, but rather by what a reasonable audience would believe those intentions to be on the basis of publicly available evidence). Anyone who sets out to write on the topic of legal interpretation will find this volume's debate between Larry and these formidable critics to be an illuminating exploration of the arguments that can be mustered both for and against today's competing defenses of originalism, as well as those that go to the defensibility of theories of interpretation that eschew altogether a concern for original understandings of legal texts.

Alon Harel's contribution constitutes a bridge between Part II's focus on Larry's constitutional jurisprudence and Part III's focus on Larry's more general jurisprudential positions. As Harel anticipates, Larry's theory of the role of law as a vehicle for achieving the settlement of disputes shapes his theory of adjudication, as well as his

44 Laurence Claus, "Vindicating Judicial Supremacy," this volume.

45 Connie S. Rosati, "Alexander's 'Simple-Minded Originalism,'" this volume.

46 Jeffrey Goldsworthy, "Subjective versus Objective Intentionalism in Legal Interpretation," this volume.

47 Lawrence B. Solum, "Simple-Minded Originalism? Simply Wrong!," this volume.

48 Frederick Schauer, "Intentions in Tension," this volume.

49 Larry Alexander, "Simple-Minded Originalism," in *The Challenge of Originalism: Theories of Constitutional Interpretation*, ed. Grant Huscroft and Bradley W. Miller (Cambridge: Cambridge University Press, 2011), 87–98.

theory of legal authority and the rationality of rule following.[50] In his chapter, Harel argues that Larry should distinguish legal authoritative settlements from constitutional authoritative settlements, for, as he maintains, while the former are instrumentally beneficial, the latter possess intrinsic value, for they make the protection of fundamental rights a matter of duty, rather than discretion, on the part of the state.

Larry was drawn to the field of general jurisprudence, to which Part III of this volume is dedicated, and specifically to the debates surrounding the nature of adjudication and the authority of law, when he hosted a gathering on the role of precedent at which he remembers finding a colloquy between Fred Schauer and Michael Moore particularly seductive. His subsequent analysis of three models of precedent[51] prompted him to argue that demands for judicial constraint either make sense of rule-like allegiance to precedents but not of the common practice of distinguishing them, or explain the practice of distinguishing precedents but only by sacrificing the values of judicial constraint to begin with.

Just as Larry found himself skeptical of the defensibility of prominent theories of precedent, so he came to reject the notion that there are principles of a distinctly legal pedigree that properly enter into a judge's reasoning. Beginning with an attack on the account of legal principles made jurisprudentially popular by Ronald Dworkin,[52] Larry ultimately expanded his critique of legal principles so as to place himself at odds with all those who seek to defend the claim that principles unique to law can be identified and employed in adjudication.[53] Among these opponents is Mitch Berman, who argues in his contribution to this volume that a distinctly positivist account of legal principles both survives Larry's existential dismissal of legal principles and poses a significant challenge to Larry's intentionalist theory of interpretation discussed in Part II above.[54]

Larry's striking claims about both precedent and legal principles stem from a common source – his deep and pervasive skepticism about equality as a discrete moral value. Larry appreciates that equality has its unique normative bite only when one is projecting moral error onto future cases. If a precedent case was rightly decided, then the reasons that make that decision correct will also make a subsequent decision in keeping with that precedent correct, so equality has no work to do. Equality can exert moral pressure only when cases wrongly decided in the past

50 Alon Harel, "Alexander's Constitutionalism: A Qualified Defense," this volume.

51 Larry Alexander, "Constrained by Precedent," *Southern California Law Review* 63, no. 1 (1989): 1.

52 Larry Alexander and Kenneth Kress, "Against Legal Principles," in *Law and Interpretation*, ed. Andrei Marmor (Oxford: Oxford University Press, 1995), 279–328.

53 Alexander and Sherwin, *The Rule of Rules*, chap. 8; Larry Alexander, "There Are No Legal Principles," in *Institutionalized Reason: The Jurisprudence of Robert Alexy*, ed. Matthias Klatt (Oxford: Oxford University Press, 2012), 115–31.

54 Mitchell N. Berman, "For Legal Principles," this volume.

are thought to demand like treatment in the future. In Larry's view, there is little to be said for perpetuating past errors, and hence, little to be said for the moral value of equality.[55]

At the root of Larry's positions on precedent, legal principles, and interpretation is a latent allegiance to a brand of legal positivism that lends support to his more explicit view that law serves one primary function: settlement. This view has implied, as William Baude describes it, a "hard-nosed but somewhat unfashionable position on judicial review"[56] – a position that Larry and Fred Schauer defended in a piece in the *Harvard Law Review* that won them a good deal of attention, if not a proportionate amount of approval.[57] Baude's contribution challenges the compatibility of Larry's uncompromising theory of judicial supremacy with his simultaneous championship of the thesis, discussed above, that the meaning of legal language is given by its author's intentions.

Beyond the contentious theory of judicial supremacy to which his functional theory of law commits him, Larry has recognized that his account of the purpose of law commits him to a perplexing theory of the authority of law and the rationality of rule following. As he has argued, if law is to serve a settlement function, law must take the form of determinate rules. But rules purport to impact the practical reasoning of citizens in a manner that invites an intractable dilemma – what Larry has famously called "the gap." "There is an always-possible gap between what we have reason to do, all things considered, and what we have reason to have our … officials … require us to do."[58] As Larry has insisted, law cannot claim an authority that justifies our blind allegiance, and yet, law may serve its ultimate good only if we follow its commands *as if* they had the authority to compel exceptionless allegiance, and only if we require others to do the same, even when the law's commands depart from what morality would have us do. In his counterintuitive formulation: "It may be morally good that we punish ourselves for breaking morally good rules for morally good reasons."[59]

In his contribution to Part III, Steve Smith explores the compatibility of Larry's theory of authority with Larry's theory of interpretation (discussed in Part II), suggesting that the well-known "aggregation problem" may prove particularly

55 Alexander, "Constrained by Precedent"; Alexander and Kress, "Against Legal Principles."

56 William Baude, "The Court, or the Constitution?," this volume.

57 Larry Alexander and Frederick Schauer, "On Extrajudicial Constitutional Interpretation," *Harvard Law Review* 110, no. 7 (1997): 1359. See also Larry Alexander and Frederick Schauer, "Defending Judicial Supremacy: A Reply," *Constitutional Commentary* 17, no. 3 (2000): 455; Larry Alexander, "Constitutional Rules," 369; Larry Alexander and Lawrence B. Solum, "Popular? Constitutionalism?" *Harvard Law Review* 118, no. 5 (2005): 1594, 1628–35.

58 Larry Alexander, "The Gap," *Harvard Journal of Law & Public Policy* 14, no. 3 (1991): 695.

59 Ibid., 696.

problematic for Larry.[60] As Smith hypothesizes, if Larry takes seriously the full scope of the aggregation problem so as to recognize how often legal texts are drafted and enacted by groups of lawmakers who do not share intentions concerning the meaning of their language, Larry will be forced to conclude that a great deal of "law" is indeed gibberish. This conclusion in turn suggests that anarchy is masquerading as the rule of law more often than Larry might want to admit (unless, as Smith slyly hypothesizes, Larry is indeed a closet anarchist!).

Larry's paradoxical thesis that the law must claim an authority it does not have so as to induce us to defer to it more often than rationality would permit is the subject of the contribution by Emily Sherwin as well as that by Leo Katz and Alvaro Sandroni. According to Sherwin, a theory of extended practical rationality offers the possibility of making sense of exclusionary reasons, and so of making rational a deference to rules.[61] According to Katz and Sandroni, while Larry is right to indict the rationality of any strategy that requires one to intend to do what one knows will be contrary to reason at some future time of action (e.g., to intend to follow a rule that one knows is overinclusive), there may be a means of constructing a "package deal" to which it is rational to commit, despite its entailing future irrationality.[62]

Larry's interest in the relationship between law and morality and the ways in which morality may exert itself in opposition to the law's demands has motivated his participation in a number of debates that are squarely within the arena of moral philosophy. It is to his work in this fourth field of inquiry that Part IV of this volume is devoted. To take but a few examples, Larry has made path-breaking contributions to discussions about the power of consent to alter moral obligations,[63] the legitimacy of paternalism,[64] the defensibility of legal moralism,[65] the scope of moral responsibility for others' immoral actions,[66] the role of equality in a theory of distributive justice,[67] and the tension between scalar values and binary choices.[68] His discriminating work

60 Steven D. Smith, "Alexander as Anarchist," this volume.

61 Emily L. Sherwin, "Exclusionary Rules," this volume.

62 Leo Katz and Alvaro Sandroni, "Larry Alexander and 'the Gap,'" this volume.

63 Larry Alexander, "The Moral Magic of Consent (II)," *Legal Theory* 2, no. 3 (1996): 165; Larry Alexander, "The Ontology of Consent," *Analytic Philosophy* 55, no. 1 (2014): 1.

64 Larry Alexander, "Voluntary Enslavement," in *Paternalism: Theory and Practice*, ed. Christian Coons and Michael Weber (Cambridge: Cambridge University Press, 2013), 231–46.

65 Larry Alexander, "Harm, Offense and Morality," *Canadian Journal of Law and Jurisprudence* 7, no. 2 (1994): 199; Larry Alexander, "The Legal Enforcement of Morality," in *A Companion to Applied Ethics*, ed. R.G. Frey and Christopher Heath Wellman (Hoboken: Blackwell, 2003), 128–41; Larry Alexander, "Plastic Trees and Gladiators: Liberalism and Aesthetic Regulation," *Legal Theory* 16, no. 2 (2010): 77.

66 Larry Alexander, "Other People's Errors," *Ethical Theory and Moral Practice* 16, no. 5 (2013): 1049.

67 Larry Alexander and Maimon Scharzschild, "Liberalism, Neutrality, and Equality of Welfare Versus Equality of Resources," *Philosophy and Public Affairs* 16, no. 5 (1986): 85.

68 Larry Alexander, "Scalar Properties, Binary Judgments," *Journal of Applied Philosophy* 25, no. 2 (2008): 85.

on discrimination in the early 1990s[69] remains among Larry's finest achievements and reflects the kind of philosophical bravery that is a signature of Larry's scholarly career, for many at the time were eager to assume (erroneously) that by raising questions about the circumstances in which discrimination is wrongful, Larry was somehow suggesting that its wrongfulness was in doubt. Larry has since abrogated his defense of the discriminator-oriented account that he advanced in that 1992 *University of Pennsylvania Law Review* piece. Where others might insist on doubling-down on a contentious but often-cited position, Larry has been willing to concede the weaknesses of that position and recognize in print the strength of competing accounts that trace the wrongfulness of discrimination to its social consequences[70] or its effects on victims themselves.[71] Kasper Lippert-Rasmussen's contribution to this volume explores the kinds of counterexamples that ultimately prompted Larry to abandon his own discriminator-oriented account of the wrongfulness of discrimination.[72] He joins Larry in hypothesizing that any disrespect-based account must be replaced by a theory that traces the moral gravamen of discrimination to the effects it has on victims or on the larger society. However, as Larry has made clear, and as Lippert-Rasmussen appreciates, such accounts are not without their own problems, for even when discrimination results in no harm – indeed, even when it results in gains to its victim and to society at large – we are still gripped with the intuition that such discrimination is morally condemnable, an intuition unexplained by consequentialist accounts.

For all his many contributions to substantive disputes in ethics, Larry is best known in moral philosophy for his work on deontology. His early article on two-level consequentialism, "Pursuing the Good – Indirectly,"[73] has been extremely influential, joining David Lyon's classic work in providing a compelling refutation of a popular alternative to deontological ethics. His unique brand of deontology constitutes a jurisdictional, patient-centered, agent-neutral theory of deontological moral constraints that focuses on the rights of victims rather than the duties of perpetrators. His view is that one right grounds all others, namely the right not to *be used* by others. This he calls "the means principle" after Kant's injunction never to use another as a means to obtaining one's own ends. Larry contrasts this patient-centered deontology

69 Larry Alexander, "What Makes Wrongful Discrimination Wrong? Biases, Preferences, Stereotypes, and Proxies," *University of Pennsylvania Law Review* 141, no. 1 (1992): 149; see also Larry Alexander, "Disparate Impact: Fairness or Efficiency," *San Diego Law Review* 50, no. 1 (2013): 191.

70 Larry Alexander, "Review of Deborah Hellman and Sophia Moreau, Philosophical Foundations of Discrimination Law," *Ethics* 125, no. 3 (2015): 872.

71 Larry Alexander, "Is Wrongful Discrimination Really Wrong?" (unpublished manuscript available from Larry Alexander).

72 Kasper Lippert-Rasmussen, "Respect and Discrimination," this volume.

73 Larry Alexander, "Pursuing Good – Indirectly," *Ethics* 95, no. 2 (1985): 315.

with the agent-centered version of his coauthor, Michael Moore, in their authoritative *Stanford Encyclopedia of Philosophy* entry.[74] While Moore's deontology focuses on duties and on the agency of those they bind, cashing out such agency partly in terms of intentions, Larry focuses on the notion of using another, construed not intentionally but causally. In Larry's view, one may impermissibly use another even if one does not intend to do so and even if one does not know that one will do so as a causal means of achieving an end.

In her contribution to this volume, Kim Ferzan develops and extends the means principle in the service of work to which she and Larry are continuing coauthors, arguing that it allows third parties to rescue those whose deaths would prevent a great many more deaths.[75] As she maintains, if those whose lives would be saved are not entitled to be shielded from death by another's sacrifice, then there can be no wrong in saving the one at the loss of many, even if the one would not otherwise have sought to remove himself from the position in which his death would have had consequential advantages. Richard Arneson, however, raises doubts about the independent defensibility and mutual compatibility of the tenets that define the moral ontology that Larry has defended and that Ferzan here expands. He takes issue with Larry's construal of the means principle, the degree to which Larry might be thought to flirt with its absolutism, and the application of the means principle to property and the use of natural resources.[76] In Arneson's view, Larry elevates the moral problems inherent in deontology to the status of dilemmas when there are reasoned bases for thinking that they are not intractable.

Among such problems are those that confront deontologists who deny that deontological constraints are absolute. Such "threshold deontologists" construe categorical maxims as overridable when the consequences of abiding by them would be catastrophic. Larry feels the pull of threshold deontology and, for this reason, he does not construe his means principle as absolute. But he has been unable to resist throwing down the gauntlet to anyone who invokes consequentially specified thresholds as means of releasing actors from consequentially blind obligations; for he is convinced that, if pressed, they must admit that their thresholds are inevitably ad hoc and arbitrary. Larry's gauntlet is taken up in this volume not only by Richard Arneson, but also by Michael Moore and Kevin Cole. Michael Moore argues that Larry's charge of arbitrariness rests on a mistake about how deontological maxims win out against consequential calculations

74 Larry Alexander and Michael S. Moore, "Deontology," in *The Stanford Encyclopedia of Philosophy*, ed. Edward N. Zalta (Stanford: Metaphysics Research Lab, Center for the Study of Language and Information, Stanford University, 2007).

75 Kimberly Kessler Ferzan, "The Means Principle and Optimific Wrongs," this volume.

76 Richard Arneson, "Deontology's Travails," this volume.

in below-threshold circumstances.[77] As he insists, once one understands that the most stringent obligation prevails below the threshold, one can appreciate that the same mechanism is at work at and above the threshold, making the notion of a threshold non-alien to a properly construed deontological account. Kevin Cole agrees but offers a distinctly different argument in support of the thesis that Larry's charge of arbitrariness is not fatal to a defensible theory of threshold deontology.[78] He then brings this volume full circle, arguing that Larry ought to take seriously the ways in which threshold deontology can be invoked to insulate his retributive theory of punishment from the concerns raised by those whose contributions comprise Part I of the volume. The volume thus ends where it begins – connecting Larry's moral philosophy to his theory of criminal justice in a manner that fittingly captures the systematic interconnectivity of Larry's work across the fields to which he has contributed.

1.4 CONCLUSION

Larry has much about which to be proud. His intellectual career is characterized by an unflagging dedication to following arguments where they take him, to defending conclusions however unpopular they may be, and to pushing others to do the same. These strengths are on display in the final chapter of this volume in which Larry responds with his characteristic enthusiasm to the contributions of colleagues who have honored his work by vigorously probing its merits.[79] Larry's generosity in sharing his ideas with others and in taking the lessons of others' work to heart has made him a prized coauthor of a veritable "who's who" in the legal academy, and numerous scholars credit him with having "made their careers" through his generous coauthorship and his fierce championship of their talents.

In my own case, Larry has been a bottomless well of intellectual inspiration. Indeed, I recall a point well into my career when I wondered if I would ever write an article that wasn't provoked by some recent piece by Larry. His invitations to unpack vexing concepts within criminal law, jurisprudence, and moral philosophy have been so tantalizing, so seductive, so intuition challenging, that I have given myself over time and again to their pursuit. Perhaps I would have found interesting things to write about had I never succumbed to the temptation to engage with Larry's puzzles, paradoxes and perplexities, but the projects to which my scholarly life has been devoted have been a succession of tributes to Larry's genius and intellectual generosity.

77 Michael S. Moore, "The Rationality of Threshold Deontology," this volume.

78 Kevin Cole, "Real-World Criminal Law and the Norm Against Punishing the Innocent: Two Cheers for Threshold Deontology," this volume.

79 Larry Alexander, "Appreciation and Responses," this volume.

Larry smiles warmly and shrugs in affable embarrassment when friends and admirers laud his life's work. It is not, he insists, the source of his greatest pride. Instead, he takes his greatest accomplishments to be his very accomplished children, who themselves have found partners of equal ambition and success. Jenny is a high-profile corporate lawyer in Buffalo, whose husband, Raj, is a bold entrepreneur in the hospitality industry. David is a successful radiologist in Seattle, whose wife, Hitomi, is an in-demand movie translator. And Jonathan is a neuroscience postdoctoral fellow at Tufts, whose impressive record gives him good reason to aspire to success within the academy that matches his father's. While Larry has found grace in the purposeful lives of his children and the enormous love they bear for him, it is a grace forged, in part, on the anvil of heartache. For his beloved first grandchild, Tej, was the tragic victim of a congenital heart defect upon which modern medicine exhausted its miracles. Today, the memory of this precious child is indelibly etched into his being, but with Elaine and their children he now finds joy in their four thriving grandchildren – Simran, Sejal, Kai, and Luka – who are themselves exhibiting all of the characteristic energy and purpose that is their legacy. There will likely be more grandchildren to come in the years ahead; and there will be great-grandchildren to follow in the generation thereafter. May they all know, through the pages of this book and the stories they are told, that determination, drive, courage, curiosity, and ingenuity are the gifts of their heritage.

PART I

Puzzles in Criminal Law

2

Kinds of Punishment

*Douglas Husak**

2.1 INTRODUCTION

I set myself a challenge when searching for a topic to contribute to this much-deserved Festschrift for my long-time friend Larry Alexander. I struggled to identify an important issue in the philosophy of criminal law about which Alexander had *not* written. Anyone familiar with Alexander's body of work could have anticipated that this challenge would be formidable. His work is not only voluminous, but also comprehensive and systematic. Even if Alexander has not addressed a particular issue explicitly, it should not be too difficult to predict what he would say about it. The only topic I was able to identify involves an issue about which virtually no contemporary philosopher of criminal law has written.[1] An issue that satisfies this description (viz., is seemingly important but currently neglected by penal theorists) should lead philosophers to ponder why so little attention has been paid to it. If the following arguments are sound, the answer is evident: The problem has not been discussed because theorists who stress the centrality of desert to questions in the philosophy of criminal law turn out to have very little to say about it. Alexander himself might even concur with my subsequent observations. I would welcome this outcome on the present occasion, inasmuch as Alexander and I have spent too much time disagreeing and too little time emphasizing our many points of agreement.

2.2 THE PROBLEM AND A LARGER THEORETICAL CONTEXT

Philosophers of criminal law who work within the retributive tradition have focused on the question of whether and how state punishment is justified. This fixation

* Thanks to Leora Katz and to members of the conference in tribute to Larry Alexander for helpful comments on earlier drafts.

[1] I say virtually no *contemporary* theorist seems to be working on this topic. As the dates in several of my footnotes attest, there was a flurry of activity about modes of punishment in the 1980s and 1990s.

is perfectly sensible; the fundamental problem remains unresolved. These penal theorists have said relatively little, however, about the *kinds* or *modes* or *types* of punishment (I will use these terms interchangeably) that should be utilized. Contemporary states execute, imprison, fine, place on probation, conditionally discharge, caution, and do a great deal more to the persons they convict.[2] What general principles govern how states should choose between the foregoing responses to culpable wrongdoing – or select an altogether different type of sanction?[3] If my subsequent reasoning is sound, it is easy to understand why retributivists like Alexander have tended to neglect this issue. They have neglected it because they have little to contribute to its resolution.[4] Since I regard some version of retributivism as the dominant school of thought among contemporary penal theorists, it should not be surprising that legal philosophers have had so little to say about the modes of punishment to prefer. In what follows, I will support this conclusion and discuss a few of the somewhat controversial positions on which it rests. I hope to make some headway on this topic by defending what I call the "deferential view about kinds of punishment" (or "deferential view" for short).

Before proceeding, I hasten to add that the relative lack of input from retributivists on this matter has not resulted in a windfall of influence for philosophers who lean towards consequentialism. Instead, contemporary sentencing policy seems to have become untethered from *any* respectable normative theory. Perhaps the actual practice of punishment has never been especially responsive to scholarly thought. It is well known that sentences in the real world almost always result from negotiated pleas, so no one should expect them to conform to abstract principles. But the sentencing guidelines that proliferated in the 1980s at least represented an (albeit crude and imperfect) *attempt* by legal philosophers to implement a normative theory. These guidelines, however, are now discretionary under federal law, and nothing coherent has emerged to replace them. The major sentencing innovations of the past quarter century – mandatory minimums, three-strike laws, and life sentences without parole, for example – are not evidence that sentencing policy has become increasingly consequentialist, but that sentencing policy adheres to no intelligible theory at all.[5] Although they uniformly complain that punishments are too severe,

2 See Nora V. Demleitner, "Types of Punishment," in *The Oxford Handbook of Criminal Law*, ed. Markus D. Dubber and Tatjana Hörnle (New York: Oxford University Press, 2014), 941.

3 Some of the most innovative and creative "punishments" are imposed on corporations pursuant to deferred prosecution agreements. See Brandon L. Garrett, *Too Big to Jail* (Cambridge, MA: Harvard University Press, 2014). Some of these innovations might be replicated when natural persons are punished.

4 As I will contend, the only nontrivial principle clearly derived from (most versions of) retributivism itself requires parity in sentencing.

5 See Michael Tonry, *Sentencing Fragments* (New York: Oxford University Press, 2016).

legal philosophers may never have played a less significant role in shaping sentencing policy in the halls of criminal justice.

Even though I hope the topic is inherently interesting and practically important on its own merits, my inquiry into modes of punishment is animated by three larger philosophical concerns. First, my discussion helps to decide *how much* of a comprehensive theory of punishment can be derived from principles of desert.[6] A comprehensive theory, I assume, would address all of the familiar normative questions about punishment: whether, whom, and how much to punish.[7] In addition, a comprehensive theory would have implications for the particular kind(s) of punishment that should be utilized. Is retributivism comprehensive in this sense? Can retributivists say a great deal, or can they say almost nothing about this matter? I will argue in favor of the latter answer.

Second, focusing on a neglected topic might provide a novel basis for adjudicating between different punitive schools. As far as I am aware, no legal philosopher has made an extended effort to assess whether retributivist or consequentialist traditions offer a more plausible basis for choosing the types of punishment to inflict. Still, I am sure that the particular problem on which I focus would generally be thought to be more difficult for retributivists than for consequentialists. Theorists who work in the latter tradition seemingly have a more straightforward response to my question: We should impose whatever modes of punishment produce the best outcomes. Admittedly, consequentialists disagree about which outcomes the criminal justice system should pursue and how to prioritize them. They also remain uncertain about how to achieve whatever results they deem to be optimal. Still, consequentialists have *some* idea of how to proceed in answering these questions. They have a research program in which a few answers are likely to be found. Does this apparent fact provide a reason to prefer their normative framework to that of their rivals? We cannot decide unless we know the parallel response from retributivists. Can they offer a distinctive approach to this issue? I will conclude that retributivists should decide what modes of punishment to impose in much the same way as consequentialists. But I deny that this conclusion gives us much of a reason to prefer their tradition. Instead, it shows only that retributivism is not comprehensive in the sense already explained. No competitive theory, including retributivism, can hope to match consequentialism in its scope and simplicity.

6 See Douglas Husak, "What Do Criminals Deserve?" in *Legal, Moral, and Metaphysical Truths: The Philosophy of Michael S. Moore*, ed. Kimberly Kessler Ferzan and Stephen J. Morse (New York: Oxford University Press, 2016), 49.

7 For an argument that retributivism must be supplemented by independent considerations to decide how to sentence defendants convicted of multiple offenses at one time, see Michael Tonry, "Solving the Multiple Offense Paradox," in *Sentencing for Multiple Crimes*, ed. Jan de Keijser, Julian V. Roberts, and Jesper Ryberg (New York: Oxford University Press, 2017).

Third, part of the rationale for identifying alternative kinds of punishment is that voices are increasingly raised against our heavy reliance on *incarceration*. Although few of these criticisms are new,[8] dissatisfaction with our prison system has grown along all points of the political spectrum, and is especially vehement in what has come to be characterized as our era of *mass incarceration*. Inasmuch as a consensus has emerged that the status quo is problematic, the time is ripe to evaluate alternatives to it. I will conclude that retributivists are unlikely to have anything distinctive to contribute in reducing the phenomenon of mass incarceration by devising alternatives to imprisonment.

My inquiry implicates these three larger philosophical themes. Clearly, however, none can be pursued without understanding what makes a punitive theory *retributive*.[9] In-house quarrels begin here. Foes of the retributive tradition tend to provide an implausible characterization of this school of thought in order to try to make their target more vulnerable.[10] I hope to evade semantic problems by offering a definition that is broad and vague by design. By a *retributive* theory, I mean any attempt to justify punishment that affords a central role to *desert*.[11] Retributivists can and do disagree over any number of questions about desert. Most notably, they disagree over the exact part it plays in the justification of punishment. But they have no business characterizing themselves as retributivists unless the role they afford to desert is somehow indispensable to their justification. As might be anticipated, however, desert plays a more central role in some particular accounts than in others. Thus, I hold the somewhat novel position that whether a theory qualifies as retributive turns out to be a matter of degree – some theories are *more* or *less* retributive than others. What makes a theory of punishment more retributive than another is not that it generally recommends more severe sentences, but that it affords a more central role to desert in identifying what these sentences should be.

What exact role *should* be assigned to desert? Radically distinct answers have been given, each of which may have different implications for the modes of punishment that are acceptable. Henceforth, I assume that retributivists endorse a *principle of proportionality*. The precise formulation of this principle is crucial for any number of controversies that may be relevant to the present inquiry. Although nothing in

[8] See, for example, Francis T. Cullen, Cheryl Lero Johnson, and Daniel S. Nagin, "Prisons Do Not Reduce Recidivism," *Prison Journal* 91, no. 3 suppl. (July 19, 2011).

[9] If communicative or expressivist theories qualify as versions of retributivism, one might derive additional implications for the kinds of punishment to impose. Such theorists might object to incarceration, for example, because it fails to ensure/express/communicate in the right way.

[10] See Douglas Husak, "Retributivism in Extremis," *Law and Philosophy* 32, no. 1 (2013): 3–31.

[11] "Retributivism without *desert*...is like *Hamlet* without the Prince of Denmark," Hugo Bedau, "Retribution and the Theory of Punishment," *Journal of Philosophy* 75, no. 11 (1978): 608 (emphasis in original).

their *definition* requires that the following version be accepted, the vast majority of retributivists appeal to desert and proportionality to help decide *how much* a culpable wrongdoer should be punished.[12] As I construe it, the principle of proportionality requires (*ceteris paribus*) that *the severity of the punishment should be a function of the seriousness of the offense*. As so understood, this principle entails parity in sentencing: Defendants who commit equally serious offenses should (*ceteris paribus*) be given equally severe punishments.[13] When all other things are equal, a culpable wrongdoer is treated contrary to her desert if the severity of her punishment deviates from the foregoing requirement.[14] To apply this principle, I make an additional (and heroic) assumption: Retributivists can (somehow) specify the quantum of punishment an offender deserves. To simplify (or, more candidly, to *over*simplify), I will refer to this quantum as Q.[15] Proportionality requires that all criminals who have committed offenses of comparable seriousness should presumptively receive a sentence of severity Q. Attempts to identify modes of punishment acceptable to retributivists must satisfy this constraint.

2.3 THE DEFERENTIAL VIEW

Armed with the foregoing presuppositions and informed by the larger theoretical context, I now describe what I believe to be the most plausible way retributivists should approach my central problem, that is, to specify the modes of punishment to be imposed on offenders. I call this position the "deferential view." If it is correct, the answer to my question turns out to be uninformative. Once the amount of punishment a culpable wrongdoer deserves (Q) has somehow been specified, retributivists who adopt the deferential view have almost nothing further to say about the particular form it should take. The deferential view holds the latter issue to be largely a matter of indifference, as long as each of the several possible options implements a principle of parity by treating each offender as she deserves. Particular defendants may indeed receive differing kinds of punishment, but these modes must be comparable in severity if each of the persons on whom they are imposed has committed an equally serious crime. If parity can somehow be established between the many

[12] Andrew von Hirsch expresses what I take to be conventional wisdom in writing: "The principle of proportionality addresses the *severity* of penalties, not their particular mode." See Andrew von Hirsch, *Censure and Sanctions* (Oxford: Clarendon Press, 1993), 5.

[13] See Andrew von Hirsch, *Past or Future Crimes?* (New Brunswick: Rutgers University Press, 1987).

[14] Despite subtle variations in its formulation, a principle of proportionality may come close to qualifying as a rock-bottom foundation of retributivist sentencing theory. Nonetheless, it should be mentioned that many of the recent sentencing innovations mentioned in Section 2.2 are obvious violations of it. As I have indicated, contemporary sentencing policy conforms to no intelligible theory at all.

[15] For further thoughts, see Douglas Husak, "The Metric of Punishment Severity" (forthcoming).

alternative kinds of available punishments, retributivists have almost no basis to prefer one to another.[16] The only nontrivial constraint that derives from retributivism itself is that each mode must impose Q, the amount the offender deserves.

An (imperfect) analogy with a theory of deserved remuneration may help to illustrate the deferential view. Suppose we have a set of principles that somehow allow us to describe how much remuneration (call it R) a person deserves for performing a particular task in a given circumstance. The kind of currency in which R should be tendered is presumably a matter of indifference. The only nontrivial requirement is that R must have *value*, and no one would expect the theory of compensation itself to specify whether this value should be expressed in Israeli shekels, sheep, Cambodian riels, olive oil, or gold bullion. Whatever normative considerations are brought to bear on the mode of currency to prefer cannot be derived from the general theory of remuneration itself. Deserved punishment is relevantly similar. The deferential view indicates that as long as each mode of punishment inflicts Q – the quantum the offender deserves – retributivists lack the resources to identify the particular mode it should take.

The deferential view, then, cedes questions about modes of punishment almost entirely to consequentialists. The kind of sanction to be used in a particular case is to be decided by identifying what is best at achieving the goals of punishment. As I have indicated, consequentialists are bound to differ over what the exact goals of punishment are and how to prioritize them when they cannot all be realized. Obviously, these disputes are not easily resolved – but if agreement can be reached about these matters, the task of settling on the kind of sanction to prefer (assuming each imposes Q) requires an expertise in empirical matters beyond the ken of most legal philosophers.[17] Retributivists should defer to social scientists and criminologists to achieve whatever objectives are worthwhile, while ensuring that offenders are given the severity of the punishment they deserve.

Let me simply mention three of the kinds of proposals defended by consequentialists that should be acceptable to retributivists who subscribe to the deferential view. Suppose two defendants are identical in their desert, but differ in that one poses a greater risk of reoffending. It would be sensible to inflict a sanction that more closely supervises and thus better incapacitates the offender who creates the greater

[16] I put aside the immense difficulties in showing that parity obtains when defendants are sentenced to the *same* mode of punishment. For a discussion of this difficulty in the context of imprisonment, see E.A.C. Raaijmakers, "The Subjectively Experienced Severity of Imprisonment: Determinants and Consequences" (forthcoming).

[17] Some legal philosophers apparently believe that the difficulty in deciding what kind of punishment to inflict places the very viability of punishment itself in doubt. See Benjamin L. Apt, "Do We Know How to Punish?" *New Criminal Law Review: An International and Interdisciplinary Journal* 19, no. 3 (2016): 437–72.

risk. Or suppose the prospects for rehabilitation are much greater for one defendant than for another. Eligibility for competitive programs that reform offenders might be governed by the likelihood of future success. Finally, suppose some of those who engage in a given kind of offense (such as domestic violence) are fueled by alcohol while others are not. As long as the former abstains from drinking, the problem is unlikely to be repeated. In light of this difference, why inflict the same mode of punishment on both? Again, I stress that retributivists should allow such factors to influence the choice of a mode of punishment *only* if each levies a punishment of severity Q.[18] Although legal philosophers tend to object when sentencing authorities appeal to factors such as age, employment history, health, family background, income, drug use and the like, their opposition should be muted if they could be convinced that a particular sentence that is affected by these variables is equal in severity to a sentence that is not. Of course, the usefulness of these factors is wholly dependent on the reliability of the empirical evidence that given modes of punishment are more or less effective in achieving their ends.[19] So-called common sense about the future effects of given responses should give way to careful empirical analysis.[20] Even the effectiveness of imprisonment itself should not be taken for granted.[21]

As I have indicated, I think the deferential view should be accepted. My rudimentary sketch of it so far, however, is clearly inadequate; the deferential view requires refinement through amendment or clarification. Although there may be no *practical* significance to whether we construe these refinements as amendments or as clarifications, the difference is important for the first of the larger *theoretical* concerns that animate my inquiry, that is, for the purpose of deciding how much of a comprehensive theory of punishment can be derived from retributivist principles. In indicating that retributivists are indifferent about the kinds of punishment the state should be permitted to impose as long as each inflicts Q, I mean only that the considerations *internal to their theory* give them no ground to prefer one to another. But any sensible retributivist will accept a number of *independent* moral principles that preclude some kinds of punishment. These principles are independent of retributivism in that they are immaterial to what offenders deserve. Even if a given number of lashes, for example, is equivalent in severity to a given monetary fine

18 See A.E. Bottoms, "The Concept of Intermediate Sanctions and Its Relevance for the Probation Service," in *The Criminal Justice System: A Central Role for the Probation Service*, ed. Roger Shaw and Kevin Haines (Cambridge: Cambridge University Press, 1989), 84.

19 The quality of empirical evidence keeps improving. See Francis T. Cullen, "Rehabilitation: Beyond Nothing Works," *Crime and Justice* 42, no. 1 (2013): 299.

20 For example, for a sophisticated analysis of how sex-offender registries affect rates of recidivism, see J.J. Prescott, "Portmanteau Ascendant: Post-Release Regulations and Sex Offender Recidivism," *Connecticut Law Review* 48, no. 4 (2016): 1053–78.

21 Peter N. Salib, "Why Prison? An Economic Critique," *Berkeley Journal of Criminal Law* 22, no. 2 (2017): 111.

("twenty lashes or fifty dollars"), no one (retributivist or otherwise) should profess to lack a basis to choose between them. Conceptions of human dignity, I assume, provide a strong rationale to rule out corporal punishments, e.g., flogging, branding, amputating, tarring and feathering, castration, drawing and quartering, stoning, and the like. And appeals to human dignity preclude more than corporal punishments; some punishments currently in place in the United States are probably ruled out as well. For example, thousands of prisoners today are held in solitary confinement, and thousands more have been sentenced to life imprisonment without the possibility of parole. In addition, the need to preserve dignity provides the best explanation of the fate of various shaming sanctions. Calls to replace more conventional modes of punishment with devices to embarrass and humiliate offenders enjoyed a period of academic respectability in the United States at the end of the twentieth century. Advocates of shaming sanctions contended that they were more effective and less expensive than imprisonment.[22] Even if their allegations were correct – which was seldom conceded – critics quickly denounced shaming sanctions as too degrading for a liberal society. It is hard to see how any of these methods of punishing offenders respects their dignity.

The unresolved theoretical question is whether the conception of human dignity that precludes these kinds of punishment is inherent in or extrinsic to the retributive tradition itself. Either answer has plausibility. If the former, their inclusion should be deemed a clarification of their theory: No person deserves to be treated in a manner that violates her dignity. If the latter, their inclusion should be deemed an amendment to their theory: Despite their compatibility with desert, respect for dignity rules out these kinds of punishment. Quite a few side-constraints to given theories can be conceptualized either way: as principles emanating from within the theory, or as considerations drawn from outside of it. Regardless of whether dignity is construed as internal or external to retributivism itself, however, it is clear that it must be preserved because it provides an important source of limitations to the kinds of punishment to be allowed. The deferential view cannot be so deferential that it fails to countenance these normative considerations.

Although the exact theoretical status of dignity may be debatable, it is beyond dispute that a number of possible responses to culpable wrongdoers *are* precluded by retributivism itself. Whether these objectionable practices should be categorized as *kinds* of punishment, however, is open to debate. For instance, punishing persons known not to be guilty of the charge is placed off the table by retributivists. Examples include not only cases of telishment – the punishment of a suspect known by the

[22] Dan M. Kahan once defended (but subsequently denounced) shaming sanctions, but eventually gave them up. For his earlier thoughts, see Dan M. Kahan, "What Do Alternative Sanctions Mean?" *University of Chicago Law Review* 63, no. 2 (1996): 591–653.

authorities (but not by the general public) to be innocent in order to deter future wrongdoing. Additional examples include *vicarious* and *collective* punishments. The former punishes one individual, typically a friend or family member, in order to deter a perpetrator, who often is difficult to apprehend. The latter punishes each member of a group, some or most of whom have not been guilty of the offense, in order to deter the behavior of one or more members of that group. Each of these clearly unjust practices has long been cited by retributivists as counterexamples to consequentialism, which is said to be committed to them in principle. Whether or not consequentialists can manage to evade the force of these apparent instances of *reductio*, my claim here is that retributivism itself contains the resources to oppose these unjust penal practices.

It is equally clear, however, that quite a few morally relevant considerations limit the types of punishment to impose even though they are almost certainly *extrinsic* to retributivism. Suppose two kinds of punishment each impose Q and thus treat offenders as they deserve. If the first is much more expensive to taxpayers than the second, it would be ludicrous to hold that anyone (retributivist or otherwise) must have no preference for one over the other. The obvious preference for the less costly option necessitates resorting to principles outside of the retributive theory. As long as we agree that these considerations are relevant, there may be little practical urgency to locate them inside or outside of the theory itself. The important point is that it is no objection to retributivism that it needs to be supplemented by nondesert considerations.

Do other principles that are *internal* to retributivism influence the mode of punishment to prefer? It might be suspected that the details of *how* retributivists succeed in justifying punishment have implications for this topic, but I am dubious. Retributivists frequently posit an intuitive *fittingness* or *appropriateness* between culpable wrongdoing and state punishment. To this point, I am in accord. Historically, however, some retributivists have gone further and claimed to intuit a similar fittingness between the kind of offense committed and the type of response deserved. Presumably, the *lex talionis* is meant to describe such a relation between crime and punishment: Those who wrongfully maim should be maimed, and those who wrongfully kill should be killed.[23] But why? What apart from intuitions supports the *lex talonis* as construed literally? Sometimes the answer invokes deterrence. In cases in which the rationale underlying the prohibited conduct may not be apparent, this idea could have some merit. If an offender is unclear over what is objectionable about, say, bullying, the most productive way to instruct him might be to bully him in turn. "Let's see how you like it!" Still, the general idea that the particular

[23] See Immanuel Kant, *Metaphysical Elements of Justice*, trans. John Ladd (Indianapolis: Bobbs-Merrill, 1965), 101.

crime perpetrated suggests a specific kind of punitive response is widely discredited as barbaric; I am unaware of a single contemporary legal philosopher who accepts the *lex talionis*. The raping of rapists is again precluded by principles that probably are independent of retributivism itself, even if one feels some intuitive pull to the suggestion that the nature of the crime committed has implications for the mode of punishment that should be imposed.

Some philosophers have sought to provide an account of why offenders are deserving of punishment that does not rely solely on intuitions of fittingness.[24] Arguably, these efforts might be thought to have implications for my project of identifying the mode of punishment to inflict. Suppose, for example, that some or all punishments are deserved because culpable wrongdoers breach a duty of fair play. Perhaps they skew the balance of benefits and burdens by claiming a liberty to perform an act they deny to others and thus incur a debt that needs to be repaid.[25] If any such account explains why some or all wrongdoers deserve to be punished, it might seem appropriate to deprive them of the very good they wrongly claim: liberty. One need not adhere to a literal *lex talionis* to appreciate that the general kind of good taken by freeriders is a candidate for the kind of good that should be taken from them in turn. Something akin to imprisonment may seem to be a natural response to the excess liberty allegedly claimed by those who violate their duty of fair play. On closer inspection, however, any such connection between retributivism and imprisonment seems untenable. First and more generally, benefits-and-burdens theories encounter a multitude of objections. Second and more to the point, *any* deprivation that qualifies as a mode of punishment would seem to involve a diminution of liberty; imprisonment itself has no special status according to fair-play theories.[26] Once again, it is hard to see how a particular version of retributivism has implications for the kind of punishment that should be utilized.

The deferential view is attractive unless we can salvage one of the foregoing attempts to derive a mode of punishment from retributive principles. If the deferential view (as suitably clarified or amended) is correct, retributivists should be encouraged to help themselves to the empirical research of social scientists about what

[24] Michael Moore defends the link between culpable wrongdoing and punishment by relying on the force of first-person retributive emotions. See Michael Moore, *Placing Blame* (New York: Oxford University Press, 1997), 104.

[25] Countless versions of this basic position have been defended. Most recently, see Peter Westen, "Retributive Desert and Fair Play," in *Legal, Moral, and Metaphysical Truths: The Philosophy of Michael S. Moore*, ed. Kimberly Kessler Ferzan and Stephen J. Morse (New York: Oxford University Press, 2016), 63n6.

[26] According to Westen, "the degree of suffering that a culpable malefactor deserves is the degree of well-being at society's hands that he previously enjoyed." Ibid., 77. This account might assist us to identify (what I have called) Q, but cannot help in specifying the *mode* that Q should take.

kinds of punishment to impose. Consequentialists prefer those modes that *work*, and have expended quite a bit of effort to identify the particular types of punishment that satisfy this criterion. Retributivists should be happy to borrow their accumulated wisdom. Just as consequentialists have a normative basis to prefer the less expensive mode of punishment, retributivists have a normative basis to prefer the more effective mode. The crucial difference between retributive and consequentialist theories is not that the former is wholly unconcerned about results such as crime reduction, but instead is that the concern about results such as crime reduction among retributivists derives from outside of their theory itself. What consequentialists tend to identify as the objective or goal of their theory is conceptualized by retributivists as a beneficial side-effect. Thus, it is false to accuse retributivists of not caring whether the punishments they inflict are effective. What *is* true is that the source of their caring is extrinsic to their theory.

2.4 THE NATURE OF PUNISHMENT

As I have indicated, I think the deferential view describes how retributivists should decide what modes of punishment to impose. But neither it nor its competitors can be assessed without taking a position on several contested questions in criminal theory. While many of these issues are familiar and have attracted a great deal of critical discussion, others are barely discussed by philosophers who write about punishment. In what follows, I mention just one such controversy and discuss how it bears on my central topic. Although I believe that the outlines of an acceptable position on this question are clear, I fear that the details of a more complete account are not. Unless these matters can be settled – which I do not pretend to accomplish here – we should remain agnostic about whether to accept the deferential view and be less sure of how to proceed in specifying the kinds of punishment retributivists should allow.

Any attempt to choose between several possible modes of punishment must be confident that each of the options on the table is indeed an instance of it. If we disagree about what punishment *is*, it is all but inevitable that we will differ about what *kinds* to prefer. To take an extreme example, would exile to a beautiful island where culpable wrongdoers are well treated be a viable candidate, as long as those individuals who remain behind are assured that those who are exiled are leading a terrible life? To answer such questions, one would *think* we must decide whether a particular response should be conceptualized as a kind of punishment in the first place. But matters are not quite so straightforward. Those who contend that culpable wrongdoers should be exiled to the beautiful island might admit that it is not really a mode of punishment, but proceed to argue that the optimal response to culpable wrongdoers is not to *punish* them at all. The long-standing fear is that questions are begged because punishment is defined so that only retributivists can suppose it is ever justified.

Notwithstanding this fear, I contend that any response we should countenance as a form of punishment involves an intentional deprivation intended to express censure. Unless a response constitutes a deprivation – or what theorists sometimes call "hard treatment" – we should not categorize it as punitive. If I am correct, the foregoing example of exile to a beautiful island (colorfully described as "funishment") is simply not a mode of punishment and should not be included among our options unless we are prepared to abandon punishment altogether.[27] In addition, according to my preferred definition, a response is not punitive unless it expresses condemnation and is designed to stigmatize. In the absence of this latter feature, an account of punishment would be wildly overinclusive. We could not distinguish a tax (which rarely is punitive) from a genuine punishment unless the latter were used to censure the person on whom it is imposed. And we could not distinguish a requirement to pay damages in tort (which is usually compensatory) from a genuine punishment.[28] This last point is especially significant, since a number of theorists propose that compensatory schemes should replace conventional modes of punishment whenever defendants are solvent.[29] Even if their proposal has merit, it is best interpreted as a plan to abolish punishment, albeit selectively.

In any event, a response does not amount to a punishment because it *happens* to deprive and to censure. Real punishments are *intended* to have these effects. Thus, we cannot categorize particular responses to wrongdoing as punitive or nonpunitive without knowing the intentions of those who impose them. This latter requirement has always proved difficult to apply. The most widely discussed problem is to divine the mental states of legislators, a problem that is magnified by the incentives to disguise a response as nonpunitive in order to circumvent the procedural protections that surround the criminal process. Other problems, however, are equally worrisome. If intentions are crucial in determining whether a response is punitive, we must decide *whose* intentions are relevant. This determination is simple, for example, when a parent punishes his child. But criminal justice is administered by multiple agents who occupy distinct roles and frequently disagree. In deciding whether a sanction is punitive, should we defer to the intentions of legislators who enact the statute, to the police and prosecutors who enforce it, or to the judges who sentence offenders – or perhaps to some combination of these

27 See Saul Smilansky, "Hard Determinism and Punishment: A Practical *Reductio*," *Law and Philosophy* 30, no. 3 (2011): 353–67.

28 Some theoretical foundation is needed for the tort/crime distinction. See the various positions in Matthew Dyson, ed., *Comparing Tort and Crime* (Cambridge: Cambridge University Press, 2015).

29 See Richard A. Posner, "An Economic Theory of the Criminal Law," *Columbia Law Review* 85, no. 6 (1985): 1204–5. I neglect the "kicker" some economists include in their account of penal sanctions.

officials? And what should we say when the intentions of whomever we identify as the relevant actors are mixed – as is likely to be true in a great many cases? To cite just two of many troublesome kinds of examples, if a legislator enacts a drug offense because she believes that those who breach it should receive treatment, but a judge sentences offenders because she is convinced they deserve retribution, are the defendants actually punished? Or suppose one judge sentences an offender to prison because of her belief in desert and another imposes the same sentence for purposes of public protection. Is only the first but not the second defendant really punished? Similar sorts of hard cases could be multiplied indefinitely. Efforts to decide whether two offenders receive an equally severe punishment Q could be derailed at the outset if our understanding of punishment entailed that only one but not the other defendant is actually punished when those who play a role in their sentencing have different intentions.

Despite the enormity of these difficulties, I put them aside. If we utilize my preferred definition, the kinds of punishment available to the state turn out to be vast, and are not restricted to the familiar modes mentioned in Section 2.2. We should also include the stigmatizing hardships that often are imposed as *collateral consequences* of some other punishment: disqualifications from various privileges such as government benefits, public housing, gun ownership, jury duty, foreign travel, voting, and a wide array of others.[30] Although some of these collateral consequences are reserved for a particular kind of offense, such as a registration requirement for sexual predators, it is conceivable that a public registry could be compiled for *all* perpetrators. A scholarly debate has emerged over whether or not some or all of these collateral consequences are a part of the "real" punishment offenders suffer.[31] This determination has obvious practical significance. For example, does the subsequent imposition of any of these collateral consequences ever violate constitutional rules precluding *ex post facto* punishments? But however these controversies are settled, I see no debate about whether these sanctions *can* be genuine punishments. If the intention to impose any of the foregoing stigmatizing deprivations by the relevant party is sufficiently clear, there should be no room for doubt. Conceivably, a culpable wrongdoer *could* be sentenced to surrender his gun, forfeit his food stamps, or relinquish his college scholarship, just as surely as he could be sentenced to three months in prison. He might even be sentenced to perform or abstain from some activity that is beneficial to him in the long run, even though he dislikes it at the time it is required.[32]

30 See Zack Hoskins, *Collateral Restrictions* (New York: Oxford University Press, forthcoming).

31 See Sandra J. Mayson, "Collateral Consequences and the Preventive State," *Notre Dame Law Review* 91, no. 1 (2015): 301–62.

32 See David Birks, "Paternalistic Punishment" (forthcoming).

For a sanction to qualify as an uncontroversial instance of punishment, however, I assume it not only must be imposed with the *intention* to censure, it also must *succeed* (or at least stand a reasonable prospect of succeeding) in stigmatizing. If this assumption is correct, new difficulties in categorizing a sanction as punitive are presented. If an authority believes a shaved head is a badge of disgrace, but almost all persons whose heads are shaved regard it with indifference, does the response constitute a punishment? This question does not simply involve persons whose beliefs are unconventional or idiosyncratic. Even when the relevant authorities have a punitive intent, entire groups within a single jurisdiction may tend to regard given kinds of treatment as not especially stigmatizing. Theorists need to decide not simply whether these treatments are effective in accomplishing whatever their objectives may be, but also whether they amount to punishments at all.

Just as controversial, I believe, are responses which are plausibly conceptualized as an *alternative to* punishment rather than as a *kind* of punishment. Although the sentence of punishment to a beautiful desert island is only the product of a fertile philosophical imagination, many existing ways to respond to offenders illustrate the same difficulty. I will mention only two. First, consider the several models of *therapeutic justice* that have proliferated in the past few decades. Various specialty courts – the most well known of which are *drug* courts – typically make punitive sanctions contingent upon the failure to complete a rehabilitative program. Some enthusiasts of drug courts conceptualize the treatment regimens they mandate as a kind of punishment rather than an alternative to it, but the question is hardly settled.[33] Second, consider the models of *restorative justice* that have actually been implemented around the world. Some of the most vocal advocates of restorative justice seemingly favor the *abolition* of punishment, and believe the responses they propose to substitute are preferable to anything correctly described as punitive.[34] Other theorists, however, admit that restorative programs *do* impose punishments, but regard them as more productive and humane than the unenlightened modes they would replace.[35] Once again, more than terminology is at stake in how these questions are answered. Are rehabilitation and restorative justice genuine punitive options? I see no prospect of resolving this uncertainty without a clear understanding of the nature of punishment itself. According to my definition, we cannot decide

[33] See Douglas Husak, "Retributivism, Proportionality, and the Challenge of the Drug Court Movement," in *Retributivism Has a Past. Has It a Future?*, ed. Michael Tonry (New York: Oxford University Press, 2011), 214.

[34] If crime is conceptualized as a social problem to be solved, the best response may not be to impose a stigmatizing deprivation (i.e., to punish) the offender at all. See John Braithwaite and Philip Pettit, *Not Just Deserts* (Oxford: Clarendon Press, 1990).

[35] For discussion, see Antony Duff, "Restoration and Retribution," in *Restorative Justice and Criminal Justice: Competing or Reconcilable Paradigms*, ed. Andrew von Hirsch, Julian Roberts, Anthony Bottoms, Kent Roach, and Mara Schiff (Oxford: Hart, 2003), 43.

without knowing the intentions of those who create and administer the programs in question.

Fascinating problems arise if I am correct that punishments necessarily involve *two* analytically distinct components: deprivation and stigma. It would be easy to find alternatives to imprisonment if the only objective were to deprive or impose hard treatment. Deprivations can be inflicted in a multiplicity of ways. The much greater difficulty, however, is to design otherwise acceptable alternatives that simultaneously *stigmatize*. At present, the vast majority of the public continues to equate genuine punishments with incarceration and regards almost all alternatives as insufficiently severe. Their perception probably derives less from their belief that nothing short of imprisonment can deprive than from their conviction that nothing short of imprisonment can stigmatize. Unfortunately, we still lack a viable means to express public condemnation against serious wrongdoing without resorting to incarceration. Dan Kahan claims this difficulty reflects what he calls "punishment incommensurability."[36] If the state imprisons one offender and fines another, for example, the quanta of punishment severity imposed on each is unlikely to equal Q, since imprisonment uniquely expresses the censure punishment necessarily requires.[37]

As I have indicated, my inquiry is partly motivated by the desire to curb mass incarceration. I am confident that retributivists have much to contribute toward this goal. They can demonstrate, for example, why some behaviors currently proscribed should not be criminalized at all,[38] why the scope of some defenses should be enlarged,[39] and why some behaviors that are and ought to be prohibited are insufficiently serious to merit severe sentences.[40] The present question, however, is whether retributivists have any special insights into how to defend modes of punishment that would reduce our reliance on imprisonment. Here my verdict is more skeptical.[41] We have little problem identifying alternatives to imprisonment when offenses are relatively petty and few of those who commit them are incarcerated in the first place. The greater challenge, I am sure, is to identify an alternative means to censure and stigmatize when an offense is relatively serious. Unless the problem of punishment incommensurability can be solved, the prospect of reducing mass incarceration is bleak.

36 Dan Kahan, "Punishment Incommensurability," *Buffalo Criminal Law Review* 1, no. 1 (1998): 5–22.

37 See R.A. Duff, *Punishment, Communication, and Community* (Oxford: Oxford University Press, 2001), 146–48.

38 Douglas Husak, *Overcriminalization* (Oxford: Oxford University Press, 2008).

39 See Douglas Husak, *Ignorance of Law* (Oxford: Oxford University Press, 2016).

40 See Andrew von Hirsch, Martin Wasik, and Judith Greene, "Punishments in the Community and the Principles of Desert," *Rutgers Law Journal* 20, no. 3 (1989): 595–618.

41 See Michael E. Smith, "Will the Real Alternatives Please Stand Up?" *Review of Law & Social Change* 12, no. 1 (1983): 171–98.

Pessimism on this matter is reinforced by recent criminological history. Calls to reduce the scale of imprisonment are hardly new and have come both from political appointees and legal philosophers. In a speech on prisons in 1983 that is eerily reminiscent of today, Attorney General William French Smith remarked: "We simply cannot afford to ignore alternative forms of punishment."[42] Such "punishment options," he continued, "should be available only in limited cases for nonviolent criminals where the sanction is sufficient to punish the offender."[43] Needless to say, this plea did not result in dramatic change; the scale of incarceration has increased fivefold since the time of Smith's remarks. The final clause in the foregoing quotation hints at why no solution was found. We have been unable to identify (otherwise acceptable) alternative modes of punishment that express sufficient censure and impose enough stigma when serious crimes are committed. Unless we are able to find them, alter the definition of punishment, or abolish punitive sanctions altogether, the epidemic of mass incarceration is likely to continue to plague us.

2.5 CONCLUSION

Retributivism, as I have defined it, requires that a central place be afforded to desert in efforts to justify punishment. I have assumed that retributivists allow desert to play a major role by adopting a principle of proportionality and its corollary of parity. According to what I have called the deferential view, retributivists are largely indifferent about the modes of punishment to utilize as long as proportionality is preserved and equally deserving offenders receive equally severe sentences. Within this constraint, they should be prepared to defer to consequentialists about the kinds of punishment to prefer – notwithstanding some uncertainty over whether the alleged options *are* genuine modes of punishment.

[42] "Remarks of the Attorney General Vanderbilt University School of Law Nashville, Tennessee March 3, 1983," DocPlayer, http://docplayer.net/17987669-Remarks-of-the-attorney-general-vanderbilt-university-school-of-law-nashville-tennessee-march-3-1983.html.

[43] Ibid.

3

Partial Responsibility and Excuse

*David O. Brink**

The criminal law is broadly retributive insofar as it predicates censure and sanction on culpable or responsible wrongdoing.[1] Wrongdoing for which the agent is not responsible and, hence, not culpable (in this sense) is excused. Responsibility and excuse are *scalar* phenomena, because the capacities constitutive of the normative competence required for responsibility can be had to different degrees and their impairment can be a matter of degree. Ideally, the criminal law would aim to deliver just deserts in cases of partial responsibility, making censure and sanction *proportional* to the degree of culpable wrongdoing. However, with some qualifications, American criminal law is *bivalent* about responsibility and excuse. It treats responsibility as all or nothing, and it is very stingy with excuse, in effect treating many cases of partial responsibility as if the individuals were fully responsible. It is normatively problematic to treat responsibility and excuse as bivalent when the underlying facts about them are scalar in nature.[2] In this essay, I want to explain this concern about

* It is my pleasure to contribute an essay honoring Larry Alexander, who has been a friend for two decades and from whom I have learned so much about the philosophy of law, especially legal interpretation and criminal jurisprudence. My debt is all the greater because of our frequent disagreements.

1 Culpability plays two very different roles within the criminal law. Culpability in a *narrow* sense concerns the mental elements of wrongdoing – elemental *mens rea* – whereas culpability in the *broad* sense concerns the agent's responsibility for her wrongdoing, without which she would be excused. I distinguish these two roles in David O. Brink, "The Nature and Significance of Culpability" (manuscript, San Diego, 2014). In this essay, I am concerned exclusively with culpability as broad culpability.

2 My focus on the normative puzzle that results from bivalent verdicts of responsibility and excuse where the facts about responsibility are scalar is the same sort of puzzle that Larry has explored for normative ethics in Larry Alexander, "Scalar Properties, Binary Judgments," *Journal of Applied Philosophy* 25, no. 2 (2008): 85–104. The underlying puzzle is the same, but our applications and morals are different. For more general discussions of the normative gap between scalar input and bivalent outcomes in the criminal law, see Douglas Husak, "Partial Defenses," *Canadian Journal of Law and Jurisprudence* 11, no. 1 (1998): 167–92 and Adam Kolber, "The Bumpiness of Criminal Law," *Alabama Law Review* 67, no. 3 (2016): 855–86.

the bivalent character of American criminal law, take partial responsibility seriously, and explore some realistic alternatives to bivalence about excuse.

My discussion will be abstract and conceptual, focusing on general features of the criminal law's assumptions about desert, responsibility, and excuse. But it will nonetheless be helpful to have some potential examples of partial responsibility in mind. Thinking about insanity, immaturity, addiction, and provocation, we might identify the following cases of potential partial responsibility.

1. The mother experiencing severe postpartum depression who commits infanticide, though knowing it to be legally wrong.
2. The adolescent who commits a property crime under intense pressure from gang members in his neighborhood.
3. The addict who commits a nonviolent crime to support his addiction, which he acquired while taking medically prescribed pain medication.
4. The battered woman who kills her abuser while he sleeps.

Whether any of these cases would be best understood as cases of full responsibility, full excuse, or partial responsibility would, no doubt, depend on further details of the cases. But it shouldn't be too hard to imagine ways of filling out the details that would raise issues of partial responsibility.

3.1 PREDOMINANT RETRIBUTIVISM

These issues about partial responsibility and excuse are framed by the broadly retributive character of the criminal law. Retributivism says that blame and punishment ought to be proportional to desert, which is itself the product of two independent variables – wrongdoing and culpability or responsibility.[3]

$$P \propto D\ (= W \times R)$$

In particular, for present purposes, I will assume that the best formulation of retributive ideas is *predominant retributivism*.[4] Predominant retributivism is a *mixed* theory of punishment in which a *backward-looking* emphasis on desert predominates over *forward-looking* rationales for punishment, such as deterrence, rehabilitation, and the expression of community norms.

Any form of retributivism insists that culpable wrongdoing serves as a *constraint* on blame and punishment. Desert is a necessary condition for blame and punishment,

[3] Here, I adapt some related ideas in Robert Nozick, *Philosophical Explanations* (Cambridge, MA: Harvard University Press, 1981), 363–66. My formula resolves some ambiguities and inconsistencies in his discussion.

[4] See David O. Brink, "Retributivism and Legal Moralism," *Ratio Juris* 25, no. 4 (2012): 496–512.

because both are impermissible in the absence of culpable wrongdoing, and desert places an upper limit on permissible punishment, which must not exceed what would be proportional to desert.

Predominant retributivism insists that desert is not just a constraint on blame and punishment but also provides an important *rationale* for these attitudes and practices. In particular, it claims that blame and punishment are *fitting responses* to culpable wrongdoing in the sense that culpable wrongdoing is sufficient for a strong pro tanto case for blame and punishment. Other things being equal, we should blame and punish culpable wrongdoers proportionately to their desert.

However, other things are not always equal. There can be non-desert-based reasons not to punish proportionately, in particular, to punish less than required by desert. Such nondesert factors can include the costs of punishment, the prospects for rehabilitation, and the value of mercy or forgiveness. The strong pro tanto case for blame and punishment based on desert must sometimes compete with these countervailing considerations and may not always carry the day. Because predominant retributivism allows that desert can compete with nondesert reasons against proportionate punishment, it is already a mixed theory of punishment.

Predominant retributivism is also a mixed theory of punishment insofar as it allows desert and nondesert factors to address different questions about punishment. A complete theory of punishment should address *whom* to punish, *why* we should punish, *how much* we should punish, and *how* we should punish. Retributivism offers a unified answer to the first three questions: We should punish culpable wrongdoers; we should do so, because they deserve punishment for culpable wrongdoing; and we should punish in proportion to the degree of their culpable wrongdoing. Though desert may *constrain* how we punish, because it constrains how much we should punish, it leaves the manner of punishment largely *underdetermined*.[5] Provided that we punish all and only the guilty, punish them because they deserve punishment, and punish them in proportion to their just deserts, we are free to and should punish them in ways likely to promote various forward-looking values, such as rehabilitation, deterrence, and moral communication and education.

Another way to reconcile forward-looking rationales for punishment and the retributivist backward-looking focus on desert is to allow consequentialist considerations to supplement considerations of desert in the determination of precisely how much to punish. Despite the apparent precision of the retributivist formula for punishment, desert may determine only an interval, rather than a precise quantum, of punishment. Indeed, interval sentencing is reflected in various sentencing guidelines, including the United States Federal Sentencing Guidelines.[6]

5 For a similar view, see Douglas Husak, "Kinds of Punishment," in this volume.

6 United States Sentencing Commission, *Guidelines Manual* (November 2016).

Whether punishment intervals reflect genuine metaphysical indeterminacy in the desert basis of particular crimes or epistemological indeterminacy in our ability to track small but genuine differences in culpable wrongdoing is an interesting question, which we need not settle here. As long as there is limited indeterminacy in the desert basis for punishment, whether metaphysical or epistemological, there is a need to specify further a precise punishment value within the deserved interval. So, it is open to us to appeal to various consequentialist rationales to fine-tune the quantum of punishment within the space of punishments set by desert.

Something like predominant retributivism has considerable intuitive appeal and fits well with important parts of criminal jurisprudence. For instance, it explains well the two main kinds of affirmative defense a defendant can offer – *justifications* and *excuses*.[7] Justifications and excuses deny the two independent variables in the retributivist desert basis for blame and punishment. Justifications, such as necessity, deny wrongdoing, whereas excuses, such as insanity or duress, deny culpability or responsibility.[8] Just as justification is the flipside of wrongdoing, so too excuse is the flipside of responsibility.

3.2 THE FAIR OPPORTUNITY TO AVOID WRONGDOING

Because the denial of responsibility is an excuse, responsibility and excuse are inversely related. Those responsible for their wrongdoing lack an excuse, and excused wrongdoing is wrongdoing for which the agent is not responsible. This allows us to model responsibility by attending to excuses.[9]

The criminal law recognizes two main kinds of excuse – *incompetence* excuses such as insanity, and *duress* excuses. Incompetence involves impairment of an agent's internal capacities. By contrast, duress involves a situational failing in which wrongful interference by another with the agent's options deprives her of the fair opportunity to act on her own deliberations about how to behave. In this

7 While justifications and excuses are the two main affirmative defenses available to defendants, there are also policy-based exemptions, such as prosecutorial immunity for diplomats. See, e.g., Paul H. Robinson, *Structure and Function in the Criminal Law* (Oxford: Clarendon Press, 1997), 96–124, 204–7 and Mitchell Berman, "Justification and Excuse, Law and Morality," *Duke Law Journal* 53, no. 1 (2003): 1–77.

8 A true justification concedes that the offense has been proven but claims that, in light of the circumstances and the law's larger purposes, the conduct in question is nonetheless not wrong. We could acknowledge this fact by distinguishing between prima facie and all-things-considered wrongdoing, and claiming that the prosecution has the burden of proving prima facie wrongdoing and that justification is an affirmative defense that denies all-things-considered wrongdoing. That shows that the wrongdoing in the retributivist desert basis for punishment is all-things-considered wrongdoing.

9 Michael S. Moore, *Placing Blame* (Oxford: Clarendon Press, 1997), 548, describes excuse as "the royal road" to responsibility. It's important to recognize that it is a two-way street.

way, standard excuses recognized by the criminal law reflect impairment of the agent's *capacities* or *opportunities*. If we treat excuse as a window onto responsibility, this should lead us to factor responsibility and, hence, culpability into two main conditions – *normative competence* and *situational control*. This conception of responsibility draws on and synthesizes two traditions of thinking about responsibility – the reasons-responsive wing of the compatibilist tradition of thinking about free will and responsibility, and the fair choice approach to criminal responsibility.[10]

Normative competence involves *reasons-responsiveness*, which itself involves both *cognitive* capacities to distinguish right from wrong and *volitional* capacities to conform one's conduct to that normative knowledge. It is important to recognize that responsibility is tied to *competence*, not *performance*. We do not excuse the weak-willed or the willful wrongdoer for failing to recognize or respond appropriately to reasons, but we do excuse the incompetent. If we excused for faulty performance, the fact of wrongdoing would itself be exculpatory, with the absurd result that we could never hold anyone responsible for wrongdoing.

Normative competence requires the cognitive capacity to make normative discriminations and recognize wrongdoing, as is reflected in the M'Naghten rule that excuses if the agent lacked the capacity to discriminate right from wrong at the time of action.[11] For instance, this cognitive conception of competence and insanity is reflected in the Federal insanity test.

> It is an affirmative defense to a prosecution under any Federal statute that, at the time of the commission of the acts constituting the offense, the defendant, as a result of a severe mental disease or defect, was unable to appreciate the nature and quality or the wrongfulness of his acts. Mental disease or defect does not otherwise constitute a defense.[12]

[10] The reasons-responsive tradition of moral responsibility on which I draw is reflected in Susan Wolf, *Freedom within Reason* (New York: Oxford University Press, 1990); R. Jay Wallace, *Responsibility and the Moral Sentiments* (Cambridge, MA: Harvard University Press, 1994); John Martin Fischer and Mark Ravizza, *Responsibility and Control* (New York: Cambridge University Press, 1998); Dana K. Nelkin, *Making Sense of Freedom and Responsibility* (Oxford: Clarendon Press, 2011); and Michael McKenna, "Reasons-Responsiveness, Agents, and Mechanisms," *Oxford Studies in Agency and Responsibility* 1 (2013): 151–83. The fair choice literature in criminal jurisprudence on which I draw is reflected in H.L.A Hart, *Punishment and Responsibility* (Oxford: Clarendon Press, 1968); Michael S. Moore, *Placing Blame* (Oxford: Clarendon Press, 1997); and Stephen J. Morse, "Culpability and Control," *University of Pennsylvania Law Review* 142, no. 5 (1994): 1587–1660 and Morse, "Uncontrollable Urges and Irrational People," *Virginia Law Review* 88, no. 5 (2002): 1025–78. A fuller presentation of the fair opportunity conception of responsibility is contained in David O. Brink and Dana K. Nelkin, "Fairness and the Architecture of Responsibility," *Oxford Studies in Agency and Responsibility* 1 (2013): 284–313 and David O. Brink, "Responsibility, Incompetence, and Psychopathy," *Lindley Lectures* 53 (2013): 1–41.

[11] M'Naghten's case, 10 Cl. & F. 200, 8 Eng. Rep. 718 (1843).

[12] 18 U.S.C. § 17(a)(2005).

However, normative competence requires more than cognitive competence. It also requires volitional capacities to form intentions based on one's practical judgments about what one ought to do and to execute these intentions over time, despite distraction, temptation, and other forms of interference.[13] Volitional impairment might take the form of irresistible urges, paralyzing phobias, severe depression, or damage to the prefrontal cortex of the brain. Recognition of a volitional dimension of normative competence argues against purely cognitive conceptions of insanity, such as the M'Naghten test, and in favor of a more inclusive conception, represented in the Model Penal Code (MPC), which conceives of insanity as involving significant impairment of *either* cognitive *or* volitional competence.[14]

> A person is not responsible for criminal conduct if at the time of such conduct as a result of a mental disease or defect he lacks substantial capacity either to appreciate the criminality [wrongfulness] of his conduct or to conform his conduct to the requirements of law.[15]

If so, normative competence involves *both* cognitive *and* volitional competence.

But excuse is not exhausted by denials of normative competence. Among the factors that may negate blameworthiness are external or situational factors that impair an agent's opportunity to act on her practical reasoning. In particular, agents may be excused for wrongdoing that is the product of coercion or duress. The paradigm situational excuse is coercion by another agent, as when one is threatened with physical harm to oneself or a loved one if one doesn't participate in some kind of wrongdoing – for instance, driving the getaway car in a robbery. The MPC adopts a reasonable person version of the conditions under which duress excuses, namely, when a person of reasonable firmness would have been unable to resist, provided the actor was not himself responsible for being subject to duress.[16] Situational duress does not compromise the wrongdoer's status as a responsible agent and does not challenge her normative competence, but it does challenge whether she is responsible for her wrongdoing.[17]

13 For skepticism about the volitional dimension of normative competence, see Morse, "Uncontrollable Urges and Irrational People." For a defense of the volitional dimension of normative competence, against volitional skepticism, see Brink and Nelkin, "Fairness and the Architecture of Responsibility," 296–302.

14 Model Penal Code § 4.01. The Model Penal Code is a model statutory text of fundamental provisions of the criminal law first developed by the American Law Institute in 1962 and subsequently updated in 1981.

15 Ibid., § 4.01(1).

16 Ibid., § 2.09.

17 Following the MPC, the conventional wisdom within the criminal law is that duress involves hard choice whose source is wrongful interference by another agent and that duress is an excuse, rather

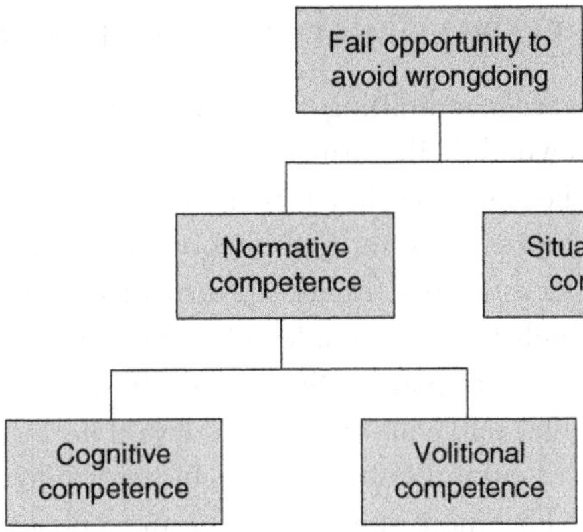

FIGURE 3.1 The Fair Opportunity Conception of Responsibility

So far, the conception of responsibility emerging here is a two-factor model twice over. Responsibility is factored into normative competence and situational control, and normative competence is factored into cognitive and volitional capacities. This kind of two-factor model seems plausible, in significant part because it promises to fit our practices of excuse in both moral assessment and the criminal law pretty well. Incapacity excuses deny normative competence, whereas duress excuses deny the opportunity to exercise those capacities free from inappropriate interference by others. But it would be nice if there were some unifying element to its structure.

One possible umbrella concept is *control*. Freedom from coercion and duress, cognitive competence, and volitional competence all seem to be aspects of an agent's ability to control her actions. But control seems important, because it seems *unfair* to blame agents for outcomes that are outside their control. This suggests that the umbrella concept should be fairness – in particular, the *fair opportunity to avoid wrongdoing* – because failure of either normative competence or situational control violates the norm that blame and punishment be reserved for those who had a fair opportunity to avoid wrongdoing. If we treat the fair opportunity to avoid wrongdoing as the key to responsibility, we get the picture of the architecture of responsibility shown in Figure 3.1.

than a justification. Interesting questions can be raised about both assumptions. I cannot address these questions here, though I hope to do so elsewhere. For some relevant discussion, see Peter Westen, "Does Duress Justify or Excuse?" in this volume. I do believe that duress excuses, rather than justifies, in some, if not all, cases. In any case, my focus in this essay is on incompetence excuses, rather than duress excuses, so the main argument of this essay is not hostage to the resolution of these issues involving duress.

3.3 PARTIAL RESPONSIBILITY AND IDEAL THEORY

Intuitively, responsibility is *scalar*, admitting of degrees. This is reinforced by the fair opportunity conception in which both normative competence and situational control are matters of degree, because their impairment is a matter of degree.

Though partial excuse makes sense for both incompetence and duress excuses, I will focus on partial incompetence excuses. Normative competence involves reasons-responsiveness, which is itself a matter of degree. This can be measured counterfactually – one is more responsive the greater the range of circumstances in which one would recognize and conform to the relevant norms, and less responsive the greater the range of circumstances in which one would not recognize or conform to those norms. The more normatively competent agent is responsive cognitively and volitionally to the relevant norms in a greater range of possible circumstances, and the less competent agent is responsive in a smaller range of possible circumstances. Moreover, competence can be understood as ease or facility of performance and incompetence as difficulty of performance. The limiting case of difficulty is impossibility, and degree of incompetence can be understood in terms of comparative difficulty of performance.[18]

If we hold the magnitude of wrongdoing constant, then, other things being equal, blame and punishment should be directly proportional to the degree of responsibility, as measured by the degree of normative competence, which is itself inversely related to degree of difficulty. So, as a matter of ideal theory, responsibility and excuse ought to be *continuously scalar* – *analog* – thereby achieving *proportionate* desert and justice, as shown in Figure 3.2.

Here, proportionate justice is represented by the diagonal. Punishment to the left of the diagonal is underpunishment, whereas punishment to the right of the diagonal is overpunishment. The degree of underpunishment or overpunishment can be measured by distance from the diagonal.

3.4 BIVALENCE

However, for the most part and with some qualifications, American criminal law treatment of responsibility and excuse is bivalent, recognizing a threshold of competence and responsibility below which one is fully excused and above which one is fully responsible.

An exception to this trend toward bivalence is the doctrine of provocation, under which intentional homicides committed with adequate provocation reduce to an

[18] For one development of this view, see Dana K. Nelkin, "Difficulty and Degrees of Moral Praiseworthiness and Blameworthiness," *Noûs* 50, no. 2 (2016): 356–78.

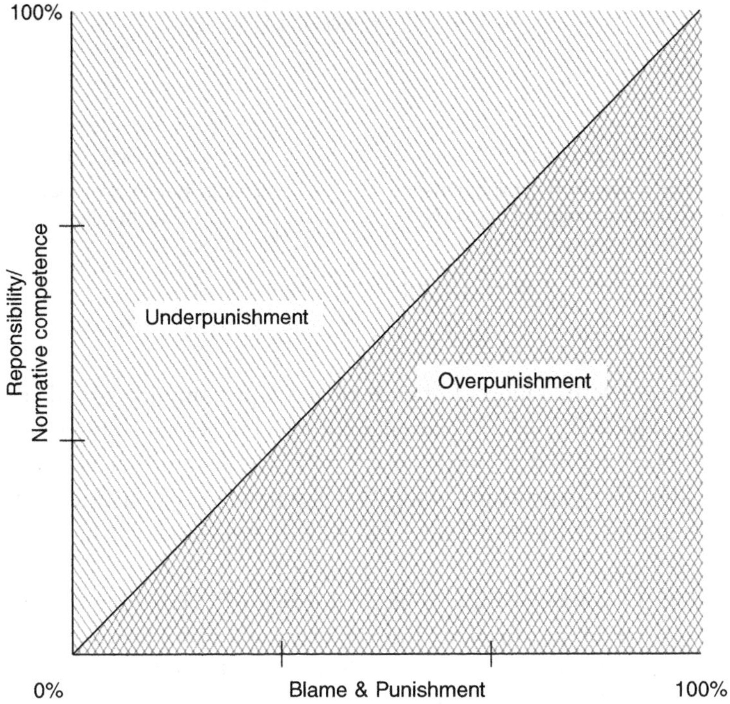

FIGURE 3.2 Proportional Justice

offense of voluntary manslaughter. But the scope of this exception is quite limited, restricted as it is to homicides resulting from provocation. Moreover, even in this limited domain, it is not clear if this is a true exception, inasmuch as it is unclear whether provocation is best conceptualized as a partial excuse (partial responsibility) or as a partial justification (lesser wrongdoing).[19]

A potentially significant qualification to this trend toward bivalence involves a division of jurisprudential labor within criminal trials. A criminal trial is *bifurcated* into *guilt* and *sentencing* phases (Figure 3.3). The guilt phase combines determinations of wrongdoing and affirmative defenses, such as excuse. The prosecution bears the burden of proof (beyond a reasonable doubt) for the elements of wrongdoing – both the objective elements (ac*tus reus*) and the mental elements (*mens rea*). Once wrongdoing is established, the defense has the opportunity to prove affirmative defenses, such as justification or excuse, and it has the burden of proof (preponderance of the evidence or clear and convincing evidence). So,

[19] My own view, for which I cannot argue here, is that provocation cases bifurcate into partial justifications and partial excuses.

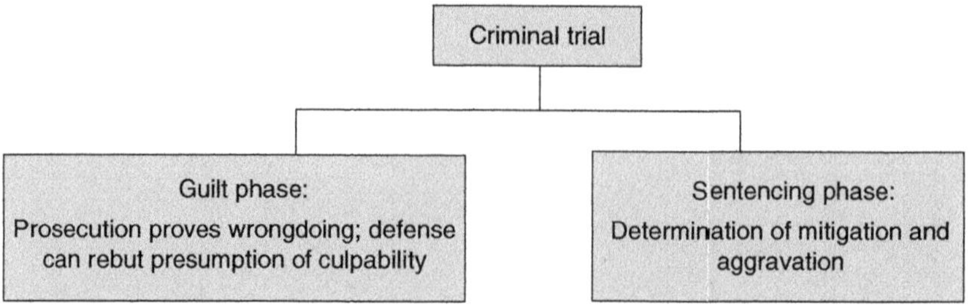

FIGURE 3.3 Bipartite Criminal Trials

in particular, a determination of offense creates a presumption of culpability for wrongdoing, which the defense can attempt to rebut, establishing an excuse. If wrongdoing is established and no excuse is proven at the guilt phase, the trial proceeds to sentencing. In principle, mitigation at sentencing can include both desert factors relevant to, but not sufficient for, excuse and nondesert factors, such as remorse or reform.

Even if the guilt phase of a trial is bivalent, one might claim that the sentencing phase is scalar, rather than bivalent. Indeed, one might claim that the scalar nature of the sentencing phase makes up for the bivalence of the guilt phase.

However, though the possibility of sentence mitigation can sometimes soften the edges of bivalence about excuse, it is an imperfect way to do so. First, there is often little or no discretion at sentencing. Mandatory minima and sentence enhancements often eliminate or severely restrict discretion at sentencing. Second, even when sentencing discretion exists and is wide, it is nonetheless discretionary. Failure to mitigate where there is lesser culpability is not seen as wronging the defendant. But from the perspective of a broadly retributive jurisprudence that insists on proportional punishment, mitigation should be mandatory, rather than discretionary. Finally, sentence mitigation is imperfect conceptually as well as practically. Excuse is an affirmative defense denying one element of the retributivist desert basis for punishment and is determined at the guilt phase. But partial responsibility and excuse concern the same dimension of desert and ought to be assessed at the guilt phase, leaving nondesert considerations to inform sentencing.

With these qualifications in mind, it is fair to say that American criminal law is predominantly *bivalent*, rather than scalar, about responsibility and excuse, and that sentence mitigation is a very imperfect remedy for the concerns that bivalence at the guilt phase of a trial raises. For the most part, American criminal law treats responsibility and excuse as all-or-nothing, setting a fairly low threshold above which one is fully responsible (Figure 3.4).

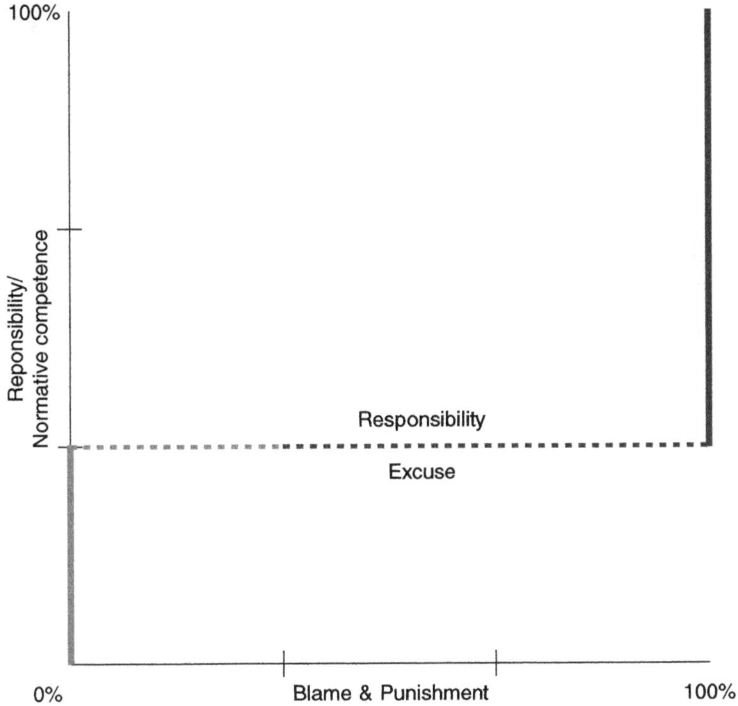

FIGURE 3.4 Bivalent Justice

It's hard to know how best to operationalize the criminal law threshold for normative competence and responsibility. Given how many criminal offenders suffer from some form of mental illness and impairment, how infrequently defendants plead insanity, and how infrequently these pleas are successful, one might think that the threshold is quite low. If anything, I've understated how inclusive the bivalent conception of responsibility is by setting the threshold, for purposes of illustration, at 33 percent competence.

We can see how bivalence results in punishment that deviates significantly from just deserts by combining the first two graphs (Figure 3.5).

By comparing bivalent and proportionate verdicts, we can see that a bivalent system introduces regions of underpunishment and overpunishment, which reflect the degree of unjust deserts, because the distance between actual punishment and the diagonal is proportional to the degree of underpunishment or overpunishment. With a comparatively low threshold for responsibility, the region of overpunishment is large both absolutely and in relation to the region of underpunishment. This is bad enough. But if we agree with William Blackstone (1723–1780) that it is worse to overpunish than to underpunish (he thought it was

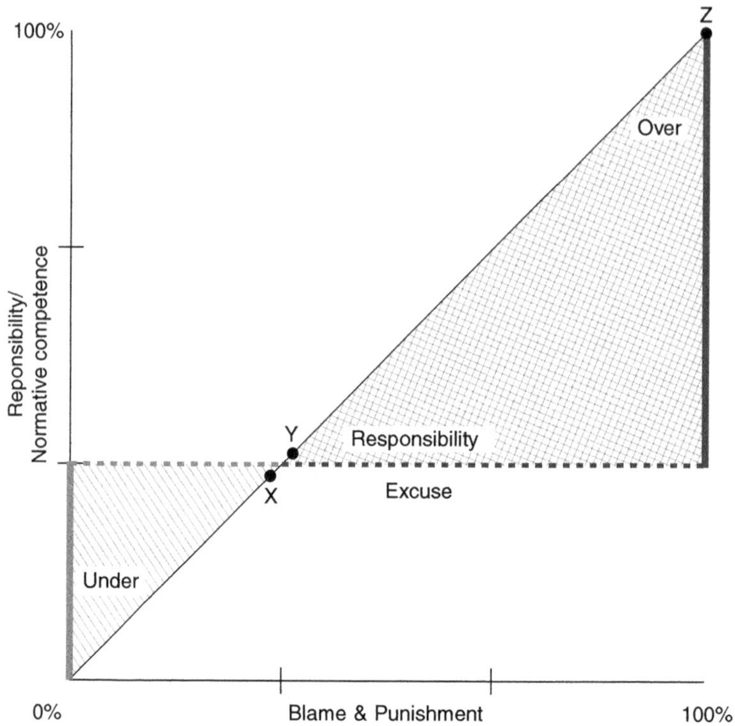

FIGURE 3.5 Proportional Justice Meets Bivalence

ten times worse), we should be especially troubled that the ratio of overpunishment to underpunishment is so high.[20]

These comparisons hold all else being equal and make no assumptions about the frequency of cases at different points on the responsibility axis. If, as seems plausible, most offenders not qualifying for a full excuse have impaired competence to some degree, this will aggravate the worry about overpunishment.

Moreover, normative thresholds are arbitrary when the relevant underlying factors are scalar. Thresholds attach enormous normative significance to small differences straddling the threshold and ignore large differences above and below

[20] Blackstone's version of this asymmetry involves a 10:1 ratio: "better that ten guilty persons go free than that one innocent party suffer." William Blackstone, *Commentaries on the Laws of England* (London: Strahan & Woodfall, 1791), 4: 358. Benjamin Franklin is alleged to have thought the ratio is 100: 1. It might be tempting to think that Blackstone's asymmetry is already recognized in the fact that the prosecution bears a high burden of proof (beyond a reasonable doubt). But that burden concerns proof of wrongdoing, not culpability or responsibility. Once wrongdoing is established, it is the burden of the defense to prove that the defendant is not culpable, because incompetent. So, the procedure for proving responsibility and excuse does not reflect Blackstone's asymmetry.

the threshold. For instance, X and Y are responsible and, hence, blameworthy to similar degrees, whereas Z is blameworthy to a much higher degree. Their comparative just deserts are represented on the diagonal. However, the bivalent system with a responsibility/excuse threshold treats them very differently. X is fully excused, and Y is fully responsible, though their underlying levels of normative competence are very similar. Moreover, Z is treated as just as responsible and, hence, blameworthy as Y, even though Z is significantly more culpable than Y. These are significant failures of just deserts.

3.5 NONIDEAL THEORY

A *perfect* moral accountant (e.g., God) would employ a fully scalar conception of just deserts, assigning blame and punishment on a case-by-case basis and making them proportionate to culpable wrongdoing. Her determinations would conform to the diagonal.[21] However, our judiciary and juries are staffed by mortals who are *imperfect* moral accountants, with the result that attempts to implement just deserts sometimes lead to overpunishment or underpunishment.

One concern is that jury studies suggest that juries tend to focus on the magnitude of the wrongdoing and are insufficiently sensitive to factors that reduce culpability, thus leading to significant overpunishment.[22]

[21] There is a problematic gap between scalar moral worth and bivalent divine verdicts – penalties and rewards – if God assigns all souls to Heaven or Hell, which are noncomparatively good or bad. See Ted Sider, "Hell and Vagueness," *Faith and Philosophy* 19, no. 1 (2002): 58–68. This problem is reduced, though perhaps not eliminated, if Dante is right that there are levels (circles) in Heaven and Hell corresponding to a person's degree of moral worth.

[22] See Catherine A. Crosby, Preston A. Britner, Kathleen M. Jodl, and Sharon G. Portwood, "The Juvenile Death Penalty and the Eighth Amendment: An Empirical Investigation of Societal Consensus and Proportionality," *Law and Human Behavior* 19, no. 3 (1995), 245–61. The questionnaire contained descriptions of cases with defendants on trial for murder whose ages ranged from ten to nineteen years. The details of the cases included a description of the crime, probable culpability of all juveniles, level of remorse, and age of the defendant. The number of respondents willing to impose the death penalty for the defendants were as follows: 96.3 percent of male respondents and 95.7 percent of female respondents were willing to impose the death penalty on the nineteen-year-old defendant; 92 percent of male respondents and 87 percent of female respondents were willing to impose the death penalty on the sixteen-year-old defendant; 87.5 percent of male respondents and 52.9 percent of female respondents were willing to impose the death penalty on the fifteen-year-old defendant; and 71 percent of male respondents and 52.4 percent of female respondents were willing to impose the death penalty on the ten-year-old defendant. Though the willingness among male respondents to impose the death penalty was not completely insensitive to immaturity, and the willingness among female respondents was more sensitive, the level of insensitivity in both men and women was striking. A similar finding about the comparative insensitivity of views about the severity of sentencing to degree of maturity and normative competence is made in Simona Ghetti and Allison D. Redlich, "Reactions to Youth Crime: Perceptions of Accountability and Competency," *Behavioral Sciences and the Law* 19, no. 1 (2001): 33–52.

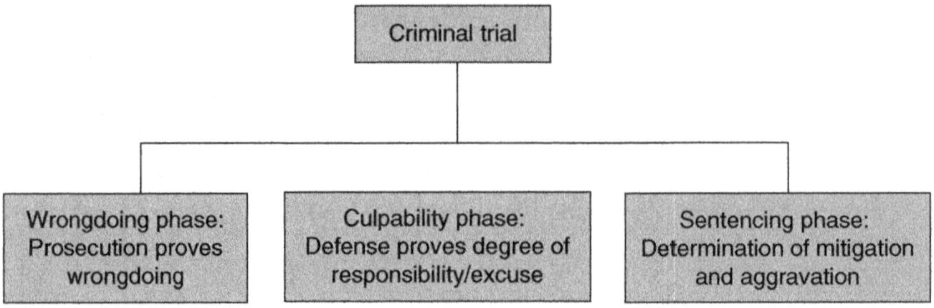

FIGURE 3.6 Tripartite Criminal Trials

One remedy for this blindspot for culpability would be to require explicit culpability determinations, involving determinations of degrees of responsibility. In principle, this could occur at the guilt or sentencing phase of a trial. But, as we saw, there are practical and conceptual obstacles to doing this at the sentencing phase. These determinations could be made at sentencing if they were made mandatory, rather than discretionary. Even so, to give effect to the grading of culpability, mandatory minima would need to be eliminated or greatly reduced. Even if these practical problems could be overcome, there would still be the conceptual obstacle that excuses deny responsibility or culpability and so should be assessed at the guilt phase of a trial, as other affirmative defenses are. Because partial responsibility and excuse concern this same dimension of desert, there is a strong argument for including assessments of partial responsibility at the guilt phase of a trial. If we require a mandatory grading of culpability at the guilt phase of a trial, we are effectively replacing a bifurcated trial with a *tripartite* trial in which determinations of wrongdoing and culpability/responsibility are separated and mandatory (Figure 3.6).

Under this proposal, once wrongdoing was proved, there would be a mandatory culpability determination, where the defense could introduce evidence of reduced competence and not just complete incompetence. There would be grades of culpability, and the defense would have the burden of establishing an excuse, whether full or partial. But each case would be required to reach a separate culpability determination. After this, there would be a separate sentencing phase where further considerations of mitigation and aggravation, including nondesert factors, would be decided.[23]

[23] I would like to think that this proposal for a trifurcated trial is similar in spirit to Robinson's elegant proposals to make the process and verdicts of the criminal law better reflect the underlying normative structure of criminal liability. For instance, Robinson argues that the simple binary verdict of guilty or not guilty obscures the different possible reasons for a not-guilty verdict. It would be better if courts were required to deliver one of five verdicts at the guilt phase of the trial: (1) no violation, (2) justified violation, (3) excused violation, (4) nonpunishable violation, or (5) guilt. See Paul H. Robinson, *Structure and Function in Criminal Law* (New York: Oxford University Press, 1997): 204–7.

However, mandatory culpability assessments are only a remedy for overlooking the role of culpability in desert if these assessments can be made with some degree of reliability. But we might doubt that this is true. An important residual concern about implementing proportionate justice is that it's very difficult to track small differences in culpability. So even if just deserts in ideal theory would be analog, perhaps just deserts in nonideal theory should be discontinuous.

There are really two issues here. First, it's hard for imperfect moral accountants to recognize small differences in culpability. This is the problem of *epistemic granularity*. Second, even when we stipulate small differences in culpability, our normative responses don't always track those differences. Suppose A and B both succumb to temptation and do wrong, but that A's temptation is slightly greater than B's. God might blame B (a little) more than A, but most of us wouldn't. This is the problem of *normative granularity*. I'm inclined to view both epistemic and normative granularity as departures from the ideal of proportionate justice.

These are real difficulties in implementing analog justice for nonideal circumstances. But they don't support adoption of the current bivalent system. Any optimal rule, principle, or norm can be misapplied. We don't show that a norm is suboptimal just because some of its applications are individually suboptimal. Instead, we have to show that there is another norm whose adoption would produce fewer suboptimal outcomes overall or whose suboptimal outcomes would be less unjust. But then, difficulty with reliably producing just deserts by an analog method is not good reason to prefer a bivalent method, unless bivalence produces fewer cases of unjust deserts or ones that involve less injustice. But since the bivalent system ignores all but the most extreme forms of incompetence, it is likely to generate greater injustice – in particular, more cases of more pronounced overpunishment. If the deviations from proportionate justice are small, an analog system might still promote just deserts best, overall.

Nonetheless, it is possible that attempts to implement analog justice, even within a trifurcated criminal trial, would seriously deviate from proportionate justice, because of significant epistemic and normative granularity. If so, an alternative would be to move to some kind of discontinuous assessment of culpability that was more coarse-grained than proportional justice but more fine-grained than the bivalent system.

3.6 TRIVALENCE

One such alternative would be a *trivalent* culpability assessment that allowed for verdicts of fully responsible, partially responsible, and nonresponsible. Here, American criminal law might take a page from some other criminal justice systems that are trivalent about excuse. Criminal laws in England and Wales, Scotland,

Ireland, and Australia recognize a defense of diminished responsibility to homicide, reducing what would otherwise be the sentence for murder to one of manslaughter.[24] For instance, in England, section 2 of the Homicide Act of 1957 provided this partial excuse for homicides committed by those with diminished capacity:

> Where a person kills or is a party to the killing of another, he shall not be convicted of murder if he was suffering from such abnormality of mind (whether arising from condition of arrested or retarded development of mind or any inherent causes or induced by disease or injury) as substantially impaired his mental responsibility for his acts and omissions in doing or being party to the killing.

Section 52 of the Coroners and Justice Act 2009 in England and Wales modified this provision, reducing an offense of murder to manslaughter in cases in which the defendant killed another as the result of "diminished responsibility" arising from a medical condition that impaired the defendant's ability "to understand the nature of his conduct, to form a rational judgement, or to exercise self-control."[25]

We might *generalize* this recognition of partial responsibility and excuse from homicides to all crimes. For instance, the German Criminal Code affords a full excuse for any offense to anyone who lacks normative competence and a partial excuse in cases of diminished responsibility in which normative competence is substantially, but incompletely, impaired.[26]

> Section 20 Insanity. Any person who at the time of the commission of an offense is incapable of appreciating the unlawfulness of their actions or of acting in accordance with any such appreciation due to a pathological mental disorder, a profound consciousness disorder, debility or any other serious mental abnormality, shall be deemed to act without guilt.[27]
>
> Section 21 Diminished Responsibility. If the capacity of the offender to appreciate the unlawfulness of his actions or to act in accordance with any such appreciation is substantially diminished at the time of the commission of the offense due to one

[24] For useful comparative data, see *Loss of Control and Diminished Responsibility*, ed. Alan Reed and Michael Bohlander (Farnham: Ashgate, 2011). The contributions by Ronnie Mackay, "The New Diminished Responsibility Plea," John Stannard, "The View from Ireland," and James Chalmers, "Partial Defences to Murder in Scotland," are especially useful.

[25] The Scottish recognition of partial excuse to homicide dates at least from HM Advocate v. Dingwall (1867) 5 Irv 466 and was enacted into statute in the Criminal Justice and Licensing (Scotland) Act 2010, § 168. Though its conception of incompetence is not as clear as it might be, the Scottish conception is arguably similar to that in the Model Penal Code and the Coroners and Justice Act 2009, recognizing both cognitive and volitional incompetence.

[26] German Criminal Code, §§ 20–21 StGB; See Michael Bohlander, "When the Bough Breaks – Defences and Sentencing Options Available in Battered Women and Similar Scenarios under German Law," in *Loss of Control and Diminished Responsibility*, ed. Reed and Bohlander (Farnham: Ashgate, 1997): 247–71.

[27] German Criminal Code, § 20 StGB.

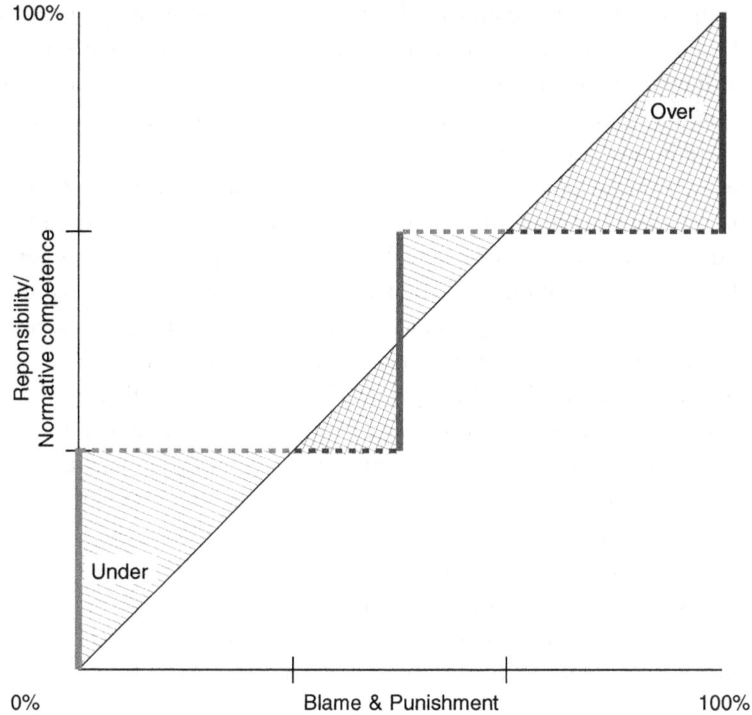

FIGURE 3.7 Trivalent Justice

of the reasons indicated in section 20, the sentence may be mitigated pursuant to section 49(1).[28]

This would be to introduce into American criminal law a generic partial excuse defense.[29] If trivalence is motivated by concerns about our inability to make the more fine-grained determinations of responsibility required by analog justice, then we might want to constrain such assessments within a finding of partial responsibility. We might insist that the punishment appropriate for partial responsibility should be *half* of what would be appropriate for full responsibility. Figure 3.7 shows one way to operationalize this proposal.

[28] Ibid., § 21.

[29] For interesting discussion, to which I am indebted, see Stephen J. Morse, "Undiminished Confusion in Diminished Capacity," *The Journal of Criminal Law and Criminology* 75, no. 1 (1984): 1–55 and Morse, "Diminished Rationality, Diminished Responsibility," *Ohio State Journal of Criminal Law* 1, no. 1 (2003): 289–308. Interestingly, Morse's defense of partial excuse in the later paper reverses his skepticism about partial excuse in the earlier paper.

Not surprisingly, if we compare the trivalent and bivalent systems correctly applied – the outcomes of conforming to their principles – the trivalent system is superior. It equalizes the ratio of overpunishment to underpunishment and reduces the magnitude of injustice done in individual cases (which reflects distance from punishment imposed to the diagonal).

Because trivalent culpability assessments make a tripartition of culpability intervals, we might conceptualize them as substantially responsible, partially responsible, and substantially nonresponsible. We could also represent these as percentage intervals of full responsibility – 0–32 percent responsible, 33–66 percent responsible, and 67–100 percent responsible. We could understand these relationships between qualitative and quantitative assessments of culpability in one of two ways depending on which we take to be explanatorily primary. We could treat the qualitative assessments as mutually exclusive and jointly exhaustive and then treat the percentage of responsibility as a way of operationalizing these qualitative differences. Alternatively, we could treat the percentage of censure and sanction as reflecting percentage of culpability and the qualitative assessment of culpability as reflecting a perception of this percentage. For our purposes, I think we can remain agnostic about whether the qualitative or quantitative assessment is explanatorily primary.

However, if we accept the Blackstone asymmetry that overpunishment is worse than underpunishment, we might want to modify the trivalent model so that we never overpunish relative to the amount of responsibility, in effect rounding punishment downward so that 67–100 percent responsibility would warrant 67 percent of the maximum punishment under proportionate justice; 33–66 percent responsibility would warrant 33 percent of the maximum punishment under proportionate justice; and 0–32 percent responsibility would warrant no punishment (Figure 3.8).

This modification of trivalence makes use of only 67 percent of the scale of proportionate justice. Though it increases the degree of underpunishment somewhat, it eliminates the sins of overpunishment, at least when trivalence is correctly applied.

3.7 TETRAVALENCE

But we might think that we are often capable of somewhat more fine-grained culpability discriminations than the trivalent system allows. Perhaps the Goldilocks standard of granularity that is still psychologically realistic would be a *tetravalent* system that divides culpability into quartiles. As with the trivalent assessment, we can remain agnostic about whether qualitative or quantitative assessment is explanatorily primary. If we accept the Blackstone asymmetry that overpunishment is worse than underpunishment, we might want to avoid the sins of overpunishment relative to the responsibility quartiles, in effect rounding punishments downward so that 75–100 percent responsibility would warrant 75% of the maximum punishment under

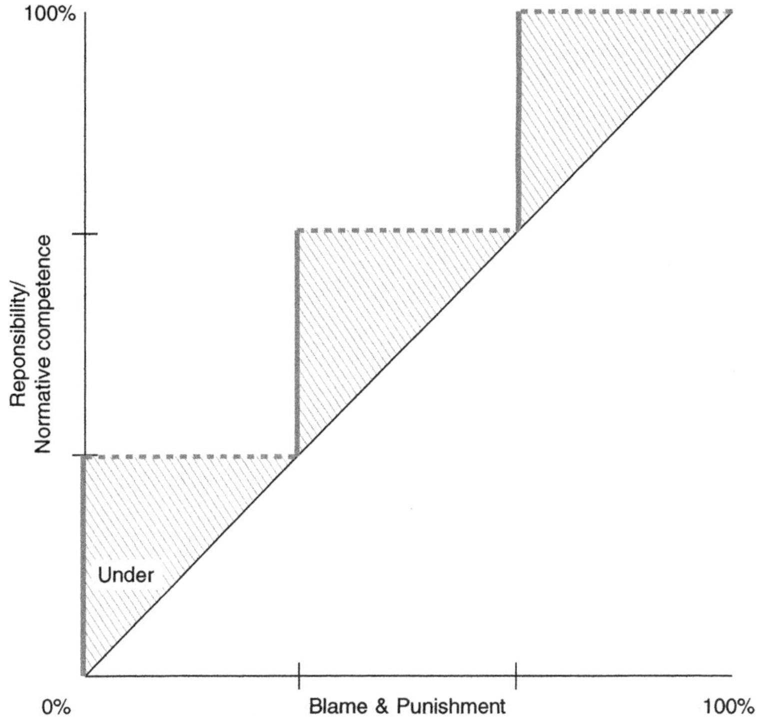

FIGURE 3.8 Trivalent Justice with Blackstone's Asymmetry

proportionate justice; 50–74 percent responsibility would warrant 50% of the maximum punishment under proportionate justice; 25–49 percent responsibility would warrant 25 percent of the maximum punishment under proportionate justice; and 0–24 percent responsibility would warrant no punishment (Figure 3.9).[30]

If we are going to employ discontinuous measures of responsibility and normative competence, tetravalence is arguably the limit of granularity that is psychologically realistic. By comparison with trivalence, tetravalence would utilize a larger percentage of the scale of proportionate justice – 75 percent. While it would still produce underpunishment, it would limit its severity. Also, though it would be less punitive than proportionate justice, it would eliminate overpunishment entirely, in recognition of Blackstone's asymmetry.

[30] This tetravalent conception of responsibility and excuse parallels the tetravalent measurement of the completion of criminal attempts that I outline in David O. Brink, "The Path to Completion," *Oxford Studies in Agency and Responsibility* 4, ed. David Shoemaker (New York: Oxford University Press, 2017): 183–205.

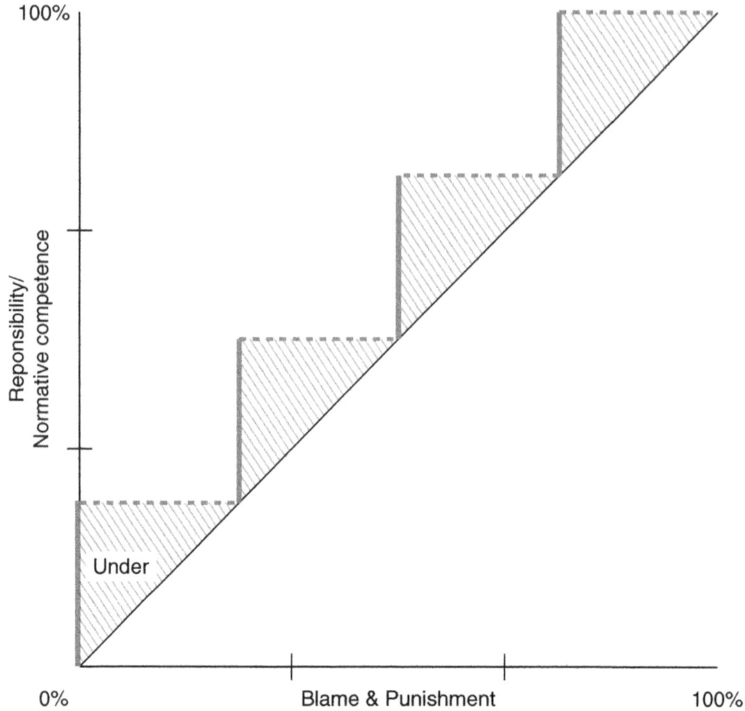

FIGURE 3.9 Tetravalent Justice with Blackstone's Asymmetry

3.8 CONCLUSION

A retributive concern with just deserts should take partial responsibility and excuse seriously. There are questions for both ideal and nonideal theory about how best to handle partial responsibility and excuse. We have briefly explored four options.

1. A bivalent system with a comparatively low threshold for responsibility/excuse operative in American criminal law.
2. A trivalent system operative in some European criminal justice systems, including a variation that rounds punishment downward in response to Blackstone's asymmetry.
3. A tetravalent system, which may approximate the Goldilocks standard of granularity and is also responsive to Blackstone's asymmetry.
4. A fully scalar analog system that aims at proportionate justice.

A bivalent criminal justice system significantly fails to deliver just deserts. This is clearly true of ideal theory, but it also very plausible for nonideal theory, because bivalence ignores all but the most extreme forms of impaired normative competence. This means that we should reject bivalence and embrace partial responsibility and excuse.

One question is *where* to do this. In principle, it could be done at sentencing, at the guilt phase of a trial, or at a separate culpability phase, which would occur after the determination of wrongdoing but before sentencing. If culpability grading were to occur during sentencing, mandatory minima and enhancements would need to be eliminated or severely restricted. Moreover, culpability grading would have to be mandatory, rather than discretionary. Even so, there would still be something conceptually problematic about separating determination of full and partial excuse into separate phases of a trial, insofar as they both bear on the same dimension of the retributivist desert basis for blame and punishment, namely, responsibility. It makes better sense, I think, to include a determination of partial excuse at the same point at which full excuses are assessed. This could be part of the guilt phase of a trial, after the prosecution establishes wrongdoing, which is where affirmative defenses are now assessed. However, it should be a mandatory assessment. Alternatively, one might introduce a separate culpability phase in trials, after a wrongdoing phase. Whereas the prosecution would be required to establish wrongdoing, the defense would be required to establish degree of culpability. Under either proposal, wrongdoing for which the agent bears some responsibility would then pass to the sentencing phase of the trial, which would be restricted to nondesert factors.

Another question is *how* to implement partial responsibility and excuse. We examined three possibilities. Analog or proportionate justice is comparatively easy to understand in principle but potentially fragile in practice. Nonetheless, aiming at proportionate justice may minimize unjust deserts. That depends on the acceptance, rather than conformity, value of proportionate justice in relation to other systems. That's a difficult question that is partly empirical insofar as it depends on the nature and extent of the epistemic granularity problem.

If the difficulties of implementing proportionate justice are severe enough, we might prefer a discontinuous system that is more fine-grained than bivalence. Trivalent and tetravalent systems that respond to Blackstone's asymmetry are alternatives worth exploring. My sympathies lean toward a tetravalent system, partly because of its promise to deliver a Goldilocks standard, balancing fuller use of the scale of proportionate justice and psychological realism. But the choice is a difficult, partly empirical one that requires fuller exploration and assessment.[31]

[31] This is an exposition of the main ideas in what will be the last chapter of a book manuscript I am working on, (tentatively) titled *Fair Opportunity, Responsibility, and Excuse*. Earlier versions of this material were presented as a Faculty Research Lecture at the University of California, San Diego, at the University of St. Andrews, the Forum for Legal and Political Philosophy at Cambridge University, and a Yale Law School conference honoring Larry Alexander. I am grateful to Larry Alexander, Mitch Berman, Reuven Brandt, Tom Dougherty, Richard Holton, Heidi Hurd, Doug Husak, Adam Kolber, Michael Moore, Stephen Morse, Dana Nelkin, Theron Pummer, Fred Schauer, Chip Sebens, Paulina Sliwa, and Peter Westen for comments on earlier versions. Special thanks to Ben Sheredos and John Dougherty for invaluable help with the graphs.

4

"Thank God I Failed"

R.A. Duff

4.1 INTRODUCTION

The breadth and scope of Larry Alexander's scholarship is enough to leave his colleagues, and admiring observers, short of breath – and a Festschrift contributor spoilt for choice: Even within the field of criminal law there are so many topics on which he has produced original and provocative work that choice is still difficult. However, since we have previously crossed swords on criminal attempts,[1] I will take up an issue about attempts on which we disagree, but which we did not then debate. The question is well worn: Does the fact of success or failure in a criminal attempt make any difference, in itself, to what the offender deserves by way of conviction and punishment? Alexander's answer to this question is a firm "No,"[2] mine is "Yes."[3]

Alexander's answer is not as iconoclastic as his other views on criminal responsibility are. Rather few theorists have been persuaded by his general account of criminal liability; many see it rather as a challenge – to show what is wrong with it, and to provide more persuasive arguments in favor of a less iconoclastic account (which is why his account is valuable even for those who reject it). But many theorists agree with Alexander that the outcome of a criminal attempt should not affect the attempter's criminal liability, because it cannot affect her penal desert. The would-be arsonist whose fire fails to light acts just as culpably, and thus deserves the same punishment, as she would have had her attempt succeeded. Many take the same view of

[1] See Larry Alexander, "Duff on Attempts," in *Crime, Punishment, and Responsibility: The Jurisprudence of Antony Duff*, ed. Rowan Cruft, Matthew H. Kramer, and Mark R. Reiff (Oxford: Oxford University Press, 2011), 215–38; R.A. Duff, "In Response," in *Crime, Punishment, and Responsibility: The Jurisprudence of Antony Duff*, ed. Rowan Cruft, Matthew H. Kramer, and Mark R. Reiff (Oxford: Oxford University Press, 2011), 367–69.

[2] See especially Larry Alexander, "Crime and Culpability," *Journal of Contemporary Legal Issues* 5 (1994): 1–30; Larry Alexander, Kimberly Kessler Ferzan, and Stephen Morse, *Crime and Culpability: A Theory of Criminal Law* (New York: Cambridge University Press, 2009), chap. 5.

[3] See R. A. Duff, *Criminal Attempts* (Oxford: Oxford University Press, 1996), chap. 12.

reckless actions: The culpability and penal desert of one who recklessly endangers another's interests are not affected by whether the threatened harm actually ensues. This is also Alexander's view, although in his case it is simply the wider version of his view of attempts: Rather than treating purpose separately from recklessness, he holds that we can "reduce purpose to recklessness," at least "normatively," even if not "conceptually."[4] Thus, if the actual result of an attempt does not affect the agent's penal desert, nor can the actual result of a reckless action.[5] I will focus, however, on attempts, because I believe that the structure of responsibility differs as between purposive and reckless wrongdoing – in which case the arguments about the significance or insignificance of resulting harm might differ in the two cases.[6] I cannot argue, and do not assume, this view here, but to avoid getting entangled in that discussion, I will focus on attempted crime.

Many of the arguments on either side of this long-running debate are by now familiar, and I do not want to rehash them here. But a good reason for discussing Alexander's arguments is that he offers some novel objections to the view that results do matter for criminal desert, and that he also helps us to see how much depends on just how we understand the nature of the judgment we are making when judging what a person deserves from the criminal law. In the remainder of this chapter I will discuss first, in Section 4.2, some of the examples through which Alexander hopes to prompt intuitions friendly to his view, and to undermine intuitions hostile to it; then, in Section 4.3, I turn to his arguments about "causal conundrums;" and finally, in Section 4.4, I discuss the significance of the idea of a "moral ledger," in which one's moral credit and discredit is to be recorded. The relief that a failed attempt might provoke in observers, or in a repentant attempter ("Thank God [you/ I] failed"), will be an important theme, to be explained in Section 4.4.

4.2 PUMPING INTUITIONS

Proponents of the "results matter" view often appeal to examples: We are to ask how we, or the agent, would or should respond to the success or failure of an attempt; this is meant to pump intuitions that favor that view.[7] Such appeals to intuition cannot, even if they produce the hoped-for results, be conclusive: Intuitions cannot

4 Alexander, Ferzan, and Morse, *Crime and Culpability*, 35–41. Since this is a Festschrift for Alexander, I refer throughout to his views, even when I am discussing *Crime and Culpability*, rather than to the views of Alexander, Ferzan and Morse: that they are indeed his own views, and not views forced on him by his coauthors (a likely story!), is confirmed by looking at "Crime and Culpability."

5 I ignore negligence here, since Alexander does not believe that it is a legitimate ground of criminal liability. Alexander, "Crime and Culpability," 6–7; Alexander, Ferzan, and Morse, *Crime and Culpability*, chap. 3.

6 See further R. A. Duff, *Answering for Crime* (Oxford: Hart, 2007), chap. 7.

7 See Daniel Dennett, *Intuition Pumps and Other Tools for Thinking* (New York: Norton, 2013).

be treated as infallible, and become less reliable even as guides to the intuiters' considered moral beliefs as the examples become more outré, or overcomplicated;[8] they can often be explained away by the proponents of opposing views. However, they provide useful starting points for reflection; and Alexander's examples raise some pressing questions for proponents of "results matter."

We can begin with the firing squad, one or more of whose rifles is loaded with a blank, so that each member can hope that he fired a blank. It is, Alexander thinks, absurd to attach any moral weight to this possibility: The "true desert" of each member of the squad is "unaffected by the fact that … he might not have actually caused the death;"[9] it would make no difference to anyone's desert if we found out which rifles had been loaded with blanks. An obvious first response to this example is to agree that each member is to the same degree responsible for the prisoner's death, whether or not he fired a blank; but to argue that that is because this is a case of collective, rather than individual, action. What each member should think is not "I (might have) killed him," but "we killed him;" the responsibility for the death is shared equally by every member of that "we."[10] Alexander seeks to avoid this response by constructing his own example of "the shooting gallery," in which each of twenty would-be gang initiates must, to gain full membership, pull the trigger of a gun that they know to be pointed at a victim who is screened from them, and to have been loaded with nineteen blanks and one live round: The initiates, Alexander emphasises, "are unknown to each other and are not in any way acting in concert."[11]

However, first, he cannot avoid the "collective action" response that easily. For the gang has set the situation up so that, as a result of the twenty trigger pullings, the victim will be killed, and "all the actors realize that as a result of their actions, an innocent person will be killed."[12] Each initiate knows that he is playing a part in this structured course of action: We can justifiably treat each not merely as an individual who is acting in a way that he knows exposes another to a one-in-twenty chance of being killed, but as a member of a group that is acting collectively in a way that they know will kill another person.[13] Second, however, even if we do treat the case as one

8 Hence the unhelpfulness of the myriad variations of the "trolley problem" that philosophers have ingeniously invented: see Frances Kamm, *The Trolley Problem Mysteries* (New York: Oxford University Press, 2016).

9 Alexander, "Crime and Culpability," 10; see Alexander, Ferzan, and Morse, *Crime and Culpability*, 176n4.

10 Likewise, should the condemned prisoner miraculously survive (all the live bullets miss), all members of the squad can share in the relief, or disappointment, that "we did not kill him."

11 Alexander, "Crime and Culpability," 8–9; see Alexander, Ferzan, and Morse, *Crime and Culpability*, 175–76, where the gang has become a satanic cult.

12 Alexander, "Crime and Culpability," 9.

13 I leave aside the question of whether we should ascribe a purpose to kill, or only knowledge that the victim will be killed.

of collective agency, I am not as confident as Alexander is that it would be irrational for individual participants (and for us) to think that it matters morally which of them fired a loaded gun.

Imagine a variant firing squad, whose members fire in turn, not knowing in advance which guns are loaded with real bullets and which with blanks. Some members, as they prepare to fire, might hope that theirs is a real bullet: They want to play a key part in the execution of a traitor. Others pray that theirs will prove to be a blank: Whilst they did not dare refuse to take part in the execution, they hope that their part will prove not to have been that of killer. The former will be disappointed if it turns out that their rifles were loaded with a blank; the latter will be relieved – even morally relieved, since they will feel less guilty, less remorseful, about their part in what was done. Is this an irrational, unwarranted response? I am not sure. We could see it as a self-deceptive attempt to avoid recognizing one's full responsibility for the death as a member of the group that caused it. But we might instead think that individuals need not be entirely subsumed into the group of which they are part – that there is room to discriminate, morally, between the parts played by each individual.

Imagine one last variant on this kind of case. A victim is to be killed, and the members of the group whose collective enterprise this is draw lots: The member who draws the short straw will be the one who shoots him. Each member is unqualifiedly ready to shoot, if he draws the short straw. But each might also hope that it will not be him – that *he* will not have to become a killer; each might feel relieved if he draws a long straw. On Alexander's account there is a significant moral difference, as to desert and culpability, between the straw drawer and the trigger puller: The latter has irreversibly unleashed the risk of death, the former still has more to do (should he draw the short straw) and thus has the capacity and the chance to withdraw from the enterprise; so only the trigger puller has committed a culpable action.[14] I don't deny this difference – though I deny the conclusion, since, unlike Alexander, I think that incomplete attempts and preparations can be culpable actions.[15] But both the straw drawer and the trigger puller might, I think, feel similar relief that the part they were prepared to play in the collective enterprise did not, as it turned out, require them to kill.

I do not, I confess, have any clear intuitions about these kinds of case – whether we should see the relief that the person who does not (directly, individually) kill might feel as expressing an appropriate response to the moral significance of actual results; or as expressing a self-deceptive attempt to distance himself from the

[14] On this "last act" test for culpable action, see Alexander, "Crime and Culpability," chap. 6.

[15] See R. A. Duff, "Risks, Culpability, Criminal Liability," in *Seeking Security*, ed. G.R. Sullivan and Ian Dennis (Oxford: Hart, 2012), 121–42.

collective action in which he is nonetheless fully involved; or as flowing from a kind of squeamishness that lacks moral force. But the uncertainties created by this kind of case (insofar as they are real, and not merely my own confusions) have more to do with normative uncertainties about collective agency than with uncertainty about the moral significance of actual results: with the extent to which those involved in collective undertakings can still see themselves (and be seen) as individual agents. If we focus purely on the collective action, we can think about the relief that those involved in it might feel if death does not ensue – "Thank God, we didn't kill him;" if we focus purely on the individual action, we can think about the relief that the individual might feel if he is not the one who directly causes death – "Thank God, I didn't kill him." In each case, the "results matter" theorist and the "results don't matter" theorist will disagree about the significance of that relief; the move to collective action does not help to settle that disagreement. Further uncertainties arise when we ask about the relationship between the collective and the individual actions, but those are not uncertainties about the moral significance of results.

However, these kinds of example do point towards a further question for the "results matter" theorist – one that has not received sufficient attention, and that is also raised by some variants of the causal overdetermination cases that Alexander discusses.[16]

A would-be killer completes her attempt: She pulls the trigger, sets the bomb, hands over the cup of poisoned tea; she puts it beyond her own power to prevent the death that she intends. But then (too late to intervene) she undergoes a Damascene conversion: She realizes the full horror of the murder that she has, as she thinks, committed; she wishes that she could have prevented it; she is wracked by remorseful guilt. But then she discovers that her attempt failed, and caused no harm: The shot missed its happily unaware target; the bomb did not detonate; the tea was spilled. "Thank God I failed!" she says to herself. "Results matter" theorists might argue that this reaction is morally appropriate, and is relevant to how the criminal law should treat failed attempts: I'll say more about this in Section 4.4. The point to note here, however, is that the reaction has two aspects: first, "Thank God, I didn't murder him;" second, "Thank God, he wasn't murdered." In ordinary cases, they go together: If I didn't murder him, he was not murdered. But in cases of collective agency, even if the individual can separate out his own agency in the way canvassed above, they come apart: The shooter whose gun was loaded with a blank might be able to say "Thank God, I didn't murder him," but cannot say "Thank God, he wasn't murdered" – for he was murdered, by the collective agency of the group. Similarly, consider a case of potential overdetermination. A fires at V, at the same moment as (unknown to A) B fires at V. Each shot, if it hit as the

[16] See Alexander, Ferzan, and Morse, *Crime and Culpability*, 182–83.

shooter intended, would suffice to cause V's death – thus producing a case of causal overdetermination. In fact, A's shot misses, whilst B's shot hits and kills V. A repents his murderous attempt as soon as he has pulled the trigger, but then discovers that his shot missed. Can he now say a consolatory "Thank God, I failed"?

He cannot now feel relief that V was not murdered: for V has been murdered. Thus, any relief he feels cannot express his revived concern for V's well-being. As far as that is concerned, there is nothing to be relieved about. His relief can only be that *he* was not V's murderer. If we are to get clear about the possible moral, or legal, significance of failure, we must think about that kind of relief, which responds to the *mere* fact that *my* attempt failed.

We will return to this issue in Section 4.4, but should first attend to some of the "causal conundrums" by which Alexander also aims to unsettle the "results matter" theorist.[17]

4.3 "CAUSAL CONUNDRUMS"

There are, as Alexander points out, familiar problems about both "factual" and "proximate" causation: familiar cases in which we may be unsure whether we should say that A caused the relevant result. Sometimes, for instance, we cannot know the relevant facts: Who fired the shot that killed V? Sometimes we know the facts, but are uncertain, or disagree, about the normative question of whether those facts suffice to justify attributing the result to A. Obvious examples are those in which the chain of events leading from A's initial action to the outcome that A intended differs radically from A's intentions or expectations as to means. As Alexander rightly points out, we may disagree, or be unsure, not just about what judgment to make in specific cases, but about the criteria that should guide such judgments. Alexander's criminal law, however, will not face such problem cases, since its courts will never have to determine whether A caused a result that he intended. In at least that respect, it simplifies the criminal law.

This would be a significant argument in favor of Alexander's view, if at least one of three things was true: first, that such problem cases are so common as to render many criminal cases problematic; second, that even if such problem cases are not common, the importance of actual results is so minor that it is an uneconomic use of resources to make verdicts and sentences depend on them, given the difficulties involved in trying to do so; third, that even if "causal conundrums" of these kinds do not actually arise in many criminal cases, our apparent inability to resolve them in any nonarbitrary way undermines the reliability or rational legitimacy of all our causal judgments, so that we can *never* say, with justified confidence,

17 Ibid., 180–88.

that A caused V's death. However, none of these things is true (in a way that could support Alexander's argument). The first is straightforwardly false: Most criminal cases pose no such problems; when they do pose some such problem, so that the attribution of causation is uncertain, *in dubio pro reo* mandates the accused's acquittal of the completed crime (she can still be convicted of attempt). To assert the truth of the second would be to beg the question at issue: How important (if at all) are actual results? The third would be iconoclastic indeed: Within the law, apart from its implications for criminal law, it would sweep away tort law;[18] outside the law, it would undermine all the modes of human thought and discourse that involve attributing causation to human actions, and most if not all of our practical reasoning (since, in deciding what to do, we often rely on predictions about the effects of this or that action – predictions of the outcomes that would be causally attributable to us). Fortunately for our ordinary ways of thinking, talking, and acting, however, the continuing irresolubility of these "causal conundrums" (if they are rationally irresoluble – I take no stand on that here) has no such implication: It shows that our causal thought becomes problematic at the periphery (as is often true of our normative thinking); but that does not undermine its reliability or rationality at the center. I can still say, with rational confidence, that Jane caused John's death when, acting on her own, she shot him in the heart – even though there are alternative scenarios in which I could not make any such confident judgment; there are hard cases, but also simple cases.

There is one other causal matter to which we should attend here: the issue of unexpected (but welcome) consequences. Sometimes these are immediate (although unforeseen by the agent and perhaps unforeseeable by her or others), and such that she would certainly have been justified in acting as she did had she been aware of them and acted because of them. A thief steals a bag that in fact contains a bomb. By taking it to a remote place (to check its contents), she saves a number of lives. A "would-be killer misses his victim and kills a terrorist who was about to kill 1,000 people."[19] Others are more remote: Perhaps in the long run what at the time looked like a clearly wrongful, and on balance harmful, action turns out to produce significant benefits, which might even outweigh the short-term harm.[20] If results matter, Alexander argues, they should matter in cases such as these: but such

18 See Alexander and Kimberly Kessler Ferzan, "Confused Culpability, Contrived Causation, and the Collapse of Tort Theory," in *Philosophical Foundations of the Law of Torts*, ed. John Oberdiek (Oxford: Oxford University Press, 2014), 406–25.

19 See Alexander, Ferzan, and Morse, *Crime and Culpability*, 178–79. The bomb thief was an actual Israeli case, described by P.H. Robinson, "The Bomb Thief and the Theory of Justification Defenses," *Criminal Law Forum* 8, no. 3 (1997): 387 (see his note 1 for sources).

20 See Alexander, "Crime and Culpability," 12–14; Alexander, Ferzan, and Morse, *Crime and Culpability*, 179–80.

fortuities cannot alter the agent's culpability, and therefore should not affect the fact or extent of his deserved punishment.

Such cases take us beyond the core of the "results matter" thesis: for that thesis concerns the significance of the (non)occurrence of results that were within the scope of the agent's intention (or, in the case of recklessness, within the scope of the risks that she foresaw). But in these cases we are dealing with outcomes that *ex hypothesi* fell outside that scope. Alexander seems to find this distinction puzzling.

> Defenders of "results matter" typically deny that results matter in the absence of culpable mental states ... But if results are morally inert in the absence of the requisite mental states, what explains their moral valence in the presence of such mental states?[21]

Now, if we begin with two separate categories – "results" and "culpable mental states" – we might indeed wonder how the culpability of the mental states can somehow affect or infect the results; and, if it can do so, why it should not affect all results – the unintended and unforeseen as well as the intended or foreseen. But that is not where we should begin; nor is the "results matter" thesis best expressed as the thesis that the occurrence of the relevant result aggravates the agent's culpability or penal desert. Rather, we begin (in our response to and judgment of the agent) with the completed action that he intended – with the murder or arson that he intended and tried to commit, with the integrated unity of intention and result that characterizes human action.[22] We can then ask whether an agent's failure to complete the action that she intended and attempted to commit should affect our judgment of her culpability and desert. So the question is not whether success aggravates, but whether failure mitigates; and it concerns only results within the agent's contemplation – no moral magic is involved.

This is not to dismiss the question raised by cases of "unknown justification," like that of the thief who steals a bomb-holding bag. It is a question, within a "results matter" framework, about what kinds of result matter and how they matter. The question is usually understood as one about the conditions of justification in criminal law (Is it enough that the justificatory fact existed, or must the agent have been aware of, or motivated by, that fact?), but that is not the best way to understand

[21] Alexander, Ferzan, and Morse, *Crime and Culpability*, 179; see ibid., 173, on the "question ... whether culpability *plus* causation has some moral magic that causation itself lacks."

[22] The claim that this "characterizes human action" does not depend for its truth on whether, as a matter of statistics, successful actions are more common than failures; it is a claim about how we understand human action. See further Duff, *Criminal Attempts*, chaps. 9–11. This is another matter on which Alexander and I differ radically, since he holds a volitionist theory of action (see Alexander, Ferzan, and Morse, *Crime and Culpability*, chap. 7); we cannot pursue this disagreement here.

it.[23] The question is whether the offense should be so defined that an element of it is negated by the justificatory fact – in which case the agent should be acquitted of the complete offense, as "deeds" theorists argue (which leaves it open whether she should be convicted of an attempt to commit that offense); or so defined that that fact can be cited as a justification for committing the offense – in which case "reasons" theorists are right that it should be a fact of which the agent was aware and by which she was motivated. In offenses of recklessness, an element of the offense is that the risk is an unreasonable or unjustifiable one for the agent to take: if the prosecution fails to prove this, it has failed to prove that the defendant committed the relevant offense; she then needs no justificatory defense to avoid conviction. Analogously, what the "deeds" theorist should argue is that the unjustifiability of the defendant's action ought to be folded into the definition of the offense: Thus, theft might be defined as involving the objectively unwarranted appropriation of another's property – in which case taking the bomb-holding bag would not constitute theft. By contrast, a "reasons" theorist must argue that the offense definition ought not to include the relevant justificatory fact: The accused has committed the offense, and if he wants to avoid conviction by offering a justificatory defense, he must do so by explaining the justificatory reasons for which he acted.[24]

I have not so far offered any arguments against Alexander's "results do not matter" view, or in favor of the "results matter" thesis. I have tried only to show that the "results matter" theorist need not be disturbed by the difficulties that Alexander aims to create for her – difficulties to do with collective agency, with "causal conundrums," and with fortuitously beneficial results. It is time now to ask what (new) can be said about the basic conflict between these two camps.

4.4 MORAL LEDGERS AND CRIMINAL LAW AS COMMUNICATION

An important aspect of the problem of outcome luck is hinted at by one phrase in *Crime and Culpability*. Is an agent's "positive moral ledger enhanced," Alexander asks, by the dramatic but entirely unforeseen benefits that his well-meaning action brings?[25] My concern here is not with the significance of unforeseen benefits, but with the tempting image of the "moral ledger," and its role in the context of criminal wrongdoing.

[23] See classically George P. Fletcher, *Rethinking Criminal Law* (Boston: Little, Brown, 1978), 555–66; Paul H. Robinson, *Structure and Function in Criminal Law* (Oxford: Oxford University Press, 1997), 95–124. For the view suggested here, see Duff, *Answering for Crime*, 277–84.

[24] This is not how Alexander would describe the matter (see Alexander, Ferzan, and Morse, *Crime and Culpability*, 91–92, on "eviscerating the offense-defense distinction"), but it is the appropriate way for those who accept that "results matter" to describe it.

[25] Alexander, Ferzan, and Morse, *Crime and Culpability*, 179.

My moral ledger records all my moral credits and debits: I accrue credits by acting rightly, or well, or perhaps heroically (we need not ask here whether I accrue credits for simply doing my minimal duty, or only for conduct that is in some way supererogatory); I accrue debits by acting wrongfully. The ledger itself, as an accurate record of my credits and debits, can be kept only by the recording angel: Only she can know the relevant truths about me. But human beings can do their fallible best to work out what credits and debits they and others have accrued; and that is what courts must do in determining criminal guilt and punishment. For criminal law is concerned with retributive justice, with ensuring that wrongdoers suffer the penal burdens that they deserve. Doing retributive justice involves ensuring that courts impose penal burdens that suitably match the relevant debits in defendants' moral ledgers. Thus, the criminal law should so define offenses (and so specify principles of sentencing) that, when a defendant is convicted of a crime, the court will be able to work out from the definition of the relevant crime (as far as is reasonably possible for a fallible human institution) the size of the debit that the defendant accrued by committing the offense. We must therefore ask what can generate moral debits (or credits, for that matter), since only then will we know what kinds of factors should figure in the law's offense definitions; and a "results don't matter" thesis might seem plausible in answering that question.

Credits and debits can accrue in my financial ledger in many ways, many of which involve substantial elements of luck: I can gain or lose money through processes over which I exercise little or no control; and whilst some of those processes might be unjust, we do not suppose that financial credits and debits either generally are, or should be, free from the influence of luck. But moral credits or debits, especially if they are to determine what kind of punishment (human or divine) I am to suffer, seem different; it is here that we find the powerful intuition that lies at the heart of the "results don't matter" thesis. Surely what is a matter of bad luck cannot accrue moral discredit for me: It would be unfair if I accrued a debit in my moral ledger for something over which I had no control; it would similarly be unfair if I could gain moral credit for something that was a matter of luck. It is only a short step from there to the familiar thesis that since the actual results of my actions, their actual impacts on the world, are always to some degree a matter of luck, those results must be irrelevant to my moral credit or discredit.

That is why the judge sentencing a man who had thrown vitriol at his former girlfriend, but had luckily caused her no (physical) harm, was obviously right to say that the fact that "you did her no harm … in truth does not redound to your credit at all." But the judge went wrong, according to this view, when he held that the defendant was nonetheless "entitled, fortunately for yourself, to have it remembered that you really only attempted to burn and disfigure this poor girl," and convicted and sentenced him only for an attempt (a sentence lighter than he would have received had his attack succeeded).[26]

It certainly seems right to say that I cannot claim moral credit for the failure of my attempt – at least if the attempt was wholehearted. But there are two possible reasons for that which do not support a "results don't matter" thesis. First, to say that I cannot *claim* credit for failing is not yet to say that others (and in particular the law) should not nonetheless *allow* me such credit: What I can felicitously claim is often not the same as what I should be given. Second, failure can affect the entries in a moral ledger without bringing credit: Rather (according to the "results matter" view), failure generates a smaller debit than would have accrued if the attempt had succeeded. The recording angel does not first record the debit appropriate to the completed crime, and then record a credit to offset part of that debit; she simply records a smaller debit in the first place. These points do not, however, get near the heart of the issue, which concerns the appropriateness of this model, or metaphor, of the moral ledger.

One question is whether that model is sustainable: Can we really draw the sharp distinction that it requires between those matters (wholly within the agent's control, wholly free from the influence of luck) that are to determine the entries in the ledger, and those matters (not within the agent's control, vulnerable to the vagaries of chance) that cannot affect the ledger? A lot depends here on the philosophy of action. The ledger records our credits and debits as agents: So we need an account of action under which our actions (or at least a significant range of them) are wholly within our control. That is why the volitionist account on which Alexander relies is important for his purposes.[27] All of the actual outcomes of our actions are subject to the vagaries of chance – including their physical manifestations, since even the movements of my limbs or contractions of my muscles could be frustrated by a sudden paralysis. If we are to find a core of agency that is wholly within my control, it seems that something like volition is the only possibility. However, I will not pursue this issue here. I want instead to ask whether, even if that model is sustainable as a model of our ultimate moral credit and discredit as agents,[28] it is a model that the criminal law should follow: Whether criminal offenses should (at least ideally) be so defined as to capture only kinds of "action" that would generate negative entries in

[26] *Carmichael* [1930] 22 Cr. App. R. 142; the quotes are from p. 143.

[27] See *supra* note 22; Michael S. Moore, *Act and Crime: The Philosophy of Action and its Implications for the Criminal Law* (Oxford: Oxford University Press, 1993).

[28] The qualification "as agents" is crucial here: there are many kinds of moral appraisal, such as appraisals of moral character or of virtue and vice, that do not depend only on what is within our control – but that also do not involve blame, or attributions of culpability. But criminal law is concerned only with that for which blame is appropriate – only with immorality that is culpable; it is thus concerned not with every kind of moral defect, but only with wrongdoing (see Moore, *Act and Crime*, 49–59).

the ledger; whether the convictions and sentences handed down by criminal courts should (at least ideally) track those entries.

That this is indeed an appropriate model for the criminal law is suggested by a familiar way of understanding retributivism. "Retributivism" picks out a range of theories that are united by the claim that punishment is to be understood and justified as an appropriate or fitting response to wrongdoing: To explain why a wrongdoer's punishment is justified, and why the practice of punishment itself is justified, we are to look back towards the wrong, and to the relationship between past wrong and present punishment – rather than looking, as consequentialists look, to the consequences of the punishment. The central task for retributivists is then to explain that justificatory relationship: How does a past wrong make a present punishment appropriate? One familiar answer is that the wrong generates "negative desert" – a quantum of suffering (whose currency could be, for instance, pain, or loss of liberty, or loss of money) that is now due to the wrongdoer. What punishment does is to impose that quantum of suffering, thus ensuring that wrongdoers "receive their negative desert."[29] If this is what punishment is about, the attraction of the ledger model is obvious: for it precisely records each person's negative and positive desert – her moral discredits and credits. That model also then generates some of the questions that, as Alexander notes, this version of retributivism faces.[30] In determining the appropriate severity of an offender's sentence (how many "units of suffering" he deserves), should the court attend only to the discredit entered in his ledger by the crime for which he has been convicted? Or should it attend as well, for instance, to any credits that he might also have earned; or to units of suffering to which he might have already been subjected (at the time, or as a result, of the crime); or to the overall balance of credits and discredits, and of suffering and doing well, in his life?

Here again, there are two questions to ask. One concerns the moral plausibility of this picture of cosmic justice. Should we really believe that there is this deep (some would say mysterious) connection between culpable wrongdoing and suffering such that the former demands the latter? Is the world really morally better to the extent that culpable wrongdoers suffer pains or hardships or harms whose severity is somehow proportional to the seriousness of their wrongdoing? Even if we do or should believe this, however, a second question arises: Should it be the responsibility of the state, or of the political community of which the state is the institutional instrument, to try to achieve that moral good? Should we agree with Moore that "the world is better if it is morally better, and to the extent legislators can achieve

[29] That this is Alexander's version of retributivism is suggested by *Crime and Culpability*, 7–12, from where the quoted phrases are taken.

[30] See Alexander, Ferzan, and Morse, *Crime and Culpability*, 10–12.

that moral betterment through law, they should do so"?[31] I will again focus on the second question.

Alexander does not share Moore's robust version of retributivism, according to which *the* function of the criminal law is to punish culpable wrongdoers.[32] For Alexander, "the criminal law's primary concern is the prevention of harm," and its distinctive contribution appears when we seek to pursue that end by "inculcat[ing] norms that are meant to guide people's choices;" for if we are to inculcate such norms, we must also "inculcat[e] reactive attitudes towards those who … violate the norms;" those reactive attitudes include "the sense that punishment is fitting;" thus, "the criminal law both creates and reflects value by announcing which conduct is sufficiently wrong to deserve blame and punishment."[33] Furthermore, his retributivism is "moderate" rather than "strong" – "negative desert is necessary and sufficient for punishment but … desert does not *mandate* punishment."[34] On his account, however, the distinctive function of criminal law is still to pave the way for punishment; the function of punishment is to inflict on culpable wrongdoers an appropriate quantum of harm or suffering; and "sometimes punishment will serve no purpose other than to see that the guilty get what they deserve."[35]

Part of this line of thought seems to me right: The criminal law (in its substantive dimension) declares a set of norms that are supposed to guide our conduct towards each other (our conduct, I would say, as members of the political community whose law it is). In so doing, it also provides an appropriate, deserved response to violations of those norms: for to take a set of norms seriously, as our norms, is to be disposed not only to guide our own conduct by them, but also to respond appropriately to violations of them (by ourselves and by others). We can also usefully talk of the "reactive attitudes" that are appropriately felt towards norm violators. But what do those attitudes include? One question – a version of the first question noted above – is whether they include a "sense that punishment is fitting," and whether that "fitting" punishment consists essentially in the infliction of a quantum of deserved suffering. The other question – the second question noted above, on which I want to focus – is whether it should be one of the guiding aims of the state to maintain an institution

31 Michael S. Moore, "Four Reflections on Law and Morality," *William & Mary Law Review* 48, no. 5 (2007): 1540. For some doubts about this claim, see R. A. Duff, "Legal Moralism and Public Wrongs," in *Legal, Moral, and Metaphysical Truths: The Philosophy of Michael S. Moore*, ed. Kimberly Kessler Ferzan and Stephen J. Morse (New York: Oxford University Press, 2015), 95–109.

32 See Michael S. Moore, *Placing Blame: A Theory of Criminal Law* (New York: Oxford University Press, 1997), 33–35.

33 Alexander, Ferzan, and Morse, *Crime and Culpability*, 4–6.

34 Ibid., 7 (emphasis added).

35 Ibid., 8.

of criminal punishment whose function is to ensure that norm violators do indeed receive that suffering.

I will not argue directly against this view here (save to suggest that when we think about the proper aims of a contemporary, liberal, secular state, it is far from clear that we should suppose the infliction of deserved suffering to be one of them). Instead, I will sketch a quite different account of an appropriate way of responding to criminal wrongdoing – a response that is in a sense more conversational, that expresses different reactive attitudes, and that incorporates (for what I will suggest is good reason) a "results matter" perspective.[36]

A liberal polity's criminal law is concerned not with the state of its citizens' souls or with their overall moral character, but with how they behave towards each other. Its substantive part defines the kinds of wrongful conduct of which the polity takes formal, condemnatory notice. These wrongs, it declares, are wrongs that merit a formal, public response. Its procedural and penal parts then provide for that formal response: Those accused of committing such wrongs are liable to be brought to trial; and, if convicted, are liable to be punished. The procedural and penal dimensions of criminal law can thus also be seen (and so far, I think, this account is along lines similar to Alexander's) as giving institutional, formal expression to the reactive attitudes that are appropriate in response to such wrongs. But what are these attitudes? They include blame, but this (as a reactive attitude) is not neatly separable from a range of moralized emotions that we are likely to feel (and should feel) in response to criminal wrongs – most obviously, emotions such as indignation and anger.[37] For blame, of the kind that figures in our civic or social lives (which is where the criminal law belongs), marks not a detached judgment on the contents of a person's moral ledger, but a response to what he has done: to what he has done in the social and material world in which we live with him as embodied social beings.

We are indignant at the wrong done to a victim of (a consummated) crime. That indignation is a response not merely to harm he has suffered (it is not the same as our sympathetic response to one who suffers harm through natural causes), nor merely to the wrongful choice, or attempt, that the perpetrator made. It is a response to the wrongful injury that the victim has suffered – to the rape, the murder (as distinct from death), the physical attack (as distinct from injury), or the theft (as distinct from loss of property), that he suffered. The perpetrator must, we should think, be called to account for what he has done – which is precisely what the criminal trial is supposed to do: He is called to answer to the charge that he committed this wrong,

[36] See further R.A. Duff, "Retrieving Retributivism," in *Retributivism: Essays on Theory and Policy*, ed. Mark D. White (Oxford: Oxford University Press, 2011), 3–24.

[37] See Bernard Williams, "Morality and the Emotions," in Bernard Williams, *Problems of the Self* (Cambridge: Cambridge University Press, 1973), 207–29.

and for this wrong if it is proved that he committed it. A core purpose of this process is that it should bring the perpetrator to face up to, to accept his responsibility for, what he has done; if we can understand criminal punishment in (at least partly) communicative terms, as part of a communicative engagement with the perpetrator that formally begins in his trial, we can say that punishment too involves an attempt to bring the offender to confront, to face up to, the wrong he has committed.

I have been talking so far of our response to consummated crimes, completed wrongs, since this is where we begin: that is to say, we see and respond to nonconsummated wrongs, to failed attempts to harm another, in the light of the consummated wrongs that they failed to become. As I emphasized above, the criminal law is concerned with our conduct towards each other in our shared, embodied, social world, and thus with our actions as engagements in, as impingements on, that world.[38] It is concerned neither merely with choice or volition (or indeed merely with *mens rea* as constituted by purpose or awareness), nor merely with the material effects of such choice or volition (with the *actus reus*), but with meaningful actions as interventions in our shared world.

It is against this background that "… but, thank God, you failed" is significant, as part of our response to failed criminal attempts: It expresses the relief we appropriately feel that the intended harm did not eventuate. That relief is not separable from, but conditions, our moral response to the perpetrator's conduct: It is not just the kind of relief that we might feel when we see someone narrowly escape a falling rock or forest fire, but a distinctive kind of relief at the noncompletion of a wrong. It is a relief that the perpetrator ought also to feel, or come to feel, in the sense that if he comes to repent his (attempted) crime, as he should, he will feel this relief that he failed. That is why the fact of his failure properly conditions both his trial and his punishment: Our response to him should signal both our condemnation of his wrongful action and our relief that it failed – a condemnation and relief that he should come to make his own.

This has been a bare sketch of a conception of criminal action (as a wrongful engagement in our shared social and material world), and of the criminal process of trial and punishment (as an appropriate response to such actions), that supports a "results matter" view. It constitutes not a direct argument against Alexander's account, but an attempt to show that there is an alternative that makes good (better?) normative sense of our practices. To finish this brief chapter, however, I should return to an important issue that is, I suggested earlier, raised by some of the examples by which Alexander hopes to confute the "results matter" theorist.[39]

38 Which is why (though I cannot pursue the issue here) it is so important to decide how we are to understand action in the context of criminal law: see *supra* notes 22 and 27.

39 See Alexander, Ferzan, and Morse, *Crime and Culpability*, 180–88.

In ordinary cases of failure, "Thank God I failed" can express a relief with two dimensions: that the intended victim did not suffer the wrong that I tried to commit and, accordingly, that I did not commit that wrong. Sometimes, however, only the latter dimension is available: for the victim suffered the wrong, but not at my own hands. Is "Thank God I failed" still appropriate, as something that the (would-be) perpetrator can properly feel, and as something that can properly condition the criminal law's response? Or would that mark a morally inappropriate concern with the extent to which his hands have been dirtied – rather than with the wrong that was done (albeit by someone else)? I need to be able to say that it would still be appropriate – and think that I can. The would-be murderer should, of course, share in our response to the wrong that was actually committed and suffered (though, in his case, that response should be conditioned by the horrified thought that that is what he tried to do to the victim). But he can still be relieved that he did not make himself a murderer,[40] and our response to him (as distinct from our response to the actual murderer) can still be conditioned by the thought "but at least you didn't kill him" (or, perhaps, "but at least *you* didn't kill him").

I have suggested that we can articulate a plausible version of "results matter" for the criminal law of attempts, in opposition to Alexander's argument that results should not matter. However, to do so we must delve not only into moral philosophy (which is where much of the debate about the significance of results is focused), but also into philosophy of action and political philosophy – we must get clear about the role of criminal law (and criminal punishment) in a contemporary liberal polity, and about what conception of action is appropriate to that role. Alexander might not have confuted the "results matter" theorists, but they have work to do if they are to respond adequately to his arguments. Here, as elsewhere, Larry Alexander provokes and challenges even when he does not persuade.

40 See Peter Winch, "Trying," in Peter Winch, *Ethics and Action* (London: Routledge, 1972), 130–50.

5

Does Duress Justify or Excuse?

The Significance of Larry Alexander's Ambivalence

Peter Westen

Why, then, do commentators characterize duress as an excuse? Many do so, I believe, because they assume that threats that are natural in origin provide the baseline for determining the harms that actors may inflict on innocent and non-threatening persons. Because they take natural threats as the baseline for justification in such cases, and because section 2.09 of the Model Penal Code (MPC) provides a defense for coercive threats that go beyond that baseline, commentators feel they must regard section 2.09 as an excuse. I have argued that commentators are mistaken. A coercive threat of an unlawful harm is a graver evil for a threatened person than an otherwise identical evil that is natural in origin; and the offense that a person is coerced into inflicting may not be as grave an evil by him as the evil of his coercer. The combination justifies coerced actors in committing offenses that would be unjustified if the threatened and inflicted harms differed in their respective origins. Larry Alexander's scholarship is distinguished by Larry's profusion of original and insightful positions across a remarkable range of moral and legal topics. It is also distinguished by Larry's resoluteness.

The subject of this essay – the essential nature of the criminal defense of duress – is one where Larry's usual resoluteness fails him. From his earliest writings on criminal law to the present, Larry has given the defense of duress a markedly prominent role. Yet he has always remained ambivalent about why duress exonerates. His ambivalence is significant because the question "*Why* does duress exonerate?" not only implicates how the defense is conceptualized as between justification and excuse but also affects the breadth of what is exonerated.

I shall argue that Larry is right to be ambivalent about duress (albeit not for the reason he gives) but wrong in believing that ambivalence is of little consequence. I shall proceed in eight parts. Section 5.1 identifies the elements of the MPC's formulation of the duress defense, including its requirement of coercion. Section 5.2 discusses Larry's distinct version of the defense. Section 5.3 discusses Larry's ambivalence regarding whether duress is a justification or an excuse. Section 5.4 identifies features that commentators agree distinguish justification from excuse. Section 5.5 analyzes the MPC's formulation of the duress defense in light of the latter distinction, arguing that duress typically functions as a justification, though, when actors suffer from insuperable infirmities, it can function as an excuse. Section 5.6 addresses three sets of commentators who should conclude that duress is a justification but, paradoxically, balk at the consequences of their own reasoning. Section 5.7 argues that an insight of Antony Duff's regarding the nature of harm supports the MPC's distinction between coercive threats and noncoercive human threats and natural threats. And Section 5.8 discusses the normative consequences of whether duress is a justification or an excuse.

5.1 THE ESSENTIAL ELEMENTS OF THE DEFENSE OF DURESS

The modern defense of duress is a product of the MPC. Prior to the MPC, most jurisdictions did not even recognize duress as a defense. And those that did typically framed the defense as a choice between specified greater and lesser evils, leading commentators to conclude that the defense sounded in justification.[1]

The MPC reforms the defense in four ways. First, MPC § 2.09 makes explicit what was previously implicit, namely, that the gravamen of duress is *coercion*.[2] Coercion is a two-party relationship in which a malefactor uses a threat of unlawful harm to pressure a reluctant actor into becoming the malefactor's instrument in a course of conduct of the malefactor's devising. The relevant course of conduct under section 2.09 is the offense with which the actor is charged, which is typically an offense against a third party. A coercer both devises the criminal act at issue and employs threats of unlawful harm to pressure a reluctant actor to commit it. The coerced party neither conceives the criminal conduct nor acts other than as the malefactor directs him to under threat of harm. What relieves actors of criminal responsibility under section 2.09 is not the presence of threats alone but the presence of coercive threats.

Second, rather than frame the defense in terms of choices between greater and lesser evils, the MPC frames it in general terms. Section 2.09 provides that an actor has a defense to *any* crime, provided he can show that he was coerced to commit the crime by *any* threat of unlawful force against the actor's person or that of another,

[1] See Wayne R. LaFave and Austin W. Scott, Jr., *Substantive Criminal Law* (Minneapolis: West, 1986), § 5.4(a).

[2] American Law Institute, *Model Penal Code and Commentaries* (Philadelphia: American Law Institute, 1971) § 2.09 ("It is an affirmative defense that the actor engaged in the conduct charged to constitute an offense because he was *coerced* to do so by the use of, or a threat to use, unlawful force against his person or the person of another, which a person of reasonable firmness in his situation would have been unable to resist" (emphasis added)).

whether imminent or not, that "a person of reasonable firmness in his situation would have been unable to resist."

Third, in contrast to prior law, section 2.09 is intended to provide victims of coercive threats with a broader defense than section 3.02 provides for victims of *natural* threats. The MPC Commentary addresses two hypothetical cases in which actors respond to respective threats of death by committing homicide, the difference being that one actor responds to a natural threat while the other responds to a coercive threat. The Commentary reasons that, although neither actor possesses a lesser evil defense under section 3.02, the victim of the coercive threat, and he alone, is entitled to an instruction on duress under section 2.09.[3]

Finally, and in contrast to prior law, which framed duress as a justification, the authors of the MPC state that section 2.09 is an "excuse" whenever it provides a defense to an actor who does not possess a lesser evil defense under section 3.02.[4] Thus, insofar as section 2.09 provides a defense of duress to a person who would have a defense of necessity were the threat of force natural rather than coercive in origin, section 2.09 replicates section 3.02 and constitutes a justification. However, insofar as section 2.09 goes beyond section 3.02 and provides a defense to a person who would not have a necessity defense were the threat of force natural in origin, section 2.09 is declared to be an excuse.

5.2 LARRY'S VERSION OF DURESS

The defense of duress occupies a prominent place in Larry's theory of criminal responsibility. Yet Larry's version of the defense differs significantly from the MPC's because he implicitly eliminates the MPC's requirement of coercion.

Duress, in Larry's theory, is just one of three defenses that persons possess who have to choose between either inflicting harm on others or suffering harm (or allowing others to suffer harm):

(1) *"Self-defense," and "defense of others."* These defenses, in Larry's view, obtain when innocent persons must choose between either suffering harm at the hands of culpable aggressors (or allowing innocent third persons to suffer such harm), or harming the culpable aggressors or other culpable persons instead. The defenses entitle innocent persons (or third persons acting on their behalf) to avoid threats of culpable harm by harming culpable persons when doing so is proportionate and necessary.[5]

3 American Law Institute, *Model Penal Code and Commentaries* (1985), pt. 1, § 2.09, 378.

4 Ibid., 373.

5 Larry Alexander, "Self-Defense, Justification, and Excuse," *Philosophy and Public Affairs* 22, no. 1 (1993): 60.

(2) *"Lesser evil" justification (or "social" justification).* This defense obtains when innocent persons must choose between either suffering harm from natural threats or from innocent human aggressors or other innocent human threats (or allowing others to suffer such harm), or harming innocent persons instead. In Larry's view, the defense entitles innocent persons (or third persons acting on their behalf) to avoid threats of harm by inflicting harm on innocent persons, provided the inflicted harm is the lesser evil under the circumstances, as measured agent-neutrally, and inflicting the harm does not violate deontological constraints.[6]

(3) *Duress.* This is the *residual* defense that remains when persons must choose between suffering harm (or allowing loved ones to suffer harm), or inflicting harm on innocent persons instead. Larry does not explicitly discuss coercive threats of the sort that section 2.09 addresses, except to say that he attaches no normative weight to coercion. He means to include coercive threats, however, because he defines duress to include all threats of harm, whether coercive or not, whether human or natural in origin, and whether unlawful or lawful. In Larry's view, an actor has a defense of duress when five conditions obtain: (1) a person or natural event – and, if a person, regardless of whether he acts voluntarily or involuntarily, lawfully or unlawfully – poses an threat of physical harm to the actor or a loved one; (2) the actor has no choice but to suffer the threatened harm (or allow a loved one to suffer it) or try to avoid the threatened harm by harming an innocent person, whether the latter is an innocent source of the threat or an innocent third person; (3) the actor elects to protect himself or a loved one by harming an innocent person; (4) the actor's conduct is not socially justified; and (5) a person of reasonable firmness in the actor's situation would have been unable to resist acting as he did.[7]

Because Larry's version of duress is not confined to coercive threats, it is considerably broader than section 2.09. It extends to what Larry calls "Innocent Aggressors" (e.g., an insane man threatens to kill an innocent actor unless the latter protects himself by killing the insane man); "Innocent Swords" (e.g., a fat man is thrown from a cliff and, like a falling sword, threatens to fall upon an innocent actor at the bottom unless the latter protects himself by vaporizing the falling fat man); "Innocent Bystanders" (e.g., a sole actor is working on a railway sidetrack onto which a bystander threatens to fatally turn a runaway trolley in order to save five, unless the

6 Ibid., 60–61; Larry Alexander and Kimberly Ferzan, *Crime and Culpability: A Theory of Criminal Law* (Cambridge: Cambridge University Press, 2009), 136.

7 Alexander, "Self-Defense, Justification, and Excuse," 63–64; Larry Alexander, "Justification and Innocent Aggressors," *Wayne Law Review* 33, no. 4 (1987): 1187; Alexander and Ferzan, *Crime and Culpability*, 125, 134–36.

actor protects himself by shooting the bystander); and "Innocent Shields" (e.g., a malefactor uses an innocent person as a shield as part of a threat to kill an innocent actor unless the latter protects himself by killing the innocent shield).[8] Moreover, because Larry draws no normative distinction between human and natural threats, he would provide a defense to an actor who, to avoid an avalanche, runs over children playing on the road, provided the actor would have a defense to running them over if a coercive malefactor threatened to kill him unless he did so.[9] And because Larry draws no normative distinction between threats of lawful and unlawful force, he would provide a defense to a fleeing felon who kills a police officer to prevent the officer from *lawfully* shooting him, provided the felon would have a defense if the police officer threatened to *unlawfully* shoot him (hereinafter "Fleeing Felon").[10]

5.3 LARRY'S AMBIVALENCE REGARDING WHETHER DURESS JUSTIFIES OR EXCUSES

The defense of duress comes into play for Larry only when an actor's conduct is not a lesser of two evils, that is, not "socially justified." Yet that does not mean that Larry regards duress as an excuse. Starting with his first article on the issue and continuing to the present day, Larry has remained ambivalent about whether duress is a justification or an excuse, because Larry is ambivalent about whether justified harms are confined to *socially* justified harms or also extend to *personally* justified harms.

Harm is "socially" justified for Larry when (i) it is a lesser evil as assessed on an agent-neutral basis, and (ii) its infliction does not violate deontological rights. Moreover, because third parties who are not under threat and who have no family relationships to others should assess their interests in relation to others on agent-neutral grounds, the rights of third parties are a direct function of whether harms are socially justified: Once a harm is determined to be socially justified, third persons may assist an actor in inflicting it (just as the actor himself may inflict it); and, because it is a lesser evil as assessed agent-neutrally, third parties may not prevent an actor from inflicting it.[11]

By contrast, harm is "personally" justified when, although it is not a lesser evil assessed agent-neutrally, it is a lesser evil from a threatened actor's agent-relative standpoint and, therefore, a harm that the actor is permitted to inflict. A harm can be a lesser evil for him because, being the person who is personally threatened, he is allowed to weigh his own interests (and the interests of his loved ones) more heavily

[8] Alexander and Ferzan, *Crime and Culpability*, 135, 141.

[9] Ibid., 142.

[10] Ibid., 141.

[11] Ibid., 104, 112, 137–39; Alexander, "Self-Defense, Justification, and Excuse," 56; Alexander, "Justification and Innocent Aggressors," 1187–88.

than society weighs them agent-neutrally. Because agent-relative interests do not transfer to third persons who are not under threat and have no family at issue, they do not affect what third persons may and may not do. Thus, if a harm is a greater evil when assessed agent-neutrally, third parties may not assist an actor in inflicting it – and they may prevent him from inflicting it – even though the actor himself may be personally justified in inflicting it.[12]

Larry recognizes that, if agent-relative interests exist, they can justify an actor inflicting otherwise unjustified harms, including in contexts of duress. Yet Larry remains ambivalent about whether duress is a justification because he is ambivalent about whether agent-relative interests do, indeed, exist.[13] If they do not exist, he says, duress is not a justification and, hence, must be an excuse.[14]

5.4 THE ESSENTIAL DISTINCTION BETWEEN JUSTIFICATION AND EXCUSE

The distinction between justification and excuse is as old as Cicero.[15] Yet it remains contested because commentators differ about practically every aspect of it. With respect to justification, commentators disagree about whether it is wholly objective, wholly subjective, or both objective and subjective;[16] whether it is confined to conduct that is positively desirable or also extends to conduct that is merely permissible;[17] whether third persons may resist conduct that is justified;[18] and whether the distinction between justification and excuse should be abandoned in favor of alternative categories.[19]

12 Alexander and Ferzan, *Crime and Culpability*, 112, 137–39.

13 Alexander, "Justification and Innocent Aggressors," 1189.

14 Alexander and Ferzan, *Crime and Culpability*, 112, 136, 138, 146.

15 Eugene R. Milhizer, "Justification and Excuse: What They Were, What They Are, and What They Ought To Be," *St. John's Law Review* 78, no. 3 (2004): 725 (citing Cicero's Laws).

16 See Paul H. Robinson, *Structure and Function in Criminal Law* (Oxford: Clarendon Press, 1997), 95–124 (wholly objective); Kent Greenawalt, "The Perplexing Borders of Justification and Excuse," *Columbia Law Review* 84, no. 8 (1984): 1907–9 (wholly subjective); and George P. Fletcher, *Rethinking Criminal Law* (Boston: Little, Brown, 1978), 556–66, 691–98 (both objective and subjective).

17 See George P. Fletcher, "The Right and The Reasonable," *Harvard Law Review* 98, no. 5 (1985): 977–80 (confined to positively desirable conduct); Mitchell N. Berman, "Justification and Excuse, Law and Morality," *Duke Law Journal* 53, no. 1 (2003): 332–37 (extends to permissible conduct).

18 See Claire O. Finkelstein, "Self-Defense as a Rational Excuse," *University of Pittsburgh Law Review* 57, no. 3 (1996): 621, 644 (third persons may not resist); Hellen Frowe, "The Justified Infliction of Unjust Harm," *Proceedings of the Aristotelian Society* 109, no. 1 (2009): 346–51 (third persons may sometimes resist).

19 See Arnold Enker, "In Support of the Distinction Between Justification and Excuse," *Texas Tech Law Review* 42, no. 2 (2009): 305 (the distinction is useful); Eric Colvin, "Exculpatory Defences in Criminal Law," *Oxford Journal of Legal Studies* 10, no. 3 (1990) (the distinction should be replaced).

With respect to excuse, commentators disagree, among other things, about whether it is a function of lack of choice, traits of character, or attitudes of respect for the legitimate interests of others;[20] whether it is entirely desert based or partly consequentialist in nature;[21] and whether it can be action-guiding.[22] In addition, commentators disagree about the issue on which Larry remains agnostic: They differ on whether duress justifies or excuses, though the great majority of them agree with the MPC that, insofar as duress is broader than choice of evils, it excuses.

Despite their disagreements, commentators nevertheless agree on one thing regarding justification and excuse. They agree with J.L. Austin[23] that a person whose conduct is justified does nothing *wrong*, while a person whose conduct is excused does, indeed, do wrong, but not a wrong for which he is *blameworthy*.[24] Moreover, by virtue of agreeing on that, they also agree on what societal judgments of justification and excuse respectively *express*. The societal message to those who are justified is: "You did nothing wrong; and should the same dilemma recur, you would not be wrong to do as you did before." By contrast, the message to those who are excused is: "You did the wrong thing. And, should the dilemma occur in the future, you would be wrong to do as you did. Yet you are not blameworthy."

For purposes of this essay, I shall focus on what commentators agree upon, because I believe their disagreements are largely irrelevant to how duress ought to be conceptualized – with two exceptions. Naturally, one exception concerns disagreement about the very subject of this essay, i.e., whether duress is a justification or an excuse. The other exception concerns disagreement about what distinguishes wrongful conduct from nonwrongful conduct. Some commentators argue that an actor's conduct

20 See Michael Moore, "Choice, Character, and Excuse," *Social Philosophy and Policy* 7, no. 2 (1990) (choice); Michael Bayles, "Character, Purpose, and Criminal Responsibility," *Law and Philosophy* 1, no. 1 (1982) (character); and Peter Westen, "An Attitudinal Theory of Excuse," *Law and Philosophy* 25, no. 3 (2006) (an attitude of lack of regard for the legitimate interest of others).

21 See Claire O. Finkelstein, "Excuses and Dispositions in Criminal Law," *Buffalo Criminal Law Review* 6, no. 1 (2002): 349–50 (excuses further the consequentialist goal of nurturing dispositions of intimate attachment by exculpating actors even when their dispositions go awry); Daniel Varona Gomez, "Duress and Antcolony's Ethic: Reflections on the Foundations of the Defense and its Limits," *New Criminal Law Review* 11, no. 4 (2008): 642–43.

22 See Peter Alldridge, "Rules for Courts and Rules for Citizens," *Oxford Journal of Legal Studies* 10, no. 4 (1990): 487–90 (excuses are not action-guiding); R.A. Duff, "Rule-Violations and Wrongdoings," in *Criminal Law Theory: Doctrines of the General Part*, ed. Stephen Shute and A.P. Simester (New York: Oxford University Press, 2002), 65–68 (excuses can be action-guiding).

23 John Austin, "A Plea for Excuses," *Proceedings of Aristotelian Society* 57, no. 1 (1956): 2.

24 Berman, "Justification and Excuse, Law and Morality," 4 (the "prevailing consensus" of what distinguishes justification from excuse is that the former is not wrongful while the latter is wrongful but nonblameworthy). Berman accepts the distinction (see ibid., 18), but forcefully argues that criminal law and morals can differ in their respective standards of wrongfulness and blameworthiness. See ibid., 11–29.

is nonwrongful – that is, justified – only if his action is positively desirable, indeed, sufficiently desirable that others may not resist it. Other commentators argue that an actor's conduct is justified if it is merely permissible, even if it is not desirable. I will not review the competing arguments in this debate because I am persuaded that an action is justified if it is permissible, and that an action may be permissible for an actor even though third parties may resist it.[25]

5.5 DOES DURESS UNDER THE MPC JUSTIFY OR EXCUSE?

MPC § 2.09 provides a defense to an actor who commits an offense when coerced by a threat of unlawful force against his person (or that of another) that a "person of reasonable firmness" in the actor's "situation" would be unable to resist. Comparing the two italicized phrases, a *person of reasonable firmness* is a wholly objective standard,[26] while *a person in the actor's situation* is a partly objective and partly individualized standard.[27]

"Reasonable firmness" is a measure of normative courage. Normative courage, in turn, is a person's willingness to respect the legitimate interests of others in relation to his own and his loved ones' interests when circumstances force him to sacrifice one in favor of the other. Reasonable firmness is the minimal courage that society demands of persons at the cost of punishment when they must choose between themselves and others.[28] It is commonly said that what is demanded is reasonable firmness, not heroic or saintly firmness.[29] And that is correct. But it is also misleading, because reasonable firmness sometimes requires heroism, e.g., where, to be reasonably firm, a soldier must refuse to hand nuclear launch codes to a terrorist even though he knows that the terrorist will shoot him for refusing.[30]

[25] See Joshua Dressler, "New Thoughts About the Concept of Justification in Criminal Law: A Critique of Fletcher's Thinking and Rethinking," *UCLA Law Review* 32, no. 1 (1984): 87–98 (reviewing the debate).

[26] American Law Institute, *Model Penal Code and Commentaries*, 275; Marcia Baron, "Justifications and Excuses," *Ohio State Journal of Criminal Law* 2, no. 2 (2005): 394; Ian Howard Dennis, "On Necessity as a Defence to Crime: Possibilities, Problems, and the Limits of Justification and Excuse," *Criminal Law and Philosophy* 3, no. 1 (2009): 40.

[27] Alexander and Ferzan, *Crime and Culpability*, 147–48.

[28] John Gardner, "The Gist of Excuses," *Buffalo Criminal Law Review* 1, no. 2 (1998): 579; Duff, "Rule-Violations and Wrongdoings," 64–66.

[29] R.A. Duff, "Rethinking Justifications," *Tulsa Law Review* 39, no. 4 (2004): 840, 840n32

[30] See Dressler, "Exegesis of the Law of Duress," *Southern California Law Review* 62, no. 5 (1989): 1374 ("A jury might also rightly expect people to manifest the utmost moral strength – even, at some point, to choose death – when they … are playing a part … in an especially barbaric scenario, such as the Holocaust"); Aristotle, *Nichomachean Ethics*, trans. Rev. D.P. Chase (London: Walter Scott, 1847), III.1, 1110-a-26–28 ("some acts, perhaps, we cannot be forced to do, but ought rather to face death after the most fearful sufferings").

By contrast, whether an actor is *responsible* for possessing such courage is assessed by reference to a person in the actor's "situation." The latter standard, which also figures in the MPC's provisions on recklessness, negligence, and elsewhere, assesses criminal responsibility by reference to a hypothetical person who possesses some, but not all, of the features that constitute an actor. I have argued elsewhere that a person in the actor's situation is one who possesses all of the actor's objective and subjective features, including his idiosyncrasies and infirmities, with one exception. The exception concerns an actor's values, that is, his views regarding the proper balance between his interests and the legitimate interests of others. A person in the actor's situation is one who, though otherwise identical to the actor, possesses the objective values that society believes persons ought to possess.[31]

Section 2.09's two standards can thus combine to provide two very different defenses, depending upon the facts. To illustrate, consider the following:

Housekeeper

A malefactor wishes to kill a rival whose house is secured by an alarm system that is routinely armed at night. The malefactor, posing as a doctor, injects the housekeeper's teenage daughter with a poison which will kill the girl within four hours unless she receives a rare antidote. The malefactor possesses the antidote but threatens to withhold it if the housekeeper follows routine and sets the alarm. The housekeeper, fearing for her daughter, deliberately refrains from arming the system. The malefactor enters the rival's home and kills him. The housekeeper receives the antidote, saves her daughter, and is charged with aiding and abetting a murder.

Phobic Manager

A malefactor wishes to steal the payroll of a company whose manager has a pathological fear of rats.[32] The malefactor and his partner enter the manager's office under false pretenses and, while his partner restrains the manager, the malefactor threatens to empty a basket of Norwegian rats onto the manager unless the manager discloses the combination of the office safe. The business manager, fearful of the rats, writes down the multipart combination and hands it over. The malefactor

[31] Peter Westen, "Individualizing the Reasonable Person in Criminal Law," *Criminal Law and Philosophy* 2, no. 2 (2008): 137–62.

[32] I take this hypothetical, as modified, from Gary Watson. See Gary Watson, "Excusing Addiction," *Law and Philosophy* 18, no. 6 (1999): 613.

opens the safe, takes the payroll, and flees, leaving the basket of rats on the floor. The manager is tried for aiding and abetting a theft.

The defendants in "Housekeeper" and "Phobic Manager" share several features. Both commit crimes that they are ordered to commit under threats of unlawful physical harm to themselves or loved ones. Both commit crimes that would fail to qualify as lesser evils if the threatened harms were natural in origin. (A person who lives in a rat-infested home may not steal from his employer merely because it is the only way he can escape living with rats; and a person who inadvertently ingests poison may not kill another merely because it is the only way he can obtain an antidote). And, though both defendants act out of fear, neither is so panicked as to be rendered "incapable of rational thought":[33] Both acted voluntarily within the meaning of MPC § 2.01 in that both of them deliberated and thereupon purposely acted to avoid evils they feared more than the crimes they committed.

Nevertheless, Housekeeper and Phobic Manager also differ in a significant respect. The housekeeper is a typical duress victim in that she is a rational person who, though she is concerned with and fears for her child, suffers from no infirmity that prevents her from understanding and complying with society's moral norms. She does not claim that her perception of the facts was impaired or her normative judgment clouded, other than that she had to choose between the evils of allowing her child to be murdered and allowing a putative murderer to kill another instead. She is a typical duress victim because coercers typically select victims whom they can count on to be able to assess ends, means, and alternatives, and to act predictably.[34] In contrast, the phobic manager is atypical because he relies for his defense on something peculiar to him that impairs his perception and normative judgment, i.e., a phobia that causes him to place excessive weight on something of relatively little consequence.

I shall take no position on whether either of our hypothetical actors is entitled to a duress defense, though I suspect that many will balk at declaring the housekeeper's omission to be wrongful, all things considered. I shall focus instead on the norms of criminal responsibility that ought to guide a trier of fact in reasoning about the two cases.

The first step is to assess the actors' respective choices solely by reference to section 2.09's objective standard of "reasonable firmness," that is, by reference to a person who possesses reasonable firmness but does not suffer from any cognitive

33 Duff, "Rule-Violations and Wrongdoings," 64.

34 Craig L. Carr, "Duress and Criminal Responsibility," *Law and Philosophy* 10, no. 2 (1991): 178n26. "If B knows his business, it makes sense to think he is treating A as a rational actor since B obviously wants A to do X and B can hardly rely on what a person whose judgment has been impaired will do."

or volitional impairment that distinguishes him from ordinary persons who must choose between suffering harm and harming others. A person of reasonable firmness is one who places proper weight on the legitimate interests of others in relation to his own, including any legitimate agent-relative interests of his own. In order to determine whether an actor satisfies that standard, the trier of fact should ask itself, "How should I address him?" In the housekeeper's case, a trier could address the housekeeper in one of two ways:

Message 1

> You faced a tragic dilemma, with terrible outcomes whatever you chose to do. Nevertheless, we must pass judgment on what you chose to do in the face of the dilemma. We need not decide what a hero or saint would have done under the circumstances. Rather, we must declare what the criminal law minimally demands of a mother in such a case – and what the law demands of you should the same situation recur. We declare that you did the *wrong* thing. You cared too much about your own daughter and not enough about your employer. You should have allowed your daughter to be murdered rather than enable your employer to be murdered. That is not to say that we blame you for what you did. We have not yet decided that. But we can say this: Your act was an act of moral cowardice, and it was sufficiently cowardly to warrant criminal condemnation. You exhibited a defect in character that you should endeavor to repair. As for mothers in the future, the message is: "*Don't* do what this mother did."

Message 2

> You faced a tragic dilemma with terrible outcomes either way. Given your choices, however, we cannot say that you did the wrong thing. This does not mean that we admire what you did or believe you should aspire to do it again if the same situation should recur. It means only that we shall tell you what we would tell anyone who seeks guidance on how to act in such situations: "Your act was not an act of moral cowardice that warrants criminal condemnation."

Message 1 is that the housekeeper acted wrongly and, hence, was unjustified. Message 2 is that the housekeeper did not act wrongly and, hence, was justified.

The second step is to determine why an actor who receives Message 1 – that is, a message that she acted wrongly – should nevertheless be excused, if, indeed, she should be excused. The actor may invoke the language of section 2.09 and argue that a person of reasonable firmness in his or her situation would have been "unable to resist" doing the wrong thing that he did. The phrase "unable to resist" (and references to an actor's "will" being "overborne"[35]) cannot be taken literally, however. They do not mean the absence of a voluntary act within the meaning of MPC § 2.01, because housekeeper and manager not only acted but engaged in conscious and goal-directed activity.[36] Nor can it mean that an actor is so petrified he that lacks volitional capacity to conform his conduct to the requirements of the law because if he did, the law would excuse him altogether, regardless of how horrific his conduct is, rather than evaluate him for proportionality between the threats he faces and the wrong he commits.[37] "Unable to resist" is a metaphor for something that could be framed in other and more literal terms. It is a metaphor because no one knows what it would be to literally have no choice with respect to what one intentionally chooses.[38]

Now Douglas Husak has argued that a person who does the wrong thing in the context of duress should nevertheless be excused if an *ordinary* person would also have done the wrong thing under the circumstances.[39] However, Husak does not explain why a person who intentionally commits a wrong should be excused merely because average persons, who could and should abstain from committing the wrong, would disregard their obligations and commit the wrong. The claim that "Everybody does it" is not an excuse anywhere else in law or morals.[40] On the contrary, the measure of non-culpability for wrongdoing is that of a "reasonable" or "law-abiding" person in the actor's situation, not that of statistically average persons regardless of their morals.

Joshua Dressler, in turn, argues that duress is and ought to be an excuse because it is an appropriate concession to "human weakness."[41] By "weakness," of course, Dressler means *normative* weakness[42] – that is, frailty that leads a person to disregard the legitimate interests of others in favor of his own – because only persons who act

35 Regina v. Hudson [1971] 2 A.B. 202, 206 (opinion of Widgery, LJ).

36 Herbert Fingarette, "Victimization: A Legalist Analysis of Coercion, Deception, Undue Influence, and Excusable Prison Escape," *Washington & Lee Law Review* 42, no. 1 (1985): 71–82; Finkelstein, "Excuses and Dispositions in Criminal Law," 333–35; Robert F. Schopp, "Justification Defenses and Just Convictions," *Pacific Law Journal* 24, no. 3 (1993): 1303.

37 Glanville Williams, *Textbook of Criminal Law* (London: Stevens and Sons, 1983), 625; Dan M. Kahan and Martha C. Nussbaum, "Two Conceptions of Emotions in Criminal Law," *Columbia Law Review* 96, no. 2 (1996): 334–35.

38 Theodore Y. Blumoff, "The Neuropsychology of Justifications and Excuses: Some Problematic Cases of Self-Defense, Duress, and Provocation," *Jurimetrics* 50, no. 3 (2010): 400–1; Carr, "Duress and Criminal Responsibility," 175.

39 Douglas Husak, "The 'But-Everyone-Does-That' Defense," *Public Affairs Quarterly* 10, no. 4 (1996): 311–12.

40 See Jeremy Horder, *Excusing Crime* (Oxford: Oxford University Press, 2004), 136–37; Dressler, "Exegesis of the Law of Duress," 1364.

41 Ibid., 1334.

42 Ibid., 1364.

wrongly are in need of excuse.[43] Which raises the question *why*. Why should the law excuse normative weakness in a person who intentionally and nonmistakenly commits a *mala in se* offense that he is wrong to commit under the circumstances?

The answer, Dressler says, is that it would be "hypocritical" and, hence, "ineffective" for judges to convict an actor of exhibiting normative weakness that the judges themselves believe they, too, would have exhibited under the circumstances.[44] But that is not so. It is not hypocritical for judges to condemn actors for doing what judges themselves would have done, so long as judges acknowledge that they, too, would deserve condemnation for doing such a thing.[45]

Other commentators maintain that moral weakness may be excused when it results from four combined factors: (1) the *difficulty* of resisting, given the harm one will suffer as a consequence; (2) the *emotional stress* of acting under fear; (3) *foreshortened time* to deliberate; and (4) the relatively *minor* nature of the normative wrong of choosing an evil that, albeit a greater evil under the circumstances, is not grossly disproportionate to the threatened harm. The authors of the 1971 proposal to reform the Federal Criminal Code took that position. They proposed that a person's conduct be excused if his conduct "would otherwise be justified … but is marginally … excessive because he was confronted with an emergency precluding adequate appraisal or measured reaction."[46]

This 1971 proposal would probably not avail the housekeeper who had four hours to deliberate before acting. More importantly, it is inconsistent with prevailing criminal norms. To illustrate, imagine that a writer momentarily leaves his laptop unattended in a coffee shop; a thief grabs the laptop and flees; the writer, afraid that he will lose his only copy of a book manuscript, shoots and grievously injures the thief within a jurisdiction that prohibits the use of lethal force to thwart a theft. The writer satisfies the aforementioned conditions that supposedly support excuse: He is forced to inflict harm or suffer harm; he labors under the fear of losing his laptop and irreplaceable manuscript; he has no time to deliberate; and the difference between what he does, i.e., shoot and seriously wound, is only marginally excessive, given that he would have been allowed to chase down, tackle and seriously wound the thief to prevent the theft, if he had been able.

How would courts treat the novelist under prevailing norms? Courts might take the aforementioned factors into account to mitigate the novelist's punishment, just as they mitigate the punishment of persons who commit intentional and wrongful homicide under extreme emotional disturbance for which there is a reasonable

43 Horder, *Excusing Crime*, 49 ("claims of true justification are inconsistent with seeking excuse").

44 Joshua Dressler, *Understanding Criminal Law, 7th ed.* (New Providence, NJ: LexisNexis, 2015), 315 (quoting the Model Penal Code Commentaries).

45 Alan Brudner, "A Theory of Necessity," *Oxford Journal of Legal Studies* 7, no. 3 (1987): 339, 358.

46 National Commission, *Final report* (1971), § 608(2).

explanation or excuse.[47] That is, they might partially justify and partially excuse the novelist's conduct because of the hard choice he faced and the stress he suffered.[48] But once society defines through law what it regards as morally excessive harm – once it defines what is wrongful force in self-defense – it does not ordinarily excuse persons who intentionally violate what they know or should know are those limits, merely because they are under pressure to marginally violate them.[49] (Significantly, the authors of the 1971 proposal itself concede that their proposal might better serve as a partial excuse than a complete excuse.[50])

Jeremy Horder and Alan Brudner have argued that, where the absence of a "lawful defense" is an element of the crime of intentional assault, an actor who knows he is using a certain force but mistakenly believes it is legally justified is presently excused in England, even if the force is excessive as a matter of law.[51] However, that assumes that England means to equate intention regarding the *fact* of excessive force with intention regarding the *legal prohibition* against excessive force. A jurisdiction may so provide, if it so wishes.[52] But, ordinarily, an actor's mistake of law regarding what distinguishes lawful from wrongful conduct does not exculpate an actor from committing *mala in se* offenses, even where he fears for himself or loved ones.

This is not to say that duress is never an excuse. An actor may be right minded and yet suffer from an infirmity or immaturity that, though it does not deprive him of normative competence altogether (as insanity does), nevertheless causes him to blamelessly exaggerate an evil with which he is threatened.[53] If an infirmity or immaturity is sufficient that the actor cannot overcome it, it could cause even a right-minded actor to give an evil more normative weight than it deserves relative to another, marginally greater evil. In that event, the actor has an excuse under section 2.09 for choosing a marginally greater evil than he should. He has an excuse because he suffers from a condition that prevents him from properly assessing a threatened evil against marginally greater evils. He is excused for doing the wrong thing because a person of reasonable firmness in his "situation" might act similarly.

47 See MPC § 210.3.1(b). I have argued elsewhere that such mitigation is a partial excuse rather than a partial justification. See Peter Westen, "How Not to Argue that Reasonable Provocation is an Excuse, *University of Michigan Journal of Law Reform* 43, no. 1 (2009): 175–92.

48 See 18 U.S.C.S. Appx § 5K2.12 (treating duress as grounds for a mitigating factor in sentencing for federal offenses). See generally Douglas Husak, "Partial Defenses," *Canadian Journal of Law and Jurisprudence* 11, no. 1 (1998): 167–92.

49 Carr, "Duress and Criminal Responsibility," 176.

50 National Commission, *Working papers* (1991), 278.

51 Horder, *Excusing Crime*, 64 (citing Alan Brudner).

52 Antony Duff argues that the duress defense should exculpate persons who, because of fear, make marginal mistakes regarding what is permissible force. See R.A. Duff, "Criminal Responsibility and Emotions: If Fear and Anger Can Exculpate, Why Not Compassion?" *Inquiry* 58, no. 2 (2015): 198.

53 Horder, *Excusing Crime*, 95n.175, 137.

With the foregoing standards in mind, we can return to our two hypothetical actors. The phobic manager would argue that, though he failed to do what an idealized person of reasonable firmness would have done, he should nonetheless be excused because he suffered from an insuperable infirmity that caused him to exaggerate the harm with which he was threatened (i.e., rats), causing him, through no fault of his own, to give it greater normative weight than it deserved relative to the harm he committed to escape it (i.e., delivering the company payroll). Being a right-minded person, he would have known that being plagued by rats would not justify killing or even seriously injuring an innocent party. But, through no fault of his own, he regarded the threat as sufficiently frightful to justify a nonviolent theft. (The same reasoning may excuse a captive soldier who, after being waterboarded once, and being physically and psychically depleted, develops such a phobia of waterboarding that he gives the threat of further waterboarding greater weight than it warrants in relation to the disclosure of military secrets.)

"Housekeeper" is the more significant hypothetical because it is more typical. Depending upon the jurisdiction's view of agent-relative interests, the housekeeper's conduct may be justified as the act of a person of reasonable firmness. If not, she may merit a partial defense because she labored under a choice of evil and under emotional stress that persons who ordinarily aid and abet criminal homicide do not. But if her conduct is, indeed, unjustified, she has no grounds for claiming a complete excuse because she possesses no insuperable infirmity that would excuse her from complying with objective norms of reasonable firmness.[54] She is a typical duress defendant and, as such, either has a complete defense of justification under section 2.09 or ought to have no complete defense at all.

5.6 COMMENTATORS WHO BALK AT THE CONSEQUENCES OF THEIR OWN REASONING

Space does not permit me to respond to many commentators who believe that duress is an excuse. But I would like to discuss three sets of commentators whose views are revealing because, while their reasoning seems to support duress being a justification, they balk at drawing the conclusion their own views appear to dictate.

John Gardner and Antony Duff both believe that an actor who faces a hard choice is justified when his conduct is normatively acceptable; that an actor has an excuse only if his conduct is decidedly wrongful; and that an actor who faces a coercive threat has a duress defense if his conduct exhibits the fortitude and regard

[54] Carr, "Duress and Criminal Responsibility," 177.

for the interests of others that society has a right to minimally demand of persons.[55] Revealingly, they confess that this appears to commit them to the position that a person typically has a defense of duress only if his conduct is normatively acceptable under the circumstances and, hence, justified rather than wrongful.[56] Yet, paradoxically, they continue to maintain that duress is an excuse – paradoxically, because, by their own admission, a defense cannot be an excuse unless it is a defense to conduct that does *not* exhibit proper regard for the interest of others.

Gardner and Duff are aware of the paradox and try to explain it. They both argue that, just as reasonable *mistakes* are an excuse, so, too, acting with reasonable *courage* is also an excuse.[57] But that analogy conflates apples with oranges.[58] Reasonable mistakes are subjective errors that produce objectively wrongful conduct, while, by Duff's and Gardner's own account, reasonable courage produces conduct that objectively "lives up to" the "standards of character" that society demands of persons.[59]

Duff further maintains that, although excuses are not ordinarily "action-guiding," duress is an exception because its message to the public is: While we do not "demand" that you act heroically, we nevertheless *urge* you to act heroically.[60] The duress defense is, indeed, action-guiding, but not because it urges heroism. It is action-guiding by virtue of what it minimally demands of actors, namely, that they manifest reasonable firmness. It thus does what justifications generally do: It defines and universalizes conduct that it declares to be objectively permissible.

A second set of commentators are Albin Eser and Stephen Garvey. Eser and Garvey agree that conduct is justified unless it is wrongful, and that conduct is wrongful only if it is disfavored by competing interests.[61] They also agree that an actor may lack a choice-of-evils defense on agent-neutral grounds and yet possess a duress defense by virtue of possessing legitimate agent-relative interests. Nevertheless, they maintain that, insofar as persons act on the basis of agent-relative rather than agent-neutral interests, they act wrongly and must beg to be excused. They claim that when a threatener, A, coerces B to harm an innocent party C, the wrongfulness of

55 Gardner, "The Gist of Excuses," 598; John Gardner, "Justifications and Reasons," in *Harm and Culpability*, ed. A.P. Simester and A.T.H. Smith (Oxford: Clarendon Press, 1996), 107–14; Duff, "Rule-Violations and Wrongdoings," 64–65.

56 John Gardner, "The Logic of Excuses and the Rationality of Emotions, *Journal of Value Inquiry* 43, no. 3 (2009): 316, 338; Duff, "Rule-Violations and Wrongdoings," 66.

57 Gardner, "The Gist of Excuses," 597–98; Duff, "Rule-Violations and Wrongdoings," 65–66.

58 Schopp, "Justifications and Just Convictions," 1306–7.

59 National Commission, *Working papers* (1991), 278.

60 Duff, "Rule-Violations and Wrongdoings," 65–68.

61 Albin Eser, "Justification and Excuse," *American Journal of Comparative Law* 24, no. 4 (1976): 621–37; S. Garvey, "Authority, Freedom, and the Guilty Mind," Cornell Legal Studies Research Paper No. 16-7 (2016), https://papers.ssrn.com/sol3/papers2.cfm?abstract_id=2729414.

B's conduct must be measured on the same an agent-neutral basis as applicable to A, regardless of whether B possesses legitimate agent-relative interests that A lacks.[62]

With due respect, Eser and Garvey mistakenly assume that what is wrong for A to coerce B to do must be equally wrong for B *himself* to do. In actuality, the interests of A and B are distinct and must be separately assessed for wrongfulness. B may have legitimate agent-relative interests that justify him in doing what A may not do.[63] If B's agent-relative interests suffice, B's conduct is not wrongful and, hence, not anything for which he is in need of excuse.

Finally, Mitchell Berman argues that, even though duress may be a justification in morals, it can be an excuse in criminal law, depending upon what a jurisdiction demands of an actor in situations of duress. Berman's argument is this: A jurisdiction may enact a "conduct rule" in its *criminal law* that requires moral heroism of actors (declaring anything less than heroism to be criminally impermissible) and, yet, simultaneously adopt a "decision rule" that excuses actors who engage in nonheroic conduct, provided that their conduct exhibits what in *morals* is "morally adequate firmness."[64]

Berman's argument is subject to the same criticism as Duff's. The state has instruments at its disposal for encouraging heroism. But criminal law is not one of them – not, at least, where criminal law simultaneously exculpates a person who, in Duff's words, lives up to the criminal law's minimal "demands"[65] or, in Berman's words, exhibits a "morally adequate degree of firmness."[66] By withholding punishment from such a person, the criminal law is expressing a conduct rule, not a decision rule. After all, the reason law withholds punishment from an actor whose conduct exhibits morally adequate firmness is not that he possessed features traditionally associated with decision rules of excuse, i.e., individualized cognitive or volitional deficits that negate the public's forming reactive emotions of resentment toward him for making the wrong choice. Rather, it withholds punishment because, given the objective alternatives open to him, he made a morally adequate choice. It withholds punishment from him because it would withhold blame from *anyone* who faced the same alternatives and made the same choice.

5.7 HUMAN THREATS VERSUS NATURAL THREATS

I have argued that the actor in "Housekeeper" may have a valid defense under section 2.09 because her conduct may have exhibited reasonable firmness, and that,

62 Eser, "Justification and Excuse," 634–37; Garvey, "Authority, Freedom, and the Guilty Mind," 48–53.

63 Watson, "Excusing Addiction," 608–10 (agent-relative interests factor into justification, not excuse).

64 Berman, "Justification and Excuse, Law and Morality," 32–38, 72–73.

65 Duff, "Rule-Violations and Wrongdoings," 66.

66 Berman, "Justification and Excuse, Law and Morality," 72.

if she does have a valid defense under section 2.09, it must be a defense of justification. Yet I have also assumed that she would lack a defense of justification under section 3.02's choice-of-evils provisions if the threat to her daughter had been natural in origin. One of two things must, therefore, follow: Either I am correct and, hence, coercive threats of harm differ normatively from other threats of harm; or, as other commentators, including Alexander, conventionally maintain,[67] coercive threats do not differ normatively from other threats and, hence, either section 2.09 is a defense of justification that should be shrunk to be coterminous with section 3.02, or it is a defense of excuse that should be expanded to encompass noncoercive and natural threats as well.

I believe that my position finds support in an argument that Antony Duff makes in another context. Duff's argument concerns the nature of harm. Duff differs from most commentators who argue that a person suffers the same harm whether another intentionally kills him or he is killed by a cause that is natural origin.[68] By contrast, Duff argues that "an intention to harm transforms the character of the harm ...; one who is injured with intent might suffer the same physical injury as someone who is injured by natural causes ...; but he suffers a distinctive harm of being injuriously attacked."

> Both the murder victim and the victim of natural causes suffer death; but the character of the harm that they suffer surely also depends upon the way in which they die. One who tries to kill me ... attacks my life and my most basic rights; and the harm which I suffer in being murdered ... essentially involves this wrongful attack on me.[69]

If Duff is correct, and I think he is, his claim affects how choices of evils are assessed for purposes of duress.[70] If intentional harms are distinctively evil in ways that natural harms are not, the conventional view of duress is mistaken in several ways: mistaken in maintaining that intentional harms are no more evil than natural harms; mistaken in maintaining that threats of intentional harm exculpate only to the extent that threats of otherwise identical natural harm exculpate; and mistaken in

[67] National Commission, *Final report* (1971), § 609; Winnie Chan and A.P. Simester, "Duress, Necessity: How Many Defences?" *Kings Law Journal* 16, no. 1 (2005): 121; Claire O. Finkelstein, "Duress: A Philosophical Account of the Defense in Law," *Arizona Law Review* 37, no. 1 (1995): 260; Watson, "Excusing Addiction," 613; Alexander and Ferzan, *Crime and Culpability*, 125, 134–36.

[68] See R.A. Duff, *Criminal Attempts* (Oxford: Clarendon Press, 1996), 132.

[69] R. A. Duff, *Intention, Agency, and Criminal Liability: Philosophy of Action and the Criminal Law* (Oxford: Basil Blackwell, 1990), 112.

[70] Contrary to what is sometimes said about it, Duff's claim does implicate the doctrine of double effect. See Peter Westen, "Is Intent Constitutive of Wrongdoing?" in *Crime, Punishment, and Responsibility: The Jurisprudence of Antony Duff*, ed. Rowan Cruft, Matthew H. Kramer, and Mark R. Reiff (Oxford: Oxford University Press, 2011), 202–8.

maintaining that threats of intentional harm do not justify conduct unless threats of otherwise identical natural harm also justify it.

Duff's insight may also be relevant to how one assesses the gravity of the *other* harm at issue in duress cases, i.e., the criminal offense that an actor commits to escape the harm with which he is being coercively threatened. If intentions are constitutive of wrongdoing, an actor who commits an offense only because he is coerced to do so under a threat of harm to his person (or to the person of a loved one) may be inflicting a lesser evil than the malefactor inflicts who devises the offense in the first place and uses coercive threats to execute it. If so, the malefactor's and actor's intentions can combine to transform both threatened evils and inflicted evils. The combined intentions aggravate the former's evils and lessen the latter's evils. And in doing so, they can justify actions that would otherwise be unjustified.

5.8 THE NORMATIVE CONSEQUENCES OF WHETHER DURESS JUSTIFIES OR EXCUSES

Larry downplays his ambivalence about whether duress is a justification or an excuse by denying that it has any "practical implications."[71] I believe Larry is mistaken. *Why* duress exonerates necessarily affects *what* is exonerated in the name of justification and excuse.

Consider the particular defense codified in MPC § 2.09. Section 2.09 provides a defense only for actors who are subjected to human coercion, not for actors who face otherwise identical, nonculpable human and natural threats. I have argued here that a malefactor's use of coercion alters the gravity of evils that an actor faces, thereby justifying conduct that would otherwise be unjustified. If that is correct, it vindicates the distinction that section 2.09 draws between coercive threats and all other threats. It accepts prevailing standards of justification and excuse by justifying actors who exhibit "reasonable firmness" and excusing persons who, because of insuperable infirmities, exhibit as much firmness as society can expect of persons in their "situation." On the other hand, if the thesis is wrong – that is, if coercion does not alter the gravity of evils – we would have to revise what we presently regard as justified and/or excused: Either we should eliminate section 2.09 as an independent defense or we should enlarge it to encompass all threats, regardless of whether they are coercive, human or natural in nature.

Larry takes the latter option. He argues that the duress defense be expanded to encompass all threats, regardless of nature or origin, including threats to inflict lawful harm. He defends the broader rule by arguing that insofar as actors possess agent-relative interests that suffice, the broader rule is a valid defense of justification,

[71] Alexander and Ferzan, *Crime and Culpability*, 138.

and that insofar as actors do not possess agent-relative interests, the broader rule is a valid defense of excuse. In either event, he says, the difference hardly matters. I believe Larry is mistaken. Larry's broader rule transgresses existing norms of justification and excuse, regardless of which norm is invoked to support it. If Larry's rule were adopted, it would require general changes in what is presently justified and excused.

Let us start with justification. Many commentators believe that agents have agent-relative interests that justify them in inflicting harms on innocents that would be unjustified if the agents were not acting to save themselves or loved ones from threatened harm.[72] Larry recognizes that, if such interests obtain, they militate in favor of his positions regarding Innocent Aggressors, Bystanders, Shields, and Swords (see Section 5.2, above). But even then, Larry's expansive rule of duress exceeds existing understandings of justification in at least two respects. First, Larry's rule is broader than it may appear. Larry's is not a rule that broadens the duress defense to include natural threats while nevertheless allowing the fact finder to *consider* whether threats are natural, human, or coercive in assessing how persons of reasonable firmness would respond. Rather, it is a rule that gives no normative weight *at all* to the origin of threats. It is a rule that victims of natural threats have a defense whenever victims of otherwise identical human, coercive threats would have a defense. This equating of such distinct threats contradicts the shared intuitions that underlie both section 2.09 and common law rules of duress,[73] both of which give some normative weight to whether threats are coercive in origin. Second, Larry proposes giving no normative weight to whether threats are lawful or unlawful. He would provide victims of lawful threatened harm with a defense whenever victims of unlawful threatened harm would have a defense. This equating of lawful with unlawful threats contradicts the shared intuition that actors who are threatened with lawful harm are not as justified as persons threatened with unlawful harm in eluding harm by harming innocent persons (see "Fleeing Felon," above).

Larry's alternative solution is to treat his proposed rule as an excuse. The alternative is more problematic still, however, because, if the essence of such an excuse were applied generally, it would mean *completely* excusing broad categories of conduct that, at present, are either *not* excused at all or only *partially* excused. An actor who faces a Hobson's choice between suffering harm himself (or allowing loved ones to suffer it) and harming an innocent third person undoubtedly experiences

[72] See, e.g., Jonathan Quong, "Agent-Relative Prerogatives to Do Harm," *Criminal Law and Philosophy* 10, no. 4 (2016): 815–29; Watson, "Excusing Addiction," 608–10.

[73] For the argument that even prior to section 2.09 the common law defense of duress placed normative weight on coercion, see Peter Westen and James Mangiafico, "The Criminal Defense of Duress: A Justification, Not an Excuse – and Why it Matters," *Buffalo Criminal Law Review* 6, no. 2 (2003): 835, 860–62.

fright and stress. But when he responds by electing to save himself or a loved, he is exercising moral agency: He is making a conscious decision to benefit himself or his own at the cost of intentionally harming an innocent third party. If, in his fear and stress, he makes what society regards as the wrong choice – that is, a choice that society would emphatically tell him not to make again if the situation were to recur – we might partially excuse and partially justify him. Moreover, if his choice is not egregiously wrong, and if he makes it while suffering from an insuperable disability or immaturity like the actor in Phobic Manager, we might fully excuse him. But nowhere in the law – or, at least, nowhere else – do we fully excuse moral agents who, while possessing *no* insuperable infirmities, intentionally, nonmistakenly, and wrongfully inflict *mala in se* harms on innocent persons merely because fear or stress renders it "hard"[74] for them to do the right thing. If we do it with duress, we must do it elsewhere as well.

5.9 CONCLUSION

A majority of commentators regard duress as an excuse rather than a justification.[75] Yet that is problematic on its face. Actions under duress share no family resemblance with complete excuses like insanity, involuntary intoxication, infancy, and mistake – all of which involve subjective cognitive and/or volitional deficits that are distinctive to individuals; all of which operate by negating society's reactive emotions of resentment for conduct that is condemnable; and all of which provide complete excuses, regardless of how horrific an actor's conduct. Actions under duress resemble complete justifications like the lesser evils defense and self-defense – all of which (i) involve competent moral agents who, while under the pressure of hard choices, intentionally and nonmistakenly harm others in order to benefit themselves or their own; (ii) obtain only when offenses are objectively proportional in some way to the harms with which actors are threatened; and (iii) are universalizable to all persons facing such choices.

Why, then, do commentators characterize duress as an excuse? Many do so, I believe, because they assume that threats that are natural in origin provide the baseline for determining the harms that actors may inflict on innocent and nonthreatening persons. Because they take natural threats as the baseline for justification in such cases, and because section 2.09 provides a defense for coercive threats

[74] But see Duff, "Criminal Responsibility and Emotions," 98, arguing that a person should be fully excused for failing to do what it is "hard" for him to do.

[75] But see Alan Wertheimer, *Coercion* (Princeton: Princeton University Press, 1987), 168; Glanville Williams, *Criminal Law: The General Part* (London: Stevens and Sons, 1961), 755–56.

that go beyond that baseline, commentators feel they must regard section 2.09 as an excuse.

I have argued that commentators are mistaken in thinking that natural threats constitute the baseline for determining harms that threatened persons may inflict on innocent and nonthreatening persons. A coercive threat of an unlawful harm is a graver evil for a threatened person than an otherwise identical evil that is natural in origin; and the offense that a person is coerced into inflicting may not be as grave an evil by him as the evil of his coercer. The combination justifies coerced actors in committing offenses that would be unjustified if the threatened and inflicted harms differed in their respective origins.

6

Alternative Lesser Evils

Gideon Yaffe

6.1 INTRODUCTION

Larry Alexander has produced volumes of important work on a wide variety of topics. This is well recognized. But the number of pages he has published may be dwarfed by another number – the number of invitations he has issued. He is constantly organizing conferences and roundtables, volumes and special issues. While I'm thankful for Larry's published works, I'm indebted to him especially for including me so frequently in his intellectual circles – and for doing so despite the fact that we so rarely, if ever, agree. It is as a result of saying yes to Larry's invitations that I have become part of a thriving community of legal theorists. In fact, it is thanks to Larry's many invitations that there is such a community to be part of.

And so it seems fitting that in this essay I will accept one of Larry's invitations. In his important paper "Lesser Evils: A Closer Look at the Paradigmatic Justification,"[1] Larry invites criminal law theorists to address a series of fascinating puzzles about the lesser evils defense. The lesser evils defense is rarely used, but it seems an essential part of a just criminal code. How could it be appropriate to punish someone for performing an act that leaves the world far better off, by the state's own standards, than noncriminal conduct would have left it? As both Larry's work on the defense and the work of others illustrates, reflection on the structure of the defense, as well as the grounds for its inclusion in a just criminal code, illuminates a lot about the nature of criminal prohibition and the justification for the state holding people to account for violating its demands.

One of the puzzles Larry identifies concerns how to think about the lesser evils defense in those cases in which the defendant had not two options, but three or more. In the standard case, there are two options: legal behavior that would result in

[1] Larry Alexander, "Lesser Evils: A Closer Look at the Paradigmatic Justification," *Law and Philosophy* 24, no. 6 (2005): 611–43.

something bad, or criminal behavior that would be, overall, less bad. The defendant can mind his own business and let a town burn from a forest fire, or he can steal a car to quickly warn the fire department so they can build a firebreak. The defendant offers the lesser evils defense to shield himself from liability for performance of the less bad, but criminal thing – in this case, stealing the car. In the cases that Larry invites us to think about, by contrast, the defendant had yet another, even less bad criminal option that he decided, for his own personal reasons, not to take. So, he did not make the world optimal, but he did prevent the world from becoming as awful as it might have been. The defendant could alert the fire department either by the petty theft of an old Ford, worth about $100, or by the grand theft of a new Ferrari, worth over $250,000. He picks the Ferrari because it's so much more fun to drive and so commits the much greater crime of grand theft. Should the defendant benefit from the lesser evils defense in such a case? Given that the Ford stealer is owed the defense, is the Ferrari stealer also? Or, if not, perhaps the Ferrari stealer should be punished as if he had committed an offense as severe as the difference between stealing a Ferrari and stealing an old Ford? My aim here is to answer these questions. As we will see, while the answers are of intrinsic interest, they also shed light on the fundamental rationale for the lesser evils defense. By thinking through Larry's question, that is, we can see what normatively relevant facts we mirror in the law with the institution of the lesser evils defense.

The central idea that I will be here sketching and defending is this: We learn from reflection on Larry's puzzle that the lesser evils defense is not a way of realizing in the law a truth about morality. It is not a way of increasing the likelihood of acquittal of agents who are either diminished in responsibility for wrongdoing or who have done nothing morally wrong. Rather, it has a fundamentally *procedural* rather than substantive rationale. It is something that we must include in any legal system with a claim to be exercising not just power, but authority, even if the laws of that system are out of line with the moral facts. This grand idea, I suggest, is what we learn from reflection on Larry's seemingly simple puzzle.

6.2 PRELIMINARIES

The discussion to follow is guided by the idea that a defense should be available to a defendant only if the fundamental function of the defense is served by its availability to him. For instance: Self-defense protection from liability should be available to a defendant who kills someone who forfeited his right not to be killed (by, for instance, culpably aggressing against the defendant), *since* the point of including the affirmative defense of self-defense in law is to shield from liability those who do not violate the rights of those whom they kill. It is because that's the point of the affirmative defense of self-defense (arguably) that it should be available when the defendant kills someone who has forfeited the relevant right. So, similarly, to know whether the lesser evils defense should be available to the Ferrari stealer, and others who opt for the second best of three (or more) bad options, we need to know whether granting the defense in such cases is in line with, or instead in discord with, the point of including the lesser evils defense in the law. But to know *that*, we need to know what that point is; we need to know the fundamental rationale of the lesser evils defense.

Let's define some terms. First, let's stipulate that the terms "crime" and "criminal act" will refer to a complex of behavior, circumstances and results such that, if shown to have occurred beyond a reasonable doubt, the prima facie case against a defendant (D) for some offense would be satisfied. So used, there is an open question whether a crime is a violation of the law. At least, this is so, given the further assumption that justified conduct is not in violation of the law, although it sometimes appears initially to be so. Self-defensive killing, for instance, on this view, is not a violation of the law against murder, although it is a crime, for it meets the definition of intentional homicide. The result is that a justified criminal act is not against the law.

Now, in the cases that interest us, there are three potential states of the world that we need to consider: Worst, Better, and Best. These are not actions, but states of the world. Worst is the world that will be realized if the defendant does nothing criminal. The word "does" here is intended to be neutral between acts and omissions, doings and allowings. In the example above, Worst is the burning of the village, which is what will take place if D engages in no criminal act. In fact, it will take place even if D is knocked unconscious and so *does* nothing, strictly speaking, at all. Better is the world that will be realized if the defendant commits a particular crime, call it C-Better. In our example, C-Better is stealing the Ferrari and Better is the world that results from that crime. C-Better is a token of type C (e.g., grand auto theft), which is a crime defined by statute. (Reminder: Given the way in which the term "crime" is being used here, there is an open question whether any particular token of type C is in fact a violation of the law.) Finally, Best is the world that will be realized if the defendant commits crime C-Best. What we will assume is that Worst is worse than both Better and Best, and Better is worse than Best.

Given all this, the question is this: On the assumption that there is sufficient reason to legally prohibit acts of type C, is there also sufficient reason not to legally prohibit acts like C-Better? If so, then a natural way to set things up so that they are as they ought to be is to allow a defendant who commits a crime like C-Better to shield himself from liability using the lesser evils defense. If, by contrast, acts like C-Better should be prohibited, given that acts of type C should be, then the lesser evils defense should not apply when a defendant commits a crime like C-Better, a crime that realizes Better despite the fact that Best was available.

It's important to see that our question cannot be answered in the absence of an account of the function or rationale for including the lesser evils defense in the law. Larry assumes that in broad outline the defense is one of a family of defenses, the justification defenses, intended to shield from liability those who perform morally permissible acts. While ultimately I want to suggest that this is mistaken, let's stick with the assumption for now. So understood, the questions are then, (a) is C-Better morally permissible? and (b) if so, is it morally permissible for the distinctive reasons that the lesser evils defense concerns? If the answer to (a) is "no," then the defendant who commits C-Better ought to be denied any justification defense, although another kind of defense might, in principle, be available to him. If the answer to (a) is "yes," but the answer to (b) is "no," then it would make sense to deny the lesser evils defense offered by the defendant who commits C-Better, but grant him some other justification defense.

6.3 AN ARGUMENT AGAINST C-BETTER'S PERMISSIBILITY

In his paper, Larry offers both an argument for the claim that C-Better is not permissible, and an argument for the claim that it is. He prefers the latter argument to the former, although it is a bit unclear from the text what his grounds are for this preference. Paraphrasing a bit to use the terminology just introduced, here is how he describes the argument for denying the defense:

> [D]efendant did not bring about the least evil possible. The evil he caused ([Better]) was greater than the minimum he could have caused ([Best]). [Better was] not *necessary* to [prevent Worst], nor did defendant believe [Better was] necessary. Only [Best] was necessary. We would have liked for him to have chosen [Best] over [Better]. These considerations appear to militate in favor of denying the defense.[2]

The argument as stated invokes two related but different ideas that should be separated. First, there's the observation that Better is not necessary for the avoidance of Worst since Best was available. Presumably, this is relevant because it undercuts a claim on D's part to the effect that the only way he could have prevented Worst was by bringing about Better. That's not true since he could have, instead, brought about Best. Second, there's the observation that "we" prefer Best to Better. Presumably, this is relevant because it undercuts a claim on D's part to the effect that he did what we would have wanted him to do.

Paired with these two different pleas that one might offer in one's defense are two seemingly different ways of construing the purpose of the lesser evils defense – the purpose that distinguishes it, that is, from other justification defenses. The advocate

[2] Ibid., 619.

of what we might call the "No Choice" rationale thinks that the lesser evils defense is a mechanism through which legal force is given to the plea, "I had no other way to prevent Worst!" The advocate of what we might call the "Social Preference" rationale thinks the lesser evils defense gives legal force to the plea, "I did what you would have had me do!" Both of these rationales have the implication that there should be no lesser evils defense for the commission of C-Better, since the defense's purpose would not be served by granting it. The defendant was perfectly capable of preventing Worst by performing C-Best, and that is what we would have had him do.

How different are these two rationales for the defense? Less different than it might appear. To see this, note that the lesser evils defense is often labeled "the necessity defense." Under the No Choice rationale, this label is apt: The defense is intended to capture the thought that the crime which D committed *must* have been committed if Worst was to be prevented. However, if the No Choice rationale is to capture even the basics of the lesser evils defense, the relevant notion of *requirement* or *necessity* cannot be exhausted by the notion of inability. It cannot be, that is, that a person enjoys the lesser evils defense only if *there was nothing else* besides C-Better that he was able to do to prevent Worst. Imagine, for instance, that he could alert the fire department either by stealing an unoccupied car or by murdering a driver and taking his car. When he steals the unoccupied car, there remained something else that he had the ability to do to prevent Worst: He could have killed the driver of the occupied car instead. But that fact does not invalidate his lesser evils defense. That is, the fact that D had the ability to prevent Worst through conduct *more* wrongful than the conduct he chose does not invalidate the defense. And so it follows that "I had no other way to prevent Worst!" does not mean "I lacked the ability to prevent Worst through any means other than C-Better." So what does it mean? Probably something like this: "Every alternative act that would have prevented Worst was either one I lacked the ability to perform, or else one that was worse than the act I performed."

But notice that, so understood, No Choice and Social Preference turn out to be equivalent. The reason is that the claim of the person who says, "I did what you would have wanted me to do!" is a claim to the effect that every other act D could have performed, including the act of allowing Worst to occur, was worse than C-Better. After all, he cannot mean that *every* act, including acts he *lacked* the ability to perform, were inferior, by "our" standards, to the one he performed. It surely would have been better if he had telepathically alerted the firemen to the fire; the trouble is that that is not something he had the ability to do. So, the person who says, "I could not have prevented Worst any other way!" and the one who says, "I did what you would have wanted me to do!" assert the same disjunction: "Every other act that would have prevented Worst was either less good than C-Better, or else not one I had the ability to perform." The only difference is that the former person emphasizes the second disjunct, and the latter the first.

Put simply, someone who says, "I had no choice!" really means "I had no *better* choice!" If the lesser evils defense functions to give legal force to this familiar plea, then we have our answer: The defense should not be available for commission of C-Better, for it is simply false that the agent performed the best act of those that he had the ability to perform; he could have performed C-Best.

But there is good reason to think that this is not the purpose of the lesser evils defense.[3] The main problem is that, on its face, to insist, in one's defense, that one took the best option one could is to offer an *excuse*. To say that one had no better option is a way of saying that one is not responsible, or culpable, for what is avowedly a wrongful act. But there is good reason to think that the lesser evils defense is not an excuse. After all, those who prevent the greater evil are worthy of praise for their conduct. But a person is worthy of praise for what she does only if she is responsible for it. And so that shows that the lesser evils defense applies even in the face of the presence of the necessary and sufficient conditions that excuses show to be absent.

A defender of the No Choice rationale (equivalent, I've suggested, to the Social Preference rationale) could resist this line of argument by denying that to assert that one had no better choice is to offer an excuse. Perhaps, for instance, one is drawing on the maxim that ought implies can and so, in asserting one's inability to do anything better, one is thereby undermining the claim that one had an obligation to do so. However, if this is right, *then there are no excuses*. Every instance in which one cites one's inability to do something would turn into a case in which one was defending oneself by noting the way in which inability undercuts obligation. While it is of course *possible* that there are no excuses, but only justifications, I must confess that I do not take this possibility very seriously. At the very least, it's a high enough price to motivate a search for an alternative rationale for the lesser evils defense.

For this reason, the proposed argument – the argument for the claim that the agent who commits C-Better should be denied the lesser evils defense – falters. It rests on an account of the defense's purpose under which either it is an excuse, or there are no excuses, and neither position is plausible.

6.4 AN ARGUMENT FOR C-BETTER'S PERMISSIBILITY

When Larry offers the argument he endorses, the argument in favor of granting the lesser evils defense to D for crime C-Better, he tacitly endorses a distinct and

[3] I've argued for this claim at greater length elsewhere. See Gideon Yaffe, "A Procedural Rationale for the Necessity Defense," *Journal of Value Inquiry* 43, no. 3 (2009): 369–89.

superior position about the purpose of the defense than that canvassed in the last section. Paraphrasing again:

> [I]n the absence of any affirmative duties, the lesser evils defense is a permission, not a mandate. Defendant can with impunity choose to do nothing to [prevent Worst]. But if the choice is between [Worst and Better], we would prefer that he choose [Better]. And if he is not motivated to [prevent Worst] by [performing C-Best], but he is motivated to [prevent Worst] by [performing C-Better], we should be thankful that he at least has some motivation to [prevent Worst]. If we tell him he will not get the defense unless he [performs C-Best], he will likely do nothing, and [Worst will be realized]. The wiser policy thus appears to have the defense be available to one who chooses a lesser evil even if he does not choose the least evil of which he is aware.[4]

Larry here considers a hypothetical person who will prevent Worst only if it is permissible to perform C-Better.[5] Why does he consider such a person? Why does he think that hypothetical person's behavior is relevant to the question of whether to grant the lesser evils defense for C-Better? Were such a person to say, "I had no better way to prevent Worst!" that would not be true. He could have performed C-Best. We would prefer that this person perform C-Best – something he is perfectly capable of doing – even if we cannot hold out any hope that he will. So, Larry cannot be accepting the view of the lesser evils defense's purpose identified in the previous section; from the point of view of someone who advocates that position, there is nothing to learn from the hypothetical person who prevents Worst only if C-Better is permissible.

Larry's language here about the "wise policy" suggests that he is trying to justify granting the lesser evils defense in cases of the kind at issue because that would incentivize a class of people, namely, those who would realize Worst if C-Better were legally prohibited, to prevent Worst. But this cannot be what Larry actually has in mind. For one thing, any time we justify allowing a defense to a class of people simply because the resulting behavior patterns are better that way than the alternative, we give up on the kind of rationales for criminal law doctrines that Larry has devoted a large chunk of his research to providing. Imagine that there is a large group of people who will commit murder if rape is illegal, but if rape is legal they will commit that crime instead and keep their murderous impulses in check. Nobody in the business of understanding the moral structure and justification of

4 Alexander, "Lesser Evils," 619.

5 Larry seems to think it clear that this person deserves the lesser evils defense. But it's not clear to me. Imagine someone who steals a car and says, in his defense, that if he were barred from stealing the car he would have committed rape; he needed an outlet for his aggression. That's no argument for granting him a defense to the theft of the car.

the criminal law would take the existence of such a group, no matter how large, to justify legalizing rape. It might be a "wise policy," in the sense that it would result in less overall harm, but it would be abhorrent. The fact that a lot of lives could be saved that way just is not to the point. This just can't be the kind of thing Larry has in mind, despite the language he uses that points that way.

Rather, Larry tacitly holds, I suggest, that the lesser evils defense is a way of giving legal force to the following plea by the defendant: "I did better than you had a right to expect me to do!" The idea is that the plea is addressed to someone who can legitimately expect only permissible conduct from the defendant, and so has a right to expect from him only the behavior that would generate Worst. The hypothetical person who will prevent Worst only if C-Better is permissible is relevant because we do not have a right to expect that the defendant be even as good as that person; we do not have a right to complain if he has no motivation at all to prevent Worst, and so we should celebrate rather than condemn any motive he has to prevent Worst, even if such motives fall far short of what we would like to see. The idea is that the lesser evils defense is a policy built for those who are motivated better than we have a right to expect, where we have no right to expect people to be at all averse to permissible behavior. Call this the "Better than Expected" rationale for the lesser evils defense.

The position to which Larry, I claim, is implicitly committed – namely Better than Expected – is different from the rationale(s) labeled above, No Choice and Social Preference. Under Better than Expected, any act better than a permissible act is shielded from liability even if there were yet better acts that would have prevented Worst and which the agent was fully capable of performing. This is why Better than Expected has the implication that the agent who commits C-Better is owed the lesser evils defense while the other position has the opposite implication. However, this is also what makes Better than Expected indefensible.

To see this, note that Better than Expected presupposes the following principle:

> If act A is permissible, and act B results in a better world than that which A results in, then B is permissible.

But every nonconsequentialist must deny this principle. Why is it permissible to allow the forest fire to destroy the village? The answer is that such conduct is merely an *allowing* and not a doing. If there were no moral difference between doing and allowing, it would be clearly impermissible to allow the village to burn since it is clearly impermissible to actively burn it down. But stealing the car is a doing, and so we learn nothing at all about its permissibility from the fact that it is permissible to allow the forest fire to burn the village. Since the permissibility of allowing the village to burn is not a function of the value of the behavior's consequences, the fact that other behaviors have better consequences tells us nothing at all about their permissibility.

The point just made is not special to the case in which the permissible but catastrophic option is an allowing rather than a doing. Consider Judith Thomson's famous Henry Fonda example. Poor Judith is dying and the only thing that can save her is for Henry Fonda to place his cool hand on her brow. But she's nothing to him and, as it happens, he's enjoying his vacation in Paris, a day's travel away, when the request arrives. It's perfectly permissible for him to decline the invitation to come to her bedside – a doing – despite the fact that he thereby commits homicide.[6] Now imagine that right there next to him at the Eiffel Tower is another famous philosopher whom he can save from being maimed by simply blowing her a kiss. Maiming is less bad than killing, and it's permissible for Henry Fonda to kill Judith (by declining the invitation) but it does not follow that it's permissible for him to decline to blow the kiss and thereby maim the Parisian philosopher. What people do and do not have the right to demand of each other is not a simple function of the values of the consequences of the behaviors. Fonda's permission to kill Judith does not derive from anything about its consequences, which are awful, but instead from something about his rights, and so the fact that another act has less bad consequences tells us nothing at all about its permissibility; it might implicate rights in a different way.

Larry discusses the bearing of deontological constraints on the lesser evils defense in his paper. However, he there asks whether the defense should be available to an actor who violates such a constraint in bringing about the lesser evil. He suggests, plausibly, that it depends on the magnitudes of the greater and lesser evils, which are, in turn, in part a function of how they are caused. The question that he is there answering is interesting, but it's a different question from the one that I am here raising. My concern is with cases in which the permission to realize the greater evil has its source in something other than the value of the consequences of such behavior. In fact, given that the evil in question is so enormous, *every* case in which it's permissible to realize the greater evil is one in which the permission is explained by something like the fact that the relevant behavior is merely an allowing, or by some other morally significant fact about it, distinct from its consequences, such as the way in which it implicates rights. What follows is that we cannot reach the conclusion that C-Better is permissible from the premises that (1) it is permissible not to prevent Worst and (2) Better is better than Worst. From (1) and (2) nothing at all follows about the permissibility or impermissibility of C-Better, assuming that consequentialism is a false moral theory. What that shows is that the plea "I did better than you had a right to expect me to do!" is severely limited in its power to shield a person from blame. We often have the right to expect people to refrain from doing things that have better consequences than other things we have no right to

[6] Judith Jarvis Thomson, "A Defense of Abortion," *Philosophy and Public Affairs* 1, no. 1 (1971): 55.

expect them to avoid. The owner of the car has no right to expect you to refrain from allowing the village to burn, but, for all we know, he has every right to expect you to refrain from stealing his car, even though the world would be a lot better if you went ahead and stole it.

In short, the price of admission to nonconsequentialism – and who would turn down the chance to attend that party? – is acceptance of the idea that deontic properties, like permissibility and impermissibility, may not be distributed among acts in a way that tracks the distribution of the evaluative properties of those acts, like having good and bad consequences. But what follows is that the lesser evils defense cannot be a way of giving legal force to the plea "I did better than you had a right to expect me to do!" If it were, then it would be highly inept, for it would shield people from criminal liability for impermissible conduct that just happened to have better consequences than some available and permissible conduct.

Taking stock of the progress made in this section and the last: It's natural to see the lesser evils defense as the legal codification of the familiar plea that one did the best one could to prevent a catastrophe. So understood, the defense ought not to shield those who could have done better and so ought not to be available in defense of the commission of C-Better. But as natural as it is, it cannot be right, since it involves painting the defense as an excuse, or else denying that any defenses are excuses. Alternatively, we might follow Larry in his tacit acceptance of the idea that the defense is grounded in the principle that it is permissible to do anything better than a permissible act. So understood, the lesser evils defense should shield the agent who commits C-Better from criminal liability, assuming that it was permissible for D to realize Worst. But the problem is that that principle is true only if consequentialism is true, which is very unlikely for well-known reasons. The result is that we still have no idea whether the lesser evils defense should shield from liability those who prevent a disaster, but not in the best way available to them. To settle that question, we need a better theory of the purpose of the lesser evils defense.

6.5 A PROCEDURAL ESTOPPEL DEFENSE

There are various legal mechanisms for shielding defendants from liability thanks to the fact that finding them or holding them liable would amount to some form of misconduct on the government's part. The defendant and his conduct, when such shields are available, is often no different from the conduct and character of others who are justifiably held liable because the government did not misbehave with respect to them. The exclusionary rule, barring from evidence a coerced confession, or evidence collected in an illegal search, for instance, is an example. The bloody knife provides proof of guilt beyond a reasonable doubt, whether or not the cop who found it had a search warrant. A criminal defense that is like this is neither an excuse nor a justification. It shields the defendant from criminal liability even if he is fully responsible and culpable for morally wrongful and illegal conduct. In what I have labeled "procedural estoppel defenses," the problem is that were the government to convict and punish, its conduct would be in conflict with itself; it would embody a contradiction.[7] Double jeopardy is like this. Trials proceed under the presupposition that the government has the authority to settle the question of the defendant's guilt. But to proceed with a trial after a verdict has already been reached in the relevant matter is to presuppose that the entity that reached that verdict lacked the authority to settle the matter. When it is one and the same government that reaches a verdict yesterday and places the defendant on trial today, then the government has inconsistent commitments or presuppositions. In such a case, the government both presupposes that it has, and that it lacks, the authority to settle the question of guilt.

Why it is that the government ought to be blocked from exercising its power in ways that involve inconsistent commitments is a question not in moral, but in political philosophy. If a defendant is falsely acquitted, that's a moral error. The only way to correct the error would be to place him in jeopardy a second time. Barring the second jeopardy, therefore, is not justified on *moral* grounds. This is generally the case with procedural estoppel defenses. There is something problematic about inconsistency in the government's commitments, and it is problematic in a way that undermines the government's authority. In fact, this is something which a theory of the source and grounds of political authority should account for and explain. Consent-based theories do a good job of explaining it, if we grant that citizen consent cannot be given to power exercised with inconsistent commitments, for instance. But any adequate theory of governmental authority should be able to accommodate this.

The state would have inconsistent commitments were it to convict and punish in standard, two-option lesser evils cases. The state is committed to preventing the great evil that would have been realized had the defendant not taken steps to prevent it. But the conviction and punishment of a criminal defendant involves the presupposition that what the defendant realized through his conduct was something that the state is committed to preventing. The result is that were the state to convict and punish in lesser evils cases, its conduct would be grounded in both a commitment to prevent the greater evil, and a commitment to prevent that which prevented it. Such exercises of government power cannot be authoritative.

Notice that this line of thought involves no claims about the moral value of that which the government is committed to preventing. For all that's been said, what the government would label "an evil" is actually a good. The defendant who steals a car in order to prevent the government's genocide machine from grinding to a halt

7 Yaffe, "A Procedural Rationale," 371.

is owed a lesser evils defense – despite the fact that the world would have been far, far better, morally speaking, if the genocide machine had, indeed, ground to a halt. The reason is that were the government to convict, its behavior would exemplify inconsistent commitments and so would fail to meet a first and basic necessary condition for authority.

This account of the lesser evil defense's rationale has immediate implications for cases in which the defendant prevents the greater evil in a nonoptimal way. The defense should be granted in such cases for the same reasons that it should be granted when there are only two options. Were the defendant to be convicted and punished, the government's conduct would involve both a commitment to preventing the greater evil and an inconsistent commitment to preventing its prevention, as the defendant did. Since an exercise of such power cannot be an exercise of authority, preservation of the government's authority requires acquittal of the defendant.

Now, it is also the case that the government is committed to preventing Better. And so the government is falling short of its commitments in declining to convict and punish the defendant who realizes it through criminal conduct. But complete success is not a necessary condition of government authority, while avoiding inconsistency is. If there is ambivalence in intuition when it comes to cases of the sort Larry invites us to look at, it is because, I suggest, we recognize that the price of government consistency in such cases is government failure.

6.6 CONCLUSION

It is an implication of the view offered in the last section that the lesser evils defense is neither an excuse nor a justification. At least, it is clearly no excuse, and it is not a justification when that term is used in a nontrivial way. The term "justification," as used to describe a legal doctrine, is used in two importantly different ways. When the term is used nontrivially, it refers to a shield to criminal liability that applies thanks to the fact that the defendant's conduct is not morally wrongful, despite belonging to a type of conduct prohibited thanks to the fact that it is ordinarily morally wrongful. It is in this sense that it is sometimes said that lethal self-defense is a justification. Intentional homicide is prohibited because it's ordinarily wrong; lethal self-defense is the rare case of morally permitted intentional homicide. To call a legal doctrine a justification, in this sense, is to identify its function: to mirror in law the moral fact about the exceptional nature of a subset of acts of an ordinarily morally impermissible type.

In the other, trivial sense, the term "justification" is used to refer to conduct that is not legally prohibited despite the fact that it is of a type that is ordinarily legally prohibited. So understood, the term is used to refer to a legal doctrine with a certain logical structure; morality has nothing to do with it. In this sense, too, self-defense is a justification. Intentional homicides committed in self-defense are not in fact in violation of the law, despite the fact that intentional homicide is a prohibited type. I call this type of justification trivial because under it legislators craft new justifications whenever they add "unless" clauses to statutes, explicitly or tacitly, no matter what the content of those clauses. If a statute says that it is illegal to do such and such unless you are a licensed pawnbroker, then being a licensed pawnbroker is a justification, in the trivial sense, for doing the thing in question. But this would not be a justification in the nontrivial sense since, ordinarily anyway, the same moral principles apply to pawnbrokers as to the rest of us.

Under the rationale for the lesser evils defense sketched in the last section, it is a justification in the trivial sense: Criminal conduct that realizes the lesser evil is not legally prohibited. But in this trivial sense, all procedural defenses are justifications, and so the designation illuminates little of interest. More importantly, if I am right about the rationale for the lesser evils defense, then it is not a justification in the nontrivial sense. The moral qualities of the defendant's conduct, not to mention the ordinary moral qualities of conduct of that type, have nothing to do with the grounds for shielding the defendant from criminal liability.

Have I offered an argument for this point of view over competitors? Only to someone who, like Larry, believes that a defendant should be shielded from criminal liability when he performs C-Better despite the fact that C-Best was available to him. Someone who holds that belief needs to explain it. He cannot explain it through appeal to any of the competing rationales for the lesser evils defense canvassed here, but can explain it through the view I propose. In this sense, then, my argument can be thought of as an invitation to Larry and others – an invitation to accept my proposed rationale for the lesser evils defense, or find an alternative that can provide a morally sound solution to Larry's puzzle. I like to think, however, that it is fitting to respond to Larry's invitation by offering him one in return.

PART II

Problems in Constitutional Law

7

Justifying Academic Freedom

Mill and Marcuse Revisited

Brian Leiter

7.1 ACADEMIC FREEDOM: PRELIMINARIES

Academic freedom, as defined influentially in 1940 by the Association of American University Professors (hereafter "AAUP"),[1] encompasses the following entitlements:

1. Teachers are entitled to full freedom in research and in the publication of the results, subject to the adequate performance of their other academic duties.
2. Teachers are entitled to freedom in the classroom in discussing their subject, but they should be careful not to introduce into their teaching controversial matter which has no relation to their subject.
3. College and university teachers are citizens, members of a learned profession, and officers of an educational institution. When they speak or write as citizens, they should be free from institutional censorship or discipline, but their special position in the community imposes special obligations. As scholars and educational officers, they should remember that the public may judge their profession and their institution by their utterances. Hence, they should at all times be accurate, should exercise appropriate restraint, should show respect for the opinions of others, and should make every effort to indicate that they are not speaking for the institution.

Freedom in research and teaching – the first two provisions – are the central components of academic freedom, and not only in the United States, a point to which I return.

Let us begin, however, by looking more closely at the striking third provision in the AAUP definition – which focuses on what is elsewhere called by the AAUP "extramural" expression. As written, it is not clear whether the right to be "free from

[1] AAUP 1940 Statement of Principles on Academic Freedom and Tenure, www.aaup.org/report/1940-statement-principles-academic-freedom-and-tenure.

institutional censorship or discipline" for extramural speech – speech "as citizens" – applies only when the various "good manners" provisions are observed, or whether the "good manners" provisions are simply recommendations to academics. The text is compatible with the more demanding reading – one favored, typically, by critics of academic extramural speech – and on one occasion a court even endorsed that reading,[2] though there is very little case law on this point. The AAUP itself, in a 1963 committee report on a controversy involving extramural speech by a faculty member at the University of Illinois, interpreted the "good manners" provision "exclusively as an admonition addressed to the conscience of the faculty,"[3] although a plurality but not a majority of the committee thought it was not simply "a precatory statement," but "was intended to recognize the legitimacy of university authority to discipline faculty members for violating norms of accuracy, self-restraint, and courtesy even in respect to professional unrelated extramural utterances."[4] As William Van Alstyne noted many years ago, this would, ironically, impose a much higher burden on the extramural political speech of academics than ordinary citizens: "[O]rdinary political rhetoric," as Van Alstyne remarked, does not generally have to answer to "the exceptionally inhibiting standards of accuracy, care, restraint, and courtesy identified with [a professor's] professional status."[5] Van Alstyne was writing decades before the emergence of social media platforms – Twitter, Facebook, blogs – that lend themselves all too easily to violating the "good manners" provisions in a way that letters to the editor of the local newspaper usually did not.[6]

I want to begin by addressing the legal status of academic freedom in the United States and elsewhere,[7] which will help us define the parameters of its moral

[2] See, e.g., Starsky v. Williams, 353 F.Supp. 900, 917 (D. Ariz. 1972), in which the court opined that "the content of the [plaintiff Starsky's] speech in calling Mr. Sumner a 'bastard,' etc., adds very little to the world of ideas. It communicates only vituperation, bad temper, and a kind of loss of personal dignity on the part of a faculty member that may be the exact kind of conduct meant to be avoided by the AAUP standard of 'appropriate' restraint. The school's interest in discipline in demanding some minimum of courtesy in a faculty member's on-campus relationships with school officials outweighs the free speech interests here." Note, however, that notwithstanding the preceding, the court concluded that Arizona State University had violated Starsky's First Amendment rights by terminating him primarily on the basis of other conduct that did enjoy constitutional protection.

[3] William Van Alstyne, "The Specific Theory of Academic Freedom and the General Issue of Civil Liberty," in *The Concept of Academic Freedom* 82, ed. E.L. Pincoffs (Austin: University of Texas Press, 1972).

[4] Ibid.

[5] Ibid., 83.

[6] The absence of an intermediary between speaker and public is the key feature responsible for the serial violation of "good manners" provisions in cyberspace – sometimes, of course, that is salutary, but it makes the AAUP's framing of the protection for extramural speech all the more important.

[7] Its legal status in the United Kingdom and Germany is usefully reviewed in Eric Barendt, *Academic Freedom and the Law: A Comparative Study* (Oxford: Hart, 2010), chaps. 4–5. I will return to these countries, below, in the text.

relevance. As a matter of American constitutional law, academic freedom's status is vexed and uncertain. As Aziz Huq memorably puts it: Academic freedom's "constitutional status is under siege in the [US] Supreme Court. It is frankly repudiated by leading circuit court judges. Jurists scoff at the prospect of indolent academics – glutted at faculty lunches on oysters, aphorisms, and *amour propre* – being granted constitutional entitlements greater than the riffraff."[8] Legal protection for academic freedom, however, also derives from American contract law, since most contracts with university professors incorporate (at least by reference) the AAUP definition of academic freedom as one of the contractual rights to which *at least* tenured faculty are entitled.[9] Indeed, the institution of tenure is typically justified, by the AAUP and others, as protection for academic freedom.[10] And academic freedom is, in turn, justified as the best mechanism for the discovery of truth, which is ultimately supposed to be in the interest of society as a whole.

Tenure is often described as "lifetime employment" – and, de facto, too often that is what it is even in cases of gross dereliction of duty – but what it really means is that a faculty member can only be terminated for *cause*, i.e., unprofessional performance of the faculty member's contractual duties as a teacher and scholar, as assessed by his or her professional peers. Since the employer must show cause to terminate the faculty member, a variety of procedural protections also apply under AAUP guidelines.[11] Tenure does help insulate academics from being punished for their ideas, including their extramural speech under AAUP rules, though the protection is imperfect,[12] but few prophylactic measures are foolproof. But tenure is also an especially unusual institution in America, where "at-will" employment relationships are the norm – that is, contractual relationships in which employees can be terminated by the employer at his or her discretion, subject primarily to limitations having to

[8] Aziz Huq, "Easterbrook on Academic Freedom," *University of Chicago Law Review* 77, no. 4 (2010): 1055, 1056–57. There are, however, federal court cases protecting academic freedom as a constitutional matter. See, e.g., Silva v. New Hampshire, 888 F.Supp. 293 (D. N.H. 1994) or Turkish Coalition of America v. Bruininks, 804 F.Supp. 959 (D. Minn. 2011). Much of the trouble stems, I suspect, from the issue raised below about extramural speech; in this regard, Van Alstyne, "The Specific Theory of Academic Freedom and the General Issue of Civil Liberty," was prescient.

[9] In some states, including Texas, courts have denied that provisions in faculty handbooks constitute contractual entitlements. See Spuler v. Pickar, 958 F.2d 103, 106 (5th Cir. 1992). There has been surprisingly little litigation over the contractual right to academic freedom as defined by the AAUP, *perhaps* because universities recognize their contractual obligations.

[10] AAUP 1940 Statement of Principles on Academic Freedom and Tenure. Note that when the United Kingdom removed tenure, they enacted a statutory protection for academic freedom in the 1988 Act. Education Reform Act of 1988, c. 40 § 202 sch. 11 (Gr. Brit.).

[11] AAUP 1940 Statement of Principles on Academic Freedom and Tenure.

[12] Recall the cases of Ward Churchill at the University of Colorado and Steven Salaita at the University of Illinois, both fired for their offensive political speech, though in both cases pretextual grounds were adduced. Both their positions were ultimately vindicated by the courts, though only Salaita received a cash settlement.

do with impermissible forms of discrimination on the basis of race, gender, age, and so on. A high-level employee of the Exxon oil company has no contractual right not to be fired for what he "speaks or writes" as a citizen. Why should a professor, when speaking as a citizen, enjoy a freedom from employment repercussions that most other citizens do not enjoy? This is the aspect of the AAUP definition of academic freedom most vulnerable to attack in a capitalist society where at-will employment is the norm.

This is also the aspect of the 1940 AAUP statement that has attracted the most critical comment from supporters of academic freedom. As Van Alstyne noted in his seminal 1972 essay, "academic freedom" has migrated "from a close association with protection of the academic in his professional endeavors and assumed a new synonymy with the general civil liberties of academics (and especially their general *political* liberties)."[13] Ordinary citizens might be forgiven for thinking it "odd" that, as Van Alstyne put it,

> professors ... insist that professors have an *extra* right to be protected in these aprofessional pursuits [i.e., extramural speech] ... a claim sublimely stronger than [ordinary citizens], insisting as professors do that such activities are part of their "academic freedom" and a special contribution to the social good, whereas such activities by others are merely an ordinary matter of common liberty to be tolerated in a liberal society but not, of course, of the same rank of special good as the protection of academic freedom.[14]

Van Alstyne, we should remember, wrote at a time when there were signs – most notably in the Supreme Court's 1968 decision in *Pickering v. Board of Education*[15] – that extramural political speech by *all* government employees would receive significant constitutional protection, which would render the situation for academics (at least those at *state* schools) under the AAUP definition less anomalous. *Pickering* proposed striking a balance "between the interests of the teacher, as a citizen, in commenting upon matters of public concern and the interest of the State, as an employer, in promoting the efficiency of the public services it performs through its employees."[16] Later cases developed and modified this test.[17] The US Court of Appeals for the Second Circuit gave a crisp summary of the state of the law in 1995:

> Whittled to its core, [the Supreme Court] permits a government employer to fire an employee for speaking on a matter of public concern if: (1) the employer's prediction of disruption is reasonable; (2) the potential disruptiveness is enough to

[13] Van Alstyne, "Theory of Academic Freedom," 62.
[14] Ibid., 64.
[15] 391 U.S. 563 (1968).
[16] Ibid., 568.
[17] See Connick v. Myers, 461 U.S. 138 (1983); Waters v. Churchill, 511 U.S. 661 (1994).

> outweigh the value of the speech; and (3) the employer took action against the employee based on this disruption and not in retaliation for the speech.[18]

All of this, alas, was before the alarming US Supreme Court decision in *Garcetti v. Ceballos* in 2006,[19] which held that "when public employees make statements pursuant to their official duties, the employees are not speaking as citizens for First Amendment purposes, and the Constitution does not insulate their communications from employer discipline."[20] *Garcetti* involved a prosecutor who claimed constitutional protection for a memo to his superiors about a warrant whose factual basis he deemed wanting. The Court rejected the attorney's claim, noting that "his expressions were made pursuant to his duties" in the prosecutor's office.[21] But are not the teaching and writing of a professor at a public university all "expressions … pursuant to his duties"?[22] After *Garcetti*, it is not certain whether *Pickering* balancing tests even protect faculty at public universities even in the core of their academic freedom.

But that leads to another important caveat: *Pickering* has no bearing on the speech of private employees and, in the United States at least, many professors are privately employed. The 1940 AAUP statement, by protecting extramural speech, actually gives faculty at private universities the same legal rights as those at public universities – assuming, again, that the AAUP protections are incorporated by private contract *and* assuming that *Garcetti* does not evolve to eviscerate the speech rights of public university faculty.

Although the legal status of academic freedom is not my main topic – what the law requires is, after all, one thing; what we ought to do is always another: the central lesson of the legal positivist tradition from Bentham to Hart and beyond – the legal quandaries surrounding academic freedom in the United States do help focus the issue. In a free and democratic society, one might hope that no citizens should suffer employment repercussions for their political speech, regardless of their employers, unless that political speech runs afoul of *general* legal regulations (e.g., prohibitions on sexual harassment or, as in many countries, hate speech). My topic, however, is only what arguments there are for *specifically* academic freedom, which is usefully defined by Van Alstyne as follows:

> Insofar as it pertains to faculty members in institutions of higher learning, "academic freedom" is characterized by a personal liberty to pursue the investigation, research, teaching, and publication of any subject as a matter of professional interest

[18] Jeffries v. Harleston, 52 F.3d 9, 13 (2d Cir. 1995).

[19] 547 U.S. 410 (2006).

[20] Ibid., 421.

[21] Ibid.

[22] Ibid., 431 (Stevens dissenting).

> without vocational jeopardy or threat of other sanction, save only upon adequate demonstration of an inexcusable breach of professional ethics in the exercise of that freedom. Specifically, that which sets academic freedom apart as a distinct freedom is its vocational claim of special and limited accountability in respect to all academically related pursuits of the teacher-scholar: an accountability not to any institutional or societal standard of economic benefit, but solely to a fiduciary standard of professional integrity ...The maintenance of academic freedom contemplates an accountability in respect to academic investigations and utterances solely in respect of their professional integrity, a matter usually determined by reference to professional ethical standards of truthful disclosure and reasonable care.[23]

I will gloss the preceding as the freedom in research and teaching that is the core of academic freedom, contrary to the AAUP definition which includes extramural speech.

When we look to some other countries with outstanding university systems that offer legal protection for academic freedom, we find that they too identify this as the real core of academic freedom. For example, Germany's postwar constitution – "the Basic Law" – enshrines core academic (and artistic) freedom in the text: "Art and science, research and teaching shall be free."[24] Protection for *Wissenschaftsfreiheit* – "scientific freedom" – dates back to the early nineteenth century, when Germany was the birthplace of the modern idea and reality of a university.[25] In German, *Wissenschaft*, or "science," has a much broader connotation than the anglophone "natural science": It includes any systematic form of inquiry into nature, history, literature, or society marked by rigorous methods that aim to secure the reliability or truth of its findings.[26] In Germany – as in Van Alstyne's account of academic freedom – it falls to academic professionals in each *Wissenschaft* to determine what constitutes failure to live up to scientific standards.[27]

In the United Kingdom, after the elimination of university tenure in 1988, academic freedom was secured by statutory provision,[28] according to which,

> academic staff have freedom within the law to question and test received wisdom, and to put forward new ideas and controversial or unpopular opinions, without

23 Van Alstyne, "Theory of Academic Freedom," 71.

24 *Grundgesetz*, art. 5(3), translation at www.gesetze-im-internet.de/englisch_gg/index.html.

25 Eric Barendt, *Academic Freedom and the Law: A Comparative Study* (Portland: Hart, 1970), 120–21.

26 Interestingly, in the German case scientific freedom has been held by the Constitutional Court to create positive entitlements, not just protection from interference: "the state is under a constitutional duty to safeguard the value by making some provisions for the effective exercise of academic freedom." Ibid., 118. It is even a right enjoyed by nonacademics, insofar as they are engaged in *Wissenschaft*. Ibid., 119.

27 Ibid., 125. Whether all disciplines in the modern university are *Wissenschaften* is a topic to which I return below.

28 Ibid., 93.

placing themselves in jeopardy of losing their jobs or privileges they may have at their institutions ...[29]

As one English commentator notes, "the freedom is not explicitly limited to the communication of ideas in lectures and seminars," so would presumably cover *some* extramural speech, at least that related to the area of academic expertise.[30] It does not appear that the protection for academic freedom in the United Kingdom encompasses as broad a protection for extramural speech unrelated to academic expertise as does the AAUP's provision.

My topic is *whether* and *why* we ought to provide a special kind of legal protection for academic freedom, even when the research and teaching of faculty are offensive to members of the polity at large or harmful to the interests of politicians or corporations or even ordinary citizens. I believe that requires us, in the first instance, to revisit the reasons why any legal protection should be provided to speech (not just academic speech) that is harmful, offensive, disruptive, and so on – in other words, I will treat the justification of academic freedom as a subset of the justification of general freedom of expression. After clarifying what I take to be the most compelling reasons for a general freedom of expression – including noting reasons for skepticism about those justifications – we will return to the question of the scope of academic freedom and, in particular, whether the justification for academic freedom for faculty also extends to students.

7.2 WHY PROTECT SPEECH? JOHN STUART MILL AND HERBERT MARCUSE REVISITED

In the nineteenth century, John Stuart Mill gave the most important defense of the liberty of expression in the modern era, one influential to the present day.[31] It is worth noting that Mill's own account was heavily influenced by Wilhelm von Humboldt's writings on this topic in the late eighteenth century. Humboldt, of course, was also primarily responsible for the idea of a modern research university and for the attendant *Wissenschaftsfreiheit* that was deemed essential to its

29 Education Reform Act of 1988, c. 40 § 202 sch. 11 (Gr. Brit.).

30 Barendt, *Academic Freedom*, 94.

31 John Stewart Mill, *On Liberty* (West Strand: John W. Parker and Son, 1859). I do not discuss here a very different tradition, loosely Kantian, according to which the protection of free speech is justified by respect for the autonomy of individual speakers, listeners, readers, and thinkers. These views depend on false views about the autonomous capacities of persons; once we correct for their metaphysical extravagance, a deflated sense of "autonomy" emerges as a pertinent consideration within the broadly utilitarian framework. For extended discussion, see my "The Case Against Free Speech," *Sydney Law Review* 38, no. 4 (2016): 407, 423–29.

success.[32] The relevance of Mill's arguments to academic freedom is not simply accidental.

Mill believed that knowing the truth would maximize human well-being or happiness; and he believed we are more likely to find out what is true – in both theoretical and practical matters – if we permit people wide latitude to express their views and opinions, even when those turn out to be mistaken.[33] Mill's core rationale for these beliefs was twofold: First, we are fallible, so we may be wrong (wholly or partially) about what we take to be true, but we are less likely to discover our errors unless others with opposing views enjoy the freedom to challenge us; and second, even if we believe what is true already, being challenged by false beliefs insures that we hold our beliefs for sound reasons, not just dogmatically. Mill's idea that freedom of expression contributes to the discovery of what is true, and that such discovery is a social good to be promoted, is, as mentioned earlier, central to the AAUP's justification for academic freedom.[34]

The intuitive resonance of Mill's rationale in post-Enlightenment Western democracies is so powerful that the countervailing considerations are rarely considered seriously. But in the Millian spirit, we should consider those doubts explicitly, especially as they come from someone quite familiar with the Humboldt tradition. In a famous 1965 essay, the German philosopher Herbert Marcuse argued against liberty of expression for those defending imperialist aggression and oppression (he was thinking, in particular, of the recent US invasion of Vietnam in 1962 and the ensuing military violence): No tolerance, according to Marcuse, should be accorded to that kind of harmful and dangerous expression. Marcuse is sometimes adduced as exemplifying the anti-Millian, purportedly totalitarian tendencies of the left. This is an ironic charge, made by those who obviously have never read Marcuse's essay (or perhaps even Mill) carefully. For Marcuse's argument – and this is the really crucial point – was explicitly Millian, so any totalitarian tendencies are there in Mill himself.[35] Marcuse's claim was that toleration of expression of

[32] See Michael N. Forster, "The Liberal Temper in Classical German Philosophy: Freedom of Thought and Expression," in *After Herder: Philosophy of Language in the German Tradition*, ed. Michael N. Forester (New York: Oxford University Press, 2010), 244, 246–47

[33] I am skeptical of this assumption, as I argued in Leiter, "The Case Against Free Speech," 430–33. As Larry Alexander succinctly puts the point: "In domains in which obtaining the truth is the principal value – for example, in legal proceedings – expression is regulated and circumscribed. Even in the area of scientific inquiry, professional journals refuse to publish claims that the editors believe are not properly substantiated …" Larry Alexander, *Is There a Right to Freedom of Expression?* (New York: Cambridge University Press, 2005), 128. See also ibid., 130 for related criticisms.

[34] See AAUP 1940 Statement of Principles on Academic Freedom and Tenure.

[35] For an example of the simple-minded understanding of Mill that misses this problem, see Michael McConnell, "Why Protect Religious Freedom?" *Yale Law Journal* 123, no. 3 (2014): 770, 790–95.

certain views harms human well-being, and so could not be justified on utilitarian grounds. As Marcuse put it:

> [S]ociety cannot be indiscriminate [in what it tolerates] where the pacification of existence, where freedom and happiness themselves are at stake: here certain things cannot be said, certain ideas cannot be expressed, certain policies cannot be proposed, certain behavior cannot be permitted without making tolerance an instrument of the continuation of servitude.[36]

Marcuse's general thought is roughly that prohibitions on public justifications for, e.g., chattel slavery, or *de jure* segregation would, in fact, have hastened the end of both horrific institutions. *If* that were true, the burden on a utilitarian justification of such expression would be very high indeed.

The key to understanding both Mill and Marcuse, in short, is to realize that neither of these thinkers believed that liberty of expression was *intrinsically* valuable. Rather, they thought that liberty of expression was only valuable *in virtue of its actual consequences* – the consequences being hostage to facts about the world in which such expression occurred. Two general kinds of facts are important in this regard, though I do not think either Mill or Marcuse adequately identified them. First, there are facts about *expression* and, second, there are facts about *regulation of expression*. Facts about expression include *what* is expressed, *how* it is expressed, *who* expresses it, and *to whom* it is expressed. Even if all the facts about expression are bad ones – harmful ideas are expressed, they are expressed in ways that discourage thought and inflict harm directly or indirectly, and hearers or readers are not equipped to understand or respond appropriately to what is expressed – it still matters what the facts are about the regulation of expression. Regulators can be sufficiently stupid or venal or unreliable that we are better off with horrible facts about expression than we are with regulation of it. Most of American free speech jurisprudence – which is singularly forgiving of libel, as well as racist, misogynistic, and neo-Nazi abuse – is only explicable on the latter assumption. Marcuse was particularly insensitive to this last point, while Mill was insensitive to the former points.

Many commentators pass over in silence one of Mill's most striking claims in *On Liberty*, one that makes absolutely clear how he *really* thought about his arguments for liberty of expression. Mill wrote that his doctrine of the Harm Principle – "that the sole end for which mankind are warranted, individually or collectively, in interfering with the liberty of action of any of their number is self-protection" or "to prevent harm to others" –

36 I cite to the online version of Hubert Marcuse, "Repressive Tolerance" (1965), 3–4, www.marcuse.org/herbert/pubs/60spubs/65repressivetolerance.htm (published in Robert Paul Wolff, Barrington Moore, Jr., and Herbert Marcuse, A *Critique of Pure Tolerance* (Boston: Beacon Press, 1969), 95–137).

> is meant to apply only to human beings in the maturity of their faculties. We are not speaking of children or of young persons below the age which the law may fix as that of manhood or womanhood. Those who are still in a state to require being taken care of by others must be protected against their own actions as well as against external injury. For the same reason we may leave out of consideration those backward states of society in which the race itself may be considered as in its nonage … Despotism is a legitimate mode of government in dealing with barbarians, provided the end be their improvement and the means justified by actually effecting that end. Liberty, as a principle, has no application to any state of things anterior to the time when mankind have become capable of being improved by free and equal discussion.[37]

It is tempting to dismiss the particulars here as Mill's rationalization for British dominance of its colony in India. To do so, however, ignores that this is merely an objection *to the empirical facts* as Mill understood them, not to his understanding of the principle. Mill also claims that "mankind" has "in all nations with whom we need here concern ourselves" now "attained the capacity of being guided to their own improvement by conviction or persuasion,"[38] but that empirical assertion deserves as little credence as his assertion about the "barbarians" on the Indian subcontinent.

One may understand Marcuse's intervention in the debate as occurring at precisely this point. Marcuse's case against broad tolerance of even harmful speech is, in short, a version of Mill's case against free speech in colonized India: The facts about expression in many modern societies, including capitalist America in Marcuse's view, make clear that its consequences are harmful – partly because the population, suffering from massive indoctrination by the media as well as massive ignorance about what their elected leaders believe and about the causal relations between policies and outcomes,[39] is unable to sort the true from the false; and partly because what is expressed overwhelmingly favors the interest of the ruling class, to the detriment of the vast majority. Let us take these points up in turn.

Free expression can maximize human well-being only if those exposed to it can evaluate what they hear and make decisions that maximize their well-being in accordance with what is true. As Marcuse put it, giving expression to the Kantian ideal of "enlightenment":

> [L]iberal tolerance was, at least in theory, based on the proposition that men were (potential) *individuals* who could learn to hear and see and feel by themselves, to develop their own thoughts, to grasp their true interests and rights and capabilities,

[37] Mill, *On Liberty*, 10.

[38] Ibid.

[39] See generally Christopher H. Achen and Larry M. Bartels, *Democracy for Realists: Why Elections Do Not Produce Responsive Government* (Princeton: Princeton University Press, 2016).

> also against established authority and opinion. This was the rationale of free speech and assembly. Universal toleration becomes questionable when its rationale no longer prevails, when tolerance is administered to manipulated and indoctrinated individuals who parrot, as their own, the opinion of their masters, for whom heteronomy has become autonomy.[40]

Marcuse's worry in 1965 – which is even more justified a half-century later – is that the rationale for unbridled free expression is now defeated, since we are not dealing with "individuals" who can think and reason "against established authority and opinion." This is perhaps the central epistemological issue of our moment in America, and maybe worldwide – that is, an issue about what knowledge is and when we have it. When significant portions of the populace view scientific consensus, as reflected in reports by the National Academy of Sciences, as counterindicators as to the truth,[41] how far are we from the Kantian ideal? The Internet, that great equalizer in access to so-called information, also eliminates all the traditional arbiters of fact and fiction. Walter Cronkite did not repeat *just anything* on television, but on the Internet; Matt Drudge and Alex Jones will repeat *almost* anything if it conforms to their simple-minded or paranoid prejudices. Neither Drudge nor Jones graduated from college. Lots of quite brilliant people in human history did not even graduate from high school, but Drudge and Jones are rather plainly not among that group: Drudge is a simpleton, and I would not be surprised if it turned out that Jones suffered from a clinical mental illness. Will freedom of expression maximize human welfare when ignorant, simple-minded or sick people expose millions of their fellow citizens to falsehoods and misleading information?

Scholars on the libertarian right have recently mounted a sustained attack on the ignorance of the electorate – *not* blameworthy ignorance, but simple ignorance resulting from the busy demands of real life. Some have even gone so far as to argue "Against Democracy" in the title of one notable academic book by one libertarian critic.[42] The evidence of massive voter ignorance – about how the world works, about cause and effect, even about what the actual policies of politicians are – is overwhelming, at least in the United States (though similar evidence comes from

[40] Marcuse, "Repressive Tolerance," 4.

[41] See the discussion in Leiter, "Case Against Free Speech," 418–19.

[42] See generally Jason Brennan, *Against Democracy* (Princeton: Princeton University Press 2016); see also Ilya Somin, *Democracy and Political Ignorance* (Stanford: Stanford University Press, 2013). The conclusions these authors want to draw are, however, rather dubious. Somin's book is a brief for limited government, a non sequitur on the evidence adduced, since, as Achen and Bartels show, everything depends on the makeup of the "elite coalition" (see below in the text). Brennan's case for "epistocracy" would be plausible if Plato had been right, or if the social sciences were more epistemically robust than they actually are. On the case for democracy even in the face of massive ignorance and indoctrination, see Leiter, "The Case Against Free Speech," 433–39.

other countries). None of this should be surprising: Most people are busy earning a living, cooking meals, caring for sick parents, getting kids to school, fighting with insurance companies, and so on – not to mention surfing pornography websites, following sports teams, and searching out shopping opportunities. As two political scientists who study democracy put it, regarding those they call "pure" independent voters[43] in the American context, that is, those who do not lean to either the Democrats or the Republicans:

> Typically less-informed, they may fail to grasp what is at stake in the choice of one party or another, much less where their overall interests lie. Thus, they are often swept along by the familiarity of an incumbent, the charisma of a fresh challenger, or a sense that it is "time for a change," even when the government did not cause the current unsatisfactory situation and cannot greatly alter it. When the party balance is close … election outcomes turn on how these "swing voters" happen to feel when they go to the polls. As Philip Converse [citation omitted] put it, "Not only is the electorate as a whole quite uninformed, but it is the least informed members within the electorate who seem to hold the critical balance of power, in the sense that alternations in governing party depend disproportionately on shifts in their sentiment."
>
> The result is that, from the viewpoint of governmental representativeness and accountability, election outcomes are essentially random choices among the available parties – musical chairs. Elections that "throw the bums out" typically do not produce genuine policy mandates, not even when they are landslides. *They simply put a different elite coalition in charge* [emphasis added]. This bloodless change of government is a great deal better than bloody revolution, but it is not deliberate policy change. The parties have policy views and they carry them out when in office, but most voters are not listening, or are simply thinking what their party tells them they should be thinking. This is what an honest view of electoral democracy looks like.[44]

These authors do not, however, address the mechanism by which a particular "elite coalition" emerges from the "musical chairs" electoral process. Marcuse, as a Marxist, had a clear view on this: The only viable elite coalitions in capitalist societies are those that do not fundamentally threaten the interests of the ruling class, i.e., those who control the majority of the wealth, the capital available for investment

[43] They here mean to exclude the "independents" who in fact, on further questioning, lean to one party or the other. They also mean to exclude quite clearly a category they don't mention, namely, "academic independents," who, as ideologues, have such well-defined views on policy questions that no existing party could be adequate to their excruciatingly "nuanced" conception of what should be done. As Nietzsche would say, "The rule is more interesting than the exception." Friedrich Nietzsche, *Beyond Good and Evil: Prelude to a Philosophy of the Future*, trans. Walter Kaufmann (New York: Vintage Books, 1989), 37.

[44] Achen and Bartels, *Democracy for Realists*, 312.

and the means by which society produces what it needs and wants. For someone like Marcuse, the crucial point about the fabled "marketplace of ideas" in capitalist societies is that the only ideas that get public traction are those unthreatening to ruling elites. Thucydides, long before capitalism, noted a similar phenomenon 2,500 years ago,[45] but most of history since confirms the pattern.

Take an obvious, and contemporary, example. Why is it that there is endless handwringing in the American media about the solvency of Medicare, Medicaid and Social Security – programs that make an enormous difference to the well-being of tens of million people in the United States – yet there is no discussion in the mass media of how confiscating the wealth of often idle billionaires – the Koch Brothers and their children, the Walton children, perhaps some hedge-fund gamblers, beneficiaries of other inherited fortunes and so on – would allow us to fund these social programs for decades to come? Why should anyone, in virtue of birth, have a billion dollars, while millions of people – again, often in virtue of birth – suffer? There are surely answers to that question, but that would not be the Marcusian point: The crucial point is that *the question is not even discussed*, not treated as a question requiring an answer. That the question simply does not exist as part of the mythical "marketplace of ideas" is what is truly astonishing. How could that be?[46]

A rather obvious explanation is that, even absent state regulation of speech, there is regulation by powerful private interests, especially through the media, of speech, in which ideas that threaten the prerogatives of the ruling class (the actual "elite") are suppressed or marginalized, since those folks actually own the media fora. Marcuse's illiberal idea, fast-forwarded to 2017, is simple: State suppression of the reactionary media like Rush Limbaugh, Matt Drudge, and Breitbart could only be salutary to human well-being, since those media outlets are the most aggressive advocates of policies injurious to the vast majority. Of course, the ideological deformity of American mass media – which, for example, prohibits discussion of the benefits of confiscating the wealth of billionaires in order to help people in need – extends well beyond the reactionary fringe of the mass media. But let us turn the Millian lens just on the fringe: Would Mill, were he familiar with the deformities of modern media expression, have disagreed about Limbaugh, Drudge, and Breitbart?

45 See Brian Leiter, "Classical Realism," *Philosophical Issues: A Supplement to Noûs* 11, no. 1 (2001): 244, 250–53.

46 Many issues are not discussed in the mass media, but it is quite clear that being *nonsensical* is not the relevant filter, as any random perusal of the mass media reveals. Consider, just off the top of my head, discussion of whether Iraq posed a military threat to the United States in 2003; discussion of whether there is massive voting fraud that requires draconian voting requirements; discussion of whether repeal of the Affordable Care Act will affect medical care available to Americans; and so on. The proposal to confiscate inherited fortunes to pay for programs that affect aggregate well-being is obviously more reasonable.

Does anyone doubt he would have been appalled? Mill imagined public discourse being carried out in discursive pamphlets and written columns in the major newspapers. He had no conception of television and radio, let alone the Internet. (Even a twentieth-century libertarian and Millian, Karl Popper, was an opponent of television, for Millian reasons![47]) The "barbarians" of the India of Mill's colonial imagination look like paragons of wisdom by comparison to Matt Drudge, Sean Hannity, Rush Limbaugh and the other purveyors of systematic misinformation in American mass media.

There are philosophical peculiarities of Marcuse's view that deserve notice, and ought to affect how we evaluate his version of the Millian arguments. Marcuse is, to start, a very unMarxian Marxist, one influenced too much by Lukcas's rereading of Left Hegelian views (ones Marx rejected) into twentieth-century Marxism,[48] as well as by Max Horkheimer's related and mistaken attack on instrumental reason (reasoning about the most effective means to our ends, which are themselves not subject to rational evaluation) – precisely the kind of reason Marx himself thought crucial to revolutionary transformation.[49] Marcuse thinks that there are knowable moral truths, not just truths about effective means to ends, which makes his view more like Plato's in the *Republic* than like anything Marx ever said. Marcuse's great virtue among Frankfurt School theorists was always to be much clearer about the concrete import of the sometimes tortured prose of Horkheimer and Adorno. Marcuse says that the difference between "human and inhuman teachings and practices" is "not a matter of value-preference but rational criteria" (8) and that free speech contributes to "improvement, of progress in liberation" precisely because "there *is* an objective truth which can be discovered, ascertained only in learning and comprehending that which … can … be done for the sake of improving the lot of mankind" (4).

Unfortunately, Marcuse, unlike Mill, runs together the metaphysics (i.e., what is true) with the epistemology (i.e., what we know): Perhaps there are objective truths about what constitutes improving human life, but we still need to find the conditions under which we can actually know what they are. Mill also thought there were knowable truths about ethical questions, but he believed that contestation among opposing views was crucial to securing our confidence that we really knew those "objective" truths. Marcuse – who, alas, took Hegel far too seriously – clearly thought that "rational criteria" for assessing these questions were immanent in existing practice and thus available to select philosophers. As he wrote:

47 See Karl Popper, *Against Television*, BBC interview on April 13, 1993.

48 See generally Georg Lukács, *History and Class Consciousness: Studies in Marxist Dialectics*, trans. Rodney Livingstone (Great Britain: The Merlin Press, 1971).

49 See generally Brian Leiter, "Why Marxism Still Does Not Need Normative Theory," *Analyse & Kritik* 37, no. 1–2 (2015): 23.

> In Plato, rationality is confined to the small number of philosopher-kings; in Mill, every rational human being participates in the discussion and decision – but only as a rational being. Where society has entered the phase of total administration and indoctrination, this would be a small number indeed, and not necessarily that of the elected representatives of the people. (10)

We can agree with Marcuse that our elected representatives are not philosopher-kings, but who then are? That remains unclear. What is clear is that Marcuse's philosopher-kings, who can rationally decide what ought to be done, are not that different from Plato's, except that they have read Hegel and also appreciate the putative laws of economic development according to Marx!

I do think, for reasons I cannot develop here, that we should reject Marcuse's latent Platonism and Hegelianism:[50] There is no reason to think anyone has privileged knowledge of ethical truths, even if there are factual truths about how economic/historical events unfold. Moral views emerge from concrete historical circumstances – a view common to the economist Karl Marx, the anthropologist Marvin Harris, and the classical archaeologist Ian Morris, among many other serious researchers – and the motor of history is not the discovery of moral truth but the conflict between what people want and the material circumstances they find themselves in.

If that is correct, then the only case for free speech that seems to me remotely plausible is that the facts about regulators of expressions – about which Marcuse is mostly silent – are such that there is no likely remedy for the harmful consequences of their mistakes that would not produce a worse outcome, at least under current conditions.[51] This bears emphasizing, since most of the trite Mill-inspired platitudes about free speech do not withstand scrutiny, though they form the crux of American free speech jurisprudence. "The remedy for bad speech is good speech" is a familiar one, so let us pause to note all the ways in which it is false, if not absurd. First, good speech can only counteract *future* harms of bad speech, and *only then if* the good speech is effective; if the listeners are ignorant, biased, or won't listen, then the bad speech will continue its travels into the world unhindered where it will continue to produce mischief. Second, good speech cannot remedy harms *already caused* by

[50] Given his general philosophical positions and rhetoric, Marcuse himself makes a remarkable concession when he says that "democratic tolerance is under all circumstances more humane than an institutionalized intolerance which sacrifices the rights and liberties of the living generations for the sake of future generations." Marcuse, "Repressive Tolerance," 7. My reading of a remark like this – with its stunning reference to "rights" – is that this is Marcuse signaling his opposition to East German totalitarianism, whatever the deficiencies of West German capitalist democracy.

[51] As Larry Alexander correctly cautions, we should also not overstate the point: "The premise that government is unduly error-prone in regulating expression appears to be an empirical rather than a conceptual one. One might imagine then that governments vary, perhaps considerably, with respect to their capacities to regulate expression well." Alexander, *Is There a Right to Freedom of Expression?* 145. I agree with Alexander, a point which would support a subtler Marcusian theorist in the future.

bad speech, just as little as better bank security *after the fact* can remedy prior bank robberies. Third, unless there is any prospect of good speech in the offing – and good speech as loud and audible as that which it wants to counteract – then bad speech is again unconstrained in its consequences. The remedy for genuinely bad speech should be the same as the remedy for genuinely bad use of guns: sanction after the fact; prevention and suppression, where possible, before the fact.

But that brings us right back to the real problem: How do we *know* which speech is the really "bad" speech? And even if we can make reasonable judgments about that as observers or scholars or students – let alone Marcusian philosopher-kings – is there any reason to trust that government will make those judgments correctly? We may need robust protection for worthless speech because, at present, we have no reason to think that regulation of putatively "bad speech" would not be even more pernicious than the effects of the speech regulated. This is not an a priori and universal truth, just an inductive inference over a lot of past experience. Some countries – Germany notably – have correctly and successfully regulated speech by Nazis, for example, but Nazism may be *sui generis* in the history of the modern world in having established its bona fides as worthless and harmful over the corpses of tens of millions of people. Just as hard cases make bad law – as the familiar juridical saying has it – so, too, easy cases do not necessarily make good law. In the United States right now, it is far too easy to imagine how aggrieved groups of all stripes would quickly seize on the opportunity to suppress speech they dislike on the grounds that it is "hate speech," even if its distance from Nazism were great.

I thus endorse, with some regret, the main theme of American free speech jurisprudence, namely, that the best case for general freedom of expression is that we have no reason to be confident that the state will suppress the speech that actually should be suppressed because it is worthless and harmful.[52] Marcuse's bad reputation on the subject of speech is due to his total inattention to the regulation question – though, as one anecdote in philosophical circles has it,[53] when asked who would decide what speech was valuable, Marcuse answered, "Who decides now?" There is an important insight in that quip. Right now, media conglomerates, those with control of the means of communication to the vast majority of people on the planet, make the decisions. Fortunately, they do not make all the decisions about what speech can be expressed. The crucial fact about capitalist media is (1) in America and many other countries, they are free from active state regulation, and (2) they no longer occupy the whole field of expression, thanks to the Internet, which gives us not only the conspiracy-minded maniac Alex Jones and the right-wing Internet propagandist

[52] See Alexander, *Is There a Right to Freedom of Expression?*; see also Frederick Schauer, *Free Speech: A Philosophical Enquiry* (Cambridge: Cambridge University Press 1982).

[53] I first heard it from T.M. Scanlon.

Matt Drudge, but also the left-wing filmmaker and Internet propagandist Michael Moore and the popular leftist blog *Daily Kos*. There is very significant regulation of speech by private enterprises in America and elsewhere, but these media do not occupy the whole field, as a result of the technology that is distinctive of our era. Assessing the impact of these developments is a crucial empirical question for those who believe, as I do, that much expression is plainly worthless and harmful and would, in an ideal world, be quarantined from the public at large.

7.3 ACADEMIC FREEDOM REVISITED

Against this theoretical background, we may now return to the question of how to think about academic freedom in teaching and research. Such freedom is typically justified, in Millian terms, as truth maximizing. Marcuse, as we have seen, accepted the Millian rationale, but doubted that the preconditions for truth-maximizing speech existed in society as presently constituted. But here there is something surprising about Marcuse's view, and too little noted, namely, that he recognized that the university was different. While he rejected "indiscriminate" toleration that "protect[s] false words and wrong deeds which demonstrate that they contradict and counteract the possibilities of liberation," he went on to write: "Such indiscriminate tolerance is justified in harmless debates, in conversation, in academic discussion; it is indispensable in the scientific enterprise, in private religion" (3–4). Marcuse, as a German, undoubtedly understood the *wissenschaftlich* enterprise quite broadly, going well beyond natural science.[54] Thus, the dispute between Mill and Marcuse about the background conditions in which utility-maximizing speech can take place actually suggests an important conclusion with respect to academic freedom. For *even Marcuse* – the Hegelian-Marxist skeptic about free expression in the political sphere – recognized the sphere of academic debate as one in which "indiscriminate" toleration, as he would put it, should prevail.

Marcuse associated academic or scientific debates with "harmless" ones, but of course they are not always, so here Marcuse's intellectual looseness betrays him. A more plausible set of claims are the following:

1. The immediate consequences of academic debate are always harmless, only affecting opinion in the journals and the seminar room (to the extent they are harmful elsewhere, the regulation of such speech falls within the purview of general norms of speech regulation in a society).

[54] Marcuse, as discussed earlier, no doubt thought that an obscurantist Christian metaphysician like Hegel was also a purveyor of a *Wissenschaft*, but that is doubtful: Hegel should be taught as a matter of intellectual history, of course, but he cannot be invoked as a guide to truth, let alone as evidence of the harm of certain kinds of speech.

2. Academic debate should still be held to the standards of professional or *wissenschaftlich* competence, of the kind emphasized in the AAUP statement on academic freedom.
3. Academic debate held to *wissenschaftlich* standards will maximize the discovery of truth for Millian reasons over the long term, and that contributes to general well-being.[55]

Here we have a Marcusian rationale – inspired by Mill – to want to ensure robust protection for academic freedom in research.[56] The special role of the universities is to provide a forum in which vigorous pursuit of knowledge and truth is free from sanction or censure, since (1) the results of such inquiry harm no one immediately, and (2) universities satisfy (or aspire to satisfy) the Millian (and Marcusian) conditions in which truth is more likely to be discovered over the long term, at least insofar as *wissenschaftlich* standards of disciplinary expertise are honored, a point to which I return.

As an empiricist and fallibilist like Mill – that is, someone who thinks knowledge comes from experience and we could always be wrong – I want to agree with Mill quite strongly that we can never be confident in the truth of what we believe, and thus our beliefs demand constant challenge. Challenge can be useful for discovering the truth, however, only if we are in a cognitive position to assess the challenge. Universities are – at least in the capitalist world – the primary sites of such challenges, the only ones, outside of courts of law, in which knowledge of the truth stands some chance of prevailing, subject to rigorous disciplinary interrogation. The unmediated Internet, with its blogs and tweets, as well as television and the mass media, are largely worthless on this score. In all these fora no one really

55 It is plausible, given the underlying mechanisms, that this last claim is true, but I am not aware of any empirical evidence that, in fact, academic freedom really does maximize discovery of truths.

56 Does that mean academic freedom should protect advocacy of Nazism or slavery, or the inferiority of certain races or religions? The answer is, "yes, it should," subject to the demand that these defenses meet the standards of a *Wissenschaft* and that they are, of course, subject to the regulation of speech beyond the academy, as relevant. I am not much worried about "scientific" Nazism gaining traction in serious universities, but it is clearly the case that there may be traction for other morally suspect views within existing university disciplines. The empirical bases for claims about racial or gender-based differences should be seriously scrutinized, and I expect they will be rejected as they have been before, but they are fit subjects for research and debate – for "indiscriminate" toleration, as Marcuse would put it. (After all, if there were cognitive differences that tracked racial, ethnic, or gender differences, that leaves wholly open what ought to be done about it.) The much harder cases will involve the kind of noncognitive normative advocacy that characterizes parts of many humanistic and social science fields. While all criteria of "scientific" inquiry are socially constructed, in many fields one hopes that the criteria must answer to the facts about the world, not facts about the community of inquirers. Of course, that way of framing the problem presupposes substantive views about the status of forms of inquiry that are themselves subjects of contestation in various disciplines – and Millian fallibilism and academic freedom suggests we should try to be agnostic about them!

listens to what anyone else says, arguments and evidence are never evaluated seriously, and the absence of mediators guarantee that any bozo with a computer, or a sympathetic billionaire backer, can be "heard."

In universities, at least while academic freedom prevails, the situation is different: Certainly, professors propagate bogus ideas, and whole dubious *Wissenschaften* – think of behaviorism in psychology, or neoclassical economics, or deconstructionism in literary studies – can flourish for decades. Partisan agendas can claim the mantle of scientific knowledge across the spectrum of political opinion, but in the end all these views have to answer to inquiry and critique, and as long as academic freedom prevails, we have reason to be optimistic that truth will win out in the long run, because serious universities meet the preconditions that both Mill and Marcuse assume are essential for free debate to be utility-maximizing.

But what are "serious" universities? It will not suffice to say they are the ones in which *Wissenschaften* prevail, since that just pushes the question back one degree. If Humboldt's ideal was to create a place where rigorous methods for the discovery of truth could flourish, then there is a serious problem for fields that deny there is such a thing to discover. Here is how Larry Alexander puts it: "If there is no knowledge … then the reasons for academic freedom have vanished. Indeed, the case for universities and their departments has vanished. If knowledge is political, why not let the duly elected politicians determine what is true?"[57] Alexander lays the blame for this theoretical state of affairs at the doorstep of what he calls "the identity politics/post-modernist crowd."[58] That may overstate the case, though we can agree that when methods of inquiry are *explicitly* subsumed to moral or political ends, rather than epistemic ones,[59] the defense of academic freedom will be in trouble. But that was not the problem with behaviorism in psychology, let alone with neoclassical economics, the only putatively scientific field in which scholars whose views contradict each other (Eugene Fama and Robert Schiller) were deemed worthy of a Nobel Prize in the same year.[60] Yet psychology underwent a major scholarly self-correction

[57] Larry Alexander, "Academic Freedom," *University of Colorado Law Review* 77, no. 4 (2006): 883, 896. For a similar worry, see generally David M. Rabban, "Can Academic Freedom Survive Postmodernism?" *California Law Review* 86, no. 6 (1998): 1377.

[58] Ibid., 896. Alexander says the problem is the idea that "criteria for measuring academic merit are 'socially constructed'" (Ibid., 891), but this can't be right since "academic merit" is not a natural kind, but a constructed one. Indeed, all epistemic standards are constructed, as even Quine would agree!

[59] I am assuming that epistemic ends can be independent of moral and political ones – and I am assuming that as a Quinean. On the Quinean view, epistemic standards earn their status in virtue of their *practical* usefulness, not their moral and political merits. See Brian Leiter, "Why Quine is Not a Postmodernist," in Brian Leiter, *Naturalizing Jurisprudence: Essays on American Legal Realism and Naturalism in Legal Philosophy* (New York: Oxford University Press, 2007), 137.

[60] Economics, as critics external to the field have frequently pointed out, has fairly obviously been subject to an ideological capture that insulates it from the failure of its predictive models, in a way no actual science could withstand. See, e.g., Daniel Hausman, *The Inexact and Separate Science of Economics*

beginning with Chomsky's critique of behaviorism in the late 1950s, and economics too has been marked precisely by ideological rifts that ensure lively competing research programs persist. Alexander's polemic is perhaps most apt with respect to those departments created in response to demands from aggrieved groups seeking "recognition," as well as the more feeble of the humanities, like literary studies,[61] not to mention many parts of academic law which often emulate the worst features of these other pseudo-disciplines.

Can we say more about what constitutes *Wissenschaften*? University administrators would no doubt welcome such guidance, since, as defenders of academic freedom, they must ensure their institution is a site of only such inquiry. There are, alas, no necessary and sufficient conditions for what makes a mode of inquiry epistemically reliable; even in the natural sciences, there is no criterion that demarcates "scientific" inquiry from nonsense.[62] A commitment to wanting to find out what is true is, needless to say, rather important; the possession of and ability to teach *methods* of inquiry is another good sign of a *Wissenschaft*; and receptiveness to critique from other *Wissenschaften* in the university is another useful indicator. But the evidential standards for truth regarding, e.g., the authenticity of ancient texts, the correct translation of Augustine, the causes of suicide bombing, and the relative contribution of natural selection and genetic hitchhiking to evolution will be multivarious, and admit only of evaluation by reference to preexisting expert opinion. This is the potentially dangerous circularity of academic freedom based on disciplinary expertise, but I see no way around it, except to require that all university disciplines be open to critique from other university disciplines.

Most fields in most Western universities these days will qualify, I suspect, as *Wissenschaften* in the relevant sense: biology, psychology, the cognitive sciences, mathematics, chemistry, linguistics, much of philosophy[63], physics, the applied

(Cambridge: Cambridge University Press, 1992); Alexander Rosenberg, *Economics: Mathematical Politics or Science of Diminishing Returns* (Chicago: University of Chicago Press, 1993). And for a fascinating history of how the quasi-Nobel Prize in Economics was created in 1969 to legitimize the discipline and resist social democracy, see Avner Offer and Gabriel Söderberg, *The Nobel Factor: The Prize in Economics, Social Democracy, and the Market Turn* (Princeton: Princeton University Press, 2016).

61 Literary studies used to be a clear *Wissenschaft* in the Humboldt sense when it presupposed a high level of technical competence with languages, diction, the history of texts, and the formal features of expression.

62 See Larry Laudan, "The Demise of the Demarcation Problem," in *Physics, Philosophy and Psychoanalysis: Essays in Honor of Adolf Grünbaum*, ed. Robert Cohen and Larry Laudan (Dordrecht: D. Reidel, 1983), 111.

63 Philosophy I know well, and here the situation is complex. Much of anglophone philosophy has adopted a *wissenschaftlich* self-conception, but there are still outliers where in-group cults, usually inspired by Heidegger or Wittgenstein, dominate and the result is not a truth-oriented community but an academic community whose goals are self-congratulation and solidarity. I wish this were only true at marginal universities, but sadly it is not.

sciences (including engineering), even most of what goes on in political science, sociology, history, and economics. And the crux of academic freedom in this context is that faculty are not censured for their views arising from their disciplinary competence; arguments and evidence are the central currency of the exchange of ideas, consistent with the *wissenschaftlich* ideal; and tolerance of minority viewpoints is actively encouraged by those who administer university life. Not all minority viewpoints need be encouraged, only those that can claim that they arise from methods of inquiry and analysis that are relevant to ascertaining what is true. Academic freedom, in short, is the hallmark of a serious university, and disciplinary competence in the *Wissenschaft* is the benchmark for the freedom in question.

Very dangerous ideas do arise from academia, needless to say, but they are less dangerous in an academic setting than elsewhere, and dangerous ideas can be defused in a university setting or subjected to regulation outside it. Think of it this way: We do not test weapons of mass destruction in residential neighborhoods. Why we should we test dangerous ideas there? The virtue of the proverbial ivory tower is precisely its insulation from immediate effects. But if we agree with Mill and Marcuse that knowing what is true is valuable, then we should firmly embrace academic freedom, even if we have doubts about freedom of expression more broadly.[64]

[64] My thanks to David Rabban for guidance on the law of academic freedom. Earlier versions of this paper were given as the inaugural Schaffer Lecture sponsored by the Department of Philosophy at the University of Iowa in April 2017, and at workshops with the law faculties at Tel Aviv and Haifa Universities in March 2017, and at the University of Chicago in May 2017. I can recall particularly helpful questions or comments from Hanoch Dagan, Chaim Gans, Gregory Landini, Itamar Mann, Mike Seidman, and Geof Stone. My thanks to Taylor Coles for research assistance.

8

Vindicating Judicial Supremacy

Laurence Claus

8.1 THE IMPORTANCE OF SETTLEMENT

Larry Alexander, writing with Fred Schauer, with Larry Solum, and alone, has argued that the Supreme Court's dispute resolving often needs to settle what the law is, not just for lower courts, but for everyone.[1] If *Marbury v. Madison*[2] is rightly read more modestly, then that modesty was misplaced. *Cooper v. Aaron*[3] is right – when the Court resolves disputes about the *law*, those resolutions can and should supplement the law that applies to everyone. The Supreme Court is a supplementary lawmaker, indeed a supplementary constitutional lawmaker: we need it to be so, for the reason we need constitutions and law at all.[4]

Alexander and Schauer argue for judicial supremacy based on a claim about why we have law. They identify a "recur[ring]" answer to the question "what is law for?" Their claim, that we have law to help us settle what is to be done,[5] shares attributes with Jürgen Habermas's observation that "the very function of law" is "to stabilize expectations."[6] Law is the solution to a universally shared problem facing those who would live together in large groups. As Alexander puts it, that problem "is not motivation but knowledge."[7] Life in community calls for a way to share understanding of

1 Larry Alexander and Frederick Schauer, "On Extrajudicial Constitutional Interpretation," *Harvard Law Review* 110, no. 7 (1997): 1359; Larry Alexander and Frederick Schauer, "Defending Judicial Supremacy: A Reply," *Constitutional Commentary* 17, no. 3 (2000): 455; Larry Alexander, "Constitutional Rules, Constitutional Standards, and Constitutional Settlement: *Marbury v. Madison* and the Case for Judicial Supremacy," *Constitutional Commentary* 20, no. 2 (2003): 369; Larry Alexander and Lawrence B. Solum, "Popular? Constitutionalism?," *Harvard Law Review* 118, no. 5 (2005): 1594.

2 5 U.S. (1 Cranch) 137 (1803).

3 358 U.S. 1 (1958).

4 Alexander and Schauer, "On Extrajudicial Constitutional Interpretation," 1371.

5 Ibid.; Alexander and Schauer, "Defending Judicial Supremacy," 457, 467.

6 Jürgen Habermas, *Between Facts and Norms: Contributions to a Discourse Theory of Law and Democracy*, trans., William H. Rehg (Cambridge: MIT Press, 1996), 201.

7 Alexander, "Case for Judicial Supremacy," 377.

each other's likely actions and expectations and a way to shape that shared understanding. Law affects behavior mainly by informing of others' likely behavior and expectations, including likely responsive or facilitative conduct. Law lets us learn about our shared tomorrow today. Communities' legal systems supply fast tracks to new social practices, backed up by layered and iterating responses to observance and disregard that form patterns of reward and punishment.[8] A constitution can succeed in distributing and contouring power in a community, but only if that community can share an understanding of that accomplishment. Alexander and Schauer conclude that "[t]he reasons for having laws and a constitution that is treated as law are accordingly also reasons for establishing one interpreter's interpretation as authoritative. *Cooper v. Aaron* thus reflects the very reason for having a constitution that is regarded as law."[9]

Comparative constitutional experience supports Alexander's conclusion that someone needs to settle the law of a constitution if that constitution is to fulfill its function, and that the constitution's designated dispute resolver is usually the most apt candidate for the task. European legal systems that generally eschew judicial opinion writing and resist the notion of judges as lawmakers have made exceptions for their constitutional courts and councils. And in many instances the Europeans have established those bodies as specialists in constitutional law and nothing else, with extensive jurisdiction to decide abstract questions of constitutional validity at the request of other participants in the constitutional scheme.[10] Even British parliamentary supremacy has a judicially expounded constitutional foundation, and from *Dr. Bonham's Case*[11] to the *Fox Hunting Case*,[12] English judges have at times treated the primacy of statutes over the common law as itself a proposition of the common law that may be subject to other fundamental principles of the common law. What

8 A highway patrol officer who never gives out speeding tickets will not keep his job for long. See Ken Binmore, *Natural Justice* (Oxford: Oxford University Press, 2011), 85: "If someone deviates and we go to one of the subgames off the equilibrium path, it remains optimal in a perfect equilibrium to stick to your original strategy provided everybody else does. In particular, if your strategy tells you to punish the deviant at some cost to yourself, it will be optimal for you to carry through on the punishment. If you deviate by trying to escape your duty to punish, you will take us to yet another subgame where it is optimal for some other player to punish you for your dereliction of duty. If he fails to discharge his duty, we go to yet another subgame – and so on forever. With only a finite number of players, these chains of responsibility are necessarily closed in the manner that Kant failed to consider."

9 Alexander and Schauer, "On Extrajudicial Constitutional Interpretation," 1377.

10 See European Commission for Democracy through Law (Venice Commission), *Study on Individual Access to Constitutional Justice*, Parts III and IV (Council of Europe, January 27, 2011). (See in particular the Constitutional Court of Germany and Constitutional Council of France.)

11 8 Co. Rep. 113b, 118a; 77 Eng. Rep. 646, 652 (1610). On the interpretation of Coke's claim, see Jeffrey Goldsworthy, *The Sovereignty of Parliament: History and Philosophy* (Oxford: Oxford University Press, 1999), 111.

12 Regina (Jackson and others) v. Attorney General, [2006] 1 AC 262, 302–3, ¶ 102 (Lord Steyn, House of Lords, decided October 13, 2005). See also the speech of Lord Hope of Craighead; ibid., 304, ¶ 107.

counts as a valid statute is ultimately a question for the courts.[13] The United States Supreme Court's willingness to decide some disputes about government power that are unripe or moot congruently reflects the recognized value of ultimate judicial settlement.[14]

Alexander and Schauer write of *authoritative* settlement of what is to be done,[15] but use the word in a way that could serve as a synonym for *legal* or could refer to a source of legality. If the law of a community serves to settle what is to be done in that community and the community's need of authority is a need for settlement, then the idea of authority may not be adding anything to the idea of law as an autopoietic settlement device.[16] Our rhetoric of authority did not come from a conventionalist account of law and government, but if a conventionalist account of law and government is right,[17] then the idea of authority becomes endogenous to the ideas of law and government. However well selected, no lawgiver has moral *carte blanche*. And a concept of exogenously-sourced authority that is coextensive with no one's power, and not clear *ex ante* about its own extent,[18] and not in itself the answer to when we should follow,[19] seems of little value to anyone. That we still embroider our accounts of law and government with the language of authority may be attributed to artifactual history – the truth that our talk of authority and duty to obey emerged

13 Sir Owen Dixon, *Jesting Pilate*, 2nd ed. (Buffalo: William S. Hein, 1997), 203–13, but see Jeffrey Goldsworthy, "The Constitution and its Common Law Background," *Public Law Review* 25, no. 4 (2014): 265, 266–68; Jeffrey Goldsworthy, *Parliamentary Sovereignty: Contemporary Debates* (Cambridge: Cambridge University Press, 2010), 14–56. The great American founding-era textualist James Iredell (see Calder v. Bull, 3 U.S. (3 Dall.) 386, 399 (1798)) wrote in a letter to Richard Dobb Spaight (August 26, 1787): "Without an express Constitution the powers of the Legislature would undoubtedly have been absolute (as the Parliament in Great Britain is held to be), and any act passed not inconsistent with natural justice (for that curb is avowed by the judges even in England), would have been binding on the people." II Griffith John McRee, *Life and Correspondence of James Iredell* (New York: D. Appleton, 1858), 172.

14 On ripeness, compare Stenberg v. Carhart, 530 U.S. 914 (2000) with Hope Clinic v. Ryan, 195 F.3d. 857 (1999); on mootness, see Roe v. Wade, 410 U.S. 113 (1973).

15 Alexander and Schauer, "On Extrajudicial Constitutional Interpretation," 1371.

16 Compare Niklas Luhmann, *Law as a Social System*, ed. Fatima Kastner, Richard Nobles, David Schiff, and Rosamund Ziegert, trans. Klaus A. Ziegert (Oxford: Oxford University Press, 2004); Laurence Claus, *Law's Evolution and Human Understanding* (Oxford: Oxford University Press, 2012).

17 "[C]onventional social rules … include, besides ordinary social customs (which may or may not be recognized as having legal force), certain important legal rules including the rule of recognition, which is in effect a form of judicial customary rule existing only if it is accepted and practiced in the law-identifying and law-applying operations of the courts." H.L.A. Hart, *The Concept of Law*, 2nd ed. (Oxford: Oxford University Press, 1994), 255–56 (Postscript).

18 Compare Joseph Raz, *The Morality of Freedom* (Oxford: Clarendon Press, 1986), 80 (describing "a piecemeal approach to the question of the authority of governments").

19 See Larry Alexander and Emily Sherwin, *The Rule of Rules: Morality, Rules, and the Dilemmas of Law* (Durham, NC: Duke University Press, 2001), 53–55; Larry Alexander, "The Gap," *Harvard Journal of Law & Public Policy* 14, no. 3 (1991): 695, 695–96; Frederick Schauer, "Rules and the Rule of Law," *Harvard Journal of Law & Public Policy* 14, no. 3 (1991): 645, 692–93.

from millennia of power struggles among dominant persons framed by a discourse about who had rights to rule.[20]

Alexander and his coauthors' argument has two features that this chapter will seek to address. First, Alexander and Schauer emphasize that their conceptual case for judicial supremacy does not depend on founding-era understandings of how the new constitutional scheme would and should work. They therefore assume, for the sake of argument, that those who mount a historical case against judicial supremacy have the history right, and contend that their conceptual argument can nonetheless contribute valuably to debate about whether we should accept judicial supremacy as intrinsic to the constitutional scheme now.[21] Second, Alexander and Solum distinguish judicial supremacy from judicial dictatorship – courts are constrained by the interpretive project in ways that limit the supplementary lawmaking it involves.[22] As discussed elsewhere in this volume, Alexander's view of the conceptual and moral constraints on legal interpretation differs from the views of his coauthors and could be expected to be especially constraining.

This chapter will identify much-overlooked elements of the historical record that support Alexander's case for judicial settlement of constitutional law. To the extent that his views may have evolved somewhat on the relevance of history to what we should accept now,[23] this may be a welcome supplement to his argument. But this chapter will also draw from the historical record evidence that the founders' structural choices were influenced by theoretical presuppositions that caused them not to appreciate the extent of the lawmaking task they were indirectly assigning to the courts. The consequence is that the history and logic of the American constitutional scheme call for judicial supremacy, but a supremacy that must be exercised to create whole bodies of constitutional law in the exercise of a policymaking discretion unguided by constitutional text and without precedent in judicial practice. In short, even under Alexander's constrained view of constitutional interpretation, judicial supremacy under the United States Constitution entails a large measure of judicial dictation.

8.2 THE FOUNDING ENDORSEMENT OF JUDICIAL SETTLEMENT

Among aspects of the constitutional scheme for which the Supreme Court is an especially apt source of supplementary constitutional law, Alexander and Solum

[20] I Karl R. Popper, *The Open Society and Its Enemies*, 4th ed. (Princeton: Princeton University Press, 1962), 121.

[21] Alexander and Schauer, "On Extrajudicial Constitutional Interpretation," 1369; Alexander and Schauer, "Defending Judicial Supremacy" 459–67.

[22] Alexander and Solum, "Popular? Constitutionalism?," 1609, 1632.

[23] Compare ibid., 1635.

identify "a modestly strong case for judicial settlement of the boundaries of federal power." They observe that "Congress itself is unlikely to be a good judge in its own cause and thus will not be trustworthy in settling those boundaries."[24]

History supports their conclusion.[25] The project of defining a boundary between the nation and the states by enumerating national powers was a localist initiative, a feature of the New Jersey Plan's response to the Virginia Plan's unqualified nationalism.[26] The Philadelphia Convention enumerated Congress's powers to limit them. And from the moment that the Convention, through its committee of detail, first enumerated national powers in the draft Constitution, the drafters showed that they contemplated judicial enforcement of the apportionment. Edmund Randolph's early committee draft of the enumerated powers ended with the following provision:

> 19. (To organize the government in those things, which)
>
> <Insert the II Article>
>
> (All laws of a particular state, repugnant hereto, shall be void, and in the decision thereon, which shall be vested in the supreme judiciary, all incidents without which the general principles cannot be satisfied shall be considered, as involved in the general principle.)[27]

Max Ferrand put the sentence fragment and complete sentence in parentheses to show that they were crossed out. In their place within James Wilson's draft we see the first recognizable version of the necessary and proper clause we have now.[28] Randolph's predecessor provision reveals that from the outset, members of the committee charged with detailing Congress's powers linked power enumeration to an arbitral role for the Supreme Court. In particular, they saw the Court as having to make judgments about the breadth of Congress's powers, and provided accordingly that those powers should be construed to include "all incidents without which the general principles cannot be satisfied." Wilson's reformulation both expressed the incidental powers principle and let Congress legislate "to organize the government," as Randolph's preliminary draft had put it.

Would *Congress's* actions be subject to Supreme Court review? Randolph and another committee colleague, John Rutledge, subsequently showed that they

[24] Ibid., 1634–35.

[25] See, e.g., Laurence Claus, "The Framers' Compromise," *American Journal of Comparative Law* (forthcoming, 2019) (reviewing Michael Klarman, *The Framers' Coup* (Oxford: Oxford University Press, 2016)).

[26] I Max Farrand, *The Records of the Federal Convention of* 1787, ed. Max Farrand (New Haven: Yale University Press, 1911), 242–45 (June 15, 1787) (Madison's notes) (hereinafter Farrand, *Records*).

[27] II Farrand, *Records*, 144.

[28] Ibid., 137n6 168. The angle-bracketed reference was inserted by John Rutledge. (See ibid., 137n6.) John Mikhail suggests that this may have been an attempt to insert Article II of the Articles of Confederation, reserving to the states all powers not expressly delegated to the nation. See John Mikhail, "The Necessary and Proper Clauses," *Georgetown Law Journal* 102, no. 4 (2014): 1045, 1092–96.

thought so. In their sights was a proposal to make the Justices removable by the President on a vote of both Houses of Congress without need to allege wrongdoing. Rutledge, whose edits appear in Randolph's early draft of the enumeration, observed: "If the supreme Court is to judge between the U.S. and particular States, this alone is an insuperable objection to the motion."[29] Randolph concurred, and "opposed the motion as weakening too much the independence of the Judges."[30] These successful objections would have made no sense if the delegates had understood judicial review to be confined to state laws. The objections presupposed that the Supreme Court needed independence from Congress, which was true only if the Court was going to decide the validity of national action too. Were Congress to have the last word on the reach of its own powers, then it would never clash with the courts over their judging "between the U.S. and particular States," because it could always preempt state laws. Earlier, Charles Pinckney had argued that the Justices would need to be financially independent because they would, among other things, "even be the Umpires between the U. States and individual States as well as between one State & another."[31]

Did the delegates understand the Court's intergovernmental dispute resolving to involve settling the content of the law for everyone? They repeatedly invoked judicial review to explain why other methods of settling the content of the law were not needed, including judicial preapproval of national laws,[32] Congressional veto of state laws,[33] and ad hoc tribunals to settle territorial and jurisdictional disputes.[34] Such records as we have of the debates through which the Convention rejected these other structural proposals suggest that the existence of judicial review as a substitute source of constitutional settlement was weighty if not decisive. These acknowledgments of judicial review culminated in William Samuel Johnson's unanimously supported motion to give the Supreme Court jurisdiction over all cases arising under the Constitution.[35] James Madison recorded himself saying that the Court's jurisdiction should be confined to cases of a judiciary nature, and reported that the delegates "generally supposed" the added jurisdiction to be so confined.[36] Whatever he meant by that – a political question doctrine, a rule against advisory opinions, or something else – during the ratification debates he assured a localist New York readership

[29] II Farrand, *Records*, 428 (August 27) (Madison's notes).

[30] Ibid., 429.

[31] Ibid., 248 (August 10) (Madison's notes).

[32] Ibid., 294–95 (August 15) (Journal). See also 298–99 (Madison's notes); I Farrand, *Records*, 97–98 (June 4) (Madison's notes); ibid., 109 (Pierce's notes); II Farrand, *Records*, 73, 74, 76–77, 78, 80 (July 21) (Madison's notes).

[33] II Farrand, *Records*, 28 (July 17) (Madison's notes); 390–91 (August 23) (Madison's notes).

[34] Ibid., 401 (August 24) (Madison's notes).

[35] Ibid., 430 (August 27) (Madison's notes).

[36] Ibid.

that the Court would actively and independently guard the boundary between the nation and the states. Although "in controversies relating to the boundary between the two jurisdictions, the tribunal which is ultimately to decide, is to be established under the general Government," the new Supreme Court was to be constituted in a way that secured its impartiality.[37]

Early in the life of the Philadelphia Convention, Johnson asked Madison how the states would survive in the proposed new constitutional system if they lacked a veto over national initiatives.[38] Johnson and other Connecticut delegates were seeking a Senate that would resemble the Confederation Congress as a true assembly of state governments.[39] Madison's response, according to his own notes, did not identify any institutional safeguard for the states' role in governing and displayed indifference to their fate.[40] Over the strong objection of Madison and his nationalist allies,[41] the Connecticut Compromise of July 16, 1787 established a robust political safeguard of federalism, a Senate composed of bloc-voting state government delegations.[42] The Compromise endorsed a national legislative structure like that under which Germany would unite a century later. As the German experience then confirmed, courts were not needed to settle the distribution of power between the nation and the states if the states' presence in the national legislature let the states settle that distribution directly.[43] After the Compromise, the Philadelphia Convention voted for an expanded general description of national power – national power was no longer a threat to the states, because they had the means to control its exercise.[44] But a few days later, the states' structural protection was fatally undermined when the Convention voted for the Senate to be composed of individually-voting state

37 James Madison, The Federalist 39, *New York Independent Journal*, in *The Documentary History of the Ratification of the Constitution* XV, ed. John P. Kaminski, et al. (Madison: Wisconsin Historical Society Press, 1976), 384, 385 (January 16, 1788) (hereinafter Kaminski, *Documentary History*).

38 I Farrand, *Records*, 355 (June 21) (Madison's notes); see also ibid., 363 (Yates's notes).

39 Ibid., 196, 201–2 (June 11) (Madison's notes), 193 (Journal); ibid., 343 (June 20) (Madison's notes); ibid., 468 (June 29) (Madison's notes); ibid., 474 (Yates's notes), 477 (King's notes).

40 Ibid., 357–58 (June 21) (Madison's notes). See also ibid., 363–64 (Yates's notes). See also ibid., 463–64 (June 29) (Madison's notes); ibid., 464n2, 471 (Yates's notes); 477 (King's notes).

41 Ibid., 490 (June 30) (Madison's notes); ibid., 551 (July 7); II Farrand, *Records*, 19–20 (July 16–17).

42 II Farrand, *Records*, 13–15 (Journal), 15–16 (Madison's notes). For evidence that this was the understood effect of the vote, see the preceding debates, e.g., I Farrand, *Records*, 468 (June 29) (Madison's notes), 474 (Yates's notes), 477 (King's notes); 489–90 (June 30) (Madison's notes); 510 (July 2); 549 (July 7).

43 German Const., Arts. 5–7, 76 (1871); see James Harvey Robinson, *The German Bundesrath* (Philadelphia: University of Pennsylvania, 1891), 62: "The jurisdiction in constitutional questions is not delegated to the courts, but, so far as it is provided for at all, it is exercised by the Bundesrath." Judicial review under the Empire was limited to subordinate rules and regulations. See Bernd J. Hartmann, "The Arrival of Judicial Review in Germany under the Weimar Constitution of 1919," *BYU Journal of Public Law* 18, no. 1 (2003) 107, 111.

44 II Farrand, *Records*, 21 (July 17) (Journal); ibid., 26–27 (Madison's notes).

appointees rather than bloc-voting state delegations.[45] Those appointees were to receive long terms, a provision that the Virginia Plan had included for senators "to ensure their independency."[46] Equal state representation under the hollowed-out Compromise served to distribute power not so much among levels of government as among dominant individuals – it became a way for political leaders from small states[47] to secure for themselves seats at the national table. Once seated, their interests were those of national leaders, not of state government agents.[48] After this change in the character of the Senate, the Convention enumerated national powers and, from the moment they did so, the drafters demonstrated that they were looking to the courts to settle the distribution of power between the nation and the states. In the words of John Marshall at the Virginia Ratifying Convention: "To what quarter will you look for protection from an infringement on the Constitution, if you will not give the power to the Judiciary?" Suggesting an absence of other sufficient structural safeguards,[49] he observed: "There is no other body that can afford such a protection."[50] And Marshall was clear about how the judiciary would afford that protection. If Congress "were to make a law not warranted by any of the powers enumerated, it would be considered by the Judges as an infringement of the Constitution which they are to guard: They would not consider such a law as coming under their jurisdiction. They would declare it void."[51]

Madison and other key founders engaged with this issue in the ratification debates to emphasize that the Supreme Court would actively and independently enforce the enumeration of national powers to limit Congress. Both Oliver Ellsworth and James Wilson joined Marshall in explicitly assuring their respective states' ratifying conventions that the Supreme Court would not just disregard unconstitutional

45 Ibid., 94–95 (July 23) (Madison's notes).

46 I Farrand, *Records*, 20 (May 29) (Madison's notes).

47 II Farrand, *Records*, 94 (July 23) (Oliver Ellsworth) (Madison's notes).

48 Ad hoc attempts by state legislatures to instruct their senators how to vote ended long before the seventeenth amendment. See William H. Riker, "The Senate and American Federalism," *American Political Science Review* 49, no. 2 (1955): 452–69. State legislators could not control senators, in part because senators' terms were much longer. And absent state control, senators' vocational interests have been served by national accomplishments that have often come at the expense of state power. In Larry Kramer's words, "State officials are rivals, not allies ..." Larry Kramer, "Understanding Federalism," *Vanderbilt Law Review* 47, no. 5 (1994): 1485, 1510–11.

49 Compare Herbert Wechsler, "The Political Safeguards of Federalism: The Role of the States in the Composition and Selection of the National Government," *Columbia Law Review* 54, no. 4 (1954): 543; Jesse H. Choper, *Judicial Review and the National Political Process* (Chicago: University of Chicago Press, 1980).

50 Virginia Convention, in X Kaminski, *Documentary History*, 1432 (June 20, 1788).

51 Ibid., 1431. This sequence of events is also recounted in Laurence Claus, "Enumeration and the Silences of Constitutional Federalism" (presented at the International Symposium on Constitutional Silence, Trinity College Dublin, September 1, 2016, and forthcoming in a dedicated issue of the *International Journal of Constitutional Law* (2018)).

Congressional actions, but would declare those actions void.[52] Limiting the supreme legislative body by issuing *declarations* that its unconstitutional actions were *void* was surely a law-settling service.[53]

Larry Kramer's account of the frequency and fervor with which the people themselves were invoked as a constitutional safeguard[54] reports rhetoric to be expected from a generation for whom revolution was a tested enforcement mechanism and judicial decision making about whether laws were inside or outside specified subjects of power was not. Patrick Henry showed that the Constitution's opponents perceived potential for judicial enforcement to work, but they also recognized that it depended on the judges acting independently[55] – something in which the founders had less basis for confidence than they had in their own capacity to rise up. Rising up was, however, as Marshall said in *Marbury*, a great exertion, not apt for regular repetition.[56] The founding debates reveal ample evidence that, in the meantime, judicial settlement of the law of the Constitution was expected to feature in America's ordinary governance.

8.3 FOUNDING PRESUPPOSITIONS

The Philadelphia Convention's two principal power-apportioning strategies each rested on presuppositions that have proved to be false. The strategy of power enumeration by subject presupposed that laws, and government actions under those laws, could readily and uncontroversially be classified by subject. The strategy of power separation by kind presupposed that the activities of governing institutions

[52] James Wilson, Pennsylvania Convention, in II Kaminski, *Documentary History*, 450–51 (December 1, 1787), 517 (December 7); Oliver Ellsworth, Connecticut Convention, in III Kaminski, *Documentary History*, 553 (January 7, 1788).

[53] Declarations that laws and other government actions are void straddle the distinction between adjudication and explanation, between resolving disputes among particular parties and expounding the law for everyone. Declaratory judgments, issued pursuant to the equitable jurisdiction with which Article III invests the Supreme Court, are *judgments*, not just opinions, but they speak not directly to the fate of parties, but to what the law is. Compare William Baude, "The Judgment Power," *Georgetown Law Journal* 96, no. 6 (2008): 1807, 1844–45.

[54] Larry D. Kramer, *The People Themselves: Popular Constitutionalism and Judicial Review* (Oxford: Oxford University Press, 2004); Larry D. Kramer, "The Supreme Court, 2000 Term – Foreword: We the Court," *Harvard Law Review* 115, no. 1 (2001): 4.

[55] Virginia Convention, in X Kaminski, *Documentary History*, 1420–21 (June 20, 1788); see also John Marshall, ibid., 1430.

[56] 5 U.S. (1 Cranch) 137, 176. (1803). Writing as Publius, James Madison observed of Congressional overreach: "*In the first instance*, the success of the usurpation will depend on the executive and judiciary departments, which are to expound and give effect to the legislative acts; and *in the last resort*, a remedy must be obtained from the people, who can by the election of more faithful representatives, annul the acts of the usurpers." The Federalist 44, *New York Packet*, in XV Kaminski, *Documentary History*, 473 (January 25, 1788) (emphasis added).

could readily and uncontroversially be distinguished from those of other institutions by essence or nature. The falsity of these presuppositions requires the Constitution's dispute resolver to create whole bodies of constitutional law to settle the actual vertical and horizontal distribution of power, with little guidance from constitutional text or history.

8.3.1 *Power Enumeration*

Near the end of the Philadelphia Convention, two delegates "moved to insert a declaration 'that the liberty of the Press should be inviolably observed.'" Roger Sherman responded in a way that would often be echoed in the ratification debates by those who argued against adding a national bill of rights.[57] "It is unnecessary," he contended. "The power of Congress does not extend to the Press." The Convention voted down the motion without further recorded debate, suggesting that Sherman's opinion was widely shared. The delegates seemed to think that laws about the enumerated subjects of Congress's power could not also be about the press.[58]

What was Sherman talking about? Why couldn't a law about commerce or taxing also be about the press? *Aboutness* is not monopolistic.[59] Laws do not have solitary subjects. Laws are multifaceted in character – they are intrinsically susceptible of multiple characterizations, even when their makers do not especially intend them to be. A law that punishes desertion from the military is about defense *and* about employment *and* about criminal law *and* about judicial process, and may implicate a range of conceivable human rights too. This truth lay ready to thwart attempts to apportion power by enumerating its subjects. If, for example, an enumerator intended to assign military matters to one government and employment issues to another, enumeration would fail to settle who could make a law that was about both.

The debates at Philadelphia make clear that the participants' purpose in enumerating subjects of Congressional power was to apportion power between the nation and the states by limiting Congress's power.[60] Power enumeration was an attempt to

57 See Section 8.4. Some of those who argued during the ratification debates that the enumerated powers did not reach important rights may have understood that conceptually those powers could reach such rights, but that courts could read down the powers to stop them from doing so. James Wilson appears to have seen things that way. But, given the founders' limited experience of judicial review and complete lack of experience with judicial review under enumerated powers, most of those who argued that the enumerated powers did not invade rights likely just did not appreciate the extent to which multisubjectivity of governing actions renders power enumeration indeterminate.

58 II Farrand, *Records*, 617–18 (September 14) (Madison's notes).

59 See Stephen Yablo, *Aboutness* (Princeton: Princeton University Press, 2014); John R. Searle, *Intentionality: An Essay in the Philosophy of Mind* (Cambridge: Cambridge University Press, 1983); Hilary Putnam, "Formalization of the Concept 'About,'" *Philosophy of Science* 25, no. 2 (1958): 125.

60 The same observations about this are made in Laurence Claus, "Enumeration and the Silences of Constitutional Federalism." As Randolph observed to the Virginia Ratifying Convention, "if its

express subjects of national power exhaustively, not just to cite some salient ones. For example, when rejecting a draft enumerated power to "emit bills," the delegates made clear that they sought to stop Congress from issuing a paper currency, and thought that omitting express power was sufficient to deny power, without the backup of an express prohibition.[61] Only state governments, whose powers were unenumerated, had to be expressly prohibited from printing money.[62] In their quest to be comprehensive, the architects of power enumeration differed from authors in the long tradition of Anglo-American rights enumeration.[63] Bills of rights set baselines for freedom and equality; they do not cap a constitutional scheme's commitment to those values. The Convention's unprecedented attempt to apportion power between a genuine national government and existing state governments was all about capping what could be done. The ninth and tenth amendments were written to remind everyone of the distinction – rights enumeration did not limit rights, but power enumeration definitely did limit powers.

powers were to be general, an enumeration would be needless" (X Kaminski, *Documentary History*, 1348 (June 17, 1788)). John Mikhail has recently argued that the necessary and proper clause's reference to all other powers vested by the Constitution in "the Government of the United States" would be surplusage if it were merely a reference to express investitures of power by provisions of the Constitution other than Article I, section 8, because the clause additionally refers to all other powers vested in "any Department or Officer" of the government. See John Mikhail, "The Necessary and Proper Clauses," *Georgetown Law Journal* 102, no. 4 (2014): 1045; John Mikhail, "The Constitution and the Philosophy of Language: Entailment, Implicature, and Implied Powers," *Virginia Law Review* 101, no. 4 (2015): 1063. Mikhail's surplusage argument assumes that "any Department" means any part, including any branch, of the government. But that is not how the Constitution uses the word "Department." The only other places where "Department" appears in the Constitution are both in Article II, section 2, which includes references to "the executive Departments" and to vesting appointments of inferior officers "in the President alone, or in the Courts of Law, or in the Heads of Departments." These uses imply that the President is not a Head of Department, so that the term "Department" as used in the Constitution does not refer to a whole branch of government. The founders had the "branches" terminology available to them too – for example, Madison referred to governments' "co-ordinate branches" at the Virginia Ratifying Convention (X Kaminski, *Documentary History*, 1413 (June 20, 1788)). The most plausible reading of the reference to "all other Powers vested by this Constitution in the Government of the United States" is that it covers other express conferrals of powers on those institutions that the Constitution itself creates and collectively calls the Government of the United States, namely, each House of Congress, the President, and the Supreme Court. These express conferrals include express conferrals of powers exercisable by some of these institutions only in combination – for example, power to appoint superior officers and to make treaties is expressly conferred on a combination of the President and the Senate. Congress can make laws necessary and proper for carrying into execution the powers to appoint superior officers and to make treaties, not because these are powers vested "in any Department or Officer," but because they are powers vested in "the Government of the United States."

61 II Farrand, *Records*, 308–10 (August 16) (Madison's notes). Even arch nationalist James Wilson, who authored the necessary and proper clause, supported the omission because it would "have a most salutary influence on the credit of the United States to remove the possibility of paper money." Ibid., 310.

62 U.S. Const. art. I, § 10, cl. 1.

63 See, e.g., Magna Carta (1215) (Eng.); Bill of Rights (1689) (Eng.); Declaration of Rights (1776) (Va.).

Had power enumeration's purpose been merely to mention some salient powers, then no one would have claimed that it was difficult to do. Yet, after enumeration was proposed, both James Madison and James Wilson made that claim. Wilson "observed that it would be impossible to enumerate the powers which the federal Legislature ought to have."[64] Madison omitted himself later saying that "[n]o Line can be drawn between the State Governments and the General Government," but several other notetakers reported him saying it.[65] Those objections made sense only if the delegates understood that enumeration's purpose was exhaustive expression. And that was how both Madison and Wilson characterized power enumeration during the ratification debates. In seeking to secure the draft constitution's safe passage through the state conventions, they each emphasized that the courts would enforce stringent limits on national power that power enumeration imposed.[66] Writing privately to Thomas Jefferson, however, Madison foresaw that attempts to enforce enumeration would encounter "the impossibility of dividing powers of legislation, in such a manner, as to be free from different constructions by different interests, or even from ambiguity in the judgment of the impartial."[67]

The localists at Philadelphia lifted power enumeration from the Articles of Confederation and introduced it via the New Jersey Plan into the new compromise constitutional scheme. Specifying subjects in a *treaty*, such as the Articles had been, helps set an agenda for that treaty's member states, who retain latitude to proceed together by consensus, however they please. Specifying subjects in a "federal" *constitution* is no more determinative of what can be done. If the purpose of constitutional enumeration is to *settle* what can be done by each level of government in a federal system, then it is predestined to fail. Many laws of each government will be capable of characterization as about subjects assigned to the nation *and* as about subjects that helped prompt the choice to continue having state governments.

64 I Farrand, *Records*, 60 (May 31) (Pierce's notes).

65 James H. Hutson, ed., *Supplement to Max Farrand's The Records of the Federal Convention of* 1787 (1987), 61 (June 8) (Butler's notes). See also ibid., 60 (Lansing's notes); I Farrand, *Records*, 169 (Yates's notes). On Madison's omission of this point from his own notes, see Mary Sarah Bilder, *Madison's Hand: Revising the Constitutional Convention* (Cambridge, MA: Harvard University Press, 2015), 76–77. According to his own notes, Madison had earlier said that he strongly favored an enumeration of national legislative powers but doubted that it was practicable. Those notes record him saying that he was unsure what his ultimate opinion would be. (I Farrand, *Records*, 53 (May 31) (Madison's notes).) William Pierce recorded him saying that "at present he was convinced it could not be done" (Ibid., 60 (Pierce's notes)).

66 See, e.g., James Wilson, Pennsylvania Convention, in II Kaminski, *Documentary History*, 450–51 (December 1, 1787), 517 (December 7); James Madison, The Federalist 39, *New York Independent Journal*, in XV Kaminski, *Documentary History*, 384–85 (January 16, 1788); James Madison, The Federalist 44, *New York Packet*, in ibid., 473 (January 25, 1788).

67 James Madison to Thomas Jefferson, in XIII Kaminski, *Documentary History*, 446 (October 24, 1787).

The Canadian Constitution makes enumeration's indeterminacy more transparent by enumerating provincial powers too. The Canadian Supreme Court regularly confronts laws, national or provincial, that could rationally be characterized as about subjects of expressly exclusive national power *and* as about subjects of expressly exclusive provincial power.[68] It would be question begging to invoke national supremacy as a reason to hold that anything we could rationally characterize as national is national, and the Canadian Court has not done so. National supremacy applies only to valid national law, and national law is not valid unless it is properly characterized as inside national power.

How, then, are disputes to be resolved among governments when those disputes are about their respective shares in a system of enumerated powers? The constitutional dispute resolver, both here in the United States and everywhere else that emulates the American model of enumerated powers, must settle those disputes somehow. As power enumeration is deeply underdeterminative, how can legislators at each level of government know what laws they can constitutionally contemplate? Constitutional dispute resolving needs to clarify and to guide – in short, to *settle* the distribution of power. The Constitution's text says nothing about how to characterize multifaceted laws in relation to abstract subjects of power. History tells us why – most of the founders just did not comprehend the extent of enumeration's indeterminacy. Their lack of comprehension reflected the degree of their innovation from past institutional design. A judicial task of deciding whether laws were inside or outside subjects of power was unprecedented. Though many of the lawyer-delegates at Philadelphia showed they were aware that judicial review would feature in the new system, they had very limited experience from which to foresee how it would work and none from which to appreciate how a court would reason in deciding what a constitutional power enumeration actually accomplished.

Where does this leave the Supreme Court, and its counterparts in other constitutional systems that emulate American power enumeration? The Constitution leaves the Supreme Court with the necessary task of creating a whole body of law – the law of constitutional characterization. The Court must decide what principles and tests it will use to specify the relation that a national law must have to an enumerated subject of national power in order for that national law to be adequately about that enumerated subject and therefore inside the power. What *express* relation to the subject of power must the law have, if any? What relevance have the law's actual or likely effects? What about the legislators' purposes, perhaps evidenced by foreseen or foreseeably likely effects? None of this is settled by the Constitution's text, nor by founding-era practice. It must be settled by a judge-made law of constitutional characterization. One option is for that judge-made law to wave through any national law that could

[68] See, e.g., Labatt Breweries of Canada v. Attorney General of Canada, [1980] 1 S.C.R. 914.

rationally be characterized as within national subjects of power.[69] Counting against choice of that principle is the structural function and historic purpose of enumeration, namely, to *apportion* power between levels of government. Implementing a rational basis test amounts to the umpire in a competition for power abdicating in favor of one of the competing teams. If such a test had been an accepted aspect of power enumeration at the founding, nationalists would not have objected to power enumeration and localists would not have proposed it. But whatever principles and tests the Supreme Court chooses for its law of constitutional characterization, that choice remains a purely judicial one, unguided as to its details by the Constitution's text and unaided by founding-era practice. Evidence of original meaning may help courts understand the enumerated subjects of national power, but does not settle what relation to those subjects national laws must have. As a constitutional project of characterizing laws under subjects of power was unprecedented, the law of constitutional characterization has had to be made by the courts from scratch.

8.3.2 *Power Separation*

The Constitution's first three Articles begin by purporting to vest "[a]ll legislative Powers herein granted," "[t]he executive Power" and "[t]he judicial Power" respectively in the three institutions that those Articles establish. This reflects a theory of power apportionment more fully expressed in the Massachusetts Constitution of 1780: "In the government of this Commonwealth, the legislative department shall never exercise the executive and judicial powers, or either of them: The executive shall never exercise the legislative and judicial powers, or either of them: The judicial shall never exercise the legislative and executive powers, or either of them: to the end it may be a government of laws and not of men."[70]

Many who read Montesquieu would have appreciated that hermetically sealing essentially different kinds of power in separate institutional silos was neither possible nor desirable. But the founders' constitutional drafting implicitly accepted Montesquieu's premise that checks and balances among institutions served to protect a primary essentialist separation and that this separation was crucial to liberty and the rule of law.[71] A more percipient analysis of the prototypical postrevolutionary English constitution would have recognized that the system's signature

69 See, e.g., United States v. Lopez, 514 U.S. 549, 617 (1995) (Breyer J, joined by Stevens, Souter, and Ginsburg JJ, dissenting) ("the specific question before us, as the Court recognizes, is not whether the 'regulated activity sufficiently affected interstate commerce,' but, rather, whether Congress could have had 'a rational basis' for so concluding").

70 Mass. Const., Part the First, art. XXX (1780).

71 Charles-Louis de Secondat, Baron de Montesquieu, *The Spirit of the Laws*, trans. Thomas Nugent (London, 1750), ed. Franz Neumann (New York: Hafner, 1946), bk. 11, chaps. 5–6.

accomplishment was power *sharing*, not power *separation*. Checks and balances promote liberty and the rule of law not merely by defending institutional turf, but by requiring more minds to concur before power can be exercised and so preventing any one among the powerful from conclusively determining the reach of her own power.

Montesquieu was beguiled by the challenge of circumventing Enlightenment orthodoxy on the indivisibility of sovereignty and distracted by the unique institution of the English jury.[72] He showed no sign of noticing that most law in England was common law, created through written reports of judicial decision making. He did not see that the doctrine of precedent through which the common law was built could be turned to exposition of statutes and constitutions. If a court says more about what a constitution requires than the constitutional document does, and if later courts defer to the first court's words when deciding disputes about that question, then the first court has added to the law of the constitution. Had Montesquieu noticed that phenomenon, he would doubtless have called it lawmaking. When Montesquieu called the power of judging politically insignificant, he meant the fact-finding function of juries.[73] Hamilton was mischievous in deploying that quotation to downplay the power that the Constitution vested in the Supreme Court.[74]

The distinction between departmentalism and judicial supremacy exists only because judges can make law. We can all see now that lawmaking occurs in all three branches of the United States Government, most of it in the so-called executive. And lawmaking is the only activity of governing institutions that is distinctively *governmental*. We all do law *applying*, at least to ourselves and often in our relations with others. Our "private" institutions apply law in their relations with us as much as our "public" ones do. Dispute resolving often happens privately too, and a familiar complaint about the social costs of widespread resort to private arbitration is that the legal system loses the precedent – private dispute resolving does not *add to the law*.

The Constitution purports to distinguish its institutions in kind, but proceeds to assign particular powers incompatible with that distinction. The President's power to say yes or no to legislation is greater than that of any individual legislator in the House or Senate, and substantively makes him a defeasible third chamber of the legislature.[75] The Senate's power to say yes or no to senior executive appointments substantively makes it as managerial as an executive board.[76] And its power to try

72 See Laurence Claus, "Montesquieu's Mistakes and the True Meaning of Separation," *Oxford Journal of Legal Studies* 25, no. 3 (2005): 419.

73 Ibid., 422, 430.

74 Alexander Hamilton, The Federalist 78, in XVIII Kaminski, *Documentary History*, 87, 88, 93n(a) (May 28, 1788).

75 U.S. Const., art. I, § 7, cl. 2.

76 U.S. Const., art. II, § 2, cl. 2.

impeachments makes it a judiciary.[77] If the Constitution's essentialist labeling does not preclude these institutional assignments, what value does it have in deciding whether other institutional innovations pass constitutional muster?

The Constitution's essentialist institutional descriptions are too compromised by dissonant, often constitutionally expressed institutional practice to settle whether additional interinstitutional checks and balances are constitutional. In deciding, for example, whether Congress through a one-house veto can supervise executive action, including executive action that is actually lawmaking, the Supreme Court is not really helped by the Constitution's essentialist typology.[78] And there is surely a strong functional argument that as the two houses of Congress must agree before new law can be made by Congress, either house of Congress should be able to say no to new law made by the executive. In substance, the Court is left to its best policymaking judgment when it decides what interinstitutional arrangements to allow and thereby creates the law of institutional competence.

8.4 THE REACH OF JUDICIAL LAWMAKING

In crafting the law of constitutional characterization and the law of institutional competence, the Supreme Court can implement its own best judgment about the optimal distribution of power among the levels and branches of American government. Suppose the Court must settle a dispute over a new national initiative that could rationally be characterized as about subjects of enumerated national power and as about other subjects that state governments already regulate. The Court could choose to be guided by the principle expressed at the very opening of the Philadelphia Convention, in the Virginia Plan, that Congress should have power to legislate in those cases "to which the separate States are incompetent."[79] Laws that could competently be chosen closer to the governed could be left to be made closer to the governed.[80] Being representation-reinforcing[81] does not necessarily call for

77 U.S. Const., art. I,' § 3, cl. 6.

78 Compare INS v. Chadha, 462 U.S. 919 (1983).

79 I Farrand, *Records*, 21 (May 29, 1787) (Madison's notes).

80 See Robert D. Cooter and Neil S. Siegel, "Collective Action Federalism: A General Theory of Article I, Section 8," *Stanford Law Review* 63, no. 1 (2010): 115 (arguing that Article I, section 8, should be construed as authorizing Congress to address collective action problems caused by interstate externalities and national markets). See also Stephen Gardbaum, "Rethinking Constitutional Federalism," *Texas Law Review* 74, no. 4(1996): 795, 836; Donald H. Regan, "How to Think About the Federal Commerce Power and Incidentally Rewrite United States v. Lopez," *Michigan Law Review* 94, no. 3 (1995): 554, 555.

81 See generally John Hart Ely, *Democracy and Distrust* (Cambridge, MA: Harvard University Press, 1980).

Thayerian deference to Congress[82] – it arguably calls for identifying which group of representatives is best situated to represent on the matter at issue. *Ceteris paribus*, the closer to us our representatives are, the more we can access and influence them; and the more we can access and influence them, the more represented we are. Through a principle of subsidiarity,[83] federalism can draw representative government as close to the ideal of *self*-government as good government can get. On the other hand, the breadth of the Court's policymaking discretion in creating its law of constitutional characterization allows weight to be given to reliance interests, to settled expectations, when deciding disputes about long-serving national measures that might fail a subsidiarity test.

The law of constitutional characterization and the law of institutional competence could even be evolved to elaborate an implied bill of rights,[84] including the sort of "substantive" liberty- and equality-based limitations on national power for which the due process clause of the Fifth Amendment has hitherto been pressed into linguistically improbable service.[85] Key nationalists gestured in that direction during the ratification debates, when resisting calls for an express bill of rights. The Constitution would authorize intrusion on important freedoms only if it did so very directly, James Wilson opined. "If indeed, a power similar to that which has been granted for the regulation of commerce, had been granted to regulate literary publications, it would have been as necessary to stipulate that the liberty of the press should be preserved inviolate, as that the impost should be general in its operation."[86] Just empowering Congress to regulate commerce was not enough to let it reach press freedom, Wilson contended. If Congress attempted to overreach, "the judges, as a consequence of their independence, and the particular powers

[82] See James B. Thayer, "The Origin and Scope of the American Doctrine of Constitutional Law," *Harvard Law Review* 7, no. 3 (1893): 129, 144; Larry D. Kramer, "Putting the Politics Back into the Political Safeguards of Federalism," *Columbia Law Review* 100, no. 1 (2000): 215, 291; John F. Manning, "Foreword: The Means of Constitutional Power," *Harvard Law Review* 128, no. 1 (2014): 1, 78.

[83] Compare Treaty on European Union, art. 5(3): "Under the principle of subsidiarity, in areas which do not fall within its exclusive competence, the Union shall act only if and insofar as the objectives of the proposed action cannot be sufficiently achieved by the Member States, either at central level or at regional and local level, but can rather, by reason of the scale or effects of the proposed action, be better achieved at Union level."

[84] Compare John Toohey, "A Government of Laws and Not of Men?" *Public Law Review* 4, no. 1 (1993): 158, 170, delivered soon after the Australian High Court's landmark implied freedom of speech decisions in Australian Capital Television v. Commonwealth, 177 CLR 106 (1992) and Nationwide News v. Wills, 177 CLR 1 (1992).

[85] See generally John Harrison, "Substantive Due Process and the Constitutional Text," *Virginia Law Review* 83, no. 3 (1997): 493; J.A.C. Grant, "The Natural Law Background of Substantive Due Process," *Columbia Law Review* 31, no. 1 (1931): 56; Roscoe Pound, "Liberty of Contract," *Yale Law Journal* 18, no. 7 (1909): 454.

[86] James Wilson, Speech in the State House Yard, Philadelphia, in II Kaminski, *Documentary History*, 168 (October 6, 1787).

of government being defined, will declare such law to be null and void."[87] The courts would hold that the enumerated subjects of national power just did not cover intrusions on important freedoms, and accordingly those courts would characterize attempts at such intrusions as not within national power.

Wilson was responsible for the "necessary and proper" formulation of the sweeping clause,[88] but during the ratification debates he was far from isolated in insisting that Congress could not properly pass laws that intruded on important freedoms.[89] Wilson was one of the few at Philadelphia who showed signs of adequately appreciating power enumeration's indeterminacy. His critique of enumeration at the Convention suggests he likely saw that laws about commerce conceptually could curtail cherished freedoms, and that expository lawmaking by the Supreme Court would be needed to stop that occurring. His inclusion of the "proper" requirement in "necessary and proper" may have been aimed at fortifying judicial power to protect rights by reading down enumerated powers.

As the ratification debates proceeded, opponents of the Constitution demanded express protection for those important freedoms that readily came to mind. Freedom of the press, they insisted, should not depend on the contestable claim that powers over commerce and taxing did not authorize laws about the press.[90] But when the first Congress added a bill of rights, it added a rule for their construction: "The enumeration in the Constitution of certain rights shall not be construed to deny or disparage others retained by the people."[91] Wherever rights would have been protected in the absence of the bill of rights, the addition of the bill of rights was not to change that. To the extent, therefore, that Wilson was right, and individual rights could be protected in the judge-made law of characterization, the addition of express rights was not to deny or disparage that protection.[92] The Supreme Court was to remain empowered to settle the sweep of its law of constitutional characterization and its law of institutional competence and to do so in ways that complemented the Constitution's express protections for rights.

87 James Wilson, Pennsylvania Convention, in II Kaminski, *Documentary History*, 517 (December 7, 1787).

88 II Farrand, *Records*, 163n17, 168.

89 See Gary Lawson and Patricia B. Granger, "The 'Proper' Scope of Federal Power: A Jurisdictional Interpretation of the Sweeping Clause," *Duke Law Journal* 43, no. 2 (1993): 267, 315–21. See also Alexander Hamilton, The Federalist 84, in XVIII Kaminski, *Documentary History*, 130, 131 (May 28, 1788) ("the constitution is itself in every rational sense, and to every useful purpose, a bill of rights").

90 See, e.g., James Monroe, The Virginia Convention, in IX Kaminski, *Documentary History*, 1112 (June 10, 1788); II Farrand, *Records*, 640 (George Mason); Thomas Jefferson to James Madison, in VIII Kaminski, *Documentary History*, 249 (December 20, 1787).

91 U.S. Const., amend. IX. See Ryan C. Williams, "The Ninth Amendment as a Rule of Construction," *Columbia Law Review* 111 (2011): 498.

92 See Lawson and Granger, "The 'Proper' Scope of Federal Power," 273.

8.5 CONCLUSION

The judicial supremacy for which Larry Alexander and his coauthors argue is supported by the history of the Constitution's adoption and by the logic of its structure. Settling the law of the Constitution requires the Supreme Court to create the law of constitutional characterization and the law of institutional competence. In doing so, the Court has engaged in largely unconstrained constitutional policymaking, because constitutional text and past practice provided little guidance. What most confines judicial lawmaking in the American constitutional tradition and distinguishes it from a judicial dictatorship is the absence of a jurisprudence of positive rights. Enforcing equality principles is as close as the American Court comes to dictating what governments *must* do, as distinct from keeping governments within judicial understandings of their proper bounds.[93]

[93] Compare Palmer v. Thompson, 403 U.S. 217, 233–34 (1971) (Douglas J dissenting) ("There is, of course, not a word in the Constitution, unlike many modern constitutions, concerning the right of the people to education or to work or to recreation by swimming or otherwise. Those rights, like the right to pure air and pure water, may well be rights retained by the people under the Ninth Amendment").

9

Alexander's "Simple-Minded Originalism"

Connie S. Rosati

Larry Alexander boasts about being a simple-minded originalist.[1] Over a long career, he has written insightfully not only about originalism, but about freedom of speech, issues in normative ethics, the relationship between law and morality, and a variety of issues in both constitutional law and theory and criminal law and theory. Given his stellar publication record, Alexander has a great many things to be boastful about. Being a simple-minded originalist, however, isn't one of them. In this essay, I undertake to explain why. As I will try to show, Alexander's principal considerations in support of his form of originalism fail to support it. An examination of these considerations suggests that originalism may be best understood as a normative thesis, rather than a semantic thesis or a thesis about the nature of interpretation. As such, it stands in need of more compelling support than it has thus far received. Beyond the difficulties with Alexander's defense of his originalism, his view faces serious problems of its own. I examine just a couple of these problems. I then go on to explain some of the reasons why his originalism is too underdeveloped and incomplete to address the questions that most interest us when we seek to answer constitutional questions.[2]

1 "I confess. (Actually I boast.) I'm a simple-minded originalist." Larry Alexander, "Simple-Minded Originalism," in *The Challenge of Originalism*, ed. Grant Huscroft and Bradley W. Miller (Cambridge: Cambridge University Press, 2011), 87. Alexander defends his form of originalism in a number of publications. See Larry Alexander, "Telepathic Law," *Constitutional Commentary* 27, no. 1 (2010): 139–50; Larry Alexander, "Originalism, the Why and the What," *Fordham Law Review* 82, no. 2 (2013): 539; Larry Alexander, "Legal Positivism and Originalist Interpretation," *Revista Argentina Teoría Jurídica* 16 (2015). See also Larry Alexander and Saikrishna Prakash, "Is That English You're Speaking? Some Arguments for the Primacy of Intent in Interpretation," *University of San Diego Law Review* 41, no. 3 (2004): 967–95; Larry Alexander and Emily Sherwin, *Demystifying Legal Reasoning* (Cambridge: Cambridge University Press, 2008), 323–352.

2 Alexander means for his originalism to apply to all legal texts (and, really, to any text or oral communication). For ease of exposition, I often talk herein simply in terms of legal texts, but I shall mainly be interested in Alexander's originalism as it concerns constitutional interpretation.

9.1 WHAT IS ORIGINALISM?

Before we can explore the problems with Alexander's originalism, we must begin by considering what originalism is. Originalist theories share the view that the meaning of the Constitution (or of any legal text) is its "original meaning" rather than, say, its contemporary meaning. Where originalist theories diverge is with respect to the kind of original meaning they take to be relevant to understanding the Constitution. According to original public meaning originalism, to understand a bit of constitutional text we must discover its "public meaning" at the time of ratification.[3] Some of what original public meaning originalists say suggests that the public meaning of a text is its *sentence meaning* or conventional meaning; some of what they say suggests that public meaning is a kind of idealized conventional meaning, or what a *reasonable* member of the public at the time would have understood it to mean. Depending on how we understand the idealization, of course, the distinction between these formulations might not come to much; I take it that the idealization would be meant to correct for confusions about language and the conventional meanings of words and sentences that an arbitrary actual member of the public might well have. According to original intended meaning originalists, the meaning of a piece of constitutional text is its *speaker's meaning*, its authorial or intended meaning. By this, they have in mind the *actual* intended meaning, rather than an idealized intended meaning.[4] From here on, for ease of discussion, I will usually refer to original public meaning originalism as "textualism" and original intended meaning originalism as "intentionalism." Alexander's simple-minded originalism is a form of intentionalism.[5]

Originalism of either variety has important strengths, although originalists don't always advertise them effectively. First, our constitutional debates and discourse typically presuppose that there are correct answers as to what the Constitution requires,

[3] For some representative work by public meaning originalists, see, e.g., Antonin Scalia, *A Matter of Interpretation: Federal Courts and the Law* (Princeton: Princeton University Press, 1997); Randy E. Barnett, *Restoring the Lost Constitution* (Princeton: Princeton University Press, 2004); Robert W. Bennett and Lawrence B. Solum, *Constitutional Originalism: A Debate* (Ithica: Cornell University Press, 2011); Lawrence B. Solum, "Originalism and Constitutional Construction," *Fordham Law Review* 82, no. 2 (2013): 453–537.

[4] But see Ronald Dworkin, *Freedom's Law: The Moral Reading of the Constitution* (Cambridge, MA: Harvard University Press, 1996), in which he sometimes seems to adopt an idealized intended meaning approach to understanding the Constitution. For discussion, see Connie S. Rosati, "The Moral Reading of Constitutions," in *The Legacy of Ronald Dworkin*, ed. Wil Waluchow and Stefan Sciaraffa (Oxford: Oxford University Press, 2016), 323–252.

[5] Other proponents of intentionalism include, e.g., Walter Benn Michaels, "A Defense of Old Originalism," *Western New England Law Review* 31, no. 1 (2009): 21–37; Alexander and Prakash, "Is That English You're Speaking?" In addition, Alexander, "Telepathic Law," mentions Paul Campos, Stanley Fish, Steven Knapp, and Steven Smith.

forbids, or permits.[6] They typically presuppose that there are constitutional facts, much as our moral debates and discourse typically presuppose that there are moral facts. But it is hard to defend the existence of constitutional facts if we do not allow that there are facts about the meaning of the constitutional text and facts about what follows from that meaning, and so facts about how to get from the Constitution's semantic content to facts about the content of the law.[7] Originalists, to their credit, recognize these points, and nonoriginalists, to my mind, have yet to supply a compelling alternative that does.[8]

Second, originalist theories rest on a plausible approach to understanding the meaning of texts, namely, that in order to understand the meaning of a text we need to understand its *original* meaning. I take it that we rely on this idea in our everyday reading and understanding of texts. Consider the theme song to "The Flintstones." As the song informs us, when we're with the Flintstones, we'll "have a yabba dabba doo time, a dabba doo time," we'll "have a gay old time." Now, I take it that we would be making a mistake if we were to interpret the last line of the stanza as informing us that we will have a homosexual time with the Flintstones. Rather, we have to understand the word "gay" as having the meaning (say, "happy") that was common when Hoyt Curtin composed the song in the late 1950s. Of course, we might be led to alter our understanding of the song. The word "gay" apparently took on a sexualized meaning as early as the fourteenth century.[9] In the twentieth century, it eventually came to refer to homosexuality (and to male homosexuals in particular), and the latter usage evidently existed in some circles even before the song was written. As intentionalists might suggest, had Curtin intended the latter meaning, rather than the common meaning, it might cast the relationships between Fred and Barney, and Wilma and Betty, in a whole new light.

9.2 THE STATUS OF ORIGINALISM

Despite its undoubted appeal, we are as yet without a fully developed and compelling version of originalism, or so I am inclined to believe, and basic questions about originalist theories remain. One set of questions about any form of originalism concerns its status. Should we understand originalism simply as a semantic thesis,

6 Connie S. Rosati, "Constitutional Realism," in *Dimensions of Normativity*, ed. David Plunkett, Scott Shapiro, and Kevin Toh (Oxford: Oxford University Press, forthcoming).

7 For reasons that I hope will become clear later, these might all turn out to be normative facts.

8 I say this as someone who is not an originalist, as least as I currently understand what that would involve.

9 At least according to that questionably reliable source, Wikipedia, s.v. "gay," https://en.wikipedia.org/wiki/Gay.

as a thesis about the nature of interpretation, or as a normative thesis? Alexander seems to waiver between the three positions.[10]

Alexander's remarks sometimes suggest that we should understand originalism as a thesis about the nature of interpretation. That is to say, he sometimes seems to be expressing a view about interpretation and *what it is* to be interpreting a text. "[W]hen one is interpreting a text, as opposed to doing other things with it, one is necessarily seeking its author's or authors' intended meaning."[11] Alexander doesn't explain the kind of necessity he has in mind in this passage, but the sentence naturally suggests that *one couldn't be engaged in interpreting a text* unless one were seeking its intended meaning. As he also expresses it, "to interpret a text just *is* to ascertain its authorially-intended meaning."[12] Call this the "interpretation claim." Intentionalism would simply follow, according to this view, from the nature of interpretation.

More often, Alexander's remarks in defense of intentionalism suggest that we should understand it as a semantic thesis, a thesis about how any text, or any spoken sentences for that matter, have meaning. Call this the "semantic claim." He frequently claims, for example, that where there is no authorial intent, there is no meaning. Consider some representative passages:

> No author communicating, no norms.[13]
>
> I would say [in the case where there is no shared legislative intent] that despite the appearance of being meaningful, the law has no authorially intended meaning. It is gibberish.[14]

[10] Alexander and Prakash, "Is That English You're Speaking?" 974–76. Alexander offers numerous other considerations in support of intentionalism, and I cannot address all of them here. But some of them strike me as confused. For example, he frequently appeals to the idea that texts do not announce the language in which they are written. Ibid. He illustrates the point using the word "canard," which means "fib" in English but "duck" in French. Alexander takes it to be a problem for textualism (or more precisely, for what he calls "intention free textualism") that it has no way to identify the language in which a text is written. For this, he claims, we need to identify or posit an author and figure out which language that author usually writes in. But the claims and the example are misleading. We can, of course, find words written in a certain alphabet that have meanings in another language that shares that alphabet. But I suspect we would be hard pressed to find entire sentences or texts of which this is true, except by considering imaginary languages, such as Alexander's "Schmenglish." What's more, linguists would presumably be able to identify the language in which a text is written without positing an author or knowing anything about authorial intent. If a linguist couldn't do this, then he or she would be hard pressed to tell us whether an author usually writes in English, French, or Chinese, and so the problem would be one not only for textualists, but also for intentionalists.

[11] Alexander, "Telepathic Law," 139.

[12] Ibid., 140.

[13] Alexander, "Simple-Minded Originalism," 87.

[14] Alexander, "Originalism, the Why and the What," 542.

> One cannot attribute meaning to marks on a page or to sounds without reference to an author, actual or idealized, who is intending to communicate a meaning through the marks or sounds.[15]
>
> 'Texts' without authors and intended meanings are not texts; and texts *with* intended meanings are texts *only with respect to the intended meanings.*[16]
>
> [W]hat makes the constitution as it appears in the back of my casebook the same Constitution as the parchment in the National Archives? … What makes them the same is that they have the same semantic meaning. But they only have that if they have the same authors and authorially intended meanings.[17]

Alexander claims that seeking the intended meaning of legal texts is "the same thing we do when we read a letter from Mom, a shopping list from our spouse, or instructions for how to assemble a child's toy made in China."[18]

In other places, Alexander's remarks suggest that we should understand intentionalism as a normative thesis. He has characterized the dispute between textualists and intentionalists as "a normative one over whether interpreters should look to the intentions of actual authors or hypothetical ones, and when, if we are to look to actual authorial intent, policy considerations (such as the rule of law concerns) should lead us to ignore certain evidence of that intent."[19] Call this the "normative claim."

As for what should decide the supposed dispute between textualists and intentionalists, Alexander repeatedly appeals to the idea that only certain persons have the authority to pronounce norms of the legal system, and so only the actual intended meaning of the legal texts they produce is authoritative.

> *The meaning of the norm that the legislative person or body has chosen and communicated symbolically is the meaning that person or body intends those symbols to communicate.* Whether we are talking about a constitutional provision, a statute, an administrative rule, an executive order, or a judicially promulgated rule, its meaning, *for purposes of the legal enterprise*, is its authorially intended meaning – in Gricean terms, its speaker's meaning.[20]

Notice that this passage would seem to allow that there are other meanings to a legal text. It's just that those meanings aren't relevant "for purposes of the legal enterprise," wherein our interest is in discovering the meaning that is authoritative.

15 Alexander and Prakash, "Is That English You're Speaking?" 974.

16 Ibid., 977.

17 Alexander, "Simple-Minded Originalism," 93.

18 Ibid., 87; see Alexander and Sherwin, *Demystifying Legal Reasoning*, 132–41.

19 Alexander and Prakash, "Is That English You're Speaking?" 968–69.

20 Alexander, "Originalism, the Why and the What," 540.

> The symbols that make up the author's text have no intrinsic meaning. They are just marks or sounds ... They either mean what their authors intended them to mean or else they mean what some imagined author might have meant by them. *But in order to be authority-preserving, the interpreter must try to discover what the actual author or authors meant by those symbols, i.e., that code.* In the context we are considering, any other meaning other than that of the actual author or authors will produce a legal norm that was not the legal norm those with authority to enact legal norms – the legislators – voted to enact.[21]

In this passage, Alexander again seems to allow that texts may have more than one meaning, though any of those meanings must be versions of authorial intended meaning. But having allowed this, he insists that only the actual authorial meaning is authority-preserving.[22]

Perhaps Alexander means to offer all three considerations in favor of intentionalism, though if he were right about any one of these claims, then he wouldn't need the others, except perhaps the normative claim, which might figure importantly in debates between intentionalists and nonoriginalists. In any case, there are reasons to doubt each of them.

The interpretation claim, according to which interpreting texts necessarily involves seeking intended meaning, seems to be question-begging against the textualist. To interpret something, in the ordinary sense, is to "explain or tell the meaning of."[23] But to say that interpretation necessarily involves seeking intended meaning is simply to assume that the meaning of a text is the intended meaning, and this is precisely what public meaning originalists reject.

Of course, if Alexander were right with regard to the semantic claim, then the interpretation claim would succeed. But it is simply false that a sentence in, say, English has speaker's meaning or no meaning at all. Alexander is fond of examples in which letters are accidentally formed by everything from blowing dirt to bird droppings to illustrate his claim that where there are no intentions, there is no meaning.[24] So let us imagine that the waves wash up onto the shore a slew of pebbles, which settle in the shape of letters in the Latin alphabet that spell out "the cat is on the mat." Now, it is certainly true that, as there is no author, there is no message being communicated, and in that sense, there is no meaning. It is nevertheless also true that someone who knows the English language could read the words and understand their conventional meaning (or meanings) and the conventional

[21] Larry Alexander, "Aggregating States of Mind: A Reply to Fallon" (manuscript, San Diego, 2017), 5.

[22] Alexander also argues that what he calls "intention free textualism" is a "conceptual impossibility." Alexander and Prakash, "Is That English You're Speaking?" 972. But if that is the case, then the issue between intentionalists and textualists is a conceptual one rather than a normative one.

[23] Merriam-Webster, s.v. "interpreting," www.merriam-webster.com/dictionary/interpreting.

[24] Alexander, "Simple-Minded Originalism," 87.

meaning (or meanings) of the sentence. Alexander seems to think there is only meaning where there is messaging, but that isn't true. Perhaps he wants to restrict the term "meaning" to words and sentences used to communicate a message, but then he would be offering a stipulative definition rather than making a point about semantics. Textualists would rightly protest that we need to recognize the existence of both sentence meaning and speaker's meaning. So Alexander arguably faces a dilemma. If he means to be offering the semantic claim as a genuine claim about semantics, then his claim is incorrect; if he is offering the semantic claim based on a stipulative definition of "meaning," then his claims about how legal texts get their meaning presuppose rather than support his intentionalism.

Even if Alexander were right that our interest as interpreters of legal texts should lie with intended meaning, I doubt that it would or should make much practical difference to our interpretation of legal texts. Presumably, the authors of legal texts mean to communicate their intentions effectively. In order to do so, they need to use language in a way that will be understood by their intended audience. But this requires using words with their conventional meanings and, where words may lack conventional meanings, including technical or stipulative definitions using words that do have conventional meanings. As a result, ordinarily, the best way to understand authorial intentions is by understanding the conventional meanings of the sentences that authors have written or ratified. And where we have evidence that authorial meaning departs from conventional meaning, it is less clear than Alexander suggests whether we ought to follow the conventional meaning or the intended meaning. Which we should follow is a matter of normative argument.

Given the foregoing considerations, I think we should conclude that originalists are offering a normative thesis, a thesis about which among the various semantic meanings of the text we ought to follow "for purposes of the legal enterprise."[25] As we have seen, Alexander does offer a normative argument in favor of intentionalism over textualism, as he characterizes it. That argument appeals to authority and what is needed to preserve it. But the argument strikes me as too underdeveloped to be persuasive. Let us suppose that certain persons have authority to enact legal norms. We can still inquire about the nature and scope of that authority and the normative constraints on its exercise. One plausible way to understand parts of Lon Fuller's "inner morality of law" is as laying out normative constraints on the exercise of law-making authority.[26] The most relevant of his eight principles for present purposes are

[25] For extended discussion of the various kinds of meaning and how choice among them involves reliance on normative considerations, see, e.g., Mark Greenberg, "Principles of Legal Interpretation," Part VI, 34–38 (2016) (unpublished manuscript), http://philosophy.ucla.edu/wp-content/uploads/2016/08/Principles-of-Legal-Interpretation-2016.pdf, https://perma.cc/HVA6-GZHB.

[26] Lon L. Fuller, *The Morality of Law* (Mew Haven: Yale University Press, 1964), 39.

the second and fourth. These concern the need to publicize, so that affected parties can be aware of the rules that they are supposed to follow, and the need to make rules understandable. We might say that lawmaking authority is subject to constraints of publicity and intelligibility. Publicity alone won't accomplish anything if the rules aren't understandable. Ordinarily, the way to make rules understandable is to write them in clear, direct language, using words with their conventional meanings and supplying definitions using words with conventional meanings for any technical terms. When a legal text has a relatively clear conventional meaning, though one that fails adequately to express the authorities' intended meaning, it isn't at all obvious that the latter rather than the former should be controlling. In favor of intended meaning is the position of certain persons as authorized to set forth the legal norms; in favor of public meaning is a recognition of the normative constraints on their authority. And this is just to scratch the surface; the normative case for either intentionalism or textualism would need to be quite complex and nuanced. The point here is not that Alexander is mistaken to think normative considerations favor intentionalism over textualism. The point is, rather, that much more argument is needed to prove that this is so.[27]

9.3 PROBLEMS FOR INTENTIONALISM

I have argued that the considerations Alexander offers fail adequately to support his intentionalism. Of course, other arguments might be offered. But rather than conjecture as to what these might be, we would do well to consider problems with the view that we would be defending.

Alexander correctly describes himself as subscribing to a view that is "considered heretical among most legal academics."[28] Originalism, in its intentionalist form, has come in for sustained criticism, perhaps most famously by Paul Brest.[29] As public

[27] Alexander and Sherwin, *Demystifying Legal Reasoning*, 173–90, argue that substantive and procedural norms for dealing with infelicities, such as in cases where intended meaning would have absurd or unjust results, must themselves be adopted by those with a higher authority than those with authority to make rules, who would thereby be restrained, because they lead to departures from the rule makers' intended meaning. So perhaps they would respond to me that any constraints on the authority of rule makers would have to come from a higher authority. But this seems to assume that we already have a clear and compelling conception of what the authority of any rule maker involves. Alexander and Sherwin might in the end be right, but more argument would be needed to persuasively establish this.

[28] Alexander, "Simple-Minded Originalism," 87.

[29] Paul Brest, "The Misconceived Quest for the Original Understanding," *Boston University Law Review* 60, no. 2 (1980), 204–238. Of course, at the time Brest leveled his criticisms against originalism, the distinction between intended meaning originalism and public meaning originalism had not been cleanly drawn. The kind of intentionalism that he criticizes isn't quite the speaker's meaning view of contemporary intentionalists. Nevertheless, his criticisms carry over to the latter view.

originalists like Randy Barnett[30] tell it, public meaning originalism is a development in originalist theory that overcomes most of the objections to intended meaning originalism. Alexander has argued that, in fact, textualism faces some of the same problems as intentionalism.[31] It isn't clear that he is right about this. But even if he were, that would hurt textualism rather than help intentionalism, unless, of course, the intentionalist can better respond to the objections than the textualist.

Alexander discusses a number of objections to intentionalism, and he is forthright about one objection in particular, which he takes to be quite serious, though not so serious as to defeat his view. That objection concerns the problem of aggregating intent when legal texts are the product of multiperson bodies, such as ratifying conventions and legislatures.[32] There is, of course, the initial difficulty of discovering the intended meaning of each individual member of that body, particularly when we are talking about a legal text ratified in the distant past, such as the Constitution. But suppose that we could discover the various individual intended meanings of the members of an authoritative group. The question then becomes what constitutes the *intended meaning of the group*. Suppose that members of the group had intended meaning M1, M2, or M3. We can imagine the following three possibilities. First, a majority might adopt the legal text, although there is no majority (and perhaps no plurality) intended meaning. Second, there is a majority intended meaning, and that majority voted in favor of adopting the legal text. Third, the persons who hold the majority intended meaning are a different portion of the group than the majority who voted for adoption of the legal text. Perhaps a simple majority voted for adoption, with those voting "aye" evenly divided as between M1 and M2, while most of those who opposed adoption of the legal text shared intended meaning M2. In the first case, assuming that the meaning of the legal text is determined by the ratifiers' intended meaning, intentionalism would entail that the text is meaningless.[33] Where there is no group intent, there is no meaning, and so there is no law. The second case might seem straightforward. But the intended meaning of those who drafted a legal text might be different from the intended meaning of

30 Barnett, *Restoring the Lost Constitution*, chap. 4.

31 Alexander, "Simple-Minded Originalism," 91; Alexander, "Originalism, the Why and the What," 542; Alexander, "Legal Positivism and Originalist Interpretation."

32 Alexander discusses this objection in a number of places (e.g., Alexander, "Simple-Minded Originalism," 91; Alexander, "Originalism, the Why and the What," 542; Alexander, "Legal Positivism and Originalist Interpretation," 8–9; Alexander, "Aggregating States of Mind," manuscript). Alexander and Sherwin further explore this objection in Alexander and Sherwin, *Demystifying Legal Reasoning*, 145–50.

33 How would this work? A majority would have a certain understanding (accurate or not) of the authorial intent of the drafters of the legal text and adopt that understanding as their own, either supporting the legal text so understood or not supporting it.

those who adopted it; and if the intentionalist is committed to *authorial* intent, then it isn't clear whether the drafters' intent or the ratifiers' intent ought to prevail.[34] Intentionalists like Alexander might appeal to the authority of the ratifiers to support the claim that it is their intent that counts. But we would need a story about why the drafters' intended meaning doesn't fix the meaning – that is, after all, the *original* meaning of the text, which ratifiers might understand either correctly or incorrectly or not at all. As for the third case, if we say that the majority vote determines the meaning of the legal text, then again there is no group intent and so no law. If we say instead that the meaning of the legal text is determined by the majority intended meaning, rather than the majority vote, then there is no legal text with that intended meaning that was adopted by a sufficient number, so, again, it would seem that there is no law.

Now, Alexander may be right that textualism faces its own problem of aggregation.[35] And intentionalists might be able to develop a plausible solution to this problem, if not in the first case, where there is no majority intended meaning, then at least in the second and third cases. Perhaps they might say that majority intended meaning, where there is one, determines the meaning of the legal text, even when the meaning-determining majority and the adoption-determining majority differ. There are two questions: One concerns the *meaning* of a legal text; the other concerns whether the *proper procedures* for adoption of that sort of legal text have been followed, such as the procedures set forth in Article I of the Constitution. Meaning is fixed by the majority intended meaning; adoption is determined by following the specified procedures. It just happens that a large number of those who voted for adopting the legal text turn out to have been mistaken about the meaning of the text they voted for. I won't consider this possible response further. My point is simply that the intentionalist would no doubt have more tricks up his or her sleeve.

As serious as the aggregation problem might be, I believe that there are yet more serious problems for intentionalism. I will explore just two of them here. One concerns how to reconcile an authoritative group's intended meaning of a legal text with that group's higher-order or interpretive intentions.[36] Of course, if intentionalism were just a semantic theory, and the correct semantic theory, then intended meaning would determine the meaning of a legal text, and there would be nothing to settle. But as I argued earlier, originalism (textualism and intentionalism)

[34] Larry Solum pressed a point like this one at the conference, though he pressed more on the fact that the members of Congress in many cases do not even read the legislation on which they are voting, and so likely had no intended meaning, in contrast to the actual drafters of the legislation. This would, if correct, pose problems for Alexander's authority argument for intentionalism.

[35] Alexander, "Simple-Minded Originalism," 91.

[36] Brest, "The Misconceived Quest for the Original Understanding," 204–38, raises a version of this worry.

is most plausibly a normative thesis. And an authoritative group's interpretive intentions might well bear on the normative question of how to settle the meaning of a legal text. It seems likely, though, that many members of authoritative groups have no particular interpretive intentions at all, and there may be no group interpretive intentions. Aside from facing another kind of aggregation problem at the level of interpretive intent, even if there were group interpretive intentions, we are, if anything, in a worse position to discover them than to discover the group intended meaning of a legal text. In the case of the Constitution, for example, we don't know (and likely couldn't know) with any degree of certainty the interpretive intentions, if any, of the framers and ratifiers.

Even if actual group interpretive intentions might have a bearing on whether to accept intentionalism as a normative thesis, their bearing would be limited for reasons related to those we considered earlier when we looked at Alexander's authority argument for intentionalism. If, as suggested, the authority of those who enact legal norms is subject to constraints, those constraints might themselves limit acceptable interpretive intentions or even prescribe a set of ideal interpretive intentions. For example, publicity and intelligibility constraints might require understanding a legal text in accordance with its public meaning or even an idealized public meaning. The latter might be more or less idealized. It might just be what a reasonable member of the relevant public would have understood the words of a legal text to mean. It might be a matter of constructing the public meaning of a legal text in light of the purposes that animated its drafting and adoption. The point is, once again, that even if adopters possess the authority to set legal norms, it may not be entirely up to the adopters of a legal text how that text is to be understood.

My suggestions might seem to be subject to at least one of the objections Alexander raises in the course of criticizing textualism. According to Alexander, the textualist must really be appealing to a hypothetical authorial intent (intention-free interpretation is impossible, he claims.)[37] This hypothetical authorial intent would be what "some hypothetical member of the public who is a contemporary of the actual authors would have believed was the actual authors' intended meaning."[38] Alexander raises a couple of difficulties for appeals to hypothetical authorial intent as determined by hypothetical members of the public. First, he claims that it is arbitrary how textualists characterize this hypothetical member of the public. The idea seems to be that there is any number of hypothetical members of the public, for there are many ways of idealizing, and choice among them would be arbitrary. Second, and what he takes to be more important, the textualist has no good answer as to why to go with hypothetical authorial intent over actual authorial intent.

[37] Alexander and Prakash, "Is That English You're Speaking?" 972–82.

[38] Alexander, "Simple-Minded Originalism," 88–89.

The main claims that Alexander makes in presenting this objection strike me as problematic. First, I think Alexander is simply mistaken to think that public meaning originalists must really be appealing to hypothetical authors and authorial intent. He seems to hold this view because he accepts the semantic and interpretive claims discussed earlier. But for reasons I have already given, those claims are either false or question-begging. Textualists, I take it, really think we must look for the public or conventional meanings of legal texts, even if they are not always consistent in how they express and defend their theories. Any idealization is to something like what a reasonable member of the public at the time of adoption would have understood the words of a legal text to mean; there is no appeal to what that hypothetical person would have considered the authorial intent to be.

The part of this objection to textualism that might seem to apply to my suggestions comes with Alexander's claim that the choice of idealizations must be arbitrary. But it would take much more argument than he offers to support this skeptical claim. Merely pointing to the various possibilities about how to idealize and various questions that would need to be addressed in selecting an idealization is not enough to show that there wouldn't be grounds for choosing some idealizations over others. Some of those grounds might come from a more adequate account of the constrained authority possessed by those who are empowered to enact legal norms. Some, as noted earlier, might simply involve correcting for an actual member of the public's misunderstandings of the conventional meanings of words and sentences. In any case, my point was not that constraints on authority would require idealization, but simply that they might.

A second worry about intentionalism concerns the relationship between the different intentions that the authors or adopters of a legal text might have had. Now, Alexander's official view is that we interpreters are after authorial intended meaning – what the authors intended to say or communicate in using the words that they did. But in addition to their intended meaning, the authors undoubtedly had other intentions. Some of these intentions might have concerned the purposes they had in mind – the ends they sought to advance or the problems they sought to remedy – in adopting a legal text. For example, the authors and adopters of the Affordable Care Act sought to remedy the problems of exploding healthcare costs, high numbers of uninsured people with limited access to healthcare, and discrimination in health insurance. In addition to their purposes in enacting a legal text, its authors and adopters might have intended or expected that certain things happen, or not happen, as a result of enacting that legal text. To take a familiar example, the ratifiers of the Fourteenth Amendment (mostly) accepted segregated schools and so did not intend that Amendment to have the result that segregated schools violate equal protection. Call these three kinds of intent the authors' intended meaning, intended purposes, and intended applications.

Important questions arise about the relationships among these kinds of intent. Alexander's position is that although authors' intended applications might be evidence of their intended meaning, only the latter is controlling.[39] (Textualists similarly take intended applications to be evidence of the original public meaning of a legal text, though only the latter is controlling.) Presumably, he would say the same thing about their intended purposes. What originalists, including Alexander, have yet to provide us with is a compelling account of when and how intended purposes or intended applications are evidence of intended (or public) meaning. This fact is liable to lead to slippage, with expected applications or purposes being treated as determining meaning when they do not. Justice Scalia was often guilty of this slippage, something for which Ronald Dworkin, among others, criticized him.[40] For example, Scalia thought that the death penalty was clearly not unconstitutional. Why? Here is what he writes:

> No fewer than three of the justices with whom I have served have maintained that the death penalty is unconstitutional, *even though its use is explicitly contemplated in the Constitution*. The Due Process Clause of the Fifth and Fourteenth Amendments says that no person shall be deprived of life without due process of law; and the Grand Jury Clause of the Fifth Amendment says that no person shall be held to answer for a capital crime without grand jury indictment.[41]

In talking about what the Constitution contemplated, Scalia is arguably relying on the intended applications of the framers and ratifiers, rather than solely on the text of the Constitution. They accepted the death penalty, and so presumably did not think that it was in violation of the Eighth Amendment ban on cruel and unusual punishments. Some evidence that they did not think so comes in the Amendments that Scalia cites. But the text of the Constitution "contemplated" the acceptability of the death penalty only insofar as it does not explicitly say, one way or the other, whether the death penalty is constitutionally permissible. The amendments that Scalia cites seem only to set *necessary* conditions on the use of the death penalty. We could nevertheless conclude, consistently with the Fifth and Fourteenth Amendments, that the Eighth Amendment does after all prohibit capital punishment.[42] The requirements that there be no death penalty without due process of law and no death penalty without grand jury indictment are consistent with the conclusion that there be no death penalty at all.

There are other views one might take besides Alexander's about the relationships among the three kinds of intent. Early originalists like Raoul Berger seem to have

39 Alexander, "Originalism, the Why and the What," 541.

40 Ronald Dworkin, "Comment," in Scalia, *A Matter of Interpretation*.

41 Scalia, *A Matter of Interpretation*, 46.

42 Glossip v. Gross, 135 S. Ct. 2726 (2015) (Breyer dissenting).

treated intended applications and purposes as qualifying the meaning of the text.[43] This sort of view about the relationships among the three kinds of intent seems to be responsible for the common rejection of originalism, even though criticisms that fairly apply to it are incorrectly leveled against contemporary versions of intentionalism and textualism. The points I mean to stress are two: (1) there is more than one view a theorist might take about the relationship among the three kinds of intent, and we would need good reasons for accepting one of these views over the others; and (2) if we are to take the particular approach Alexander accepts, we would need to know much more about how that approach is supposed to work.

Some of these problems may well afflict textualists as much as intentionalists, as Alexander himself insists with respect to the aggregation problem. If that is the case, then originalists of all stripes have their work cut out for them. But, again, it is of no particular help to intentionalism if its originalist competitors suffer from similar shortcomings.

9.4 FURTHER DEVELOPMENT

I want now to draw together the various threads of this exploration of Alexander's intentionalism. The main takeaways, I think, are these. First, originalism – whether intentionalism or textualism – is best understood as making a normative claim, in the sense specified earlier. Second, Alexander's arguments in favor of intentionalism fail to provide adequate support for it. Third, intentionalism faces serious problems of its own and is underdeveloped.

The mains ways in which intentionalism is underdeveloped are these. First, insofar as intentionalism, as a normative thesis, depends on its claim to be authority-preserving, the intentionalist owes us a much better developed account of the authority possessed by those empowered to enact legal norms. An adequate account must include a specification of what constraints operate on the exercise of that authority. And the intentionalist must then explain why intentionalism better preserves this constrained authority than its competitors. This, I think, is no easy task.

Second, the intentionalist must explain what intentionalism really contributes to our understanding of legal texts, like the Constitution, given that (1) we have at best limited access to authorial intentions; (2) we have, as of yet, no adequate solution to the aggregation problem; and (3) as a practical matter, the best way to understand authorial intent is ordinarily to understand the conventional meaning of a legal text.

Third, even if we accept intentionalism, intentionalists owe us an account of how cleanly to separate intended meaning from intended purposes and intended

43 Raoul Berger, "Ronald Dworkin's The Moral Reading of the Constitution: A Critique," *Indiana Law Journal* 72, no. 4 (1997): 1109–1114.

applications, as well as an account of how precisely these three kinds of intent are connected to one another. Without this, as I have explained, intentionalism is subject to a problematic slippage. This slippage may lead the interpreter to mistake intended purposes or intended applications for intended meaning, or to see them as identifying the intended meaning in ways that they do not or in ways that simply reflect the moral or policy positions of the interpreter. As a consequence, intentionalism would lose one of the principal claimed advantages of originalism, namely, that it constrains judges better than its competitors, though this assumes that in fact originalism has this supposed advantage.

We might add that intentionalism can be, at most, but one part of a broader theory of adjudication.[44] By itself, it tells us little about how to answer the constitutional questions that confront judges. Alexander draws a distinction between two kinds of legal norms – rules and standards – which would seem to be relevant to how judges should proceed. As he depicts them, rules are "rather determinate norms, or at least they are norms that require no moral or other practical reasoning to apply … In other words, whatever their differences in values, all can understand what the rule requires." Standards, by contrast, "are norms that do require moral or other practical reasoning to apply. As I sometimes put it, a standard is a norm that requires for its application that its audience do the right thing, morally or prudentially, within the constraints set by the rules."[45] He provides as examples of each type of legal norm a stop sign or speed limit (rules) and norms such as "drive reasonably" and "pay your fair share in taxes" (standards). He contends that whereas rules require interpretation, standards require not interpretation but, rather, practical reasoning. Why this difference? Because, he claims, "what interpretation seeks are authorially-intended meanings, and the deliverances of practical reasoning are independent of such meanings."[46] He also claims that "interpretation itself ends when the interpreter discovers that the authors intended to promulgate a standard."[47]

I think these claims cannot be what Alexander really means to say. First, as Alexander himself recognizes, according to his view interpretation is needed to discern whether a bit of legal text enacts *either* a rule or a standard. Second, interpretation doesn't quite end once it has been determined that the legal text enacts a rule rather than a standard (or vice versa), for interpretation requires, both in the case of rules and standards, that we understand the *intended meaning*, and so

44 Contemporary forms of textualism have the virtue of recognizing the need for something more than public meaning, and so have appealed to forms of constitutional construction to supplement original meaning. See, e.g., Barnett, *Restoring the Lost Constitution*, chap. 5; Solum, "Originalism and Constitutional Construction," 453–537.

45 Alexander, "Legal Positivism and Originalist Interpretation," 4.

46 Ibid., 4–5.

47 Ibid., 5.

understand the *content* of the intended rule or the intended standard. Interpretation ends when the interpreter determines that the authors intended to enact a *particular* standard, or when the interpreter determines that the authors intended to enact a *particular* rule Having proceeded this far, the next step is to get from the intended meaning to the content of the law. This requires, at least in part, application of the rule or standard. Third, practical reasoning cannot be independent of authorially intended meaning, at least not if the practical reasoner is to be implementing the intended standard. Finally, although there may be differences in the kind of practical reasoning involved in the application of rules and standards, one must engage in practical reasoning, if not moral reasoning, to apply either type of legal norm.[48] In the case of rules, the practical reasoner must figure out, among other things, which cases fall under the rule and which do not. And this may require attending not only to the intended meaning of the rule but the intended purpose of the rule, as well as intended applications. The practical reasoner may also need to engage in means-end reasoning in the application of rules. Perhaps the point that Alexander really means to make is that standards leave it to the practical reasoner, in a way that rules do not, to figure out what makes sense given the relevant standard, which will involve kinds of practical reasoning (such as moral reasoning) that may not be involved in the application of rules.

Alexander, and his coauthor Emily Sherwin, are on record with the view that "legal reasoning is just ordinary reasoning applied to legal problems."[49] So perhaps Alexander does not think that the intentionalist needs to say anything in particular about how to get from intended meaning to the content of the law: Just consider how our ordinary reasoning works. But I'm not sure things are that easy. Hard cases are, after all, hard. I think the intentionalist needs to say more about how he would supplement intentionalism in order to develop a theory of adjudication. This would include saying more about how the adjudicator is to get from intended meaning to the content of the law and to the resolution of a particular case.

9.5 CONCLUSION

Bernard Williams, in his attempt to deliver a deathblow to utilitarianism, ultimately dubbed it "simple-minded." As he explained, "Simple-mindedness consists in having too few thoughts and feelings to match the world as it really is."[50] Intended meaning

48 See Alexander and Sherwin, *Demystifying Legal Reasoning*, 3, which makes clear that Alexander recognizes the role of practical reasoning in applying legal rules.

49 Ibid.

50 J.J.C. Smart and Bernard Williams, *Utilitarianism: For and Against* (Cambridge: Cambridge University Press, 1973), 149.

originalism, I fear, is simple-minded – at least in its current state of development. It tells us too little of what we need to know in order to understand legal texts and reason our way to what the norms they enact may entail. And it may in the end, for reasons given earlier, be of little practical import in our efforts to understand and implement legal norms. In at least its current state of development, it thus seems unable to match the "legal world" as it really is.

Having raised a number of worries about Alexander's intentionalism, I want to conclude by emphasizing the important contributions his writings on originalism have made. Alexander has shown us that legal scholars and theorists have been too quick to dismiss intentionalism in the wake of criticisms by Brest and others. He has exposed the attractions of intentionalism by showing how it seems to line up with our ordinary efforts to understand one another and by exploring some of the resources that intentionalists have for supporting their approach to interpretation. He has shown us that the contemporary move to public meaning originalism may depend both on underestimating the power of intentionalism and overestimating its own power to avoid difficulties critics have raised for originalism. And he has done all of this in an admirably lucid, thoughtful, and engaging manner. Any effort to develop an intentionalist theory to address the kinds of worries explored herein will have to begin with Alexander's pioneering work.

10

Subjective versus Objective Intentionalism in Legal Interpretation

Jeffrey Goldsworthy

10.1 INTRODUCTION

Larry Alexander has long been a leading proponent of the thesis that the meaning of a law is the meaning that the lawmaker intended it to communicate. He has argued frequently and powerfully against nonintentionalism, which denies either that a multimember lawmaker can have an intention, or that its intentions inform the meanings of its laws. In this paper I will say only a little about that debate, although I agree with Alexander that nonintentionalism (thus defined) is implausible.[1] Instead, I will discuss a disagreement within the intentionalist camp, between "strong" or "subjective" intentionalists – such as Alexander – and "weak" or "objective" intentionalists – such as me. I take Larry Solum's public meaning originalism to be a version of the latter position. I will explain and assess what I take to be the main arguments for and against these positions.

For convenience, I will use the following acronyms throughout:

SI for subjective intentionalism;
OI for objective intentionalism; and
PMO for public meaning originalism.

10.2 FRAMING THE DEBATE

It may help to avoid misunderstandings if I set out some basic premises that help frame the debate between SI and OI.

1. The way in which written constitutions and statutes should, as a matter of law, be interpreted is ultimately determined by legal norms established

[1] See the first and concluding paragraphs of Section 10.3.

wholly or partly[2] by the conventional practices of legal officials, especially judges.[3] It cannot be determined merely by philosophical truths about linguistic meaning, although they can be made relevant by practice-based norms. These norms may include statutory or common law interpretive norms, as well as deeper constitutional norms including Hartian rules of recognition or fundamental principles identified through Dworkinian "interpretation."[4]

2. As for the interpretation of statutes, Anglo-American practice-based norms include the principles that:
   (a) in making or changing statutes, a legislature possesses legislative "supremacy" within its constitutionally allocated domain of lawmaking authority;[5]
   (b) a legislature, by enacting a statute, makes new laws or changes old ones, and simultaneously attempts to communicate to the community what these new laws or changes are;[6]
   (c) when interpreting a statute, judges should first and foremost seek to ascertain the linguistic meaning that it communicates – its "communicative content" – which is either identical to or depends heavily on what the legislature intended it to be (the difference between these alternatives is the subject matter of this paper);
   (d) judges may also supplement the meaning of a statute if its communicative content is insufficiently determinate to settle a legal dispute, and in limited and unusual circumstances may correct or rectify that content by changing it or adding to it. These circumstances are arguably confined to ones in which judges should act creatively to serve as the legislature's "faithful agents," consistently with principle (a): for example, obeying a later statute that requires the "reinterpretation" of earlier ones, correcting scriveners' errors, "reading down" a statute to ensure that it is constitutionally valid, or fabricating so-called implications to ensure that a statute achieves the legislature's obvious and immediate purposes in enacting it

2 The word "partly" accommodates Dworkinian interpretivism.

3 Jeffrey Goldsworthy, "Originalism in Constitutional Interpretation," *Federal Law Review* 25, no. 1 (1997): 1, 8.

4 For agreement, Larry Alexander, "Constitutional Theories: A Taxonomy and (Implicit) Critique," *San Diego Law Review* 51, no. 3 (2014): 623, 641–43.

5 See Jeffrey Goldsworthy, *Parliamentary Sovereignty, Contemporary Debates* (Cambridge: Cambridge University Press, 2010), 226–28.

6 Compare Heidi Hurd, "Sovereignty in Silence," *Yale Law Journal* 99, no. 5 (1990): 945; Mark Greenberg, "Legislation as Communication? Legal Interpretation and the Study of Linguistic Communication," in *Philosophical Foundations of Language in the Law*, ed. Andrei Marmor and Scott Soames (Oxford: Oxford University Press, 2011), 217, 230–32, 241–50.

or complies with its presumed standing commitments to important legal principles (such as that of *mens rea*).

I doubt that Alexander would dispute principles (a)–(c), which have been frequently and explicitly recognized by the judiciary. Principle (d) has rarely been explicitly recognized, and is more controversial, but is – I believe – implicit in judicial interpretive practices.

3. In Australia, somewhat similar norms – although principle (d) only in a very truncated form – have been adopted in relation to its constitution (substituting "the founders" for "the legislature," etc.), unsurprisingly since that constitution is a statute of the UK Parliament. Regarding the United States Constitution, principles equivalent to (b), (c), and (d) are more controversial. Originalists subscribe to principles (b) and (c), but nonoriginalists either reject one or both of them, or endorse a very expansive version of principle (d), authorizing the judiciary to rectify or update the Constitution when it is deemed no longer compatible with contemporary values.

10.3 NONINTENTIONALISM

Principle (c) is denied absolutely by strong nonintentionalists. Some have denied that Anglo-American practice-based norms make lawmakers' intentions partly determinative of the meanings of statutes or constitutions, but that denial has been refuted.[7] Others deny that multimember lawmaking bodies can have intentions, which seems implausible given that (a) such intentions are often plainly perceptible, and statutory interpretation would lead to absurd conclusions if they were ignored (I will shortly provide an example); (b) we all naturally and commonly ascribe intentions to groups; and (c) emerging new philosophical theories of group intentions have either already vindicated that practice or are on the verge of doing so.[8]

Alexander's main argument against nonintentionalism has long been that without assumptions about authorial intentions we could not determine that a meaningful text even exists, or the language in which it is written.[9] I tend to agree, although John

7 See Goldsworthy, "Originalism in Constitutional Interpretation," 8–12; Robert G. Natelson, "The Founders' Hermeneutic: The Real Original Understanding of Original Intentions," *Ohio State Law Journal* 68, no. 5 (2007): 1239.

8 See the theories discussed in Richard Ekins, *The Nature of Legislative Intent* (Oxford: Oxford University Press, 2015), chap. 3, which he then develops.

9 See, e.g., Larry Alexander and Saikrishna Prakash, "'Is That English You're Speaking?' Some Arguments for the Primacy of Intent in Interpretation," *San Diego Law Review* 41, no. 3 (2004): 967, 974–76.

Searle disagreed and I am loathe to take on Searle regarding matters of language.[10] But Alexander has also pointed out that language usage is much more versatile than simply adopting linguistic meanings fixed by social conventions (as recorded in a dictionary); for example, speakers can use words nonliterally, or idiosyncratically.[11] Indeed, the conventional meanings of sentences chronically underdetermine the meanings of utterances of those sentences if contextual evidence of authorial intentions is not used to contextually enrich them.[12]

As legal theorists have long known, and linguists and philosophers of language now confirm, meanings determined solely by linguistic conventions are much thinner than what we understand utterances to express and imply.[13] The literal meaning of a context-free sentence usually (and arguably always) underdetermines what its utterance in a particular context expresses and implies.[14] The sentence in itself is just a template or skeleton that must be contextually enriched in order to ascertain what its utterance expresses and implies. Enrichment involves inferring speakers' or authors' likely communicative intentions not only from the conventional (literal) meaning of the sentence, but also from background knowledge of their beliefs and values and the context in which they uttered the sentence.[15]

The underdeterminacy thesis is true by definition in the case of implied meanings, which, since they are not expressed by words alone, cannot be derived solely from the conventional meanings of words. What is perhaps surprising is that the literal meaning of a context-free sentence also often underdetermines what an utterance of the sentence expresses. Paradoxically, even express meanings often include inexplicit content.

[10] See John R. Searle, "Literary Theory and Its Discontents," *New Literary History* 25, no. 3 (1994): 637.

[11] Larry Alexander and Emily Sherwin, *Demystifying Legal Reasoning* (New York: Cambridge University Press, 2008), 135–36; Alexander and Prakash, "Is That English You're Speaking?" 978.

[12] Alexander and Sherwin, *Demystifying Legal Reasoning*, 136–38.

[13] For legal theorists, see the works cited in ibid., 137n13, 140n19, and in Jeffrey Goldsworthy, "Implications in Language, Law, and the Constitution," in *Future Directions in Australian Constitutional Law*, ed. Geoffrey Lindell (Sydney: Foundation Press, 1994), 150–51. For philosophers of language and linguists, see, e.g., Scott Soames, *Philosophical Essays: Natural Language*, vol. 1 (Princeton: Princeton University Press, 2009), chap. 15; Robyn Carston, "Legal Texts and Canons of Construction: A View from Current Pragmatic Theory," in *Law and Language: Current Legal Issues*, vol. 15, ed. Michael Freeman and Fiona Smith (Oxford: Oxford University Press, 2013), 8.

[14] The "always" argument is that even a sentence that appears to state a proposition could, when actually uttered, be used nonliterally, for example, ironically or metaphorically: see Kent Bach, "Context ex Machina," in *Semantics versus Pragmatics*, ed. Zoltán Gendler Szabó (Oxford: Oxford University Press, 2005), 15, 26–27.

[15] Goldsworthy, "Implications in Language," 150–51; Jeffrey Goldsworthy, "Legislative Intentions, Legislative Supremacy, and Legal Positivism," *San Diego Law Review* 42, no. 2 (2004): 669; Ekins, *Legislative Intent*, chap. 7; Andrei Marmor, *The Language of Law* (Oxford: Oxford University Press, 2014), chaps. 1–2, esp. 24–34.

For example, utterances – including legal utterances – often include ellipses, a term I use to refer to an omission of a word or words in an uttered sentence that the audience "fills in" through contextual enrichment.[16]

Some sentences are inherently elliptical because they require contextual enrichment to express complete propositions: for example, "She is ready" [for what?], or "I've had enough" [of what?]. Section 92 of the Australian Constitution provides that "trade, commerce, and intercourse among the States … shall be absolutely free," without explicitly specifying what it is to be absolutely free from. The High Court's attempts to fill in this ellipsis were long hindered by its refusal to consider most of the available historical evidence of the framers' intended meaning. In 1988, it changed course, examined that evidence, and was able to fill in the ellipsis. The section was understood to mean "absolutely free [from discriminatory protectionism]," rather than the absurd "absolutely free [from all legal constraint]" or the unworkable "absolutely free [from all unreasonable legal restraint]."[17]

Other uttered sentences need completion to avoid absurdity: For example, an utterance of "Everyone has gone to Paris" would usually be understood nonliterally to mean "Everyone [in some contextually defined group, such as a family or group of friends] has gone to Paris." Section 51(ii) of the Australian Constitution gives the national Parliament power to make laws "with respect to taxation." This cannot have been intended to refer to all taxation, including State taxation; otherwise, the national Parliament could amend and repeal State tax laws. What lawyers naturally understand the section to (have been intended to) mean is: "with respect to [national] taxation." Moreover, I suggest that although this is not its literal meaning, it is its express meaning, rather than that the express meaning is qualified by an unexpressed implication. This is, incidentally, an example of what I described earlier as intentions that are "plainly perceptible," if only as a matter of common sense, which must be taken into account to avoid absurdity.[18]

Many other uncontroversial examples could be given of contextual evidence of authorial intentions enriching the meanings we ascribe to legal texts, examples not only of ellipses but also of semantic and syntactic ambiguities, relational terms ("citizen" or "alien" in relation to what country?), presuppositions, and various kinds of implications.[19] The collective force of such examples makes strong nonintentionalism implausible.

[16] Ellipses are sometimes called "implicitures," from the adjective "implicit": see Kent Bach, "Conversational Impliciture," *Mind & Language* 9, no. 2 (1994): 124.

[17] Cole v. Whitfield (1988) 163 CLR 360.

[18] See text accompanying note 8.

[19] Jeffrey Goldsworthy, "The Implicit and the Implied in a Written Constitution," in *The Invisible Constitution in Comparative Perspective*, ed. Rosalind Dixon and Adrienne Stone (New York: Cambridge University Press, forthcoming).

10.4 SUBJECTIVE VERSUS OBJECTIVE INTENTIONALISM

We therefore turn to the disagreement within the intentionalist camp, between SI and OI. Both accept principle (c) in Section 10.2 above: When interpreting a statute or constitution, judges should seek to ascertain the intention of the lawmaker. But they understand this in different ways. SI maintains that judges should seek the lawmaker's actual subjective intentions, whereas OI holds that those intentions are relevant only insofar as they were publicly manifested, in that sufficient evidence of them was made readily available to the public or at least to legal advisers.

This disagreement can be conducted at two different levels. One level is that of linguistic meaning and communication in general, rather than the meanings of laws in particular. For Alexander and his allies, SI is true of laws partly because they believe it is true of linguistic communications in general (given that constitutional norms require laws to be interpreted as communications[20]). Legal and literary theorists who defend SI at the general level include, in addition to Alexander, literary theorists Stanley Fish, Stephen Knapp, and Walter Benn Michaels, and legal theorists Saikrishna Prakash, Paul Campos, Richard Ekins, and Richard Kay.[21] They can claim the support of various philosophers of language including Stephen Neale[22] and Kent Bach.[23]

OI, on the other hand, can be propounded either – like SI – as a general thesis about the meaning of any linguistic communication (a position I will call "general OI"), or as a distinctively legal thesis about actual and/or desirable restrictions on what evidence of legislative intentions legal interpreters should take into account (which I will call "legal OI"). General OI has been defended by me, Andrei Marmor,[24] and the philosopher of language Scott Soames.[25]

[20] See Section 10.2, principle (b), above.

[21] For many references, see Alexander and Sherwin, *Demystifying Legal Reasoning*, 180n10, 186n20; Ekins, *Legislative Intent*, chap. 7.

[22] Stephen Neale, "Pragmatism and Binding," in *Semantics Versus Pragmatics*, ed. Zoltán Gendler Szabó (Oxford: Oxford University Press, 2005), 165–285.

[23] Kent Bach, "The Top 10 Misconceptions About Implicature," in *Drawing the Boundaries of Meaning*, ed. Betty J. Birner and Gregory Ward (Amsterdam: John Benjamins, 2005), 21.

[24] Andrei Marmor, "Truth in Law," in *Law and Language*, ed. Michael Freeman and Fiona Smith (Oxford: Oxford University Press, 2013), 45, 52–53, 55. Here, without citing my prior defense of it, Marmor adopts OI, despite previously having regarded it very differently: see Andrei Marmor, *Interpretation and Legal Theory*, 2nd ed. (Oxford: Hart, 2005), 22n20, in which he refers to my defense of OI in a long, critical review of the first edition of his book, Jeffrey Goldsworthy, "Marmor on Meaning, Interpretation, and Legislative Intention," *Legal Theory* 1, no. 4 (1995): 439, 441–42, 450–51, 458.

[25] Scott Soames, "Deferentialism: A Post-Originalist Theory of Legal Interpretation," *Fordham Law Review* 82, no. 2 (2013): 598.

Legal OI can be defended on rule of law or judicial economy grounds. It is therefore possible to accept both SI at the general level and legal OI. Richard Ekins, for example, vigorously defends SI,[26] and brusquely dismisses general OI, as the best theory of communicative meaning.[27] Nevertheless, he advocates a form of legal OI that has similar, if not identical, consequences to general OI.[28]

The disagreement between SI and OI is one reason why Mark Greenberg rejects what he labels the "communicative theory" of legal meaning.[29] There are, he argues, too many candidates for the communicative intentions to which intentionalists appeal. But it is unsurprising that lawyers are somewhat confused, uncertain, and in disagreement about the nature of the communicative contents of laws. Very few lawyers are adept in the philosophy of language, which is complex and difficult, and they might not agree with one another even if they were. Eminent philosophers of language disagree among themselves about the nature of communicative content,[30] but that does not show that linguistic communications do not have communicative contents, or that those contents are not determined partly by evidence of authorial intentions. If theoretical disagreement about the nature of something were a good ground for disbelieving that the thing exists, there would be nothing we could believe in.

10.5 THE ARGUMENT FOR OI

As noted in Section 10.2, how written constitutions and statutes should, as a matter of law, be interpreted is ultimately determined not by philosophical truths about the meaning of linguistic communications in general, but by practice-based norms. In Anglo-American law, OI fits much better than SI with the interpretive norms enunciated by the courts. At least in recent times, they have frequently said that they are interested in "objective" intentions, rather than the "subjective" intentions of legislators.[31] Well before that, their interpretive practices (especially the refusal of courts throughout the British Commonwealth to consult legislative history) were more consistent with OI than SI. British and Australian courts – and I presume American ones as well – have often drawn a distinction between lawmakers' actual

[26] Ekins, *Legislative Intent*, 194–95.

[27] Ibid., 210; see also his "Objects of Interpretation," *Constitutional Commentary* 32, no. 1 (2017): 1, 9.

[28] For detailed discussion, see Jeffrey Goldsworthy, "Legislative Intention Vindicated?," *Oxford Journal of Legal Studies* 33, no. 4 (2013): 821, 836–41.

[29] Greenberg, "Legislation as Communication?," 217, 230–32, 241–50.

[30] For example, Neale and Soames apparently disagree with one another on this point: see Neale, "Pragmatism and Binding"; Soames, "Deferentialism."

[31] Richard Ekins and Jeffrey Goldsworthy, "The Reality and Indispensability of Legislative Intentions," *Sydney Law Review* 36, no. 1 (2014): 39, 46–51; Antonin Scalia, *A Matter of Interpretation, Federal Courts and the Law* (Princeton: Princeton University Press, 1997), 17.

subjective intentions, which might be unknowable or too difficult to retrieve, and intentions that – given publicly available evidence – they seem to have "expressed" or "manifested" in making a law.[32] The courts do not hold themselves bound either by the literal (purely conventional) meanings of the words of a statute, or by subjective intentions that the legislature failed to enable its intended audience to discern. They seek to give effect to the "objective meaning" of a statute, which is evidenced by both the linguistic conventions that determine literal meanings and other evidence of the legislature's intentions that it is readily available to the statute's intended audience. That other evidence can include common-sense understandings of the legislature's likely purposes and intentions, the historical circumstances in which the statute was enacted, and (to a limited extent) legislative history.[33]

Richard Ekins and I recently argued that these judicial statements and practices are best understood as endorsing a version of OI, although we did not attempt to choose between general OI and legal OI.[34] What follows are arguments based on both linguistic theory and legal principle for these positions.[35]

10.5.1 *The Argument for General OI*

SI's claim that the meaning of any communication just is what its speaker intended it to mean seems false, because it seems possible for the meaning that people intend to communicate to differ from the meaning they succeed in communicating. It surely cannot be the case that, whenever we speak or write with the intention of expressing or implying something, we are guaranteed to successfully express or imply that thing simply by virtue of having that intention. People can intend to say or imply something but fail to do so, and conversely, they can say or imply something they did not intend. When we are told that we have misunderstood what someone meant, we often defend ourselves by replying: "I now realize what she meant to say, but that's not what she did say," or "He may not have intended to imply that, but he did."[36] SI must deny that such replies can be strictly correct: If the meaning of someone's utterance is identical to the meaning she intends it to have, then she can only appear to, but cannot really, say something other than what she intends to say. That strikes me as counterintuitive.

[32] Ekins and Goldsworthy, "Reality and Indispensability," 46–47.

[33] See also Jeffrey Goldsworthy, "Legislative Intentions, Legislative Supremacy, and Legal Positivism," *San Diego Law Review* 42, no. 2 (2005) 493.

[34] Ekins and Goldsworthy, "Reality and Indispensability," 46–51.

[35] Much of the following is taken from Jeffrey Goldsworthy, "Moderate versus Strong Intentionalism," *San Diego Law Review* 42, no. 2 (2005): 669.

[36] Goldsworthy, "Moderate versus Strong Intentionalism," 677. See also Mitchell Berman, "Originalism is Bunk," *New York University Law Review* 84, no. 1 (2009): 1, 44–46, 52.

When people fail to communicate the meaning they intend to communicate, the meaning they do communicate must be something else. In such cases, the meaning of their utterance – of their speech act – is surely the meaning they communicate, not the one they intended to communicate. Defending SI, Stanley Fish replies that "having your meaning misunderstood doesn't mean that your meaning is something other than what you have determined it to be."[37] That is true, but misses the point, which is that when your utterance fails to communicate your meaning to your intended audience (through your fault not theirs), but communicates some other meaning to them instead, that other meaning – and not your meaning – must be the meaning of your utterance. That meaning will be what your meaning appears to your intended audience to be, given evidence that is readily available to it, including the conventional meanings of your words and other clues such as context.[38]

The meaning of an utterance is surely not something hidden within the speaker's mind and inaccessible to its intended recipient, such as an intended meaning that is made clear only to the speaker's spouse or in a private diary entry.[39] We conceive of the meaning of an utterance as something essentially public, and not – like desires, pains or other mental states – as something essentially private of which we can have only indirect evidence. We do so partly because it is important for many practical purposes that utterances have meanings that are publicly accessible. We hold people responsible for what they have communicated, which is what they appear to have intended to communicate, whether or not it is what they actually intended to communicate. OI therefore holds that what people appear to say or imply, in the light of all the evidence readily available to their intended audience, is what they do say or imply. For an utterance to mean what its author intends it to mean, its intended audience must be capable of ascertaining that meaning. This requires that the audience have access to persuasive evidence of the intended meaning, provided partly by the conventional meanings of the words uttered, and partly by other clues to the author's intention, such as shared background knowledge of the author's beliefs and values, and the context in which the utterance was made. It follows that Humpty Dumpty was wrong to say, in *Alice in Wonderland*, that his words mean whatever he intends them to mean.[40] We can use words to mean something quite different

[37] Stanley Fish, "The Intentionalist Thesis Once More," in *The Challenge of Originalism: Theories of Constitutional Interpretation*, ed. Grant Huscroft and Bradley Miller (New York: Cambridge University Press, 2011), 99, 101.

[38] See Goldsworthy, "Moderate versus Strong Intentionalism," 670–71; Goldsworthy, "Implications in Language, Law and the Constitution," 150–52.

[39] See Goldsworthy, "Marmor on Meaning, Interpretation."

[40] Compare Larry Alexander, "Simple-Minded Originalism," in *The Challenge of Originalism, Theories of Constitutional Interpretation*, ed. Grant Huscroft and Bradley Miller (New York: Cambridge University Press, 2011), 87, 92n12.

from their conventional meaning only if we ensure that our intended audience has ready access to sufficient contextual evidence of our intention to do so. Because our audience must have evidence that it can understand, our attempt to convey our intentions is subject to constraints that must be respected if we are to succeed. Those constraints help determine the meaning of our utterances, whatever our intentions might be.

Alexander objects that when I interpret an ordinary communication, such as a shopping list written by my wife, I want to know what she intended to communicate to me – what she intended me to buy at the supermarket.[41] That may be true, but it does not show that what she intended to communicate by writing her list is the same as the meaning of the list. It shows that I am more interested in her meaning than in the meaning of the list as such, and I use the latter only as evidence of the former. If, for example, my daughter happens by chance to be with me in the supermarket, and convinces me that my wife intended an item on the list to mean x rather than y, I would buy x even if the item as written indicates that she intended y (she does have appalling handwriting!). The fact that in interpreting some utterances we may be seeking the speaker's or author's meanings does not show that utterance meanings and speaker's meanings are one and the same thing. In many other cases – including when we are interpreting legal texts – we have good reason to be more interested in their utterance meanings (as defined by OI) than their author's meanings.

But Alexander is right that "objective" legislative intentions are conceptually dependent on subjective intentions.[42] An "objective" intention is what a reasonable audience would conclude was the author's "subjective" intention, given all the publicly available evidence of it. Indeed, the existence of a subjective intention is a crucial presupposition of an attribution of an objective intention to the author of a text. If we knew that the creators of a text had no relevant subjective intention (for example, they were monkeys pounding randomly on keyboards), we would have no rational basis for attributing any objective intention to the text either.[43]

10.5.2 *The Argument for Legal OI*

The main arguments for legal OI have often been employed by opponents of legislative history being used to interpret statutes. One objection is that legislative history

[41] Alexander and Sherwin, *Demystifying Legal Reasoning*, 132–33.

[42] See, e.g., Caleb Nelson, "What is Textualism?" *Virginia Law Review* 91, no. 2 (2005): 347, 353–57; and for detailed discussion of other possible understandings of "objective intentions," Ekins and Goldsworthy, "Reality and Indispensability," 46–51.

[43] Compare Hurd, "Sovereignty in Silence," 966.

is inherently unreliable, but, as Alexander has observed, no intentionalist is interested in inherently unreliable evidence of authorial intentions.[44] But other familiar objections favor OI over SI. They raise concerns about the rule of law, and judicial economy – the importance of the meanings of laws being publicly ascertainable without excessively time-consuming and expensive investigations into obscure evidence of the lawmakers' intentions.

Lawmakers have authority to make laws, but it is the laws they make that inherit their authority, not – when there is a difference – the laws they intended to make. If the will of the lawmaker were binding, then it would be the true law, and what we currently call laws – which are promulgated by the lawmaker – would merely be evidence of the true law. But the will of the lawmaker is only authoritative insofar as it is communicated – expressly or impliedly – by the laws that it makes. That is the truth in Scalia J's observation, which Alexander criticises, that "[i]t is the law that governs, not the intent of the lawgiver … [We have] a government of laws, not of men."[45] And that is why Scalia maintains that legal interpreters seek "a sort of 'objectified intent.'"[46]

This is not just a point about the meaning of the term "the law." It is, more fundamentally, about the importance of the law being open and transparent to those required to obey it, so they can plan their lives with confidence that their expectations will not be upset by the unpredictable application of hidden intentions. As Scalia also observed, that would be "one step worse than the trick the emperor Nero was said to engage in: posting edicts high up on the pillars, so that they could not be easily read."[47]

This is why Richard Ekins, who rejects general OI, endorses legal OI.[48] Despite insisting that the meaning of a statute is the meaning the legislature intended it to communicate, he requires that legislative intent be inferred only from "publicly available evidence, which is to say evidence that is open to the community."[49] Because it is not open and transparent to the community, "the secret diary or private correspondence of the … [lawmaker] is irrelevant (even if discovered and published) to the legal meaning and effect of his enactments."[50]

44 Alexander and Sherwin, *Demystifying Legal Reasoning*, 204.

45 Scalia, *A Matter of Interpretation*, 17. Criticized by Alexander and Sherwin, *Demystifying Legal Reasoning*, 193ff.

46 Scalia, *A Matter of Interpretation*, 17.

47 Ibid. Richard Kay points out that this "trick" is usually attributed to Caligula, not Nero: "Original Intention and Public Meaning in Constitutional Interpretation," *Northwestern University Law Review* 103, no. 2 (2009): 703, 719n70.

48 See Ekins, *Legislative Intent*, 194–95; Ekins, "Objects of Interpretation," 1, 9; Goldsworthy, "Legislative Intention Vindicated?" 821, 836–41.

49 Ekins, *Legislative Intent*, 247.

50 Ibid., 269–70.

Hence he denies that his main thesis entails that interpreters should consult legislative history, which British Commonwealth courts have been very wary of using partly because it "threatens to unsettle what is transparent to the community."[51] He believes that even if legislative history is excluded, there is often enough other contextual evidence from which the legislature's intended meaning can be inferred.[52] What is open and transparent to the community includes the overall statutory scheme, the rest of the law, especially that which the legislature aims to change, and the nature of the mischief it addresses.[53]

Alexander takes his commitment to SI seriously, for example, in saying that when lawmakers have chosen symbols to communicate their intended meaning, "the symbols that they chose for that purpose – *however aptly or inaptly* – must be deemed to mean what they intended them to mean."[54] On the other hand, he has often discussed the possibility that a legal system might adopt special rules of procedure or form, limiting the evidence of legislative intention that may be taken into account, to protect the rule of law by ensuring that the meanings of laws are publicly accessible or not subject to manipulation. For example, such rules might confine that evidence to standard dictionary meanings of the lawmakers' words, or exclude legislative history.[55] He even says that a community "probably should have rules of form, such as a rule that prefers the dictionary meaning of [a law] to intentions that are markedly in conflict with the ordinary understandings of the words [the lawmaker] has used."[56] But he denies that such rules concern the interpretation of laws in the strict sense of aiming to discern their true meaning; rather, they require recrafting those laws in order to serve extraneous values such as the rule of law.[57] This comes close to Ekins' position, which tempers SI with legal OI.

51 Ibid., 272.

52 Ibid., 256.

53 Ibid., 236, 256–57. For further discussion, see Goldsworthy, "Legislative Intention Vindicated?" 836–41.

54 Larry Alexander, "Originalism, the Why and the What," *Fordham Law Review* 82, no. 2 (2013): 539, 540 (emphasis in original); see also Larry Alexander "Telepathic Law," *Constitutional Commentary* 27, no. 1 (2010): 139, 141.

55 E.g., Larry Alexander and Emily Sherwin, *The Rule of Rules: Morality, Rules, and the Dilemmas of Law* (Durham, NC: Duke University Press, 2001), 120–21; Alexander and Sherwin, *Demystifying Legal Reasoning*, 179–82; Larry Alexander, "All or Nothing at All? The Intentions of Authorities and the Authority of Intentions," in *Law and Interpretation; Essays in Legal Philosophy*, ed. Andrei Marmor (Oxford: Clarendon Press, 1995), 384–86.

56 Alexander and Sherwin, *The Rule of Rules*, 122.

57 Ibid., 122; Alexander and Sherwin, *Demystifying Legal Reasoning*, 138, 189.

10.6 ARGUMENTS AGAINST OI AND PMO

Public meaning originalism (PMO) is often a version of OI. Larry Solum, for example, defines original public meaning as "the meaning that (i) the drafters of the text would have reasonably expected (ii) the audience to whom the text is addressed (iii) to attribute to the drafters (iv) based on the evidence (public record) that was publicly available at the time the text was promulgated."[58]

Alexander and Richard Kay have both defended SI against OI and/or PMO. Although Kay seems to understand PMO as a form of textualism rather than of OI,[59] some of his arguments could be aimed at OI as well. Their arguments can be divided into (a) attempted rebuttals of arguments made in favor of OI or PMO, and (b) arguments aimed directly against OI and PMO.

10.6.1 *Attempted Rebuttals of Arguments in Favor of OI and PMO*

Alexander dismisses the possibility of secret or hidden intended meanings, a major concern of OI and PMO, as a red herring. Authors necessarily intend their audience to recognize the meaning they intend to communicate to it – otherwise they would not be attempting to communicate – so they would never intend to keep their intended meaning hidden.[60] But that merely shows that, rather than being deliberate, hidden meanings must result from mistakes. Speakers and authors sometimes fail to provide their audience with adequate accessible evidence of their communicative intentions. That is when a gap opens between SI and OI. It raises concerns of unfairness to the audience, which necessarily relies on the meaning apparently communicated (regarded by OI as the meaning communicated) when it cannot know the meaning that was intended to be communicated.

Alexander argues that there is no good reason to favor the apparently communicated meaning on grounds of "fair notice" or upset expectations,[61] but I do not understand why. Not only members of the public, but public officials and governments, must be able to rely on competent legal advice about the meanings of laws, advice that can only realistically be based on publicly available evidence

[58] Lawrence Solum, "Pluralism and Public Legal Reasons," *William & Mary Bill of Rights Journal* 15, no. 1 (2006): 7, 15 (quoted by Alexander and Sherwin, *Demystifying Legal Reasoning*, 215 (emphases added)).

[59] Kay, "Original Intention and Public Meaning," 706, 718; Richard Kay, "Construction, Originalist Interpretation and the Complete Constitution," *University of Pennsylvania Journal of Constitutional Law* 19, no. 4 (2017): 1, 15.

[60] Alexander and Sherwin, *Demystifying Legal Reasoning*, 216; Alexander, "Simple-Minded Originalism," 90; Alexander, "Constitutional Theories," 640.

[61] Alexander and Sherwin, *Demystifying Legal Reasoning*, 216; Alexander, "Simple-Minded Originalism," 90–91.

of legislative intention. Very important expectations and arrangements may be based on that advice; if they are later upset due to previously inaccessible or very obscure evidence of the lawmakers' communicative intentions, then surely unfairness becomes a concern. Alexander replies that the application of any interpretive theory can lead to mistakes and upset expectations, and adds: "Detrimental reliance on erroneous interpretations is a problem, but it is not solved by denying that erroneous interpretations are erroneous."[62] But that begs the question by assuming that SI is correct, so that any interpretation that departs from its conclusions is a mistake.

Alexander claims that PMO was developed partly to avoid the difficulty of showing how collective intentions are possible.[63] If so, he is right to point out that PMO cannot avoid that difficulty, because the original audience would also have been seeking the lawmakers' collective intentions.[64] As noted at the end of Section 10.5.1, objective originalism assumes the existence of subjective intentions, and therefore inherits the philosophical difficulties of explaining how a multimember lawmaker can have them.

10.6.2 *Arguments against OI and PMO*

10.6.2.1 Authority

Kay objects that PMO "severs the connection between the Constitution's rules and the authority that makes us care about those rules in the first place"; in America, "[t]he Constitution is binding because it is the expression of the will of 'the people.'"[65] But as we have seen, a lawmaker has authority to impose its will only through the laws it makes; only those laws, and what they express and imply, and not the lawmaker's unexpressed will, inherit its authority.[66] This is just as true of "the people." According to OI, what a law expresses or implies is informed by textual and contextual evidence of the lawmaker's will that was readily accessible to its intended audience, but not by esoteric evidence of its will. Kay's objection may be effective against a narrow textualist version of OPM, which excludes most evidence of the lawmaker's will, but it does not count against OPM as a form of OI.

62 Alexander, "Simple-Minded Originalism," 90–91.

63 Alexander, "Constitutional Theories," 639.

64 Alexander, "Constitutional Theories," 641; Alexander, "Simple-Minded Originalism," 91; Larry Alexander, "Legal Positivism and Originalist Interpretation," San Diego Legal Studies Paper No. 15-200 (November 8, 2015), https://papers.ssrn.com/sol3/Papers.cfm?abstract_id=2691740, 7–8.

65 Kay, "Original Intention and Public Meaning," 714, 716.

66 See Section 10.5.2.

Kay and Alexander both complain that OI and PMO infer the meaning of legal texts from "hypothetical" or "fictional" authors – constructs of interpreters rather than the actual authors – who lack any lawmaking authority.[67] As Kay puts it, PMO relies on "an artificial concept instead of on an actual historical event."[68] This is not an illuminating depiction of OI, which does endeavor to construct the intention of the actual lawmaker – but only insofar as that intention can be discerned by the intended audience from publicly available evidence. The question is: What has the actual lawmaker succeeded in communicating to its audience? OI, and versions of PMO that adopt OI, do indeed treat laws as "the work of real human beings who possessed qualities – legitimacy, intelligence, wisdom, skill, and sensitivity – that make us ready to defer to their judgment long after they have concluded their work."[69]

Alexander complains that, by interpreting laws otherwise than as their makers actually intended, OI will sometimes produce a "mindless" or "accidental" law that no one intended.[70] That is true, but it will be a consequence of the lawmakers' mistake – their accident. Also, OI is unlikely to adopt an absurd meaning because, as Alexander has observed, absurdity is a good, albeit defeasible, reason to assume that such a meaning could not have been intended.[71]

10.6.2.2 Arbitrariness, Indeterminacy, and Multiple Meanings

Critics of OI object that different members of an audience might reasonably attribute different meanings to an utterance due to differences in their access to relevant contextual information. If each of their interpretations is reasonable, given the contextual information available to them, then, according to OI, the utterance must have more than one meaning, each of them equally correct. Steven Knapp and Walter Benn Michaels object that, if so, we are "left without any way of understanding what people are up to when they think they are disagreeing about what a text means." OI therefore:

> misses the main point of intentionalism: we can only make sense of what people are doing when they disagree with each other about the meaning of a text if we suppose that they regard the text as meaning what its author actually (and not just apparently) intended.[72]

[67] Alexander, "Simple-Minded Originalism," 89, 91n10; Alexander, "Telepathic Law," 144; Kay, "Original Intention and Public Meaning," 718.

[68] Ibid., 725.

[69] Ibid., 726.

[70] Alexander, "Legal Positivism and Originalist Interpretation," 8.

[71] Alexander and Sherwin, *Demystifying Legal Reasoning*, 168.

[72] Steven Knapp and Walter B. Michaels, "Not a Matter of Interpretation," *San Diego Law Review* 42, no. 2 (2005): 651, 664.

But in these rare cases, unless the speaker or author was deliberately sowing confusion, she must have been mistaken about the contextual information available to all the members of her intended audience. Whatever she intended to communicate, she failed to do so with respect to some of them and, instead, communicated something else. The meaning she intended to communicate – her meaning – is something they can sensibly disagree about, and they are all attempting to infer it partly from the contextual information readily available to them. But if they do not have access to the same contextual information, her utterance will have different meanings. If this is a bullet – and note that SI must also accommodate multiple meanings if an author intends an utterance to have them – then OI must bite it.

Alexander and Kay both argue that in the case of laws, there is no nonarbitrary way of identifying a representative member of the intended audience.[73] "Each member of the public would differ, even if only slightly, in terms of their linguistic facility, their understanding of the general purposes motivating the language of [the law], their familiarity with the debates in Congress ... and so on."[74] Moreover, which of these differently situated and equipped people are selected will determine which of many different possible meanings will be chosen. Interpreters will be able to impose the meaning they prefer on normative grounds simply by selecting "a suitable hypothetical reader."[75]

This seems to me an exaggeration. There are at least two reasons to ask what a well-informed, intelligent, and competent lawyer at the time of enactment would have understood the law to communicate. First, statutory and even constitutional provisions sometimes have technical legal meanings fixed by prior laws, judicial decisions, or conventional legal understandings. Only lawyers are equipped to identify which words have technical legal meanings. The courts have therefore often treated lawyers as the lawmakers' intended audience, or at least laypeople only through the medium of professional legal advice. "Public meaning" should be understood accordingly. Secondly, this is the most charitable test for the actual author – the lawmaker – because well-informed, intelligent, and competent lawyers are much more likely than ill-informed or unintelligent laypeople to discern the lawmaker's intended meaning. But there can be no guarantee: The lawmaker may have erred either in choosing its words, or in anticipating what contextual information will be available to lawyers.[76]

73 Alexander, "Constitutional Theories," 639; Alexander, "Simple-Minded Originalism," 89n6; Alexander and Prakash, "Is That English You're Speaking?" 976; Alexander and Sherwin, *Demystifying Legal Reasoning*, 210; Kay, "Original Intention and Public Meaning," 721–22.

74 Alexander, "Simple-Minded Originalism," 89n6.

75 Kay, "Original Intention and Public Meaning," 723.

76 Compare Alexander and Sherwin, *Demystifying Legal Reasoning*, 217.

Alexander and Kay also object that PMO may generate too many alternative possible meanings.[77] This is because when evidence of actual intention is restricted, a higher number of ambiguities and other indeterminacies are likely to remain unresolved, leaving more than one possible meaning available, with no discernible authorial intention able to determine which one is right.[78] This may be true, but adherents of OI are not altogether disabled from enquiring into the actual subjective intention of the lawmaker. If interpretation leaves indeterminacies unresolved, interpreters must then shift into what Solum calls the "construction zone," and choose which of the alternative possible meanings should be preferred.[79] There is no reason why, at that stage, interpreters could not take into account extra evidence of authorial intention that was excluded at the interpretation stage. Doing so might help explain aspects of the law that would otherwise remain puzzling, and suggest a sensible and attractive construction. Admittedly, interpreters (or rather, "constructors") would not be bound to do this, but neither would they be precluded from doing so.[80] The criticism must therefore be that interpreters are left with more discretion to prefer an unintended meaning.[81] But since an intention that the lawmaker failed to communicate lacks legal authority, that discretion is inescapable – even if in some cases it is used judiciously to identify and apply an uncommunicated intention.

10.6.2.3 "Mistakes"

Alexander asserts that if there is a difference between what the author actually intended to communicate, and what the audience reasonably understands the author to have intended, then the audience is mistaken about the meaning of the text, and its mistake should not prevail over the intended meaning.[82] "[W]hy have legislators," he asks, "if we are going to ignore their enacted norms and substitute instead norms that a hypothetical person would have mistakenly thought the legislators enacted?"[83]

77 Ibid., 201–11; Kay, "Original Intention and Public Meaning," 720.

78 Alexander and Sherwin, *Demystifying Legal Reasoning*, 211n11; Kay, "Original Intention and Public Meaning," 719–20, 721; Kay, "Construction, Originalist Interpretation," 17.

79 Lawrence Solum, "The Interpretation-Construction Distinction," *Constitutional Commentary* 27, no. 1 (2010): 95.

80 But doing so routinely would amount to adopting OI.

81 See Kay, "Construction, Originalist Interpretation." He denies that interpretive discretion is ever required in the case of the American Constitution; ibid., 18–22, esp. 19, 22n111. Alexander is more amendable to interpreters acting creatively when laws have indeterminate meanings: see, e.g., Alexander and Sherwin, *The Rule of Rules*, 119–20.

82 Alexander and Sherwin, *Demystifying Legal Reasoning*, 216; see also Kay, "Original Intention and Public Meaning," 713.

83 Alexander, "Originalism, the Why and the What," 539, 541.

This criticism seems inconsistent with his concession – previously noted – that communities should "probably" have special rules of form restricting the evidence of legislative intention that may be taken into account, in order to ensure that the meanings of laws are publicly accessible.[84] In addition, the criticism begs the question in favor of SI. If OI is right, and the audience has exercised due diligence in seeking the author's intended meaning, it has not made any mistake. It has correctly discerned the meaning that the author communicated to it. It is the author, not the audience, who has made a mistake by not successfully communicating what it intended to communicate.

Kay, like Alexander, wonders "why interpreters should prefer the public meaning, which, by hypothesis, we believe the constitution-makers did not intend."[85] He discusses scriveners' errors as one example. "In this case, no one seems to think it proper to apply the apparent but unintended mistake."[86] That is true, but only in cases where both the mistake and the intended meaning are obvious. If not, Anglo-American courts do not allow themselves to correct the mistake.[87] The requirement of "obviousness" brings the correction within the scope of OI, since intelligent and competent lawyers would identify obvious errors and advise their clients accordingly.

Alexander also argues that, because members of the intended audience would seek the lawmaker's intended meaning, they would prefer that meaning to prevail over any "mistake" they may have made.[88] I doubt it. As previously observed, when people are told that they have misunderstood someone's utterance, they often defend themselves by replying: "I now realize what she meant to say, but that's not what she did say."[89] And they often rightly insist – for reasons of fairness that are particularly pertinent to law – that the speaker be held to what he said, even if he did not intend to say it.

A related criticism is that PMO, despite aiming to avoid common objections to SI, reintroduces subjective legislative intent through the back door.[90] Since the representative audience member will seek evidence of authorial intention, why not go straight to the source?[91] PMO is therefore "merely an abstraction that filters authorial intention."[92] OI would reply that the "filter" is essential to our reliance on

84 See the last paragraph of Section 10.5.2.

85 Kay, "Original Intention and Public Meaning," 713.

86 Ibid., 713.

87 See Antonin Scalia and Bryan A. Garner, *Reading Law: The Interpretation of Legal Texts* (St Paul: Thomson/West, 2012), 237–38.

88 Alexander and Sherwin, *Demystifying Legal Reasoning*, 216; Alexander, "Constitutional Theories," 640.

89 Goldsworthy, "Moderate versus Strong Intentionalism," 677; see also Berman, "Originalism is Bunk," 44–46, 52.

90 Alexander and Sherwin, *Demystifying Legal Reasoning*, 208.

91 Alexander, "Legal Positivism and Originalist Interpretation," 7.

92 Alexander and Sherwin, *Demystifying Legal Reasoning*, 208–9.

communicative meanings being essentially public rather than private, which in the legal context is essential to the rule of law.

10.7 IS THE CHOICE BETWEEN SI AND OI OF PRACTICAL SIGNIFICANCE?

Kay suggests that, in practice, application of SI and PMO (and, by extrapolation, OI) will usually reach the same result.[93] This is partly because their interpretive methodologies are very similar.

> Seeking that shared meaning [of lawmakers] does not require [SI] combing through the speeches, correspondence, and diaries of each member of every necessary majority ... [I]t calls for an investigation almost identical to that described by most proponents of public meaning. Mainly, we know someone's intended meaning by examining the typical meaning attached to the words they used.[94]

It is also due to the care that lawmakers (or at least constitution-makers) usually take in their attempt to craft clear laws; Kay claims, I think overoptimistically, that "lawmaking bodies rarely speak casually or impetuously"[95] and make mistakes in expression "only in exceptional circumstances."[96]

There is a legitimate question as to whether the choice between SI and OI makes enough practical difference for the debate between them to be worthwhile. I believe it does. If it did not, why would judges so often repudiate the search for "subjective" intentions and claim, instead, to be seeking some kind of "objective" intention? Moreover, practical matters such as the admissibility of legislative history may turn partly on this choice. But this is not the occasion to investigate the practical importance of the choice.[97]

93 Kay, "Original Intention and Public Meaning," 712.
94 Ibid., 708, 714, 720.
95 Ibid., 712.
96 Ibid., 712.
97 I thank Rick Kay for comments and apologize for having insufficient space to respond adequately to them.

11

Simple-Minded Originalism? Simply Wrong!

Lawrence B. Solum

11.1 INTRODUCTION

In "Simple-Minded Originalism,"[1] Larry Alexander offers an elegant version of originalism that implicitly relies on two simple propositions. I will articulate these propositions in language different from Alexander's, but I believe that the conceptual content of my version is very close (or identical) to propositions that he would be willing to endorse explicitly:

Proposition One: Meaning is essentially intentional. For a text to have actual meaning (in the sense of communicative content), that meaning must be the meaning that the author intended to communicate to the readers of the text.

Proposition Two: Constitutional legitimacy requires a legitimate author. For a text to have legitimate authority, the meaning of the text must have been produced by the author vested with legitimate authority.

These two propositions are the core of what Alexander calls "Simple-Minded Originalism" (which I shall abbreviate as SMO). The actual meaning of the constitutional text must be the meaning that the authors (framers or ratifiers) intended to communicate: There may be other meanings, but they would be counterfactual and not actual.[2] The only legitimate content of the constitutional text is content that was

[1] Larry Alexander, "Simple-Minded Originalism," in *The Challenge of Originalism*, ed. Grant Huscroft and Bradley W. Miller (Cambridge: Cambridge University Press, 2011), 87. Where the phrase "Simple-Minded Originalism" is enclosed in quotation marks (as in the text accompanying this footnote) or abbreviated as SMO, it refers to Alexander's article. Where it is capitalized without quotation marks, it refers to Alexander's theory. Similarly, phrases like the "Fixation Thesis" and "Public Meaning Originalism" (abbreviated as PMO) are capitalized to indicate they are used as proper nouns that name the specific version of the idea or theory as defined in this essay.

[2] The word "actual" is being used in the sense associated with possible worlds semantics. An actual meaning is one that exists in this world – the world that is actual as opposed to merely possible.

produced by the legitimate authors. Given these two propositions, it would seem to follow that constitutional practice ought to be found by the original meaning of the constitutional text – that is, the actual meaning created by the authors of the text.

In this essay, I will show that both of Alexander's premises are false and that if they were true they would create an irresolvable dilemma for original intentions originalism. Either the constitutional text is meaningless but legitimate, or the text is meaningful but illegitimate. Alexander can escape the dilemma via the notion of second-order communicative intentions, but if Alexander takes this path, he will find that his arguments provide grounds for rejecting original intentions originalism and support for its most important rival, Public Meaning Originalism (PMO).

Here is the roadmap. Section 11.2 situates simple-minded originalism in the landscape of contemporary constitutional theory. Section 11.3 lays bare the fallacy that underlies Alexander's first premise: Intentions are essential for meaning, but this does not entail the conclusion that the meaning of a text must be the meaning the author intended to communicate. Section 11.4 examines Proposition Two and shows that it does not establish the legitimacy of original intentions as the source of constitutional law. Section 11.5 examines Alexander's possible resort to second-order intentions and demonstrates that this "escape hatch" leads to an originalism that emphasizes public meaning. Section 11.6 concludes.

11.2 SITUATING SIMPLE-MINDED ORIGINALISM

Before saying more about Alexander's two propositions, SMO can be situated in the context of contemporary constitutional theory. Originalism is best understood as a family of constitutional theories. Almost all originalists agree on two ideas:

The Fixation Thesis – The linguistic meaning or communicative content of the constitutional text is fixed at the time each provision is framed and ratified.[3]

The Constraint Principle – Constitutional practice, including the decision of constitutional cases and the judicial articulation of constitutional doctrines, should be constrained by the original meaning of the constitutional text.[4]

The meaning of the constitutional text is fixed, and that fixed meaning is binding on constitutional actors, including judges, presidents and other executive officials, and members of legislative bodies. SMO is a member of the originalist family of constitutional theory. SMO affirms the Fixation Thesis because the meaning that

3 Lawrence B. Solum, "The Fixation Thesis: The Original Meaning of the Constitutional Text," *Notre Dame Law Review* 91, no. 1 (2015).

4 Lawrence B. Solum, "The Constraint Principle: Original Meaning and Constitutional Practice" (unpublished manuscript, Draft 71, dated March 16, 2017), https://papers.ssrn.com/sol3/papers.cfm?abstract_id=2940215.

an author intended to convey by a text is fixed when the text is drafted by the author; Proposition One entails fixation of meaning. SMO affirms the Constraint Principle because it claims that legitimacy requires adherence to the fixed meaning created by an author with legitimate authority; although Proposition Two, by itself, does not entail constraint, it would entail constraint when combined with other plausible propositions that justify the claim that constitutional practice should be guided by a constitution with legitimate authority.

Although originalists agree on fixation and constraint, they disagree on other matters. One disagreement concerns the nature of original meaning. The range of views on this question include the following:

Public Meaning Originalism – The original meaning of the constitutional text is the meaning that the text had for "We the People," the citizens who constituted the United States.[5]

Original Intentions Originalism – The original meaning of the constitutional text is the meaning that the framers intended to convey.

Framers' Understandings Originalism – The original meaning of the constitutional text is the meaning conveyed to the ratifiers of each provision.

Original Methods Originalism – The original meaning of the constitutional text is the meaning produced by application of the original methods of constitutional interpretation and construction to the text.[6]

Original Law Originalism – The law in effect at the time the Constitution was ratified is legally binding unless it was changed by methods authorized by the original law.[7]

SMO is either a version of Original Intentions Originalism or a closely related view. If the framers are the authors of the constitutional text, then SMO is a framers' intent theory, but if some other individual or group is the author (e.g., the individual drafter of a provision or the ratifiers), then SMO is a version of drafter's intent originalism or ratifiers originalism.

Although different versions of originalism may produce different outcomes at the margins, it seems likely that they will converge when applied to most of the constitutional text. Because the framers intended to communicate to the public and the

5 Public meaning originalists include Justice Antonin Scalia, Randy Barnett, and myself. See Antonin Scalia, *A Matter of Interpretation: Federal Courts and the Law*, ed. Amy Gutmann (Princeton: Princeton University Press, 1997), 47; Randy E. Barnett, *Restoring the Lost Constitution* (Princeton: Princeton University Press, revised ed. 2014); Solum, "The Fixation Thesis."

6 John McGinnis and Michael Rappaport, "Original Methods Originalism: A New Theory of Interpretation and the Case against Construction," *Northwestern University Law Review* 103, no. 2 (2009): 751.

7 See William Baude, "Is Originalism Our Law?," *Columbia Law Review* 115, no. 3 (2015): 2349.

ratifiers were members of the public, the first three forms of originalism are likely to produce identical results except in cases where there was a failure of constitutional communication. The versions of originalism that focus on original methods and original law may diverge more substantially, because they do not ground their theory of meaning on the idea that the constitutional text was intended to be understood by "We the People."[8]

Because of the differences between and among originalists, we can distinguish between two modes of originalist theory and practice. The first mode is "sectarian": Sectarian originalism adopts a particular version of originalism, such as PMO or one of its rivals. The second mode is "ecumenical": Ecumenical originalism aims to develop theories and engage in practice that is neutral on the questions about which originalists disagree. The arguments that Alexander advances in favor of SMO in his essay "Simple-Minded Originalism" are sectarian; they argue for SMO and against its rivals. Likewise, the arguments advanced in this essay are sectarian in nature; they support PMO and undermine SMO and related forms of original intentions originalism.

Many contemporary originalists embrace the interpretation-construction distinction,[9] which can be stated as follows:

Interpretation – Constitutional interpretation is the activity that discovers the communicative content of the constitutional text.

Construction – Constitutional construction is the activity that determines the legal effect of the constitutional text, including the decision of constitutional cases and the legal content of constitutional doctrines.

Although the interpretation-construction distinction can and should be embraced by all originalists, some originalists may prefer to use the terms "interpretation" and "construction" synonymously, using other vocabulary to describe the difference between the discovery of linguistic meaning and implementation of that meaning, for example, via the decision of cases or the articulation of constitutional rules.

[8] The relationship between public meaning originalism and original methods requires extended discussion, but the divergence between these approaches should not be exaggerated. Public meaning originalism recognizes that some provisions of the constitution have technical legal meanings; for this reason, the cases where original methods and original law provide the most distinctive meanings can be incorporated via the notion of a publicly accessible meaning and the division of linguistic labor. Original methods originalists can argue that the public would have understood that the constitutional text was to be given its legal meaning, and hence that the legal meaning is the public meaning in a derivative sense: the public do not directly understand the constitutional text and are not the readers who are intended to comprehend the text.

[9] Lawrence Solum, "The Interpretation-Construction Distinction," *Constitutional Commentary* 27, no. 1 (2010): 95.

Alexander does not take a position on the interpretation-construction distinction in "Simple-Minded Originalism."

Originalists differ on other questions, including the extent to which the constitutional text is underdeterminate. Some originalists believe that at least some provisions of the constitutional text create substantial "construction zones," because these provisions are vague or open textured.[10] Other originalists believe that the text is almost fully determinate; such determinacy might result from application of the original methods of constitutional interpretation and construction, or it might result from the application of default rules, for example, a rule that requires deference to democratic institutions when the text is not clear. Alexander takes no stand on the degree of underdeterminacy of the constitutional text. Presumably, his position is that the answer to this question depends on the authorial intentions that give meaning to particular constitutional provisions.

If the constitutional text is underdeterminate, then constitutional construction will require some method that goes beyond direct translation of the communicative content of the constitutional text into the legal content of constitutional doctrine. Almost all originalists agree that constitutional construction should follow the determinate meaning of the constitutional text. But if the text is underdeterminate, a question arises as to what should be done within the area of underdeterminacy (or "construction zone") created by vague or open-textured communicative content. For example, originalists might adopt a default rule of deference to democratic institutions;[11] another method of construction would look to the original purpose of the vague or open-textured provision and adopt the construction that is consistent with the letter and best realizes the spirit of the constitution.[12] SMO does not address the question as to how constitutional construction should proceed when the meaning of the constitutional text underdetermines the shape of constitutional doctrine.

Alexander's version of originalism is best characterized as a partial or incomplete constitutional theory. It addresses some of the questions that a complete version of originalism must answer, but it takes no stand on others. Nonetheless, it is a version of originalism, because it endorses fixation and constraint.

[10] Underdetermination, and hence construction zones, can also result from situations in which the text is irreducibly ambiguous or if the text has gaps or contradictions. "Irreducible ambiguity" refers to situations in which ambiguity is not resolved by context.

[11] This possibility is discussed in Lawrence Solum, "Originalism and Constitutional Construction," *Fordham Law Review* 82 (2013): 511.

[12] For an example of this approach, see Randy E. Barnett and Evan D. Bernick, "The Letter and the Spirit: The Judicial Duty of Good-Faith Constitutional Construction" (unpublished manuscript, 2017), https://papers.ssrn.com/sol3/papers.cfm?abstract_id=2913223.

11.3 THE ROLE OF AUTHOR'S INTENTIONS IN THE PRODUCTION OF MEANING

Recall that Proposition One asserts that authorial intention is essential to meaning. Here is how Alexander states a similar idea in "Simple-Minded Originalism":

> Suppose someone shows you a piece of paper with marks on it and tells you that the paper contains normative propositions (instructions, do's and don'ts). He asks you to tell him what those normative propositions are (they are to govern him, not you). What would you do?
>
> First of all, you would not think of paper and marks as by themselves constituting normative propositions. If you knew that the paper fell off a paper truck, and that the marks were made by blowing dirt and bird droppings – that is, that no *author communicating norms* had been involved in its production – then you would tell your interlocutor that no normative propositions were to be found on the paper. No author communicating, no norms. (God would count as a possible author if one thought he might be attempting to communicate through the blowing dirt and bird droppings.)
>
> On the other hand, if you believed that the marks were in fact made by some person or persons – possibly including God – intending to communicate norms, then you would naturally ask the following: Who were the authors, in what circumstances and with what purposes were they communicating the norms, and what language were they using to do so –English, Esperanto, some idiosyncratic idiolect, a code, and so on?[13]

The argument here is that intentions are required for the production of meaning. For a text to be meaningful, the causal processes that produced the text must include intentions. Without any intention to create meaning, the marks on a piece of paper would not actually be a text at all – even if the shape of the marks was identical to marks that would have had meaning if they had been used intentionally by an author to convey meaning.

Alexander recognizes a possible rejoinder to this argument. He continues:

> Now at this point, someone will surely point out to the simple-minded originalist – that would be me – that there are other "meanings" of a text's meaning besides the intended meaning of its author. There is its meaning in, say, standard English (its Gricean "utterance meaning"). There is its "original public meaning." And so on.
>
> Well, yes and no. Yes, in that I don't deny one can intelligibly speak of utterance meanings in a given language or of original public meanings. But no, in that in

[13] Alexander, "Simple-Minded Originalism," 97–98 (emphasis in original).

> doing so, one has not so much departed from the original, authorially intended meaning as merely substituted hypothetical authors for the real ones.
>
> Take, for example, the so-called textualist, who eschews seeking authorially intended meanings in favor of looking to standard utterance meanings. The textualist is hypothesizing authors who speak in a given language (as of a particular date and perhaps a particular place) – how would we know what standard meanings to look to if we did not know the language our authors were using? – and who speak it perfectly. (We would also have to hypothesize that when there is more than one definition of a word, the hypothesized authors always choose, say, the first definition given – which might also entail that we hypothesize their dictionary of choice when there are warring dictionaries.) Moreover, a really pure textualist would never look to the circumstances and purposes of the actual authors in resolving ambiguities, for that would be deferring to authorially intended meanings and thus raise the question, why not defer to them entirely?[14]

At this point, Alexander has made a conceptual error. I will explain the error in the following paragraphs, but the gist of my argument is that Alexander has moved illicitly from a true premise (that intention must play a role in the production of meaning) to a false conclusion (that meaning is reducible to intention).

We can unpack Alexander's error by taking a step back and putting his points in the context of Paul Grice's distinction between speaker's (or utterer's) meaning and sentence meaning. Because we are discussing written texts, I will substitute author for speaker in Grice's formulation of speaker's meaning:[15]

> *Author's Meaning* – The author's meaning of a text is the meaning the author intended to convey to the reader via the reader's recognition of the author's communicative intention.

Alexander's understanding of meaning is substantially the same as Grice's notion of author's meaning. How do authors convey such meanings in written texts? In the usual case, when an author uses a natural written language to convey meaning to a reader, the author will rely on the conventional semantic meanings of the words and phrases and similar conventions that govern syntax and punctuation. Authors also rely on shared context (what the author knows that the reader knows about context) for disambiguation and enrichment of the semantic (or literal) meaning of what the author has written.

Grice also put forward the notion of *sentence meaning*.[16] I will use a different formulation of what I believe to be the core of Grice's idea:

[14] Ibid., 98–99.

[15] Paul Grice, *Studies in the Way of Words* (Cambridge, MA: Harvard University Press 1989), 24–26.

[16] H.P. (Paul) Grice, "Utterer's Meaning, Sentence-Meaning, and Word-Meaning," *Foundations of Language* 4, no. 3 (1968): 225.

> *Sentence Meaning* – The sentence meaning of a written text is the conventional semantic meaning of the words and phrases as structured by the conventions of syntax and punctuation.

Sentence meaning is acontextual (or "timeless," as Grice put it). Whereas, the author's meaning of a text is the meaning the author intended the audience to grasp based on the audience's recognition of the author's communicative intentions in context, the sentence meaning of the text is the meaning of the words without reference to context and, therefore, without consideration of the communicative intentions of the author. Lawyers tend to use the phrase "literal meaning" to refer to what I am calling "conventional semantic meaning" and Grice called "sentence meaning."

The existence of conventional semantic meanings is entirely consistent with the notion that intentions must play a role in the production of meaning. Words acquire conventional semantic meanings via a complex process of interaction between individual speakers (and authors) and their audiences (and readers). Intentional action by individual speakers (or authors) is necessary to get conventional semantic meanings going, but once such a meaning is established, it is not reducible to the communicative intentions of individual speakers (or authors). Conventional semantic meanings are produced by regularities of usage and supporting linguistic behavior. When an individual speaker deviates from the convention, they may be corrected. For example, I made it into my thirties without realizing that "averse" and "adverse" were two different words. I was corrected by my students when I used the phrase "risk adversion" instead of "risk aversion" when discussing law and economics in class. My use was mistaken. Of course, if a mistake becomes the dominant usage, then the conventional semantic meaning of a word can change: Thus, "tortuous" (originally "twisty") may now have acquired the same meaning as "torturous" (inflicting torture). If sufficient numbers of competent speakers of a natural language accept and endorse the change in meaning, it becomes conventional.

The existence of conventional semantic meanings is more than just consistent with the idea of author's meaning; conventional semantic meanings are required for speaker's meanings to function as they do. It may well be possible for an individual author to create their own language, introducing vocabulary through ostensive definition and stipulation. Esperanto and other invented languages are not quite the same, as they are created using natural languages to define terms – a substantial shortcut. But the invention of a new language would be a very cumbersome way to communicate, and in practice it would severely limit the richness and range of linguistically mediated communication. Imagine having to create Esperanto (without relying on any natural language for definitions) as a step in the process of drafting a

Constitution. Conventional semantic meanings enable authors to form communicative intentions. Without the resource provided by a preexisting vocabulary, constitutional communication would be very difficult and perhaps impossible.

Author's meaning frequently relies on conventional semantic meanings, but this is not always the case. An author can coin a new word, as Paul Brest did when he coined the word "originalism."[17] Or an existing word can be repurposed, creating a "modulation" – a new (and usually related or more precise) meaning for an old word.[18] And, of course, authors make mistakes about conventional semantic meaning. But these exceptions are not inconsistent with the fact that author's meaning usually depends on the use of conventional semantic meanings. Authors enter a linguistic world in which conventional semantic meanings already exist and are available for their use.

The claim that conventional semantic meanings are not reducible to the communicative intentions of authors should be clarified. We can distinguish among relationships between conventional semantic meaning and communicative intentions, including *identity*, *reduction*, *dependence*, *supervenience*, and *grounding*. Conventional semantic meanings are neither identical to nor reducible to individual communicative intentions, because patterns and norms of usage, which only emerge at the social level, are what make them conventional. Conventional semantic meanings are not independent of communicative intentions, because they cannot come into being without communicative intentions, and patterns of communicative intentions are required for conventionality. Conventional semantic meanings do not supervene on communicative intentions, because it is at least possible that the same pattern of communicative intent, when accompanied by two different sets of usage norms (e.g., dispositions to correct usage), would produce two different conventional semantic meanings. For example, "tortuous" may not have the conventional semantic meaning as "torturous" if a significant deviant usage produces correction, but the same quantity of deviant usage might not be sufficient to establish the new meaning if it produces acceptance and endorsement. Depending on one's theory of what *grounding* is,[19] conventional semantic meanings may be grounded on communicative intentions.

In sum, conventional semantic meanings are not identical with or reducible to individual communicative intentions, nor are they supervenient on such meanings. But conventional semantic meanings are not independent of individual communicative intentions and can be said to be grounded on such intentions.

[17] Paul Brest, "The Misconceived Quest for the Original Understanding," *Boston University Law Review* 60, no. 2 (1980): 204.

[18] Francois Recanati, *Literal Meaning* (Cambridge: Cambridge University Press, 2003), 131.

[19] "Grounding" is a complex topic, and for the purposes of this chapter, I am bracketing the question as to what relationship the word "grounding" refers.

Recall the formulation of what I call Alexander's "Proposition One":

Proposition One: Meaning is essentially intentional. For a text to have actual meaning (in the sense of communicative content), that meaning must be the meaning that the author intended to communicate to the readers of the text.

Sentence meanings are meanings in the sense that is relevant here. The conventional semantic meaning of a text yields content. We refer to this content when we say that someone did not actually say what they meant. Alexander's arguments demonstrate that the meaning (in the sense of linguistic meaning or communicative content) is dependent on individual communicative intentions, but Proposition One says more than this. It asserts that all meaning is individual communicative content – that is, that meaning reduces to communicative content – but that conclusion does not follow from his argument.

The crux of Alexander's argument is in the following sentence (from a passage quoted in full above):

> I don't deny one can intelligibly speak of utterance meanings in a given language or of original public meanings. But no, in that in doing so, one has not so much departed from original authorially intended meaning as merely substituted hypothetical authors for the real ones.

As I understand this argument, the work is being done by the word "hypothetical." Alexander is implicitly distinguishing between the *actual* meaning of a constitutional provision and a *counterfactual* (hypothetical or fictive) meaning. The actual meaning is the meaning yielded by the communicative intentions of the author. Alexander asserts that the conventional semantic meaning of the same text is counterfactual: It exists in some possible world in which the constitutional provision was produced by an author whose communicative intentions coincide with the conventional semantic meaning of the provision, but it is not the meaning of the provision in the actual world. And it follows that it is only a *possible* meaning and not *the* true meaning of the text.

The problem with this argument is that conventional semantic meanings are part of the actual world. They are produced by the patterns of usage that give rise to conventional semantic meanings. These linguistic events are not hypothetical, counterfactual, or fictive. They actually happened. The conventional semantic meanings to which they give rise are not located in some nonactual possible world; they are part of the actual world. Conventional semantic meanings are actual meanings. The actual conventional semantic meaning of a writing is no less actual because it is not the author's meaning.

There is one additional point that needs to be made before we leave our discussion of Alexander's Proposition One. So far, I have been discussing conventional semantic meanings ("literal meanings" or "sentence meanings") and not "original public meaning" or "plain meaning." The original public meaning of a constitutional provision is neither its sentence meaning nor its author's meaning.

Why does public meaning differ from author's meaning and sentence meaning? The public meaning of a constitutional provision is the meaning that the provision had for the public at the time the provision was framed and ratified. The public meaning of a constitutional provision is not acontextual; it takes the public context of constitutional communication into account. To the extent that the public context adds pragmatic enrichment or contextual disambiguation, the public meaning of the constitutional text will vary from the literal meaning (sentence meaning or conventional semantic meaning). But the public meaning of the constitutional text is not necessarily the author's meaning either. The public context of constitutional communication sometimes excludes information that is relevant to the author's meaning; for example, the public context of constitutional communication in the case of the constitutional text drafted in 1787 did not include the record of deliberation at the Philadelphia Convention. For that reason, the public meaning of the constitutional text may not be identical to the author's meaning.

Although author's meaning and public meaning may differ, there are good reasons to believe that they will converge most (or almost all) of the time. Assuming that the drafters of the constitutional text intended to communicate to the public, they had very good reasons to rely on conventional semantic meanings, standard grammar and punctuation, and the public context of constitutional communication. It would be very odd indeed for the authors of a constitutional text to say to themselves, "We will use this word in an idiosyncratic way, even though our audience will have no way to access this peculiar meaning." If the authors of a constitutional text intend to communicate to the public, their success depends on their use of public meanings and the publicly available context of constitutional communication. Given that most constitutional provisions are drafted with care by competent speakers of English (in the case of the United States Constitution), we would expect that the communicative intentions of the authors and the public meaning of the text will converge.

Although the author's meaning of the constitutional text and the public meaning can be expected to converge most (or almost all) of the time, there are situations where the two meanings can diverge. For example, it is possible that the drafters of a given provision made a linguistic mistake – because they had a false belief about the conventional semantic meaning of a word or phrase. Because constitutional drafting usually involves many stages with input from many readers of draft language, it is unlikely that many such mistakes will occur, but it is possible. For example, it is at least possible that conversations among those involved in the drafting process will produce an "echo chamber effect," where a linguistic mistake by a drafter changes the linguistic perceptions of others involved in the drafting process and the linguistic mistake goes unnoticed. It is also possible that the drafters of a constitutional provision would engage in deliberately deceptive communication, attempting to "pull a fast one" by using language that appears to mean one thing on first impression and casual inspection, but yields a different meaning when subject to careful parsing.

Alexander recognizes these points when he writes,

> It is incoherent for one to say, "When I said A, I intended meaning X, but I intended that my audience believe that I intended meaning Y." An intended meaning of an utterance is the uptake the speaker intends in his audience. Secret meanings of the type the OPM proponent fears don't exist.[20]

When there is a divergence between author's meaning and public meaning, a choice must be made. Using the language of the interpretation-construction distinction, we could put the choice this way. When interpretation yields two different meanings (author's meaning that varies from public meaning), constitutional construction requires that we make a choice. Both meanings are actual meanings, but only one can be put into legal effect.[21]

If Alexander's argument for Proposition One had succeeded, there would still be a choice, but it would be between the actual meaning of the text and a fictitious meaning. Although some constitutional theorists might argue for the fictitious meaning, others might believe that it is obvious that judges have no authority to disregard the actual meaning of the constitutional text and substitute a fictitious meaning. If the choice is between two actual meanings, then (at least on the surface), it looks like some normative justification must be offered for choosing one meaning over the other – "actuality" can no longer do the work of discriminating between meanings.

11.4 AUTHORITY AND AUTHORSHIP

Alexander does have a normative justification for preferring author's meaning over public meaning. That justification is expressed in Proposition Two:

> *Proposition Two: Constitutional legitimacy requires a legitimate author.* For a text to have legitimate authority, the meaning of the text must have been produced by the author vested with legitimate authority.

[20] Alexander, "Simple-Minded Originalism," 100.

[21] I owe thanks to Greg Klass for helping me to see this point clearly. See Gregory Klass, "Interpretation and Construction in Contract Law" (May 1, 2017), 16–26. Available at SSRN: https://ssrn.com/abstract=2913228.

Alexander does not state Proposition Two in these words, but I believe that this proposition is necessary for us to make sense of the arguments that Alexander does make in passages like the following:

> I have, up to this point, attempted to make the case that if we are to attend to the normative propositions in the Constitution, we should seek the intended meanings of its actual authors (the ratifiers), not the intended meanings of any of an indefinite number of possible hypothetical authors. Why otherwise would we care about that particular document? It is decidedly odd to care about a document the markings on which were produced by actual people intending to communicate thereby some instructions to others if one is going to disregard *those* instructions in favor of seeing what the instructions would be had they been issued by hypothetical persons of various descriptions. It is not that one cannot do the latter. But it nonetheless is an enterprise the justification of which escapes me.
>
> But should we care about the norms intended by the actual authors of the Constitution? Even if I am right that caring about the document in the National Archives only makes sense if we care about the intended meaning of its actual authors, that does not itself establish that we *should* care about that document any more than we do care about the Articles of Confederation, the Constitution of the Confederate States of America, or Justinian's Code. Of course, the Constitution, in Article VI, declares itself to be the supreme law of the land, which, if true, would be a good reason to care about it and its originally intended meaning. But merely declaring itself to be the supreme law, which was what its authors intended it to be, cannot make it true that it *is* the supreme law.[22]

Proposition One has substantial intuitive appeal. Why does the communicative content of the constitutional text have authority? It seems silly to argue that the piece of paper itself is authoritative; pieces of paper are not the kind of thing that can have authority. Alexander's thought seems to be that the authority of the communicative content of the constitutional text derives from the authority of its authors.

The framers and ratifiers of a given constitutional provision have authority to promulgate the constitutional text; the authority of the communicative content of the text is derivative from their authority. The only content with legitimate authority is the content created by authors who themselves have legitimate authority to create that content. From these premises, the conclusion expressed by Proposition Two seems to follow: "For a text to have legitimate authority, the meaning of the text must have been produced by the author vested with legitimate authority."

There is, however, a puzzle about this argument for Proposition Two. Alexander's theory focuses on the authors of a text – or, to use the legal terminology, the drafters. The legitimate content of the constitutional text is that content created by a drafter

22 Alexander, "Simple-Minded Originalism," 103–4.

who has legitimate authority to draft the text. The puzzle results from the gap between the individuals who draft constitutional text and the institutions with legitimate authority to propose and ratify constitutional provisions.

This puzzling gap can be brought into clear focus by considering the analogous case of ordinary legislation. Modern statutes are almost always drafted by persons without legitimate authority. For example, many statutes are drafted by industry groups or lobbyists.[23] It is rare for members of Congress to draft statutory language and, in many cases, even staff play only a supporting role in the drafting process. Moreover, with respect to complex regulatory statutes, it is very likely that the members of Congress will not even have read the statute; in some cases, a statute may be enacted without any staff member having read the statute from start to finish – and some provisions may never have been read by any staff member. There is no sense in which the actual author of such a statute has legitimate authority.

Proposition One would require us to give effect to the content created by the communicative intentions of the authors with legitimate authority, but it may well turn out that the members of Congress did not have communicative intentions of the sort that would directly provide the actual content of the statute. Alexander's theory would seem to lead to the conclusion that the meaning of many statutes is the meaning provided by the communicative intentions of lobbyists or industry groups, but that these meanings lack legitimate authority. This would seem to lead to the conclusion that many statutes should simply be ignored. Without authority, they should not be binding on judges and other officials.

The case of the text of the United States Constitution is different. In the case of the constitutional text drafted at the Philadelphia Convention, most of the drafting work seems to have been done by Gouverneur Morris and James Wilson, in connection with their work on the Committee of Style and the Committee of Detail, respectively.[24] Neither Morris nor Wilson was authorized to create constitutional content. Indeed, the Philadelphia Convention was not authorized to create a new constitution. The relevant legitimate authorities would be the ratifying conventions, but they are not the authors of the text. The same holds for constitutional amendments. The text of amendments is drafted by individuals who lack legitimate authority to amend the constitution. State legislators arguably do have legitimate authority to ratify and hence enact constitutional amendments, but members of state legislatures are not the authors of constitutional amendments. It seems quite likely that many or most of the ratifiers of the various parts of the original constitution and its amendments did not form communicative intentions sufficiently rich and precise for Alexander's

[23] For an extended example, see Jessica Litman, *Digital Copyright* (Amherst: Prometheus Books, 2001).

[24] My understanding is based on published work by William Treanor.

purposes, and even if they did, these intentions would not be the intentions of the authors – the only intentions that Alexander admits as providing content.

Thus, Alexander's two propositions lead to the conclusion that the meaning of the constitutional text lacks legitimate authority. This is a rather large bullet to bite. Can Alexander avoid this *reductio* of his position?

11.5 SECOND-ORDER INTENTIONS

One possible escape route for Alexander appeals to what I will call "second-order intentions." Let us stipulate that a first-order communicative intention provides the communicative content of a text *directly*. Thus, in the first sentence of this paragraph, I use the name "Alexander" and my first-order communicative intention is to refer to Larry Alexander, who is a member of the law faculty of the University of San Diego and the author of "Simple-Minded Originalism." Second-order communicative intentions are intentions about intentions. Alexander might argue that persons with legitimate authority can have second-order communicative intentions that provide content based on the first-order communicative intentions of other persons who lack such authority. Thus, a member of Congress could have a second-order communicative intention to enact the meaning created by the first-order communicative intentions of the individuals who drafted a statute. The members of Congress have legitimate authority and their second-order communicative intentions provide the content indirectly by adopting the first-order communicative intentions of the staff member, lobbyist, or industry group that did the actual drafting work. Similarly, in the case of the Constitution, members of the ratifying conventions or state legislatures could have a second-order intention to enact whatever content is provided by the first-order intentions of the drafters of the provision.

Because one can have second-order intentions without knowledge of the first-order intentions of the drafter, we seem to have a solution to the problem of legitimacy created by the conjunction of Proposition One and Proposition Two. Thus, we would have a kind of delegation of the authority to create communicative content: So long as the delegation itself is authorized and legitimate, the content would be legitimate and hence the reduction discussed above is avoided.

In order to avail himself of the escape hatch provided by second-order intentions, Alexander could amend Proposition Two as follows:

> *Proposition Two: Constitutional legitimacy Rrquires a legitimate author*. For a text to have legitimate authority, the meaning of the text must have been produced by the first-order communicative intentions *or endorsed by the second-order communicative intentions* of an author vested with legitimate authority.

I do not know whether Alexander will wish to avail himself of this escape hatch, but if he does, it immediately leads to the collapse of his case against PMO.

If Alexander opens the door to second-order communicative intentions as an escape route from the *reductio* outlined above, he will also open the door to second-order intentions that take the public meaning of the constitutional text as their object. If ratifiers can intend to ratify the private first-order communicative intentions of drafters, they can intend to ratify the public meaning of the constitutional text. Even this possibility creates a serious problem for Alexander, as it would result in a serious gap in his argument. Proposition Two would now be neutral as between SMO and PMO.

But the problem for Alexander is much worse than the opening of a gap in his argument. Recall Alexander's answer to the problem of secret intentions: "An intended meaning of an utterance is the uptake the speaker intends in his audience. Secret meanings of the type the OPM proponent fears do not exist."[25] Notice that Alexander is implicitly appealing to a second-order intention here: Authors intend the reader to grasp content based on the reader's recognition of the author's communicative intention.[26] Constitutional communication is aimed at the public; the meaning that the ratifiers of a constitutional provision intend the public to grasp is necessarily the public meaning. That is, a second-order intention is built into the situation of constitutional communication, and that second-order intention points to public meaning and not to author's meaning. Alexander's argument entails the conclusion that the relevant second-order communicative intention must be to communicate to the relevant "audience" and, in the constitutional context, that audience is the public. If Alexander is right when he says that "Secret meanings … do not exist," his reason should lead him to reject SMO and endorse PMO.

Even if PMO were not entailed by Alexander's argument against secret intentions, there are independent reasons to believe that the second-order intentions of ratifiers would be focused on public meanings rather than the communicative intentions of the drafters. Ratifiers are themselves members of the public, and they stand in a similar relationship to drafters as does the public at large. Members of the ratifying conventions lacked access to records of the deliberations at the Philadelphia Convention. Given this communicative situation, what they ratified is the public meaning and not some nonpublic meaning to which they lacked epistemic access. Similarly, members of state legislatures ratify the text of constitutional amendments

[25] Alexander, "Simple-Minded Originalism," 100.

[26] Alexander is using second-order intentions because he is appealing to the Gricean understanding of communicative intentions as reflexive. Francois Recanati, "On Defining Communicative Intentions," *Mind & Language* 1, no. 3 (1986): 213.

proposed by Congress in light of those portions of the drafting record that are publicly accessible.

As a normative matter, there are good reasons to prefer public meanings over non-public meanings discovered on the basis of evidence that was not within the publicly accessible context of constitutional communication. The Constitution itself announces that it is an act of "We the People." The process of ratification of the Constitution drafted in 1787 was public in nature, with public political debate and ratifying conventions elected by voters representing the public. The public meaning of the constitutional text possesses legitimacy that is absent in the case of the non-public communicative intentions of the drafters of particular provisions.

11.6 CONCLUSION

Simple-Minded Originalism has substantial intuitive appeal rooted in an analogy between one-on-one, face-to-face communication between individuals and the complex communicative situation in which constitutional provisions are drafted by individuals, proposed to the public by one set of institutions, and ratified on behalf of the public by another set of institutions. On the one hand, the analogy is illuminating: We cannot understand constitutional communication without taking individual communicative intentions into account. On the other hand, the analogy is misleading: Constitutional interpretation and construction necessarily have a more complex structure than the simple case of one-on-one communication between individuals. Simple-Minded Originalism is simply wrong.

12

Intentions in Tension

*Frederick Schauer**

Most human actions are intentional. Sometimes, of course, people wind up doing things accidentally, negligently, mistakenly, unthinkingly, but for most people most of the time most of their actions are mostly the product of their intentions.

The fact that most human actions are produced by intentions does not entail the conclusion that those intentions are necessarily or even usually relevant in assessing the legal (or social) consequences of those actions. Oliver Wendell Holmes's dog may have been able to distinguish between being kicked and being stumbled over,[1] but I am less sure that the distinction is even always understood by *my* dog, whom I have always thought of as pretty smart. More importantly, the fact that people and, more controversially, institutions[2] have intentions says little about the contexts in which,

* I am grateful to Heidi Hurd, the University of Illinois College of Law, and the Yale Law School for organizing and sponsoring this volume and the conference that preceded it, and especially to Larry Alexander, a friend (and occasional coauthor) of long standing, whose intellectual honesty, intellectual courage, and open-mindedness embodies a model of the scholarly disposition at its best.

[1] "Even a dog distinguishes between being stumbled over and being kicked." Oliver Wendell Holmes, Jr., *The Common Law* (Boston: Little, Brown, 1881), 3. See Michael C. Dorf, "Even a Dog: A Response to Professor Fallon," *Harvard Law Review Forum* 130, no. 2 (2016): 86–94, responding to Richard H. Fallon, Jr., "Constitutionally Forbidden Legislative Intent," *Harvard Law Review* 130, no. 2 (2016): 523–89.

[2] A large and important literature addresses the question whether there can be collective intentions, and thus whether multimember groups like legislatures, appellate courts, families, and basketball teams can have intentions as groups rather than serving merely as the aggregators of the intentions of their members. Among the more prominent affirmative answers to the question are John Searle, "Collective Intentions and Actions," in *Intentions in Communication*, ed. Philip R. Cohen, Jerry Morgan, and Martha Pollack (Cambridge, MA: MIT Press, 1990), 401–15; Raimo Tuomela, "We Will Do It: An Analysis of Group-Intentions," *Philosophy and Phenomenological Research* 51, no. 2 (1991): 249. And on the other (negative) side, see, for example, Frank H. Easterbrook, "The Role of Original Intent in Statutory Construction," *Harvard Journal of Law & Public Policy* 11, no. 1 (1988): 59; Kenneth A. Shepsle, "Congress is a 'They,' Not an 'It': Legislative Intent as Oxymoron," *International Review of Law and Economics* 12, no. 2 (1992): 239. The question of the existence (or not) of group intentions is important and relevant in numerous contexts, but in this essay I will simply assume that the right answer to the question whether they exist is "yes." Alexander believes to the contrary, Larry Alexander, "Aggregating States of Mind: A Response to Fallon," San Diego Legal Studies Paper No.

and the purposes for which, those settings do or do not matter. And thus in law, as elsewhere, the question of what consequences, if any, turn on someone's or some entity's intentions is different from the question of whether those intentions exist.

In two different domains of Larry Alexander's enormously valuable and influential scholarship, intentions play a central role. In writing about freedom of speech both as a topic in political philosophy[3] and as a doctrinal topic under the positive law of the First Amendment,[4] Alexander has argued that the triggering event (and more or less the primary focus for an adjudicator) for a free speech question is government (or some other putative restricter) having intentions of a certain kind. Although governments might do all sorts of things that turn out incidentally to have the effect of restricting or inhibiting communication, only those governmental actions, Alexander has argued, that are motivated by a certain kind of governmental intent[5] will bring those actions within the purview of a free speech principle and the theories and doctrines of the First Amendment. For Alexander, making sense of freedom of speech requires that both courts and commentators put the intentions of government at the center of any inquiry.

Alexander has also made enduring contributions to the study of statutory and constitutional interpretation, and here again intentions play a vital role in his approach. Because the interpretation of law necessarily involves the interpretation of language, acts of legal interpretation presuppose some account of what language is and how it works. And for Alexander, this is an inquiry that again leads him to the centrality of intentions, and to the view, to oversimplify, that understanding language requires understanding the intentions of those who use it.[6] To interpret

17-258, https://sssrn.com/abstract=2916864, but virtually nothing that I say in this essay depends on this disagreement or on my position about the issue.

3 And here see especially Larry Alexander, *Is There a Right to Freedom of Expression?* (New York: Cambridge University Press, 2005). See also Larry Alexander, "The Misconceived Search for the Meaning of 'Speech' in Freedom of Speech," *Open Journal of Philosophy* 5, no. 1(2015): 39; Larry Alexander and Paul Horton, "The Impossibility of a Free Speech Principle," *Northwestern University Law Review* 78, no. 5 (1984): 1319.

4 In addition to articles cited below, see Larry Alexander, "Compelled Speech," *Constitutional Commentary* 23, no. 2 (2006): 147; Larry Alexander, "Low Value Speech," *Northwestern University Law Review* 83, no. 3 (1989): 547; Larry Alexander, "Banning Hate Speech and the Sticks and Stones Defense," *Constitutional Commentary* 13, no. 1 (1996): 71.

5 At least for purposes of this essay, I will ignore potentially important distinctions among the concepts of intent, purpose, and motive, and will here simply assume that each of those terms designates the kind of mental state that is Alexander's concern.

6 See Larry Alexander, "Originalism, the Why and the What," *Fordham Law Review* 82, no. 2 (2013): 539. As I note below, Alexander at times appears to believe that interpreting any language requires knowing (or hypothesizing) the intent of the speaker, and at other times he seems to adopt the more modest and more plausible position that language in general can be understood by reference to linguistic conventions and without necessary recourse to real or hypothesized intentions, but that *legal* interpretation, because of the nature of law and not because of the nature of language, requires interpretation

the language of a written legal item, therefore, whether that item be a constitution, a statute, or an administrative regulation, it is necessary, Alexander has maintained, to take account of the intentions of the entity that has written or otherwise produced[7] the language.

In what follows I will argue that Alexander is correct about the first and mistaken about the second – that he is right to take governmental intentions as vital to making sense of a free speech principle and to interpreting the First Amendment, but wrong in thinking that authorial intention is essential (or even desirable) in interpreting legal language. In what follows I will explain why I believe this to be so, and in the process offer a sketchy prolegomenon to a more comprehensive view about the relationship between law and intention more generally.

12.1 ALEXANDER ON INTENTIONS AND FREEDOM OF SPEECH

In one of Alexander's most widely-cited and justifiably influential articles, he laid the foundation for his conclusions with the premise that all or virtually all governmental actions will have some proximate or not-so-proximate effect on who can say what, and when, and how.[8] A rise in the corporate tax rate, for example, will likely decrease the amount that the *Washington Post* can publish; a decrease in the speed limit may make it more difficult for reporters to report breaking news; changes in downtown parking regulations may stifle the ability of individuals to speak in the

of the lawmaker's intent. Because I take the latter position to be more plausible (although, as shall be seen, not plausible enough), it will be the focus of my analysis and critique in this essay.

7 Interpretive intentionalists must deal with the question of exactly which (or whose) intentions matter, but I will not deal extensively with that question here. Still, the example of the United States Constitution illustrates the issue and the problem. For a constitutional amendment, say, to become law in a technical sense (putting aside the convention method of amendment), there must be approval by a two-thirds vote in each house of Congress followed by ratification by at least (now) thirty-eight (three-quarters) of the fifty states. But what, then, is the shared intention of those forty different bodies? And if, following H.L.A. Hart (*The Concept of Law*, ed. Penelope A. Bulloch, Joseph Raz, and Leslie Green (Oxford: Clarendon Press, 3rd ed., 2012)) and perhaps Hans Kelsen (*Pure Theory of Law*, trans. Max Knight (Berkeley: University of California Press, 1967)), we understand that the Constitution itself is law today only by virtue of its contemporary and continuing validation by a contemporary and continuing rule of recognition or *Grundnorm* (see, ironically, Larry Alexander and Frederick Schauer, "Rules of Recognition, Constitutional Controversies, and the Dizzying Dependence of Law on Acceptance," in *The Rule of Recognition and the U.S. Constitution*, ed. Matthew Adler and Kenneth Einar Himma (New York: Oxford University Press, 2009), 175–92) that must be accepted by officials (or the public, or the army?), the complexities of whose intentions are relevant to constitutional validity and constitutional interpretation, then the problems increase exponentially.

8 Larry Alexander, "Trouble on Track Two: Incidental Regulations of Speech and Free Speech," *Hastings Law Journal* 44, no. 4 (1993): 921. See also Alexander, *Is There a Right to Freedom of Expression?* 13–37.

public square; and a cutback in education funding will affect what people know and thus what they can or will say.[9]

Because there is no governmental action that does not have some effect of some sort on communicative capacity and often on communicative content, Alexander maintains that the effect of a governmental action on communication – Track Two in Laurence Tribe's influential typology[10] – can never trigger First Amendment scrutiny. To conclude otherwise, Alexander argues, is to allow the First Amendment to swallow up the entirety of governmental action and to make all government actions subject to First-Amendment-inspired constitutional review.

The larger implication of this view, to Alexander, is that even for those topics that should properly be subject to constitutional review under the First Amendment, the focus in evaluating the constitutionality of some speech-related state action or rule must be on governmental intent and not on the effect of a governmental action. The focus, Alexander insists, must be on *why* government is taking the action under challenge.[11] For him, neither the speaker's intent[12] in speaking nor the consequences of the government action are especially germane, at least as a theoretical matter, although they might be relevant as a result of strategic or pragmatic empirical

9 See San Antonio Independent School District v. Rodriguez, 411 U.S. 1 (1973), rejecting the argument that the First Amendment required a particular form and level of public school funding because of the relationship between education and speech.

10 Laurence H. Tribe, *American Constitutional Law*, 2nd ed. (New York: Foundation Press, 1988), § 12-2, 791. The basic idea of there being different degrees or levels of judicial scrutiny depending on whether the government is or is not aiming at the "communicative impact" of a restricted communication – the difference between restricting flag burning because it conveys an unpatriotic message and restricting flag burning under a general no-public-burning ordinance designed to reduce the risk of fire – stems from the Supreme Court's influential decision in United States v. O'Brien, 391 U.S. 367 (1968), and was applied specifically to flag burning in Texas v. Johnson, 491 U.S. 397 (1989), and United States v. Eichman, 496 U.S. 310 (1990). Tribe's justifiably influential analysis and typology was preceded by John Hart Ely, "Flag Desecration: A Case Study in the Roles of Categorization and Balancing in First Amendment Analysis," *Harvard Law Review* 88, no. 7 (1975): 1482. Perhaps the best example of the idea in application can be found in Clark v. Community for Creative Non-Violence, 468 U.S. 288 (1984), in which the Supreme Court upheld the conviction of a group of protesters under a general "no sleeping in the park" regulation, even though the protesters were camping out in the park for the sole purpose of engaging in protest activity.

11 See Larry Alexander, "Low Value Speech," *Northwestern University Law Review* 83, no. 3 (1989): 547, 553n22.

12 See Larry Alexander, "Free Speech and Speaker's Intent," *Constitutional Commentary* 12, no. 1 (1995): 21. Alexander's conclusions about the irrelevance of speaker intent are challenged in Leslie Kendrick, "Speech, Intent, and the Chilling Effect," *William & Mary Law Review* 54, no. 5 (2013): 1633, and Alexander's response is Larry Alexander, "Free Speech and Speaker's Intent: A Response to Kendrick," *Columbia Law Review Sidebar* 115 (2015): 1. And see also Larry Alexander, "Redish on Freedom of Speech," *Northwestern University Law Review* 102, no. 3 (2013): 593. On the same topic, and substantially in accord with Alexander's conclusions, see Frederick Schauer, "Intentions, Conventions, and the First Amendment: The Case of Cross Burning," *The Supreme Court Review* 2003 (2004): 197.

concerns about overregulation and related phenomena, concerns typically discussed under the heading of the "chilling effect."[13] If government is attempting to stifle (a certain kind of[14]) communication or shape (some part of) the communicative environment, then its actions are presumptively unconstitutional, or at least presumptively subject to close scrutiny. But if government's goals are speech-independent, he argues, then the theoretical irrelevance of the First Amendment is not altered by the existence or nature of any communicative intent on the part of the subject of a regulation, nor by any effect that the regulation may produce on the communicative environment more generally.

12.2 WHY ALEXANDER IS RIGHT ABOUT INTENTIONS AND FREEDOM OF SPEECH

Alexander's conclusions about the First Amendment are correct, but it is worth discussing three different reasons why that might be so.

First, Alexander may be correct for reasons that arise out of his "Trouble on Track Two" article,[15] and that might be best understood as strategic or pragmatic. More specifically, the focus on governmental intent may arise out of necessity as a result of the facts that a vast quantity – and likely a significant proportion – of human behavior involves speech or communication in some literal sense, that another vast quantity of actions (including government regulation) that are not speech in a literal sense nevertheless have a communicative component, and that almost all regulatory actions by the state have some effect on communication. And if each of these observations is correct, then it turns out that almost every governmental action could support a First Amendment challenge, a consequence that courts, with good reason, would want to avoid.

This reason for limiting First Amendment challenges to those cases in which government intended to inhibit communication because of its content resembles one

[13] Thus, Alexander need not disagree with the test emerging from New York Times Co. v. Sullivan, 376 U.S. 264 (1964), in which the Supreme Court imposed a publisher/speaker intent requirement of actual knowledge of falsity as a way of preventing publishers and speakers from being excessively deterred in a world of legal uncertainty by the risk of liability for theoretically protected speech about public officials. See Frederick Schauer, "Fear, Risk, and the First Amendment: Unraveling the Chilling Effect," *Boston University Law Review* 58, no. 5 (1978): 685.

[14] The inquiry into governmental intent or purpose remains dependent on an initial determination that we are dealing with the kind of communication with which the government may not interfere. See Frederick Schauer, "The Boundaries of the First Amendment: A Preliminary Exploration of Constitutional Salience," *Harvard Law Review* 117, no. 6 (2004): 1765; Frederick Schauer, "The Aim and the Target in First Amendment Methodology," *Northwestern University Law Review* 83, no. 3 (1989): 562.

[15] See *supra* note 8.

of the considerations that influenced the Supreme Court in *Washington v. Davis*.[16] There, the Court articulated what we might call the floodgates fear. In the context of the claim in *Washington v. Davis* that discriminatory effect or impact alone should at least create grounds for a constitutional equal protection challenge,[17] the Court observed that close judicial scrutiny of discriminatory impact, without more, "would raise serious questions about, and perhaps invalidate, a whole range of tax, welfare, public service, regulatory, and licensing statutes ..."[18]

When transposed to the First Amendment, the floodgates concerns are even greater. Not only are pretty much the same considerations that are applicable to equal protection also relevant with respect to the ubiquity of an effect on communication, as Alexander has argued, but now there is also the added feature of the fact that most human actions either have or can be argued to have a communicative dimension. I might drive above the speed limit not only to get to my destination earlier, but also to demonstrate to my passenger that I am a highly competent driver, or that I do not care that much for legal restrictions. And I might drive at or below to speed limit in part to demonstrate to that passenger that I am cautious, or that I am law-abiding, or both. Similarly, not only did car-buyers in the 1960s buy cars with enormous engines and (otherwise) pointless tail fins in order to demonstrate their coolness, sexiness, or whatever, but contemporary car-buyers also buy and own a Tesla or a Prius to display their environmental consciousness (and, in the case of Teslas, their wealth) or buy and own a Volvos to demonstrate their concern with safety. I pick up after my dog to avoid inconveniencing others, but also, at times, to communicate to others that I am a good citizen. And so on for a vast universe of actions that do not on their face appear to be communicative, but nevertheless have a significant communicative component – one that is sometimes intended and sometimes not.

All of the foregoing suggests that a largely intent-exclusive First Amendment doctrine might have much to recommend it pragmatically, simply as a necessary way of keeping every action from becoming an action of free speech concern, and thus as a way of preventing every case from becoming a First Amendment case. In

[16] Washington v. Davis, 426 U.S. 229 (1976).

[17] The Supreme Court in Washington v. Davis did allow that under some circumstances discriminatory impact might provide evidence of discriminatory intent, but rejected the argument that discriminatory impact could itself provide the basis for any form of heightened equal protection scrutiny. And although Washington v. Davis involved a claim of racial discrimination, the same conclusions apply to sex discrimination as well. See Personnel Administrator v. Feeney, 442 U.S. 256 (1979).

[18] 426 U.S. at 248. On the same point, see Robert W. Bennett, "Reflections on the Role of Motivation under the Equal Protection Clause," *Northwestern University Law Review* 79, no. 5/6 (1985): 1009, 1010–11. See also Arlington Heights v. Metropolitan Housing Development Corporation, 429 U.S. 252 (1977), observing that the absence of proof that discriminatory purpose was a "motivating factor" "ends the constitutional inquiry."

addition, however, there might also be deeper theoretical reasons for insisting on an intent focus in the domain of free speech. One such reason might be free-speech-specific, in the sense that the very idea of free speech might be about not wishing government to have motives or intents or purposes of a certain kind. Thomas Scanlon's influential account of the justifications for a free speech principle is of this variety,[19] because, under one interpretation, a citizen's autonomy is jeopardized when government tells her she may not receive a certain type of information in order that she should not have reasons of a particular type. And although arguments might be offered against Scanlon's account,[20] and although Scanlon himself has rounded off some of the sharper corners of his original proposal,[21] the basic idea is that there are plausible conceptions of the idea of free speech that appear to hinge on what some putative restricter ought not to do, rather than on what the speaker or listener chooses to do. Insofar as such conceptions are valid, a government-intent-focused understanding of freedom of speech and the First Amendment might be justified on more than simply floodgates or related pragmatic grounds.

Apart from the possibility of a restricter-intent-focused conception of freedom of speech itself, we might even imagine a restricter-intent-focused conception of constitutionalism generally. Especially for a constitution that, unlike the constitutions in South Africa, Eastern Europe, and some American states, for example,[22] contains few positive rights,[23] we might understand constitutional rights and constitutional adjudication generally as being more about disabling government than about empowering citizens. And if this understanding is correct, as it well may be as a historical matter for the Constitution of the United States,[24] then it is only a short

[19] Thomas Scanlon, "A Theory of Freedom of Expression," *Philosophy and Public Affairs* 1, no. 2 (1972): 204–23.

[20] See Frederick Schauer, *Free Speech: A Philosophical Enquiry* (Cambridge: Cambridge University Press, 1982); Frederick Schauer, "On the Distinction Between Speech and Action," *Emory Law Journal* 65, no. 2 (2015): 427.

[21] T.M. Scanlon, Jr., "Freedom of Expression and Categories of Expression," *University of Pittsburgh Law Review* 40, no. 4 (1979): 519; T.M. Scanlon, "Comment on Baker's Autonomy and Free Speech," *Constitutional Commentary* 27, no. 2 (2011): 319; T.M. Scanlon, "Why Not Base Free Speech on Autonomy or Democracy?" *Virginia Law Review* 97, no. 3 (2011): 541; T.M. Scanlon, "Comment on Shiffrin's Thinker-Based Approach to Freedom of Speech," *Constitutional Commentary* 27, no. 2 (2011): 327.

[22] See Mila Versteeg and Emily Zackin, "American Constitutional Exceptionalism Revisited," *University of Chicago Law Review* 81, no. 4 (2014): 1641.

[23] That is, rights requiring government to do something rather than simply requiring government to refrain from doing something. For application of the distinction to free speech issues, see Frederick Schauer, "Hohfeld's First Amendment," *George Washington Law Review* 76, no. 4 (2008): 914.

[24] I mention the history as an aside, and decidedly not to suggest any sympathy with an originalist view of constitutional interpretation, a view I reject in all of its versions. And although it is relatively uncontroversial that the Constitution was not originally understood as granting entitlements to citizens, whether the Constitution is principally an enabling or disabling document vis-à-vis the government is

step from the premise that disabling government is the principal purpose of the Constitution to the conclusion that governmental motives ought to be the touchstone of the inquiry, whether we are talking about freedom of speech, freedom of religion,[25] equal protection,[26] state restrictions on interstate commerce,[27] state taxation of federal entities,[28] or pretty much anything else.[29] This is not the place to explore in depth this potential understanding of the entirety of the American constitutional tradition, but I mention it here only to suggest that a government-intent-focused understanding of the First Amendment might be justified not only on pragmatic grounds, and not only on free-speech-specific theoretical grounds, but also on theoretical grounds that go to the very essence of just what (some) constitutions are designed to do, and just what those constitutions, at their deepest, are all about.

12.3 ALEXANDER ON INTENTIONS AND LEGAL INTERPRETATION

In a more or less different strand of scholarship, Alexander has argued that constitutions, statutes, regulations, and most (all?[30]) other canonical legal items should be interpreted according to the original intentions of the authoritative authors of those items.[31] This position – original intent originalism, as opposed to

a source of continuing political and rhetorical controversy, a controversy I have no need to address on this occasion.

[25] See Wallace v. Jaffree, 472 U.S. 38 (1985); Church of the Lukumi Babalu Aye, Inc. v. City of Hialeah, 508 U.S. 520 (1993); Edwards v. Aguillard, 482 U.S. 578 (1987).

[26] See *supra* notes 16–18 and accompanying text.

[27] See Hunt v. Washington State Apple Advertising Commission, 432 U.S. 333 (1977); Bacchus Imports, Ltd. v. Dias, 468 U.S. 263 (1984); Kassel v. Consolidated Freightways Corp., 450 U.S. 662 (1981); Donald H. Regan, "The Supreme Court and State Protectionism: Making Sense of the Dormant Commerce Clause," *Michigan Law Review* 84, no. 6 (1986): 1091.

[28] North Dakota v. United States, 460 U.S. 300 (1983).

[29] See Cass R. Sunstein, "Naked Preferences and the Constitution," *Columbia Law Review* 84, no. 7 (1984): 1689.

[30] Would Alexander apply his original intent originalism to authoritative precedents? If he views both vertical and horizontal precedents as authoritative (see Larry Alexander, "Constrained by Precedent," *Southern California Law Review* 63, no. 1 (1989): 1), and if he views the source of precedential authority as substantially textual (ibid.), he then seems committed to the conclusion that interpreting a precedent requires recourse to the intentions of the judge or the court that decided the earlier (precedent) case. On the question, see Charles Barzun, "Impeaching Precedent," *University of Chicago Law Review* 80, no. 7 (2013): 1625; Adrian Vermeule, "Judicial History," *Yale Law Journal* 108, no. 6 (1999): 1311.

[31] See Larry Alexander and Emily Sherwin, *Demystifying Legal Reasoning* (New York: Cambridge University Press, 2008), 131–219; Larry Alexander, "Simple-Minded Originalism," in *The Challenge of Originalism: Theories of Constitutional Interpretation*, ed. Grant Huscroft and Bradley W. Miller (Cambridge: Cambridge University Press, 2011), 87–98; Larry Alexander, "The Search for Legislative Intent," *University of Queensland Law Journal* 33, no. 2 (2014): 397, Alexander, "Originalism, the Why and the What," 539; Larry Alexander, "Of Living Trees and Dead Hands: The Interpretation

the now ubiquitous original public meaning originalism – can exist in weak and strong forms. The weaker form of original intent originalism would hold that vague or ambiguous texts (but only vague or ambiguous texts) should be interpreted by recourse to evidence of the original intentions of the enactors, and thus the use of original intentions is interstitial. But the stronger form would conclude that even clear text should give way in the face of extrinsic evidence that the text did not accurately capture what we know the authorial intent to be, thus making the use of original intentions pervasive.[32]

At least in constitutional interpretation, original intent originalism, whether in its strong or its weak form, is out of fashion these days,[33] having been largely supplanted by so-called original public meaning originalism.[34] But no one has ever accused Alexander of being fashionable, or of choosing his academic positions in order to sail with the shifting winds of academic popularity. And thus, although original intent originalism in the constitutional context is at times embarrassed by discoveries about the original intentions of those who drafted the equal protection clause (and who seemed explicitly to have not intended that the clause be used to desegregate the public schools[35]) and the First Amendment (who may not

of Constitutions and Constitutional Rights," *Canadian Journal of Law & Jurisprudence* 22, no. 2 (2009): 227.

[32] Or, for that matter, necessary. If even plain text is defeasible in the face of evidence that the plain text did not accurately capture the original intentions of the drafters or enactors, then every use of plain text involves the implicit presupposition that no contrary intention exists. And thus the existence or nonexistence of contrary intentions is on the table in every case of interpretation. For a similar point but not in the context of originalist interpretation, see Ronald Dworkin, *Law's Empire* (Cambridge, MA: Harvard University Press, 1986), 353–54, 449n14 (arguing that seemingly easy cases involve the implicit conclusion that the plain text is not inconsistent with the result generated by the full interpretive method); Duncan Kennedy, "Legal Formality," *Journal of Legal Studies* 2, no. 2 (1973): 351 (maintaining that every application of formal law presupposes the conclusion that nonformal sources would not indicate a different result).

[33] In reality, original intent originalism was never really *in* fashion, at least in the context of constitutional interpretation, but at least it was more in fashion when the leading opponents of so-called noninterpretivism included, for example, Raoul Berger, *Government by Judiciary* (Cambridge, MA: Harvard University Press, 1977); Robert H. Bork, "Neutral Principles and Some First Amendment Problems," *Indiana Law Journal* 47, no. 1 (1971): 1; Henry P. Monaghan, "Our Perfect Constitution," *New York University Law Review* 56, no. 2/3 (1981): 353. In the context of statutory interpretation, interpretation according to original (legislative) intent (often under the label of "legislative history") remains more actively supported than does its counterpart in constitutional interpretation. See Caleb Nelson, *Statutory Interpretation* (New York: Foundation Press, 201), 231–362.

[34] The contemporary literature is vast, and includes, for example, Antonin Scalia, *A Matter of Interpretation: Federal Courts and the Law* (Princeton: Princeton University Press, 1997); Keith E. Whittington, *Constitutional Interpretation: Textual Meaning, Original Intent, and Judicial Review* (Lawrence: University Press of Kansas, 1999); Lawrence B. Solum, "District of Columbia v. Heller and Originalism," *Northwestern University Law Review* 103, no. 2 (2009): 923.

[35] See Berger, *Government by Judiciary*.

have intended to invalidate any speech restrictions other than prior restraints[36]), Alexander's theoretical defense of original intent originalism as an approach to interpreting the Constitution and ordinary statutes rests on deeper theoretical grounds.

Part of Alexander's argument appears at times to rest on a view about the nature of language. He appears to believe, and has sometimes argued, that we cannot understand language without at least presupposing a conscious intender, a real or hypothetical agent whose actual or presumed intent makes it possible to understand language in the first place, and thus to understand some set of noises or marks as being made *in* a language. Because the use of language is itself an intentional human act, the argument goes, we can understand language only by understanding the communicative intentions of those who are using language to communicate, or at the very least understanding that there was someone who intended to communicate something in a language.[37]

In defending original intent originalism, Alexander occasionally professes allegiance to the related accounts offered by Stanley Fish, Walter Benn Michaels, and various other literary theorists.[38] But all too often those accounts, especially in the literary theory genre in which they were spawned, seem to rest simply on a definitional fiat about just what it is to "interpret." But even accepting Alexander's occasional sympathy with such a position, it still seems unfair to Alexander to saddle him with arguments that appear to be so unsatisfactory. To be fair to Alexander, therefore, we should focus on whether his arguments are sound or mistaken, and not on whether he is sound or mistaken in selecting his allies. Consequently, a far more formidable target is presented by Alexander's arguments connecting his approach to understanding language as intentional with his view about the nature of law itself and legal authority, rather than the nature of language or the definition of "interpretation."

[36] See Patterson v. Colorado, 205 U.S. 454 (1907). And compare Leonard W. Levy, *Legacy of Suppression: Freedom of Speech and Press in Early American History* (Cambridge, MA: Harvard University Press, 1960), with David A. Anderson, "The Origins of the Free Press Clause," *UCLA Law Review* 30, no. 3 (1983): 528. Levy has produced a revised version, Leonard W. Levy, *Emergence of a Free Press* (New York: Oxford University Press, 1985), which softens his original claims somewhat, but even the softening has not satisfied his critics. See David M. Rabban, "The Ahistorical Historian: Leonard Levy on Freedom of Expression in Early American History," *Stanford Law Review* 37, no. 3 (1985): 795.

[37] See Larry Alexander, "All or Nothing at All? The Intentions of Authorities and the Authority of Intentions," in *Law and Interpretation: Essays in Legal Philosophy*, ed. Andrei Marmor (Oxford: Clarendon Press, 1995), 357–404; Larry Alexander and Saikrishna Prakash, "'Is That English You're Speaking? Some Arguments for the Primacy of Intent in Interpretation," *San Diego Law Review* 41, no. 3 (2004): 967.

[38] Larry Alexander, "Telepathic Law," *Constitutional Commentary* 26, no. 1 (2010): 139.

More specifically, Alexander, aligning himself with, most prominently, Joseph Raz,[39] but also with Richard Posner[40] and many others, sees law as an essentially authoritative practice, one in which certain authorities give guidance, instructions, or orders that the rest of us are expected to follow.[41] And from this premise Alexander derives the conclusion that relying on anything other than the intentions of the instruction-giver is unfaithful to the authoritative nature of law.[42] At times, the interpreter will find it relatively easy to divine those instructions from the conventional linguistic meaning of the instructions themselves,[43] but when that conventional meaning is vague or ambiguous (the weak version of original intent originalism) – and possibly even when it is clear but clearly at odds with what we otherwise know about the instructor's intentions (the strong version of original intent originalism) – the job of the interpreter is to reach the conclusion that is most consistent with the intentions of the author or the enactor (the constructive author, even if not the one who wrote the words in the first place) of the relevant legal language.

Although Alexander at times leans in the direction of believing that intention-free understanding of language is simply impossible, at other (and better) times he accepts that meaning is conventional, and thus that we might understand language in light of linguistic conventions, even absent an actual human intender. He recognizes that texts produced by multiple monkeys, by the patterns of the clouds, or by the arrangement of seashells on the beach[44] might have conventional meanings – clouds in the shape of C-A-T will mean (putting aside the question of what it means to mean something) cat and not dog – and that is because the existing rules and conventions of language can generate meaning.

Although Alexander in his better moments thus accepts the possibility of intender-independent meaning, he rejects such a possibility for law, and here is where Alexander's Razian understanding of law as authority takes center stage. For Alexander, law itself is simply about the use of authorities to give us moral guidance,

39 See especially Joseph Raz, *The Authority of Law: Essays on Law and Morality* (Oxford: Clarendon Press, 1979); Joseph Raz, *The Morality of Freedom* (Oxford: Clarendon Press, 1986); Joseph Raz, "The Problem of Authority: Revisiting the Service Conception," *Minnesota Law Review* 90, no. 4 (2006): 1003.

40 Richard A. Posner, "Legal Formalism, Legal Realism, and the Interpretation of Statutes and the Constitution," *Case Western Reserve University Law Review* 37, no. 2 (2006): 179.

41 And that is why Posner, ibid., equates legal interpretation with the attempts by an army private to interpret the orders of the sergeant, because the private wants to do what the sergeant wants him to do just because the sergeant wants him to do it. The same conclusion follows if we understand the subject as desiring to follow these instructions or orders for the subject's own good, as in the Razian "service conception" of authority. Raz, "The Problem of Authority."

42 Alexander, "All or Nothing at All?"; Alexander, "Telepathic Law."

43 But see *supra* note 32.

44 See Frederick Schauer, "An Essay on Constitutional Language," *UCLA Law Review* 29, no. 4 (1982): 797.

an approach to moral human action that is preferable (that is, will produce better moral results in the long term) to letting each of us apply morality directly.[45] Because a host of moral and cognitive failures might produce morally suboptimal results were citizens simply told to do the morally right thing, law, recognizing this potential for suboptimality, provides the justification for creating lawmaking institutions and empowering lawmaking officials whose directives, when followed, will produce a morally better array of outcomes and decisions than would be produced were citizens to make moral decisions directly and without law's rule-based intermediation. And if law is thus about having authorities who will tell us what, morally, to do, then, for Alexander, the central aspect of law is the direction of the authorities. To ignore those directions, Alexander says, is to ignore the very point of law in the first instance. And because the touchstone is therefore what the authorities are telling us what to do, their intentions in doing so must, according to Alexander, be the focus of legal interpretation.

12.4 BUT ...

Alexander's arguments for the primacy of lawmaker intent are deeper and more sophisticated than any intentionalist arguments that now exist, and for that he deserves enormous credit. But Alexander's argument also provides the platform for the strongest argument against his position. And for that we have to return to the monkeys.

[45] See Larry Alexander and Emily Sherwin, *The Rule of Rules: Morality, Rules, and the Dilemmas of Law* (Durham, NC: Duke University Press, 2001). Alexander and I agree about the importance of the "settlement function" of law (Larry Alexander and Frederick Schauer, "On Extrajudicial Constitutional Interpretation," *Harvard Law Review* 110, no. 7 (1997): 1359; Larry Alexander and Frederick Schauer, "Law's Limited Domain Confronts Morality's Universal Empire," *William & Mary Law Review* 48, no. 5 (2007): 1579), but in a sense I take the settlement argument one step further. Yes, we might achieve preferable (to individual determination in the face of moral disagreements) settlement by deferring to an authority and his, her, or its intentions, but we might also achieve settlement by deferring to the conventional meaning of legal texts and thus to the authority of that conventional meaning. Such an approach might produce mistakes, but whether the mistakes produced by such an approach are greater in expected (frequency multiplied by magnitude) consequences than those produced by deferring to the intentions of an authority will vary with the nature of the issues and the characteristics of the authorities. The point here, however, is only that if we accept that suboptimal authorities might produce better results than individual interpretation, then we can see why, in some contexts, conventional meaning divorced from intentions might be better still. And if taking the argument to this next step seems fanciful, consider the cases that have invalidated search warrants because of obvious errors in the identification of the addresses of the premises to be searched. E.g., United States v. Constantino, 201 F. Supp. 160 (W.D. Pa. 1962); United States v. Kenney, 164 F. Supp. 89 (D.D.C. 1958). Although the majority rule would not invalidate the warrants under such circumstances, the fact that some courts hold otherwise suggests that it is far from fanciful to believe that following literal meaning even in the face of contrary intent may be appropriate in some contexts.

Recall that law, for Alexander, is ultimately an institution of the second best. In an ideal world, he argues, people would make their own first-order moral decisions, which decisions, because those people are ideal decision makers in an ideal world, would produce a morally ideal society. Prisoners' dilemmas and related problems of coordination and cooperation admittedly complicate the picture, but the basic idea is still that law itself emerges primarily as a consequence of the fact that real people in the real world are far from ideal decision makers, and as a result real societies use law to produce the best possible moral results under circumstances of widespread moral nonideality.

So now let us think about Alexander's monkeys. He acknowledges that a brigade of monkeys could produce symbols that might look like words in a language – English, say – and would thus have meanings in that language.[46] But because those monkeys would not have intended anything, they cannot be said to have authority over anyone and anything. And because the monkeys did not have any authority over anything or anyone, Alexander argues, their emanations would be of no consequence, even if, purely by coincidence, their emanations might have conventional meanings in a language.

Alexander uses his monkeys to make the point that conventional meaning, even assuming (properly) that it exists, might be morally, normatively, and institutionally irrelevant, and he uses that point to say the same about intention-free conventional meaning in law. But recall Alexander's argument for law in the first place: Law is a second-best substitute in a world of suboptimal moral decision makers who make suboptimal moral decisions when left to their own devices. But if law can serve as the second-best solution in a morally suboptimal world, then there seems no reason why literal, conventional, nonintentional meaning could not serve the same function vis-à-vis authoritative law that law serves vis-à-vis morality. If we use law (and its human and authoritative lawmakers) when we lose confidence in individual and dispersed moral decision makers, then it seems as if, *mutatis mutandis*, we could at one remove use conventional (non-intent-based) meaning when we lose confidence in decision makers who seek to divine legislative (or any other authority) intent in interpreting the law.[47]

Based on the full corpus of the Alexander *œuvre*, he ought to be receptive to this challenge. He has, after all, been an astute and persuasive defender of rules, whether

46 Alexander, "Telepathic Law."

47 On the possibility that a strategy of relying on thin, superficial, and possibly mistaken literal (conventional) meaning might in some contexts be optimal over a run of decisions, see John Manning, "The Absurdity Doctrine," *Harvard Law Review* 116, no. 8 (2003): 2387; Frederick Schauer, "The Practice and Problems of Plain Meaning: A Response to Aleinikoff and Shaw," *Vanderbilt Law Review* 45, no. 3 (1992): 715; Frederick Schauer, "Statutory Construction and the Coordinating Function of Plain Meaning," *Supreme Court Review* 1990 (1991): 231.

stated as canonically inscribed rules[48] or understood as the best way to understand the constraints of precedent.[49] And in his defense of rules, Alexander understands their suboptimality, and thus understands that what they provide is not a set of ideal results, but a set of results that may be superior to the set of results that would be obtained by direct application of their background justifications, especially those background justifications that would be misunderstood or otherwise misapplied by people attempting to apply those justifications directly.

But if this is so, which Alexander believes,[50] then there is no reason why literal conventional meaning could not serve the same function. Conventional meaning might poorly reflect the goals of the actual authorities, but so too might legal rules poorly reflect the goals and norms of first-order morality. In arguing against intention-free conventional meaning, Alexander appears to express an optimism about the ability of interpreters to discover and interpret intentions that he rejects about the ability of law's subjects to discover, interpret, and apply morality. Or, to put it more bluntly, conventional meaning textualism might suck, but at some times and in some places and on some subjects it might suck less than original intent originalism, and exactly for the reasons that Alexander, more than anyone, has helped us to appreciate.

12.5 CONCLUSION: WHERE ALEXANDER IS RIGHT

In an interesting way, Alexander's consistency between his largely sound sympathy for intent with respect to freedom of expression and his largely mistaken sympathy for intent in legal interpretation reflects a deeper and correct insight. Unlike those who might say that intentions are always and necessarily relevant in understanding, interpreting, and applying any act, including but not limited to speech acts, and unlike those who would say that intentions are never relevant, Alexander understands that the relevance of intentions is a function of the enterprise within which they exist and within which they might be used. Intentions matter in the interpretation of wills because the intentions of the testator are the touchstone for and the point of the enterprise.[51] But speaker intentions (as opposed to ordinary or public meaning) do not matter in the common law of defamation because the point of the enterprise is focused on the reactions of unknown and unanticipated listeners or readers.[52]

48 Alexander and Sherwin, *The Rule of Rules*.

49 Alexander, "Constrained by Precedent," 1.

50 As do I, by the way. Frederick Schauer, *Playing by the Rules: A Philosophical Examination of Rule-Based Decision-Making in Law and in Life* (Oxford: Cambridge University Press, 1991); Frederick Schauer, "Formalism," *Yale Law Journal* 97, no. 4 (1988): 509–48.

51 See, for example, Saylor v. Saylor, 169 So.3d 998 (Ala. 2014); Canaday v. Baysinger, 152 N.W. 562 (Iowa 1915); Kellam's Executor v. Jacob, 148 S.E. 835 (Va. 1929).

52 See, for example, Siegel v. Thompson, 181 Ill. App. 164 (1913); Rodgers v. Kline, 56 Miss. 808 (1929).

And the very difference between common law fraud and so-called antifraud actions under the Securities Act of 1933 and the Securities Exchange Act of 1934 is that the latter makes issuer (speaker) intent irrelevant in a way that it was essential under the former, and that is precisely because the securities laws are designed to shift the burden of disclosure and investigation from buyer to seller.[53]

What these examples show, and there could plainly be many more,[54] is that the use or nonuse of intent in legal interpretation is not a function of the nature of language. Language can be interpreted according to the intentions of the language user, and language can be interpreted according to linguistic conventions alone without reference to the intentions of the speaker (or listener). The very idea of language is thus agnostic on the question of the role of intentions in its interpretation. Once we understand this, we can see that the use or nonuse of intentions in constitutional, legal, statutory, contract, literary, or other interpretation is dependent not on the nature of language, but instead on the nature of the enterprise whose language or acts we are trying to interpret. Alexander's reliance on intent with respect to both freedom of speech and the interpretation of canonical legal language is, as I have argued here, sound on the former and mistaken on the latter, but the very fact that he offers distinct arguments for each demonstrates that he properly understands that the importance of intentions is domain dependent, and not a function of the nature of language or even the nature of law.[55] And in this, minor disagreements aside, Alexander is plainly correct.

53 See generally Alan R. Bromberg, Lewis D. Lowenfels, and Michael J. Sullivan, *Bromberg and Lowenfels on Securities Fraud* (New York: Clark Boardman Callaghan, 2016).

54 Including the long-standing debates between objective and subjective theories of contract, with the former stressing the surface meaning of the contract and the latter the intentions of the parties. See Wayne Barnes, "The Objective Theory of Contracts," *University of Cincinnati Law Review* 76, no. 4 (2008): 1119; Joseph M. Perillo, "The Origins of the Objective Theory of Contract Formation and Interpretation," *Fordham Law Review* 69, no. 2 (2000): 427.

55 And thus I distinguish the nature of law from the enterprise of interpreting legal texts.

13

Alexander's Constitutionalism

A Qualified Defense

Alon Harel

13.1 INTRODUCTION

In a few words, Larry Alexander and Fred Schauer capture elegantly the primary function of law in society. Under their review: "Law provides the benefits of authoritative settlement, as well as the related but still content-independent benefits of inducing socially beneficial cooperative behavior and providing solutions to Prisoner's Dilemmas and other problems of coordination."[1] This observation is further developed to explain the supremacy of judicial interpretations of the constitution. Alexander and Schauer argue that: "When the Constitution is subject to multiple interpretations, a pre-constitutional norm must referee among interpretations to decide what is to be done. One such norm is that the Supreme Court's interpretation is authoritative and supreme,"[2] and they add: "To see judicial supremacy in settlement terms, as we do, is thus to see constitutional law as serving an essentially stabilizing and constraining function."[3] The supremacy of constitutional norms as well the supremacy of judicial interpretation of the Constitution serve therefore the same function served by legal (nonconstitutional) norms: They both serve the purpose of providing authoritative settlement of disagreements which, in turn, facilitates coordination, cooperation, and stability.

In this paper, I wish to examine and develop the concept of authoritative settlement. More specifically, I differentiate between *legal* (nonconstitutional) authoritative settlement and *constitutional* authoritative settlement. I argue that, while the former advances instrumental goals identified by Alexander such as coordination,

[1] Larry Alexander and Frederick Schauer, "On Extrajudicial Constitutional Interpretation," *Harvard Law Review* 110, no. 7 (1997): 1371; Larry Alexander, "Introduction," in Larry Alexander, *Constitutionalism: Philosophical Foundations* (Cambridge: Cambridge University Press, 1998), 1–2.

[2] Alexander and Schauer, "On Extrajudicial Constitutional Interpretation," 1377.

[3] Alexander and Schauer, "Defending Judicial Supremacy," *Constitutional Commentary* 17, no. 3 (2000): 437.

cooperation, stability, and predictability, constitutional authoritative settlement has in addition intrinsic value; it is the settlement itself rather than its contingent consequences that is valuable. More specifically, constitutional authoritative settlement is valuable because it transforms and restructures the relations between the state and its citizens.

Legal authoritative settlement serves the purpose of guiding individuals to act harmoniously and thereby inducing beneficial cooperation. Its primary goal is *to create* rights and duties which will settle disagreements and thereby contribute to the well-being of society. In contrast, constitutional authoritative settlement does not create rights but *recognizes* or *acknowledges* preexisting rights. Constitutional authoritative settlement embodies the understanding that the settlement of certain disagreements cannot rest merely on the discretionary powers of the polity or its institutions. Instead, the authoritative constitutional settlement typically entrenches prepolitical moral duties which must be acknowledged and complied with by the polity. The division of labor between legal authoritative settlement and constitutional authoritative settlement is crucial for the protection of freedom, as the latter type of authoritative settlement signifies the understanding that moral rights are mandatory and that their normative force does not depend upon the preferences, judgments, or inclinations of members of the polity. Citizens protected by constitutional provisions interpreted and enforced by the courts do not live at the mercy of the legislature, and their rights are not merely protected de facto; instead, the constitutional protection signifies the mandatory force of prepolitical moral rights – force which does not hinge upon the inclinations of the polity or its citizens.

This observation also explains why courts rather than representative institutions such as legislatures are in charge of interpreting the Constitution. Representative institutions are designed to give effect to our preferences and judgments, to enhance our autonomy, and to make us the masters of our own destiny. But we are not masters of our destiny when human rights are at stake. Consequently, there is a fundamental difference between legal settlement and constitutional settlement: The former serves an instrumental role promoting stability and predictability, while the latter has in addition intrinsic value – it serves to publicly acknowledge that the protection of prepolitical moral rights by the state is obligatory, not discretionary. The overriding power of constitutional norms and of the judicial interpretations of the Constitution provide public recognition that the protection of rights is the state's duty rather than merely a discretionary gesture on its part. Hence, the institutional division between the legislature, on the one hand, and the courts, on the other, does not serve merely instrumental goals (of the type served by legal settlement); it has an important role in recognizing publicly the limits of the powers of the polity and the mandatory force of rights.

Section 13.2 describes the main arguments provided by Alexander to justify the supremacy of the Constitution and judicial supremacy in constitutional interpretation. In particular, it examines the nature and value of authoritative settlement, legal authoritative settlement, and constitutional authoritative settlement. This part also challenges, refines, and develops the concept of authoritative settlement. Section 13.3 differentiates between legal and constitutional authoritative settlement and identifies the distinct value of constitutional authoritative settlement. More specifically, I argue that the Constitution is designed primarily to incorporate what Alexander labels "real moral rights," as contrasted with created rights. It is the former type of rights and the ways of incorporating them into the legal system that is the central question addressed in this paper. Section 13.4 develops brief speculative suggestions concerning the source of the disagreements between proponents and opponents of legal settlement.

13.2 LEGAL AND CONSTITUTIONAL SETTLEMENT

Alexander believes that the primary function of the legal system is authoritative settlement of disagreements.[4] He extends his analysis also to the Constitution and uses the concept of authoritative settlement to justify judicial supremacy in constitutional interpretation.[5] This part presents and refines the concept of authoritative settlement. I first examine why settlement as such is valuable. Then I turn to examine the distinctive virtues of legal settlement and, finally, I explore the distinction between legal and constitutional authoritative settlement.

Assume a society in which all individuals are motivated to honor their moral obligations and act in accordance with moral reasons. Some may believe that in such a society law (or any other means of settlement) is redundant. In particular, authoritative settlement is not needed, as individuals would act harmoniously in accordance with the relevant moral norms. Hence, they will reap the benefits of cooperation without establishing a legal system.

Many have argued in the past against this naïve view. Joseph Raz, for instance, argued that even in a society of angels "law would exist for the purposes of assisting in coordination, dispute resolution, and damage recovery."[6] Alexander refines this argument by stressing the epistemic difficulties in reaching coordination and argues that:

> Because of our moral disagreements, we could not predict with any certainty what others were going to do; and because what is the morally correct conduct for me

4 Larry Alexander, "Of Living Trees and Dead Hands: The Interpretation of Constitutions and Constitutional Rights," *Canadian Journal of Law and Jurisprudence* 22, no. 2 (2009): 229.

5 Alexander and Schauer, "On Extrajudicial Constitutional Interpretation."

6 Joseph Raz, *Practical Reasons and Norms* (Oxford: Oxford University Press, 1975), 159.

> often depends upon what others are doing, my inability to predict and coordinate with others will lead me to do what is morally wrong even if I am trying to do what is morally right. Legal settlement of what I and others are obligated to do allows me to coordinate my acts with others' acts and avert the moral costs of colliding good intentions.[7]

Settlement is needed, therefore, not only to solve motivational deficiencies but also epistemic deficiencies.[8] Legal settlement is one effective means of settlement and, consequently, legal settlement provides individuals with reasons for action. This analysis raises two questions: first, why (and whether) settlement is so valuable and, second, why (and whether) *legal* settlement is valuable. Let me address separately each of these questions.

Alexander identifies three reasons for the significance of settlement. First, settlement "allows me to coordinate my acts with others' acts and avert the moral costs of colliding good intentions."[9] Second, settlement also "can improve moral decision making by means of giving decision makers the benefits of others' expertise ... Legal settlement can improve our moral decision making if the law makes use of expertise."[10] Third, "legal settlement also makes moral decision making more efficient in terms of time and other resources."[11] It exempts decision makers from the need to make decisions on their own and allows them to depend upon judgments of others. Given these "individually and socially beneficial goods," coordination and settlement of disagreements "provide content-independent reasons for the existence of the state, of law, and of the obligation of obedience to the law."[12] While Alexander refers in these paragraphs to legal settlement, it is evident that these beneficial consequences are relevant to any settlement, irrespective of whether it is legal or not.

Once the value of settlement has been clarified, one could ask whether *legal* settlement has any advantages over nonlegal settlement. At times Alexander asserts that "agreement and settlement appear to be the peculiar and special province of law, and the peculiar and special province of constitutions."[13] Yet I do not think that this claim can be substantiated and, further, it is clearly not necessary for Alexander.

7 Alexander, "Of Living Trees and Dead Hands," 227–28.

8 I think this explains why, according to the Jewish tradition, one of the laws of Noah (laws that bind non-Jews) requires non-Jews to establish a legal system. It is not enough to comply with the rules prohibiting murder or theft; it is also necessary to establish a legal system. This is because without such a system, even good-willing individuals will not be able to reap the benefits of cooperation.

9 Alexander, "Of Living Trees and Dead Hands," 228.

10 Ibid.

11 Ibid.

12 Alexander and Schauer, "On Extrajudicial Constitutional Interpretation," 1374.

13 Alexander and Schauer, "Defending Judicial Supremacy," 469.

One may think of three possible routes to justify the distinct role of law in settling disputes. First, one could deny that *legal* settlement is particularly valuable and simply maintain that legal settlement is the current dominant means of authoritative settlement and, once this means of settlement is established, it ought to be honored (like any other conventional and effective means of settlement). Hence, the only virtue of *legal* settlement over other forms of settlement is that it is the dominant conventional existing means of settlement. Law does not only settle disputes; it is in itself a settled mechanism for settling disputes and its virtue is simply that it is a settled mechanism. Second, one could argue that legal settlement is valuable because the law and/or legal reasoning is particularly likely or successful in settling disagreements. Alexander defends this view and says: "[W]e rely on the proposition that law-based institutions serve stability and settlement fostering functions more than do other social institutions."[14] He repeats this argument when he defends judicial supremacy in constitutional interpretation by establishing that the courts are the most effective mechanism for settling constitutional controversies.[15] Last, one can conjecture that legal settlement is superior to other forms of settlement, not because it is more likely to succeed in effectively settling disagreements, but because it is more likely to settle disagreements in the right way. Legal reasoning, ideally at least, is impartial and grounded in reason and, consequently, is more likely to settle disagreements justly.

Settlement of disagreements is clearly valuable for the reasons identified by Alexander: coordination, cooperation, efficiency, expertise, etc. *Legal* settlement can also be valuable for the reasons we pointed out above. In particular, I believe that legal settlement is superior because it is more likely to settle disagreement in a just or correct way. Let me elaborate.

Settlement cannot be all that there is to law. It is not enough to settle disputes; it is also necessary to settle them, as much as possible, justly. To justify the use of legal norms and, in particular, to justify the role of courts in determining what law is, one needs also to resort to the virtues of courts in making right or correct settlements. Alexander is not indifferent to this concern. Despite the significance given to settlement as such, Alexander also distinguishes between "those questions that a court is more likely to answer correctly and those questions that a majoritarian body is more likely to answer correctly."[16] Courts are desirable not only because they settle but also because they often settle reasonably justly or correctly and, to the extent that

[14] Ibid., 472.

[15] Ibid., 473–78.

[16] Larry Alexander, "Constitutional Rules, Constitutional Standards, and Constitutional Settlement: *Marbury v. Madison* and the Case for Judicial Supremacy," *Constitutional Commentary* 20, no. 2 (2003): 375.

they do not, Alexander also concedes the possibility that other institutions can be in charge of settlement.[17] Perhaps the most evident indication of Alexander's awareness of the importance of just settlement is the extensive discussion of the "challenge of Dred Scott."[18] In cases in which judicial interpretations of the Constitution are pernicious, officials ought to reject them and act on their own understanding of the Constitution. Settlements that are pernicious are worse (or, at least, may be worse) than no settlements whatsoever.

To succeed in its primary mission – the settlement function – law has to consist of determinate rules. Settlement presupposes therefore specificity and determinacy of the legal norms. In Alexander's view: "It is determinateness that produces the moral benefits of coordination, expertise and efficiency. Standards – those legal norms that are not determinate rules – leave matters unsettled ... They fail to fulfill the settlement function. Rather, they defer settlement."[19]

It is time to turn from legal settlement to constitutional settlement. Alexander maintains that despite the prevalent view that "arguments from coordination, cooperation or settlement have less relevance to constitutions," such arguments are central to the justifiability of constitutions.[20] They are central in two respects: First, they justify the supremacy of the Constitution, and second, they justify the supremacy of the judicial interpretation of the Constitution. With respect to the former issue (the supremacy of the Constitution), Alexander argues:

> Just as a rule of precedent recognizes the value of settlement for settlement's sake, so too does a constitution exist partly because of the value of uniform decisions on issues as to which people have divergent substantive views and personal agendas. The decision to create a single written constitution, and thus depart from a model of parliamentary supremacy, is based on the possibility of varying views about fundamental questions, and the undesirability of leaving their resolution to shifting political fortunes. Moreover, one reason for being suspicious of shifting political fortunes is that they shift so frequently. Without a written constitution as a stabilizing force, there is a risk that too many issues needing at least intermediate term settlement will remain excessively uncertain.[21]

This is a compelling argument. The one minor disagreement I have is that I see no reason why a written constitution serves better this purpose than a nonwritten one.[22]

17 Larry Alexander, "What is the Problem of Judicial Review," *Australian Journal of Legal Philosophy* 31, no. 1 (2006): 7.
18 Alexander and Schauer, "On Extrajudicial Constitutional Interpretation," 1382–83.
19 Alexander, "Of Living Trees and Dead Hands," 228.
20 Alexander and Schauer, "On Extrajudicial Constitutional Interpretation," 1372.
21 Ibid., 1376.
22 Alon Harel, *Why Law Matters* (Oxford: Oxford University Press, 2014), 153.

As Dicey has shown us, "conventions, understandings, habits, or practices" can be as effective in settling constitutional disputes as written norms.[23]

And, with respect to the latter issue (the supremacy of judicial interpretation), Alexander argues:

> When the Constitution is subject to multiple interpretations, a pre-constitutional norm must referee among interpretations to decide what is to be done. One such norm is that the Supreme Court's interpretation is authoritative and supreme ... Its chief alternative is the norm that each official decide for herself what the Constitution requires. But the chief alternative's chief weakness is its failure to take seriously the settlement's function ability to explain much of the importance about law in general and constitutions in particular.[24]

While all legal norms serve the function of settling disputes, Alexander believes that constitutional settlement differs from legal settlement in two respects. First, constitutional settlement is particularly significant because the Constitution "governs all other law, it is especially important for the matters it covers to be settled."[25] Given the special status of the Constitution as the foundation of the legal system, it is especially important to settle constitutional issues. Second, "[a] constitution, because of the difficulty of altering it, attempts to effect a more permanent settlement of what ought to be done than do statutes and common law decisions."[26] Legal (non-constitutional) norms are subject to frequent alterations and, consequently, are not always effective in settling disagreements and bringing about certainty, stability, and predictability. In contrast, constitutional norms are stable and stringent and practically unamendable and, therefore, can better serve this purpose. This argument is also used by Alexander to justify the supremacy of judicial interpretations concerning the Constitution. Given the different structure of courts and legislatures, judicial interpretations of constitutional norms are more likely to be stable than legislative initiatives.[27] Note that both differences between legal and constitutional norms identified by Alexander are quantitative rather than qualitative differences. Both legal

[23] A.V. Dicey, *The Law of the Constitution*, 10th ed. (London: Wildy & Sons, 1959), 24.

[24] Alexander and Schauer, "On Extrajudicial Constitutional Interpretation," 1377.

[25] Ibid.

[26] Alexander and Schauer, "Defending Judicial Supremacy," 457.

[27] Many theorists criticized this latter view. Keith Whittington, "Extrajudicial Constitutional Interpretation: Three Objections and Responses," *North Carolina Law Review* 80, no. 3 (2002): 794–96. Andrei Vermeule also argued: "Would legislative supremacy produce more or less stability than judicial supremacy? Inertia or structural status quo bias is built into legislative institutions by voting rules, bicameralism and other features. Is this stronger or weaker than the status quo built into judicial institutions?" Adrian Vermeule, *Judging Under Uncertainty: An Institutional Theory of Legal Interpretation* (Cambridge, MA: Harvard University Press, 2006), 249. I believe this question is an empirical one and given that I am skeptical with respect to the ability to address empirical questions of this sort, I will not address this issue. For reasons for my skepticism, see Harel, *Why Law Matters*, 3–4.

norms and constitutional norms are means for settling disputes. The latter are only more so in two respects: They settle more important or foundational issues, and they settle them more stringently. It is precisely this observation, namely the claim that the difference between constitutional settlement and legal settlement is merely a matter of degree, that I challenge in the next part. I will argue that constitutional settlement has special significance that is not shared by legal settlement.

13.3 THE VALUE OF CONSTITUTIONAL AUTHORITATIVE SETTLEMENT: WHY *CONSTITUTIONAL* SETTLEMENT MATTERS

It was shown that authoritative settlement is valuable because it facilitates coordination, expertise, and efficiency.[28] Both legal norms and constitutional norms serve to settle disagreements. This section establishes that constitutional authoritative settlement differs from legal authoritative settlement and, further, this difference accounts for the significance of using courts in constitutional adjudication, namely, it accounts for judicial supremacy in constitutional interpretation.

Constitutional authoritative settlement facilitates public recognition that the protection of rights is a duty of the polity, rather than a mere discretionary gesture that hinges upon the goodwill of the polity. By invalidating a statute on the grounds that it conflicts with a constitutional right, the court announces that the state has a duty to honor the right, namely, that honoring it is not a matter that is governed by the state's will, judgment, or its inclinations. Hence, authoritative *constitutional* settlement is not merely valuable because it facilitates coordination, or brings about better decisions, or is more efficient and less costly. In addition, authoritative constitutional settlement is valuable as a pronouncement concerning the normative status of the settlement – its status as a settlement concerning preexisting moral rights whose force does not hinge upon the will of the state. The constitutional order consisting of binding constitutional directives facilitates a clear differentiation between duty-based decisions and discretionary decisions – decisions which depend on the will or the judgment of the state.[29] Let me elaborate.

Many disagreements require settlements that hinge primarily or exclusively on the will of the polity. For instance, the polity ought to settle disagreements with respect to the procedures required to bequeath property. The resulting settlement reflects preferences and judgments balancing between the need for flexibility on the one hand, and reliability on the other. The more stringent and rigid the procedure

[28] Alexander, "Of Living Trees and Dead Hands," 228.

[29] I developed an earlier version of this argument in Harel, *Why Law Matters*, chap. 5. While my discussion there does not use the term settlement, I see now that the concept of settlement developed by Alexander is presupposed by my analysis there.

is, the more reliable it is, but, at the same time, it imposes greater costs on the relevant agents and vice versa. It is important to settle the disagreement concerning the procedure and to settle it in ways that are publicly salient. This example illustrates the need, identified by Alexander, to create rights or make rights more determinate.[30] Once society has selected a settlement, it has created a right which did not exist before the settlement took place. Once the right has been created, it provides reasons to comply with it simply because it has been created and has become salient.

By contrast, other disagreements have to be resolved by incorporating prepolitical moral rights into the legal system.[31] In such cases, the polity settles disagreements concerning what rights we have and makes them legally binding (and, often, also enforceable by the judiciary). In doing so, the polity ought to identify what the content of the prepolitical moral rights is – a content which does not depend on its will. The former category is the category of created legal rights, while the latter category can be labeled replicated or incorporated moral rights. We can sum up the difference between the two categories in the following way: Created legal rights are desirable because they settle disagreements, while replicated or incorporated legal rights are settled because they are desirable independently of the legal or constitutional incorporation of these rights.

The dichotomy between the two types of rights is not always as sharp as it may seem at first sight. To the extent that people have a prepolitical right to bequeath property, they also have a right that the procedure required in order to bequeath property be reliable and flexible. If this is so, one can argue that there is a preexisting right to have a procedure which balances these two considerations. Let me, however, pursue the analysis by assuming that, even if the distinction is not always sharp and precise, it is often sufficiently clear for practical purposes.

When real moral rights are replicated, i.e., incorporated into the legal system, they are often transformed. The legal or constitutional entrenchment of preexisting moral norms results in greater specificity and determinacy than that characterizing the preexisting moral norms. This is because legal or constitutional directives purporting to incorporate moral norms typically select one norm among the many morally permissible or acceptable moral norms. This norm is not necessarily the best norm but it is a reasonable one. It follows, therefore, that that even when legal or constitutional directives entrench preexisting moral norms, the legally or constitutionally entrenched norms are not a mere exact replica of the moral norm. In the process of incorporation, the polity makes choices and selects among the infinite number of potentially acceptable moral norms one specific norm that serves to guide decision makers.

30 Alexander, "Of Living Trees and Dead Hands," 229.

31 Ibid., 228.

Sometimes the norm that is incorporated is abstract and indeterminate, using terms such as "due process," "equal protection," "dignity," "'cruel and unusual," etc. In such cases, the legal or constitutional incorporation of the moral norm does not settle the disagreements effectively. But even in such cases, the legal or constitutional incorporation is conducive to settlement. What settles the disagreements is the continuous interpretation of the norm, which gradually transforms it into a clear and determinate rule. The standard becomes a rule (or, at least, more rule-like) as a result of its continuous interpretation.

Once the choice of the incorporated norm has been made, it typically has further moral consequences. Constitutions, as Joseph Raz pointed out, are often "self-validating." More specifically, Raz argued that as long as constitutions "remain within the boundaries set by moral principles, constitutions are self-validating in that their validity derives from nothing more than the fact that they are there."[32] Hence, while the initial choice made by the polity to select a norm is underdetermined by morality, once the norm is in place, it (typically) gains normative weight as a result of its being incorporated. It gains normative weight precisely for the reasons identified by Alexander. Once a provision has been incorporated into the Constitution, it facilitates settlement and, as long as the content of the settlement is reasonable (even if not ideal), it promotes the values of settlement.

Let me turn back to the distinction drawn by Alexander between the two types of rights: created rights and replicated (incorporated) legal rights. The former gain normative weight by being incorporated by the legal system, while the latter have normative weight independently of whether they are incorporated. Should this distinction affect the mode of incorporation? Should created rights be protected in a different way from incorporated rights?

The primary claim of the rest of this section is that while created rights are typically (although not always) subject to legal settlement, incorporated prepolitical rights should be subject to constitutional settlement. To the extent that rights are our creation, it is permissible (at least typically) to revise them or abolish them if the polity wishes to do so. The legal entrenchment of these rights is attributed to the will or judgment of the polity. Hence, in principle, created rights can be determined by a body which represents the will of the polity, namely, the legislature. This is not so with respect to prepolitical moral rights: The incorporation of these rights is not "up to us," and the mode of their incorporation ought to signify their status as prepolitical moral rights.

32 Joesph Raz, "On the Authority and the Interpretation of Constitutions: Some Preliminaries," in *Co nstitutionalism: Philosophical Foundations*, ed. Larry Alexander (Cambridge: Cambridge University Press, 1998), 173.

Note the qualification made above consisting of the words "in principle." Sometimes there are pragmatic reasons, in particular reasons that rest on the importance of rigid settlement to entrench created rights constitutionally. Alexander points out various norms that have been incorporated into the US Constitution which require settlement but do not involve norms that can be categorized as "real moral rights."[33] Such norms could, in principle, be settled by law but, to the extent that legal settlement is less stable, it may be that there are good reasons to settle such matters constitutionally. Created rights should be settled constitutionally when the created rights require stability and the legal settlement fails to guarantee stability. Most typically, such created norms include norms that establish legal institutions and determine their powers. Without a constitutional entrenchment of these norms, they are subjected to manipulative attempts to redesign these norms in ways that benefit powerful interest groups. Yet, most created rights are legally rather than constitutionally incorporated.

In contrast to the case of created legal rights, when the legal system incorporates prepolitical moral rights, constitutional rather than legal entrenchment is valuable for principled reasons, as only the constitutional entrenchment of such rights facilitates public recognition that the protection of these rights is the state's duty and that the state lacks the power to decide otherwise. Moral rights, so to speak, are not created by us and therefore they cannot be left to institutions that are designed to represent *our* preferences or judgments.

This last observation seems enigmatic. Both legal and constitutional settlements are the byproduct of decisions made by humans. How can one say that they are "not for us to decide"? After all, they are inevitably decided by us or, at least, by some person or institutional entity. There is no available authoritative source other than us that can settle these disagreements or, for that matter, any other disagreements.

To state that such disagreements "are not for us to decide" does not mean, of course, that ultimately they are not decided by us, or at least by some person or institution. Yet, in contrast to created rights, we have no power to settle disagreements in a way which deviates from real moral rights. In settling disagreements concerning moral rights, the polity must acknowledge the existing mandatory force of these rights – force that is independent of its will. The institution that is in charge of entrenching and interpreting these rights is crucial for this purpose. Legislatures, I maintain, are not the right institutions to incorporate prepolitical moral rights because they are primarily structured to give effect to our will.

To explain this observation, note that some institutions gain normative meaning from the values associated with these institutions. Such a link between institutions and values is a prevailing feature of our political and legal culture. Institutions are

[33] Alexander and Schauer, "Defending Judicial Supremacy," 469.

not merely tools for producing just decisions; they are inextricably linked with certain values of the political community. Legislatures and courts signify different values: Legislatures signify commitment to majoritarian sentiments, while courts signify commitment to reason. Legislatures are institutions which represent and promote interests, preferences, judgments, etc. They are charged with crystallizing the collective will of society; they are subject to public pressures from various sectors of the population and, at least ideally, give voice to conflicting interests and preferences. Legislative decisions are created by us and legislatures are, therefore, not the right institutions to convey the mandatory force of real moral rights binding the polity.

To provide an analogy, assume that there is a dispute as to whether A has a particular duty towards B, or what the content of A's duty to B is. Typically, it would be preposterous to let A resolve this dispute. A may be highly conscientious and he may resolve the dispute justly. B may even trust the conscience of A and rightly believe that A is impartial. But, even if this is so, it is still the case that A cannot make decisions with respect to *his* duties towards B. The reason A cannot make such decisions is because, even if A is likely to make the right decision, it is wrong that B's rights are governed by A and, consequently, that B is at A's mercy and depends on his goodwill. The *de jure* slave whose master realizes that slavery is wrong (and therefore does not exercise his powers over the slave) is still a slave. He is a slave not because the master orders him around or is likely to do so in the future (as, under our hypothesis, this is not the case). He is a slave because his master *can* order him around, regardless of what he will in fact do or is likely to do.

Similarly, it seems preposterous to grant a representative body charged with the duty to represent the people to make determinations with respect to the limits of its own powers. Even if the legislature is most likely to make the right decision with respect to my right to free speech, it is wrong that the scope of my right hinges on its discretion, namely, that it *can* limit my right if it so wishes. This is because the very power it has to determine what my rights are is inimical to freedom in the same way that the very power the master has to issue commands to the slave is inimical to freedom, irrespective of whether he exercises this power.[34]

This is why the *constitutional* entrenchment of real moral rights and *judicial supremacy* of constitutional interpretation is essential to the protection of freedom. Citizens are freer in a society in which such rights are recognized as duties independently of the inclinations of the legislature. They are freer in a constitutional polity because judgments concerning their rights do not result from the mere judgments or preferences of legislatures. The supremacy of the Constitution and the supremacy of the judicial interpretations of the Constitution signify that citizens do not live at

[34] Harel, *Why Law Matters*, 170–85.

the mercy of their legislature and are not subject to its whims. By granting the power to legislatures to interpret the Constitution, we imply that incorporated rights are not real moral rights to which the polity is subject but rather created moral rights – the products of our own preferences and judgments.

Let me illustrate the difference by using a specific case. In *Texas v. Johnson*, the US Supreme Court examined the constitutionality of a law prohibiting the burning of the US flag. Mr. Johnson burnt the flag to protest the policies of Ronald Regan and was arrested and charged under a Texas law that prohibits the desecration of a venerated object. The Supreme Court affirmed the decision of the Texas Court of Criminal Appeals, which reversed the conviction on the grounds that the law violated the First Amendment.

The First Amendment is understood by many to be a real moral right rather than a created one and I shall assume that this is indeed so. If the decision concerning *Texas v. Johnson* had been made by the legislature, namely, if the legislature had decided to abolish the prohibition, this would have implied that the decision to abolish the prohibition was based on the inclinations of the polity. In such a case, we could say that the legislature *decided* to allow the burning of the flag. By contrast, although in one sense, by interpreting the Constitution, the court can be said to have made a decision allowing the burning of the flag, there is a sense in which it made no decision whatsoever. Instead, the court merely *declared* that such a right exists.

This is not merely a semantic difference. It is the fact that the interpretation is made by a court – a court which does not create rights but merely declares their existence – that gives Johnson what he is entitled to: namely, the recognition that he has a constitutionally incorporated moral right to burn the flag even if the polity wishes he would not have such a right. The contrast between the legislature and the courts is precisely the contrast between deciding that such a right exists – i.e., creating the right – and merely declaring that it exists. The meaning of a permission to burn the flag would be radically different if the legislature were to decide to abolish the statute prohibiting the burning of the flag. The right to burn the flag would in this case be protected because we, as a polity, wish it to be protected and decide to permit it, rather than because it ought to be protected regardless of our judgments or preferences.

This claim rests on a more general observation concerning legal institutions. Legal institutions are not mere contingent means to facilitate the realization of valuable ends, for example, identifying the right decisions. It is often the case that different legal institutions are valuable for noninstrumental reasons.[35] The legislature and the courts are not merely mechanisms for producing good and just laws. If

[35] Ibid., 2.

they were, one could determine which institution is more appropriate by examining the quality of the settlement of disagreements of each of these institutions and divide the powers between them accordingly. Instead, these institutions have (at least in principle) distinct roles: The legislature is the institution designed to promote our ends and thereby facilitate the mastery over our destiny, while the Constitution and the courts engaged in constitutional interpretation are designed to mark the limits of the powers of the polity. In the absence of constitutional duties, legislative decisions could always be attributable to the legislature's judgments or inclinations, rather than to its duties.

Why is it so crucial to sharply differentiate the mechanisms for settling disputes with respect to these two types of rights? More specifically, why is the publicly salient differentiation between legislative decisions and constitutional decisions so important? Is it not sufficient to guarantee that real moral rights are adequately protected? Arguably, as long as an institution is sufficiently protective of moral rights, we should not care which institution it is.

The answer to this question was provided earlier, but it needs to be elaborated upon. The significance of the Constitution and judicial supremacy is that it protects individual freedom. The public recognition of rights-based duties (by means of constitutional entrenchment) is essential for the protection of freedom, as freedom does not require merely that the legislature refrain from actually violating rights, but also that it be bound to refrain from doing so. This implies that the decision to refrain from violating rights should not be based on the legislature's judgments or inclinations. Johnson, under this view, is not merely entitled to burn the flag without being subjected to criminal sanctions; he is entitled to a decision with respect to his right that is not subject to the judgments or preferences of the majority.

Legal and constitutional settlements of disputes therefore differ fundamentally from each other. Legal settlement is designed to achieve instrumental benefits identified by Alexander: coordination, efficiency, and expertise. Constitutional settlement signifies the subjugation of the polity to prepolitical moral norms. It implies, therefore, that citizens' rights are not at the mercy of the legislature.

And what about democracy? Do the people not have a right to participate – a right to make choices with respect to their lives?[36] Alexander argued persuasively that democracy does not always outweigh urgent moral considerations. If people's fundamental moral rights are violated, "I … cannot see why that decision [the democratically accepted decision] should be given more moral weight than its credentials warrant."[37]

36 Jeremy Waldron, "The Core of the Case Against Judicial Review," *Yale Law Journal* 115, no. 6 (2006): 1346.

37 Alexander, "What is the Problem of Judicial Review," 11.

This is a sound answer; democracy is not a consideration which overrides all considerations. But it seems to me that democratic concerns still pose a challenge for Alexander. This is because the value of constitutional settlement has to be balanced against democratic concerns, and the latter may perhaps at times override the former.

To examine this issue, note that there are two ways for constitutionalists to address the challenge of democracy – the challenge that constitutions violate the right of democratic participation. Under the balancing approach, individual rights are balanced against democratic concerns, and the latter may at times override the former. Hence, denying Texas citizens the power to prohibit the burning of the flag is a loss for democratic values – a loss which has to be balanced against the importance of the right to burn the flag. In making a constitutional determination that a statute is unconstitutional, one has to establish that the benefits outweigh the costs (in terms of loss for democratic values).[38] By contrast, a proponent of constitutionalism can endorse a categorical view. Under the categorical view, if individuals have real moral rights, there is no reason whatsoever to honor the democratic decision at the expense of the right.[39]

I cannot see in Alexander's arguments any clear indication as to whether he supports the balancing or the categorical approach. Yet the value of settlement, as understood by him, supports the balancing approach rather than the categorical approach. While the moral right is important, its importance is not necessarily greater than democratic concerns. But, according to my view of constitutional settlement, this is false: Democracy cannot be balanced against the need to protect moral norms. The value of constitutional settlement identified above provides reasons to adhere to the categorical rather than the balancing approach. This is because this argument demonstrates (or at least purports to demonstrate) that democracy is not only contingently oppressive (when the democratic decisions in fact violate moral rights), but it is necessarily oppressive (because the democratic decisions *can* violate moral rights, and therefore the moral rights are at the mercy of the majority). To protect freedom, one needs to protect real moral rights, irrespective of what citizens want or judge to be just.

It is common to point out that democracy can prioritize the interests of majorities over those of minorities (and, at times, the interests of well-organized powerful minorities over those of dispersed unorganized majorities). The potential conflict between democratic procedures and the protection of basic rights was already

[38] Corey Brettschneider, *Democratic Rights: The Substance of Self Government* (Princeton: Princeton University Press, 2007), 144.

[39] Alon Harel, "Judicial Review and the Value Theory of Democracy," *Representation* 46, no. 1 (2011): 66.

understood in the nineteenth century. Much work in political theory aims to resolve this conflict.

Yet, the analysis above points out an additional concern: The rights of individuals in a democracy (understood in procedural terms) are always contingent on the inclinations and judgments of the majority. Even if the majority protects these rights vigorously, and even if it is likely to do so in the future, it is still the case that individuals' rights are a byproduct of the choice or discretion of the legislature. This is a noncontingent deficiency of democratic institutions: It does not depend on the prospect that these institutions will effectively protect rights. Even if the legislature is enlightened and devoted to the protection of rights and justice, the mere fact that our rights are at its mercy is a deficiency that needs to be addressed, and it is only the Constitution and the supremacy of courts that can address this concern. Hence, it is false to maintain that democratic procedures *can be* oppressive (when they happen to result in unjust laws); instead, it should be recognized that democratic procedures *are necessarily* oppressive (simply because they may result in unjust laws).[40] Democratic procedures are oppressive if and when they empower democratic institutions to violate preexisting moral rights. It follows, therefore, that democratic concerns cannot be balanced against moral rights; the willingness to balance is in itself an oppressive practice which implies that our rights hinge upon popular sentiments.

In a constitutional polity, the legislature does not merely protect rights; it is constitutionally bound to protect rights. The decision concerning incorporated moral rights does not hinge on the inclinations of the legislature. Citizens are not subject to its preferences, judgments, or whims. Even if the legislature is goodwilled and most likely to honor individual rights, the dependence of citizens on its goodwill is inimical to freedom. Precisely as it is inimical to be a slave, even if one's master does not exercise his rights of domination, so it is inimical for freedom to be subject to the whims of the majority, even if the majority does not abuse its powers. Citizens ought to be independent of the popular will; their moral rights ought to be publicly recognized irrespective of what their legislature desires or believes is desirable. If, instead of being constitutionally entrenched, rights are protected by the legislature (even if effectively protected), their force hinges on the sentiments of the majority or on judgments of representatives.

This implies that constitutional settlement matters *as such*. It matters not as a means of protecting rights; it matters as public confirmation that the protection of rights is mandatory. A legislature that complies with binding constitutional directives is not considered to having made a free choice to comply with them; instead, such a legislature does what it must do, irrespective of its wishes or judgments as to what is desirable. Constitutional settlement differs, therefore, from legal settlement not

[40] Harel, *Why Law Matters*, 188–90.

because the former is more stringent or more likely to be stable, but because it does not hinge on the inclinations of the legislature.

Constitutional settlement therefore differs fundamentally from legal settlement. It does not merely rest on the contingent beneficial results of settlement.[41] It is the authoritative settlement itself that is valuable, rather than its contingent consequences. It implies also that the proper scope of using constitutional rather than legal settlement is in cases of incorporated moral rights. Created rights are typically the province of legal (nonconstitutional) settlement.

13.4 CODA: ON SETTLING THE DISPUTE BETWEEN ADVOCATES AND OPPONENTS OF LEGAL SETTLEMENT

While settlement is evidently desirable, legal settlement has its drawbacks. Alexander is well aware of the vices of legal settlement. He mentions and addresses the opposition to legal settlement. More particularly, he discusses the argument that settlement may "truncate precisely the public debate and deliberation that lies, or should lie, at the heart of the constitutional tradition."[42]

Alexander's objections to the anti-legal-settlement camp are compelling objections. He argues that "it appears to us far from certain that a constitution is either a necessary or a sufficient condition, or even a significant causal contributor, to fruitful public debate about matters of great political and moral moment."[43] But the anti-legal-settlement camp still has its own appeal. Arguably, even if settlement is desirable, legal settlement is a coercive settlement; it deprives people of the opportunity to settle disagreements in informal ways, to resolve disagreements informally and consensually. And, although, as Alexander argues on the basis of US experience, constitutional settlement does not preclude political deliberation, it may influence its intensity and depth.

This is an empirical conjecture and, like all empirical conjectures concerning major issues, it is, in my view, irresolvable.[44] While Alexander's claims concerning

[41] This view has implications with respect to the understanding of the concept of authority. Joseph Raz famously argued for the normal justification thesis under which A is an authority over B if and only if B would be likely to comply better with reasons that apply to him independently already were he to accept as binding and act on the directives of A than he would if he were to act on his own assessment of reasons. Joseph Raz, *The Morality of Freedom* (Oxford: Oxford University Press, 1986), 53. By contrast, my view implies that authority can be justified not merely on instrumental grounds. Constitutional authority does not rest merely on the likelihood that it guides citizens to act justly or correctly. It seems that the implications of my view are closer to the views of Darwall concerning authority. See Stephen Darwall, "Authority and Reasons: Exclusionary and Second-Personal," *Ethics* 120, no. 2 (2010).

[42] Alexander and Schauer "Defending Judicial Supremacy," 467–68.

[43] Ibid., 468.

[44] Harel, *Why Law Matters*, 3–5.

the virtues of settlement are plausible, they also rest on empirical conjectures which, Alexander himself concedes, cannot be substantiated.

But, in addition to the empirical conjectures, the debates between proponents and opponents rest on different normative premises. The more one values political debate and public deliberation, the more one would be opposed to constitutional settlement. The more one values the tangible benefits of settlement – cooperation, expertise, and efficiency – the greater the inclination to resort to constitutional settlement. Ultimately, therefore, the disposition to settle disagreements by using constitutional means rests not only on empirical conjectures but also on normative sensibilities.

Constitutionalism is an elusive concept. One of the great virtues of Larry Alexander's theory of constitutionalism is that, unlike much of what is often labeled constitutional theory, it is not grounded in any particular constitution. It is generalizable and touches upon the very idea of a constitution and its underlying justification. This article accepts the foundations of Alexander's view, namely, that both law and constitutions serve to settle disagreements. However, it differs from Alexander's framework in that it maintains that legal and constitutional settlement are very different phenomena. Constitutions settle disagreements in ways that are distinctive and radically different from other instances of legal settlement.

PART III

Perplexities in Jurisprudence

14

For Legal Principles

Mitchell N. Berman

14.1 INTRODUCTION

By any measure, Larry Alexander ranks high among the day's widest-ranging, most original, and most rigorous legal theorists. Beyond his lasting and profound scholarly contributions across diverse fields, Larry is also a mentor and a mensch. In my own (far from isolated) case, not only was Larry instrumental in my landing an entry-level job twenty years ago, he has, in ways large and small, overseen much of my continuing legal education since. I realize that, were it not for Larry Alexander, none of us would be contributing to this volume. But I'm tempted to say that that's doubly true for me. I am profoundly in his debt.

Although I owe Larry more than I could repay, my task in this essay is to try to put a dent in my arrears. I'll do so in the fashion customary among our ilk: by highlighting and endeavoring to correct one of his errors. My topic is Alexander's well-known rejection of legal principles.

Most legal thinkers – judges, litigators, legal scholars, legal philosophers – believe that legal rules and legal principles are meaningfully distinguished. Many folks may have no very precise distinction in mind, and those who do might not all agree. But it is widely believed that legal norms come in different logical types, and that one difference is reasonably well captured by a nomenclature that distinguishes "rules" from "principles."

Alexander has campaigned against this legal orthodoxy for nearly forty years,[1] elaborating his case at greatest length in "Against Legal Principles," an influential article coauthored two decades ago with Ken Kress.[2] "Against Legal Principles" pressed a

[1] See Larry Alexander and Michael Bayles, "Hercules or Proteus? The Many Theses of Ronald Dworkin," *Social Theory and Practice* 5, no. 3/4 (1980): 267.

[2] Larry Alexander and Ken Kress, "Against Legal Principles," in *Law and Interpretation: Essays in Legal Philosophy*, ed. Andrei Marmor (Oxford: Clarendon Press, 1995), 279, reprinted in *Iowa Law Review* 82, no. 3 (1997): 739. I will cite to the journal article.

strikingly ambitious thesis – not merely that this or that conception or deployment of legal principles is misguided, but that there is no coherent, meaningful account of legal principles to give: "[L]egal principles cannot exist except perhaps as theoretically possible but practically inert entities."[3] Shorn of a hedge for the theoretically-possible-but-practically-inert, the thesis becomes: "Either legal principles are just (correct) moral principles, or they are nothing."[4]

I believe that Alexander is mistaken. I believe that there are distinct types of legal norms; that one type of legal norm has features – particularly "weight" – widely attributed to what we call "principles"; and that the rules/principles distinction, when properly construed, is centrally important to legal theory.

I cannot fully establish my affirmative claim in this limited space. Instead, I will sketch the rudiments of my account of what legal principles are, how they are constituted, and what functions they serve, and then show how that conception of legal principles survives Alexander and Kress's arguments for their categorical rejection.

The basic idea is this: Legal principles are legal norms that are grounded in social facts that make up legal practices and that serve to *metaphysically determine* or *constitute* the legal rules. This picture contrasts with Ronald Dworkin's account in which legal principles constitute or determine the legal rules by *morally justifying* them. It also contrasts with a common view of legal principles as norms that *supplement* legal rules, rather than constituting them, and are to be used by judges when rules "run out."

Although Alexander and Kress claim to defeat legal principles generally, they focus on Dworkin's account. I will first observe that, even if legal principles cannot do the work Dworkin attributes to them, Alexander and Kress's arguments for that conclusion cause no trouble for accounts that put principles to different use. I will then argue that additional arguments that purport to reach beyond the Dworkinian *conception* of legal principles (so to speak) to the very *concept* are unpersuasive.

That's not all. In addition to denying legal principles, Alexander affirms a form of constitutional originalism that he describes as "simple-minded."[5] According to his account, the law is (to a first pass) what the constitutional text's authors intended to communicate by means of its enactment.

Alexander's rejection of principles and his embrace of intentionalist originalism are intertwined. I will argue that Alexander's case for originalism founders if the universe of legal norms includes fundamental norms that are grounded directly in social facts and that participate in the production or determination of legal rules.

3 Ibid., 739.

4 Ibid., 767.

5 Larry Alexander, "Simple-Minded Originalism," in *The Challenge of Originalism*, ed. Grant Huscroft and Bradley W. Miller (Cambridge: Cambridge University Press, 2011), 87.

14.2 "AGAINST LEGAL PRINCIPLES": A SUMMARY

Acknowledging "the ubiquity of references to legal principles in jurisprudential literature, legal scholarship, and case law,"[6] Alexander and Kress begin by describing belief in legal principles as central to "an entire jurisprudential tradition, a tradition that has shaped not only academic thought on these matters, but also how lawyers and judges think and operate."[7] They also recognize, albeit cursorily, a diversity of viewpoints regarding precisely what distinguishes these two norm types.[8]

Lack of agreement regarding just what legal principles consist in or what functions they serve makes defense of a universal negative challenging. Because the error theorist about legal principles cannot reasonably address every theoretically possible conception of legal principles, at least two distinct argumentative strategies are available. The standard move is to try to establish that there is enough agreement on the core concept so that features can be identified that must be shared by *any* purported account of "legal principles" for it to *be* an account of *legal principles*, and show that no account with those features is possible. An alternative is to identify the most plausible account, show that that account fails, and then conclude that all other accounts fail a fortiori. Alexander and Kress adopt both strategies.

Their argument begins with a general account of the rule/principle distinction. Legal rules are posited by specific institutions at specific moments; they have canonical form; and they "are determinative of the outcomes of whatever transactions come within their terms,"[9] which is to say that they "have all-or-nothing application."[10] Legal principles cannot be posited, lack canonical formulation, and have the dimension of "weight," which is to say that they may "bear on" the proper legal characterization or treatment of a dispute without even purporting to deliver decisive resolution.[11] For Alexander and Kress, these three features are not merely representative of the two distinct norm types, but definitional. They deny any room for intermediate norms – e.g., norms that are promulgated but have weight.[12]

Although the three features just mentioned were first limned by Dworkin, Alexander and Kress treat them as essential to *any* account of legal principles. Weight

[6] Alexander and Kress, "Against Legal Principles," 739.

[7] Ibid., 745.

[8] Ibid., 746–47. For a survey of the terrain, see Humberto Ávila, *Theory of Legal Principles* (Dordrecht: Springer, 2007), chap. 2.

[9] Alexander and Kress, "Against Legal Principles," 740.

[10] Ibid., 747.

[11] Alexander and Kress sometimes describe rules as having infinite weight and (supposed) principles as having finite weight. Sticking with convention, I'll describe principles as having weight, and rules as being determinative.

[12] Alexander and Kress, "Against Legal Principles," 741n6, 741n8.

is the critical feature: "[W]eight is essential to their being principles, since they have neither canonical form nor dependence on particular persons' datable intentions to govern their application."[13] The crux of their objection holds that norms with weight cannot emerge from legal practice. "What weight will [legal] principles have, and how will such weight be determined?" they ask. Referencing Quine, they conclude that "[n]o set of past cases, no matter how large the set, can fix as a matter of logical entailment the weight in the context of a present case of any principles that would explain those past cases."[14]

While Alexander and Kress treat the features that Dworkin attributes to legal principles as true of *any* account of legal principles, they also recognize that Dworkin's rendering is special – "the most powerful," "clearest," and "most careful" account.[15] What makes Dworkin's account *an* account of legal principles, rather than *the* account? His account is distinctive not in terms of the formal qualities that legal principles are supposed to possess (weight) or to lack (canonical form), but in terms of their contents and functions. Dworkinian legal principles (say Alexander and Kress) are "the morally best principles that would justify the promulgation of a high percentage of the extant legal rules."[16] They "are the theoretical entities that justify the legal rules, determine how they should be extended and modified, and resolve conflicts among them."[17]

Alexander and Kress aim most of their critical fire at features that make Dworkin's account of legal principles special, and not those that are purportedly true of all accounts. At bottom, Alexander and Kress insist that legal principles understood in this fashion are normatively unattractive.

> Moral principles have the virtue of moral correctness; legal rules have the virtues of being the creations of those with authority to make law and of giving clear guidance. Legal principles, however, have none of these virtues. They are neither morally correct nor uncontroversial in application … They represent the worst of all worlds.[18]

The supposedly distinct virtue of legal systems that Dworkin calls "integrity" cannot render legal principles attractive, for "there cannot be a coherent reason in terms of the true moral value of equality for ever departing from the requirements of the correct moral theory."[19] Finally, and for reasons that we can skip past, use of

13 Ibid., 761.
14 Ibid.
15 Ibid., 739, 746, 752.
16 Ibid., 747.
17 Ibid., 748.
18 Ibid., 753–54.
19 Ibid., 755.

legal principles cannot, as Dworkin claims, "protect legal rights against retroactive upsets."[20]

In sum, legal actors would never have reason to follow "legal principles, which offer neither the guidance virtues of rules nor the virtue of moral correctness."[21] Despite its multiple failings, however, Alexander and Kress maintain that "[i]f there are legal principles that are morally incorrect principles, then Dworkin's account of them is the best there is."[22] Therefore, the failure of Dworkin's account of legal principles dooms *all* accounts.

14.3 A POSITIVIST PICTURE OF LEGAL PRINCIPLES AS LEGALLY FUNDAMENTAL NORMS

I am not a disinterested observer of debates over the existence of legal principles; I have an account to peddle. In my view, in brief, legal principles are the fundamental norms of a legal system; they are grounded directly in behaviors and attitudes of members of the legal community (chiefly judges); and they function not only to guide judges when called upon to exercise judicial discretion, but to participate in the production of legal rules.

I elaborate on this picture of legal principles elsewhere.[23] My modest aim here is to make the basic idea intelligible and not implausible. I'll start not with legal principles but with legal rules.

While Alexander and Kress are error theorists about legal principles, they're realists about legal rules: "[L]egal rules exist and belong to the ontological realm of fact." Assuming arguendo this is true, however, legal rules are not, of course, ontologically fundamental. In virtue of what do legal rules exist? What grounds legal rules? In what do they consist? (Throughout this essay, I use language of metaphysical determination – grounding, determination, constitution, emergence, etc. – loosely and somewhat interchangeably. I'm trying to present a rough picture, not to commit myself to any particular and controverted metaphysical theses.) "Their existence," say Alexander and Kress, "consists of their canonical formulation and the possibly complex, combined intentions of the rules' authors that their canonical formulation represents."[24]

Let's put a label to this thesis. Call it "intentionalism," and define it (to a first pass) as follows: The law is whatever norms the authors of a legally authoritative

20 Ibid.

21 Ibid., 786.

22 Ibid., 764.

23 See Mitchell N. Berman, "Our Principled Constitution," *University of Pennsylvania Law Review* 166, no. 6 (2018): 1325.

24 Alexander and Kress, "Against Legal Principles," 763n96.

text intended to communicate by means of their enacted text. Alexander and Kress appear to affirm intentionalism (or a close relative).

Even if true, intentionalism is not itself ontologically fundamental or ultimate. We can ask what are the grounds or determinants of intentionalism, or what makes intentionalism true? For a positivist, the answer, at some point down this path of regress, will be: social facts. On the simplifying yet plausible assumption that the chain of regress ends here, intentionalism would be directly grounded in social facts. Hart's rule of recognition is the dominant account of how this could be: If intentionalism is true, it is true in virtue of a convergent practice among legal officials of accepting intentionalism in the way described by the internal point of view.[25] But that's only one possible way; the particulars of Hart's account are not *definitional* of positivism. Perhaps intentionalism arises from social facts other than by means of a convergent practice of officials that Hart describes. It may arise from a different type of convention or agreement among legal practitioners. Or it may arise from other sociolegal practices, paradigmatically including, but not limited to, its explicit invocation by judges to explain and (legally) justify the announcement of legal rules and the issuance of legal rulings.

It's not essential now to embrace any particular positivist account of the mechanisms or manner by which social facts ground or determine legal norms. (I'll say a little more later.) Abstracting from the particulars of the Hartian account, two general points are important. First, intentionalism (if true) is grounded in social facts, not in other legal norms; it is, let us say, a "fundamental" rather than "derivative" legal norm. Second, the function of intentionalism is to contribute to the existence of other legal norms – namely, the derivative ones. If legal rule R1 exists, that is in virtue of the conjunction of intentionalism and the fact that the authorially intended meaning of a statutory text S is R1 (along, no doubt, with other facts too).

Thus far, this section tries merely to make explicit details of the picture of legal rules that Alexander's own account suggests, at least when located in a positivist frame. Now, I'll add a third idea: Intentionalism is not the *only* legal norm that is legally fundamental and serves to participate in the determination of derivative legal rules. There could be many others, and in a complex and mature legal system there are bound to be. Here are examples of other possible legal norms that have these features. I'm not asserting that any are *actual* fundamental norms in the American legal system; I'm introducing familiar and plausible examples to convey a flavor of the norms we might expect to see at the fundamental legal level of a legal system:

[25] H.L.A. Hart, *The Concept of Law*, 3rd ed. (New York: Oxford University Press, 2012).

- *desuetude* – legal rules that have not been obeyed or enforced for substantial time lose force;
- *derogation* – statutes in derogation of the common law are narrowly construed;
- *practice counts* – distributions of governing power that have become accepted have legal force;
- *negative retributivism* – persons should not be punished in excess of their moral blameworthiness or desert;
- *federalism* – national legislation must respect the special role of states as distinct sovereigns;

and, for any reader who's not yet certain about where I'm going,

- *wrongdoers shouldn't profit* – persons shouldn't be allowed to profit from their own wrongdoing.

All of these norms – desuetude, practice counts, federalism, intentionalism, and so on – are what I propose to call legal principles. Together with numberless others, they comprise a disparate lot. One may be tempted to describe some as "substantive," and others as "formal" or "procedural." Some may strike you as morally attractive, others as neutral or morally objectionable. Yet they all have this in common: They are legally fundamental (not posited or determined by other legal norms), grounded in social facts, lacking canonical formulation, and essential to the existence of legal rules. Legal rules are produced by the interaction or combination of legal principles and the facts that they make relevant.

Notice that I did not claim that these purported principles all possess weight. And I didn't because intentionalism itself looms as a counterexample. As initially formulated – "the law is whatever the authors of a legally authoritative text intended to communicate by means of their enacted text" – intentionalism appears determinative, or rule-like.

But that earlier formulation cannot stand as is. If even a small handful of legal norms operate at the fundamental level, then intentionalism must be reformulated, for it won't be true, as our first cut at intentionalism conveys, that the intentions of some group of authors determine or constitute the content of our legal rules, full stop. A revision of some sort is called for.

Two possible revisionary routes are most obvious: either a determinative norm qualified with exceptions (intentionalism$_E$) or a nondeterminative norm with weight (intentionalism$_W$). I endorse the latter, something like the following:

- *intentionalism* – the norms that the authors of an authoritative legal text intended to communicate by means of its promulgation have substantial force.

So, yes, according to the positivist account I'm offering, legal principles have weight.[26]

How do weighty norms ("principles"), along with the nonlegal facts that they make relevant or operate upon, interact to produce determinate norms ("rules")? What are the underlying mechanisms? That's a very fair question that philosophers of law and other metanormative theorists should strive to resolve. I cannot take on that project here. In the meantime, consider that principles are types of norms and that norms are, or are comfortably analogized to, forces. So if you want a possible and loose model of their interaction in mind, think vector addition. The essential point is that legal principles are plural and play a functional rule in the production of legal rules. In a bumper sticker: Legal principles are grounded in social facts; legal rules are constituted by legal principles (and the facts they make relevant). Call this picture "principled positivism."

I will add a little detail to this barebones sketch in the remaining two sections. At this stage, it's enough to reiterate how this account of legal principles differs from the chief competitors.

Start with Dworkin. For Dworkin, legal principles depend upon moral principles. To be sure, legal principles are not *identical* to moral principles, or even a true subset: "[L]egal principles will not be moral principles but will deviate from them because of morally infelicitous legal materials with which they must cohere."[27] But nor are legal and moral principles entirely distinct, or related only as a matter of empirical contingency. As Alexander and Kress characterize them, Dworkinian legal principles are "the morally best principles … among all possible principles that meet or exceed the threshold of 'fit.' "[28] They "are connected to moral principles in that moral principles determine which set of legal principles among those sets that 'fit' the legal rules is the morally best set of principles."[29]

However it may be best to characterize Dworkinian legal principles – say, as "nonideal" moral principles,[30] or not – more important and less ambiguous is what function they are thought to serve. They are what they are – they have the content and force that they do – in virtue of their ability to morally justify rules and practices of the legal system. As Dworkin explained, "rights and responsibilities flow from past

[26] At least characteristically. The defining feature of principles, on the account I'm presenting, is their legal fundamentality. Weight characteristically goes with fundamentality, but I do not dismiss the possibility of norms that are fundamental and determinative. On a simplifying rule/principle binary, these would be principles.

[27] Larry Alexander, "The Method of Text and ?: Jack Balkin's Originalism with No Regrets," *University of Illinois Law Review* 2012, no. 3 (2012): 619.

[28] Alexander and Kress, "Against Legal Principles," 744.

[29] Ibid., 747.

[30] Ibid., 748n44.

decisions and so count as legal, not just when they are explicit in these decisions but also when they follow from the principles of personal and political morality the explicit decisions presuppose by way of justification."[31]

That is no part of the positivistic picture of legal principles I have sketched. Legal principles are part of the complex normative architecture of legal systems. They help mediate between the social factual grounds of the system and the determinate rules that the system generates, maintains, and enforces. They do not serve to *justify* the rules of the system from any extralegal normative vantage point. The principles don't morally justify the rules; they participate in their production.

Or consider a second, non-Dworkinian, account of legal principles as norms that judges should deploy when rules run out. Gary Lawson described this familiar view well: "adjudicators must be able to decide cases even when the rules give out, so we have to supplement the rules with something. That 'something' might be moral principles if they are capable of doing the job, or it might be legal principles if moral principles are insufficiently robust."[32] Again, on the view I am pitching, legal principles do not – or do not *only* – offer guidance when the rules run out; they are part of the rules' grounding.

This is not a novel or idiosyncratic account. Roscoe Pound advanced a recognizably similar view nearly a century ago. "We deceive ourselves grossly when we devise theories of law or theories of judicial decision that exclude such things from 'the law'," he wrote, speaking of "a body of philosophical, political, and ethical ideas as to the end of law."[33]

> When such ideal pictures have acquired a certain fixity in the judicial and professional tradition they are part of "the law" quite as much as legal precepts. Indeed, they give the latter their living content and in all difficult cases are the ultimate basis of choosing, shaping, and applying legal materials in the decision of controversies.[34]

Replace "legal precepts" with "legal rules," and call the fundamental stuff grounded in "judicial and professional" practice "legal principles," and you've got the basic picture. Alexander and Kress ask: "In what sense are legal principles 'legal'?"[35] They are legal in that they are brought into existence by legal practice, and they serve as grounds for the more determinate norms that it is the function of a legal system to generate, maintain, and enforce.

[31] Ronald Dworkin, *Law's Empire* (Cambridge, MA: Harvard University Press, 1986), 96.

[32] Gary Lawson, "A Farewell to Principles," *Iowa Law Review* 82, no. 3 (1997): 898.

[33] Roscoe Pound, "The Theory of Judicial Decision," *Harvard Law Review* 36, no. 8 (1923): 645.

[34] Ibid.

[35] Alexander and Kress, "Against Legal Principles," 745.

14.4 PRINCIPLED POSITIVISM SURVIVES ALEXANDER AND KRESS'S CRITIQUE

As I have already stressed, most of Alexander and Kress's arguments target Dworkin's account of legal principles and other possible accounts that share these features: Legal principles are derivative variations on moral principles whose function is to morally justify legal rules and practices. Alexander and Kress's central complaint is that imperfect or "incorrect" moral principles cannot provide the moral justification that proponents of such principles promise.

I believe that Alexander and Kress score points against Dworkin. Indeed, the "one-system picture" that Dworkin advanced in his final major jurisprudential work, *Justice for Hedgehogs*, might help vindicate Alexander and Kress's contention that "Dworkin's case for legal principles is nothing more than a case for correct moral principles."[36]

Be that as it may, these criticisms lack force against any account of legal principles that eschews the features central to and distinctive of Dworkin's. And there may be many. Lawson pressed this very concern sharply. Observing that the role Dworkin assigns to moral principles in the generation of legal principles renders his account "decidedly unrepresentative of modern understandings of legal principles," Lawson complained that, "by focusing on Dworkin's account of legal principles, Alexander and Kress may have selected the most rather than the least vulnerable target for their attack."[37]

What arguments do Alexander and Kress present against legal principles conceived as described in Section 14.3 – namely, as fundamental legal norms that are grounded in social facts, have the dimension of weight, and participate in the determination of the derivate and more determinate legal norms customarily termed "rules"? Brian Leiter thought none, charging that "Against Legal Principles" "is actually devoid of any arguments against the *existence* of legal principles, and consists entirely of *normative* arguments against employing legal principles."[38]

I think that Leiter overstates his case.[39] But it remains true that individuating and clearly specifying Alexander and Kress's arguments against non-Dworkinian

[36] Ibid., 764; see Ronald Dworkin, *Justice for Hedgehogs* (Cambridge, MA: Harvard University Press, 2011), chap. 19. For my criticism of the one-system picture, see Mitchell N. Berman, "Of Law and Other Artificial Normative Systems," in *Dimensions of Normativity: New Essays on Metaethics and Jurisprudence*, ed. David Plunkett, Scott Shapiro, and Kevin Toh (Oxford University Press, forthcoming).

[37] Lawson, "A Farewell to Principles," 894, 893.

[38] Brian Leiter, "Explanation and Legal Theory," *Iowa Law Review* 82, no. 3 (1997): 906.

[39] As revealing is Alexander and Kress's response: "Our ontological argument against legal principles is an argument against their existence as normative *justificatory* entities. Whether such entities might exist in some other ontological mode is a question we reserve for another occasion." Larry Alexander and Ken Kress, "Replies To Our Critics," *Iowa Law Review* 82, no. 3 (1997): 927. This qualification

principles is not easy. Although their argumentative barrage can be parsed in varied ways, I'll identify five more or less distinct contentions: (1) legal principles "have a problematic metaphysical status"[40]; (2) even if legal principles could exist, they would require an agreement among practitioners that manifestly does not obtain; (3) even if legal principles could exist and arise without agreement, their weight cannot be determined by social facts in the way that a positivist account requires; (4) even if weighty principles can emerge from social facts, they cannot interact to serve their supposed function of helping to determine legal rules; and (5) even if principles have weight and can interact to produce determinate legal norms, we cannot gain knowledge (or true belief) of them. I address Alexander and Kress's arguments for these contentions in order.

The first objection to legal principles – concerning their "problematic metaphysical status" – is not developed at length, but centers on the claims that legal principles contrast unfavorably with legal rules on the one hand and with moral principles on the other. Hand one:

> [L]egal principles cannot unproblematically claim the same ontological status as legal rules. Though legal principles, like legal rules, are formulated by judges and legislators, the formulation and the legal principle are ontologically distinct. The formulation of a legal principle *refers* to it, whereas the formulation of a legal rule *is* the legal rule.

Hand two:

> Legal principles have the following metaphysical oddity. They arise not from the realm of fact, and not from the realm of value, but from the combination of fact and value. Unlike the straightforward supervenience on facts that many philosophers claim is the best ontological account of moral values, the supervenience of legal principles is on a combination of facts (legal rules) and moral values.[41]

Neither contrast that Alexander and Kress draw withstands scrutiny. On the first hand, it is incorrect that "the formulation of a legal rule *is* the legal rule." The formulation of a rule and the rule itself are distinct, for the same rule can be formulated in varied ways. "No vehicles are allowed in the park" and "Vehicles are not permitted inside this park" are distinct verbal formulae but plausibly refer (and, in a given context of utterance, can give rise) to the identical rule. To reformulate a rule

backtracks so conspicuously from the arresting ambition their initial article announces that I can treat it only as a momentary failure of nerve. To credit it as their settled position is to give up the game to all genuinely positivist conceptions of legal principles. Alexander's current view is unqualified: "There are no legal principles." Alexander, "The Method of Text and ?" 621 (emphasis omitted).

40 Alexander and Kress, "Against Legal Principles," 762.

41 Ibid., 763n96.

need not change its content. It is critical to remember, yet easy to forget, that a text, a text's meaning, and the normative entity (say, a "rule") to which the text gives rise are of different metaphysical kinds.[42] Because the relationship between a formulation of a rule and the rule itself is both more complex and less well understood than Alexander and Kress let on, they have not substantiated their claim that the metaphysical status of legal principles is problematic whereas the metaphysical status of legal rules is straightforward.[43]

On the second hand, even if the "metaphysical oddity" Alexander and Kress note is true of legal principles according to the Dworkinian account, in which "the construction of [legal principles] is guided by correct moral principles,"[44] recall that, according to the positivist picture I'm presenting, legal principles are constructed only by social facts, not by moral principles.[45] Thus, positivist legal principles as I have described them are not metaphysically odd in the way that Alexander and Kress claim.

If Alexander and Kress have identified no deep metaphysical obstacle to the possibility of legal principles grounded in social facts, the nonexistence of legal principles would nonetheless be secured if the conditions necessary for their emergence do not, and could not plausibly, obtain. That's Alexander and Kress's next move. Assuming arguendo that "[l]egal principles and their weights are whatever competent practitioners would agree they were,"[46] it's obvious that competent practitioners in modern complex legal regimes do not all agree about the principles that supposedly populate the system, and they're not about to.

Although agreement admits of degrees, Alexander and Kress mean by "agreement" unanimous or near-unanimous consensus or accord. I agree that "agreement," so construed, is not our lot. What remains to be established is that positivist theories of law require agreement of this character for principles to emerge. Alexander and Kress announce that they "have serious doubts that conventionalism can ever

42 See Mitchell N. Berman, "The Tragedy of Justice Scalia," *Michigan Law Review* 115, no. 6 (2017): 786–99.

43 Is there a more charitable understanding of the contrast between legal rules and legal principles that Alexander and Kress are trying to mark here? Possibly this: Whereas the formulation of a legal rule contributes to the existence and content of the rule itself, the formulation of a legal principle does not contribute to the principle's existence. Yet even this is too pat. It is not the "formulation" of a legal rule that makes it so, but rather the promulgation or enactment of a text that states a rule. And the invocation of principles by legal decision makers contributes to the existence of the rule. Legal rules and principles alike are brought into being by complex speech acts.

44 Alexander and Kress, "Replies to Our Critics," 932.

45 This does not mean that moral principles are entirely out of the picture. People's beliefs about moral principles may have a causal effect on the behaviors that, on my account, ground legal principles. I'm focusing on constitutive relationships here, not causal ones.

46 Alexander and Kress, "Against Legal Principles," 767.

dispense with agreement" (by which they mean nearly full agreement).[47] But a declaration of doubts, even if well founded, is not an argument.[48]

How could fundamental legal norms arise if *not* by near-unanimous agreement among practitioners regarding their existence and contents? Maybe this way: They are grounded in or constituted by their being "taken up" by legal actors in legal reasoning and decision making. The paradigm, I have said, involves invocation of principles by judges as legal grounds for a legal ruling or for a holding regarding the existence and shape of a more determinate legal norm. This happens all the time. In addition, principles can be taken up without being explicitly invoked. And they are taken up by persons other than judges – lawyers, elected officials, and ordinary citizens – as they endorse, criticize, or reaffirm either the principles themselves or rules or rulings that rest on and manifest given principles.

In short, principles are theoretical entities that are the objects of belief by legal actors and that are constituted by the legally relevant behaviors that are explained by those beliefs, and that express acceptance or endorsement. They are much like trails: "They continually change – widen or narrow, schism or merge – depending on how, or whether, their followers elect to use them."[49]

Plainly, this is only a rough sketch of how social facts could ground legal principles. It is nonetheless striking that Alexander and Kress marshal no explicit argument against something like it. Rather, after announcing doubt that a positivist principle can arise without near-unanimous agreement regarding its existence and content, they immediately shift tack. "In any event," they continue, "against these conventionalist theories, we would urge the normative superiority of following correct moral principles rather than conventional legal principles."[50] That might be so. But on a positivist picture of law, the move signals a retreat from debates about legal metaphysics (whether the class of legal norms includes a norm type that has weight and arises by practice), and into ethics (whether judges, and others, should follow law that is constituted partly by means of legal principles that arise by convention). This is why Leiter worries that the *existence* of legal principles is not among Alexander and Kress's true targets.

We come, then, to the argument that, I think, Alexander and Kress consider their strongest: Weights cannot arise by practice. But *if* my arguments to this point are successful, then the supposed problem of *weight* should seem an unpromising place to make a stand, for although content and weight are distinct attributes of a principle, they plausibly come about in roughly the same way. (Contrast, say, the shape

[47] Ibid., 767n106.

[48] Accord Lawson, "A Farewell to Principles," 896.

[49] Robert Moor, *On Trails: An Exploration* (New York: Simon & Schuster, 2016), 17.

[50] Alexander and Kress, "Against Legal Principles," 767n106.

of a jigsaw puzzle piece and the pattern of colors on its surface.) Presumably, the weights of principles, like their contents or contours, are brought about by members of the legal community taking them up and deploying them in legal reasoning and decision making. Weights are relative to one another, and are given by what members of the legal community say about them and how they use them. They are also conferred, as it were, by battle – by the rules that are adjudged victorious, and thus made so, when principles press in opposing directions. None of which is to say that the weights of principles, any more than their contents and contours, are always sufficiently determinate to yield rules covering all matters of legal dispute. I'm certain they aren't.

It is not entirely clear why Alexander and Kress believe that weights cannot arise this way. One precise objection, however, concerns the supposed context-sensitivity of principles' weights. "Because principles' weights vary in different concrete contexts, a complete account of principles requires differing weights for every conceivable context. But we cannot establish principles by agreement because we cannot establish their weight by agreement."[51]

Ignore references to "agreement," and focus only on the claim that principles' weights vary context to context. I find this characterization misleading for failing to recognize that the magnitude of the force a principle exerts in a given context is a function of (at least) two variables, not one: the weight of the principle, and the extent to which the principle is (as I call it) "activated."[52] Weight may be constant across contexts – though *not* over time[53] – while *activation* is context-sensitive. Compare: The mass of two bodies, and thus the gravitational force that they have the capacity to exert, is not contextually variant, though the gravitational force that they exert on an object in a given context also depends on their distances from that object, which *is* context-variant.

Readers who remain skeptical that practice can confer weights on principles might reflect on the alternatives. Return to the purported fundamental legal norm I dubbed intentionalism, and to its variants: a determinate norm qualified by exceptions, or a nondeterminate norm that has the quality of weight. If these fundamental norms arise somehow from messy social facts, I, at least, find it far easier to imagine the emergence of intentionalism$_W$ – a norm with possibly jagged contours and not precisely specified weight – than the emergence of intentionalism$_E$ – an

[51] Alexander and Kress, "Replies to Our Critics," 924–25.

[52] See Berman, "Our Principled Constitution"; compare Robert Alexy, "Formal Principles: Some Replies to Critics," *International Journal of Constitutional Law* 12, no. 3 (2014): 513 (defining the "concrete weight" that a principle exerts in context as a function of, inter alia, the principle's "abstract weight" and the "intensity of interference" with the principle under the circumstances).

[53] For an argument that we lack power to fix the fundamental legal stuff that plays a role in determining legal rules against gradual, evolutionary change, see Berman, "The Tragedy of Justice Scalia," 794–96.

algorithmic norm replete with (possibly) many exceptions, (possibly) intricately nested.

Let us take stock: Alexander and Kress have not yet shown that legal norms, with weight, cannot arise or emerge from social practices, and in a fashion that does not require near-unanimous practitioner agreement regarding the norms' contents and weights. Though I have not established that they can, Alexander and Kress have provided scant reason to dismiss it as a live possibility.

This leads to the fourth contention: Even if principles with weight can emerge from practice, they cannot function as I have suggested they do – namely, by combining or interacting to generate distinct legal norms that differ in content from the other principles and belong to a different normative type (a "rule"). Alexander and Kress do not advance this particular objection in "Against Legal Principles," but Alexander has in other writings challenged pluralistic nonoriginalist theories of constitutional interpretation in terms that either explicitly endorse or strongly suggest this objection. As a representative passage puts it:

> No one – not even lawyers – can meaningfully "combine" fact and value, or facts of different types, except lexically ... Any non-lexical "combining" of text and intentions, text and justice, and so forth is just incoherent, like combining pi, green, and the Civil War. There is no process of reasoning that can derive meaning from such combinations.[54]

Admittedly, it is not entirely clear, in this passage and others like it, that Alexander intends to advance precisely the objection under consideration. He says that different types of facts – facts about texts, intentions, justice, etc. – cannot combine to yield what he calls "meaning," a semantic notion. The question on the table, however, is whether legal principles and the variety of facts that they concern or make legally relevant – semantic facts, psychological facts, historical facts, moral facts, etc. – can collectively ground or constitute other, derivative legal norms. A negative answer to this question is not entailed by Alexander's disparate-facts-can't-collectively-constitute-meaning thesis.

But insofar as Alexander would deny that legal principles and the facts to which they refer can combine to produce other legal norms ("rules"), Kevin Toh and I have argued at length elsewhere that no persuasive reasons have been provided, by Alexander or others, for that skeptical conclusion.[55] So-called thick concepts (e.g.,

54 Larry Alexander, "The Banality of Legal Reasoning," *Notre Dame Law Review* 73, no. 3 (1998): 521 (footnotes omitted); see also, e.g., Larry Alexander, "Telepathic Law," *Constitutional Commentary* 27, no. 1 (2010): 144.

55 See Mitchell N. Berman and Kevin Toh, "Pluralistic Nonoriginalism and the Combinability Problem," *Texas Law Review* 91, no. 7 (2013): 1739.

courage, cruelty) are thought to combine evaluative and nonevaluative criteria. Much of social ontology (think of a university) concerns phenomena that seem to be constituted by elements made of disparate stuff. The contention that it is *impossible* for legal norms to be constituted by similarly disparate grounds requires fuller argument than Alexander's suggestive comparisons deliver.

Lastly, Alexander and Kress maintain that, even if legal principles exist, have weight, and are grounded in legal practice, we cannot gain knowledge (or true belief) about them. "No set of past cases, no matter how large the set, can fix as a matter of logical entailment the weight in the context of a present case of any principle that would explain those past cases, as Quine's indeterminacy thesis demonstrates."[56]

I will not spend long on this challenge from epistemology. Just what Quine has demonstrated is controversial.[57] Moreover, the truth that evidence underdetermines theory does not take Alexander and Kress where they wish to go. Most fundamentally, "logical entailment" is not the relevant standard. The question should be whether we can infer legal principles with adequate reliability, not whether we can deduce them. And because inference is the name of the game, it's important that the data set from which we seek to infer the contents and weights of legal principles is not limited to the outcomes of past cases but includes facts about what judges and lawyers say about putative legal principles. This is a signal difference between principled positivism and Dworkin's account. For Dworkin, legal principles morally justify the rules and therefore need neither to be invoked by legal actors nor even to explain their decisions, making the underdetermination problem loom large. It reduces to manageable size on a positivist account in which the principles are grounded in actual speech acts that are visible to participants in the practice.

At root, the epistemic objection threatens to prove far too much. It is not clear why the Quinean doubts that Alexander and Kress voice do not similarly entail that we cannot acquire true beliefs about the entire range of social phenomena that are grounded in behavioral and psychological facts – local customs, rules of fashion or etiquette, rules of informal games, conventional word meanings, etc. If we have adequate epistemic access to these other social phenomena, more argument is required to establish that persons well socialized into legal practice cannot gain adequate (though imperfect) access to legal principles.[58]

56 Alexander and Kress, "Against Legal Principles," 761.

57 See, e.g., Peter Hylton, "Willard van Orman Quine," *Stanford Encyclopedia of Philosophy* (Winter 2014), ed. Edward N. Zalta, https://plato.stanford.edu/entries/quine/ (first published April 9, 2010; substantive revision December 1, 2014).

58 Accord Lawson, "A Farewell to Principles," 896–97.

14.5 CODA: PRINCIPLED POSITIVISM CONFRONTS ORIGINALISM

Alexander and Kress target legal principles because they believe that their existence or nonexistence has jurisprudential and practical consequences.[59] I think they're right. This final section buttresses that supposition by sketching implications for Alexander's originalist theory of constitutional interpretation.

According to Alexander's brand of originalism, constitutional law is the set of legal norms that (Supreme Court holdings aside) the ratifiers of the constitutional text intended to communicate by means of ratification. This follows from two premises: first, that Americans today have in fact conferred legal authority to make constitutional law upon the ratifiers; and second, that what it is for a person or institution to have lawmaking authority simply is for the legal norms that that agent intends to communicate or bring about by means of specified speech acts to be law.[60]

One might worry that this picture of legal authority is a little *too* "simple," too all-or-nothing. One might think either that lawmaking authority is the power to have significant *influence* over the content and shape of legal norms (contra the second, conceptual, premise), or that we have invested ratifiers of the constitutional text with only partial or incomplete lawmaking authority (contra the first, empirical, premise). By one path or the other, critics of Alexanderian simple-minded originalism might deny that we have committed ourselves to our constitutional norms being *fully* determined or constituted by ratifiers' legal intentions.

This nonoriginalist retort is at least superficially plausible. We often describe actors as having lawmaking authority even when their power over our legal norms is less than plenary or conclusive. We believe that Congress has lawmaking authority even though its power to create legal norms is limited by legal norms of constitutional status. And even Alexander, while conceding that the legal authority of the Constitution's ratifiers might be limited or trumped by the authority of Supreme Court justices to displace originally intended meanings or norms,[61] doesn't thereby conclude that the ratifiers lack lawmaking authority entirely.

Anticipating that nonoriginalists would paint the ratifiers' authority over our constitutional norms as less than all but more than nothing, Alexander attributes to them the view that "the authority to make … constitutional law is the authority to make the *texts* – the set of symbols – but *not* the authority to determine what those symbols mean."[62] This, he thinks, would be a "decidedly odd" way to run a

59 Alexander and Kress, "Against Legal Principles," 763n96.

60 For a concise statement of this view (albeit one that, to my eyes, occasionally conflates the meanings of texts with the legal norms to which those texts, and their meanings, contribute), see generally Alexander, "Telepathic Law."

61 Ibid., 144.

62 Ibid., 141.

legal system, although not an impossible one.[63] The problem for nonoriginalists, he concludes, is an empirical one: In this hypothetical system, it's those who give meaning to the text, not those who authored the symbols, who enjoy lawmaking authority – an upshot that contradicts the accepted premise that ratifiers possess some genuine lawmaking power.

I share Alexander's rejection of the picture that he attributes to nonoriginalists. The question, however, is whether he has imagined the most plausible middle-ground account that nonoriginalists have to offer. I think he hasn't, and that legal principles point us in a more promising direction.

Suppose that legal practices over time have produced a large number of fundamental legal norms – norms concerning the legal force of ratifiers' legal intentions, of judicial precedents, and of extrajudicial historical practice; norms regarding the scope of national power and the weight due state prerogatives; norms about the respect government owes to particular conceptions of liberty, dignity, or equality; and so forth. So long as their legal intentions matter, ratifiers possess some measure of lawmaking authority. And that power to shape the law's content need not be total to be very much worth wanting – not everything, but a far cry from nothing. Alexander's premise that, if the ratifiers' "intended meaning does not govern" – always and fully – "then they necessarily lack lawmaking authority,"[64] is far too rigid.

If you still doubt the possibility of imperfect authority, reflect on the constitutional text that was ratified in 1789, as opposed to the later-enacted amendments. Nobody had legal authority *at the time* to make constitutional law – not the members of the Philadelphia Convention, not the persons who voted in state ratifying conventions. Alexander concludes, accordingly, that the ratifiers "had that authority only if we, today, at this moment, accept that they did."[65] But if we *now* confer authority retroactively upon the framers (or ratifiers), treating them as though invested with legal authority *ab initio*, it is peculiar to infer from our practices – including widespread and robust approval of at least some constitutional judgments that do not plausibly cohere with the norms that ratifiers intended to enact or communicate – that we have conferred the unfettered authority that Alexander claims to be baked into the very concept, rather than some version of the more qualified form of lawmaking authority that I have gestured toward.

14.6 CONCLUSION

Alexander, recall, boasts that his originalism is "simple-minded." Pound, by contrast, had cautioned readers not to believe that law is a "simple thing."

63 Ibid., 145.
64 Ibid., 144.
65 Ibid., 145.

> It is not something established definitely and absolutely by the will of the sovereign. It is not something given absolutely by logic on a basis of authority … It is a highly complex aggregate, arising socially from the attempt of men in politically organized society to satisfy the claims involved in civilized social life … Looking at law in this way we perceive at once how change takes place continually without being aware of it."[66]

I'm with Pound. Legal norms are not simply what some text says or what some persons intended to promulgate. Ordinary meanings and legal intentions are part of law's story, but not its entirety. The full story assigns a prominent role to fundamental norms grounded in legal practice – "legal principles" – that are plural and dynamic. The second Justice John Marshall Harlan had it just right: Our constitutional rules "are grounded upon fundamental principles whose content does not change dramatically from year to year, but whose meanings are altered slowly and subtly as generation succeeds generation."[67]

[66] Pound, "Theory of Judicial Decision," 660.

[67] Desist v. United States, 394 U.S. 244, 263 (1969) (Harlan J dissenting).

15

The Court, or the Constitution?

*William Baude**

15.1 JUDICIAL SUPREMACY

Twenty-five years ago, in a pair of articles written with Fred Schauer, Larry wrote an important defense of judicial supremacy.[1] Alexander and Schauer defended the most famous twentieth-century articulation of that view, the Supreme Court's opinion in *Cooper v. Aaron*. In *Cooper*, the Court refused to postpone a desegregation order against the Little Rock schools. In so ruling, the Court observed that much of the difficulty in peacefully effectuating integration was because of intransigence by state officials, and it determined that it should "answer the premise of the actions of the Governor and Legislature that they are not bound by our holding in the *Brown* case."[2]

The Court's answer to this premise was that its own majority interpretations, such as its recent decision in *Brown v. Board of Education*,[3] were due just as much obedience as the Constitution itself. As the Court put it, in almost syllogistic form:

> Article VI of the Constitution makes the Constitution the "supreme Law of the Land." In 1803, Chief Justice Marshall, speaking for a unanimous Court, referring to the Constitution as "the fundamental and paramount law of the nation," declared in the notable case of *Marbury v. Madison*, 1 Cranch 137, 177, that "It is

* I thank Sam Bray, Chad Flanders, Richard Re, and Steve Sachs for helpful suggestions, and of course Larry Alexander for endless inspiration and provocation.

[1] Larry Alexander and Frederick Schauer, "On Extrajudicial Constitutional Interpretation," *Harvard Law Review* 110, no. 7 (1997): 1359; Larry Alexander and Frederick Schauer, "Defending Judicial Supremacy: A Reply," *Constitutional Commentary* 17, no. 3 (2000): 455. For subsequent discussions by Alexander, see Larry Alexander, "Constitutional Rules, Constitutional Standards, and Constitutional Settlement: *Marbury v. Madison* and the Case for Judicial Supremacy," *Constitutional Commentary* 20, no. 2 (2003): 369; Larry Alexander and Lawrence B. Solum, "Popular? Constitutionalism?," *Harvard Law Review* 118, no. 5 (2005): 1594, 1628–35.

[2] Cooper v. Aaron, 358 U.S. 1, 17 (1958).

[3] Brown v. Board of Education, 349 U.S. 294 (1954).

> emphatically the province and duty of the judicial department to say what the law is." This decision declared the basic principle that the federal judiciary is supreme in the exposition of the law of the Constitution, and that principle has ever since been respected by this Court and the Country as a permanent and indispensable feature of our constitutional system. It follows that the interpretation of the Fourteenth Amendment enunciated by this Court in the *Brown* case is the supreme law of the land, and Art. VI of the Constitution makes it of binding effect on the States "any Thing in the Constitution or Laws of any State to the Contrary notwithstanding."[4]

As a matter of doctrinal logic, the Court's opinion is wanting. Article VI of the Constitution, the Supremacy Clause, proclaims that "[t]his Constitution, and the Laws of the United States which shall be made in Pursuance thereof; and all Treaties made, or which shall be made, under the Authority of the United States, shall be the supreme Law of the Land."[5] Judicial opinions, even opinions by the Supreme Court, are not on that list.

To squeeze judicial opinions into the Supremacy Clause, the Court relies on an egregious overreading of *Marbury v. Madison*. The Court said there that it was "emphatically the province and duty of the judicial department to say what the law is."[6] But "emphatically" is not "exclusively," nor even "supremely." *Marbury* holds that there is a judicial role in constitutional interpretation; it does not discuss what the role of other branches might be.[7]

Nor was it true that this supposed principle of judicial supremacy had "ever since been respected by this Court and the Country as a permanent and indispensable feature of our constitutional system."[8] Thomas Jefferson denied it.[9] Andrew Jackson defied it.[10] Abraham Lincoln demolished it.[11] There might well be good arguments for judicial supremacy, but they are not the ones that the Court gave in *Cooper*, and

4 Cooper, 358 U.S. 18.

5 U.S. Const., art. VI.

6 Marbury v. Madison, 5 U.S. (1 Cranch) 137, 177 (1803).

7 Michael Stokes Paulsen, "The Irrepressible Myth of Marbury," *Michigan Law Review* 101, no. 6 (2003): 2706, 2715–16; see also Daniel A. Farber, "The Supreme Court and the Rule of Law: *Cooper v. Aaron* Revisited," *University of Illinois Law Review* 1982, no. 2 (1982): 387, 404.

8 Cooper, 358 U.S. 18. To be sure, Justin Driver has documented that "widespread adherence to notions of judicial supremacy emerged at least as early as 1956, more than two years before the Court decided *Cooper*." Justin Driver, "Supremacies and the Southern Manifesto," *Texas Law Review* 92, no. 5 (2014): 1053, 1058. But 1956 is not 1803.

9 Michael Stokes Paulsen, "The Most Dangerous Branch: Executive Power to Say What the Law Is," *Georgetown Law Journal* 83, no. 2 (1994): 217, 255–56; William Baude, "The Judgment Power," *Georgetown Law Journal* 96, no. 6 (2008): 1807, 1822–24.

10 Andrew Jackson, "Veto Message (July 10, 1832)," in *A Compilation of the Messages and Papers of the Presidents*, vol. 2, ed. James D. Richardson (New York: Bureau of National Literature, 1897), 576; Paulsen, "Most Dangerous," 258–59.

11 "Lincoln Douglas Debates," excerpted in Michael Stokes Paulsen, Steven Gow Calabresi, Michael W. McConnell, Samuel L. Bray, and William Baude, *The Constitution of the United States*, 3rd ed.

they were not, as *Cooper* claimed, "basic constitutional propositions which are settled doctrine."[12]

Alexander and Schauer proceeded to reclaim *Cooper*'s reasoning in a much more sophisticated way. It was true, they argued, that Supreme Court opinions should be equated with the Constitution itself, but the reasons were philosophical rather than doctrinal. Alexander and Schauer argued that a central purpose of law is its ability "to settle authoritatively what is to be done."[13] And they argued that the same is true for constitutional law in particular: "The decision to create a single written Constitution … is based on the possibility of varying views about fundamental questions, and the undesirability of leaving their resolution to shifting political fortunes."[14]

The authors then extended this reasoning about the importance of settlement to judicial supremacy: "The reasons for having laws and a constitution that is treated as law are accordingly also reasons for establishing one interpretation as authoritative. *Cooper v. Aaron* thus reflects the very reason for having a constitution that is regarded as law."[15] Thus they defended "an obligation to follow judicial interpretations, not because they are, by definition, correct, but despite the fact that they may be incorrect."[16]

Now again, these arguments are in tension with – indeed, in the teeth of – the text and history of the written Constitution, as a number of their critics pointed out. For instance: The text of the Constitution contains "no traces" of "the *Cooper* principle of judicial interpretive finality."[17] The "overriding value promoted by the framers was a system of checks and balances, with each branch asserting its own powers and protecting its own prerogatives."[18] This implied a system of generally coordinate review, with each branch independently exercising its own constitutional prerogatives.

Some of those critics (including me) were willing to concede one slight but important form of judicial finality – the supremacy and finality of judgments in specific cases. At the Founding, the judicial power vested by Article III was understood as "the power to make authoritative and final judgments in individual cases."[19] The

(St. Paul: Foundation Press, 2016), 391–99; Michael Stokes Paulsen, "Lincoln and Judicial Authority," *Notre Dame Law Review* 83, no. 3 (2008): 1227.

12 Cooper, 358 U.S. 18.

13 Alexander and Schauer, "On Extrajudicial Constitutional Interpretation," 1371.

14 Ibid., 1376.

15 Ibid., 1377.

16 Ibid., 1381.

17 John Harrison, "Judicial Interpretive Finality and the Constitutional Text," *Constitutional Commentary* 23, no. 1 (2006): 33–34.

18 Neal Devins and Louis Fisher, "Judicial Exclusivity and Political Instability," *Virginia Law Review* 84, no. 1 (1998): 83, 85–90. Larry D. Kramer, *The People Themselves: Popular Constitutionalism and Judicial Review* (New York: Oxford University Press, 2004), 128–44.

19 Baude, "Judgment Power," 1815.

one exception was for judgments that were outside of the Court's jurisdiction, and thus exceeded the judicial power.[20] This is the best understanding of the constitutional text, its ratification, and its historical background, and it was also reflected in subsequent Founding-era practice.[21]

The original Constitution's rule of judgment supremacy thus accomplishes a more modest version of the settling function that Alexander and Schauer rely on.[22] Any particular litigated dispute will still receive a final resolution, one that is binding even on other branches of government who disagree with the outcome. But the binding force of federal judgments is limited to the case and parties that are lawfully before the court. This means that the resolution of one dispute does not automatically bind others – not until they, too, properly come before the courts, are subject to the judicial power, and receive their own adjudication.

(The original rule of judgment supremacy also explains some of the Founding-era expectations alleged by others, like Laurence Claus in this volume, about the role the Supreme Court would play in settling interpretive disputes at the Founding.)[23]

In any event, the bottom line is that *Cooper v. Aaron* cannot ultimately be grounded in the original Constitution, and no Article V amendment has added it to the Constitution since.[24] To their credit, Alexander and Schauer were willing to concede all of this.[25] They did not try to shoehorn their theory of judicial supremacy into the original Constitution or reconcile it with originalist premises. Instead, they argued that judicial supremacy was a "preconstitutional" legal rule that rested on its own bottom.[26]

20 Ibid., 1828–34.

21 Ibid., 1814–41.

22 See generally ibid., 1844–46.

23 See generally Laurence Claus, "Vindicating Judicial Supremacy," in this volume.

24 Farber, "*Cooper v. Aaron* Revisited," 408–11, creatively defends *Cooper* as a form of federal common law valid under the premises of Erie Railroad v. Tompkins, 304 U.S. 64 (1938). If such judicial lawmaking were itself valid under the original Constitution, then that would indirectly justify *Cooper*. Stephen E. Sachs, "Originalism as a Theory of Legal Change," *Harvard Journal of Law & Public Policy* 38, no. 3 (2015): 817, 855–58. But I doubt that it is. Compare William Baude and Stephen E. Sachs, "The Law of Interpretation," *Harvard Law Review* 130, no. 4 (2017): 1079, 1138–39; Caleb Nelson, "A Critical Guide to *Erie Railroad Co. v. Tompkins*," *William & Mary Law Review* 54, no. 3 (2013): 921.

25 Alexander and Schauer, "Defending Judicial Supremacy," 459 ("We thus accept that the Framers did not intend the Supreme Court to be the Constitution's supreme interpreter, that the ratifiers in the states did not understand the Supreme Court to be the Constitution's supreme interpreter, and that the text does not designate the Supreme Court as the Constitution's supreme interpreter. Consequently, we accept that such a role for the Supreme Court cannot itself be based on the Constitution textually or historically understood. Indeed, we shall go even further and assume, for the sake of argument, that the Constitution actually repudiates such a role.").

26 Alexander and Schauer clarified that they meant preconstitutional "in the logical rather than the temporal sense." See Alexander and Schauer, "Judicial Supremacy," 462–63 (citing Richard S. Kay, "Preconstitutional Rules," *Ohio State Law Journal* 42, no. 1 (1981): 187).

In making this argument, Alexander and Schauer made an important and correct point about the legal status of the Constitution: As a matter of positive law, the Constitution's authority today does not ultimately rest on its own say-so, or on the fact that it was ratified by a quasi-representative group of people from 1787 to 1790. Instead, as Alexander and Schauer put it, "The Constitution's authority – its status as fundamental law – ultimately rests not on facts about the past, but on the Constitution's acceptance as authoritative in the present."[27]

As Alexander and Schauer noted, this kind of "preconstitutional" rule can be variously put in terms of Wittgensteinian self-reference, Hans Kelsen's "*grundnorm*," or H.L.A. Hart's "rule of recognition."[28] (For that matter, one could invoke other positivist legal theories as well.[29]) But in whatever philosophical clothing, constitutional law is ultimately grounded on a norm of present legal authority, "a norm that determines not what was adopted then, but how what was adopted then should be regarded now."[30]

Alexander and Schauer were entirely correct in this search for a preconstitutional rule that governs the authority of the Constitution. To take an example, each of the Articles of Confederation, the United States Constitution, and the Confederate Constitution purport on their face to be the binding supreme law of portions of the United States.[31] Each of them was adopted by a group of people who purported to represent the American people. But which of them is law, and to what extent, is a question of that document's "acceptance as authoritative in the present."[32]

Alexander and Schauer's more aggressive claim was their argument that our particular preconstitutional rule is one of judicial supremacy. As they saw it, *Cooper v. Aaron*'s articulation of judicial supremacy was directly accepted as law by the public: "In *Cooper*, the Supreme Court ran that rule up the flagpole. If we like it, all we have to do is salute. And it appears that most of us have in fact done so. And if that is so, then that makes the *Cooper* rule as 'constitutional' as the Constitution itself."[33]

[27] Alexander and Schauer, "Defending Judicial Supremacy," 460.

[28] Ibid., 460–61 (citing, inter alia, Ludwig Wittgenstein, *Philosophical Investigations*, 3rd ed., trans. G.E.M. Ascombe (New York: Macmillan Publishing, 1958)); Hans Kelsen, *Pure Theory of Law*, trans. Max Knight (Berkeley and Los Angeles: University of California Press, 1967); H.L.A. Hart, *The Concept of Law*, 2nd ed. (New York: Oxford University Press, 1994).

[29] William Baude, "Is Originalism Our Law?" *Columbia Law Review* 115, no. 8 (2015): 2349, 2365n80. But see Charles L. Barzun, "The Positive U-Turn," *Stanford Law Review* 69, no. 5 (2017): 1323.

[30] Alexander and Schauer, "Defending Judicial Supremacy," 460–61.

[31] Articles of Confederation of 1781, art. XIII, para. 1 ("And the Articles of this confederation shall be inviolably observed by every State"); U.S. Const., art. VI, cl. 2 ("This Constitution … shall be the supreme Law of the Land"); Const. of the Confederate States of 1861, art. VI, cl. 3 ("This Constitution … shall be the supreme Law of the Land"); Baude, "Our Law?" 2408.

[32] Alexander and Schauer, "Defending Judicial Supremacy," 460.

[33] Ibid., 466.

Thus, they concluded, there is widespread support, and rightly so, for requiring "those outside the Supreme Court" to take the attitude that "the Constitution is what the Supreme Court says it is."[34] This was "but the recognition that at times good institutional design requires norms that compel decision-makers to defer to the judgments of others with which they disagree. Some call this positivism. Others call it formalism. We call it law."[35]

This positivist defense of judicial supremacy may work fine for Fred Schauer, who is not an originalist. But will it work for Larry?

15.2 POSITIVE LAW ORIGINALISM

In a different line of work, Larry has also ably defended originalism. Larry's particular variant of originalism focuses on the original intent of the Constitution's authors, or, more precisely, the "speaker's meaning" or "the uptake the [authors] intended us to have."[36] This variant may end up equating to "original public meaning" in many cases,[37] but the variant is not important for present purposes.

What is most important for present purposes is Larry's view of the *authority* of the original Constitution. In a 2014 essay on originalism, he once again addressed what he called "one of the two most difficult questions in legal philosophy" – namely, "what is our rule of recognition?"[38] This is the same preconstitutional inquiry that will be familiar to readers of his judicial supremacy articles.

As he put it there: "[O]ur constitutional law, like all law, turns on what we, the people, recognize as the ultimate ground of legal authority – what Hart calls the rule of recognition."[39] (And while there is a dispute in legal positivist circles about the relative weight of official and citizen views, Larry argued "that citizens as well as officials would have to accept those criteria.")[40] And he concluded with this analysis:

34 Alexander and Schauer, "On Extrajudicial Constitutional Interpretation," 1387.

35 Ibid.

36 Larry Alexander, "Originalism, the Why and the What," *Fordham Law Review* 82, no. 2 (2013): 539–40 (citing Paul Grice, *Studies in the Way of Words* (Cambridge, MA: Harvard University Press, 1989)).

37 Alexander, "Originalism, the Why and the What," 540; see also ibid., 540n7 (rejecting "secret authorially intended meaning").

38 Larry Alexander, "Constitutional Theories: A Taxonomy and (Implicit) Critique," *San Diego Law Review* 51, no. 3 (2014): 623, 642.

39 Ibid., 641.

40 Ibid., 642. For the dispute, see sources cited in Baude, "Our Law?" 2365n81, 2388nn224–27. See also Alexander and Solum, "Popular? Constitutionalism?" 1603–4 ("popular recognition bears a constitutive relationship to the lawfulness of a constitution. If The People ignore a purported constitution, then it is not law – no matter how much The People might like it if it were law. But if The People accept a purported constitution, acting in ways that bear the right sort of systematic relationship to the content of that constitution, then the purported constitution is law. The lesson is quite simple: popular acceptance of a certain kind is the sine qua non of the status of a constitution as law").

> How then can we tell what rule of recognition the people have accepted? Have, for example, the people accepted the Supreme Court's departures from the originalists' Constitution? They have generally acquiesced in those departures, even ones that they have disliked. But have they been aware that those departures were departures? Claims, such as those by Ackerman, that the Constitution has been amended outside of the process it prescribes for its own amendment, to be vindicated must be based on more than mere popular acquiescence and more even than acquiescence plus approval on policy grounds. But how do we test for that and discover what our rule of recognition is? Until we know our rule of recognition, we cannot know the content of our Constitution. But until we know otherwise, I, for one, am betting on the originalists' Constitution.[41]

Larry's concluding bet – that our ultimate rule of recognition points to the validity of the "originalists' Constitution" – is consistent with another essay he wrote a year earlier, arguing that "originalism of the authorially intended meanings variety is really the only game in town."[42] He argued there that to "ignore the authorially intended meanings if we don't like them," is to "become the authors of the legal norms" ourselves.[43] "That describes a revolution, a change of the rule of recognition, albeit a peaceful one."[44] In other words, we choose to accept the authority of the original Constitution's authors, and so the original Constitution is our supreme law today.

On this conclusion, I think Larry is quite right – though, as with other contributors to this volume,[45] I will admit that it took me an entire article to work through on my own what Larry managed to say in a few pungent paragraphs. In both separate and joint work, Stephen Sachs and I have argued that our law today is a form of originalism, one in which "the original meaning of the Constitution is the ultimate criterion for constitutional law, including of the validity of other methods of interpretation or decision."[46] More specifically, "[o]ur law is still the Founders' law, as it's been lawfully changed."[47]

Among other things, we have observed that our present attitude toward the constitutional document,[48] and legal officials' persistent preference for original meaning

41 Alexander, "Taxonomy," 642–43.

42 Alexander, "Originalism, the Why and the What," 543.

43 Ibid., 543n13.

44 Ibid. An earlier coauthored piece addressed these issues as well, though its bottom line is somewhat more ambiguous. See Larry Alexander and Frederick Schauer, "Rules of Recognition, Constitutional Controversies, and the Dizzying Dependence of Law on Acceptance," in *The Rule of Recognition and the U.S. Constitution*, ed. Matthew D. Adler and Kenneth Einar Himma (New York: Oxford University Press 2009), 175.

45 Kimberly Kessler Ferzan, "The Means Principle and Optimific Wrongs," in this volume.

46 Baude, "Our Law?" 2355.

47 Sachs, "Legal Change," 838.

48 Baude, "Our Law?" 2366–68; Sachs, "Legal Change," 872.

over other methods of adjudication,[49] suggest that the original Constitution is still our law today. Another especially important point is our legal culture's reluctance to acknowledge any official legal breaks from the Founding.[50] This lines up with Larry's observation that even "departures" from the Constitution's original meaning by the Supreme Court have not been widely accepted by those who were "aware that those departures were departures."[51] The ultimate rule invoked by our legal system is the Founders' law, even if we live up to that rule imperfectly in practice.

As with Alexander and Schauer's preconstitutional rule of judicial supremacy, this grounds the Constitution's authority not in history, but in the present: "The original meaning of the Constitution continues to control precisely because we the living continue to treat it as law and use the legal institutions it makes, and we do so in official continuity with the document's past. So the decisions of the dead still govern, but only because we the living, for reasons of our own, receive them as law."[52]

Given Larry's insistence on the authority of originalism, and his comments on the original Constitution as likely validated by our rule of recognition, I take it he would not (and should not) disagree.

15.3 TRYING TO SERVE TWO MASTERS

So here's the rub. We now have two competing candidates for the preconstitutional rule, the ultimate rule of recognition of our constitutional system. One view is judicial supremacy. The other view is originalism. But one of the two has to trump the other.

It is true that one can have *Cooper v. Aaron*-style judicial supremacy and *most* of the original Constitution. After all, the Constitution needs to be refracted through some institutional lens, and in principle that lens could be judicial supremacy. But still that is not the institutional lens directed by text or history. The text of our particular Constitution contains several strong indications that judicial opinions are not to be treated as the supreme law of the land.[53] And as a historical matter, the Constitution was not intended, understood, or enacted to create the rule of *Cooper v. Aaron*.[54] So to treat the rule of *Cooper* as fundamental law is to reject, at least in part, the original Constitution and the legal regime it created.

49 Baude, "Our Law?" 2374–86; Sachs, "Legal Change," 860–64; see also William Baude, Adam Chilton, and Anup Malani, "Making Doctrinal Work More Rigorous: Lessons from Systematic Reviews," *University of Chicago Law Review* 84, no. 1 (2017): 37, 54–57.

50 Sachs, "Legal Change," 838, 864–71, 873–74.

51 Alexander, "Taxonomy," 642–43.

52 Baude, "Our Law?" 2408.

53 Harrison, "Judicial Interpretive Finality," 33–34.

54 Devins and Fisher, "Judicial Exclusivity," 85–90; Baude, "Judgment Power," 1814–41.

Just the same, one can have the original Constitution and a *certain limited kind* of judicial supremacy. The original Constitution vested the federal courts with "the judicial Power" to decide "Cases" and "Controversies,"[55] and that included the power to conclusively bind other branches of government. But it binds them only to obey the judgments in particular cases, not to pre-obey the judicial opinions addressed to the world at large. So to treat the original Constitution as fundamental law is to reject, at least in part, the judicial supremacy claimed by *Cooper v. Aaron*.

Larry Alexander has made plausible cases for both positions, but Larry Alexander is one of the few scholars capable of painting Larry Alexander into a corner.[56] He has to pick one. (Here, it is worth noting a third of Larry's hard-nosed contributions to constitutional theory: his rejection of constitutional pluralism as incoherent.)[57] So which should he pick? Which is really the ultimate commitment, the bottom turtle, of our constitutional regime? The authority of the Supreme Court? Or of the Founders' law, and the original Constitution?

There is a plausible case for picking judicial supremacy. As Alexander and Schauer suggest, the Court's claim to ultimate interpretive authority in *Cooper v. Aaron* – even if it was a power grab – seems to have been successful. President Eisenhower and eventually Congress lined up on the Court's side, seeming to ratify the Court's authority, or at least not to rebuke it. As Larry Kramer, a critic of *Cooper*'s claim to judicial supremacy, laments, "here is the striking thing: after *Cooper v. Aaron*, the idea of judicial supremacy seemed gradually, at long last, to find wide public acceptance."[58]

Moreover, it is not even clear that *Cooper v. Aaron* is fairly described as a power grab. As Justin Driver has shown, for the two years before *Cooper* was decided, debates about the "Southern Manifesto" revealed that there was surprisingly widespread support for judicial supremacy outside the courts: "[M]embers of both houses of Congress, President Eisenhower, leading law professors, journalists, and, yes, even a few ordinary citizens all offered hearty endorsements of judicial supremacy."[59] *Cooper* may not have been accurately stating settled doctrine, but it may still have reflected broader popular and political understandings. This historical snapshot is of a piece with broader arguments in political science that the judiciary did not

55 U.S. Const., art. III.

56 Alexander and Schauer, "Dizzying Dependence," 184–85, *might* be read to say that Larry has chosen the Court, but the passage is ambiguous, at least to me.

57 Alexander, "Taxonomy," 631; Larry Alexander, "Telepathic Law," *Constitutional Commentary* 27, no. 1 (2010): 139, 146–47; Larry Alexander, "The Banality of Legal Reasoning," *Notre Dame Law Review* 73, no. 3 (1998): 517, 521. But see Mitchell N. Berman and Kevin Toh, "Pluralistic Nonoriginalism and the Combinability Problem," *Texas Law Review* 91, no. 7 (2013): 1739.

58 Kramer, *The People Themselves*, 221.

59 Driver, "Southern Manifesto," 1102.

so much grab the power of judicial supremacy as receive what others were willing to dump into its lap.[60] So maybe our fundamental rule of recognition really has become that "the Constitution is what the Supreme Court says it is."[61]

Still and all, I think the original Constitution has the deeper claim to authority. Judicial supremacy may be popular, but it is a conclusion, not an axiom. And the structure of legal discourse suggests that even the Supreme Court's interpretations are subordinate to the Constitution. Hence Caleb Nelson's observation that we can say: "'The Constitution plainly establishes Rule X, but the Supreme Court has interpreted it to establish Rule Y instead, and the Court is not going to overrule that interpretation.' All modern lawyers would understand the distinction that this statement draws, and relatively few would consider it completely artificial or incoherent."[62]

Moreover, arguments about judicial supremacy can reveal the original Constitution's authority. Those that still criticize judicial supremacy usually do so, at least in part, on the grounds that it contradicts the original Constitution. But so too, public defenses of judicial supremacy often seek their sanction in the original Constitution. *Cooper v. Aaron* tried to justify its articulation of judicial supremacy in orthodox originalist terms: the constitutional text and very early practice, liquidated by subsequent history. It was wrong about the original Constitution, but reminded us of the Constitution's authority.[63] *Cooper* thus seems to recognize that the usual saying should be reversed: The Supreme Court is what the Constitution says it is.

At the surface level, our seeming commitments to judicial supremacy and to the original Constitution have managed to coexist up until now for two reasons. First, many people today may be unaware that judicial supremacy and the original Constitution are irreconcilable. Second, the Supreme Court and the political branches have not recently forced the issue. In most cases, the conflict doesn't arise. The correct understanding of the original Constitution yields both judicial review and judicial finality. Under the original Constitution, the federal courts still have the ultimate power to resolve disputes within their jurisdiction, albeit case by case instead of diktat by diktat. And even judicial opinions may receive a certain measure

60 See generally Keith E. Whittington, *Political Foundations of Judicial Supremacy: The Presidency, the Supreme Court, and Constitutional Leadership in U.S. History* (Princeton: Princeton University Press, 2008).

61 Alexander and Schauer, "On Extrajudicial Constitutional Interpretation," 1387.

62 Nelson, "Guide to *Erie Railroad*," 937.

63 William Baude and Stephen E. Sachs, "Originalism's Bite," *Green Bag 2d* 20 (2016): 103, 104–5 ("We maintain that originalist arguments are fundamental to American legal practice, and also that many of these arguments are mistaken. We point out many Supreme Court opinions consistent with originalism by way of demonstrating the ubiquity of originalist arguments … But the fact that lawyers and judges invoke originalism doesn't show that their specific claims are right, any more than a man's waving a yardstick shows that he is tall. To make an argument is to risk falsification").

of practical, not-constitutionally-required, deference from other actors, who interpret in the shadow of future litigation. So what appears to be support for judicial supremacy may really reflect support for the more modest, more constitutional, regime of binding judgments and persuasive opinions.

But the peace is unstable. There will likely come a time when the conflict between judicial supremacy and the original Constitution becomes open and notorious. It may well be soon. And when that happens, ultimately we will all have to choose among Larry's two accounts of who has been given the authority to govern our country and constitutional order. But one cannot pick both the Court and the Constitution, not unreservedly, without courting civil war. And if we do pick the Court, that will mark a fundamental revolution in our constitutional order.

16

Alexander as Anarchist

Steven D. Smith

To outward appearances, my friend and colleague Larry Alexander would seem to be a kind of paragon. Several decades into his career, he still dutifully studies the law reviews, conscientiously reads workshop papers and colleagues' drafts, and makes quick and exhausting trips around the world to participate in conferences, arriving back in San Diego just in time to teach his classes, to which he continues to show admirable dedication. Larry continues to write prolifically, provocatively, probingly. He remains an energetic contributor to the governance of a law school that he more than anyone else has raised to a level of academic excellence. In the civic area, Larry studies the issues, writes op-eds, and votes. He stalwartly supports the university's basketball and soccer teams and serves on the Board of Directors for the San Diego Master Chorale. He takes the dog for a walk every day.

In short, Larry Alexander would seem to be an exemplary scholar, teacher, citizen, and human being. And he is. I, for one, feel blessed to know and work with him. And yet … well, there are complications.

For example, who would have guessed that beneath this thick veneer of respectability, Larry is actually a subversive? Indeed, an anarchist?

That's my suspicion anyway. As with other secretive subversives, of course, it would be pointless just to ask Larry to confirm or deny this suspicion, which may, I admit, seem extravagant. But I remind you that appearances can be deceiving. A person, like a text, can have hidden purposes, meanings, and agendas. A person can write slyly or tongue-in-cheek – can even shift back and forth between earnest and playfully ironic. So Larry's scholarship may appear to be straightforward and relentlessly analytical, but who's to say that he does not write with concealed (and perhaps subversive) purposes?

What are we supposed to make of the fact, after all, that, almost regardless of what subject he writes about (whether it's free speech[1] or legal

[1] Larry Alexander, *Is There a Right of Freedom of Expression?* (New York: Cambridge University Press, 2005).

principles[2] or religious freedom[3] or tort law[4] or the unconstitutional conditions doctrine[5] or liberalism[6] or antidiscrimination norms[7] or the doctrine of precedent[8]), Larry's analysis almost invariably leads to conclusions that are skeptical and deconstructive? Nihilistic even. It's true that, after carefully demonstrating the incoherence or unsupportability of some cherished traditional commitment (to freedom of speech, for example), Larry may protest in Humean fashion that he accepts the commitment anyway, though no justification in reason is available.[9] Are we really supposed to take such protestations at face value? Larry is never accused, it seems, of being a closet Crit, as I have been.[10] And yet, in view of both the remarkable breadth and the penetratingly subversive character of his work, it seems to me that Larry is far more deserving of the epithet, or the honor.

In this short essay, I want to focus on, and to try to expose, one particular aspect of Larry's subtle subversiveness – namely, his profound, if mostly concealed, anarchism.

16.1 THE ELUSIVENESS OF AUTHORITY

By anarchism, I mean the rejection or subversion of legal or political authority. And by legal or political authority (which, for present purposes, I am treating as essentially interchangeable concepts), I understand two things. One is what is sometimes called the "right to rule," or the right to preside over and direct some institution of governance. The other aspect of legal or political authority is the capacity to impose obligations on others who fall within that institution's jurisdiction.[11] Thus,

2 Larry Alexander, "What Are Principles, and Do They Exist?" San Diego Legal Studies Paper No. 13-119 (June 10, 2013), https://ssrn.com/abstract=2277787.

3 Larry Alexander, "Good God, Garvey: The Inevitability and the Impossibility of a Religious Justification of Free Exercise Exemptions," *Drake Law Review* 47, no. 1 (1998): 35.

4 Larry Alexander and Kim Ferzan, "Confused Culpability, Contrived Causation and the Collapse of Tort Theory," in *Philosophical Foundations of the Law of Torts*, ed. John Oberdiek (Oxford: Oxford University Press, 2014).

5 Larry Alexander, "Impossible," *Denver Law Review* 72, no. 4 (1995): 1007.

6 Larry Alexander, "Illiberalism All the Way Down," *Journal of Contemporary Legal Issues* 12, no. 2 (2002): 625.

7 Larry Alexander, "What Makes Wrongful Discrimination Wrong? Biases, Preferences, Stereotypes, and Proxies," *University of Pennsylvania Law Review* 141, no. 1 (1992): 149.

8 Larry Alexander, "Constrained by Precedent," *Southern California Law Review* 63, no. 1 (1989): 1.

9 See, e.g., Alexander and Ferzan, "Confused Culpability," 193.

10 See Paul Horwitz, "More 'Vitiating Paradoxes': A Response to Steven D. Smith – and *Smith*," *Pepperdine Law Review* 41 (Special Issue 2014): 943.

11 Compare Joseph Raz, "Authority and Justification," in *Authority*, ed. Joseph Raz (New York: New York University Press, 1990), 115 ("It is common to regard authority over persons as centrally involving a right to rule, where that is understood as correlated with an obligation to obey on the part of those subject to the authority").

Judge Jones has legal authority a) if she has the right to wear the robes and sit in the judge's chair and direct court proceedings, and b) if her orders or judgments impose obligations on people within her courtroom and her jurisdiction. An anarchist, conversely, is someone who rejects or works to subvert the authority of Judge Jones and other officials.

The phenomenon, or the possibility, of legal and political authority presents familiar and vexing problems for jurisprudence and political theory. How does such authority come to exist? How can it be justified?

In premodern times, when people thought of the universe as forming a kind of natural hierarchy or Chain of Being,[12] authority seemed an unremarkable facet of the world order: It was only fitting that beings lower down in the hierarchy would be properly subject and subordinate to beings higher up in the hierarchy. Such explanations typically had a religious component: A ruler's authority was ultimately grounded, in direct or indirect ways, in the decrees or the designs of God, or of the gods.[13] With the official rejection of that theistic and hierarchical worldview in favor of a flatter, more secular, and more egalitarian social and political ontology, though, authority came to seem problematic and enigmatic.

Some thinkers have maintained that in a world in which every person is deemed to be autonomous and equal, authority no longer makes any sense: Robert Paul Wolff's defense of anarchism is a well-known expression of this view.[14] More commonly, authority has been justified anyway, but on nonreligious grounds. Or at least that has been the project.

Probably the most familiar modern accounts of authority have been variations on the theme that political authority must be based on, as Jefferson and the Declaration of Independence said, "the consent of the governed."[15] A different kind of approach seeks to ground authority in more pragmatic imperatives, such as the need for authority to provide order and coordination, or the value of authority in helping

12 See generally Arthur O. Lovejoy, *The Great Chain of Being* (Cambridge, MA: Harvard University Press, 1936).

13 See generally Joseph Canning, *A History of Medieval Political Thought* (New York: Routledge 1996), 300–1450.

14 Robert Paul Wolff, *In Defense of Anarchism* (Berkeley: University of California Press, 1998), 18 ("The defining mark of the state is authority, the right to rule. The primary obligation of man is autonomy, the refusal to be ruled. It would seem, then, that there can be no resolution of the conflict between the autonomy of the individual and the putative authority of the state. Insofar as a man fulfills his obligation to make himself the author of his decisions, he will resist the state's claim to have authority over him. That is to say, he will deny that he has a duty to obey the laws of the state simply because they are the laws").

15 Compare Kent Greenawalt, "Promissory Obligation: The Theme of Social Contract," in *Authority*, ed. Joseph Raz (New York: New York University Press, 1990), 268 (observing that "[f]or most of the history of liberal democracies, the dominant theory about why citizens are obligated to obey the law has been social contract").

us to act on our own reasons more effectively than if we attempted to consider all of those reasons from scratch and purely with our own unaided judgment. John Finnis's natural law account[16] is an example of the first of these more pragmatic theories; Joseph Raz's "service conception" of authority[17] is an example of the second.

But the fragility of such accounts is well known.[18] Often they are based on dubious factual premises: the claim that we have meaningfully consented to a particular government or form of governance is probably the most notorious instance.[19] Leslie Green remarks that:

> consent theory may offer a correct conception of what it would be for the authority of states to be justified while at the same time offering an explanation of why it is not. Just as the best conception of free will may support the conclusion that we do not have it, the best conception of authority may show that it does not exist.[20]

Or the accounts can seem circular. For example, Finnis's explanation says that authority arises from the *need* for social coordination combined with the *power* of some person or institution to supply such coordination. Alright, but then how does a person or institution acquire such power in the first place? The most plausible answer, in many contexts, is that a person or institution has power because people believe that he, she, or it has ... authority. So authority depends upon power, and power depends upon authority, or perceived authority.[21] This seemingly circular account may actually work well enough for governments already in place, but it seems only to postpone the fundamental question. What actually gives rise to and justifies authority in the first place?

And then there is the problem that even if an account is factually plausible (or even if we manage to ignore its implausibility), what the account yields may not seem, upon close inspection, to be ... well, authority. It may seem to be something a bit different – some kind of authority substitute or imitation. H. L. A. Hart's famous analysis showed that the gunman who threatens you with "Your money or your life" may *oblige* you to act, but he does not impose any actual *obligation*.[22] And so he has no actual authority. Same for a government based mostly on coercive power.

16 John Finnis, *Natural Law and Natural Right* (Oxford: Oxford University Press, 1980), 231–59.

17 See, e.g., Raz, "Authority and Justification,"115.

18 For a helpful review of objections, see Abner S. Greene, *Against Obligation: The Multiple Sources of Authority in a Liberal Democracy* (Cambridge, MA: Harvard University Press, 2012), 35–113.

19 See ibid., 35–40.

20 Leslie Green, *The Authority of the State* (Oxford: Oxford University Press, 1990), 166.

21 I have tried to develop this criticism at greater length in Steven D. Smith, "Radically Subversive Speech and the Authority of Law," *Michigan Law Review* 94, no. 2 (1995): 348.

22 H.L.A. Hart, *The Concept of Law*, 2nd ed., ed. Joseph Raz and Penelope A. Bulloch (Oxford: Oxford University Press, 1997).

And a similar dismissive analysis might be extended to other sorts of accounts, including consent or contractual accounts (even if we treat these as factually plausible). Suppose I promise my wife that I will dutifully comply with the advice that Dear Abby gives her readers in the daily newspaper. I now have an obligation to follow the counsel of Dear Abby, but does this mean that Abby (or whoever writes her columns) has authority over me? It seems not. What obligates me, rather, is my promise: Abby's advice only contingently provides material for my promise to work on. I might instead have promised to do the opposite of what Abby advises; in that case I would still be under obligation, but we surely would not say that Abby has authority over me. So if instead of Dear Abby I promise to obey the orders of gray-suited people in Washington, doesn't the same conclusion follow? If I promise my mother to carry my umbrella whenever it rains, does that mean that the sky and the clouds have authority over me? In all of these instances, I may have obligations, or morally-based reasons to act; but these obligations seem to derive from my promises, not from anybody's "authority."

In a similar way, Raz's "service" account may convey a good sense of the possible practical implications of what we sometimes call "epistemic" authority. So if for some investment or other practical decision I need to know the answer to a complex math equation, I will likely do better to trust a mathematician than to rely on my own rudimentary and rusted-over skills lingering fitfully on from math classes that ended in my sophomore year of high school. I might even say that I trust and follow the mathematician because she is an "authority" in the area of math – an epistemic authority, that is. But even if the answer to the math problem will influence some decision I have to make, it seems an abuse of terms to suggest that the mathematician has *practical* authority, or "authority *over me*." Thus, the "service" conception, even if its conditions are met, seems not to be a good account of *legal* or *political* authority.[23]

Such corrosive considerations may seem to dissolve the very notion and possibility of legal and political authority.[24] To put the point in more general terms: We

[23] Kenneth Himma, "Just 'Cause You're Smarter Than Me Doesn't Give You a Right to Tell Me What to Do: Legitimate Authority and the Normal Justification Thesis," *Oxford Journal of Legal Studies* 27, no. 1 (2007) (commenting on Raz's account, Kenneth Himma explains: "Suppose that right reason demands always that we comply with moral standards. Suppose further that A is infallible in determining what is required by moral standards and is morally impeccable in the sense that A always directs what is required by those standards. And suppose that there is no other fact that might legitimate A's authority apart from A's impeccability. While I am morally obligated to comply with the correct moral judgments that are expressed in A's directives, it is false that I am morally obligated *by* A's directives. If A's directives always demand what is required by morality, I am morally obligated to do as A says – but not for the reason that A says it").

[24] I have tried to develop this point more extensively and carefully in Steven D. Smith, "Hart's Onion: The Peeling Away of Legal Authority," *Southern California Interdisciplinary Law Journal* 16, no. 1 (2006): 97.

say that someone has authority if we have reason to do what she commands "just because" she said to do it.[25] But how could that "just because" condition ever be satisfied? What would it even mean to do something "just because" someone else said to do it? Wouldn't the ostensible authority's commands always need to connect with some need or desire or obligation that we already and independently have – the need or desire to avoid coercive sanctions (like those threatened by the gunman), perhaps, or the independent obligation to keep promises we ourselves have made (like those in the putative social contract)? If so, isn't it our need or desire or obligation that is the normative ground giving us reason to act, with the command merely working as a contingent fact which the real normative ground incorporates or acts upon?[26] The very idea and possibility seem to be slipping away.

And thus we may come to suspect that Hannah Arendt was correct when she observed that "authority has vanished from the modern world," and that "[p]ractically as well as theoretically, we are no longer in a position to know what authority really *is*."[27] Arendt's observation was reminiscent of Kierkegaard's declaration that "the concept of authority has been entirely forgotten in our confused age."[28] In a similar vein, the philosopher Michael White argues that "natural authority has largely disappeared from our most common worldviews."[29] Such conclusions seem aggressively or perhaps regretfully anarchist in character, working to deny or negate the claims of legal and political authority.

Of course, the judgment that authority has been dissolved can be delivered in different tones. The announcement can be made joyously: "Free at last! Free at last! Authority is dead, and thank God Almighty" (to use a figure of speech), "we are free at last!" Or the judgment can be delivered complacently: There is no obligation or authority, but then there never was, so we are no better or worse off than we have

25 See Raz, "Authority and Justification," 121. Compare Jules Coleman, *The Practice of Principle* (Oxford: Oxford University Press, 2001), 121 (suggesting that "the law purports to govern our conduct by telling us that we have an obligation to act in a certain way for no reason other than that the law commands it"); R.B. Friedman, "On the Concept of Authority in Political Philosophy," in *Authority*, ed. Joseph Raz (New York: New York University Press, 1990), 63 ("we describe such situations [of authority] by saying that an order is obeyed … simply because X gave it or made it").

26 Compare A. John Simmons, "The Duty to Obey and Our Natural Moral Duties," in *Is There a Duty to Obey the Law?* ed. R.G. Frey (Cambridge: Cambridge University Press, 2005), 91, 94–95 (explaining that "[a] moral duty to obey the law would be a duty to do as the law requires *because* it is required by valid law, … a duty to obey the law as such, not to do as it requires just insofar as it happens to overlap with independent moral duties").

27 Hannah Arendt, "What Was Authority?," *Authority*, ed. Carl J. Friedrich (Cambridge, MA: Harvard University Press, 1959), 81–82.

28 Friedman, "On the Concept of Authority," 56–57.

29 Michael J. White, "The Disappearance of Natural Authority and the Elusiveness of Nonnatural Authority," in *Civilizing Authority: Society, State, and Church*, ed. Patrick McKinley Brennan (Lanham: Lexington Books, 2007), 21–22.

always been. My colleague Laurie Claus's recent book is more or less in this vein,[30] I would say; so, it seems to me, is Abner Greene's.[31]

But the dissolution of authority can also be viewed as lamentable, alarming, even catastrophic. In personal ruminations late in life, H. L. A. Hart described his inability to solve the problem of obligation as "[q]uite panic-generating," and he worried that his failure might have the consequence of "wrecking the book" – namely, his classic *The Concept of Law*.[32] For Hannah Arendt, the loss of authority was "tantamount to the loss of the groundwork of the world."[33] "Mere anarchy is loosed upon the world," as Yeats famously put it, and the prospects are far from pleasant. And so, from this perspective, it may seem that we suffer today from a "crisis of authority" – or of the lack thereof.

16.2 ALEXANDER'S DISSOLUTION OF AUTHORITY

On the face of his writing, Larry Alexander does not come across as an anarchist. On the contrary, he seems to suggest that authority is a good and necessary thing. Although I cannot claim complete familiarity with the formidable corpus of Larry's work, so far as I know, he has not offered either any extensive defense or any explicit deconstruction of authority in general or in the abstract; nor has he expressly and systematically addressed the question of anarchism, either pro or con. But the subject of authority comes up often enough in Larry's writing, typically obliquely as part of the exploration of some other, related theme. And at least on first reading, these oblique treatments might lead us to suppose that Larry values authority, and that he believes in it and accepts it in a fairly familiar or conventional sense.

Thus, in their important book *The Rule of Rules*,[34] Larry and his coauthor Emily Sherwin are primarily interested (as their title suggests) in the nature, importance, and interpretation of rules. But their treatment of rules leads them to make observations about the nature and necessity of authority. In this respect, Larry and Emily seem to be what we might call happy Hobbesians.[35] In order to avoid social chaos, citizens in a diverse society need to find a means of reaching "authoritative settlements" of their moral disagreements. And citizens will obtain such settlements,

30 Laurence Claus, *Law's Evolution and Human Understanding* (Oxford: Oxford University Press, 2012).

31 Greene, *Against Obligation*, 35–113.

32 Nicola Lacey, *A Life of H.L.A. Hart: The Nightmare and the Noble Dream* (Oxford: Oxford University Press, 2004), 336.

33 Arendt, "What Was Authority?" 112.

34 Larry Alexander and Emily Sherwin, *The Rule of Rules: Morality, Rules, and the Dilemmas of Law* (Durham, NC: Duke University Press, 2001).

35 See, e.g., ibid., 12 ("Moral disagreement over concrete courses of conduct, coupled with the motivation to do the right thing, can lead to the Hobbesian state of affairs as expeditiously as naked self-interest").

Larry and Emily posit, by choosing one among their number – Lex – and investing him with the function, or the authority, of settling disagreements by issuing "authoritative rules."[36] Lex gains authority primarily from acceptance by the citizens[37] – – in that respect, Larry's view (like Jefferson's) seems to be that authority derives from the consent of the governed – and secondarily because Lex is likely to have expertise in the matters requiring settlement: That is why the citizens choose him rather than someone else to settle their disagreements.[38]

Of course, Lex will not be able to govern a complex society single-handedly, so he will need to create additional rules and additional institutions and officials to whom he will delegate some of his authority.[39] But Larry and Emily appear optimistic that the citizens will be able to join not only in appointing and accepting Lex, but also in supporting the many refinements and complications that will be necessary. These hypothetical citizens, despite their fundamental moral disagreements, are presented as rational and cooperative. So Larry and Emily suggest that the differently minded citizens will simply rank their various governance preferences and then concur in converging on the most acceptable common preference.[40] Suppose that in choosing someone for the role of Lex, I rank Spence first, Bernard second, and Grump third, while you rank Grump first, Bernard second, and Spence last. We disagree on our first choices, but we can agree that Bernard is preferable as a second choice; so we will cheerfully concur in choosing him. Something like that.

Especially after the depravity of the recent political campaigns and their aftermath, one may wonder whether Larry can really be as optimistic as his discussion in *The Rule of Rules* seems to be. Might he not be sending us a tacit, more subversive message? In order to avoid Hobbesian chaos, the community needs authoritative settlements, and hence authority; but the possibility of such authority depends upon a convergence that may in fact be almost impossible to achieve.

This is a possible interpretation. But then of course the book was not written during the recent campaigns but rather in what seems, at least in retrospect, to have been a less contentious and polarized period – during that happy and harmonious time when Americans could set aside their differences and converge in not impeaching Bill Clinton and in accepting the election of George W. Bush. And in any case, Larry would not be the first reasonable, good-hearted person who generously if overoptimistically projected his reasonableness and good-heartedness onto the human race generally.

36 Ibid., 12–17.

37 Ibid., 16 (explaining that the rule conferring authority on Lex "is based on its *acceptance* as normative" (emphasis in original)).

38 Ibid.

39 Ibid., 17–21.

40 Ibid., 41–42.

So I admit that I have not yet provided any adequate evidence for my suspicion that beneath a facade of respectability Larry is subtly advancing the cause of anarchism. The crucial evidence comes, rather, from Larry's work on a subject that he has written about as much as any other – namely, constitutional interpretation, and legal interpretation generally.[41]

In this area, Larry is among a small group of intentionalists – of theorists who contend that the meaning of a constitutional provision or a statute (or any text, actually) is supplied and determined by the semantic intentions of the text's author or authors. Larry has argued for this position over and over again, in a variety of ways and forums.[42] Some of his arguments consist of common-sense observations on the nature of communication generally. If your spouse is baking a cake and sends you to the grocery store with a list that enumerates "eggs," "milk," and "flower," the last item means the white dust-like substance made from wheat. That is what the author of the list – namely, your spouse – almost surely intended, and so that is what the marks mean. If you instead bring back a tulip or a daffodil, you will be justly censured for being obtuse – and for failing to understand the intentionalist nature of "meaning."[43]

Perhaps Larry's most central and frequent argument for intentionalism, however, comes directly from an account of authority. If we have decided to invest legal authority in some person or institution – Lex, or Congress – then it seems to follow from that investment that we should interpret edicts or instructions or rules in accordance with the intentions of that person or institution (as best we can discern those intentions). Otherwise, we will not be treating them as having the authority that we wanted and purported to give them.[44]

Critics of intentionalism (like Justice Scalia) will sometimes insist that the authority invested in Congress or a constitutional convention consists merely of authority to enact laws, or texts, not to dictate those texts' meanings. But Larry replies that if we let Congress or the convention enact words but then interpret those words in accordance with what someone else – a later court, the legal professoriate – would

[41] Larry Alexander, "The Gap," *Harvard Journal of Law & Public Policy* 14, no. 3 (1991): 695.

[42] See, e.g., Larry Alexander, "Legal Positivism and Originalist Interpretation," San Diego Legal Studies Paper No. 15-200 (November 8, 2015), https://papers.ssrn.com/sol3/Papers.cfm?abstract_id=2691740; Larry Alexander, "Originalism, the Why and the What," *Fordham Law Review* 82, no. 2 (2013): 539; Larry Alexander, "Telepathic Law," *Constitutional Commentary* 27, no. 1 (2010): 139; Larry Alexander, "Simple-Minded Originalism"; Larry Alexander and Saikrishna Prakash, "Is That English You're Speaking? Some Arguments for the Primacy of Intent in Interpretation," *University of San Diego Law Review* 41, no. 3 (2004): 967.

[43] See, e.g., Alexander, "Telepathic Law," 139–40; Alexander, "Simple-Minded Originalism," 9 ("shopping list").

[44] See, e.g., Alexander, "Legal Positivism and Originalist Interpretation," 4–5 ("human artefact"); Alexander, "Originalism, the Why and the What," 540.

understand or want the words to mean, we have effectively divested the supposedly authoritative body of the authority we had decided to confer on it.

"[T]he reason we should seek the actual authors' intended meaning," he explains,

> is that the actual authors possessed the legal authority to promulgate norms, and their texts just *are* their communications of the norms they intended to promulgate. If we ignore their intended meanings in favor of any of the infinite possible meanings someone else might have intended through this set of symbols, then we are ignoring the legal norms promulgated by those with legal authority in favor of norms promulgated by persons who lack that authority. If, for example, Congress has the legal authority to make federal statutory law, then to ignore the congressionally-intended meaning of a federal statute in favor of a meaning that was not congressionally intended is to construct a federal law that lacks constitutional authorization. So, too, if the ratifiers of the Constitution and its amendments are the persons with authority to make and change constitutional norms, then to "interpret" the Constitution as if it had been authored by someone other than its ratifiers is to make constitutional "law" without authority to do so.[45]

Think of it this way: What is the good of saying that Lex has authority – authority to utter words – if those words get interpreted to mean not what Lex intended and understood by them but rather what Anthony or Ruth would want them to mean? If we do that, we displace Lex and in effect make Anthony or Ruth into the real authorities. Or, as Larry puts it, "[a]ny meaning given [to a law] other than its authorially-intended meaning renders nonsensical designating its authors as having the authority to determine the norms to govern us."[46]

This seems to me a powerful and even compelling argument. And thus far, it seems that Larry is not undermining authority but rather upholding it – and indeed struggling heroically to keep authority where it is supposed to be. But now the troublesome complication arises. Although Larry admits that authorial intentions will sometimes be difficult to discern, and that mistakes in discernment will sometimes occur, his intentionalism still seems relatively unproblematic – "simple," as he sometimes self-deprecatingly insists[47] – so long as we are talking about single authors, like Lex. But what if we have two authors – or three, or five hundred – and they do not share a unified semantic intention? What happens then?

This is of course a familiar problem, and so-called textualists or original public meaning theorists (like Justice Scalia) invoke it as a principal reason for preferring textual or public meaning over intended meaning. Larry responds – persuasively,

45 Alexander, "Telepathic Law," 140–41.

46 Alexander, "Originalism, the Why and the What," 540.

47 Ibid., 579 ("This paper is short and simple – like its author"); Alexander, "Simple-Minded Originalism," 87 ("I confess. (Actually, I boast.) I am a simple-minded originalist").

I think – that textual or public meaning approaches do not solve the problem and may even aggravate it.[48] But to say that a different approach does not solve a problem is not to make the problem go away. So, what *is* the answer to the problem of multiple and potentially divergent authors?

A possible answer might be to devise some method for selecting the relevant intention to ascribe to multiauthor documents. Among a diverse group, one or a few persons might be designated the meaning makers, so to speak. One proponent of this approach to collective meaning puts the point this way: Suppose that "Σ represents one key figure within the group." Then, "[i]f Σ intends X, and [if] a majority of group members defers to the intended meaning of Σ, then a majority of group members intends X."[49] In this vein, we might say that when a law is adopted by Congress, for example, the intention that gives the law its meaning is that of the principal sponsor, or maybe the Speaker of the House, or the President who signed it into law.

But Larry proposes no such method. Nor could he. That is because, once again, the goal is to keep authority where it was placed. The Constitution does not confer lawmaking authority on particular members of Congress, or on the President; such authority belongs to Congress *as a whole* (subject to a possible presidential veto). And Congress has not delegated its lawmaking authority – or its meaning-determining authority – to any single member, or subset of members, or to the President. Moreover, even if Congress tried to make such a delegation, the attempt would be constitutionally problematic. Although Congress has been permitted to delegate ample legislative powers to administrative agencies, for example, it has not been permitted to assign lawmaking power to some subset of itself.[50] So the relevant intention – the intention that gives a law its meaning – needs to be the intention of *Congress*, not of any subset thereof.

Let me put the point in a slightly different way. The central thrust of Larry's authority-based argument for intentionalism is that a *law* and its *meaning* are not two different things; they are one and the same. So if Congress cannot delegate *law-making* authority to one of its members, or onto some subclass of itself, it cannot confer *meaning-making* authority either.

As a result, Larry embraces the only conclusion that his authority-based argument for intentionalism would seem to permit: He says that collective intentions (and thus meanings) exist only when the authors agree in what they are trying to express – or when at least as many of the authors agree as are necessary to enact the

[48] E.g., Alexander, "Simple-Minded Originalism," 91 ("collective authorship").

[49] W. Matt Morgan, "What Did They Mean? How Principles of Group Communication Can Inform Original Meaning Jurisprudence and Address the Problem of Collective Intent," *William & Mary Bill of Rights Journal* 23, no. 4 (2015): 1233–34.

[50] INS v. Chadha, 462 U.S. 919 (1983).

law.[51] A group (like a legislature, or a convention) can speak and mean only when its meaning is in fact shared.

But, then, what about the situation in which the requisite number of legislators agrees to *vote for* a bill (or at least for a collection of words or marks described as a "bill"), but they do not agree on *what those marks mean*? In that situation, how does the law acquire its meaning? The answer, it turns out, is that the law *doesn't* acquire any meaning. It is meaningless. Larry's analysis on this point is admirably candid, and consistent with his intentionalist logic: In such situations of authorial disagreement, the law means … nothing. It is, as he says, "gibberish."[52]

You might expect that an intentionalist with Larry's integrity might quietly admit this disconcerting possibility and then make a quick strategic retreat, in the hopes that not many readers will notice the embarrassment. Not so: Larry dwells on the problem – revels in it, even. He does not allow us to overlook or pass by the conundrum. Rather, he cheerfully provides a nice, convincing illustration. Suppose that by a 2–1 vote a three-person legislature enacts a law providing that "there shall be no meetings by the bank." Unfortunately, one of the supporting legislators intends "bank" to indicate the river bank – he understands the prohibition to be based on concerns about flooding – while the other, supposing "bank" to refer to the town's financial institution, thinks the point of the law is to avoid interference with people who are trying to deposit or withdraw money. In this case, Larry says, there is no shared semantic intent, and so the law does not actually mean anything at all; it is "gibberish."[53]

So, shouldn't Larry – and shouldn't we – be troubled by this conclusion? Doesn't it present a glaring risk that a great deal of our law is in fact meaningless, "gibberish," and thus incapable of being viewed as an expression of authority that imposes any obligation on us? Larry suggests that situations of divergent authorial intentions will be unusual,[54] but it is hard to suppose that he can really be so sanguine.

True, stark cases like Larry's "bank" example, in which, unbeknownst to each other, different authors innocently intend two completely different meanings, may be anomalous. What seems overwhelmingly likely, though, and much more pervasive, is that laws will be enacted although only a minority of legislators have bothered to inform themselves about what the laws actually say. Take the Affordable Care Act, or Obamacare as it is popularly known. The law was massive and notoriously complicated, and it seems likely that most members of Congress never read

51 Alexander, "Legal Positivism and Originalist Interpretation," 19 ("shared intended meanings").

52 Ibid., 20 ("gibberish").

53 Alexander, "Originalism, the Why and the What," 542. For a similar example, see Alexander, "Legal Positivism and Originalist Interpretation," 20–21 ("three-person").

54 See Alexander, "Legal Positivism and Originalist Interpretation," 19 ("In many instances, a shared intended meaning will exist").

through it and had little inkling about much of what it contained. As Speaker of the House Nancy Pelosi famously remarked, "We have to pass the bill so that you can find out what is in it" (a wonderful comment that may, to be sure, have been misconstrued).[55] The Affordable Care Act may seem an extreme and unrepresentative instance; but if so, it probably leads to an underestimate of the phenomenon I refer to here. Thus, the vast hosts of laws that, unlike the Affordable Care Act, receive little or no public attention seem even less likely to be read and studied by most legislators.

In such instances, we arguably have not two completely different semantic intentions, as in Larry's "bank" example, but rather a semantic intention that may possibly be shared by the handful of legislators who have written or paid attention to a law, together with relative ignorance (and thus, realistically, no semantic intentions) by the majority of legislators. Could we say, then, that in such cases the law's meaning is determined by the semantic intentions of the relatively few legislators who have paid attention to it? Not, I think, according to Larry's account. To say this, it seems, would be to embrace the same sort of lawmaking and meaning-making delegation that was unacceptable when the proposal was to let the meaning be determined by the law's sponsor, or the Speaker of the House, or somebody else. It would separate the law's meaning from the source of its authority – which is *Congress* (not some *subset* of Congress). And, once again, that sort of separation is the basis of Larry's most insistent objection against nonintentionalist theories of interpretation.

And so, according to this logic, it would seem that large chunks of our statutory law – most of it, possibly – is reduced to gibberish. Judges and scholars and lawyers have argued about the constitutionality of the Affordable Care Act under the commerce power, the spending power, the taxing power. But it now seems that there is a much easier way to dispose of the law. A court might simply declare the law invalid, or not really law at all, not because it exceeds congressional powers, but rather because it is … meaningless. Gibberish. Gibberish in Larry's somewhat technical sense (and perhaps in a popular sense as well).

16.3 THE CONSEQUENCES OF ANARCHISM

To some, of course, in the case of Obamacare this conclusion may seem happy beyond anything we could have hoped for. But whatever you may think about the Affordable Care Act, it should be at least sobering to ponder the possibility of large

[55] Tommy Christopher, "The Context Behind Nancy Pelosi's 'We Have to Pass the Bill' Quote," *Mediaite*, November 17, 2013, www.mediaite.com/tv/the-context-behind-nancy-pelosis-famous-we-have-to-pass-the-bill-quote/.

sections of our law being peremptorily swept away – not as unconstitutional, but as meaningless.

So, does it follow that Larry is an anarchist? To be sure, he does not embrace the sort of philosophical anarchism of theorists who reject legal authority or obligation but tell us not to worry: People will have plenty of incentive to follow the laws even though, technically, the laws do not impose any actual obligation. They will be, as Heidi Hurd approvingly puts it, "law-abiding anarchists."[56] In that gentle version of anarchism, after all, the laws are at least still meaningful: They are something that we *can* follow if we want to. And we *will* want to; or at least so the more optimistic theorists tell us. After all, as responsible moral agents who care about our fellows (themselves responsible moral agents) and who realize that those fellows will be counting on us to follow the laws, we will want to behave morally and civilly. Won't we? So, although we may not *obey* the laws, exactly – because obedience implies obligation – we will *conform* to them. That at least seems to be the sanguine assumption of good-hearted people like Heidi Hurd and our colleague Laurie Claus.

Larry's position seems more threatening. True, unlike the philosophical anarchists, Larry concedes the possibility of authority as a theoretical matter; he even seems to acknowledge its necessity. But in practice, if it turns out that large swaths of our law are in fact devoid of meaning, then what is there for us to conform to, even if we are so inclined? In contrast to the rarified philosophical anarchism, Larry's more practical anarchism is a kind that, if it came to be widely understood and accepted, could actually lead to … anarchy.

So, is anarchy Larry's actual, if subtle, agenda? Or is he an unwitting and accidental anarchist? One familiar school of interpretation holds that when a careful thinker advocates positions that, although respectable and reassuring on their face, carry subversive implications when carefully examined, there is a divergence between the esoteric and the exoteric meanings: The esoteric meaning is authentic and deliberate, though concealed from the uncomprehending masses by the exoteric meaning.[57] Larry is nothing if not a careful thinker. So, what are we supposed to conclude? I admit it: On the face of his writings, Larry does not seem to be any sort of bomb-thrower. On the contrary. But as I have already noted, it is possible for a person to write on more than one level: Though apparently serious, and though sometimes *actually* serious, he might also and at times write ironically, or tongue-in-cheek, or with concealed meanings or intentions.

56 Heidi Hurd, "Why You Should Be a Law-Abiding Anarchist (Except When You Shouldn't)," *University of San Diego Law Review* 42, no. 1 (2005): 75.

57 See Leo Strauss, *Persecution and the Art of Writing* (New York: The Free Press, 1952).

For example, a certain kind of scholar or theorist – one with a latent Augustinian streak, perhaps – might in a strategic way make arguments similar to Larry's on the unspoken and currently unacceptable supposition that all earthly authorities, though necessary and deserving of our support and perhaps even divinely ordained, can be no more than shadows or imitations of the only real and genuine authority, which is transcendent in character. This sort of author might believe – but in a concealed way, because in our times the belief would be deemed absurd or scandalous – that without the real, transcendent authority, all authority would disappear.[58] According to this view, Hannah Arendt might be right in saying that "[p]ractically as well as theoretically, we are no longer in a position to know what authority really *is*"[59] – even if her particular account of how we came to be in this predicament is less than compelling.

Still, this seems an unlikely interpretation of Larry's position and purpose. Or at least if Larry has Augustinian tendencies, he has done an exceptionally impressive job of concealing them.

What Larry has *not* concealed is that when he was younger and more naively idealistic, he openly participated in the subversive SDS movement.[60] Knowing the mature Larry, some of us remember that fact with amusement. Larry of course gave up that radical agenda long ago.

Or did he?

58 But compare Arthur Allen Leff, "Unspeakable Ethics, Unnatural Law," *Duke Law Journal* 1979, no. 6 (1979): 1231 ("It is of the utmost importance to see why a God-grounded system has no analogues. Either God exists or He does not, but if He does not, nothing and no one else can take His place").

59 Arendt, "What Was Authority?," 81–82.

60 As it happens, when I was younger I was also referred to by some of my friends as "SDS" – but for my initials, not my political affiliations.

17

Exclusionary Rules

Emily Sherwin

I have had the good fortune to work with Larry Alexander as a colleague and coauthor over many years. Larry's spectacular talent is his ability to look over a field of study and immediately perceive its major faultlines. Maybe he has a solution to offer, maybe he does not; but in any event he points unerringly to the central problem. This is magic to me and I have often profited from it.

One of Larry's great insights of this kind is the existence of what he has called "the gap."[1] The gap refers to the inevitable divergence between the perspective of those who draft, impose, ratify, or accept a set of rules to govern future conduct and the perspective of those who must follow or apply the rules in particular cases. As Larry first put it, "There is an always-possible gap between what we have reason to do … and what we have reason to have our rules … require us to do."[2] One result of the gap is to cast serious doubt on exclusionary reasons as a rational strategy for self-governance or governance of others.[3]

17.1 RULES

A rule, for present purposes, is a directive that describes a type of situation in general and relatively determinate terms and prescribes some action or inaction in

[1] Larry Alexander, "The Gap," *Harvard Journal of Law & Public Policy* 14, no. 3 (1991): 695. The gap is discussed at length in Larry Alexander and Emily Sherwin, *The Rule of Rules: Morality, Rules, and the Dilemmas of Law* (Durham, NC: Duke University Press, 2001). Frederick Schauer makes a similar point in Frederick Schauer, *Playing by the Rules: A Philosophical Examination of Rule-Based Decision-Making in Law and in Life* (Oxford: Clarendon Press, 1991), 128–44 (discussing the "asymmetry of authority").

[2] Alexander, "The Gap," 695.

[3] On exclusionary reasons, see generally Joseph Raz, *The Morality of Freedom* (Oxford: Oxford University Press, 1986), 57–62; Joseph Raz, *The Authority of Law* (Oxford: Oxford University Press, 1979), 16–19, 22–23, 30–33.

response.[4] General, determinate rules have significant instrumental benefits. The most prominent of these are guidance and coordination. If the rule maker has special expertise that most of its subjects lack, the response prescribed by the rule is likely to be superior, on average, to the response that subjects would select on their own. Even if the rule maker brings no special skills to bear, rules enable agents to anticipate what others will do in the circumstances governed by the rule and to adjust their own conduct accordingly.

Of course, not all rules are instrumentally beneficial; some are poorly conceived or obsolete. In this essay, I assume that the rules at issue are good rules – if regularly followed, they will lead to a better set of outcomes than agents would achieve if they followed their own judgment about what to do in each case. Any rule that does not meet this test should be discarded or revised.

Because rules are general and determinate, even good rules will sometimes prescribe outcomes that are wrong when judged according to the rule's purposes or the agent's reasons for action. Yet, this fact about rules does not defeat their instrumental value. As long as the rules produce better outcomes on average than unconstrained judgment, a world in which all agents follow the rules in all cases is better than one in which agents follow their own judgment about reasons for action.

It may seem that a better world is available, in which rules guide conduct in most cases but are subject to a general exception whenever the rule prescribes a bad result. Properly applied, the exception would take account of any adverse effects a rule violation might have on coordination or other benefits of regular rule following.[5] Agents could then choose the ideal response to each case, given the existence and value of a normally sound rule, rather than the nonideal set of outcomes required by the terms of the rule. This ideal response, however, is not available to ordinary decision makers. Human reasoners are not omniscient and do not always draw accurate and complete inferences from evidence. Nor can they accurately judge the extent of their own cognitive limitations and the effect of those limitations in particular cases.

If mistakes about reasons for and against following rules in particular cases were evenly distributed between mistaken compliance and mistaken violation, the effects of an open-ended general exception on coordination and other values associated with rules might not be significant. Cognitive studies suggest, however, that salient or emotionally charged features of a decisional context have a greater impact on deliberation than equally important background probabilities or long-term consequences such as the capacity of a rule to provide coordination.[6] Accordingly,

4 An excellent source on the nature and benefits of rules is Schauer, *Playing by the Rules*.

5 See ibid., 94–100 (Schauer refers to this strategy as "rule-sensitive particularism").

6 For discussion and examples of "availability" and other common cognitive biases, see generally Amos Tversky and Daniel Kahneman, "Availability: A Heuristic for Judging Frequency and Probability,"

individual agents are likely not only to err, but to err systematically, against compliance with rules. It follows that in any case in which the rule outperforms individual judgment on average, a requirement of strict compliance is instrumentally superior to a qualified requirement that allows agents to depart from its terms when they believe this is best, all things considered.

This line of reasoning defines the forward-looking perspective of a rule maker or an agent considering whether to adopt a rule. Rules must be authoritative in the sense that they impose constraint on individual, case-by-case judgment, either by prescribing what agents must do in all covered cases or by prescribing what they should do subject to predefined exceptions. Another way to put this is that rules should have an exclusionary effect on their subjects' deliberation about what to do.[7] They should operate both as first-order reasons for action and as second-order reasons not to act on some range of first-order reasons that otherwise would inform the agent's choice. A general exception that relies on the rule subject's judgment in particular cases is not helpful from this point of view.

The question of rule following looks different from the perspective of agents who are called on to apply rules in particular cases. At the point of application, the agent may understand and agree with all the reasons that led the authority to issue an authoritative rule, including the impact that a rule violation may have on the coordination value of the rule. The rule subject may also be aware of her own cognitive limitations. At the same time, she will understand that because the rule is general and determinate, it will cover some individual cases in which the prescribed outcome is not ideal. Knowing this, she may conclude that her current situation is one in which the rule prescribes the wrong result.

For example, assume that S is subject to a rule, R, which requires her not to use a cell phone while driving a car. S endorsed rule R when it was first enacted, formed the intention to follow it regularly, and fully understands the reasons why, from the authority's long-term point of view, all persons should follow R in all cases. At the point of application, S continues to believe that R is a good rule overall; that, if regularly followed, R will prevent accidents and allow all drivers to drive more confidently; and that drivers, including herself, often underestimate risks and overestimate their ability to perform several challenging tasks at once. At the same time, she understands, as she understood when she initially endorsed rule R, that general, determinate rules are overbroad and will sometimes prescribe the wrong outcome.

in *Judgment Under Uncertainty: Heuristics and Biases*, ed. Daniel Kahneman, Paul Slovic, and Amos Tversky (Cambridge: Cambridge University Press, 1982), 163; Thomas Gilovich, Dale W. Griffin, and Daniel Kahneman, ed., *Heuristics and Biases: The Psychology of Intuitive Judgment* (Cambridge: Cambridge University Press, 2002).

7 See Raz, *Morality of Freedom*, 57–62; Raz, *Authority of Law*, 16–19, 22–23, 30–33.

There may be cases in which current driving conditions, the individual driver's skills, and a pressing need to communicate may justify a violation of R.

All these beliefs are fully consistent with the authority's point of view and with the authority's conclusion that all agents should always follow R. Currently, however, S faces a particular case covered by R. She is stuck in slow-moving traffic about one hour from home when she hears on the radio that a lockdown is in place at her daughter's middle school. There is no way to pull over and no exit coming up soon. S knows that her daughter has a phone with her at school. She also knows that her husband is in a meeting at his office near the school and is likely to be monitoring incoming texts. S would like to text her daughter, to see if she is OK, and her husband, to alert him and tell him to go to the school.

S normally is disposed to follow the rules of the road and other sensible, duly enacted rules without questioning their merits as applied. In this case, however, if S paused to consider whether she should now follow R, she might conclude that she should not. Assuming that R is a good rule that outperforms individual judgment, S's conclusion would likely be wrong. Yet from S's present vantage point, if her current evidence – the news she has heard, her desire to comfort and protect her daughter, her assessment of her own driving skills, her understanding of the imperfections of general rules, and her awareness of human cognitive limitations – appears to favor using the phone, it is difficult to see how she could reach the conclusion that she ought to follow R. The result is an irreconcilable division between the general perspective of the rule maker and the particular perspective of rule followers.

A presumption in favor of rule following does not solve the problem.[8] From the authority's point of view, it is still best for all to follow the rule in all cases. From the subject's point of view, presumptive rule following still requires her to do, in some cases, what her evidence says she should not do. A general practice of presumptive rule following may also tend to erode over time: A presumption in favor of compliance assumes that subjects will weigh the immediate reasons to break a rule against reasons to follow the rule, including maintenance of coordination and other benefits of the rule. Each decision to violate the rule slightly decreases the perception that the rule is generally followed, and therefore decreases the weight that other potential rule followers will assign to the benefits associated with the rule.

17.2 PROMISES

Although Larry associated the gap with rules, and particularly legal rules, the problem he identified affects any decision made at some time t_1 that purports to

[8] This is Schauer's preferred solution. See Schauer, *Playing by the Rules*, 202–5; Frederick Schauer, "Rules and the Rule of Law," *Harvard Journal of Law & Public Policy* 14, no. 3 (1991): 645, 674–79.

control action at a future time t_2. One example is a promise. A sincere promisor intends to impose limitations on her future choice of action by assuring the promisee that she will do or not do an act at t_2. The act may be described in fairly specific terms but the circumstances of performance, and therefore the promisor's reasons for action at t_2, cannot be fully delineated in advance. In this way, a promise is similar to a general rule.

There is no consensus on the question of whether a promise alters the normative relationship between the promisor and the promisee, or, if it does, how the alteration comes about. On one view, there is no mental act whereby a promisor can impose a new moral obligation on herself.[9] Promises become binding, if at all, by virtue of social practices or interaction between the parties that lead the promisee to expect performance and to rely on the promise.[10] To the extent that an obligation arises, it is not willed into existence by the promisor but is based instead on background principles that govern what one person owes another when her actions generate expectations.

Others have asserted, on various grounds, that individual agents have the capacity to impose binding obligations on themselves by acts of will.[11] Seana Shiffrin, for example, argues that promissory obligations play an important part in maintaining "morally decent" relationships with others, which in turn are necessary to autonomous life.[12] Shiffrin assumes that people are capable of morally decent relationships, and reasons from this premise that they must have normative power to impose promissory obligations on themselves. She describes the exercise of this normative power as a transfer from promisor to promisee of the right to determine whether the promisor will perform the promised act.[13]

9 David Hume, *A Treatise of Human Nature*, 2nd ed., ed. L.A. Selby-Bigge and P.H. Nidditch (Oxford: Oxford University Press, 1978), 516–25. For a recent defense of the position that promises do not create moral obligations independently of the harm that may follow from a breach, see Heidi M. Hurd, "Promises Shmomises," *Law and Philosophy* 36, no. 3 (2017): 279.

10 T.M. Scanlon, *What We Owe to Each Other* (Cambridge, MA: Harvard University Press, 1998), 295–317 (basing obligation on invitation to expect performance).

11 Charles Fried, *Contract as Promise: A Theory of Contract Obligation* (Cambridge, MA: Harvard University Press, 1981), 16 (basing promissory obligation on the value of autonomy and mutual trust); David Owens, "Does a Promise Transfer a Right?," in *Philosophical Foundations of Contract Law*, ed. Gregory Klass, George Letsas, and Prince Saprai (Oxford: Oxford University Press, 2012), 78, 79–80, 89–95 (basing promissory obligation on an interest in controlling rights and obligations); Seana Valentine Shiffrin, "Promising, Intimate Relationships, and Conventionalism," *The Philosophical Review* 117, no. 4 (2008): 481.

12 Shiffrin, "Promising," 497–98, 502–10, 517–19.

13 Ibid., 517; see Immanuel Kant, *The Metaphysics of Morals*, ed. Mary J. Gregor (Cambridge: Cambridge University Press, 1996), 93, § 20; Andrew S. Gold, "A Property Theory of Contract," *Northwestern University Law Review* 103, no. 1 (2009): 1.

For those who deny that agents can will a normative obligation into effect, the problem of promising is much like the problem of rule following. At t_1, the time of the promise, the promisor may have reason to make a reliable promise, either because the promise is part of a mutually beneficial transaction or because she wants to confer a benefit on the promisee. She may also anticipate that weakness of will or cognitive bias may distort her judgment at t_2 and cause her to break the promise when she should not. Thus, from the promisor's perspective at t_1, the best strategy is to treat the promise as an exclusionary reason to perform the promised act at t_2.[14]

Yet, because circumstances at t_2 cannot be fully specified at t_1, it is possible that performing the promised act will not be instrumentally justified at t_2. After taking into account the possibility of reliance, potential harm to promissory conventions, and the promisor's own cognitive limitations, the promisor may conclude that this is such a case. She may be wrong, but from her current perspective this is how her evidence appears.

The problem becomes more complicated if individuals are able to impose new normative obligations on themselves by making promises. The obligations generated by promises are sometimes described as content-independent obligations, meaning that they arise from the promise itself, without reference to what was promised or what consequences a breach of promise may cause. Yet, as Joseph Raz has pointed out, a content-independent reason is at risk of being also a bare reason, which carries no weight in an overall balance of reasons.[15]

If a promise generates an obligation with no weight in the ordinary sense, or an obligation that is difficult to weigh against ordinary reasons for action, there is an even greater risk that the promisor will undervalue reasons to perform the promise at t_2. From the promisor's perspective at t_1, this means the promisor has an additional ground for treating the promise as exclusionary. At t_2, however, her current evidence, even when discounted to allow for the risk of error, may suggest that her reasons for action favor breaking the promise. Thus, there is a persistent gap between the

14 See Joseph Raz, "Promises and Obligation," in *Law, Morality, and Society: Essays in Honour of H.L.A. Hart*, ed. Peter Michael Stephan Hacker and Joseph Raz (Oxford: Clarendon Press, 1977), 221–23. Exactly what range of reasons a prior promise would block is unclear. A promise is not a conclusive reason for action; on the other hand, Raz indicates that a promise should at least rule out self-interested reasons to break the promise. See Joseph Raz, "Is There a Reason to Keep a Promise?," in *Philosophical Foundations of Contract Law*, ed. Gregory Klass, George Letsas, and Prince Saprai (Oxford: Oxford University Press, 2014), 58, 64.

15 Raz, "Is There a Reason?" 63–71. Raz's answer to the problem is that the weight of the promissory obligation, as such, depends on the value that the promisor's assurance provides to the promisee in context. The value of assurance is not simply the value of performance, but the value of having the power to choose whether or not the promised act will occur. This is, of course, an elusive type of value. Ibid., 71–77.

promisor's perspective at the time of the promise and her perspective at the time of performance.

17.3 RATIONALITY

The problem posed by rules and promises can be restated as a problem of rationality. A traditional understanding of practical rationality holds that a rational agent must respond to her reasons for action at the time of choice.[16] On this view, when an agent must decide at t_2 whether to follow a rule or perform a promise, the only practically rational response is to make the choice that current reasons for action recommend.

A number of writers, however, have proposed that practical rationality can and should be extended over time, so that it is sometimes rational to act on a prior intention although the action does not match the agent's current reasons for action. Edward McClennen, for example, rejects the assumption that practical rationality requires agents to privilege reasons for action applicable to the agent's present self. Instead, it is rational to act on a prior "resolute" choice if the prior choice maximizes benefit to all the agent's selves over time and fairly apportions the benefit among them.[17] David Gauthier defines practical rationality in terms of rational courses of action rather than particular acts. If the agent expects at t_1 that a course of action will be beneficial overall, and continues to believe at t_2 that the course of action is beneficial, then it is rational for her to complete the course of action even if the act that completes it, standing alone, is not supported by the agent's current reasons for action.[18] Scott Shapiro endorses a plan-oriented theory of practical rationality, arguing that to obtain the long-term benefits of planning, it is rational for agents to treat prior plans as binding on their current choices of action.[19] While the plan is in place, contrary actions are not rationally "feasible."[20] For Shapiro, this form of rationality explains the authority of legal rules.[21]

16 Edward McClennen calls this the principle of "separability" and illustrates with a decision tree in which each new decisional node starts fresh with current forward-looking reasons. A decision tree of this type separates rationality into slices of time and rationality at each slice tied to current reasons for action. See Edward F. McClennen, "Pragmatic Rationality and Rules," *Philosophy & Public Affairs* 23, no. 3 (1997): 229.

17 McClennen states this most succinctly in Edward F. McClennen and Scott J. Shapiro, "Rule-Guided Behavior," in *III New Palgrave Dictionary of Economics and the Law*, ed. Peter Newman (New York: Stockton Press, 1998), 367.

18 See David Gauthier, *Morals by Agreement* (Oxford: Clarendon Press, 1986), 167–70; David Gauthier, "Intention and Deliberation," in *Modeling Rationality, Morality, and Evolution*, ed. P. Danielson (Oxford: Oxford University Press, 1998); David Gauthier, "Assure and Threaten," *Ethics* 104, no. 4 (1998).

19 Scott J. Shapiro, *Legality* (Cambridge, MA: Harvard University Press, 2011), 122–24.

20 Scott J. Shapiro, "The Difference that Rules Make," in *Analyzing Law: New Essays in Legal Theory*, ed. Brian Bix (Oxford: Clarendon Press, 1998), 39–40.

21 See Shapiro, *Legality*, 169–88.

Each of these approaches to practical rationality extends rationality over time and so allows agents to capture the benefits that accompany firm decisions. In each case, however, the cognitive mechanism by which the agent overrides her own best judgment about current reasons for action is left unexplained. More specifically, these theories fail to explain how an agent who understands the benefits of a long-term plan, but also understands that the plan will not yield benefits in every case, can privilege the prior plan over current evidence about current reasons for action, all things considered. The problem is not whether an agent who follows a plan is practically rational over the long term: If the plan is a good plan and the agent's judgment in particular cases is imperfect, then following the plan is practically rational. The problem, instead, is how an agent can proceed to follow a plan if she believes that following it now is a mistake. A standard of practical rationality that requires agents to do this is not one that agents can knowingly meet.

Michael Bratman has proposed a somewhat different theory of temporally extended practical rationality that comes closer to explaining how agents might achieve long-term practical rationality.[22] Bratman's account of practical rationality begins with the cognitive role of intentions. Intentions, for Bratman, are not simply composites of beliefs and desires but independent mental states that carry with them two forms of commitment.[23] "Volitional" commitment means that if a prior intention remains in place at the time of action, it will lead the agent to perform the intended act.[24] "Reason-centered" commitment means that in any deliberation the agent's deliberative options are limited to choices consistent with any prior intentions that remain in place at the time of deliberation.[25]

Bratman constructs a series of "historical principles" governing when it is rational for an agent to hold and act on an intention.[26] In the most basic type of case, the agent first forms an intention to act in the future, then proceeds to act on the intention without further deliberation. This sequence is rational as long as the agent formed the intention rationally at t_1, then rationally retained the intention up to the time of action without reconsidering its practical justification.[27] Retaining an intention without reconsideration is rational if the agent is guided by reasonable dispositions toward retention and reconsideration of intentions.[28] The reasonableness of the

22 Bratman sets out the framework for his theory in Michael E. Bratman, *Intentions, Plans, and Practical Reason* (Cambridge, MA: Harvard University Press, 1987).

23 Ibid., 10.

24 Ibid., 15–16.

25 Ibid., 16–17.

26 Ibid., 55. Bratman beings with an "intention-action" principle holding that, because current intentions volitionally control actions, actions and intentions should be judged by the same standards. Therefore, an agent who is rational in holding an intention is also rational in acting on it.

27 Ibid., 81–83.

28 Ibid., 64–65.

agent's dispositions toward reconsideration of intentions depends in turn on whether they tend to be instrumentally successful over the long run. Typically, reasonable dispositions toward prior intentions include a disposition not to revisit intentions unless circumstances have changed in some significant way. The result is that intentions acquire a reasonable degree of stability over time.[29]

A related principle of rationality applies to general "policies," a term Bratman uses to describe intentions to perform a type of action in recurrent situations.[30] An intention to follow a rule fits this description, as do some forms of promissory intention. Bratman's principle for intentions of this type allows the agent to act unreflectively on the prior intention if she is reasonably disposed not to reconsider the intention and also not to block its application to a particular case. Reasonable dispositions toward policies normally include both a disposition to retain the policy and a disposition not to block it in most cases.[31]

By incorporating reasonable dispositions to retain prior intentions without reconsideration into his principles of practical rationality, Bratman allows for an extension of rationality over time. Moreover, he does this without requiring the agent to engage in actions that contradict what she believes to be her current reasons for action. Instead, the agent simply acts without reflecting about reasons for action, propelled by a combination of her prior intentions and her practically reasonable dispositions to retain them.

Bratman's theory of "non-reflective (non)-reconsideration"[32] does not imply that prior intentions are rigid and indefeasible.[33] Bratman assumes that it remains open to the agent to deliberate about current reasons for action and to either reconsider and abandon prior intentions or block their application to particular cases. He also he suggests that whenever an agent spontaneously reflects on reasons for an action, she effectively reconsiders prior intentions relating to that action.[34] At this point, the volitional commitment associated with her prior intentions is dispersed and the agent must conform her action to her current reasons.

Thus, Bratman's argument is only that it is rational for an agent to bypass deliberation and act unreflectively on a rationally formed intention if she is reasonably (rationally) disposed to do so. The combination of volitionally charged intentions

[29] Ibid., 72–73.

[30] Ibid., 87.

[31] Ibid., 83–86, 88–91. Bratman also formulates a historical principle for deliberation. Assuming the agent is rational in holding a set of prior intentions at the time of deliberation, Bratman's deliberative principle requires that any new intentions the agent forms must be consistent with her prior intentions.

[32] Ibid., 61.

[33] Ibid., 5.

[34] Ibid., 60.

and reasonable dispositions to retain intentions provides a plausible cognitive explanation for how an agent rationally can perform one act when current reasons for action favor another. In this way, Bratman's theory improves on alternatives that rely on the assertion that past decisions somehow override current calculations about reasons for action.[35]

17.4 THE EPISTEMIC SIDE OF RATIONALITY

Ultimately, however, any attempt to explain the rationality of carrying out prior intentions and long-term plans in particular cases, including Bratman's, is vulnerable to the problem of the gap. There is no question that stable intentions have important instrumental benefits for agents; these benefits are particularly evident in the cases of rule following and promising. Requirements of epistemic rationality, however, threaten to undermine these benefits in particular cases.

Epistemic rationality is the rationality of belief. By most accounts, epistemic rationality aims in one way or another at beliefs that are true rather than false. Beliefs must conform to evidence or derive from processes likely to produce beliefs that are mostly true. Either way, the standard of epistemic rationality is a synchronic standard, evaluating current beliefs according to the likelihood that they are currently true.[36] The instrumental benefits of practical rationality can plausibly be allocated among multiple selves over time. Truth-oriented reasons for belief cannot be spread over time in this way. The reasons that justify a belief must indicate that the belief is true now.

This suggests that practical rationality and epistemic rationality may sometimes conflict. A proponent of temporally extended practical rationality, however, might argue that when an agent forms a practically rational intention to follow a rule or keep a promise, has a practically rational disposition to carry out her prior intentions without reflection, and later acts on her intention, epistemic rationality never comes

[35] A drawback of Bratman's theory is that it imposes only a limited form of constraint. If the agent, for one reason or another, focuses on the question of what to do, extended rationality gives way to time-slice rationality, which is vulnerable to error. Thus, the theory may be restricted to cases in which reasons for and against an action are close to equipoise, or in which so little turns on the choice of action that deliberation is not worthwhile. On the other hand, if we commonly are disposed to follow prior intentions unreflectively in a wide and significant range of cases, Bratman's account of practical rationality may have important instrumental consequences.

[36] In a sense, process reliabilism is a historical standard, referring to the reliability of the processes by which beliefs are formed. The objective, however, is to justify current beliefs, not a pattern of beliefs over time: the process is reliable if it leads to beliefs that are true now. In fact, Alvin Goldman, a leading process reliabilist, concedes that even a reliably formed belief is not justified if it is defeated by the believer's current evidence. Alvin Goldman, "Toward a Synthesis of Reliabilism and Evidentialism," in *Evidentialism and Its Discontents*, ed. Trent Doherty (Oxford: Oxford University Press, 2011), 275–76.

into play. As long as the agent forms no new beliefs about reasons for action, she is epistemically free to do what practical rationality recommends. Therefore, there is no genuine conflict between practical rationality and epistemic rationality.

17.5 EPISTEMIC RESPONSIBILITY

Whether this argument is correct depends on the extent to which epistemic rationality incorporates a standard of responsibility that requires agents to process available evidence and form corresponding beliefs.[37] On a narrow view of epistemic rationality, there is no such responsibility. Epistemic rationality pertains only to the grounds on which an agent forms and holds beliefs. Whatever beliefs the agent forms must match her evidence or satisfy certain other truth-favoring criteria.[38] Beyond this, however, epistemic rationality does not require the agent to advert to evidence, draw inferences from evidence, or form beliefs.[39] This approach to epistemic responsibility allows agents to follow Bratman's principles for temporal extension of practical rationality: If it is practically rational to plan to follow a rule or keep a promise, and if the agent's practically rational dispositions lead her to carry out her intention without reflection, epistemic rationality presents no obstacle to the practically rational choice. A narrow understanding of epistemic responsibility, however,

37 The idea of epistemic responsibility dates at least to W.K. Clifford, who told the story of a shipowner who had doubts about the seaworthiness of his ship. The shipowner suppressed his doubts and sent the ship on its way. The ship then sank with passengers aboard. Clifford said that "although in the end [the shipowner] may have felt so sure about it that he could not think otherwise, yet inasmuch as he had knowingly and willingly worked himself into that frame of mind, he must be held responsible for it." W.K. Clifford, "The Ethics of Belief," *Contemporary Review* 29 (1877): 289. This passage can be read to suggest that agents have an epistemic responsibility not only to match their beliefs to the evidence they consider, but also to consider available evidence.

38 For the purposes of this essay, I take an evidential internalist approach to epistemic justification. See generally Earl Conee and Richard Feldman, *Evidentialism: Essays in Epistemology* (Oxford: Oxford University Press, 2004), 57, 83, 178, 232; Earl Conee and Richard Feldman, "Replies," in *Evidentialism and Its Discontents*, ed. Trent Dougherty (Oxford: Oxford University Press, 2011), 302–3. With some adjustments, however, the arguments I make will accommodate a process-reliabilist point of view. See generally Alvin Goldman, "What is a Justified Belief?" in *Justification and Knowledge*, ed. George Pappas (Dordrecht: D. Reidel, 1979). I also assume that evidence available to the agent includes perceptual experience, occurrent memories and beliefs, stored background beliefs that inform occurrent beliefs, and inferences to the best explanation for any of these. Compare Richard Feldman, "Having Evidence," in *Evidentialism: Essays in Epistemology*, ed. Earl Conee and Richard Feldman (Oxford: Oxford University Press, 2004), 232 (taking a narrow view) with Thomas Kelly, "Evidence: Fundamental Concepts and the Phenomenal Conception," *Philosophy Compass* 3, no. 5 (2008): 950 (taking a broad view) and Timothy Williamson, *Knowledge and Its Limits* (Oxford: Oxford University Press, 2002), 185 (equating evidence with knowledge).

39 Feldman asserts a view of this kind, but later qualifies it by requiring agents to take account of defeating evidence, to a limited extent. Richard Feldman, "The Ethics of Belief," in *Evidentialism: Essays in Epistemology*, ed. Earl Conee and Richard Feldman (Oxford: Oxford University Press, 2004), 178, 186–88.

does not seem adequate to ensure that the agent is managing evidence and beliefs in a rational and truth-oriented way. In particular, it does not require agents to adjust their beliefs in light of evidence that indicates their current beliefs are wrong.

At the opposite extreme, epistemic rationality might be understood to require that agents must advert to all evidence in their possession, draw inferences from that evidence, and form beliefs that fit the evidence.[40] The difficulty with this comprehensive view of epistemic responsibility is that it places too great a burden on agents. We acquire far more evidence than we reasonably can process in a reflective way and translate into beliefs. Instead, we simply ignore much of our evidence, or note its presence but rightly decline to think it through.

A third, more moderate view of epistemic responsibility would limit an agent's responsibility to advert to evidence and form beliefs to cases in which the evidence tends to defeat a belief the agent currently holds. For example, Richard Feldman, who otherwise takes the narrow view that epistemic rationality requires only that beliefs must conform to evidence, makes an exception for clear cases of defeat.[41] He gives the example of an agent who believes that ginkgo biloba can improve one's memory. The agent then notices the following article title on the cover of a reputable magazine: "Ginkgo Biloba Shown to Be Ineffective." At this point, the agent has evidence contrary to his belief and ought to give up, or at least reconsider, the belief. Feldman adds that the agent has no duty to investigate ambiguous evidence or to pursue new evidence. An article titled "Some New Information on Ginkgo" would not have the same effect. With this limitation, however, an agent who ignores evidence that is likely to defeat an existing belief is epistemically irrational.[42]

This intermediate standard, imposing an epistemic responsibility to advert to evidence that promises to defeat prior beliefs, is a distinctly epistemic standard because it pertains to the truth of the agent's beliefs; therefore, it is independent from questions of instrumental benefit. The burden it places on agents is comparatively

[40] Thomas Kelly, for example, states the view that all evidence is epistemically normative. An agent in possession of evidence must respond with belief, whether or not she is interested in forming a belief on the matter. Thomas Kelly, "Epistemic Rationality as Instrumental Rationality: A Critique," *Philosophy and Phenomenological Research* 66 (2003): 625. There are indications, however, that Kelly might modify his position in some circumstances. For example, the agent might not be required to take account of evidence for or against a proposition the agent had never considered. See Thomas Kelly, "Evidence and Normativity: Reply to Leite," *Philosophy and Phenomenological Research* 75, no. 2 (2003): 468.

[41] Feldman, "Ethics of Belief," 186–88.

[42] Alvin Goldman, a process reliabilist, also endorses a standard of epistemic responsibility to process defeating evidence. An agent reads a normally reliable weather forecast in the morning and forms a belief that the afternoon will be sunny. That afternoon he is caught in a rainstorm but ignores his evidence and continues to believe that it is sunny. Goldman says that although the agent's belief initially was justified under process-reliabilist standards, it is now defeated. Goldman, "Toward a Synthesis," 23.

modest because it is limited to evidence that places prior beliefs in question. The agent is not called on to enlarge or improve her set of beliefs or to seek out new evidence that might undermine prior beliefs. She is required only to correct fairly obvious defects in her current beliefs, based on evidence in her possession.

The standard of epistemic responsibility just described may also seem a good fit for cases of rule following and promise keeping. The problem in these cases is that the agent, having adopted a general rule or made a commitment in general terms, may confront new evidence in a particular case. The new evidence indicates that her intention to follow the rule or honor the commitment does not match her reasons for action. In a typical case, the evidence of current circumstances is not subtle or obscure: It is more like the "Shown Ineffective" title than the "New Information" title. Thus, for example, S, who has formed the intention to follow a no-texting rule, is frantic over news of a lockdown at her child's school and wants to text. Her new evidence is perfectly salient; the only question for S is whether to assess its impact on current reasons for action or simply follow her practically rational general intention to follow the rule.

In another example, P's elderly neighbor is about to move to a retirement home. P promises that P will help the neighbor sort and pack belongings in preparation for the move. At the last minute P receives a call from her daughter, begging P to watch the grandchildren while she handles a crisis at work. Again, P's evidence is salient and its relevance is clear; the question is whether to sift and process it or simply keep the promise. In each case the agent believed, when she formed an intention to follow the rule or honor the promise, that she would do best on average by treating the rule or promise as an exclusionary reason for action. Her current evidence, however, threatens to defeat that belief. Therefore, by the standard under consideration, epistemic rationality requires her to review the evidence, reconsider her intention, and form a new belief about reasons for action.[43]

This conclusion, however, may be too quick. In each of the cases described, the agent's new evidence raises questions about whether she should follow her prior intentions, but it does not actually defeat the beliefs on which those intentions rest. At t_1, the agent believed that she would do better over time if she followed the rule or kept the promise than if she followed her own judgment case by case, because her judgment would more often than not be faulty. Yet she also believed that, owing to the generality of rules and promises, cases could arise in which she would correctly judge that she should not follow the rule or keep the promise. At t_2, the agent's new evidence, indicating that she should not now act on her prior intention, is consistent

[43] The agent can still choose either path, but her prior intention no longer has volitional force, and in judging what to do she may undervalue the long-term benefits of rule following or the elusive values associated with honoring a promise.

with her beliefs at t_1. She continues to believe that she will not always judge correctly when to break the rule or breach the promise, and so will do better over time by following the rule or keeping the promise without reflection. Her new evidence suggests only that she might now do better by abandoning her intention to follow the rule or keep the promise – a possibility she contemplated at t_1. Technically, the evidence does not defeat the agent's prior beliefs.

The intermediate standard of epistemic responsibility, however, can be reformulated in a way that fits the problems of rule following and promising without significantly increasing the epistemic demands it places on agents or changing the nature of its justification. The function of this standard of responsibility is to protect the integrity of the agent's current set of beliefs by requiring the agent to advert to evidence and adjust her beliefs when new evidence calls them into question in a particular context. In the examples, the agent's prior beliefs are not defeated, but the evidence suggests that they are overbroad: The agent is now in a position to assess particular facts rather than average probabilities over time. Consequently, from an epistemic standpoint, her prior beliefs can and should be corrected. In effect, the agent's new evidence tells her to replace her prior beliefs with a better belief – that she generally should follow rule R or keep her promise, but not now.

A standard of epistemic responsibility requiring agents to respond to evidence that challenges the application of prior general beliefs in particular cases serves the same epistemic values as the standard Feldman supports, which requires agents to respond to evidence that defeats prior beliefs. In each case, conforming to the standard enables the agent to restore epistemic order in a new factual context. Both standards can be stated narrowly so that agents are responsible only for ordinary inferences from readily accessible evidence. They need not advert to all evidence in their possession or draw all possible inferences from evidence, nor form all beliefs that match their evidence.

Thus, the principle drawback of this standard of epistemic responsibility is not the burden imposed on agents but the inconvenient consequences it has for temporally extended practical rationality. If agents must correct their general beliefs to match the evidence presented by particular cases, they cannot act unreflectively on prior intentions, and so cannot pursue the type of practical strategy proposed by Bratman. As a result, there may be no rational way to obtain the benefits that come from authoritative rules, reliable promises, and meaningful plans. Thus, although Bratman's theory of extended rationality offers a creative solution to the cognitive problems raised by rules and promises, it does not avoid the problem of the gap. If, as I have argued, agents have an epistemic responsibility to advert to evidence indicating that their prior general beliefs do not fit a particular case, then they cannot treat rules and promises as exclusionary reasons for action. Instead, they must modify their beliefs about reasons for action to fit current evidence. Over time, the results may not be practically rational because the agent's evidence may be incomplete and her inferences may be imperfect. This is why she decided initially that the rule or promise should have an exclusionary effect. Epistemically, however, what matters is that the agent's current beliefs should match her reasonable assessment of current evidence.

17.6 ASSIGNING PRIORITY

I have argued that the gap can be restated in terms of rationality: Because the agent's perspective changes between the time she forms an intention to follow a rule or honor a promise and the time she is called on to act on her intention, it is not possible both to pursue practically rational long-term strategies and also to maintain epistemic rationality. This raises the question, which form of rationality should take precedence?[44] Long-term instrumental strategies and binding commitments are essential to coordination, advance planning, joint endeavors, mutually beneficial exchange, and interpersonal trust. It may seem obvious, therefore, that extended practical rationality should prevail.

One difficulty with this conclusion is that in the context of rule following and promising, practical rationality may depend on epistemic rationality in ways that complicate the choice of one form of rationality over the other. In a simple case of conflict between epistemic rationality and practical rationality, an epistemic lapse does not affect the agent's practical choice. If a demon has threatened to destroy the world unless the agent believes that Utah is the capital of Massachusetts, and the agent is somehow able to comply, the agent's false belief does not affect the practical conclusion that the agent should make the trade.[45]

In the case of a rule, promise, or plan, however, practical rationality and epistemic rationality are more closely related. Bratman's theory of practical rationality involves

[44] A related issue is whether epistemic rationality is understood as a form of instrumental rationality in which the agent's goal is accuracy of belief or as a form of noninstrumental rationality that depends on the connection between an agent's evidence and her beliefs. Compare, e.g., Richard Foley, *The Theory of Epistemic Rationality* (Cambridge, MA: Harvard University Press, 1987), 6–10 and Richard Foley, "The Foundational Role of Epistemology in a General Theory of Rationality," in *Virtue Epistemology: Essays On Epistemic Virtue and Responsibility*, ed. Abrol Fairweather and Linda Zagsebski (New York: Oxford University Press 2001), 217 with Jonathan E. Adler, *Belief's Own Ethics* (Cambridge, MA: MIT Press, 2002), 1–14; Thomas Kelly, "Epistemic Rationality as Instrumental Rationality: A Critique," *Philosophy and Phenomenological Research* 66, no. 3 (2003): 621–30; Nishi Shah, "A New Argument for Evidentialism," *The Philosophical Quarterly* 56, no. 225 (2006): 447–48, 469–70 (2003); Nishi Shah, "How Truth Governs Belief," *Philosophical Review* 112, no. 4 (2003). If epistemic rationality is a form of practical rationality, then conflicts might be resolved by weighing the importance of different goals in context; if not, then direct comparison becomes more difficult.

[45] This is, roughly, Foley's example of a case in which epistemic rationality should give way to practical rationality. See Foley, *Epistemic Rationality*, 213.

webs of intentions that, together, permit rational agents to obtain the benefits of planning and coordination. In Bratman's terms, intentions carry not only a "volitional" commitment to perform the intended act but also a "reasoning-centered" commitment, such that prior intentions constrain later deliberation. When an agent deliberates about forming a new intention, the options from which she can choose are limited to options consistent with whatever prior intentions she rationally retains at the time of deliberation. It is practically rational for the agent to retain her prior intentions without reconsideration if, in doing so, she is guided by reasonable dispositions that will serve her well over time. If this condition is met, then, according to Bratman's theory of temporally extended practical rationality, the agent can and should conform her new intentions to her prior intentions without consulting evidence or forming beliefs that might cast doubt on prior intentions.

Thus, at each stage in what may be a long chain of intention, deliberation, further intention, and action, it is practically rational for the agent to disregard evidence that might lead to a different assessment of reasons for action. Yet, without the check of epistemically rational reflection on current reasons for action, there is no ground to assume that the agent's dispositions toward intentions are reliable over time. The agent may achieve workable outcomes, but it is possible that she would have done better, on at least some occasions, by attending to all relevant evidence.

Another difficulty is that, although Bratman's theory may work well in some ordinary dimensions of life, favorable dispositions toward prior intentions may not be enough to support practices such as rule following and promising. When the stakes involved in following a rule or performing a promise are high, the agent may be disposed to consult evidence even when, in fact, potential reasoning errors make it practically rational to act blindly. In cases of this kind, the agent's epistemically rational disposition to process evidence may overcome her practically rational disposition to act on her prior intentions. The alternative to Bratman's theory is a theory such as McClennen's, Gauthier's, or Shapiro's, which depends on the capacity of agents to bind their own future selves by forming intentions. As described earlier, these theories offer no plausible explanation of the cognitive process by which the t_1 self can do this and the t_1 self can in fact be bound.

17.7 CONCLUSION

Alexander rightly concluded that rule following presents an inescapable dilemma: There will always be a gap between the perspective of the rule-making authority and the perspective of individual rule makers confronting particular applications of the rule. The same is true of promising and other practices that are central to personal, social, and political life. We benefit greatly from these practices, but the change in our perspective between the time we commit to future action and the time we are called on to act in particular circumstances makes it difficult for us to honor them.

One initially promising solution is to extend our understanding of practical rationality over time. Rather than assessing reasons for action at the point of action, rational agents should act on prior intentions whenever doing so is instrumentally beneficial in the long run. The difficulty with this solution is that a parallel dilemma arises at the level of rationality. We form intentions, adopt rules, and make commitments because we need to coordinate our actions with others and because we expect to err in our all-things-considered judgment about what to do in particular cases. Intentions, rules, and commitments, however, cannot determine our future conduct unless we treat them as exclusionary reasons that somehow prevent us from forming epistemically rational beliefs about reasons for action in particular cases. Consequently, there is no rational way to circumvent the gap. Individually and collectively, we must be irrational to navigate successfully through life.

18

Larry Alexander and "the Gap"

Leo Katz and Alvaro Sandroni

A rule and its purpose often diverge, leading to a problem for the judge and other rule appliers: Should they apply it blindly or temper it by recourse to its purpose? "Doing law" versus "doing justice" is how that contrast is often expressed. Inasmuch as jurists have been aware of this phenomenon since time immemorial, one might think that everything there is to say on the subject has been said. Far from it. What Larry Alexander, along with Emily Sherwin – following on a path first trod by Fred Schauer in *Playing by the Rules*[1] – has shown, in a series of seminal articles and a landmark book, *The Rule of Rules*, is that there are some fundamental paradoxes lurking here that we are only starting to understand.[2]

One reason these paradoxes have been overlooked until Alexander helped bring them to light is that, at first glance, the source of the divergence between rule and purpose seems obvious: Practical considerations make it hard to get a rule just right. We cannot anticipate every contingency in which it will be applied, and sometimes we will find it hard to tell whether a contingency we did anticipate has in fact arisen, perhaps because it would require us to peer inside someone's mind to unearth well-concealed motivations.

But there turn out to be far deeper reasons for the divergence, the one of interest here being the one to which Fred Schauer has given the label "the asymmetry of authority" and Larry Alexander "the gap."[3] Rules have the odd and surprising property of routinely giving rise to circumstances in which it is both rational for someone to promulgate and insist on the exceptionless application of a rule and yet it would

1 Frederick Schauer, *Playing by the Rules: A Philosophical Examination of Rule-Based Decision-Making in Law and in Life* (New York: Oxford University Press, 1991).

2 Larry Alexander and Emily Sherwin, *The Rule of Rules: Morality, Rules, and the Dilemmas of Law* (Durham, NC: Duke University Press, 2001).

3 Schauer, *Playing by the Rules*, 128–34.

also be irrational for the subjects of the rule to abide by it. Or, as Fred Schauer puts it, there is an "asymmetry between the irrationality of obedience from the subject's perspective and the rationality of requiring it from the authority's."[4] This would be perfectly unremarkable in cases in which the rule creator and the rule subject have different goals: The rule creator wants peace and respect of rights, and the rule subject wants to get as much of other people's property has he can lay his hands on. Here, too, it might be rational for one to propose a rule that it is irrational for the other to obey, but that's to be expected. No, the interesting situation is one in which their objectives are identical, and yet this clash of rationalities arises. That is not what one expects.

How exactly might this happen? Let's consider a deliberately homely example offered by Alexander and Sherwin in *The Rule of Rules*.

> Suppose … that a library has a hundred regular patrons. Most of them find it useful to mark books as they read. At the same time, most prefer to read unmarked books, and most of these would prefer to forgo marking in exchange for assurance that no one else would mark in books. Further, some of the patrons strongly dislike reading marked books and have taken to checking out new books as they arrive and hoarding them for periods of time. The marking and hoarding of books produces acrimony among the patrons.
>
> If all patrons were perfect moral reasoners with perfect information, this situation would not arise. No one would mark in books unless his reason for doing so were strong enough to justify all resulting harm to others, and no one would hoard books because all would know that others marked only when justified. There would be no cause for discord. But these are obviously impossible conditions. Stephen, contemplating marking in a book, cannot accurately assess the harm it will cause without knowing how many others will read the book, what their preferences will be regarding marks, and whether any other readers will have reason to mark the same book. And if Stephen is likely to err in his calculation, Fred, who is thinking of hoarding a book, cannot assume that others will mark only when justified. And Donald, who would like to mark in a book, cannot predict the harm his own marks will cause without assessing the possibility that Stephen or others like him, rightly or wrongly, mark in the book. Thus, cooperation is not possible, even if all parties are willing.
>
> [A rule maker whom we will call] Lex might now intervene with a rule "No Marking in Books." Assuming general compliance, this rule will prevent unjustified harm and eliminate the incentive for hoarding …
>
> Nevertheless, the results of the rule are not ideal. Stephen may in fact have good reason to mark in a book (time is short, the book is obscure, and he is working on

4 Ibid., 131.

something of great social and political import). Yet if Lex qualifies the rule – "No marking in library books unless your reasons for doing so outweigh any harm the mark will cause." – the same errors will occur and the rule will fail to have the desired effect. Thus, there is a gap between what Lex has reason to demand of Stephen and what Stephen has reason to do.[5]

To repeat: *Thus, there is a gap between what Lex has reason to demand of Stephen and what Stephen has reason to do.* In other words, it is rational for Lex to demand of Stephen that he not mark the book, but it is also rational for Stephen to ignore that demand.

Here is another example *The Rule of Rules* provides of such a gap:

> Brian knows that there is a chance that over the course of the summer, his house will suddenly be invaded by ants, and he will need to call an exterminator. This is something Brian would very much like to avoid, and he can prevent it from happening by spraying ant poison outside the house at the beginning of the summer. The difficultly is that on any given day, he has better things to do than kill ants; and one day's delay is unlikely to make the critical difference. As a result, he never sprays, and sooner or later the ants arrive inside his house.
>
> Assume that Brian can persuade Lex to provide him with a personal rule: "Spray for ants on the first day of May." The rule solves the internal coordination problem by designating (arbitrarily) a point in time at which Brian must act to protect his long-term interest. A perfect reasoner with perfect information would not need such a rule. He would know precisely when ants were due to arrive, would anticipate his opportunity costs at all points during the intervening period, would be free from any bias, and would spray at the optimal time. An ordinary reasoner lacks information both about when the threat will mature and what opportunities will arise in the interim, and may unduly prefer present over future satisfaction.
>
> Thus if Brian possesses only ordinary powers of reason, and if his long-term interest in avoiding extermination is greater than the interest it preempts on May 1, he will be better off complying with Lex's rule. Yet the rule is not perfect; there may be a better time to spray, when opportunity costs are not as high. If, on May 1, Brian believes the time is not ideal, there is a gap between what Brian thought best when he asked for a rule and what he thinks best when the time comes to follow it.[6]

Once again there is a gap, between what Lex has reason to ask Brian to do when he sets up the rule and what Brian has reason to do when it comes to actually following it. What it is rational for Lex to insist Brian do, it would not be rational for Brian to actually do!

5 Alexander and Sherwin, *The Rule of Rules*, 59–60.

6 Ibid., 56–57.

A crucial move in Alexander's exploration of this paradoxical situation is the connection he draws between it and two other well-known paradoxes in the rationality literature – Gregory Kavka's nuclear deterrence paradox, and Warren Quinn's paradox of the self-torturer – which turn out to exhibit the same kind of gap.[7] Let's recall each of them in turn.

Kavka's nuclear deterrence paradox arises as follows. We, the United States, are threatened with a potential attack by another nuclear power – at the time Kavka wrote his famous articles, the Soviet Union. The most effective way to deter them from a first strike against us is to threaten a devastating retaliatory strike. The problem is that the actual carrying out of such a retaliatory strike once we have been victimized would seem both irrational and immoral. We would be destroying many innocent civilian lives with no further gain to be expected since (by assumption, at least) they have already done all the harm they mean to do. Should we therefore abstain from putting such a system of deterrence in place? No, of course not. Or at least it isn't obvious that we shouldn't. For if we put in place such a system, we make it extremely likely that there will be no attack on us in the first place and we in turn will never have reason to launch a retaliatory attack, however immoral or irrational, and therefore no one, most likely, would come to harm; whereas if we fail to put such a system in place, it is far more likely that such an attack will be launched and that there will be correspondingly many victims – us. We are presupposing of course, quite realistically in fact, that simply bluffing, and pretending to have put such a system in place without actually doing so, would not work, because the other side is bound to find out about it, through espionage and such.

The reason such a situation is regarded as paradoxical is that it would appear as though putting such a regime in place is both rational and moral, but that for someone to actually implement it, should the unlikely contingency of a strike arise, would seem to be neither rational or moral. And in this, of course, it exactly parallels *The Rule of Rules* paradox, the gap, the asymmetry of authority: It is rational to put in place a regime (a rule!), but it is irrational to actually conform to it.

Warren Quinn's paradox of the self-torturer has the same structure, but exhibits it in an unexpectedly different context. The paradox goes as follows: You are faced with a gadget that is going to subject you to increasing amounts of pain, depending on how many notches you move a pain-controlling knob. But there are some all-important fine points to the setup. First, every time you move the knob one notch, the amount of pain you will be subjected to – permanently, for the rest of your life, actually – is quite small, just barely perceptible, and only by the most strenuous of

7 Gregory S. Kavka, *Moral Paradoxes of Nuclear Deterrence* (New York: Cambridge University Press, 1987); Warren S. Quinn, "The Puzzle of the Self-Torturer," *Philosophical Studies: An International Journal for Philosophy in the Analytic Tradition* 59, no. 1 (1990): 79–90.

efforts. Second, every time you agree to move the knob by one of the available 1,000 notches, you are paid $1,000. How far will you turn the knob? How far should you turn the knob? The paradox arises out of the fact that at any given moment you really cannot defend not turning the knob another notch, since you are weighing the receipt of a very tangible benefit, $1,000, against a barely perceptible downside, adding a tiny increment of pain to your burdens. And yet, if we do this again and again and again, we will end up in a situation we would have vetoed from the very outset: ending up in agonizing pain, with a lot of insufficiently compensatory money to our credit.

This is one surprising thing *The Rule of Rules* shows us with great felicity – that most legal rules have this paradoxical structure of Kavka's nuclear paradox and Quinn's self-torturer.[8]

The question then arises as to whether there is anything one can do to bridge the gap and somehow evade the bite of the paradox? Alexander believes there is nothing, and the most pivotal chapter of *The Rule of Rules* is devoted to showing how all plausible attempts to close the gap fail. It is this claim that we are going to take issue with, not disprove, just cast doubt on it, and necessarily leave its final disposition for another day, for reasons to be explained. But, first, let us get a clear picture of the difficulty that arises as soon as one tries to do something to close the gap.

One suggestion the book considers is what is called "rule-sensitive particularism" – closing the gap by taking into account the particulars of a situation when we decide whether to apply a rule in a given context or not. That way one can be rational both in adopting the rule and in implementing it. In other words, the suggestion is that "the best response to rules is neither to follow them unthinkingly nor to engage in a full particularist assessment of reasons for action but to give rules a special presumptive weight in decision-making."[9] The best way to see why this won't do is to exploit the analogies between the gap and the nuclear deterrence paradox and that of the self-torturer. Quite evidently rule-sensitive particularism will not work with those. It won't make the problem go away for the implementer of a retaliatory strike to engage in some kind of semi-particularized inquiry as to whether he should launch a retaliatory strike, because if he is known to do so, the entire deterrence setup collapses. Nor will this kind of inquiry work for the self-torturer, because inevitably it would result in his turning the knob one more notch.

Another suggestion the book considers is an approach favored by Joseph Raz that employs "exclusionary reasons": "Joseph Raz has argued that legal rules can be understood as exclusionary reasons for action. In his view, legal rules function as second-order reasons that exclude various first-order reasons from the process of

[8] See ibid.

[9] Alexander and Sherwin, *The Rule of Rules*, 68.

moral deliberation."[10] Thus, somehow, the blind application of the rule, because of its "exclusionary" quality, is said to become rational. Once again, the analogy with Kavka's and Quinn's examples shows that to be a chimerical idea. Yes, it would be nice to treat the retaliatory setup as an exclusionary reason for the soldier who is called upon to launch the pointless retaliatory strike, but that's solving the problem by fiat rather than argument: The soldier finds himself in the situation he finds himself in, and simply declaring consideration of the fact that his retaliatory strike no longer serves any end to be "excluded" by the original setup does not seem to make rational what was not rational to begin with.

A third suggestion involves deception. That is, we might try to close the gap by inculcating in the rule followers a blind worship of rules, such that they no longer question the rationality of following the rule in a given circumstance. That might well be a desirable thing to do, but it scarcely removes the gap. We would simply be deceiving the rule follower about what is rational in order to get him to act irrationally. Deceiving the soldier about whether it is rational to launch a retaliatory strike when it isn't might cause the system to work, but it does not render his actions at that moment rationally defensible.

Perhaps the most intuitively appealing suggestion that has been made to close the gap involves sanctions. Set things up in such a way that the person who fails to follow a rule blindly will be subject to severe punishment. Setting up such punishment will then be rational, and abiding by the rule will be rational as well, since not abiding by it will result in severe sanctions to the person violating it. The problem is that ordinarily there has to be someone who has to administer the sanction, and while the rule follower might now find it rational to follow the rule, it is the administrator of the punishment who would now no longer be acting rationally. The gap has simply been displaced slightly.

This does not exhaust the possibilities, but it gives the gist of Alexander's argument.

Now there have been objections to this approach to the matter, not in the context of Alexander's argument about rules, but in the context of the debate about Kavka's nuclear paradoxes. David Gauthier has suggested that Kavka has a wrong-headed conception of rationality, and consequently of morality as well.[11] He does not agree that it is rational to set up a regime which it is then irrational for its participants to implement. He argues that the rationality of the entire setup carries over to the rationality of the actions of its implementers – that if it is rational to set up a retaliatory revenge regime, anyone implementing it cannot be regarded as acting irrationally. Rationality is a "package deal," as it were. And so is the morality of the participants,

[10] Ibid., 73–74.

[11] See, e.g., David Gauthier, "Assure and Threaten," *Ethics* 104, no. 4 (1994): 690–721.

which here seems to follow closely on the heels of its rationality: The actions of the implementers, being rational, are also moral.

In response to this claim, Kavka posed the famous toxin puzzle, not really intended as a puzzle but as a *reductio* of Gauthier's claim, but a *reductio* Gauthier decided to dodge by swallowing its seemingly absurd conclusion.[12] Kavka asks us to envision the following scenario: A man offers us $1 million if at midnight of a certain day we intend at some fixed future time to swallow a toxin that will make us feel noxious (nothing worse). He doesn't ask us to actually take the toxin. In fact, taking it at midnight is not an option. All that can and must be done at midnight, if one wants to receive the $1 million, is to entertain the intent. The point of the example is to show that such an intent would be impossible to form for a rational person, because he knows that at the predetermined point in the future he will no longer have any reason to follow through on that intent, which in turn makes it impossible for him to entertain now the intent to do so in the future.

The larger lesson meant to be drawn from the example is that one cannot argue that it would be rational for the soldier to launch a retaliatory strike against the Soviet Union just because it is part of a package deal which it would be rational to adopt, namely the overall deterrence plan. The package deal of intending now to take the poison in the future so as to receive the $1 million and then actually following through is also advantageous and the only possible way for a rational person to acquire the intent to take the toxin, and yet, says Kavka, this clearly would not render the consumption of the toxin rational once midnight has passed and the $1 million has been received.

Derek Parfit, drawing on an example of Thomas Schelling's, has further elaborated on Kavka's view. Parfit imagines a robber who threatens his victim with the death of the victim's children unless the victim reveals to the robber the combination to a safe containing a lot of gold bars.[13] It is unclear that compliance will in fact save the man's children, though it might. But there is a more promising strategy the victim has at his disposal: an irrationality pill which will make him temporarily crazy and unresponsive, at least in a rational way, to any threats the robber might utter. All right, so the optimal thing to do is another package deal: swallow the irrationality pill and then behave irrationally. Does being wrapped into this rationally conceived package render the irrational behavior rational? Pretty clearly not. From these types of examples Kavka and Parfit draw the lesson that sometimes it is rational to cause yourself to behave irrationally, without thereby rendering the caused irrational behavior rational. What they are saying, moreover, fits hand-in-glove with what economists writing in game theory have said about dynamic consistency and

[12] Gregory S. Kavka, "The Toxin Puzzle," *Analysis* 43, no. 1 (1083): 33–36.

[13] Derek Parfit, *Reasons and Persons* (New York: Oxford University Press, 1984).

subgame perfection.[14] Kavka and Parfit then draw a further lesson from this, namely that, contra Gauthier and others following his lead, such package deal reasoning does not apply in the realm of morality either. That is, Kavka wants to say about his nuclear deterrence examples that it is moral to put in place such a scheme, but not to carry it out. Parfit constructs an illuminating further example to make the same point: Imagine a prosecutor who is being subjected to a special punishment conceived by a man he long ago put in jail for a crime the man committed. The man kidnaps the prosecutor's daughters and threatens to kill them unless the prosecutor submits to the making of a highly humiliating movie about himself. This movie will then be used, the prosecutor is given to understand, to pressure him into committing various acts of corruption. Unless he performs those corrupt acts, he will be told, the movie will be disseminated. This example, for all its artificiality, rather nicely represents the structure we are interested in, i.e., a moral act that morally causes immoral behavior. To see this clearly, let us examine the prosecutor's options at various moments in time. There first is the moment at which the prosecutor faces the threat to have his daughters killed unless he agrees to have that highly embarrassing movie made. The moral course of action here is clearly to agree to have the movie made so as to achieve their release. This is true even if one takes into account the fact that once this movie is made it will be successfully used to elicit various corrupt (i.e., criminal) acts on the part of the prosecutor. The lives of the girls obviously outweigh the harm wrought by those corrupt actions (or so we will assume). Now consider the later point in time. Assume the prosecutor has successfully achieved the release of his daughters and is now faced with the dilemma of engaging in the requested corrupt actions or having the movie disseminated. If he gives in, he is acting criminally, immorally, and the fact that this misconduct is part of a larger plan, a package deal, that is moral does not seem to untaint his actions. The situation seems exactly parallel to the rationality/irrationality scenario embodied in the robber-irrationality pill hypothetical.

Alexander and Sherwin then understandably argue that rule situations track this logic, that there is the morally defensible decision to put in place a regime that necessarily involves downstream immoral rule applications – that's "the gap."

But there are reasons to doubt that the parallel holds. Let us explain. There is some reason to doubt that rationality here exactly parallels morality. The package

[14] The idea here is that as we move backwards through an unfolding game-theoretic situation, starting at the very end, and working our way through to the beginning, each subsidiary portion of the game tree should look rational all by itself, not just in the context of portions of the game tree not yet examined. In the context of an ordinary contract, in which A promises to do something for B, and B promises to do something for A, and A performs first and B second, B's actions will only qualify as "subgame-perfect" if they would be rational to perform in light of what he could expect to happen as a result of his performance or nonperformance, not in light of anything that preceded his performance.

logic, which does not work in the rationality context, shows some sign of being perfectly sensible in the moral context. Let us consider some intuitive examples of this claim and subsequently back it up with a broader argument.

There are in fact numerous examples in morality in which we clearly take the package deal view; or, more precisely, in which the kind of "look back" that is required for a package deal and that is regarded as irrational when we simply assess the rationality of an action is permitted by morality, even if not by rationality. These cases come in two varieties. One involves evaluations of actions that appear on their face moral, as well as rational, but which, once we "look back" at some earlier actions the defendant took to create the situation he finds himself in, no longer look moral (though they will still appear rational!).These are cases in which the look-back inculpates the defendant. The second variety of such cases involves defendants who are doing something that looks ostensibly immoral (although rational!), but once we look back at how they got into those circumstances, their actions no longer look immoral (although still perfectly rational!).

The first variety of these cases is exemplified by the so-called defense cases, in which a man creates a situation in which he then is in a position to act out of necessity or self-defense or duress or some other justifying or exculpating reason. The simplest would be one in which a defendant who could perfectly easily escape the harm he is threatened with deliberately forecloses all of his means of escape, such that killing his attacker becomes his only means of survival. Here, the law says he has forfeited his right of self-defense by reason of his earlier actions.

The second variety of these cases requires a bit more artifice to construct. Here is an instance of it. A man wants to try out a drug that promises to have many therapeutic properties. He wants to test it out by self-experimentation. The drug effectuates a personality shift, which in some indeterminate number of people will lead them to become severely violent. There may be ways of fixing that problem, but only if he first gets to experience the drug's effects personally. He surrounds himself with an army of bodyguards and enters – let us say that this is the kind of test the science here requires – a shopping mall. He has a violent impulse and pounces on someone. The bodyguards prove inadequate to their task and, before they can prevent it, he has seriously injured (or even killed, or attempted to kill) someone. In fact, for the dilemma to stand up perfectly, we can leave out the actual injury. The point is that in situations like this the frame would seem relevant to evaluating what came to pass, contrary to the rationality dogma.

Now there might seem to be a ready reply to this analysis, and it has been made repeatedly by those analyzing the contrived defense cases. It is to defend the rationality dogma as being applicable to morality but to argue for the wrongfulness of defendants contriving to create the conditions of their own defense by an alternative route. The argument would go thus: When the defendant inaugurates the incident that eventuates in harm, e.g., death, he does not yet have a defense, such as duress, self-defense, etc. and, hence, is guilty of causing that harm, if causing is the required *actus reus*. With regard to the second set of examples, those in which looking back might exculpate the defendant, those who make this argument might simply bite the bullet and say that in fact the defendant is guilty. Earlier actions are irrelevant.

But there are reasons to be skeptical of this approach and, in particular, to question the parallel between rationality and morality when it comes to looking back, a parallel presupposed by both Gauthier and his opponents. Work that we have done together suggests that the two settings are actually quite different and that arguments that are applicable in the ordinary settings in which rationality is invoked do not apply with regard to plausible moral reasoning.[15]

What this work does is to prove a formal result that identifies the nature and root cause of this lack of parallelism. Our focus there is on an overlooked phenomenon that characterizes all moral and legal decision making and sets it apart from the standard decision making models of economics, in which someone is simply maximizing something, typically expected utility. Many standard principles of rationality turn out to fail once intransitivity enters the picture. And all kinds of unexpected oddities make their appearance. For instance, it becomes routinely possible, in a world in which intransitivity reigns, to circumvent a legal prohibition by slightly restructuring a legal interaction, much in the way a defendant does when he contrives to create a defense, although such a strategy is subject to important limitations.

What do we have in mind when we speak of intransitivity? A simple example will help to tell the story most clearly. Consider the defense of duress. Consider a defendant who is given the choice by some gangsters between helping them in the commission of some serious crime (e.g., a bank robbery) or being subjected to some terribly painful treatment (e.g., being subjected to a partial burning). This being a standard case of duress, it would be legitimate for the defendant to choose to participate in the crime rather than be subjected to torture. Consider now a different choice the defendant might confront. Suppose that the threat he faced were a milder one. He is simply threatened with having a manuscript he values highly, because he has worked on it a long time, destroyed if he does not oblige the gangsters in their request. What will he do? If he were to give in and participate in the robbery, he would not qualify for the duress defense, and therefore he does not give in (let us suppose). Finally, imagine one last choice situation this defendant might face: His manuscript is threatened by a fire and the only way he can rescue it is by suffering some burns, in fact exposing himself to something fairly equivalent to what the

[15] Leo Katz and Alvaro Sandroni, "The Inevitability and Ubiquity of Cycling in All Feasible Legal Regimes: A Formal Proof," *The Journal of Legal Studies* (forthcoming).

gangsters in the prior example threatened him with if he did not help them. Let us suppose that he values the manuscript sufficiently that he is prepared to make that tradeoff – not an illogical, or even wildly implausible, assumption. What we now have is an instance of intransitivity.

Now in this world in which intransitivity reigns all sorts of intuitions, seemingly self-evident truths based on customary ideas about rationality, go out the window. What goes, what stays? Self-defense gives us a clue. One can think of instances of contrived self-defense that work and instances that don't work. The person who is under attack and has an easy means of egress but locks it, throws away the key, and now no longer can escape, presumably forfeits his right to self-defense, and is thus without a justification when he resorts to deadly force against his enemy. The person who acts much more antecedently, however, is in a different position. What do we mean by "more antecedently"? Well, suppose he joins the police force, hoping that at some point a criminal will have the temerity to attack him and he will then get to kill him in self-defense. Presumably, that is sufficiently antecedent. In this world then, a great deal depends on how events are clumped together for their evaluation. That opens up the possibility of viewing cases in which a regime is set up with a certain justification and its unjustified downstream consequences as standing in much the same relationship as the person who shuts off his own means of escape. If we feel hesitant, it is because the relationship might conceivably be too distant for the exoneration to travel that far. But if it does travel that far, it would close the gap.

The gap exists in the world of ordinary rationality. Law and morality, mercifully we would claim, operate according to rules that may be partially exempt from the gap. That's a large claim. More remains to be said to justify it. If we are right, that scarcely undermines the fundamental value of Alexander's insight, but it does subject it to a necessary qualification.

PART IV

Paradoxes in Moral Philosophy

19

Respect and Discrimination

Kasper Lippert-Rasmussen

19.1 INTRODUCTION

What makes wrongful discrimination wrong? This question forms the title of a 1992 article by Larry Alexander[1], which has been very important for much work on the ethics of discrimination. In it, he makes two claims. First, some forms of discrimination are not wrongful at all. Second, there are two distinct sources of the wrongness of discrimination.[2] Generally, discrimination is contingently wrong in virtue of its consequences, e.g., irrational statistical discrimination is typically wrong because of the "unnecessary social costs" involved in acting on the basis of "inaccurate stereotypes."[3] However, when "a person is judged incorrectly to be of lesser moral worth and is treated accordingly, that treatment is morally wrong regardless of the gravity of its effects. It represents a failure to show the moral respect due to the recipient, a failure which is by itself sufficient to be judged immoral."[4]

In recent work, Alexander retreats from this position.[5] He now believes that, setting aside the complications of promises and fiduciary duties, mental states are irrelevant to moral permissibility, and, with some reservations, embraces a consequence-based account of the wrongfulness of discrimination.[6] I am skeptical about the force of the

1 Larry Alexander, "What Makes Wrongful Discrimination Wrong? Biases, Preferences, Stereotypes, and Proxies," *University of Pennsylvania Law Review* 141, no. 1 (1992).

2 Ibid., 155.

3 Ibid., 169.

4 Ibid., 159.

5 Larry Alexander, "Review: Deborah Hellman and Sophia Moreau, ed., Philosophical Foundations of Discrimination Law," *Ethics* 125, no. 3 (2015): 878–79; Alexander, "Is Wrongful Discrimination Really Wrong" (forthcoming): 2.

6 Alexander, "Review: Hellman and Moreau," 873; Alexander, "The Means Principle," in *Legal, Moral, and Metaphysical Truths: The Philosophy of Michael S. Moore*, ed. Kimberly Kessler Ferzan and Stephen J. Morse (Oxford: Oxford University Press, 2016), 251, 258; compare T.M. Scanlon, *Moral Dimensions* (Cambridge, MA: Harvard University Press, 2008), 19–20; J.J. Thomson, "Physician-Assisted Suicide: Two Moral Arguments," *Ethics* 109, no. 3 (1999): 515–16.

arguments by Alexander and others in favor of the view that mental states do not bear directly on moral permissibility.[7] However, I am sympathetic to Alexander's present view that the wrongfulness of discrimination results from how discrimination harms people. Hence, I will explore the possibility of rejecting accounts of the wrongness of discrimination focusing on disrespectful mental states without commitment to any across-the-board dismissal of the relevance of mental states for moral permissibility.

Section 19.2 expounds Alexander's 1992 account. Section 19.3 argues that it is vulnerable to a counterexample. Section 19.4 presents an alternative disrespect-based account of the wrongness of discrimination offered by Benjamin Eidelson, which builds on Alexander's work. In some respects, it is superior to the latter. Yet, it is vulnerable to a counterexample similar to the one that threatens Alexander's (Section 19.5). Section 19.6 explores an additional problem to which Eidelson's account gives rise. Because Eidelson, unlike Alexander, contends that certain forms of statistical discrimination are inherently disrespectful, his view is implausibly bifurcated between a fact- and an evidence-relative account of disrespect. Hence, the overall line of this argument supports Alexander's present skepticism about disrespect-based accounts of wrongful discrimination, though for more specific reasons than those on the basis of which he holds this position.

19.2 ALEXANDER'S ACCOUNT

My focus in this section is on discrimination that Alexander in 1992 thinks is disrespectful, and, thus, intrinsically wrong.[8] What counts as *disrespectful* discrimination? Alexander suggests that discrimination "premised on the [false] belief that some types of people are morally worthier than others," where for some to have greater moral worth than others is for them to merit "greater moral concern" than others, is disrespectful towards those who are premised to have lower moral worth.[9] Or, as I shall formulate Alexander's view (probably allowing myself some exegetical liberties):[10]

X disrespectfully discriminates against Y relative to Z if, and only if:

1) Y and Z are persons;

[7] Kasper Lippert-Rasmussen, "Scanlon on the Doctrine of Double Effect," *Social Theory and Practice* 36, no. 4 (2010); Jeff McMahan, "Intention, Permissibility, Terrorism, and War," *Philosophical Perspectives* 23, no. 1 (2009).

[8] In this section and the next I take "1992" as read whenever I refer to Alexander's views.

[9] Alexander, "What Makes Wrongful Discrimination Wrong?" 160–61.

[10] Kasper Lippert-Rasmussen, *Born Free and Equal?* (Oxford: Oxford University Press, 2013), 113–27, distinguishes between three interpretations of Alexander's account.

2) X treats Y worse than Z;
3) and 2), because X falsely believes that Z has greater moral worth than Y.

This account captures well some paradigmatic cases of disrespectful discrimination, which appear wrong in part because of the disrespect they involve. Take Alexander's case of the Nazi who treats Jews worse than people whom he perceives to be Aryans, because he believes that Aryans have greater moral worth than Jews. Even if, surprisingly, this discriminatory act has no harmful effects on anyone, we might still think that there is something morally objectionable about the act; it is disrespectful and this makes it morally wrong.[11]

In the next section, I shall explain why this account is not right; but first I want to draw attention to three features of Alexander's account. First, "moral worth" is standardly used in philosophy to refer to a Kantian idea, which implies that persons have a special moral status compared to nonpersons. So construed, two features of moral worth are important. First, it is a superior moral status to whatever moral status nonpersons (e.g., severely demented human beings) possess. Second, all persons have equal moral worth, irrespective of how they vary in other respects (e.g., in terms of their level of rationality or their deeds).

Both aspects of the Kantian idea are controversial.[12] In any case, Alexander plausibly does not mean *Kantian* moral worth, but something different, and, thus, steers clear of the controversy surrounding the Kantian idea of moral worth.[13] Admittedly,

[11] Adam Parr and Adam Slavny, "Harmless Discrimination," *Legal Theory* 21, no. 2 (2015); compare Richard J. Arneson, "Discrimination and Harm," in *Routledge Handbook to Ethics of Discrimination*, ed. Kasper Lippert-Rasmussen (London: Routledge, 2017), 151–163. Some – Alexander, "Review of Hellman and Moreau" included – would argue that while, undeniably, there is something objectionable about the pertinent Nazi official, it is not that his action is wrong in the sense of being impermissible. Rather, what is morally objectionable is something about the Nazi's character or his moral deliberations (Lippert-Rasmussen, *Born Free and Equal?*, 160, 173; compare Alexander, "Review of Hellman and Moreau," 877; Alexander, "The Means Principle," 258.

[12] Richard J. Arneson, "What, if Anything, Renders All Humans Morally Equal?" in *Singer and His Critics*, ed. Dale Jamieson (Oxford: Blackwell, 1999), 151–163; Ian Carter, "Respect and the Basis of Equality," *Ethics* 121, no. 3 (2011); Jeff McMahan, *The Ethics of Killing* (Oxford: Oxford University Press, 2003); Peter Singer, *Animal Liberation*, 2nd ed. (New York: Random House, 1990); Bernard Williams, "The Idea of Equality," in *Problems of the Self*, ed. Bernard Williams (Cambridge: Cambridge University Press, 1988).

[13] There is an additional attraction of interpreting his view in a non-Kantian way. Suppose I am an anti-Kantian who rejects the notion of moral worth. Thus, I do not believe that anyone has greater moral worth than others for the simple reason that I do not believe that *anyone* has moral worth. According to Alexander's view, interpreted along Kantian lines, I could not engage in intrinsically wrong, because disrespectful, discrimination. However, given that disrespectful discriminatory acts are intrinsically wrong, this view seems implausible, e.g., in light of a case where I treat people differently on the basis of their moral virtuousness and believe that a praiseworthy action by a white person boosts his or her moral virtuousness more than an otherwise comparable act by a black person. Admittedly, Alexander ("What Makes Wrongful Discrimination Wrong?" 200) places himself in the company of "we good Kantians," but that is in a different context, where he submits that "[m]oral worth must be based on moral choices" and not "immutable traits" – a view which has a Kantian flavor, because of

his account of discrimination is person-centric in that he only considers discrimination against "people." However, even though he contends that all people have equal moral worth, he does so setting aside the possibility of "differential moral concern for the especially virtuous and vicious."[14] Moreover, he submits that the trait of "being a criminal" is "a trait that more plausibly reflects lower moral worth."[15] Neither the reservation nor the conjecture makes sense if he had in mind the Kantian notion of moral worth.

Second, while I have introduced Alexander's account as an account of the wrongfulness of certain kinds of discrimination *against* someone, suitably extrapolated it also offers an account of why certain kinds of discrimination *in favor of* someone are disrespectful and, thus, intrinsically wrong. Suppose that a benevolent slave owner treats his slaves better than others for the condescending reason that he believes that, due to being substandardly rational, they have a lower moral status than persons and that this obliges him to care more for them than for persons. This appears no less disrespectful than a comparable case of discrimination against them. Rather than saying that disrespect in Alexander's sense only interacts with discrimination *against* to produce wrongness, given the wider framework it seems better to say that such discriminatory acts *in favor of* can be intrinsically wrong as well.

Third, sometimes people assume that things that are intrinsically wrong are more wrong than things that are not.[16] However, this need not be the case, as Alexander surely agrees, despite the morally serious nature of his example of intrinsically wrongful acts of discrimination. According to his account, it would be strange if intrinsically wrongful discrimination were more wrong, per se, than extrinsically wrongful discrimination. Disrespect, according to Alexander's account, is a scalar thing. There is a difference between thinking that the moral status of some person is just slightly lower than that of another and thinking that it is much lower. Moreover, the latter view seems much more disrespectful than the former. Hence, if wrongness of discrimination results not from disrespect in an either/or fashion, but varies with the degree of disrespect, plausibly some disrespectful acts of discrimination are only slightly wrong, albeit intrinsically so, and might be much less wrong than nondisrespectful acts of discrimination that are extrinsically wrong.

its rejection of moral luck, but still is different from Kant's view on moral worth, since moral worth is grounded in the capacity for autonomous choice, not in the choices actually made.

14 Alexander, "What Makes Wrongful Discrimination Wrong?" 161.

15 Ibid.

16 If "wrong" means "impermissible," it makes no sense to talk about degrees of wrongness. Impermissibility is an either/or matter in the exclusive sense. However, in a looser sense it is intelligible, because often one can order the reasons by virtue of which something is wrong in a scalar way.

I now move on to what I think is a forceful counterexample to Alexander's account of the wrongness of disrespectful discrimination.[17]

19.3 AN OBJECTION

Suppose – counterfactually if you like – that animals and human beings have the same moral status.[18] Compare, then, the following two cases in which an experimenter conducts painful experiments on animals that confer minor benefits on human beings:

Inegalitarian Belief – The experimenter conducts his experiments on animals, falsely believing that human beings have greater moral worth than animals. He picks his experimental objects partly on the basis of a desire to conform to social expectations, but reckons he would have chosen differently had he believed that animals and human beings have equal moral status.

Egalitarian Belief – The experimenter conducts his experiments on animals, correctly believing that animals and human beings have equal moral worth. He picks his experimental objects partly on the basis of a desire to conform to social expectations, but reckons that he would have chosen differently had he believed that animals have higher moral status than human beings.

If Alexander's account is correct, the inegalitarian experimenter acts in a way that is disrespectful – he harms animals on the basis of his false belief about the unequal moral status of animals and human beings – unlike the egalitarian experimenter, who holds true beliefs about the comparative moral status of animals and human beings. Since the two cases are identical in terms of harmful consequences, and since *Inegalitarian Belief* involves Alexanderian disrespect, unlike *Egalitarian Belief*, the former case should be more wrongful than the latter. However, intuitively, *if* there is a difference in terms of wrongfulness between the two acts of experimentation, the case involving what I stipulated to be true – egalitarian beliefs about moral status – is morally more wrong.[19] It follows that we must reject Alexander's

17 Kasper Lippert-Rasmussen, "The Badness of Discrimination," *Ethical Theory and Moral Practice* 9, no. 2 (2006); Lippert-Rasmussen, *Born Free and Equal?*, 120–21.

18 Since Alexander's exclusive focus on discrimination against persons is not motivated by a Kantian view of worth, there is no reason why his account cannot be extended to apply to animals. Furthermore, the present counterexample is the one Eidelson discusses. In any case, the present counterexample could be formulated in such a way that it involves human beings only, e.g., by substituting "severely mentally handicapped people" for "animals." This would accommodate those who worry that the egalitarian experimenter, unlike the inegalitarian, must harbor some form of irrational bias and that this explains why the latter case is more wrongful than the former. Many who are not irrational believe in the moral equality of all human beings, including the severely mentally handicapped.

19 I write "*if* there is a difference in terms of wrongfulness" because I want to bracket whether mental states affect the wrongness of actions. Henceforth, I ignore the conditionality of my claim, but note that

account. According to his account, *Inegalitarian Belief* is wrong in a way in which *Egalitarian Belief* is not, that is, it involves treating some individuals worse than others on the basis of false beliefs about their moral worth. And since the two cases are morally identical in terms of all other wrong-making properties, according to Alexander's account *Inegalitarian Belief* should be more wrong.

Some might object to the previous claim on the following ground: The latter, unlike the former, experimenter acts in a way that clashes with his beliefs about moral worth (and the implied beliefs about wrongness of actions). But to the extent that mental states determine wrongness of action, plausibly the more morally objectionable a mental state, the more wrongful the resulting action is; and it seems morally more objectionable, *ceteris paribus*, to do what you think is wrong, or to do what clashes with your beliefs about moral status, than not to do so. Moreover, the normative effect of this difference might be stronger than the normative effect of the difference Alexander highlights – acting or not acting on the basis of false beliefs about status – and thus drown and thereby hide the moral significance of Alexander's difference. Hence, the relevant intuition does not show that Alexander's difference is not morally relevant to wrongness, as opposed to its not being the most important factor vis-à-vis intrinsically wrongful discrimination.

In response, note, first, that Alexander cannot press this objection without significantly revising his own account of the wrongness of disrespectful discrimination and the relevant disrespect-base. Second, consider a third experimenter – one who is in all relevant respects like the two others except that he is agnostic on the moral status of animals and human beings and reckons that he would have experimented on humans only if he had thought they had a lower moral status than animals. If we think, as I am inclined to do, that the agnostic experimenter acts no more wrongly than, or roughly as wrongly as, the egalitarian experimenter, this would go against the "drowning" hypothesis.

Third, while the proposed explanation of the moral difference between the two cases has some force, it cannot be the basis for a general disrespect-based account of intrinsically wrongful discrimination.[20] Suppose that all members of a racial minority give all members of the majority permission to treat them on the basis of

you do not object to what I claim here if you simply say, unconditionally, that the two experimenters' actions are equally wrong. While Eidelson and many others share my intuitions about the two cases, not everyone I have asked does so.

[20] It might not fit all intuitions. Compare a sexist agent who acts in accordance with the false belief that men have greater epistemic worth than women and, thus, only listens carefully to men, with an unreflectively sexist agent, who, being unreflective, holds no beliefs about the relative epistemic worth of men and women, and yet only listens carefully to men. In this case, my intuitions do not align well with the proposed account, but align well with Alexander's view. It would be nice to know why this is so. However, to offer a counterexample one does not need to offer a *theory* of why the counterexample is one.

whatever beliefs about their moral status they have, however false or irrational these beliefs are, provided that they do not act in ways, thinly described, in which they would not be permitted to act independently of their motivation. Hence, members of the minority have not given members of the majority permission to kill them, since this is impermissible regardless of motivation, but they have given members of the majority permission not to hire them for jobs on the grounds of their false beliefs about moral status, when it would be permissible not to hire them anyway on different motivations (e.g., because they were not the best qualified). Arguably, members of the racial majority no longer *wrong* members of the minority by treating them disrespectfully when they act on their false beliefs about moral worth, because of the permission that they have been granted. Still, this case is possibly no less morally objectionable than the original case – for example, because the permission, though noticed, plays no role in the deliberations of the discriminators – in which case this suggests that the relevant moral objectionableness does not bear on wrongness of actions after all, but on the nature of the agent's character or the objectionableness of her deliberations, etc.

However, if we go along with Alexander, this is not what we want to say. In his view, false beliefs about moral worth bear directly on moral permissibility. Having mentioned the problem pertaining to persons who consent to being treated disrespectfully, I set it aside. If Alexander's account captures the essence of respect and if my claim about the conditional comparative wrongness of the *Egalitarian Belief* and the *Inegalitarian Belief* is correct, this would generate problems for disrespect-based accounts in general – but things change if we revise our understanding of disrespect. This is a possibility I explore in the next two sections.

19.4 EIDELSON ON DISRESPECT

In his recent book *Discrimination and Disrespect*, Benjamin Eidelson proposes, inter alia, a sophisticated account of the wrongness of discrimination. Like Alexander in 1992, he thinks that paradigmatic forms of discrimination are all disrespectful in a way that makes them intrinsically, pro tanto wrong: "[A]cts of discrimination are intrinsically wrong when and because they manifest a failure to show the discriminatees the respect that is due to them as persons."[21] However, he conceives of disrespect differently from Alexander. In part this reflects an ambition to offer a disrespect-based account that is immune to the previous section's counterexample[22], and in part it reflects that, in one respect, he takes a more critical view of statistical discrimination than Alexander does.

[21] Benjamin Eidelson, *Discrimination and Disrespect* (Oxford: Oxford University Press, 2015), 73.

[22] Ibid., 104.

Eidelson's account of disrespect builds on Stephen Darwall's notion of recognition respect, according to which recognition respect amounts to "a disposition to weigh appropriately in one's deliberations some feature of the thing in question and act accordingly."[23] According to Eidelson, two such features are crucial: 1) that "persons are of value in themselves, and equally so,"[24] and 2) that "persons are autonomous: they possess a faculty of self-control through which they can make their lives, in significant part, their own."[25] Or, as I shall put it:

X disrespectfully discriminates against Y relative to Z if, and only if:

1) Y and Z are persons and, thus, are a) ends in themselves, and equally so, and b) autonomous;
2) in X's deliberations behind his discriminatory act, X fails to give appropriate weight to the fact that Y is an end in himself, but does not fail to do so in the case of Z, or does so to a lesser extent in the case of Y than in the case of Z; or
3) in X's deliberations behind his discriminatory act, X fails to give appropriate weight to the fact that Y is autonomous, but does not fail to do so in the case of Z.

How does this account relate to Alexander's? First, like Alexander's account, it is person-centric[26] and, thus, does not apply to cases where, say, people inappropriately give greater weight to the interests of pets rather than cows in their deliberations. Also, unlike Alexander's, this account stands and falls with the moral-equality-of-persons thesis.

Second, unlike Alexander's account, the site of disrespect according to Eidelson's account is not beliefs, but deliberations. Thus, an act can be disrespectful in his account while not being disrespectful in Alexander's account, though the reverse is not possible. It is easy to see that the former can be the case. I believe that men and women have equal moral worth. Suppose that, against my own better judgment, I suffer from an implicit bias such that I consistently give greater weight to the interests of men than to the interests of women.[27] In this case, I act disrespectfully according to Eidelson's account by, say, unconsciously giving greater weight to the interests of men, even if I do not act disrespectfully according to Alexander's

[23] Ibid., 76; compare Stephen Darwall, "Two Kinds of Respect," *Ethics* 88, no. 1 (1977); Stephen Darwall, *The Second-Person Standpoint* (Cambridge, MA: Harvard University Press, 2006).

[24] Eidelson, *Discrimination and Disrespect*, 79.

[25] Ibid.

[26] Compare ibid., 97.

[27] According to ibid., 99, you can fail to give equal weight to people's interests without having formed any "explicit judgment of comparative value."

account.[28] Eidelson thinks that this feature of his account is an advantage, since, plausibly, such cases involve disrespect.

There is another reason – pertaining to the role autonomy plays in Eidelson's account – why an act might be disrespectful in Eidelson's account and not in Alexander's. Suppose I believe, consciously as well as unconsciously, that Y and Z have the same moral worth. Suppose, moreover, that I treat Y worse than Z. For example, in my capacity as a police officer, I stop and search Y, but not Z, regularly, on grounds of reliable statistics showing that people like Y are more likely than people like Z to be engaged in certain kinds of crime. Moreover, in doing so, I fail to pay any heed to Y's and Z's self-presentations, which unequivocally suggest that Y is a law-abiding citizen and Z is not. Suppose, finally, that there is no interest-based ground for saying that I treat Y worse than Z. In this case, I engage in disrespectful discrimination according to Eidelson's account, but not according to Alexander's.

Consider next why a discriminatory act cannot be disrespectful in Alexander's sense and not disrespectful in Eidelson's sense. It is possible that an agent believes that Y has a lower moral worth than Z and yet is not disrespectful in Eidelson's sense. After all, the agent might simply bracket his beliefs about differential worth in his deliberations about how to treat Y and Z and proceed from the assumption that they have equal moral worth and, thus, give appropriate weight in his deliberations to their being ends in themselves and to their being autonomous. This, however, does not show that an act can be disrespectful in Alexander's sense but not in Eidelson's. The case is not one in which the relevant discriminatory act is *motivated* by the agent's false beliefs about moral status – but then it is not disrespectful in Alexander's sense either. To make it so, it would have to motivate the agent's discriminatory act, and for it to do that, the relevant belief must play *some* role in the agent's deliberations about what to do. But in that case, it would also qualify as disrespectful in Eidelson's account.

I want to refine Eidelson's account in one way before I move on to consider whether it is immune to the counterexample described in Section 19.3. In relation to people's status as ends in themselves, Eidelson's account includes both a noncomparative element – an agent in her deliberations should treat each individual person as an end in herself – and a comparative element – for any pair of persons, an agent should treat them as ends in themselves to an equal degree. However, when it comes to the autonomy component, Eidelson's account only takes a noncomparative form. This strikes me as an error. Suppose I treat both Y and Z as autonomous individuals. I take into account the evidential values of their self-presentational behavior to at least the degree to which Eidelson thinks "giving

[28] Ibid., 97 ("To respect a person's equal value relative to other persons one must value her interests equally with those of other persons, absent good reasons for discounting them").

appropriate weight" to their being autonomous individuals requires.[29] However, I give even more weight to the evidential value of self-presentational behavior in the case of Z than I do in the case of Y. If I find the slightest evidence deriving from Z's self-presentational behavior that, despite the fact that he belongs to a group that is strongly overrepresented in a certain category of crime, Z is law-abiding in every way, I immediately infer that Z is not engaged in any criminal conduct. However, it takes more evidence for me to infer something similar with regard to Y. I would find it odd if someone persuaded by the Eidelsonian account of disrespect did not see this as a disrespectful differential treatment by me of Y. Fortunately, it is easy to give a relevantly comparative twist to 3):

3*) in X's deliberations behind his discriminatory act, X fails to give appropriate weight to the fact that Y is autonomous, but does not fail to do so in the case of Z, *or fails to give equal weight to X and Z being autonomous.*

This completes my presentation of Eidelson's account of disrespect.

19.5 IS EIDELSON'S ACCOUNT VULNERABLE TO A SIMILAR OBJECTION?

Consider Eidelson's account of disrespect in light of the pair of examples offered against Alexander's account in Section 19.3. Is Eidelson's account also vulnerable to it? Surprisingly, it is. The egalitarian experimenter clearly does not to a greater degree than the inegalitarian experimenter fail to give proper weight to the interests of animals, in part because both experimenters give much less weight to the interests of animals in their deliberations than they should, assuming, as I did, that animals and persons have the same moral status, in part because the egalitarian experimenter correctly acknowledges the comparative moral status of animals. Yet, Eidelson thinks that what the egalitarian experimenter does is more wrongful. Accordingly, to accommodate my counterexample he introduces a notion of contempt.

> [C]ontempt seems to involve a refusal to respect something – a kind of defiance of what you at some level realize its significance to be … it is too charitable to think of most textbook racists as simply holding false beliefs about the value or moral status of those whom they disfavor … it seems far more common that racists repudiate the equal personhood of those they disfavor than that they simply fail to grasp it. To take an extreme case, the genocidaires in Rwanda clearly did not mistake Tutsis for the evaluative equivalents of cockroaches … Rather, they chose to treat them *as if* they were.[30]

[29] Presumably, "appropriate weight" means "no less than appropriate weight." In giving more weight than what is minimally required, one does not fail to show respect for the person in question.

[30] Eidelson, *Discrimination and Disrespect*, 105.

Given the following three assumptions, the introduction of contempt helps Eidelson. First, greater disrespect results in being morally more wrong, *ceteris paribus*. Second, contemptuous disrespect is more disrespectful than noncontemptuous disrespect, *ceteris paribus*. And, third, *Egalitarian Belief* involves contemptuous disrespect, whereas *Inegalitarian Belief* only involves noncontemptuous disrespect. Given these assumptions, it follows that the egalitarian experimenter's act is more disrespectful and for that reason is more wrong, even if, as far as the part of Eidelson's account of disrespect that I presented in Section 19.4 goes, both agents act disrespectfully by failing to give the interests of animals proper weight in their deliberations. Hence, provided that the three assumptions are correct, Eidelson's account is immune to the counterexample, which, so he agrees, defeats Alexander's account. Are they correct?

For present purposes, I grant Eidelson the first assumption. Disrespect comes in different degrees, and, given that disrespect is a wrong-making feature of actions, greater disrespect plausibly results in greater wrongness. The only concern I have is that embracing this assumption means that Eidelson has to explain why a similar line of reasoning is not available in relation to equal moral worth. If, say, our being rational and autonomous individuals is what our moral worth results from, then why does moral worth not also come in degrees, given that rationality and autonomy do?

The second assumption – i.e., that contemptuous disrespect is more disrespectful than noncontemptuous disrespect – seems problematic in a more direct way. For while contempt in an ordinary sense is more disrespectful than noncontemptuous disrespect, it is unclear that Eidelson's contempt really is more disrespectful. As Eidelson points out, contempt involves *some* recognition of – some respect for? – the moral status of the individual whom you hold in contempt: "You can only show contempt for something that you recognize, in a minimal way, to make a normative claim on you, which you then go on to wilfully reject."[31] So, in one respect at least, contemptuous disrespect is better than noncontemptuous disrespect. It is better in that it involves some recognition of the moral status of the object of contempt, whereas noncontemptuous disrespect involves no recognition of moral status whatsoever. The slaveholder who really believes that his slaves are subhuman is, in one respect, worse than the slaveholder who believes that his slaves are his own moral equals, but then goes on to "wilfully reject" their human equality.

One might respond that, while contempt involves a willful rejection of what one recognizes at another level, it also involves more than that. For one thing, contempt is usually taken to involve ill will or outright hostility towards the individual whom one holds in contempt.[32] Similarly, contempt in Eidelson's sense is likely to be

[31] Ibid., 106.

[32] This is not a feature of contempt in Eidelson's sense, e.g., at some level X recognizes that Y is an autonomous being and yet X goes on to willfully deny Y's status as an autonomous being by assisting

understood to involve a greater flaw in the agent's deliberations than does the case of noncontemptuous disrespect. Unlike the noncontemptuous disrespectful person, the contemptuous person is willing to entertain a contradiction in his deliberations – something which, in the case at hand, involves a failure to give appropriate weight in one's deliberations to what one recognizes to be a feature of persons.

This defense of the second assumption takes me to the third assumption. Suppose – falsely, in my view – that contempt also involves ill will and flaws in deliberations. That might render the second assumption more defensible. However, it undermines the third assumption, since hostility and differential flaws in deliberations are not part of my counterexample to Alexander. I did not stipulate that the egalitarian experimenter who conducted painful experiments on animals harbored any hostility towards his experimental objects. Indeed, he might regret that his desire to conform to social expectations leads to a preference for experimenting on animals forming his will. Moreover, noncontemptuous disrespect can also involve hostility. Accordingly, insofar as we want to test whether contemptuous disrespect is worse than noncontemptuous disrespect, we should stipulate that neither, or both, of the inegalitarian and the egalitarian experimenter have ill will towards their experimental objects. A similar point applies to epistemic flaws. If the experimenter in *Egalitarian Belief* is epistemically blameworthy for not fully believing what, at some level, he knows to be the case, then we should similarly stipulate that the experimenter in *Inegalitarian Belief* is equally epistemically blameworthy, for example, for failing to infer from available evidence that animals have the same worth as persons.[33]

In light of the arguments in the four paragraphs above, I conclude that Eidelson is unable to defend the three assumptions needed for his contempt-based supplement to enable his account to accommodate my counterexample. Suppose, however, that I am wrong about this. It might not matter much, since Eidelson's account, even when suitably supplemented, is vulnerable to a revised version of my counterexample. Consider the following two cases in which the agent engages in painful experimentation on people:

Contemptuous Experimenter – The experimenter falsely believes that Y-people have a higher moral status than Z-people and yet, partly out of conformist

Y in all sorts of ways that make sense only if Y were not an autonomous being. In short, X willfully infantilizes Y. Typically, we experience the opposite of hostility towards those whom we infantilize.

33 Since contemptuous disrespect by definition involves epistemic blameworthiness, whereas noncontemptuous disrespect may or may not involve epistemic blameworthiness, contemptuous disrespect is arguably worse than noncontemptuous disrespect per se, even if an individual case of noncontemptuous disrespect might be as bad as an individual case of contemptuous disrespect and where the two cases do not differ in terms of any properties that are not definitional properties of either form of disrespect.

motivation, he only experiments on Y-people, thus manifesting contempt towards Y-people.

Noncontemptuous Experimenter – The experimenter falsely believes that Y-people have a higher moral status than Z-people and, partly out of conformist motivation, only experiments on Z-people, thus not manifesting any kind of contempt for anyone's value.

In Eidelson's sense, both agents disrespect the individuals on whom they experiment, since both experimenters fail to give proper weight in their deliberations to the value, as perceived by them, of those persons they experiment on. Both cases, we can assume, involve the same amount of harmful consequences (e.g., harm to the experimental subjects). Only the former case involves contempt. Yet it is unclear that the former case is more wrongful than the latter.

Assuming that the preceding claim is correct, this implies that Eidelson's amended disrespect-based account may need to be rethought in light of a pair of examples very similar to the one he accepts defeats Alexander's account. Perhaps there are ways this can be done. Perhaps contempt only boosts the disrespectfulness and, consequently, the wrongness of an action when the agent's belief about the moral status of those for whom he displays contempt is correct. However, I do not see any reason why this should be so, given that we accept that mental states determine the wrongness of actions. Hence, in light of the arguments put forward in this section, I conclude that more work needs to be done for Eidelson's disrespect-based account of the wrongness of discrimination to be satisfactory and for it to serve as a superior replacement of Alexander's account.

19.6 ASYMMETRY IN DISRESPECT

In this section I present an additional problem to which Eidelson's account of disrespect gives rise and to which Alexander's account does not. This problem reflects Eidelson's view that certain forms of statistical discrimination are intrinsically wrong – a view which Alexander does not share, at least not in the form Eidelson gives it.[34]

The problem I want to explore is this: Eidelson oscillates between a fact- and an evidence-relative account of disrespect.[35] According to the fact-relative account, X treats Y disrespectfully if X fails to give appropriate weight in X's deliberations to

34 Alexander, "What Makes Wrongful Discrimination Wrong?" 161.

35 I borrow the terminology from Derek Parfit, *On What Matters*, vol. 1 (Oxford: Oxford University Press, 2011), 150–51. Parfit's taxonomy is tripartite, but for present purposes I can ignore Parfit's third taxon, i.e., belief-relative.

features that Y actually has. According to the evidence-relative account, X treats Y disrespectfully if X fails to give proper weight to evidence about features Y has.

The fact-relative account is especially salient in Eidelson's account of the ends-in-themselves component and in his appeal to Darwall's account of recognition respect. That is, I treat someone disrespectfully if I fail to give the weight to their interests that I should give them, given how they in fact are and not in light of the evidence I have regarding their status as ends in themselves.

The evidence-relative account is particularly salient in Eidelson's examination of racial profiling and, more generally, in his critique of statistical discrimination. Here, I treat someone disrespectfully by not giving the proper evidential weight to their self-presentational behavior, because in doing so I do not treat them in accordance with the evidence I have of their status as autonomous beings.[36] Eidelson does not think treating people on the basis of generalizations is pro tanto disrespectful, because, unavoidably, doing so will result in treating them based on the assumption that they are likely, or more likely than others, to have certain features that, in a number of cases, will turn out to be false.[37]

However, this asymmetric treatment could be reversed. Take the ends-in-themselves component first. Suppose Agent gives greater weight to Seemingly Superior's interests than Truly Superior's (for short: Seemingly and Superior).[38] Suppose also that Agent has overwhelming evidence that Seemingly's moral status is more elevated than Truly's, in fact so much higher that in not giving even greater weight to Seemingly's interest it would seem that, by his own lights, Agent would contemptuously repudiate the superior moral status of Seemingly. Yet suppose that, as a matter of fact, Truly has a higher moral status than Seemingly has. According to Eidelson's fact-relative account of disrespect, Agent discriminates disrespectfully against Truly, because in giving somewhat greater weight to Seemingly's interests than to Truly's, he is not giving the weight he should give to Truly's interests. However, it is also the case that, by his own lights, Agent fails to give appropriate weight to Seemingly's, not Truly's, interests. Hence, according to an evidence-relative account of disrespect, it is Seemingly, not Truly, towards whom Agent is disrespectful.

36 Eidelson, *Discrimination and* Disrespect, 144–50.

37 One assumption underlying this view might be that it is extremely costly (either relative to the benefits to the target of the generalization or absolutely) or outright impossible not to treat people on the basis of generalizations; that no one has a moral claim to be treated in ways that are extremely costly or outright impossible; and that one does not treat people disrespectfully if one does not treat them in ways in which they have no moral claim to be treated. Note, however, that the very same factor bears on the end-in-themselves component.

38 Suppose Seemingly only appears to be a person and Truly appears not to be but really is.

Take next the autonomy component. Suppose there is no self-presentational evidence that a certain person is autonomous – for example, we have strong reason to believe she is brain-dead, but as a matter of fact she is fully conscious though paralyzed. I have every reason to think of her as a nonautonomous being. However, her mind and perceptual capacities function as well as anyone's. In not treating her as autonomous, I do not disrespect her according to Eidelson's evidence-relative account of disrespect. Yet I do according to a fact-relative view of the autonomy component in Eidelson's disrespect account.[39]

To treat the end-in-themselves and the autonomy components asymmetrically in relation to the fact- versus evidence-relative distinction strikes me as untenable. Why should disrespect engage differently with different features of persons? Yet if we should treat the two components symmetrically, the question becomes *how*. Should we give fact-relative accounts of both components, or should we give evidence-relative accounts of both? Or should we, alternatively, say that there are two different forms of disrespect involved? I see problems whichever way we go.

Suppose we adopt a fact-relative treatment of both components. Barring a cosmic coincidence, this would render any instance of statistical discrimination disrespectful, and in a way that fits badly with Eidelson's account. After all, he thinks that when we act on the basis of generalizations, we do not act disrespectfully in failing to take into account all facts about how someone is autonomous or has exercised her autonomy, provided evidence about these facts is not "reasonably available."[40] However, according to the fact-relative account, we would. This suggests that we adopt the evidence-relative account instead.

If we do so, we run into another problem, this time in relation to the ends-in-themselves component. Consider the case I described four paragraphs ago. According to the evidence-based account, Agent disrespects Seemingly, even though Agent treats Seemingly better than Truly, and Truly, as a matter of fact, has a more elevated moral status than Seemingly. This does not seem right either. The mere fact that the evidence available to Agent warrants the view that Seemingly's status is much superior to Truly's and, thus, merits better treatment than Agent in fact provides Seemingly with does not seem enough to conclude that Agent disrespects Seemingly all things considered.[41] In any case, this is not the way that Eidelson wants to go.[42]

39 In theory, there could also be situations where, conversely, self-presentational evidence (falsely) suggests that the discriminatee is exercising his or her autonomy, whereas this is not in fact the case.

40 Eidelson, *Discrimination and Disrespect*, 144, 156–57.

41 Perhaps this is the place to introduce Parfit's third taxon, belief-relative (disrespect).

42 These two objections mean that it is not a way out simply to go for a conjunctive account, where you say that both forms of disrespect matter. One could hold that if I am right that there is a problem with both ways of treating the two components symmetrically, that is an argument for asymmetric treatment. Note, however, that it is a purely negative argument, i.e., it offers no positive reason for

19.7 CONCLUSION

In view of the argument in the previous section, I conclude that there is an unresolved problem in the midst of Eidelson's account of disrespect. Perhaps we are not entitled to conclude from it that the wrongness of discrimination cannot, in part at least, be accounted for in terms of disrespect, but at least we can conclude that his account is not satisfactory. Note that the schism between fact-relative and evidence-relative disrespect does not arise in the case of Alexander's account, because Alexander does not believe that certain forms of statistical discrimination are intrinsically disrespectful and, thus, does not include a component in relation to which the evidence-relative account seems much more attractive.[43] The wider upshot of this chapter is that we still do not have a satisfactory disrespect-based account of the wrongness of discrimination, and that attempting to extend its reach to statistical discrimination makes the task of providing one even more daunting.[44]

This, I take it, provides some vindication of Alexander's present view of the wrongness of discrimination, though on less grand grounds than those on the basis of which he himself holds it.

asymmetric treatment but simply offers negative reasons against symmetric treatment, and, thus, does nothing to undermine the view that there is something odd about why respect should relate differently to different features of persons.

43 The reason why the act of the egalitarian experimenter seems more disrespectful than that of the inegalitarian experimenter might be that we assess the two acts in terms of evidence-relative disrespect. If so, it is telling that Eidelson, as far as his official presentation of the ends-in-themselves component of his disrespect account is concerned, gives an account of fact-relative respect. Perhaps he overlooks this issue, because he thinks that cases where people have conclusive evidence for not ascribing equal moral worth to persons are extremely unlikely and, thus, fails to consider them.

44 Previous versions of this chapter were presented at the Minerva Centre for Human Rights, The Hebrew University of Jerusalem, December 15, 2016; KJuris, Kings College London, February 8, 2017; Nuffield Political Theory Seminar, University of Oxford, February 27, 2017; and CELPA, University of Warwick, March 7, 2017. I am grateful to Andreas Albertsen, Larry Alexander, Richard Arneson, Jessica Begon, Paul Billingham, Ian Carroll, Matt Coakely, Leora Dahan-Katz, David Enoch, Cecile Fabre, Gina Gustavsson, Kat Hadjimatheou, Deborah Hellman, Clare Heyward, Keith Hyams, Kristian Jensen, Hwa Kim, Cecile Laborde, David Miller, Lasse Nielsen, Tore Vincents Olsen, David Owens, Tom Parr, Avia Pasternak, Viki Pedersen, Felix Pinkert, Joseph Raz, Massimo Renzo, Daniel Schwartz, Re'em Segev, Adam Slavny, Daniel Statman, Julie Suk, Adam Swift, Victor Tadros, John Tasioulas, Jens Damgaard Thaysen, and Kartik Upadhyaya for helpful comments on an earlier draft.

20

The Means Principle and Optimific Wrongs

*Kimberly Kessler Ferzan**

It has been a tremendous pleasure to write with Larry for over two decades. Even when I was a law student,[1] Larry treated me as his intellectual equal and playmate, and we delighted in puzzles together. Sometimes, I find that Larry simply gets to the answer more quickly and more concisely than I do. For instance, when he sent me a draft of his first cut of one of our book chapters for *Crime and Culpability*, I found that I wasn't sure I agreed with an answer he gave to a puzzle. I deleted the two paragraphs he wrote and then sat typing furiously.[2] (I think as I write.) Five pages later, I had reached the same conclusion he reached in two paragraphs. Alas, I deleted my five pages and reinserted his perfectly concise two paragraphs. At least I was confident that I agreed with him.

Sometimes, however, it is the job of a coauthor to further develop and defend a line of argument that her coauthor has underexplained. I like to think that that is what I am doing here. In a footnote to his paper "The Means Principle," Larry argues that in deciding whether to rescue the Fat Man, who is about to be used as a means to rescue five, "what we must not do is count the consequences of the use of someone in violation of [the means principle] in our justificatory calculus."[3] Thus, putting aside cases of easy rescue, where one might be required to rescue the Fat

* For helpful discussion of this paper, I thank Alec Walen, the participants at the Roundtable on the Influence of Larry Alexander, and the participants at the New Directions in Deontology panel at the APA Pacific Division annual meeting. I am grateful to Peter Westen for his detailed and insightful written comments.

1 We wound up coauthoring because of Heidi Hurd's matchmaking. I was never Larry's student.

2 Another great thing about Larry. He has no objection to your deleting his paragraphs. On the other hand, when coauthoring with him, one should never ever use "since" when one means "because."

3 Because of space constraints, this particular footnote did not make it into Larry Alexander, "The Means Principle," in *Legal, Moral, and Metaphysical Truths: The Philosophy of Michael S. Moore*, ed. Kimberly Kessler Ferzan and Stephen J. Morse (Oxford: Oxford University Press, 2016), 251–64, but the longer version is available online at https://papers.ssrn.com/sol3/papers.cfm?abstract_id=2378608, 51-2n44 (hereinafter "The Means Principle, SSRN version").

Man (and hence it is impermissible *not* to rescue him), "we still do no wrong if we rescue him, even at the cost of the five."[4] I concur. Indeed, I agree with the paper. (Surprise, surprise.) Still, one might think that a one-sentence assertion needs a bit more support. And, helpful coauthor that I am, I aim to provide it here. Recent scholarship, as we shall see, has argued in the opposite direction.

20.1 THE PUZZLE OF PREVENTING USE AS A MEANS

Consider the following hypothetical cases:

Tracks[5] – Alex, a large man, has fallen asleep on some trolley tracks. The presence of his body will prevent a runaway trolley from hitting and killing five trapped workmen farther down the track, but Alex will die. Betty sees what is going to happen to Alex and has time to wake Alex and get him off the tracks, but she cannot free the five trapped workers.

Push – Carl sees that a runaway trolley is about to run down five trapped workers. He can stop the trolley by pushing Diane, a large woman, in the path of the trolley. Ed sees what Carl is about to do and can stop him by (a) yelling something that distracts him, (b) reasoning with him that pushing Diane is wrong, or (c) grabbing his arms to prevent the push.

It seems to me that Betty may permissibly wake Alex and that Ed may distract, reason with, or use force against Carl to prevent Diane from being pushed in front of the trolley.[6] In other words, in Push, it is permissible to prevent what is called an "optimific wrong," that is, a wrong that would otherwise be consequentially justified. And, I maintain that it is permissible for Betty to wake Alex in Tracks even though Alex will not otherwise be the victim of another person's wrongdoing. Recently, however, both Andreas Mogensen and Re'em Segev have suggested the contrary. Indeed, both conclude that Ed may not intervene to rescue Diane!

Mogensen sets forth his argument thus:

(1) If we should prevent optimific wrongs, I should intervene in [Push].
(2) If I should intervene in [Push], I should intervene in Tracks.
(3) It is not the case that I should intervene in Tracks.

[4] Alexander, "The Means Principle, SSRN version,"51–52n44.

[5] Andreas Mogensen introduced a variation of this hypothetical. Andreas L. Mogensen, "Should We Prevent Optimific Wrongs?," *Utilitas* 28, no. 2 (2016): 215–26, 219. Mogensen cites Shelly Kagan, but, importantly, Kagan only maintains that one is permitted to allow Alex to be run over. Kagan does not state that one is required to do so. Shelly Kagan, *The Limits of Morality* (Oxford: Clarendon Press, 1991), 164.

[6] I put to the side whether Ed must commit the lesser or the least evil. For discussion, see Larry Alexander and Kimberly Kessler Ferzan, with Stephen J. Morse, *Crime and Culpability: A Theory of Criminal Law* (Cambridge: Cambridge University Press, 2009), 104–08.

Therefore, it is not the case that we should prevent optimific wrongs.[7]

Let's start with a few preliminaries. First, I concur with Mogensen that Tracks and Push should stand and fall together. That is, I reject, as he does, possible ways to distinguish these cases that include what he calls the Scope Principle (that Alex is in danger and Diane is not) and the Wrong Preventing Principle (one has greater reason to prevent a moral wrong than a harm).[8] Where I part company with Mogensen is that he takes it to be impermissible to wake Alex in Tracks, and I do not.

Here's how I'd approach the analysis. Deontology includes positive and negative agent and patient claims. For analysis here, note that we have negative agent claims not to be required to rescue; we have negative patient claims not to be used as a means.[9] Hence, it is possible that one may allow Alex to die in Tracks but that it is nevertheless permissible to wake him.[10] Such a view is consistent with the position that one may turn the trolley but is not morally required to do so. Although, absent a special duty to Alex or Diane, I maintain that Betty and Ed are permitted to allow Alex and Diane to die, for present purposes I am going to assume that Betty and Ed are Good Samaritans and they would like to rescue. They aim to stop the deaths, but now must inquire as to whether they are even permitted to do so given that, by intervening, they will cause harm to five people by removing the obstacle to their impending deaths.

With these preliminaries out of the way, it is easy to identify the root of my disagreement with Mogensen. I reject premise 3 of his argument. His complete argument for premise 3 is as follows:

> In fact, it seems to me that it would be seriously wrong to intervene in this case because of the manner in which this would implicate you in the death of the five. Here, the needs of the many outweigh the needs of the few. Thus premise 3 in my argument seems true. The soundness of the argument hinges, then, on premise 2.[11]

I demur. I accept premise 2 and reject premise 3.

7 Mogensen, "Should We Prevent Optimific Wrongs?" 218–19.

8 Ibid., 218. Perhaps there are times when this is true. But, generally, a parent has as much reason to rescue one child from being murdered as to rescue the other from being killed by a bear.

9 See Alexander, "The Means Principle," 251; Kimberly Kessler Ferzan, "Omissions, Acts, and the Duty to Rescue," in *The Ethics and Law of Omissions*, ed. Dana K. Nelkin and Samuel C. Rickless (Oxford: Oxford University Press, 2017); Alec Walen, "The Restricting Claims Principle Revisited: Grounding the Means Principle on the Agent-Patient Divide," *Law and Philosophy* 35, no. 2 (2016): 211–47.

10 Accord Re'em Segev, "Should We Prevent Deontological Wrongdoing?" *Philosophical Studies* 173, no. 8 (2016): 2049–68, 2050.

11 Mogensen, "Should We Prevent Optimific Wrongs?" 219.

Before offering my explanation of Tracks, let me introduce Re'em Segev's analysis, wherein, after noting the intuitive position that one ought to intervene in Push, he fails to find a deontological account that supports that position. Segev surveys doing/allowing, intentions, and the means principle. He finds that none of these deontological accounts can vindicate common intuitions.[12]

First, Segev maintains that the doctrine of doing and allowing fails as an explanation. This is because Ed's action is merely allowing Diane to die. True enough. Still, I would refine the analysis in the following regard. As I have argued,[13] much of the moral force of the doing/allowing distinction is best understood as the difference between positive and negative agent claims. Ed certainly has a negative agent claim such that he is not morally required to rescue Diane. But the person who switches the trolley has the same claim – he just chooses to act anyway – and few theorists doubt that this is permissible. Still, even reformulated this way, I agree that this is not where the explanation lies.

Second, Segev finds the relevance of intentions to fail as an explanation. To Segev, the deontological constraint on intending, as opposed to foreseeing, harm seems ill-suited to address these allowing cases. I do not believe the doctrine of double effect reflects a moral constraint.[14] Thus, I agree with Segev that it cannot provide the correct explanation.

Finally, Segev rejects that the constraint against using someone as a means can explain these cases. He believes it is strange to say that Ed is using Diane by not saving her. He also thinks that, in order to cover Push, we could not construe the deontological constraint as agent-relative, but he takes the means principle to be an agent-relative constraint. Because I believe that the means principle is the proper prism for viewing this puzzle, I will demonstrate why, contra Segev, the means principle can illuminate not just Push but also Tracks.

20.2 WHY IT IS PERMISSIBLE TO INTERVENE

With these preliminaries out of the way, let's begin with the observation that Tracks and Push appear to implicate the means principle. Although Jeff McMahan worries that "using" is an intention-drenched verb,[15] what I mean here is that the causal process that creates the good consequences cannot include the use/appropriation of another person's body, talents, property, or labor to produce those consequences.

12 See generally Segev, "Should We Prevent Deontological Wrongdoing?"

13 See Ferzan, "Omissions, Acts, and the Duty to Rescue"; see also Alexander, "The Means Principle."

14 See Alexander and Ferzan, *Crime and Culpability*, 97–98.

15 Jeff McMahan, "Intention, Permissibility, Terrorism, and War," *Philosophical Perspectives* 23, no. 1 (2009): 345–72, 369.

This is because people cannot be appropriated for the general good. To do so fails to respect people as people.

Some theorists have objected to a causal understanding of the means principle, reasoning that causation itself cannot have a moral valence.[16] For instance, usings don't seem wrong when they are not committed by people. Consider Victor Tadros's Asteroid II:

> *Asteroid II* – A trolley is hurtling down a track and the brakes have failed. Five people are on the track in front of it. No one can do anything to alter the situation. A large person is on a bridge between the trolley and the five. An asteroid falls on the large person causing him to fall in front of the trolley which prevents it from killing the five, but kills the large person.[17]

As Alexander has argued, we can perhaps maintain that it is a good thing that the asteroid will topple the one as its doing so will save the five.[18] This as an event that does not implicate wrongdoing because the means principle isn't a rule about natural events; it is a rule about human actions. You can't use the one as a means to save the five, but if, as it happens, the one's death will save the five, there is no wrong here.

Indeed, the means principle is a patient claim that one cannot be co-opted for the general good. One is not merely a mechanism by which others can achieve good things. Underlying the causal relation, then, is the normative grounding that we are not each other's property. This claim is the converse of the agent claim that morality cannot force us to engage in actions for the general good either.[19] Hence, there is nothing mysterious in thinking that Asteroid II simply does not implicate agent or patient claims in a way that violates a person's rights, because there is no agency against which the patient is making his claim.

The complication arises because if we think that it is permissible to stand by and cheer in Asteroid II,[20] then how could it possibly be permissible to reach out a hand to rescue the person about to be toppled when such an action will result in the deaths of the five? Or, back to Tracks, how is it that Betty is permitted to wake Alex?

16 E.g., ibid., 368, 369.

17 Victor Tadros, *The Ends of Harm: The Moral Foundations of Criminal Law* (Oxford: Oxford University Press 2011), 154.

18 Larry Alexander, "Can Self-Defense Justify Punishment?" *Law and Philosophy* 32, no. 2 (2013): 159–75, 166.

19 See Alexander, "The Means Principle"; Ferzan, "Omissions, Acts, and the Duty to Rescue"; Walen, "The Restricting Claims Principle Revisited."

20 See Alexander, "Can Self-Defense Justify Punishment?" 166.

At first glance, we might simply ask what Betty is permitted to do. But, it appears that what Betty is doing is rescuing one and harming five. This seems impermissible. (Appearances, however, are deceiving in this case.)

Another approach to this question would be to start from the perspective of the would-be victim. In Tracks, if Alex wakes up and sees the trolley hurtling toward him, must he stay? Of course not. Alex need not require himself to serve as a resource to achieve good consequences.[21]

Now, what if we ask whether Betty may assist Alex given that Alex is permitted to leave? This way of thinking about the matter may generate a puzzle. If Alex's right is agent-relative, then the answer appears to be no. Given that one is not permitted to help a person who is excused,[22] it seems that one should not help someone who just has an agent-relative prerogative. For instance, even if we assume that a mother ought to steer a runaway trolley away from her own child and toward another child (and this is not an assumption everyone would share), it would still be the case that a third party may not assist the mother. For the third party has no reason to take the mother's weighted reasons as weighted for her.

At this point, it appears that Betty may not rescue Alex. From her perspective, it appears that she is harming five to save one. And if we begin with the rights that Alex has, it seems as though all he may have is an agent-relative prerogative, which cannot explain or justify a permission for Betty to assist him.

The answer lies in looking at this from the perspective and entitlements of the five. What if the five see that Alex is awake and is about to move off the tracks? Surely, they may not stop him from doing so. That would be using him as a means. They have no right that he remain and protect them from the trolley.

This means that if Alex were about to get up, Betty would act wrongfully in trying to keep him there. Then, she would be using him as a means. Specifically, she would be assisting the five by treating Alex like a mere resource that may be exploited for their benefit.

Now, it appears that Betty may not assist the five or Alex. Can it be the case that Betty acts impermissibly by assisting either party? I don't deny that cases can exist where one ought not to aid either side. After all, if George wants to kill Harry and Harry is trying to kill George, Ingrid may be best advised to help neither of them.

[21] Alexander, "The Means Principle"; Ferzan, "Omissions, Acts, and the Duty to Rescue."

[22] Accord Segev, "Should We Prevent Deontological Wrongdoing?" 2065 ("It is not only logically possible but also normatively plausible to distinguish the victim and the secondary agent in this respect. For natural rationales for the victim's right to resist wrongdoing do not apply to another person. These include the idea that the victim is excused (as opposed to justified) when he resists wrongdoing whose overall consequences are good and the idea that the victim has an agent-relative permission not to do what is morally best when this involves significant personal sacrifice. These options are irrelevant when considering what another person – the secondary agent – should do").

But Betty's doesn't seem to be that sort of case. It seems to me that the five simply aren't entitled to Alex's presence and thus Betty cannot act wrongfully by returning them to their moralized baseline, a baseline that does not include Alex's presence.

To see this, let us consider ducking cases more closely. First, let's be clear on the metaphysics. Ducking cases are double preventions.[23] In these cases, the actor prevents the preventer from stopping the harm. When Alex gets up, he prevents the preventer (his body) from preventing the death. Tracks deals with the permissibility of one person (Betty) preventing another person (Alex) from being the preventer.

Importantly, not all double preventions are permissible. If Culprit tackles Lifeguard, thus preventing Lifeguard from rescuing Drowning Victim, Culprit acts impermissibly. Culprit's preventing the preventer does drop Drowning Victim below her moralized baseline. Drowning Victim is harmed and that action is unjustified.[24] (Call this case Culprit.)

By contrast, other instances are clearly permissible. If Albert sees that a gunman is about to shoot him, he is entitled to duck even if he knows that the bullet will then hit Beatrice behind him.[25] The reason why Albert is allowed to duck is because of a negative agent claim that he has not to be Beatrice's shield.[26] (Call this case Duck.)

Notice that the difference between Culprit and Duck lies not in the metaphysical structure but in the entitlement to the preventer. In Culprit, Drowning Victim has an entitlement to the preventer. Hence, Culprit brings Drowning Victim below her moralized baseline when he tackles Lifeguard. By contrast, Beatrice is not entitled to have Albert serve as a human shield that protects her from bullets. Accordingly, Albert does not drop Beatrice below her baseline by moving.

In seeing this as a question about the entitlements of the (ultimate) "victim," it also seems that viewing Alex's right to get off the track as an agent-relative prerogative is somewhat misleading.[27] The claim is not that the person is entitled to give his life (or a loved one) greater weight. Rather, the idea is that the agent is simply not required to act in a specific way, and thus there is no morally cognizable harm for the injuries he fails to prevent. When considering why an agent does not need to rescue absent a duty, the typical analysis does not begin with the premise that the

[23] Michael S. Moore, *Causation and Responsibility: An Essay in Law, Moral, and Metaphysics* (Oxford: Oxford University Press 2009), 62.

[24] Ibid.; Ferzan, "Omissions, Acts, and the Duty to Rescue."

[25] For a survey of ducking cases, see generally Christopher Boorse and Roy A. Sorensen, "Ducking Harm," *Journal of Philosophy* 85, no. 3 (1988): 115–34.

[26] Alexander, "The Means Principle"; Ferzan, "Omissions, Acts, and the Duty to Rescue."

[27] This is a view that Alec Walen has pressed repeatedly in conversation, but does not appear to have articulated in print. See generally Tom Dougherty, "Agent-Neutral Deontology," *Philosophical Studies* 163, no. 2 (2013): 527–37. This view also seems in accord with Mogensen, who says of agent-neutral rankings that "the ordering of outcomes as better or worse does not vary from agent to agent." Mogensen, "Should We Prevent Optimific Wrongs?" 111. It is my position that this is true here as well.

agent has a prerogative not to act, but rather that the agent is not required to act, and thus the harms she fails to prevent are not harms attributable to her. If she had an enforceable duty, others can enforce it. If not, not. Here, too, if Beatrice is not entitled to Albert shielding her from bullets, it is not that Albert has an agent-relative prerogative. It is simply that the harm to Beatrice is not one Albert was ever required to bear.

Moreover, because Beatrice is not entitled to Albert's protection, anyone can recognize this normative relationship between the two and act accordingly. Similarly, the normative relationship between Alex and the five sleeping workers is that the workers are not entitled to Alex's protection. And, if they are not entitled to his protection, then not only does Alex not drop them below their moral entitlements by getting up, but also Betty does not do so either if she wakes up Alex. Hence, the reason why this is transferable beyond Alex is because this was never a matter of just weighing the alternatives. The five were never entitled to be better off by Alex's presence and thus the five are not morally cognizably harmed by Alex, or Betty, or anyone else's removal of Alex's body.[28] Alex's body was a benefit to which they were not entitled and the removal of that benefit merely brings them back to the appropriate baseline.

20.3 A SECOND LOOK AT THE MEANS PRINCIPLE, DUCKING CASES, AND THIRD-PARTY INTERVENTION

The argument of the prior section moved quickly, and I think we ought to pause so that I can explicate a bit more precisely what the takeaways are. I think we've learned more about what the means principle is, how to think about ducking cases, and how these two claims interact with what others may do.

First, as addressed in the prior section, it is a long-standing issue with the means principle that it relies on verbs like "using" that seem to require a human action and intention. At the same time, stripped of the action of a third party, it is hard to see why the causal mechanism matters.

What we learn from Tracks is that this deontological constraint is after the notion that one person cannot be the mechanism by which another person is better off. My body, my labor, my talent is not here to serve your greater good. This means that in Asteroid II the five have no claim on the one that he be hit by the asteroid. Similarly, the five have no claim on Alex that he remain on the tracks to prevent harm to them. The means principle reflects the idea that we are not resources for the benefit of

[28] Appealing to moralized baselines is nothing new. Coercion cases, and the idea of something as a threat, often turn on the idea that the coercer is threatening to place the coercee below where she has a right to be.

others, like fruit on trees. So, the causal mechanism matters because it is wrong to see people as just cogs in a wheel.

Now, one particularly salient instance of this general principle is when one person engages in an action that creates a situation where another person is the cog in the wheel. That is what happens when Carl pushes Diane in front of the trolley. Carl intentionally deploys Diane as a resource to make the five trapped workers better off. And, because these cases are particularly salient, we tend to think that what we are after are only those situations in which one agent is actively appropriating another.

But this is not so. Ducking cases reveal that even when the source of a threat is a third party or nature itself, the relationship between persons yields that one is not required to serve another's good just because otherwise a harm will result to the second party. As Judith Thomson illustrates, if the violinist is attached to me, I may unplug him, and by similar logic, Laura is not required to provide sustenance to her twin embryos.[29] And David is entitled to outrun a bear, even if that means that the bear will eat Doug.[30] The moral principle that underlies this is not that the violinist, or the embryos, or Doug, intentionally chose to use me, Laura, and David as a means, but rather that the causal mechanism by which they are better off just is me, Laura, and David, and unfortunately for them, we aren't the unclaimed property of the universe fully at their disposal. It is for this reason that causal structure matters, and not the intention (or action) of an agent. We don't need the violinist, the embryos, or Doug to be agents who intend to benefit by the causal mechanism. We just need them not to be entitled to benefit from the causal mechanism, so that removing the benefit to which they are not entitled does not count as a harm in determining whether, all things considered, one is permitted to unplug, abort, or run.

When we introduce another person into the mix, such as Alice, she ought to recognize the moral relationship between the two sets of patients. Moral relationships between patients should be respected by all agents and patients. If Michael consents to Kim punching him (even if, given his age and frailty, this is not, all things considered, a good thing to do because of the harm to him), then Heidi, too, must recognize Michael's consent in weighing whether to intervene. The normative relationships between the two patients are relationships that an agent must respect.

This argument reveals that an agent is entitled to help a ducker. In other situations, I think we take this for granted. If I am entitled to remove the IVs that connect Thomson's violinist to me, then Gideon is allowed to hand me the scissors. If Laura

[29] Judith Jarvis Thomson, "A Defense of Abortion," *Philosophy and Public Affairs* 1, no. 1 (1971): 47–66.

[30] Boorse and Sorenson, "Ducking Harm."

may abort her twins, then a doctor may assist Laura. If David is entitled to outrun the bear, then Fred may throw David his sneakers.[31]

20.4 COMPLICATIONS

Let's complicate matters. First, I have placed significant emphasis on entitlements, and this means that I need to say more about them. Second, we should address the role of the choices of the patient: Does it matter whether Betty wakes up Alex or whether she just rolls his sleeping body off the tracks? Third, we need a principle that explains why everything that is permissible for a patient to do is not thereby permissible for an agent to aid. Finally, I should turn to the (ir)relevance of culpability for these determinations.

20.4.1 *When It Is Impermissible to Prevent the Preventer*

One worry here is that most double prevention cases we've considered to this point involve a preventer that belongs either to the remover or to the "victim." Drowning Victim is harmed by Culprit because Drowning Victim has a right to the preventer. Conversely, Beatrice is not harmed by Albert because Beatrice does not have a right that Albert block bullets for her. Culprit makes Drowning Victim worse off because Culprit drops Drowning Victim below the baseline at which she is entitled to be.

But consider:

Good Samaritan[32] – Good Samaritan is under no duty to rescue Drowning Victim because doing so will result in the loss of one of her legs. However, once she sees Drowning Victim, she decides to rescue Drowning Victim and starts to walk down the beach. Culprit tackles Good Samaritan and prevents the rescue.[33]

Predictably Good Samaritan[34] – Predictably Good Samaritan is walking down the beach. She is about to spot Drowning Victim. Just before she does so, Culprit tackles Predictably Good Samaritan such that she never forms the intention to rescue Drowning Victim.

Persuasive Culprit – Virtuous Libertarian sees Drowning Victim. Just as she is about to decide to rescue, Persuasive Culprit points out to Virtuous Libertarian

[31] In conversation, Alexander has suggested that this case confuses matters because one cannot outrun a bear, so David is effectively using Doug. If that is true, then Fred shouldn't throw the sneakers any more than Fred should throw fish at Doug to draw the bear to Doug and away from David.

[32] I thank Peter Westen and Heidi Hurd for pressing me on this question.

[33] As I discuss below, I do not think intentions matter. Hence, you could imagine that Culprit tackles Good Samaritan to induce her to play a friendly game of football.

[34] I thank Will Baude for this hypothetical and the one that follows.

that any rescue will make them late to the "Rescue Not Required" rock concert down the beach. (Sometimes) Virtuous Libertarian is persuaded not to rescue.

Before addressing these cases, I think we are also constrained by this:

Flip-Flop Samaritan – Flip-Flop Samaritan is under no duty to rescue Drowning Victim. However, once she sees Drowning Victim, she forms an intention to rescue Drowning Victim and starts to walk down the beach to rescue her. No other person at the beach has seen Drowning Victim or Flip-Flop Samaritan. As Flip-Flop Samaritan walks down the beach, she smells hot dogs and decides to buy one instead of rescuing Drowning Victim.

Here are some things I believe we would all agree on. Flip-Flop Samaritan is entitled to change her mind and prevent the preventer, so long as no one has relied on Flip-Flop's initiation of rescue. Hence, Drowning Victim is not brought below the baseline at which she has a right to be because Flip-Flop Samaritan has no duty to rescue. By contrast, in Culprit, Drowning Victim is brought below the baseline at which she has a right to be because Lifeguard does have a duty to rescue.

But now the problems. In Good Samaritan, Drowning Victim is not entitled to the rescue. Indeed, Good Samaritan could convert to Flip-Flop Samaritan. If this is true, how can it be wrong for Culprit to tackle Good Samaritan (and prevent the preventer) if it is not wrong for Good Samaritan herself to prevent the preventer? My argument to this point is that the wrongfulness of the agent's behavior piggybacks off of the normative relationship between the rescuer and the drowning victim.

That is, to briefly review, if Betty wakes Alex, because the five have no right to his presence, she does not act wrongfully in rescuing him because they were not entitled to be rescued in the first place. In Culprit, because Drowning Victim has a right to Lifeguard's rescue, Culprit acts impermissibly and kills Drowning Victim. The question then is why, if Good Samaritan may change her mind, and thus Drowning Victim does not have a right to her prevention, Culprit can be acting wrongfully in tackling Good Samaritan.

The immediate difference between Good Samaritan and Flip-Flop Samaritan is that when Culprit acts, Good Samaritan has exercised her agency and has chosen to rescue. Although Good Samaritan is entitled to revoke her rescue, while her decision is in place Culprit is interfering with the normative baseline of Drowning Victim.[35]

Notice that this way in which Culprit must respect the moralized baseline is no different from the consent case earlier. If Michael consents to Kim's punching him,

[35] Given what I say below, it is more precise to say that Culprit acts wrongfully so long as Good Samaritan would not have changed her mind.

Heidi must respect that, even if Michael may revoke that consent and render Kim's action impermissible at a later time.

We might think of it this way: When someone waives a claim right that another not touch him, third parties must respect this waiver. When someone grants another a right that she act (as Lifeguard does), third parties must recognize this normative entitlement. When someone waives her agent claim and chooses to act for another's benefit, then the beneficiary will be harmed if anyone interferes with the waiver, despite the fact that the person making the waiver is entitled to return to the baseline. (Similarly, if Alex knew he was on the tracks and told Betty not to rescue him, then Betty would act wrongfully if she "rescued" Alex over his objection, because she would fail to recognize Alex's decision to act for their benefit.)

So far, so good. But what about Predictably Good Samaritan? In this case, Predictably Good Samaritan has not decided to rescue Drowning Victim, so how could Drowning Victim have a moralized baseline that includes Predictably Good Samaritan's rescue? The answer, I believe, lies in the fact-relative nature of the inquiry. We need to widen our angle. For instance, in Culprit, if it turned out that if Culprit had not tackled Lifeguard, Drowning Victim would have drowned anyway, then Culprit can't have acted impermissibly. (Culprit would still be culpable.) To make these assessments, we need all the facts.

Here's a case that shows us how risk relates to moralized baselines. Assume that at t_1, I tell Peter that if he does not let me punch him, I will throw out his lottery ticket. Is this an offer or a threat? Well, let's assume that if the lottery ticket does not have a winning number, then I am making him better off because I am throwing it out for him. Then, my statement would be akin to saying, "Hey, if you let me punch you, I will throw out your ticket for you." On the other hand, if the ticket is valuable, then my statement is a threat. But we won't know which of these two is true until t_2 when the lottery numbers are drawn.

On the fact-relative view of morality that (Alexander and) I adopt, there is already a truth of the matter at t_1 – we just don't know what it is yet. And so the moralized baseline at t_1 is already set, and my statement is already an offer or a threat. I could be wrong – I could think the ticket is a loser and my conduct is an offer, or vice versa. But the moralized baseline is set before the numbers are drawn.

Similarly, unless one believes that other people's behavior is not also deterministic (and I don't), there is already a truth at t_1 as to whether Predictably Good Samaritan will decide to rescue Drowning Victim. It is true that Predictably Good Samaritan has not herself decided to act. However, if, but for Culprit's intervention, Predictably Good Samaritan would have decided to rescue and not revoked her decision, then Culprit acts wrongfully in tackling Predictably Good Samaritan because she harms Drowning Victim.

Persuasive Culprit, however, raises questions about whether we should similarly just predict how Virtuous Libertarian will exercise her agency. Persuasive Culprit does not preempt the exercise of Virtuous Libertarian's agency in deciding to rescue; Persuasive Culprit engages with it. Let's assume that Virtuous Libertarian would have rescued but for Persuasive Culprit's interaction with her. But now, notice that Persuasive Culprit, although ultimately interacting in a way that causes injury, interacts in a way that respects the normative relations between Virtuous Libertarian and Drowning Victim. That is, Persuasive Culprit's behavior alerts Virtuous Libertarian to her negative agent claim not to have to rescue and the revocability of her decision to rescue. Similarly, Heidi can certainly yell at Michael, "Are you crazy? You are old and weak and feeble. You'd have to be nuts to let her hit you. Revoke that consent!" Each of these cases can thus be resolved by attending to the nature of the normative relationships between the various parties and the fact-relative nature of the inquiry. Ultimately, the underlying moral relations between patients are as intricate as is the agent's relationship thereto.[36]

20.4.2 *Giving the Choice to the Preventer*

In analyzing the permissibility of Betty's behavior, we should recognize that Betty may have a range of options and then ask whether the permissibility of her conduct hinges on which option she takes. Betty can leave Alex sleeping but roll his body off the tracks. Betty can wake Alex, thus giving him the choice of whether to move or not. Betty can assist Alex after he requests her help in getting off the tracks.

To my mind, the last case is the easiest because Alex has opted not to rescue, he is permitted to leave, and Betty is permitted to help him. The question then becomes whether Betty may engage in either of the first two options.

We might be tempted to say that Betty should just wake Alex because his choice not to rescue will break the causal chain between her action and the harm to the five. This option should be appealing to those who otherwise would condemn Betty for moving Alex. The idea would be this. Forget moralized baselines and forget the intrapatient claims. Rather, Betty would act wrongfully in just rolling Alex off the tracks, but if she just wakes him and gives him the option, then his decision breaks the causal chain of her responsibility for the deaths.

[36] Here is one more hypothetical to demonstrate the complexities (courtesy of Mitch Berman and Gideon Yaffe): *Blocker* – Culprit is standing so Predictably Good Samaritan cannot see Drowning Victim. Culprit is unaware of the fact that he is blocking her view. To start, as between the two patients, if Good Samaritan would have rescued, then Culprit is interfering and harming Drowning Victim. Next question, is Culprit doing anything? Here, I'd say yes. At t_1, Culprit places himself in a spot that leads to the harm to Drowning Victim. Because morality is fact-relative, Culprit acts impermissibly but nonculpably.

I think we should reject every aspect of this reasoning. First, I think we do cause harms even if they occur through the downstream voluntary human actions of another person.[37] Second, this view takes the situation to be that Betty does harm the five unless the choice is Alex's. But I think that Alex is not best seen as opting out of rescuing (where the baseline is that there will be a rescue), but as opting in. Alex's choice to stay is a choice he can make, but absent that choice, the five have a date with a deadly trolley.

There is, though, one reason to think that it is better, all things considered, for Betty to wake Alex instead of simply moving him. Assuming, of course, that she can wake him in time for him to still get out of the way, it seems that the choice of whether he wants to sacrifice himself is a choice he is entitled to make. And so, Betty's decision to move him without asking him fails to respect his autonomy: He should have the choice of whether he wants to self-sacrifice. Generally, we may have no objection to another moving our sleeping bodies out of the way of speeding trolleys rather than waking us and letting us move on our own, but the decision whether one wants to behave in a supererogatory way is a decision that we ought to be given when available. Indeed, if Alex, awakened, would choose to stay, then Alex is akin to Predictably Good Samaritan. But if Alex, had he been awakened, would have opted to get off the tracks, then Betty does not act wrongfully vis-à-vis the harm to the five trapped workers, although she may have harmed Alex in preempting his opportunity to choose.

20.4.3 *Distinguishing among Permissions*

The argument that I have presented so far seems to lead to the rule that if A has a permission to φ then B may help A φ. But now consider:

> *Phone Ringer*[38] –Mitch is one of the five trapped workers who will benefit from Alex's body. Mitch is expecting a call in five minutes. He realizes that if his phone rings, it will wake up Alex. Mitch turns his ringer off.

Does my view entail that Mitch acts wrongly in turning off his ringer? And if not, then what should we say about the following?

> *Phone by the Tracks* – Mitch is one of the five trapped workers who will benefit from Alex's body. Mitch is expecting a call in five minutes. He realizes that if his phone rings, it will wake up Alex. He can't reach his phone, which is resting a couple of feet from Alex. Mitch asks Betty to turn off his ringer for him.

[37] Alexander and Ferzan, *Reflections on Crime and Culpability*, chap. 2.

[38] Thanks to Mitch Berman and Heidi Hurd for suggesting and discussing this hypothetical and the one that follows.

Intuitively, we may be inclined to say that Mitch may turn off his ringer, but it does not seem to follow that Betty may turn it off for him. Why?

Here, we need to distinguish between the sorts of cases that I have been discussing and true agent-relative prerogatives. (It also further reveals that duckings aren't agent-relative in the way that Phone Ringer is.) What Mitch wants to do is engage in an action that will keep Alex asleep so that Alex will die. In some instances, these sorts of actions are clearly impermissible. I can't use you as a human shield. Using someone as a shield wrongs him. Here, Alex just happens to be Mitch's shield. Mitch did not plan it. Here, the point is that Mitch is just not entitled to benefit from Alex's body. And so the question is, given that Mitch's agency has yet to be implicated in this sad state of affairs, do we allow Mitch to give his life a bit more weight if all he wants to do is turn off his darn ringer? I'm tempted to say he gets to put that thumb on the scale. It is simply too much to ask him to give up his current safety, even if it is safety to which he is not entitled.[39]

However, if the reason why Mitch may turn off his ringer is truly agent-relative, then Betty can't turn it off for Mitch. Betty's agency may not be implicated in appropriating Alex's body for the greater good. If she helps Mitch, she is no longer recognizing the relationship between two patients. She is acting so that one will benefit the other. Betty may not turn off the ringer, even if Mitch may.

20.4.4 *Culpability Doesn't Matter*

Do the actor's intentions matter? To put my bottom line first, the answer is no. Alexander and I have both consistently argued against the doctrine of double effect. We do not believe that the actor's evil intentions can turn a permissible act impermissible. If Flip-Flop Samaritan is permitted not to rescue Drowning Victim, then it does not matter whether she changes her mind because she sees that Drowning Victim is actually her ex-boyfriend, whom she wants to drown.

However, the evil intentions of the person who prevents the preventer are often thought to matter. McMahan argues that if a fireman puts a net out for a person who will need to jump from a burning building, and then another actor moves it to kill the jumper, then this is a killing. If the fireman moves it, it is a letting die.[40] Yet, Sam Rickless thinks that McMahan trades on an actor's malicious intent, and this is what gives many of McMahan's cases their explanatory force.[41]

39 For a discussion of the conflict between the means principle and agent-relative prerogatives, see Kimberly Kessler Ferzan, "Self-Defense, Permissions, and the Means Principle: A Reply to Quong," *Ohio State Journal of Criminal Law* 8, no. 2 (2011): 503–513.

40 Jeff McMahan, "Killing, Letting Die, and Withdrawing Aid," *Ethics* 103, no. 2 (1993): 250–79.

41 Samuel C. Rickless, "The Moral Status of Enabling Harm," *Pacific Philosophical Quarterly* 92, no. 1 (2011): 66–86.

These questions aren't about intentions. They are simply a matter of who is entitled to remove the preventer. Consider *Barber*, a passive euthanasia case, wherein the question was whether the doctor could be charged with homicide for removing life support.[42] The court analyzes Barber's potential liability in two steps. The first is to say that disconnecting the life support is akin to withholding medical treatment. The second is to say that doctors do not have a duty to rescue when medical treatment is futile, so they are entitled to withhold.

But what distinguishes the interloper? If this is a question of metaphysics, then it appears that it shouldn't matter whether the person who pulls the plug is the doctor or some culpable agent. The *Airedale* court thought that "an interloper who maliciously switches off a life support machine [was distinguishable] because, although the interloper may perform exactly the same act as the doctor who discontinues life support, his doing so constitutes interference with the life-prolonging treatment then being administered by the doctor."[43] One has to wonder, though, whether the interloper's wrongful intention is infecting this analysis.[44] The case is complicated by the fact that we are to think the doctor has no duty to rescue if rescuing is futile. So, too, a lifeguard could have no duty to rescue a drowning swimmer if it is clear the swimmer will be dead by the time the lifeguard gets there.

The question, though, is not about futility. Rather, the interloper acts as Culprit does, and the doctor acts as Lifeguard or Good Samaritan. Good Samaritan may opt out, and still, Culprit may not tackle her. It remains true, however, that even if Culprit is just Friend, and the tackle is just horseplay, Friend does act impermissibly. By contrast, if Friend persuades Virtuous Libertarian, but only because Friend wants Drowning Victim to die, Friend still acts permissibly. Ultimately, it does not matter whether Betty wakes Alex because she loves him or hates the five. She acts permissibly in any event.

20.5 CONCLUSION

The "means principle" is both helpful and a misnomer. The animating idea that we are not resources for the benefit of others undergirds not only what actors may do but also how we should understand the relationship between patients. The focus on the former has obscured the latter, leading to the counterintuitive conclusions that not only is it impermissible for Betty to rescue Alex, but also that it is impermissible for Ed to stop Carl. A focus on the intrapatient relationships, however, yields a more

42 Barber v. Superior Court, 195 Cal. Rptr. 484 (Cal. Ct. App. 1983).

43 Airedale National Health Service Trust v. Bland, 1 All ER 821 (HL 1993).

44 Compare John A. Humbach, "Criminal Prosecution for HMO Treatment Denial," *Health Matrix* 11 (2001): 147–87.

nuanced account of when, why, and how agents may intervene. It is permissible not just to duck, but to aid the ducker, because of the lack of a claim that the third party has of benefitting from the ducker's body. This is just another instance of the grounding of the means principle. And it is the one that explains why Alexander is right to conclude that we can't count the harm to the five in our justificatory calculus as to whether to rescue the Fat Man.

Larry Alexander is a giant in many fields. In my little criminal law and philosophy nook, it has been an honor and a pleasure to write together and to be right together. I hope this essay is a contribution to both.

21

Deontology's Travails

Richard Arneson

Deontology is a work in progress. The project is to specify what we owe one another by way of moral concern and consideration in terms of a set of fundamental moral rules that constitute constraints on morally permissible conduct (sometimes one may not do what would bring about greater good) and options (sometimes one is permitted not to do what would violate no constraint and bring about greater good). Successful completion of the deontological project would involve elaborating a particular mixture of constraints and options that fit together into a coherent view of what we morally owe to each other, one that yields implications of choice of conduct and policy on any circumstances in which we might find ourselves that accord with our considered judgments in an ideally reasoned reflective equilibrium.

Successful completion of the project is not visible on the horizon. Recent discussions meander into dead ends, impasses of thought, and small niches where a few like-minded individuals wrangle about minor details of doctrines that, to put it mildly, do not appear to be on the verge of commanding general allegiance.[1]

The tangles of deontological discussions have significance for the broader issue of the dispute between consequentialism and nonconsequentialism in ethics, because deontology looks to be the most promising version of nonconsequentialism. The consequentialist holds that one ought always to do an act, among those available for choice, that would bring about an outcome no worse than the outcome of anything else one might instead have done. The standard for assessing outcomes as better or worse is given by impartial evaluation. There are endless wrinkles and minor qualifications to be considered, as well as the major issue of determining the appropriate outcome assessment standard, but, by and large, the structure of

[1] This is not to say that considerable progress has not been made in the vast literature on the structure of nonconsequentialism in recent years. See the able discussions in F.M. Kamm, *Intricate Ethics: Rights, Responsibilities, and Permissible Harm* (Oxford: Oxford University Press, 2008) and the many references she cites.

consequentialist morality is fairly well understood. However, it is likely that the most compelling alternatives to consequentialism have not yet been identified, so it is not possible to make a sensible definitive judgment in favor of consequentialism or nonconsequentialism. The sensible view is "wait and see." So all of us, whatever our moral leanings on the consequentialism versus nonconsequentialism issue, should welcome progress on the project of articulating the best and most plausible deontological morality.

Enter Larry Alexander, a distinguished legal theorist whose recent work on the morality of self-defense touches on fundamental problems in the articulation of moral constraints on permissible action. Throughout his career Alexander has been a restless as well as an innovative and creative thinker. He is continuously moving onto new theoretical ground. Building on some skeptical probes in the area of moral theory attempts to characterize the tradeoff ratios that determine when it is morally acceptable to act against someone's moral right in view of the really bad consequences that refraining from this violation would allow to happen[2], Alexander has boldly elaborated a new deontological doctrine[3] that seeks to improve on the Lockean libertarian doctrine of morality as side-constraints worked out by Robert Nozick.[4] (It is a profound tribute to Nozick's achievement that it has not been superseded in the more than forty years since its publication.)

The core of Alexander's proposal is what he calls the "means principle" (MP). This principle "forbids actors from achieving otherwise good consequences by using, without their consent, others' bodies, labor, talents, or the resources that are rightfully theirs." Regarding the last phrase, Alexander explains that the MP "forbids unconsented-to use of resources that could not have been obtained except by the possessor's use of his body, labor, or talents, or resources conveyed to him by others who obtained them similarly."

The MP takes a stand both as to the content of moral constraints and as to the content of moral options. Each person is morally at liberty to act as she chooses, using her own body, labor, talents, and the resources that are rightfully hers, so long as she does not thereby violate the moral constraint embedded in the MP. I take it that "forbids actors from achieving otherwise good consequences" in the formulation of the MP is a rhetorical flourish. The MP equally forbids nonconsensual use of the bodies and so on of others in ways that achieve bad consequences as well as good consequences.

[2] Larry Alexander, "Deontology at the Threshold," *San Diego Law Review* 37, no. 4 (2000); Larry Alexander, "Scalar Properties, Binary Judgments," *Journal of Applied Philosophy* 25, no. 2 (2008).

[3] Larry Alexander, "The Means Principle," in *Legal, Moral, and Metaphysical Truths: The Philosophy of Michael S. Moore*, ed. Kimberly Kessler Ferzan and Stephen J. Morse (Oxford: Oxford University Press, 2016).

[4] Robert Nozick, *Anarchy, State and Utopia* (New York: Basic Books, 1974).

Alexander follows Nozick and others in proposing that the core of deontological constraints establishes limits on being coerced or forced to contribute to production of good consequences. Being morally at liberty to save my bandages and medicines for my own future use even though you desperately need them right now, it would be wrong to force or coerce me to assist you by providing you with the bandages and medicine you urgently need, and wrong for the state or any individual to impose punishment (that deprives me of any moral rights I otherwise possess) for my failure to aid you. However, I might legitimately be vulnerable to criticism by appeal to unenforceable moral principles.

Alexander proposes the means principle as the sole deontological constraint on the pursuit of good consequences. The constraint on using others does not forbid doing what will cause harm to others, so long as one does not thereby benefit from the presence of these others. Gaining such a benefit would constitute using others in the ways the MP forbids. This spare feature of the doctrine is one of its two highly controversial features; the other will be mentioned shortly. Alexander affirms a highly streamlined deontology. He illustrates this feature of his doctrine by rehearsing some trolley problems. Turning a runaway trolley that is hurtling down a track toward five who are about to be run over and killed onto a side track where the trolley will kill only one person is permissible, says Alexander. What one does harms the one but is not a causal means to advancing any good cause. One does not benefit from the presence of the one on the track; one would proceed in the same way even if he were not unfortunately present. The same verdict would hold if one exploded a bomb, destroying the tracks along which a trolley is hurtling toward five, and also killing a bystander. A rough test for permissibility is that one would do the same even if the person to be harmed were not there at all; one gains no benefit from his presence. By contrast, jiggling a bridge that spans the trolley tracks, causing a fat man to fall onto the tracks and block the trolley from hurtling along its path toward killing five who are stuck on the tracks ahead, would be a case in which the presence of the person harmed provides an opportunity for saving the five. The body of the fat man is used in ways that bring about greater good. This using violates the means principle.

These examples might call to mind the doctrine of double effect[5], but Alexander upholds the MP as a non-state-of-mind principle. Nether one's intentions nor one's beliefs play a role in determining whether one's actions are morally permissible.[6]

5 See Warren S. Quinn, "Actions, Intentions, and Consequences: The Doctrine of Double Effect," *Philosophy and Public Affairs* 18, no. 4 (1989): 334–351.

6 If I believe I am killing you and intend to be killing you but am only stroking your cat, my act is not morally impermissible provided it does not involve an appropriation of the cat you own in ways that causally work to my advantage. So Alexander, denying the relevance of intention to permissibility, will assert.

The first controversial feature of Alexander's deontology is its spareness – what it leaves out. The second controversial feature is its absolutism, and more important, the underlying reasons that drive Alexander toward absolutism. Alexander is open to the possibility that the means principle is an absolute, exceptionless moral principle. The MP holds at all times and places and it is always morally wrong, all things considered, to act against it. The MP is exceptionless. This means that there are no values that compete against MP, and might be balanced against it, such that in some circumstances it makes sense to say that the MP is morally outweighed by these considerations so that in these circumstances, all things considered, one morally ought to do what the MP prohibits.

Here I am bowdlerizing Alexander's stated position, but bear with me. In his essay "The Means Principle," Alexander does not commit to upholding it as an absolute, exceptionless principle. He leaves open the possibility that it might be outweighed, perhaps in the situations of moral catastrophe invoked and then set aside by Nozick (What if by forcing someone to wiggle his nose just once you could save the planet from all global-warming woes?). But there are reasons that drive Alexander toward an absolutist construal of MP, never repudiated by him. The reasons are forcefully articulated in an earlier essay, "Deontology at the Threshold," and they constitute perhaps his most interesting contribution to the project of constructing a plausible conception of deontological ethics. His skeptical thoughts on moral thresholds join together with the means principle to make a formidable doctrine.

21.1 PRELIMINARY STATEMENT OF PROBLEMS IN ALEXANDERISM

This essay raises some objections to Alexander's views. In this assessment of Alexander on deontology, I ignore the momentous background issue of consequentialism versus nonconsequentialism in moral theory.[7] Coming to terms with the case for and against consequentialism is a venture left for another day. If I am right, any such assessment must anyway be provisional pending a full articulation and evaluation of the varieties of deontology and their merits.

This essay focuses on intramural criticisms of Alexander from within the deontological camp. I narrow the topic further by setting aside the large division between those who believe and those who deny that the state of mind of an agent, in particular her intention, plays a role in determining the permissibility of what she does.

7 For an introduction, see J.C.C. Smart and Bernard Williams, *Utilitarianism – For and Against* (Cambridge: Cambridge University Press, 1973); R.M. Hare, *Moral Thinking: Its Levels, Method and Point* (Oxford: Oxford University Press, 1981), chap. 3; Peter Railton, "Alienation, Consequentialism, and the Demands of Morality," *Philosophy and Public Affairs* 13, no. 2 (1984): 134–171; Samuel Scheffler, *The Rejection of Consequentialism*, 2nd ed. (Oxford: Oxford University Press, 1994).

First, I interpret Alexander as finding support for his view that the means principle might well be exceptionless and absolute in his view that, under examination, threshold deontology proves to be very implausible and likely incoherent. But threshold deontology is plausible and coherent. The support collapses. Furthermore, a plausible position in this domain is *aggregation*. This holds that for any wrong, however horrendous, that one person might to do a single other person, there is some quantity of trivially small benefits accruing to a sufficiently large number of other people, such that if doing the wrong brings about that amount of offsetting benefit, and all else is equal, then doing it is, all things considered, morally permissible. Benefits and wrongs trade off against each other in the space of moral reasons. But threshold is less controversial than aggregation, and uncertainty about the latter should not incline us to take seriously Alexander's objections against the former.

Stripped of the support of the rejection of threshold, the claim that the MP is absolute and exceptionless rests on an appeal to intuitions about cases, and on this terrain Alexander has no argument against anyone who has the intuition that in some circumstances we are morally bound by enforceable duties to help others in need and sometimes by enforceable duties to allow others to appropriate our bodies and talents to provide such help.[8] If I refuse to carry out an easy rescue of a child drowning in a shallow pond, and you can save the child only by credibly threatening to impose costs on me if I balk at the rescue, you are morally permitted to coerce me in this way and to carry out your threat if I fail to save the child, given some further

[8] The statement in the text follows Alexander's exposition, but it is not quite correct as it stands. Alexander supposes that on the threshold view he considers, if it is permissible for someone to override someone's right not to be used for the benefit of others, this is tantamount to affirming that the individual whose right has been overridden has an affirmative duty to supply by his own agency whatever another is permitted to take from him. For example, if it is permitted to take someone's car and use it to protect some third party's moral rights or well-being, then that individual has a moral duty to turn over his car for this purpose. I doubt this moral equivalence obtains. The reason for this lack of equivalence was pointed out by Thomas Nagel long ago. Imposing on someone a positive duty to make a large sacrifice for the sake of helping some others puts an enormous burden on his will. It can be psychologically very difficult to bring oneself voluntarily to undertake such a sacrifice, and requiring an individual to make this effort of will may be more than should be morally required of him. By contrast, in some settings, permitting a third party (for example) to kill a person for the sake of saving some number of others may place no strain at all on the person's will. I may be just sitting near the trolley track, and the third party can just shoot me, or push me onto the track, resulting in my demise and the saving of some other people from peril. This is unfortunate for me, a distressing occurrence, but need not call on me to make any decision or effort of will at all, much less a difficult or heroic effort. The further question arises, whether the person who has no affirmative duty to sacrifice his life by voluntary undertaking for the sake of several others in the circumstances just described would be morally permitted to resist a third party's using him (permissibly) for the sake of the greater good. If I am sitting on the trolley track and happen to see the third party about to shoot me or push me to advance the greater good, and I discern that he is acting permissibly, may I seek to stop him to save my life, since *ex hypothesi* I have no positive duty to sacrifice my life here? My sense is that this question could be answered either negatively or positively, in keeping with the Nagel-type position being sketched.

uncontroversial premises are in place. Suspicion that once enforceable Good Samaritan obligations are countenanced, they will be incapable of being cabined, and will inevitably obliterate claimed moral options for practical purposes, fuels the libertarian denial that any Good Samaritan obligations should be countenanced. But this is just the same radical skepticism about threshold deontology in another guise that we will have already seen reason to reject.

A second objection to the Alexander version of deontology is that from the standpoint of seeking to develop and explore the most plausible versions of nonconsequentialism, Alexander's doctrine is too concessive to consequentialism along contestable fronts. In particular, Alexander's view is both aggressive, in suggesting that what the means principle taken by itself forbids could never be permissible all things considered, and timid, in holding that in situations in which the means principle does not apply, it is always morally permissible to do what would bring about even slightly better consequences than would be brought about by scrupulously adhering to any other claimed deontological constraint. This position makes too much of the MP and too little of other candidate deontological considerations.

Alexander's enterprise appears to be driven in part by the hope that by simplifying and streamlining deontology we might well be strengthening the fortress. Less can be more. There is an undoubted attraction to leaving behind the endless coils and complications of present-day deontological theories. I shall suggest that the promise and attraction largely turn out to be illusory. (Readers will have to judge whether I am mistaken in attributing to him any commitment to the claims I am contesting.) In a nutshell, the problem is that unwarranted skepticism about commensurability proves to be the main reason to jettison claims that individuals have rights not to be harmed by others in certain ways, even when the harmful actions claimed to be wrongful would not be causal means to gaining advantages for the harming agents so that they benefit from the presence of the harmed victims.

A third criticism, made in passing, is that Alexander's defense of his right-wing libertarianism takes a swipe at left-wing libertarianism that does not inflict damage on its target. Here, Alexander invokes the means principle to place limits on permissible appropriation of unowned stuff as privately owned resources. Quite aside from any doubts one might entertain regarding the acceptability of the means principle, its invocation in this context, we should agree, is misplaced.

21.2 THRESHOLD CONSTRAINTS

A threshold deontologist holds that moral constraints on permissible action are significant pro tanto considerations that do not necessarily determine in all circumstances what is morally permissible, all things considered. A constraint might be counterbalanced by other constraints or by other types of moral considerations. Especially salient here are lesser evil justifications. Acting in accordance with a constraint in some particular circumstances might bring about a lot of harm or prevent a lot of good, and when these consequences are sufficiently bad, acting against the constraint is the lesser evil.

If the means principle is the sole deontological constraint, the problem of balancing constraints against constraints does not arise. Alexander holds that when lesser evil justifications are clearly articulated, they reveal themselves to be implausible and of doubtful coherence.

Any moral view that includes a threshold, a precise point, on one side of which acts are morally permissible, and impermissible on the other side, will be affirming a discontinuity. Is this troublesome? How can a tiny, tiny difference in value make the difference between an act's being permissible and impermissible?

It is not clear at the outset that we should see any problem here. There are discontinuities in nature; why not in ethics? A boulder precariously balanced on a slope is not moving at all. Pushed by a tiny, tiny force, it crashes hundreds of feet to the canyon floor. This can happen. Perhaps similar phenomena occur in ethics.

One might hold that any characterization of a concept will be tracing thresholds or boundaries in thought. When the characterization concerns moral concepts that figure in moral principles of right and wrong, there will be discontinuity at the threshold. If the set of moral constraints includes a prohibition on lying, there will be some specification of what qualifies as a lie, so that within the range of deceptive behaviors some deceptions will fall on one side and some on the other side of the boundary dividing lies and non-lies. One might be skeptical that the line drawing is always arbitrary.

The problem that troubles Alexander is slightly different. He imagines that, for example, we know what is appropriation or using of what belongs to another and what is not and concur in considering these appropriations as morally impermissible. We are affirming threshold deontology when we add that when refraining from doing what the constraint against appropriating prohibits would bring about consequences that are sufficiently bad, then a tipping point is reached, and what had been morally wrong and impermissible becomes morally permissible, all things considered. The picture is that there is a standard of outcome or consequence assessment and that consequences vary in degree continuously in value and disvalue as so many points along a line. At a threshold, the tipping point, the impermissible becomes permissible. Alexander proposes that the most promising version of threshold deontology will specify a ratio, exceeding which swings open the door of permissibility. The ratio might be how bad it will be for rightholders if a moral constraint is not respected, to how bad it will be for non-rightholders if the constraint is respected. The ratio might vary by type of constraint.

If there is a problem here, a further feature of any sensible deontology insightfully treated by Alexander in another context may go some way toward easing it.[9] Suppose a threshold for permissible infringement of a moral right in deontology is just barely passed. The act that just barely crosses the threshold is just barely permissible. If a further very small consideration pops up that tells against permissibility, this very slight consideration might push the act back into the impermissible range. Moreover, acts that would infringe the moral right and that lie just barely below the threshold of impermissibility are just barely impermissible. Lying to a friend about some small matter such as the exact location of my socks might be wrong, but just barely wrong. I should not feel more than just barely perceptibly guilty for doing this act, and if compensation is owed to the person to whom the lie is told, the compensation will be very small. The moral discredit that accrues to me in virtue of doing this wrong act will be very small. By contrast, if, just for the fun of it, I lie to someone about the exact location of the cliff edge she is trying to avoid, knowing that this will cause her, along with several friends tied to her, to plummet to their undeserved deaths, what I do is a long way from the boundary of the permissible, and calls for guilt on my part, indignation on the part of others, and punishment of me for the misdeed.

Rightness and wrongness are scalar notions. They vary by degree. This is fully compatible with the existence of thresholds separating rightness and wrongness.

Why resist the idea that moral permissibility is an either-or notion that supervenes on underlying considerations that vary by degree? It might be thought that that this picture of ethics leaves no room for moral constraints that are anything but conventions. Here's a line of thought:

1. The means principle is a significant, substantial constraint on what it is morally permissible to do.
2. If a magnitude of value or disvalue exceeds a certain point, the means principle constraint is overridden, and acting against it is morally permissible.
3. There is no nonarbitrary way of selecting the certain point at which the means principle constraint is overridden.
4. If there is no nonarbitrary way of selecting as the certain point at which the means principle constraint is overridden, it is not unreasonable to select a lesser magnitude, rather than any point previously selected.
5. If it is not unreasonable to select a lesser magnitude, rather than any point previously selected, as the certain point at which the means principle constraint is overridden, it is not the case that the means principle is a significant, substantial constraint on what it is morally permissible to do.

9 See Alexander, "Scalar Properties, Binary Judgments."

Propositions 3, 4, and 5 are hard to deny according to Alexander, but proposition 1 must be true, so proposition 2 must be false. Hence, we must suppose the means principle to be absolute and exceptionless. The advocate of threshold deontology denies proposition 3, and can then consistently affirm propositions 1, 2, 4, and 5.

In support of 3, Alexander appeals to an argument advanced by Anthony Ellis:[10]

1. There is some number [N] at which the act that was wrong becomes right.
2. There is no nonarbitrary way of specifying [N].
3. The difference between what is morally right and what is morally wrong cannot be arbitrary.

The three claims cannot be true together. The argument is that 2 and 3 are unimpeachable, so 1 must be false.

Response to Ellis and Alexander: The argument seems to just presuppose that a substantive judgment, for example, to the effect that kicking someone in the shins to prevent someone else suffering exactly that same harm is wrong but kicking someone in the shins to prevent someone else from suffering a much greater harm is permissible, must be arbitrary in a way that renders the judgment indefensible. I do not see any basis for this presupposition except a general skepticism about moral intuition. The idea that the fact that an act one is contemplating would inflict harm on someone is a reason not to do it rests on a substantive moral judgment, which could coherently be denied. So does the idea that the fact that an act that one is contemplating would inflict a greater rather than a smaller harm on someone is a greater rather than smaller reason not to do it. But if the former idea can be defensible, why not the latter? Next step: The fact that an act one is contemplating, that would inflict harm on someone, would also bring about benefit for another person lessens the moral reason one has not to do the contemplated action, based on its inflicting harm on someone. If one accepts this, then we should also accept that the fact that an act one is contemplating, that would inflict harm on someone, would also bring about a greater rather than smaller benefit for another person lessens to a greater extent the moral reason one has not to do the contemplated action, based on its inflicting harm on someone. The threshold deontologist holds that when the ratio of harm that would accrue to the rightholders if the right in question is not respected, to the harm that would in the aggregate accrue to non-rightholders if the right is respected, becomes sufficiently favorable, the impermissible rights-infringing act becomes permissible.

The skeptic then presses the question: Exactly where does this threshold point lie? I take it that the skeptical question lacks purchase against range judgments.

[10] Anthony Ellis, "Deontology, Incommensurability, and the Arbitrary," *Philosophy and Phenomenological Research* 52, no. 4 (1992): 855–875.

Kicking someone in the shins, when the individual has done nothing to forfeit her general right not to be harmed, is not permissible to avert similar shin-kicking harm to another that is in the range of 1.00001 to 1.00050 times larger, but is permissible to avert shin-kicking harm to another that is in the range of 3.00000 to 3.50000 times greater, says the threshold deontologist. These range judgments may be vague, and not exactly specifiable. This inexactitude that current intuitive judgment leaves might be deemed an epistemic matter or a matter of moral fact. Either way, the fact, if it is a fact, that we cannot confidently precisely fix the thresholds that are operative in threshold deontology at precise points, but only within a range, does not call into question the plausibility of range judgments or the coherence of claiming some to be true.

A complication here is that the means principle as construed by Alexander prohibits unconsented-to appropriation, not unconsented-to appropriation that harms. The MP forbids using someone against her will even when she benefits from the use. So if the MP is overridden at some threshold, the threshold point cannot strictly be a point at which a set ratio of harms to rightholders to harms to non-rightholders is exceeded. See discussion three paragraphs down in the text.

Alexander endorses the suggestion that the explanation why one could not, without arbitrariness, draw a line at some determinate point and hold that action against a deontological constraint is impermissible up to the line and permissible beyond it is that any such procedure would involve "the weighing of incommensurables." Deontological constraints say that acting against the stated constraint is intrinsically wrong, whereas in consequentialist calculation all consequences trade off against one another, and all that matters is achieving the best overall consequences. But in this context, appealing to this pronouncement against the threshold deontologist is just straightforwardly begging the question at issue.

Alexander: "For the threshold deontologist's claim is that at N [the border of permissibility], consequences *justify* acts that are otherwise intrinsically wrong. But it is difficult to see how consequences could do this unless consequences and intrinsic wrongness were commensurable on some scale." I have trouble reading this as anything other than a flat, blanket rejection of threshold deontology. Its basic thought is that good consequences that arise by infringement of deontological constraints are to be discounted, to some degree, by that very fact. A more stringent deontological constraint imposes greater discounting. From the get-go, consequences and intrinsic wrongness are being balanced against each other, and balancing implies measurement. (Moreover, intrinsic wrongness itself is woven partly from harm, a bad consequence.)

This seems to be the nub of the issue for Alexander, so I should explicitly state the view he appears to be rejecting. There is a moral constraint, for example a moral rule that forbids lying. This rule generates moral reasons of a strength that varies depending on what is at stake. (It is morally worse to lie to my sister about the character of the person she is planning to marry than to my wife about the exact sweetness of the ice cream she is planning to consume.) Think of the moral reasons as giving the moral disvalue of doing the act I am considering doing. There might be counterbalancing considerations, good consequences the lie would bring about. The moral constraint bars me from doing an act that would bring about the best reachable outcome but at the cost of violating the constraint. But, as the good consequences of telling the lie are gradually increased, at some tipping point the lie becomes just barely permissible. The consequences properly weighted give reasons for lying that amount to moral value points that offset the moral disvalue of telling the lie. There is a common scale of moral reasons that vary in strength, or moral value and disvalue scores if you prefer.

Although the view just sketched is obviously coherent, one could be skeptical that the moral reasons measurements it relies upon can actually be made. Such a skepticism is possible. I do not attempt here to argue against it. All I claim is that a skepticism so corrosive as to rule out any commensurability in this sort of case will eat away and destroy any claims of commensurability in ethics, including ones on which Alexander needs to rely to get his own position off the ground.[11]

Alexander suggests that complementing the MP is some form of consequentialist reasoning. But weighing consequences involves balancing different types of consequences against each other. There are plural consequentialist values. The vacation we have planned will provide fun and boost our virtue but damage our friendship. How do we weigh these disparate goods and bads against each other?[12] If we can rely on ordinary methods of reflective equilibrium judgment here, why not when balancing constraints of varying moral stringency against better and worse outcomes of complying with constraints and infringing them?

Alexander writes: "If there is a deontological threshold or thresholds at which deontological rights give way to affirmative duties, then one might expect that

[11] To be fair to Alexander, it should be noted that he sees clearly the rumbling menace of an expansive skepticism about commensurability that cannot be rationally cabined. He is aware of the threat of skepticism and open to it. Here, I simply report that my own conviction that it is worse (for example) to refrain from telling a lie about a small matter when refraining would bring about significant bad – not on the scale of moral catastrophe, just a garden-variety everyday bad occurrence – is far stronger than my doubts that incommensurability is pervasive in normative judgment calls. The reasons given by the wrong of the small lie added to the small harm that telling it would bring about are smaller than the reasons given by the wrong of the significant harm that not telling it would bring about. On this issue, see Ronald Dworkin, "Objectivity and Truth: You'd Better Believe It," *Philosophy and Public Affairs* 25, no. 2 (1996): 87–139.

[12] For that matter, there are different dimensions of such values as fun and friendship and virtue, so merely arriving at an all-things-considered fun assessment, for example, requires the weighing of disparate things.

moral outcomes in the neighborhood of such a radical discontinuity might seem weird or counterintuitive. And that expectation is borne out."[13] Alexander provides examples to illustrate the weirdness, which he takes to provide evidence against the threshold view.

A first comment is that such discontinuities are pretty much bound to occur in any ethics that countenances sharp cutoffs for decision. Consider an act-consequentialist view that says one ought always to do whatever will bring about best consequences. Consider a range of cases, in each of which one might harm an individual, producing a negative consequence of exactly 10 to that individual. The act will also produce downstream good consequences and, in an array of cases, these good consequences gradually increase by small increments up to 10.01. Here, there is a radical discontinuity. When one has the option of gaining 9.99 at a cost of –10, the harmful act is forbidden, but if instead one can gain just over 0.01 more gain at the exact same cost, the act switches to morally required. I do not know whether this feature of act-consequentialist calculation qualifies as weird, but I see nothing counterintuitive here. With a slight increase in resultant good consequences, an act's moral status can shift from forbidden to required.

Any trace of moral oddity here just results from the application of an either/or decision question – What is one required to do? – to a situation in which the underlying moral phenomena are scalar and we are considering very small incremental shifts in the magnitudes of these underlying scalar phenomena. Sensible ethics will superimpose scalar judgment on the either/or schema. When the net balance of consequences shifts from barely negative to barely positive, and one's choice is limited to doing the act that produces this net balance of consequences or refraining from doing so, the act shifts from just barely wrong to just barely right. Here, the shift in moral status from forbidden to required is not a big shift.

Same goes in deontology, one would suppose. A sensible deontology, applied to decision problems in which the moral difference between one act and another is slight, should not hold that the moral difference between the two acts is great. One might (barely) qualify as forbidden and another (barely) qualify as required, but doing the wrong act that is just barely wrong is not very wrong, and choosing the right act rather than another option that is just slightly worse is just barely right.

Here is an example that conveys the flavor of Alexander's discussion on this point:

> A terrorist has captured and hidden 100 hostages in a number of locations. At each location he has planted a bomb that will automatically detonate at noon. The terrorist reveals this to the police and demands certain concessions from the government before noon; otherwise, he will allow the bombs to kill the hostages.

[13] Alexander, "Deontology at the Threshold," 900.

> Luckily, the police have grabbed the terrorist's mother, who is in no way implicated in her son's terrorism. If they torture her, however, they believe that the terrorist will relent. And because 100 lives are at stake, the mother's right not to be tortured is overridden. So they begin torturing her on live television. Sure enough, after some severe suffering by his mother, the terrorist calls the police asking them to relent. The police ask him for the location of the hostages and the bombs, and he tells them where one, and only one, hostage and bomb are located. Because only 99 hostages now remain at risk, the police can no longer torture the terrorist's mother.[14]

Alexander has stipulated that we are to suppose the threshold for torturing an innocent person is 100 lives at stake. One unit of torturing an innocent person (presumably combining severity of torture and duration of torture episode) is permissible to save 100 lives.

In his example, the police believe that they can inflict one unit of torture on an innocent person and thereby save 100 lives. As it turns out, this belief is wrong. The torture unit only brings about the saving of one life. In the example, the torture of this person is wrong in the fact-relative sense. If the evidence available to the police warrants the belief that inflicting one unit of torture on the mother in these circumstances will save 100 lives, their act is justified in the evidence-relative sense.

Perhaps I am tone-deaf to deontological nuance, but I do not see anything in the example that suggests that thresholds for permissible infringement of rights are inherently counterintuitive, weird, or incoherent. The odd feature of the example turns entirely on the discrepancy between what the police believe and what the facts in the situation actually are. But this feature can also crop up in a straight act-consequentialist assessment of the situation. The police might believe that torturing an innocent to a certain degree will bring about good consequences such that this act is the one, among the alternatives, that would bring about the overall best outcome, but in fact their belief is incorrect, and their act of torture is not fact-relative justified.

Worse, similar discontinuities seem inevitably to be part of Alexander's preferred deontological morality that eschews thresholds. Alexander says morality categorically forbids using a person in certain wrongful ways as a means to bring about one's goals, no matter how morally valuable these goals might be. Alexander will have to provide some characterization of wrongfully using a person in the forbidden way, and this characterization is bound to admit a line between an act that just barely qualifies as using a person in the forbidden way and an act that just barely fails to qualify. This line might be almost indiscernibly thin, and the difference between a forbidden act and a permissible act according to Alexander's favored nonthreshold morality will be very slight. I doubt that Alexander will be troubled by this feature of

[14] Ibid., 900–901.

his view, and I doubt he should be troubled. But, *mutatis mutandis*, the same goes for the threshold deontology he criticizes. Discontinuity is not a deal-breaker or knockdown objection to a deontological morality.

Of course, one might soften the discontinuity, the sharp line between forbidden and permissible, by introducing a gray zone in which the act being contemplated is neither permissible nor impermissible but has a morally inbetween, ambiguous status. And one may introduce shades of gray, further softening the discontinuity. (The darker the shade of gray, the closer we are to impermissible status; the lighter the shade, the closer we are to permissible.) Perhaps one should carry out this maneuver. But if it is desirable, it will be just as available to a threshold deontologist as to a nonthreshold deontologist of the Alexander school, and just as available to an act-consequentialist.

21.3 USING A PERSON AS A MEANS VERSUS RUNNING ROUGHSHOD OVER A PERSON

An intriguing feature of Alexander's deontological doctrine is that the constraint against using the person or property of another to advance one's purposes is far more restrictive than the constraint against harming another when the presence of the other, or the presence of the other given there is some constraint against impinging on him in a way that harms him, is an obstacle to one's acting to advance one's purposes. In the cases that trigger Alexander's means principle constraint, the presence of another person or what belongs to him is an opportunity for the agent; she can do something to the victim that brings about benefit to her that would not have been available in the absence of that victim or of what belongs to him. If one is not appropriating what belongs to another in a way that benefits oneself, but rather doing something one would do, and do just as well, even if the other or his property were not present at all, then, if what one does brings about damage to the other, the doing of it is morally permissible, just in case the consequences of doing it are better than the consequence of refraining from doing it.

To see how Alexander's principles work together to constrain permissible action, consider two examples:

Rescue I – Jose is driving a truck bringing medical supplies to injured persons who will die if they do not swiftly obtain these medicines. There is only one road to the location of the injured, and Jose is driving along it. Sally, through no fault of her own, has fallen onto the narrow roadway, blocking it. She cannot be moved for several hours. To save the imperiled persons, Jose would need to drive his truck over Sally, killing her, since the roadway is very narrow and lacks a driveable shoulder.

Rescue II – Same as Rescue I except that there is a pothole in the road, which makes it impassable. Jose cannot complete his rescue mission, except that it so happens that Sally, through no fault of her own, has fallen into the pothole, filling the gap in the roadway with her body. She is stuck there and, for now, cannot be moved. With Sally filling the pothole, the roadway is just barely useable at that spot. Jose can drive over the pothole and complete his rescue mission, but the weight of his truck driving over the pothole will bear down on Sally, harming her.[15]

Rescue I is governed by Alexander's mild consequence-regarding constraint against eliminative harming. In this example, the presence of Sally is no benefit to Jose, just an obstacle. Or more exactly, Sally's presence is no benefit to Jose, and the constraint against harming her in this situation is an obstacle to his acting to advance his ends. According to Alexander, the constraint that applies to this situation prohibits Jose from harming Sally unless the overall consequences of harming her are better than the overall consequences of refraining from harming her.

Rescue II is governed by the means principle, so the constraint against harming binds in a dramatically more restrictive fashion. Given that Jose would benefit from the presence of Sally on the roadway if he used the opportunity provided by her presence in a way that harmed her, harming her is absolutely forbidden. Whatever the consequences, it would be morally wrong, all things considered, for Jose to advance his ends by harming Sally. Doing so would be an instance of opportunistic agency, which is strictly forbidden (unless Sally has done something morally wrong that brings about forfeiture of her right not to be used by another without her consent to advance the other's ends). Let there be a million imperiled persons who can be rescued only if Jose proceeds; that detail makes no difference; the moral prohibition still binds. Let there be a billion imperiled who can be saved only if Jose arrives at the accident site in time; no matter. Let the harm to Sally be as slight as you can conceive; same verdict.

In fact, we can imagine an example in which Sally is not harmed at all by being run over by the rescue vehicle. Its only effect on her might be to give her ailing back a slight jolt, which greatly lessens her chronic back pain permanently and so, in objective well-being terms, makes her much better off. No matter, according to the stern judgment of MP. Her body is being appropriated against her will, and this is absolutely forbidden by MP, which Alexander interprets as ruling out paternalistic appropriation. Each person is free to live as she chooses, using whatever she legitimately owns, without being used by others, provided she does not use others

[15] For another assessment of such cases, see Helen Frowe, *Defensive Killing* (Oxford: Oxford University Press, 2015), chaps. 1–2.

(and does not harm them in ways that are not defensible by an overall calculation of consequences).[16]

Proceeding in Rescue I would fall into the category of what Judith Thomson has called Running-Roughshod-over-a-Bystander.[17] She distinguishes this case from the category she calls Use-of-a-Bystander. Thomson sees the cases as morally similar.[18]

Thomson reports her opinion that the distinction between harmful agency that uses a person and harmful agency that does not has no moral significance in rendering what one does morally worse. Alexander opines that this distinction makes all the difference. According to Alexander, in Substitution-of-a-Bystander and Riding-Roughshod-over-a-Bystander, it would be wrong to force someone to substitute or ride in order to advance the overall greater good. That would be to use the forced person in violation of the means principle. But if someone voluntarily chooses to do what would produce better consequences in these types of situations, there is no moral constraint against doing so, provided what one chooses to do really does bring about better consequences. By the same token, if this do-gooder could instead do something else that would bring about even better consequences, she is permitted to do that instead, but it would be wrong to force her to do what would bring about best rather than merely better consequences.

By contrast, there is an absolute, exceptionless moral bar against proceeding in Use-of-a-Bystander cases. The difference that Thomson says does not add to moral wrongness (moral taint) at all draws for Alexander a line in the sand marking out what is absolutely prohibited.

Insofar as I can muster any deontological convictions at all, I simply report that Rescue I and Rescue II seem to me, at most, slightly different. Granting that the difference between eliminative and opportunistic agency makes a difference, and that Sally's situation in Rescue II imposes a greater constraint on Jose's proceeding to complete his rescue mission than does Sally's situation in Rescue I, the difference

16 I myself see Alexander's commitment to paternalism – and not merely to paternalism but to an unbending absolutist paternalism – as another intuitively unappealing feature of his view. The paternalism at issue here is roughly restriction of a person's liberty for her own good against her will. But mere assertion here is not going to gain those of us who are pro-paternalistic any argumentative leverage against Alexander and his followers. They are perfectly well aware of this implication and regard it with equanimity. A qualification: Alexander reports that he regards the absolute exceptionless character of the MP as intuitively troublesome in Larry Alexander, "The Jurisdiction of Justice: Two Concepts of Political Morality," *San Diego Law Review* 41, no. 3 (2004). He clearly regards embrace of the MP as nonetheless all things considered plausible, because the only candidate alternative view that does not just repudiate the MP altogether, namely, threshold deontology, proves under examination to be an unstable position, ultimately indefensible. Although this essay defends threshold deontology, the defense leaves open the possibility that in the end this doctrine *does* prove to be an unstable position, swept away by the attractive pull of the best version of act-consequentialism.

17 Judith Thompson, "Self-Defense," *Philosophy and Public Affairs* 20, no. 4 (1991).

18 Ibid., 291.

is slight. In this judgment I am largely, though not entirely, echoing Thomson's judgment.

In passing, I note that it is not clear to me that Alexander's casuistical reasoning regarding these varieties of cases is really true to his master principle. Consider:

Alcove – Two innocent people are fleeing from a tiger who intends to kill and eat them. They can save themselves by jumping together into an alcove, but by doing so they will dislodge a large man already standing in the alcove, causing him to fall to his death.

The consequences of jumping together are better than the consequences of refraining from jumping. Two deaths would be worse than one. But I would suppose that, from Alexander's perspective, the case is underdescribed. If the large man has a right to be in the space he is occupying, what sort of right is this? If the alcove is unowned land or a public park, or private land whose owner has permitted the large man to come onto it, one might think the large man has a temporary property right over the land (and the space immediately above it) that he is currently occupying. Pushing him or otherwise causing him to exit the space violates his temporary legitimate property right, and this looks to be a violation of the means principle.[19] But if this analysis is right, it applies in many, at least, of the cases Alexander seems to regard as governed by a mild consequentialist constraint rather than the fiercely demanding means principle constraint. In Rescue I, why not say the person who falls on the road is occupying space she has a right to occupy, and running over that space with her occupying it then looks to be a violation of the means principle. Same goes for many of the standard trolley cases.

One might resist this conclusion by maintaining that a pedestrian who crosses a roadway has a right to occupy the space her body traverses as it passes across the road only for the standard time it takes to cross. Falling on the road, one exceeds one's right to use and has no property right to be where one is. Or we might take a more driver-friendly view and say the pedestrian has a right to be on the roadway only insofar as this does not interfere with vehicle traffic flow. But then one needs an inquiry into the temporary use rights of space in virtually every case in which the Alexander apparatus is deployed, to determine what rights people have and what moral constraints are binding on agents in these circumstances.

Also, it looks as though, however this inquiry develops, the results will lead to counterintuitive implications for cases. In one case, one could turn a runaway trolley from a track where it is heading toward a child onto another track where it will also kill a child whose head on the tracks is positioned just slightly differently so that it will suffer just ever so slightly less than the child on the initial track would have

[19] See Jonathan Quong, "Killing in Self-Defense," *Ethics* 119, no. 4 (2009): 507–537.

suffered. The slight gain in consequences renders turning permissible. In another case, one could turn a runaway trolley from a track where it is heading toward – horror of horrors – a million children, who happen to be innocent trespassers and who will all be killed if the trolley rumbles ahead on its present path. If one turns the trolley, it will unfortunately strike and kill one child, who has a right to be sitting on the track. The means principle will grind out the conclusion that turning the trolley in the second case is impermissible.

If the MP is the sole deontological principle, then property rights will be set by consequentialist considerations, so long as those considerations are not themselves countenancing violations of MP. (For example, according to Alexander's version of libertarianism, one could not endorse a property ownership principle that dictates that able individuals shall work to provide self-sustaining gardens that will be owned by individuals unable to labor for themselves and that will provide them with food they need to live.) But if these property arrangements, justified by the consequences of their operation, then yield property rights in resources, which shelter under the strong protection of the means principle, then takings of property legitimately owned by an individual will be absolutely impermissible, even though what makes the property rights legitimate is that their overall long-term operation satisfies whatever (MP-constrained) consequentialist principles we should accept. I am unclear exactly how these interactions of the MP and consequentialism will play out, but I am doubtful that their implications for permissible action and policy will attract our considered endorsement in ideally extended reflective equilibrium.

21.4 A PUNCH AIMED AT LEFT LIBERTARIANISM

In an interesting aside, Alexander takes a swipe at left libertarians, who might be presumed to be his close allies. The left libertarian combines the ideas of private ownership of each person by that very person and equal ownership of the rest of the natural world. (There are complications here about the moral status of non-human animals that we can leave aside as irrelevant to present purposes.) The rough thought is that each individual person has a special moral status. She is entitled to live as she pleases so long as she does not thereby harm others in certain ways that intuitively count as wrongful. The natural world of land and minerals and oceans and air has a different status. It has no rights or entitlements; it is simply a good thing that it happens to be there, available for our use. No one has initial rights to this stuff more than anyone else, and since human individuals (who comprise all the persons we have encountered) enter the world at different times and need access to stuff in order to survive and thrive, a natural position is that each person, no matter when he is born, has an equal right to a fair share of natural resources unimproved by human labor. This equal world ownership claim is separate and distinct from the self-ownership idea; you could affirm the one without the other. But the libertarian clearly needs to take some view as to how individuals might come to have rights to use and control stuff in the natural world. The left libertarian takes the view just sketched. It's a sketchy position; it needs to be filled out, and this could be done in different ways. One issue will be to balance the need for stability in property rights with the transformation of rights that occurs upon each birth of a new person having her own entitlement to equal rights to a share of the unimproved earth. For property in things to be useful, there must be stability: I must know that if I plant crops, I will still own the land when harvest time comes. But maybe the reshuffling of rights that newborns occasion will give some newborns rights in what I had supposed was my land.

Alexander thinks the left libertarian project is misconceived from the start, because its initial idea about everyone initially having the same rights to all of the earth violates the means principle. He proposes an example along this line, which is supposed to reveal a deep problem in left libertarianism. Suppose the natural resources consist of fruit-bearing trees. You are short and can only reach the low-lying branches. Being taller, I can reach the higher branches. Alexander stipulates that any system of private ownership appropriation that allows you to appropriate the higher branches or to have a share of ownership of the higher branches straight-away violates the means principle, because in effect you are being given power to deny access and power to force those who can reach the high branches to labor for the benefit of the owners. The individuals who can reach the high branches but can only have access to them by sharing the fruits of labor with the owners unable to take any use of the branches themselves are being treated as means to advance the purposes of others. So left libertarianism dissolves in contradiction. So says Alexander.[20] An alternative way of putting his point would be to say that the left libertarian must repudiate the means principle, which shows that her true colors are not libertarian at all.

We should be puzzled by these Alexander assertions, and our puzzlement should ripen into flat denial of them. First of all, there is no forcing of some to work for the benefit of others in the world in which all adhere to left libertarian principles. Let's suppose, in a two-person world, the equal division of unimproved resources gives each of the two persons property ownership in one-half of each tree from roots to treetop. Call the two persons Able and Unable. Unable owns property he cannot use. (If he were extremely unable, he would be unable to reach even the low-lying

[20] The situation is more complicated than is hinted at in the text. Alexander is alert to the complications. For one thing, in a world with more than two persons, a resource may be inapt for common distribution with respect to C but apt with respect to A and B; and with more persons, more complications ensue. One must also consider natural resources improved by creative inventions introduced by one person that would have been produced anyway by later persons.

branches; according to Alexander, it would be a violation of libertarianism to allow him to appropriate any natural resources at all as his own.) What then? Unable has no right to force Able to work for his benefit or pick the ripe fruit on the high branches owned by Able. No wrongful forcing occurs, we stipulate.

The property Unable has in the high tree branches may still be of use to him. He might just like looking at the fruit, enjoying the sight of swaying branches laden with brightly colored objects. Able might happen to want to help Unable, and might do so by picking some fruit from Unable's high branches (with his permission) and handing the produce to the owner. Here, we should discern no insidious violation of self-ownership. Matters would be no different if Able and Unable reach an agreement, whereby Able picks the fruit from Unable's high branches and the fruit is divided in some agreed ratio between the two of them. Is there some subtle violation of self-ownership here? No. Each person is entitled to do whatever she wishes with whatever she legitimately owns (so long as she does not wrongfully use or harm others), and, *ex hypothesi*, Able does not legitimately own Unable's high branch property. She gains legitimate access to it only with the consent of the rightful owner, Unable. Able's lacking legitimate access to these high branches, that according to our stipulated version of left libertarianism belong to Unable, unless she secures the owner's consent, is not tantamount to forcing some to labor for the benefit of others.

Alexander's position also seems to make too much of too little. Suppose Unable is just barely able to reach the high branches, at great effort and cost. He can pick the fruit, but almost all of it drops from his hands and is wasted as he descends. In this respect, he is just barely able. He then is not barred from being assigned ownership of the branches as part of some initial distribution of unimproved stuff, according to the view Alexander suggests. If the natural resources available are extremely valuable, this slight difference between being strictly unable to use resources to which you might be assigned initial ownership and being just barely able to make use of them might make the difference between having no property and starving, and having a generous share of property and living high on the hog. If we try to avoid this result by stipulating that your entitlement to appropriate unowned land varies continuously with the degree to which you could make productive use of the land if you had access to it, we are heading toward a view that gives most property rights to the most productive, and in which your entitlement to even a bit of natural resources can disappear if someone turns out to have sufficiently greater productive talent than you for putting the land to use.

Alexander's objection to left libertarianism, thought through, seems to involve assigning a vague and arbitrary right to natural ability. If this is what is going on, I see no reason to follow Alexander in embracing this ability entitlement.[21]

[21] Suppose we have a variant of Alexander's two-person world. We can call the two persons Industrious and Lazy, in recognition of their traits. Both are able to reach all branches of the fruit trees that make

The modest conclusion to be drawn from this discussion is that acceptance of the means principle does not constrain the range of appropriation rules open to the libertarian in the way that Alexander supposes. Left libertarianism might be vulnerable on various fronts, but not this one.

21.5 CONCLUSION

Alexander's bold foray into the problem of formulating a plausible version of libertarianism is notable for its suggestions (1) that a single deontological constraint captures the properly enforceable limits on doing whatever would improve the world by an impartial measure of good consequences, and (2) that this constraint is absolute and exceptionless, to be upheld whatever the consequences. Alexander is keenly aware that this unbending norm yields counterintuitive implications about permissible conduct in many scenarios. The claim that these implications for cases are truly counterintuitive presupposes that threshold deontology makes good sense. Alexander mounts a challenge to this presupposition. This essay has argued that the challenge cannot be sustained. Whether or not this is so, we should all recognize that Alexander's discussion illuminates issues that lie at the center of the deontological project. In particular, the idea that we can boil down deontology to a single common-sense idea, the means principle, is provocative and promising. However, under scrutiny, this provocation looks less promising. Finally, Alexander's spirited attempt to use the means principle as a club for clobbering left libertarianism also fails. For all that has been said, something in the neighborhood of the means principle might yet prove to be part of a plausible deontological doctrine, but not its entirety.

up the natural world. Lazy has extreme aversion to work and would not want to labor even if the alternative were slow death from starvation. Industrious wants to work and save and build up his wealth. As I understand Alexander, his animadversions on left libertarianism do not rule out assigning initial property ownership to both Industrious and Lazy. The predictable result is then that the two reach a deal whereby Industrious picks the fruit on the trees or tree branches Lazy owns and they share the picked fruit according to some agreed ratio. This social arrangement does not violate the means principle; the scenario depicted is just a libertarian society in operation. What then entitles Lazy to appropriate is that he has the ability to make some use of the thing he appropriates; he could use it, even though he certainly won't. Lacking the ability to make some use of the thing, Unable lacks any right to appropriate.

22

The Rationality of Threshold Deontology

Michael S. Moore

22.1 INTRODUCTION

There is a pretense in much academic writing that many of us have been guilty of fostering at one time or another. This is the pretense of certitude that many academics affect even when, in their scholarly hearts, they harbor serious doubts about their conclusions or their arguments. Larry Alexander's well-known article,[1] written in response to my theory of threshold deontology,[2] is free of this common pretense. For, as a practicing deontologist himself, Alexander shares with me the bottom-line judgment that absolutist versions of deontology are implausible in the extreme.[3] Kant's version of the famous Latin saying that justice should be done even though the Heavens fall was: "Better the whole people should perish" from the earth than that an injustice be done.[4] This is the kind of stirring hyperbole that gets people to the barricades; but it is surely utter rubbish if taken as the kind of moral philosophy that any of us should actually live by.

1 Larry Alexander, "Deontology at the Threshold," *San Diego Law Review* 37, no. 4 (2000): 893–912.

2 Alexander's article was written in response to Michael Moore, "Torture and the Balance of Evils," *Israel Law Review* 23, no. 2/3(1989): 280–344, revised and reprinted as Michael Moore, *Placing Blame: A General Theory of the Criminal Law* (Oxford: Oxford University Press, 1997), chap. 17. I have since elaborated my view of deontology in Michael Moore, *Causation and Responsibility: An Essay in Law, Morals, and Metaphysics* (Oxford: Oxford University Press, 2009), chap. 3, and in Michael Moore, "Targeted Killings and the Morality of Hard Choices," in *Targeted Killings: Law and Morality in an Asymmetrical World*, ed., Andrew Altman, Claire Finkelstein, and J.D. Ohlin (Oxford: Oxford University Press, 2012), 434–66.

3 We jointly say so in Larry Alexander and Michael Moore, "Deontological Ethics," *Stanford Encyclopedia of Philosophy* (Winter 2016), ed. Edward N. Zalta, https://plato.stanford.edu/entries/ethics-deontological/.

4 Kant, Metaphysical Elements of Justice, 2nd ed., trans. J. Ladd (Indianapolis: Hackett, 1999), 100.

Given Alexander's need to have thresholds in any plausible deontology, his own included,[5] his critique of threshold deontology should be seen in the spirit in which it was written: as an invitation to help in overcoming objections to threshold deontology that Alexander was honest enough to say he could not answer alone. I thus see the present article as answering that invitation.

When I teach Alexander's deservedly influential article on threshold deontology in my ethics seminars, I usually have my students tease out the roughly fifteen or so overlapping problems raised for threshold deontology by Alexander. In their contributions to this volume, Kevin Cole[6] and Dick Arneson[7] do a good job of combining these related problems into just two or three items. Cole sees Alexander as raising two problems: (1) the arbitrariness problem, which is that there seems to be no nonarbitrary way of specifying the threshold (of awful consequences, the avoidance of which justifies violating deontological norms); and (2) the moral ballast problem, which is the seeming problem that everyone's harms that are below the threshold are mere "moral ballast," ("moral ballast" consists of items without moral import save that they allow those whose harms are threatened to occur once the threshold has been reached, to justify violating deontological norms to prevent those above-the-threshold harms). Arneson raises both of these problems, although he characterizes the moral ballast problem as the more general problem of the supposed "weirdness" of threshold deontology's treatment of cases where the bad consequences prevented are very close to the threshold. Arneson goes on to distinguish a third problem for threshold deontology that he sees Alexander as raising: this is (3), the problem of incommensurability between the badness of states of affairs (the focus of consequentialist ethics) and the wrongness of an agent violating a norm (the focus of deontological ethics).

The adequacy of Arneson's and Cole's taxonomies of Alexander's fusillade of problems for threshold deontology, and the cogency of Cole's and Arneson's responses to those problems, free me to do what I intended to do in this essay anyway – which is to answer a doubt about threshold deontology that is something of a generalization of those raised explicitly by Alexander or by Cole's and Arneson's interpretations of Alexander. This is the doubt that I shall call the "ad hocery" doubt.[8] The worry is that nothing supports the existence of the thresholds posited to

5 Alexander's patient-centered version of deontology is laid out in his "The Means Principle," in *Law, Morals, and Metaphysics: The Philosophy of Michael S. Moore*, ed. Kimberly Ferzan and Stephen J. Morse (Oxford: Oxford University Press, 2016).

6 Kevin Cole, "Real-World Criminal Law and the Norm Against Punishing the Innocent: Two Cheers for Threshold Deontology," this volume.

7 Richard Arneson, "Deontology's Travails," this volume.

8 "Ad hocery" was Jonathan Schaffer's charge against my use of a closeness doctrine to distinguish causal from noncausal relations (if x caused y, and if z is *close* to y, then x caused z too). Such use of closeness was ad hoc, Schaffer complained, because it was only an afterthought added on

exist by threshold deontology, except naked, isolated intuitions in particular cases. More particularly, the worry is that the existence of such thresholds is not demanded or even supported by any deep nature of deontology but is rather an alien, ad hoc add-on posited in order to avoid the absurdity of Kantian absolutism.

This more general concern involves the three more specific concerns investigated by Arneson and Cole. As we shall see, incommensurability (of deontological and consequentialist obligations) figures centrally in what follows. Also, both the charge of arbitrariness and the charge of weirdness at the border are involved in the more general charge of ad hocery; I intend my answer below to the ad hocery charge to also aid in the disposal of these more particular charges as well. The ad hocery worry is in a sense a charge of arbitrariness, but the arbitrariness worried about is not, or is not only, the arbitrariness in picking some determinate level at which to set a threshold; nor is it the supposed weirdness that results once one does that. Rather, the worry focused on here is whether there can be any support for the idea that there is some threshold (of awful consequences) over which one is permitted to do what otherwise one is categorically forbidden to do, some support that flows naturally from the nature of deontology itself and not just from a desire to avoid the counter-intuitive implications of that nature.

22.2 THE NON-ALIEN NATURE OF THRESHOLDS IN DEONTOLOGY

In what follows, I shall lay out seven features of morality that, I shall urge, render the idea of thresholds unsurprising and untroubling. Moreover, I shall urge that these features combine with an eighth to make thresholds in deontology not only unsurprising and untroubling but also to make the existence of such thresholds a necessary implication of deontology's true nature. I shall treat these features seriatim.

22.2.1 *Deontic Morality Consists of Consequentialist as well as Deontological Obligations*

It is not plausible to think that the agent-centered restrictions and prerogatives that constitute deontology exhaust our objective reasons for action. Most decisions in our life are not governed by such heavy-duty moral machinery. This is surely true of

to my theory of causation to avoid otherwise troublesome counterexamples; it was not a principled doctrine based on my theory of the nature of the causal relation. Jonathan Schaffer, "Disconnection and Responsibility," *Legal Theory* 18, no. 4 (2012): 399–435, 413. I responded to Schaffer's use of the "ad hocery" objection in the causal context, as well as expanded the discussion of ad hocery in relation to the closeness doctrine's use in the context of intentions rather than causation, in Moore, "Four Friendly Critics: A Response," *Legal Theory* 18, no. 4 (2012): 491–542.

those many decisions not governed by obligations of any sort, such as our decisions about where to go to lunch, whom to marry, whether to have children, etc. But it is as surely true of actions that are governed by that subspecies of reasons for action we call obligations.[9]

As an example, consider positive duties of rescue. Except for a few, unregenerate libertarians (which may include Alexander), most of us think that we have a positive duty to rescue strangers when we can do so at little risk or inconvenience to ourselves. This duty is deontic and not merely aretaic.[10] Yet this positive duty seemingly cannot be a deontological obligation, because it lacks categorical force. We know this latter fact because we can justify not saving one person by directing our resources anywhere else where they will produce consequences better than the prevention of the loss of one innocent life; for example, we can forego saving one in order to both save another's life and to prevent a third person's arm from being broken.[11]

Deontic ethics – the ethics of choice and action, as distinguished from the aretaic ethics of disposition and character – is thus comprised of consequentialist obligations as well as deontological obligations. On this Larry Alexander and I have long agreed. I have urged that the right way to see this combination is to regard consequentialist reasons as omnipresent in life and thus to see deontological reasons as a kind of side-constraint or override. There are two kinds of such overrides, obligations and prerogatives:[12] (1) sometimes our deontological obligations (not to torture an innocent, for example) override the good reasons we may have to torture on this occasion (say, the prevention of even more torture by others in the future by our torturing one now); (2) sometimes our deontological permissions (to defend ourselves against a culpable aggressor, for example) override the good reasons we may have not to

9 I argue for this in Moore, *Causation and Responsibility*. Alexander shares with me this eclectic view of deontic morality. See Alexander, "The Means Principle."

10 On the notion of aretaic duties, see Heidi Hurd, "Duties Beyond the Call of Duty," *Annual Review of Law and Ethics* 6 (1998): 3–39.

11 I adopt this test for when an obligation is consequentialist from Heidi Hurd, "What in the World Is Wrong?," *Journal of Contemporary Legal Issues* 5 (1994): 152–216. Deontological obligations "patrol the borders of permissible consequentialist calculations," in this view of things, so if an obligation does no such patrolling, it is a consequentialist obligation. See Michael Moore, "Patrolling the Borders of Consequentialist Calculation," *Law and Philosophy* 27, no. 1 (2008) 35–96.

12 Moore, *Causation and Responsibility*, chap. 3. Phil Montague accurately perceives that this way of combining deontology and consequentialism owes much to Bob Nozick's view in his *Anarchy, State, and Utopia* (New York: Oxford University Press, 1974) that deontological obligations operate as "side-constraints" on achieving consequentially desirable states of affairs. Phil Montague, "Moral Dilemmas and Moral Theory: Towards a Viable Deontology," in *Legal, Moral, and Metaphysical Truths*, ed. Kimberly Kessler Ferzan and Stephen J. Morse (Oxford: Oxford University Press, 2016). Montague is critical of this Nozick-inspired way of seeing deontic ethics, but I seek to defuse such criticisms in Michael Moore, "Responses and Appreciations," in *Legal, Moral, and Metaphysical Truths*, ed. Kimberly Kessler Ferzan and Stephen J. Morse (Oxford: Oxford University Press, 2016).

defend ourselves on this occasion (say, the fact that we will have to inflict a greater harm on the attacker than he (or they) would inflict on us if we forego self-defense). On either of these occasions, the right action is not what it usually is – a maximizing of good consequences and a minimizing of bad consequences.[13] Rather, the right action is to conform to the deontological norms of obligation or permission.

Notice that on this picture the surprise offered up by threshold deontology is not the surprise that deontological obligations and permissions often compete with consequentialist obligations. Rather, the surprise is that sometimes the consequentialist obligations are not overridden by deontological obligations and permissions; what usually overrides (deontology) is on these occasions itself overridden, and what is usually overridden (consequentialist reasons) on these occasions does the overriding. What needs explaining about threshold deontology is how this reversal of priority can be conceptualized and justified.

22.2.2 *Conflict of Obligations Is Endemic to Everyone's Moral Experience*

A basic principle of Freudian psychology was that conflicts between the mental states of belief, desire, intention, and emotion that constitute our subjective reasons for action were endemic in our mental life.[14] An analogous principle of ethics is that conflict of objective reasons is also endemic to the morality that governs how we should choose and act, and that such conflict also exists between those stringent, objective reasons for action we call obligations. True enough, Kant famously proclaimed that conflicts in our obligations was "inconceivable."[15] Yet what he meant was that conflict in our end-of-the-day obligations was unacceptable. And in this he was surely right. If we are obligated both to do some action A at time t, and to refrain from A-ing at t, then morality demands the impossible from us. It thus guarantees our moral failure, no matter what we do. While some malevolently playful Greek

[13] The vagueness in specifying the consequentialist principle is deliberate. Neither Alexander nor myself have worked out in detail what the consequentialist part of deontic morality looks like. The deontological part interests us more, and besides, there is an extensive literature written by those with a more exclusive interest in consequentialism than we have. The one aspect that we do take a position on, naturally enough for deontologists, is a firm rejection of rule (or any other form of two-level) consequentialism. See Larry Alexander, "Pursuing the Good – Indirectly," *Ethics* 95, no. 2(1985): 315–32. While I early-on rejected indirect consequentialism in my "Torture and the Balance of Evils," my most detailed rejection of it will be found in my email debate with Dan Dennett more recently, reproduced verbatim in Moore, *Mechanical Choices: The Responsibility of the Human Machine* (New York: Oxford University Press, forthcoming), chap. 10.

[14] The role conflict plays as an organizing principle of Freudian psychology is examined by me in Moore, "Mind, Brain, and Unconscious," in *Mind, Psychoanalysis, and Science*, ed., Peter Clark and Crispin Wright (Oxford: Basil Blackwell, 1988).

[15] Kant, *The Metaphysics of Morals*, trans. Mary Gregor (Cambridge: Cambridge University Press, 1996), 16.

God might foist off such an unfair morality on the human race, it is surely too unfair to be taken seriously in the absence of such malevolently divine origins.[16]

So when we say that conflict of obligations is a familiar feature of morality, we do not mean that all-out or end-of-the day obligations can and do conflict. Rather, such situations of conflict – usually called "moral dilemmas" – exist in the sense that a familiar feature of moral experience is the seeming or experienced conflict in the demands of two or more obligations. The standard, decades-old example is Jean Paul Sartre's: Sartre's student was obligated to join the Resistance and in this way fight injustice, and he was obligated to stay home to help his ailing mother; the student could not do both, and he knew that.[17] Sartre's famous injunction to his student does exemplify the kind of conflict of ultimate obligations that Kant feared: "Just decide," Sartre told his student, because there was no answer to be found in such conflicting obligations.

Few serious moral philosophers would accept Sartre's existentialist answer to moral dilemmas. Rather, one obligation or the other is thought to prevail in such situations of conflict. There are two different ways one obligation can prevail over another: (1) by creating an exception to the content of the losing obligation, which exception has the content of the prevailing obligation; or (2) by outweighing (or being in some other sense prior to, such as excluding, preempting, etc.) the losing obligation. The first is the route of the "specificationist";[18] the second is the route of those holding all obligations to be of "prima facie" or "pro tanto" force only.[19]

Notice that on the specificationist view, Kant was right: Obligations never really conflict. For if in cases of seeming conflict the content of one of the obligations contains an implicit exception making that obligation not applicable to the situation at hand, then the other obligation unproblematically governs and dictates the right course of action. For example, if the obligation is not simply to take care of a parent

16 Heidi Hurd and I explore why a morality countenancing conflict of obligations when they apply to one and the same person, or countenancing conflict of obligations when they apply to two or more persons, would be an unfair morality, the possibility of which a properly conceived deontic logic should reject. Heidi Hurd and Michael Moore, "The Hohfeldian Analysis of Rights," in *The Legacy of Wesley Newcomb Hohfeld: Edited Major Works, Select Personal Papers, and Original Commentaries*, ed. Shyam Balganesh, Ted Sichelman, and Henry Smith (Cambridge: Cambridge University Press, 2018).

17 Jean Paul Sartre, "Existentialism is a Humanism," Paris lecture, 1945, translated into English and published as *Existentialism and Humanism* (London: Methuen, 1948).

18 Although this strategy for dealing with apparent conflict of obligations is at least as old as Kant (see Barbara Herman, *The Practice of Moral Judgment* (Cambridge, MA: Harvard University Press,1993)), the label "specificationist" appears to originate with Judy Thomson. See Judith Thomson, "*Self-Defense and Rights*," the 1976 Lindley Lecture at the University of Kansas (Lawrence: University of Kansas Press, 1977).

19 The tradition begun in modern ethics by Sir W. David Ross, *The Right and the Good* (Oxford: Oxford University Press, 1930).

in need, full stop, but is rather an obligation to care of such a parent unless one can significantly aid the world in ridding itself of an unjust regime, Sartre's student faces no real conflict; he has his answer in the one obligation that applies to his particular situation.

I have in the past speculated that some degree of specificationism is called for.[20] Yet I doubt that one can be specificationist enough to show that all apparent conflicts of obligation are not real conflicts. For the content adjustments needed to render our obligations nonconflictual would be as rich as the highly nuanced moral world itself. Ethics would then be like a cartography that eschews the simplifications of traditional maps in favor of "maps" that are full size reproductions of the world mapped.

So some recourse needs be had to the second strategy showing seeming conflicts of obligation to be resolvable: hold all obligations – even categorical ones – to be prima facie ("defeasible," "pro tanto") only. Then one's overall, all-out obligation can be univocal even though it is created by a balance between two or more prima facie obligations in conflict. For this second strategy to work it needs to be the case that prima facie obligations have differential degrees of stringency (or obligating force). Such differential stringency is what allows one prima facie obligation to outweigh (override, take precedence over, be prior to) another. The nature of such stringency of obligation is the third aspect of morality needed to sustain threshold deontology as not being ad hoc.

22.2.3 *Stringency of Obligation Is Required Independently of Its Ability to Resolve Moral Dilemmas*

There is a well-known conundrum in the philosophy of mind about how one conceptualizes and measures the comparative strengths of different desires.[21] In explaining intentional action, one often wants to explain why that action was chosen and done in terms of the actor most wanting the good(s) served by the action chosen. Yet, for this explanation to be significant, what is most wanted – the strongest desire – cannot simply be defined in terms of its propensity to win out in situations of conflict. Some independent definition of "strength" must be supplied, or else the supposed empirical truth that we generally do what we most want to do when we act intentionally becomes a mere tautology.[22]

[20] Moore, *Placing Blame*, 706.

[21] A.C. Ewing, "Can We Act Against Our Stringent Desire?," *The Monist* 44, no. 1 (1934): 126–43.

[22] I pursue the ways in which, in cases of volitional excuse, we do not do what we most want to do, even though we do what we do intentionally, in Michael Moore, "The Neuroscience of Volitional Excuse," in *Philosophical Foundations of Law and Neuroscience*, ed. Dennis Patterson and Michael Pardo

Likewise, in ethics we need some independent specification of strength ("stringency") of obligation for it to be significant to explain (in terms of the greater strength or stringency of the prevailing obligation) why one obligation overrides another in situations of conflict between the two. Fortunately, that independent account of stringency of obligation is ready to hand. It is a well-known and accepted feature of deontology that, despite the uniformly categorical nature of deontological obligations, breaches of such obligations are constitutive of various degrees of wrongdoing, which differential wrongdoing in turn demands differential punishments.[23] Greater wrongdoing demands greater punishments, on any plausible rendering of the principle of proportionate punishment. Intentional killing demands more punishment than intentional theft, for example.

Such differential wrongdoing, when holding the conditions of breach constant, can only be explained by the differential stringency in the obligations breached: the more stringent the obligation breached, the greater the wrongdoing involved in breaching that obligation and vice versa. This familiar feature of our punishment practices gives us the independent specification of stringency of obligation which we need for present purposes.

22.2.4 *Stringency of Consequentialist Obligations to Do or Not Do Some Action Is a Direct Function of the Net Goodness/Badness of the Consequences of That Action*

Consequentialist obligations are founded on the avoidance of bad consequence/ promotion of good consequences. Each bad consequence avoided and each good consequence promoted creates a prima facie consequentialist obligation to do such an act, the degree of stringency of each such prima facie obligation being a direct function of the degree of badness/goodness of the relevant consequence. It should thus be no surprise that the stringency of an all-out consequentialist obligation is directly a function of the net goodness/badness of the consequences of any act. The worse the net consequences of some act, the more we are obligated not to do such act. When the downside costs are held constant, we are more stringently obligated to rescue two drowning stranger babies than we are obligated to rescue one.

(Oxford: Oxford University Press, 2016), 179–230. I accordingly pursue a definition of strength of desire that is not simply behavioral.

23 Alexander and I present this as one of the well-known puzzles of deontology, in Larry Alexander and Michael Moore, "Deontological Ethics."

22.2.5 *Stringency of Deontological Obligations Not to Do Some Action Is Only Imperfectly Correlated with the Net Badness of Consequences of Doing That Action*

As the literature on the theory of criminal legislation has examined in detail, actions that cause harm to other people, and actions that are (deontologically) wrong to do, are extensionally overlapping sets in the sense that many harm-causings are wrong and many wrongs are harm-causings.[24] Yet the relationship is one of overlap only,[25] not of congruence; there are, after all, both harmless wrongs and wrongless harm-causings.

The stringency of deontological obligation is thus only partly a function of the badness of states of affairs caused (or failed to be prevented, in the case of positive obligations) by an actor subject to such obligation. What else goes into the determination of stringency of deontological obligations is an interesting question. Joel Feinberg's "free-floating evils" provide convenient examples with which to work:[26] When one defames the reputation of the dead, or when one tortures an animal, abuses a corpse, sponsors a dwarf-tossing contest, or despoils a pristine lake, these can be done in circumstances where no nonconsenting person is harmed. Yet these can be seriously wrongful actions to perform, nonetheless. Of course, one might urge that there still are bad states of affairs (making the actions causing them wrong) in these examples. Yet in some of such examples, at least, the badness of the state of affairs is just the doing of the wrongful action. And even in cases where there are independently bad states of affairs, the degree of wrongness of the action seems imperfectly responsive to the degree of badness of those states of affairs.

An alternative construal of such examples would be to think that the degree of wrongness for each of them is largely a function of the degree of aretaic failure (lack of virtuous character or disposition) necessarily present in the actor who does such actions. Such construal is not the view that these are only instances of aretaic failure and that these are not instances of deontic failure (breach of obligation). This last idea would be contrary to our common sense about these actions: We are obligated not to torture animals, not to defame the dead, etc.; it is not just that we

24 Joel Feinberg, *Harmless Wrongdoing* (New York: Oxford University Press, 1988).

25 Insofar as the stringency of deontological obligation not to do some action A *does* depend on the badness of the consequences of A, that involves no contradiction or even unseemliness for the deontologist. As Phil Montague nicely lays out, one can allow consequences of an act to be wrong-making features of that act without turning one's obligation not to do such an action into a consequentialist obligation. Montague, "Moral Dilemmas and Moral Theory: Towards a Viable Deontology."

26 Joel Feinberg, "Legal Moralism and Free-Floating Evils," *Pacific Philosophical Quarterly* 61, no. 1/2 (1980): 122–55.

lack virtue when we do these things. The idea considered here is thus not that the aretaic displaces the deontic but rather that the aretaic measures the deontic. More precisely, the idea is that the stringency of the admittedly existing deontic obligation depends on the strength of the virtue flouted by actions breaching such an obligation. Yet this construal requires a reduction or dependency of the deontic on the aretaic that many, including myself, have rejected.[27]

This last construal suggests a third: Perhaps the degree of stringency of a deontological obligation is partly dependent on the degree of agential involvement of the actor breaching such obligation. Agent-relative obligations depend mightily for their scope on a specification of when human agency is involved in their violation. Constituting such agency (as I have urged elsewhere in detail)[28] are factors such as: acting (versus failing to prevent); doing (versus allowing); intending (versus foreseeing or risking); causing (versus merely accelerating); causing by initiation (versus causing by redirecting); causing (versus enabling another to cause); etc. The standard take on these factors defining agential involvement is that they operate bivalently, so that the actor who acts (not omits or allows) so as to cause (not accelerate, enable, or redirect) an evil he intends (not foresees or risks) to bring about violates the relevant deontological norm. An alternative, nonstandard take, however, is to construe such factors as operating in a scalar manner: The more one acts, causes, or intends, the more agential involvement there is and the more stringently one is obligated not to do the act in question.

My own form of deontology does not construe these agential involvement factors as scalar in their implications for the scope of obligation.[29] Yet, even if one went the other way here, such a construal would not fully answer the puzzle about the stringency of deontological obligation. Something besides degree of harm done and degree of agential involvement would still be necessary to fully determine stringency of deontological obligation.

So what the properties are on which the stringency of deontological obligation rests is a bit of a mystery. Undeniable, however, is the fact that we assign differential stringency to deontological obligations and that such stringency is not simply a function of the badness of consequences.

[27] I have long resisted any Hume-like reduction of the deontic to the aretaic. See, e.g., Moore, "Choice, Character, and Excuse," *Social Philosophy and Policy* 7 (1990): 219–48, reprinted and revised as Moore, *Placing Blame*, chap. 11. In Michael Moore, "Liberty and Supererogation," *Annual Review of Law and Ethics* 6 (1998): 111–43, I explore the distinctively aretaic categories of evaluation – the supererogatory, the suberogatory, the quasi-erogatory, and the indifferent – and argue for their nonreducibility to the deontic categories of evaluation, the obligatory and the permissible.

[28] For a convenient overview with citations to other writings, see Moore, "Responses and Appreciations."

[29] Moore, *Causation and Responsibility*.

22.2.6 *Because of Their Common Possession of the Property of Stringency, Obligations Are Not Incommensurable When They Conflict So That the Most Stringent Obligation Determines Right Action*

The obvious thing to say about how one should act when facing a conflict of obligations such as that faced by Sartre's student is that one should obey the most stringent obligation. If the obligation to fight injustice is more stringent than the obligation to take care of an ailing parent, then doing the former and not the latter is the right course of action. This obvious enough recommendation does not depend on there being some general, lexical ordering of all obligations. Sometimes there may be a lexical ordering between two obligations, but even when there is not, one obligation, given the features present on some particular occasion, may be more stringent than another. My old analogy for this point was with weight: Even if it is indeterminate whether Frenchmen are on average heavier than Englishmen, that would be no ground on which to doubt that some particular Frenchman is either heavier or lighter than some particular Englishman.[30]

Larry Alexander worries that this happy resolution of conflicting obligations is impossible because the obligations in conflict are incommensurable with one another. Presumably Alexander does not think this about conflicts *inter se* between prima facie consequentialist obligations – for in such cases the common coin is the goodness/badness of the consequences governing the stringency of each prima facie obligation, so that one can simply net out the balance of consequences to see what one ought to do. Likewise, presumably Alexander does not think that conflicts *inter se* between prima facie deontological obligations are incommensurable either – for, as a monist in his deontology (where all deontological obligations and permissions are governed by one principle, the means principle), Alexander is seemingly committed to there being no unresolvable conflicts of obligations here either.[31]

The main incommensurability worry relevant here is thus about conflicts between consequentialist obligations and deontological obligations. The worry, crudely put, is that this involves comparing apples and oranges to determine, say, the best fruit. Put less metaphorically: Although both deontological and consequentialist obligations

[30] Michael Moore, "Moral Reality," *Wisconsin Law Review* 1982, no. 6 (1982): 1061–156, 1152n204, reprinted in Moore, *Objectivity in Law and Ethics: Essays in Moral and Legal Ontology* (Aldershot: Ashgate, 2004), 3–98.

[31] For deontologists, such as myself, who are pluralists and not monists about the variety of our deontological obligations, things are not so happily unproblematic. The incommensurability of conflicts *inter se* of deontological obligations, however, is not the main worry relevant to the ad hoc worry about threshold deontology. (Incidentally, monists like Alexander may well have to say something more about conflicts of prima facie deontological duties – for even their one deontological principle can lead to conflicts, such as those created by inconsistent promises.)

come with differential degrees of stringency, what determines that stringency for each is different, as we have seen. The stringency of consequentialist obligation is wholly a function of the goodness/badness of consequences, whereas the stringency of deontological obligation is only partly a function of such consequences.

One cannot eliminate this difference between the two kinds of obligation by transforming the non-consequence-based determinants of deontological stringency into some agent-neutral values. Suppose, for example, one were to urge that the degree of agential involvement (a determinant of deontological stringency on the scalar view described earlier) simply be added to the badness of a state of affairs to produce a composite, a kind of agency-weighted badness for states of affairs. This would be the view that the state of affairs of Jones being killed by Smith is worse than the state of affairs of Jones dying – for the former state of affairs has the killer's agential involvement adding to the badness of Jones' death, whereas the latter has only the badness of the death.

This is a hopeless reconciliation because it transforms deontological obligations into consequentialist obligations. It purchases a common denominator for stringency of obligation at the price of eliminating deontology. For what such a move produces is a kind of agency-weighted consequentialism.[32] Whereas a truly deontological view of ethics – on either the bivalent or scalar view of agential involvement – does not cash out the determinants of deontological stringency into the goodness or badness of states of affairs. To keep deontology intact, one needs to preserve the "paradox of deontology,"[33] viz., that an agent is categorically obligated not to do some act A even if A produces the best consequences, all things considered.[34]

So we are unable to cash out the bases of deontological stringency to some bad states of affairs (which one could then net out against the bad states of affairs determining the stringency of conflicting consequentialist obligations). Still, the familiar moral experience of all of us is that we treat the stringencies of these two kinds of obligations as commensurable. We do this when we make decisions in situations of conflict: If two children, both strangers to me, are drowning, but I can satisfy my (consequentialist) obligation to save them only if I breach my (deontological) obligation to save my own child, we are not bereft of an answer as to what we should do. My own view is that my agent-relative obligation to my own child is more stringent than my agent-neutral obligation to the two stranger children, so I ought to save my

[32] Amartya Sen "Rights and Agency," *Philosophy and Public Affairs* 11, no. 1 (1982): 3–39.

[33] Alexander and Moore, "Deontological Ethics."

[34] This feature of deontology is why there is such a difference between one's obligation not to *do* some forbidden action (such as torture) and merely noncausally enabling another to do such an action. In the latter case, your obligation is consequentialist because you treat the other violating the deontological norm against torture as just a bad state of affairs you are obligated not to cause but not as an act of yours that you were categorically obligated not to do or enable.

kid.[35] Even if you disagree with me here, such disagreement would show that you too commensurate your consequentialist obligation against your deontological obligation. The only disagreement that wouldn't show this is for you to adopt Sartre's maddeningly unhelpful stance: You must just decide because there is no prioritizing one obligation over another.

The other part of our moral experience relevant here is how we regard degrees of wrongdoing for purposes of determining retributive desert and retributive punishment. We do not divide our proportionality principle up into consequentialist desert schedules and deontological desert schedules. Rather, we have one mode of punishment (typically deprivation of liberty) and we mete out that one mode of punishment proportionately to one, univocal desert. By my lights, the mother who breaches her obligation to save her own child deserves more punishment, did more wrong, than another who breaches her obligation to save two children that were strangers to her. And again, even if you disagree with me here, that would equally well show that you too place the two deserts on a common scale and compare them. Comparable deserts, comparable degrees of wrongdoing, comparable breaches of obligation, comparable degrees of stringency in the obligations breached.

22.2.7 *The Degree of Stringency in One's Overall, End-of-the-Day Obligation Is a Netting of the Stringency of the Winning Prima Facie Obligation over the Stringency of the Losing Prima Facie Obligation*

One of the intuitions on which Alexander preys is the large moral difference (in degree of wrongdoing and thus of blameworthiness) that some small difference (in differential stringency between two conflicting obligations) can make.[36] Arneson rightly rejoins that slight differences in the stringency of competing obligations in fact make only slight differences in degrees of wrongdoing and blameworthiness for breach.[37] I here register my agreement with Arneson.

In the rescue situation posited earlier, even if I am right that a mother should save her own in preference to saving two stranger children, the mother who gets it wrong doesn't get it very wrong. More accurately put, the stringency of her obligation to save her own child gets reduced by the stringency of the obligation she flouts, viz., the obligation to save the two stranger children. All-out obligation doesn't "forget" one-half of that of which it is made,[38] namely, the weaker obligation that loses out.

[35] Not a purely hypothetical or academic question for me, incidentally, albeit one faced by me in slightly less draconian circumstances.

[36] Alexander, "Deontology at the Threshold."

[37] Arneson, "Deontology's Travails."

[38] This is reminiscent of the way in which aretaic ethics does not "forget" the losing obligation when the more stringent obligation is acted upon. Years ago Bernard Williams persuasively charted how a

It still counts for something that the mother who fails to save her own child did so to save two stranger children. She did less wrong – lots less wrong – than the mother who deliberately fails to save her child when the lives of no stranger children hang in the balance.

Matching degrees of wrongdoing to net differences in the stringency of conflicting obligations removes any charge of arbitrariness directed against threshold deontology because of its disproportionate treatment of close cases. Small differences in the net stringency of competing obligations make for small wrongs when the actor chooses against the more stringent obligation, and this is as it should be.

22.2.8 *There is No Lexical Priority of Deontological Obligations over Consequentialist Obligations When They Conflict; Since All Conflicts of Obligation Are Determined by the Relative Stringency of the Obligations in Conflict, Sometimes the Consequentialist Obligation Will Prevail*

There are three versions of the lexical priority claim that should be distinguished: (1) a strong version, according to which every instance of every deontological obligation wins out over (is more stringent than) every instance of every consequentialist obligation; (2) a moderate version, according to which there are some deontological obligations (the very stringent ones like that against torture), every instance of which wins out over (is more stringent than) every instance of every consequentialist obligation; and (3) a weak version, according to which some instance(s) of some deontological obligation(s) win out over (are more stringent than) every instance of every consequentialist obligation.

None of these three versions of priority is right. As to version (1), if not lying and not breaking a promise are taken to be the content of deontological obligations (as they often are), then it is implausible in the extreme to think that some consequentialist obligation (e.g., to save a stranger from being murdered by the murderer enquiring as to the stranger's whereabouts)[39] could not outweigh them on some occasion. Version (2) is more plausible; many think that obligations like that forbidding torture are "absolute," that is, not subject to being overridden no matter what the consequences. Yet the torture debate reveals that this too is not true. Where discussants were saying what they believed was true – as opposed to saying what they thought would have the best consequences – most would admit that even torture

decent and virtuous person still feels regretful in such situations, even as he recognizes that he made the right choice of action. Bernard Williams, "Ethical Consistency," *Proceedings of the Aristotelian Society Supplementary* 39 (1965): 103–38.

[39] Kant's familiar example in his essay, "On the Supposed Right to Lie from Altruistic Motives," originally published in 1797.

could be justified by the avoidance of immediate and horrendous consequences.[40] And version (3) ultimately is no more plausible than version (2): Even torture done in horrific manners ("torture-heavy" as opposed to "torture-lite") might be justified by our obligation to attain good enough consequences.

In any case, denial of all three versions of the priority of deontological obligations over consequentialist obligation amounts to assertion of the truth of threshold deontology. And the point here is not to reargue the intuitive plausibility of threshold deontology. We are here assuming that threshold deontology is intuitive; the ad hocery worry is that it is only that. Rather, the ambition of this article is to show how the threshold deontological conclusion flows naturally from familiar positions in deontological ethics. These positions are the ones I have argued for above: that consequentialist obligations are an integral part of deontic ethics, conflict of obligations is a fact of life for us as moral agents, obligations must be differentially stringent if their force in such conflicts is to have rational resolution, and such stringency is in any case required to account for our very intuitive sense that some wrongdoing is more wrong than others; that while stringency of consequentialist obligation has a simpler metric than does stringency of deontological obligation, we trade each off against the other in situations of conflict and in situations requiring judgments of comparative desert; also that the most stringent prima facie obligation determines what our overall obligation must be, and the wrongfulness of breach of that overall obligation takes into account not only the stringency of the prima facie obligation that one violated but also the stringency of the prima facie obligation one conformed to by so acting. These considerations do not "prove" threshold deontology to be true; but on the reasonable supposition that no obligation or kind of obligation always prevails in situations of conflict with other obligations – i.e., the supposition that no version of the lexical priority thesis is true – they make threshold deontology a reasonable conclusion from a perfectly familiar and plausible view of ethics.

Indeed, we can now see that threshold deontology is a natural part of any plausible deontology. Just as deontology's distinctive "categorical force" amounts to no more than the fact that ordinarily deontological obligations are more stringent than are consequentialist obligations, so that when they conflict the deontological obligation prevails, so deontology's "threshold feature" amounts to no more than the fact that extraordinarily consequentialist obligations can be more stringent than deontological obligations, so that when they conflict the consequentialist obligation prevails. My "three-layer cake" view of deontic ethics – layer one, an omnipresent

40 I take this to be true of my long-term interlocutor on this topic, Jeremy Waldron. See Jeremy Waldron, "Torture and Positive Law: Jurisprudence for the White House," *Columbia Law Review* 105, no. 6 (2005): 1681–750.

background of consequentialist obligations, side-constrained by layer two, deontological obligations and permissions, itself overridden by layer three, the consequential trumping of deontology over some threshold[41] – is only an epistemic, not an ontological, rendering.[42] Ontologically, there is but one layer to this cake: We often face conflicting prima facie obligations, each possessing some measure of stringency; this stringency is univocal even when one of such obligations is consequentialist and the other is not; unsurprisingly, the most stringent prima facie obligation prevails in situations of conflict between two or more obligations, recognizing that most often deontological obligations are most stringent but also that sometimes that is not the case.

Threshold deontology, like most things in ethics, comes in different flavors. It remains to describe briefly the flavor of threshold deontology these considerations support. A main line of division that I have addressed before[43] is between those threshold deontologists who regard the threshold as a fixed amount of bad consequences and those who regard it as a "sliding scale," one where the stringency of the prima facie deontological obligation violated determines the amount of bad consequences needed to justify violating it. I have before defended the sliding scale version of threshold deontology, and this is the version Alexander too finds more plausible, although he calls it the "ratio" version. Rather clearly, such a version is the one supported by my invocation of the just described eight familiar features of ethics. If threshold deontology is no more than the idea that the more stringent of two conflicting, prima facie obligations prevails (and the caveat that there is no lexical priority by kinds of obligations), then a quite stringent deontological obligation will require an even more stringent consequentialist obligation if the latter is to prevail; likewise, a less stringent deontological obligation will require less stringency in the competing consequentialist obligation for the latter to prevail.

22.3 CONCLUSION

Once one answers the big question of deontic ethics – whether one is a consequentialist or a deontologist – and answers that question in favor of deontology, it might seem like a minor, subsidiary question as to whether one should be an absolutist or a threshold deontologist. Yet this is not how the question of threshold deontology presents itself to me. Deontology without thresholds – whether my agent-centered kind or Alexander's patient-centered kind – is too counterintuitive to

[41] The three-layer cake metaphor is used to describe my view in Moore, *Causation and Responsibility*.

[42] This is to construe the "prima facie-ness" of prima facie duties as epistemic and not ontological. For the difference, see Moore, "Responses and Appreciations."

[43] Moore, *Placing Blame*, 722 n132.

be countenanced as a real possibility. If the choice comes down to consequentialism versus absolutist deontology, threshold deontology not being an option, then some form of consequentialism must be the correct ethics. So the stakes with threshold deontology are high, as high (because the same) as the stakes about deontology generally.

My aim in this paper has been modest and preliminary. It is not to argue decisively for there being thresholds within deontology, thresholds over which consequentialism again holds sway. It is rather to make the idea that there could be such thresholds seem natural and familiar. I seek thus to lower the burden that must be met to justify belief in threshold deontology – not to meet that burden by actually justifying threshold deontology itself.

23

Real-World Criminal Law and the Norm Against Punishing the Innocent

Two Cheers for Threshold Deontology

*Kevin Cole**

Deontological retributivists distinguish themselves from utilitarians and other consequentialists in significant part by focusing on how criminal law should treat the innocent. A utilitarian might oppose punishing a known innocent because the practice will cause net social harm. Deontological retributivists respond, "You lost me at 'because.'"[1] The utilitarian objection to punishing the innocent is contingent. But even if the facts always worked out so that utilitarians would not punish the innocent, a deontological retributivist – I'll generally shorten this to "retributivist" henceforth – objects that the utilitarian has misdescribed why people object to punishing the innocent. The utilitarian approach, retributivists argue, fails to capture our moral intuitions.[2]

One problem for retributivists is to explain how they can support any real-world punishment system. After all, not even the criminal law's elevated reasonable-doubt burden of persuasion eliminates all wrongful convictions. Here the retributivist sometimes invokes the "means principle" or "doctrine of double effect" (henceforth "DDE"). The norm against killing innocents arguably is not offended during war when a munitions plant is bombed, notwithstanding that neighboring innocents will predictably be killed. On the other hand, if the innocents are bombed in

* Thanks to Doug Husak and Don Dripps for helpful comments. As always, Larry Alexander has been a wonderful sounding board. Special thanks are due in this case, given the subject matter. Thanks also to Asal Alipanah for research assistance. In a recent piece, Kevin Cole, "Sex and the Single Malt Girl: How Voluntary Intoxication Affects Consent," *Montana Law Review* 78, no. 1 (2017): 155–86, I refer to an earlier draft of this article, which was then titled, "Mushy Morality and Exacting Criminal Law Theory."

1 See R.A. Duff, *Trials and Punishments* (Cambridge: Cambridge University Press, 1986), 160 ("The crucial charge is not that a consequentialist will in fact punish the innocent, but that she is ready to contemplate it as an open moral possibility").

2 See Duff, *Trials and Punishments*; see also, e.g., R.A. Duff, "In Defence of One Type of Retributivism: A Reply to Bagaric and Amarasekara," *Melbourne University Law Review* 24, no. 2 (2000): 441.

hopes of coercing their government into surrender, the norm is violated. Likewise, retributivists do not desire punishment of the innocent when they design a system that, regrettably, sometimes punishes the innocent. The DDE, however, is controversial in general and in its application to the inevitable punishment of innocents, leading some to continue to maintain that the inevitable factual mistakes in any imaginable system of punishment doom retributivism as a real-world guide.

The real world poses other problems for retributivists too. Some of the problems become clear only after the norm against punishing the innocent is fully elaborated. That elaboration is one goal of this paper. In addition to illustrating the problems that retributivism must address, elaborating the norm also helps to unify what otherwise could appear to be unconnected positions about the proper scope of the criminal law. In particular, retributivism might be thought to entail an obligation that the state define its crimes and its defenses in a way that tracks moral responsibility. Even some who invoke the DDE when confronted with inevitable fact-finding error may hesitate to license the state intentionally to choose legal definitions that make moral fault irrelevant.

For example, consider proxy crimes. These crimes aim at social harm indirectly, by punishing conduct that is often preparatory to causing the harm, or correlated to the harm. Affirmative-consent standards and "no-means-no" rules are examples of proxy crimes.[3] If a jurisdiction required a verbal "yes" as a predicate to sex, some partners might have sex without satisfying the predicate, but also without either of them suffering the serious social harm of sex in the absence of willingness. Likewise, a person might say "no" to sex while actually eager to have sex. Some retributivists object to proxy crimes, and the objections can be viewed as a corollary of the norm against punishing the innocent. Proof of the proxy crime does not demonstrate that the defendant acted immorally by culpably causing a social harm, as the crime itself is not defined in terms of the social harm. But proxy crimes are common, and absolute rejection of them by a retributivist principle will strike some as exposing retributivism as incapable of guiding law in the real world.

If retributive fault is thought to turn on an actor's subjective thought processes, other real-world challenges are apparent. The subjective focus has some appeal. Many a routine case involves an actor who perceives the moral wrong in a crime only opaquely. The more thoughtful mugger realizes that mugging does more than deprive the victim of property. It also affects the victim's sense of well-being, generates fear in the community, and so forth. The more thoughtful thief realizes that a stolen computer might not only have resale value but also store work that

[3] See Kevin Cole, "Better Sex Through Criminal Law: Proxy Crimes, Covert Negligence, and Other Difficulties of Affirmative Consent in the ALI's Draft Sexual Assault Provisions," *San Diego Law Review* 53, no. 3 (2016): 507.

is hard to recreate. If we knew that a criminal stole a victim's heirlooms not just because of what they would fetch from the fence, but also because their loss would inflict psychic pain on a reviled neighbor, would we not believe that the offender had done something worse than the run-of-the-mine burglar? But we know that real-world criminal law doesn't draw such fine distinctions among offenders. Does that fact demonstrate the folly of retributivism?

After tracing out the possible implications of the norm against punishing the innocent, this article explores whether the concept of "threshold deontology" might make retributivism compatible with real-world criminal law. Nozick famously argued that "absolute" rights might be overridden to avoid moral catastrophes. While we might be obligated not to kill the innocent or to engage in torture, those obligations might yield if a terrorist credibly threatened to blow up New York City unless we execute the mayor. The approach differs from utilitarianism in that simple net social benefit is insufficient to override the absolute norms. Michael Moore explored this idea and named it "threshold deontology." While Moore most extensively elaborated his views in addressing torture, he also suggested that the concept might come into play on lesser showings – far short of those brought to mind by the phrase "moral catastrophe" – when the norm being violated is less important than those against killing innocents and torture. For example, he suggested that threshold deontology could justify granting immunity to a guilty party to secure conviction of other guilty parties.[4] Having the guilty escape justice is an evil, but it is hardly the kind of evil that comes to mind when one hears the phrase "moral catastrophe."

This article addresses in detail an often-cited, careful, and creative critique of threshold deontology by Larry Alexander. This exercise may prove useful even to

4 Michael Moore, *Placing Blame: A General Theory of the Criminal Law* (Cambridge: Cambridge University Press, 1997), 158 (footnote omitted) (threshold deontologist might "qualifiedly disavow the practice except when it is needed to punish some very deserving criminal(s)"); Moore's later work suggests another possible approach to inducing a criminal's assistance by offering a sentence reduction: "It is plausible to think that those who design the general shape of legal institutions are necessarily consequentialist in their ethics. For such system designers necessarily adopt an agent-neutral view; such legal designers cannot justly regard *their* agency as the special source of their ('agent-relative') obligations. This is in contrast to actors within legal systems. Such institutions may require each agent to regard her obligations as categorical, that is, not to be traded off against others keeping or not keeping their like obligations … One might thus condemn … those judges who lighten the punishment of one guilty person in order to induce him to turn state's witness, and thus to secure the conviction and punishment of more guilty persons. But this would be at most a kind of 'government house' deontology, a 'deontology' to be followed by agents because the legal institution requiring their adherence to it will produce the best consequences overall." Michael S. Moore, "Four Reflections on Law and Morality," *William & Mary Law Review* 48, no. 5 (2007): 1523, 1551–52. Moore acknowledges this conclusion as "troublesome" for a "life-long committed deontologist," but argues, "at the level of allocating scarce social resources, I think the concession is inevitable." Ibid., 155 2n79. It is unclear whether Moore's view would vary in the (likely rare) case in which we can be sure that convictions of codefendants could not be achieved even in the absence of resource constraints.

those unconvinced about retributivism's need for it, as Alexander's argument calls into question whether threshold deontology can function coherently even in moderating absolute norms against torture and killing innocents.

After concluding that Alexander's critique does not doom threshold deontology, the article then considers the benefits of elaborating the retributive norm against punishing the innocent with threshold deontology in mind. The approach can explain many real-world deviations from retributive ideals. It may also reduce the impulse among some theorists to tweak ideal moral theory to make it fit real-world practices. Tweaking theory to fit our practices risks that the tweaked theory will migrate to realms in which the practicalities that motivated the tweaking are absent. Better to keep the theory ideal and focus on when the practicalities require an accommodation than to lose sight of what is ideal.

Finally, the article concludes with some doubts about the consequences of deploying threshold deontology as suggested. Perhaps it is better to reserve the concept for cases that fit the phrase "moral catastrophe" more comfortably. Though it may seem odd for a deontologist to worry about consequences, doing so in this setting does not involve compromising principles, but simply how we explain them. The persuasiveness of this concern will depend on how one assesses the problems associated with available alternatives.

23.1 THE RETRIBUTIVE NORM AGAINST PUNISHING THE INNOCENT

23.1.1 *The Factual-Error Problem*

Absolute rejection of punishing the innocent is a central feature of retributivism. As critic Russell Christopher observed, "retributivism is pitched as the only theory which, in justifying punishment, does justice by … not justifying punishment of the innocent."[5]

Attacks on retributivism have often suggested that this defining characteristic poses insurmountable difficulties for the theory. Even the milder, negative strand of retributivism – which does not recognize a deontological obligation to punish the guilty – still is argued to be violated by any imaginable system of real-world punishment. To observe an absolute norm against punishing the innocent would reject any real-world system of punishment altogether.[6] To balance the evil of punishing innocents against the good done by punishing would convert retributivism into a

5 Russell L. Christopher, "Deterring Retributivism: The Injustice of Just Punishment," *Northwestern University Law Review* 96, no. 3 (2002): 843.

6 See, e.g., George Schedler, "Can Retributivists Support Legal Punishment?" *The Monist* 63, no. 2 (1980): 185.

consequentialist theory. We might think of this as the "factual error" objection to retributivism.

Retributivists offer a familiar response, invoking the DDE or the means principle. For example, Michael Moore argues that "[a]gent-relative moral norms bind us absolutely only with respect to evils we either intend or (on some versions) knowingly visit on identified individuals."[7] This application of the DDE and the "analogous doctrine distinguishing knowing visitation of harms on specified people versus risking harm to some unidentified part of a class of persons"[8] leads Moore to conclude that the inevitability of punishing some innocents under any real-world punishment scheme is "not much of a worry"[9] for retributivism. Because such conduct does not violate an absolute norm, justification of real-world punishment can involve consequential tradeoffs among the intrinsic evil of (mistakenly) punishing the innocent, the intrinsic good of punishing the guilty, and the welfare gains accomplished through deterrence and the like.

While many retributivists invoke similar themes, the critics have not been placated.[10] I take no position on the palatability of the DDE generally or as applied to retributivism's factual-error problem. But as I argue below, retributivism might be saved from DDE critics by elaboration of the idea of threshold deontology.

23.1.2 *The Immoral-Law Problem*

Even those who accept something like Moore's approach to the factual-error problem may have qualms about extending it to related settings. For Christopher, the DDE becomes not retributivism's savior, but an instrument of its destruction. He argues that if the DDE cures retributivism's factual-error problem, it also liberates legislatures to embrace strict criminal liability statutes – also anathema for retributivists. The more general problem is one that I will somewhat misleadingly call the problem of "immoral law."[11]

7 Moore, *Placing Blame*, 157.

8 Ibid., 158n12.

9 Ibid., 158.

10 See, e.g., Louis Kaplow and Steven Shavell, "Fairness versus Welfare," *Harvard Law Review* 114, no. 4 (2001): 1274 (DDE's distinction between necessary and incidental effects "depends on arbitrary statements of the actual facts").

11 The phrase is a useful shorthand but it is misleading because, if threshold deontology or some other theory can justify criminal law that would otherwise deviate from our morality about whom to punish, then punishing that person no longer seems immoral. Compare Kenneth W. Simons, "Is Strict Criminal Liability in the Grading of Offences Consistent with Retributive Desert?" *Oxford Journal of Legal Studies* 32, no. 3 (2012): 445, 447 (distinguishing "formal" from "substantive" strict liability based on relationship of statutory elements to underlying wrong and canvassing authorities).

By "immoral law," I mean criminal law that, even if correctly applied, will punish those who are not morally deserving. The problem is not factual error. A strict-liability crime can impose liability on those who do not meet the moral conditions of blame, even when correctly applied. Proxy crimes of the type discussed earlier can cause the same result even when they include *mens rea* requirements. A robust "affirmative consent" regime, for example, may well require for conviction that an actor know or be reckless regarding whether the partner has failed to say "yes"; that requirement does not entail that the actor be culpable with respect to whether the partner was willing to have sex, or even whether the partner believed assent had been manifested or felt harmed in any way.[12]

Retributivists have often criticized strict-liability crimes and proxy crimes. These criticisms can be viewed as simple corollaries of the norm against punishing those known in fact not to have offended a validly enacted law (although some of the criticisms are less widely supported).[13] In his excellent recent book on mistake of law, Douglas Husak denies law's power to transform moral into immoral conduct.[14] Moore agrees:

> Staring at a red light stopped at an intersection in the middle of the night, and staying there until the light changes for no other reason than that the law says you should, is blind, stupid, irrational rule-worship. Good for sheep, bad for people.[15]

Whether so-called morals crimes are permissible, according to this view, depends on the correctness of the morality. For example, Moore objects to making bestiality a crime (without taking a position on whether doing so is good for sheep). For those, like Moore, who believe that private sexual activity among consenting adults is not immoral, legal moralism is a dispositive argument against criminalizing it.[16]

If the crime strongly correlates with immorality, however, but does not require proof of all of the requisites of immorality, matters are more complicated. Does such a crime offend an "absolute" agent-relative moral norm. Or does the DDE mean that such statutes escape retributivism's condemnation? Christopher argues

12 Consider, for example, a situation in which neither participant was aware of the law.

13 For example, some retributivists argue that fault is established by showing that an actor violated a known criminal prohibition. See Dan Markel, "Retributive Justice and the Demands of Democratic Citizenship," *Virginia Journal of Criminal Law* 1, no. 1 (2012): 1–133.

14 Douglas Husak, *Ignorance of Law: A Philosophical Inquiry* (Oxford: Oxford University Press 2016).

15 Michael S. Moore, "Legal Moralism Revisited" (a paper presented to the Conference on Legal Moralism, Institute for Law and Philosophy, University of San Diego, San Diego, California, 2016), 5 (copy on file with author).

16 See also Duff, *Trials and Punishments*, 154 ("A system of punishment is most obviously defective if it involves the deliberate punishment of the innocent"; one example is when "[t]he law prohibits and punishes what cannot properly be seen as an offence").

that the DDE cannot address retributivism's factual-error problem without causing this immoral-law problem.

Christopher's argument works only if retributivists' positions against proxy crimes are conceived as part of the core objection to punishing the innocent. If that objection is limited to punishing those who have not in fact violated a duly enacted law, a retributivist could still object to immoral law on consequentialist grounds, recognizing the punishment of the morally innocent as an evil but weighing it against the welfare gains accomplished through deterrence and the like and (for some) the intrinsic good of punishing the guilty. Distinguishing legal and moral responsibility in this way may seem unpalatable, however. It certainly would be in tension with the way retributivists have typically pitched their arguments against strict-liability offenses. But if distinguishing legal and moral responsibility is problematic, the DDE needs to be considered more carefully. Does it actually liberate legislatures to enact immoral law, because we can never be sure whether any particular person who is convicted is not actually a person who deserves moral blame?

Arguably, immoral law generates mistakes that are, for purposes of the DDE, relevantly different from factual errors. Willful blindness doctrine provides an analogue. When a jury mistakenly thinks that a defendant killed the victim, the jury has tried to figure out whether the act occurred. At least when other actors, like the sentencing judge, lack authority to take account of a morally relevant fact, the legislature's decision to take that fact off the table involves a decision to look the other way. Perhaps the absolute norm is that we may not punish those whom we know are morally innocent. If the state has avoided asking the morally pertinent questions – and indeed precludes evidence on those questions – it is willfully blind regarding the defendant's innocence.

As a legal matter, willful blindness often is defined as requiring a high probability of a fact before requiring inquiry into the fact. If this legal requirement is viewed as having moral implications for what constitutes knowledge for purposes of the DDE, it might sort immoral law into categories. Statutes defined so that legal guilt strongly correlates with moral guilt might be viewed as acceptable, while those offering only a looser fit would offend the retributive norm against punishing the innocent (because the risk of moral innocence is so high that we regard the state as willfully blind regarding that possibility, and hence unable to invoke the DDE). At the very least, this sorting is not conspicuous among retributivists who have objected to strict-liability and proxy crimes.[17]

[17] The outcome might be similar to the idea espoused in Duff, *Trials and Punishments*, 159 ("A practicable system of punishment cannot [entirely avoid punishing the innocent]; it can take all 'reasonable', but not all possible, precautions against the risk").

It is not obvious that the "high probability" requirement is sound, however.[18] If it is not, then the DDE may not help the legislature defend immoral law. But the implication is not that all proxy crimes are suspect and that every criminal law must be written precisely to jibe with moral responsibility. Threshold deontology might justify some legislative deviations from ideal morality if the DDE does not.

23.1.3 *Bargain Justice*

Retributivism has been criticized as inconsistent with the prevalence of plea bargaining in our system.[19] If bargaining is inevitable, then bargain justice is another challenge to retributivism's ability to provide real-world guidance – though a challenge that implicates the norm against punishing the innocent only indirectly.

Regardless of what one thinks about the DDE as applied to the problems of factual error and immoral law, the DDE cannot square retributivism with bargain justice. Prosecutors know that some people with whom they cut deals are getting less punishment than they deserve – or no punishment at all – to permit focusing resources on more deserving targets. The phrase "bargain justice" understates the problem. Sometimes prosecutors cut defendants loose without getting anything from the defendant in return.

Moore invoked threshold deontology as a possible justification for this practice.[20] Bargain justice does not invariably implicate the norm against punishing the innocent – though it might.[21] But it does show the importance of threshold deontology to squaring retributivism with the practicalities of contemporary criminal law enforcement.

23.2 THE MORAL BALLAST CRITIQUE OF THRESHOLD DEONTOLOGY

Threshold deontology has been subjected to critical reexamination in scholarship generated by recent reports of harsh interrogation techniques by agents of the United States. Much of the scholarship critical of the practice cites an article by

[18] See Alexander F. Sarch, "Willful Ignorance, Culpability, and the Criminal Law," *Saint John's Law Review* 88, no. 4 (2014): 1023, 1050 (objecting to high-probability requirement). However, Sarch would equate willful blindness with knowledge when the actor fails to undertake "reasonable" investigation, and the reasonableness of an investigation partially depends on the likelihood that the fact is true, reintroducing this issue at another point in the analysis.

[19] See, e.g., Russell L. Christopher, "The Prosecutor's Dilemma: Bargains and Punishments," *Fordham Law Review* 72, no. 1 (2003): 93.

[20] See Moore, *Placing Blame*, 158; Moore, "Four Reflections," 1523, 1551–52.

[21] To encourage pleas, legislatures may authorize sentences that exceed the desert of offenders. In addition to inducing some innocents to plead guilty, this technique can punish in excess of desert the guilty who stand trial.

my colleague Larry Alexander.[22] That article questions the moral attractiveness of threshold deontology. But while often cited and relied on, the article has not often been subjected to careful examination.

23.2.1 *The Critique*

Alexander makes two arguments against threshold deontology. One is the claim that setting N is arbitrary. Since the difference between what is morally wrong and morally right cannot be arbitrary, threshold deontology should be abandoned in favor of an absolute deontology or consequentialism. To those who argue that "categorical objections to even our clearest moral wrongs (e.g., murder, torture) should be overridden" to avoid "the destruction of New York City,"[23] Alexander might respond, "How about Newark?"

In making the arbitrariness claim, Alexander expressly follows an argument developed by Anthony Ellis.[24] But Ellis's elaboration of the arbitrariness argument comes to different conclusions. After stating that nonabsolutist deontology "is the form that appeals to most people,"[25] Ellis concludes that absolutist deontology suffers the same arbitrariness problem.[26] Indeed, in the end, Ellis rejects both absolutist deontology and consequentialism, preferring "the middle ground" staked out by threshold deontology to either absolute theory, each of which "simply strains moral belief."[27]

[22] Larry Alexander, "Deontology at the Threshold," *San Diego Law Review* 37, no. 4 (2000): 893. The article has been cited in at least forty law review articles, including Michael T. Cahill, "Retributive Justice in the Real World," *Washington University Law Review* 85, no. 4 (2007): 815; Russell L. Christopher, "The Prosecutor's Dilemma: Bargains and Punishments," *Fordham Law Review* 72, no. 1 (2003): 93; Christopher, "Deterring Retributivism," 843, which rely on Alexander's critique in dismissing threshold deontology as a means of squaring retributivism with real-world practices.

[23] Carol S. Steiker, "No, Capital Punishment is Not Morally Required: Deterrence, Deontology, and the Death Penalty," *Sanford Law Review* 58, no. 3 (2005): 751, 783.

[24] Anthony Ellis, "Deontology, Incommensurability and the Arbitrary," *Philosophy and Phenomenological Research* 52, no. 4 (1992): 855.

[25] Ibid., 857.

[26] Ibid., 871. Ellis cautions of the "need to be sure that [absolutist] theories [do] not generate inconsistencies of the sort I have claimed non-absolutist deontology will generate." He doubts that absolutist deontology can pass muster. Consider Alexander's absolute deontological alternative to threshold deontology: "the best conception of deontology would deem its core principle to be that one may never use another as a resource without his consent. In other words, a person's body, labor, and talents do not exist for others' benefit except to the extent that he freely chooses to benefit others." Alexander, "Deontology at the Threshold," 911. Just as one example, how would Alexander distinguish between police questioning of a suspect that is permissible and conduct that crosses the line? How much coercion is sufficient to preclude free choice? This determination seems no less arbitrary than those called for by threshold deontology.

[27] Ellis, "Deontology, Incommensurability and the Arbitrary," 871.

My focus here is on Alexander's other argument – that threshold deontology treats people as "pure moral ballast, serving no purpose other than to create a duty to save someone else, or to override a right that stands as an obstacle to saving someone else."[28] He gives two examples. The first he calls "The Terrorist's Mother." A terrorist has captured and hidden N hostages in different locations. At each location is a bomb that will automatically detonate at a specified time unless the terrorist's demands are met. So the police grab the terrorist's mother and torture her on live TV, believing this will lead the terrorist to reveal the location of the hostages and the bombs. Moved by the police conduct, the terrorist phones police headquarters, but reveals the location of only one of the bombs and one of the hostages. Since the lives now at risk number less than N, Alexander argues, the police must stop torturing the terrorist's mother. All the remaining hostages have just been used as moral ballast, authorizing torture of the mother to save the one hostage, which would not have been permissible if only the single hostage's life had been at stake in the first place.

Alexander's other example, "The Rescue," is structurally similar. Alexander argues that if the negative duties of morality can be overridden by sufficiently good consequences, then sufficiently good consequences should similarly be capable of imposing positive duties, like duties to rescue. He plausibly argues that the N required to override a negative duty might often be greater than the N required to impose a positive duty to perform a simple, low-risk rescue. He hypothesizes 20 people trapped on a housetop as flood waters rapidly rise to engulf them. Rescuer has a large boat that can easily and safely accommodate the imperiled 20. Assume that the N to impose a duty to bring this boat over to perform the rescue is 20. As Rescuer draws nearer, one of the stranded persons jumps into Rescuer's boat. Realizing that only N–1 lives are now at risk, Rescuer pulls away from the house, leaving the other 19 people to die.

What is the nature of threshold deontology's moral ballast problem? It differs from the arbitrariness objection, in Alexander's view.[29] Presumably, it also differs from the deontological critique that consequentialism uses people as means for others' ends. Obviously, such a critique could sometimes be directed at a theory that sometimes uses an approach that can always be so faulted. So Alexander must think that the moral ballast problem taps into some other intuition that will lead us to object to threshold deontology – perhaps that threshold deontology justifies norm violations when fewer than N lives are actually saved, perhaps something else.

[28] Alexander, "Deontology at the Threshold," 901.

[29] Ibid., 905. Alexander discusses the moral ballast objection before turning to his arbitrariness point. When he begins his discussion of arbitrariness, he states that the prior sections of his article, including the moral ballast discussion, involved "identifying puzzles and raising questions about deontological thresholds without assuming … that the numbers of the various Ns are themselves arbitrary."

23.2.2 *Critiquing the Critique*

Alexander's moral ballast arguments depend on the conclusion that the threshold deontologist would, before N can be reached, require the torture to stop in The Terrorist's Mother and the duty to cease in The Rescue. In one set of cases, the conclusion is not troubling. In the other, it is wrong.

The nontroubling set involves mistakes about the likely utility of the planned course of action. If we knew *ex ante* that torturing the terrorist's mother would not yield any benefit, then of course we would prefer not to violate the norm against torture. But even pure deontological theories can lead to mistaken conduct. Self-defense against a perceived aggressor may turn out to be a deadly misunderstanding. If that possibility poses no problem for the deontologist, then why does the possibility of undertaking a mistaken course of conduct pose a problem for the threshold deontologist? Just as a person acting in perceived self-defense must stop striking blows if it becomes obvious that his "attacker" is not really a threat, a threshold deontologist must stop torturing when it becomes clear that N cannot be reached. If people are used as "moral ballast" when the threshold deontologist saves one person before realizing his mistake, why isn't the person who acts in perceived self-defense also using his "attacker" as moral ballast to save himself until he realizes his mistake?

The other set of cases requires more discussion. The torturer thinks *ex ante* that a course of conduct will lead to the release of N hostages, or we think *ex ante* that imposing a duty in a particular situation will lead to the saving of N lives. Assume the hardest case to defend. The torturer thinks that torturing the terrorist's mother will save exactly N lives (for otherwise he can't start the torture), but the torturer also thinks that the terrorist will only release one hostage each hour. Does that mean the torturer cannot begin, because he knows that after an hour he'll have to stop, and only one person (not N) will have been saved?

Alexander's assertion that the torture must stop in The Terrorist's Mother also implies that it should not begin in the example above. These conclusions make sense if two assumptions are true: first, that the norm against torture is a single, indivisible prohibition; and second, that the N for any violation of the norm is a constant.[30]

Fortunately, our everyday experiences do not force us to develop nuanced approaches. Most of us are never in a situation in which the torture or intentional killing of an innocent seems even remotely defensible. If we were in such situations, however, surely we would draw distinctions among different degrees of torture. And perhaps we would develop intuitions about what N would be necessary to subject

[30] See ibid., 904–5. Alexander acknowledges that N might vary, but does not discuss how that fact affects his moral ballast critique.

the terrorist's mother to 20 lashes, what N would be necessary to subject the terrorist's mother to 40 lashes, and the like. We would not assume that the N to apply the first lash is exactly half of the N needed to apply two – the awfulness of torturing at all implies that the N for the first unit of torture would be higher than the N that would justify the next, even if that second N should be significant.

If one approaches the inquiry in this way, then it is plausible to argue that the torturer could begin mistreating the terrorist's mother even if fully cognizant that the terrorist might release one hostage right away. In thinking about whether to begin the torture, the torturer would need to think about the course of conduct necessary to effect release of the hostages. This would be an agonizing process, one that would not even be needed until a quite high N were plausible. But if saving N40 lives by 40 lashes is acceptable, it may remain acceptable regardless of whether all N people are released at once or if 1/40 are released in response to each lash. Accordingly, the torturer might proceed even if he perceives that the terrorist is likely to trickle out hostages.

This is not to say that the torturer can administer 40 lashes whenever it appears that completing the plan will result in the saving of N40 hostages. Suppose the terrorist releases all the hostages but one after the first lash (the last hostage is the President, whom the terrorist is especially reluctant to release). Even if the torturer remains convinced that the terrorist will release the President if the remaining 39 lashes are administered, the torturer needs to make a calculation: Does the life of the President equal N39? In other words, even if N1 is less than half of N2, at some point the lives at stake in continuing the course of torture is too small to justify its continuation. If the torturer anticipated all of this before beginning, and if the President's life does not equal N39, then, before beginning, the torturer would need to think not about what constitutes N40, but about what constitutes N1.

If the above is correct, then Alexander is wrong to assume that the threshold deontologist must stop torturing in The Terrorist's Mother after the first hostage is released. Whether he must stop depends on whether continuing the course of conduct will satisfy a different and possibly lower N from the one required to begin torturing in the first place. If not, he must stop. But if he anticipated this chain of events, he should not have started in the first place, and his mistake raises no problem for the threshold deontologist that doesn't also face the absolute deontologist.

The Rescue is similar. The imposition on liberty associated with a positive duty may not be distributed equally across the time required to perform the duty. When Rescuer is told he must rescue the 20, he needs to get out of his chair, switch off the TV, perhaps tell his spouse that the opera will have to wait, gas up the boat, and spend time getting to the housetop. Whether he rescues 1 or 20, he must then navigate back to safety, and perhaps undertake some paperwork or lobbying to get reimbursed for his expenses. Accordingly, even if we fully anticipated that our survivors would board the boat seriatim, we might impose a duty on Rescuer to stay long enough to rescue everyone. The original calculation should entail assessment of the degree to which the required rescue would impose on Rescuer's liberty, including the rescue's duration. One can imagine a case in which rescuing all 20 would not be justified. Perhaps one survivor's foot is stuck in the roof, requiring considerable time and effort to extricate the person. If known in advance, this fact might preclude imposing the duty (because saving the 19 would not justify the necessary imposition on liberty). If discovered during the rescue, the trapped survivor might justifiably be left on the roof (because the extra time and effort associated with imposing a positive duty is not offset by an N of 1). Or the duty might make sense, given that the boat is already at the house, the opera has been missed, and so forth. Just as the harm in torture might be front-loaded, the imposition on liberty of requiring rescue might be front-loaded. It accordingly does not follow – and is even unlikely – that a barely sustainable duty to rescue would cease once the first person is saved.

Threshold deontology might be conceived of differently. We could imagine that a single N governs any instance of torture, and that beginning on a course of torture requires that N will be achieved, but that once that belief has been established, the torturer should think like a simple consequentialist. Obviously, this is not the approach Alexander is critiquing. If it were, then his thought experiments would not conclude with the torturer being required to stop and the rescuer being relieved of a duty. This alternative approach to threshold deontology has the virtue of simplicity. It also has the vices of simplicity. For even if the wrong in torture is front-loaded, plenty of wrong can still be done in the middle and at the end. Just because a person has been compelled by circumstances to become a torturer does not mean that he should be free thereafter to be a consequentialist.

What I hope to have shown is that threshold deontology survives Alexander's arguments against it. I now proceed to how threshold deontology might be deployed in more common situations. While torturing and intentionally killing the innocent may require a nearly unimaginable N even in the least severe instances, punishing the morally innocent might satisfy an N that is all too common. Moore himself has suggested that threshold deontology might have something to say about "moral catastrophes" far less catastrophic than even the destruction of Newark.[31]

23.3 THRESHOLD DEONTOLOGY AND THE NORM AGAINST PUNISHING THE INNOCENT

If threshold deontology remains viable, its intersection with the retributive norm against punishing the innocent is in some respects obvious. For example, the

[31] See Moore, *Placing Blame*, 158; Moore, "Four Reflections," 1523, 1551–52.

factual-error problem has a solution even for those who reject the DDE in its most plausible form.[32] As two critics of retributivism argued, "retributivists who believe that schemes of punishment can never countenance punishment of the innocent must defend a regime that is tantamount to anarchy."[33] But whatever N means in the context of punishing the innocent, one surmises that N < anarchy. Requiring proof of crime that cannot be disputed would enable so much crime that threshold deontology would override the norm against punishing the innocent.

Other exceptions to the norm against punishing the innocent pose closer questions. On litigating culpability and strict-liability crimes, the cost of assessing mental state generally may not meet the N that would be required to enact Lady Wootton's famous proposal to dispense with those determinations. The case for particular strict-liability crimes may be closer, but retributivists may be right to think it never surpasses the threshold to justify the practice.

Crimes defined using proxies for immorality will more often be justifiable, but threshold deontology offers no blank check for such provisions. When possession crimes are justifiable, the fact of possession is strong proof of the possessor's intention to bring about the harm that the crime seeks to avoid. In such cases, a jury can be asked to draw the inference of nefarious purpose. If the penalty for possession of a given drug quantity is set as if the possessor planned to distribute, even though the quantity is consistent with personal use, the incremental punishment imposed on the possessor innocent of the intent to distribute should be justified by a showing of N, which may be less than the N needed to risk punishing the altogether innocent, but still a significant threshold.

On the other hand, consider a crime like statutory rape. Even if the crime dispenses with the historical strict-liability approach on the age element, one could object that it is an instance of immoral law. What we care about, the argument runs, isn't the age of any particular sex partner, but rather the maturity of the person, or the possibility that the person has been coerced. We could forbid sex with an immature person, or through coercion. By using age as a proxy, we create the risk that an actor will be punished notwithstanding the lack of social harm in the activity (because the young person is unusually mature or impervious to coercion), or that the actor will be punished notwithstanding a lack of culpability with respect to those harms (because the actor was mistaken as to the young person's maturity or malleability).

32 But see Duff, "In Defence of One Type of Retributivism," 441 ("a retributivist response must appeal to some version of the 'doctrine of double effect' ").

33 Kaplow and Shavell, "Fairness versus Welfare," 1269.

Like the analysis above, the consequences of requiring proof of the morally relevant facts need attention. Wishful thinking about the partner's maturity might be especially likely, and the actor's culpability regarding that issue would be harder to prove even than the actor's culpability about an adult partner's willingness. If the harm to victims is particularly acute, smaller deterrent losses might be thought to satisfy N. Moreover, the vagueness of a standard written in terms of "adequate maturity" would inevitably result in the discriminatory enforcement sought to be avoided by the legality principle.[34]

The example permits discussion of another reason that what some will regard as immoral law might sometimes satisfy N. People will disagree on morality, at least at the margins. How mature is mature enough to consent to sexual relations? Any verbal formulation on which people can agree will include open-ended concepts like reasonableness that people would apply differently in concrete cases. Framing the crime in abstract terms, then, will punish the innocent from the standpoint of those who agree with the verbal formulation but disagree with how most people would apply it. Framing the crime in more precise terms – by picking a somewhat arbitrary age of consent of 16 – will strike some as convicting the morally innocent too often, but strike others as still underprotecting too many victims. To identify social consensus on moral commitments may require adopting statutes that don't jibe with anyone's moral commitments precisely.[35] The alternative is to eschew any law that cannot capture perfectly our moral intuitions. Like an overly high burden of proof, an overly exacting requirement of morally precise social consensus in drafting the criminal law would invite anarchy, and N < anarchy when it comes to immoral law.[36]

Husak's mistake-of-law proposals permit a final, somewhat extended discussion of how threshold deontology can translate the norm against punishing the innocent into real-world criminal law. Husak's proposals are made with full recognition that moral theory might not translate directly to criminal law.[37] The problem is even

[34] Compare Moore, *Placing Blame*, 172 (retributivists are not "monomaniacally focused on the achievement of retributive justice. The retributivist like anyone else can admit that there are other intrinsic goods, such as the goods protected by the rights to life, liberty, and bodily integrity. The retributivist can also admit that sometimes some of these rights will trump the achieving of retributive justice").

[35] Compare Duff, *Trials and Punishments*, 275. ("I do not suppose that we could hope to identify a determinate set of moral demands which everyone must or will agree are necessary, in every detail, to the existence and survival of the community. Any set of determinate criminal laws must therefore take particular – and contestable – moral demands"); see also Cass R. Sunstein, "Incompletely Theorized Agreements in Constitutional Law," *Social Responsibility* 74, no. 1 (2007): 1.

[36] For a different and helpful discussion, see Kenneth W. Simons, "Understanding the Topography of Moral and Criminal Law Norms," in *Philosophical Foundations of Criminal Law*, ed. R.A. Duff and Stuart Green (Oxford: Oxford University Press, 2011), 228.

[37] Husak, *Ignorance of Law*, 19 ("Almost certainly we need to retreat from the ideal I defend, but it is instructive to identify the ideal from which retreat must occur").

greater than Husak's description suggests, for his moral theory implies the relevance of facts he does not discuss. The extension, however, actually strengthens the case that a threshold deontologist could recognize an "absolute" prohibition on immoral law but justify the compromises Husak supports.

Rejecting "quality-of-will" approaches to responsibility, Husak endorses a "reason-responsiveness" theory. His approach has a substantially more subjective focus than does a quality-of-will theory. Husak worries about the palatability of his conclusions in extreme cases. "The specter that serial rapists would escape their just deserts because they manage to convince themselves that nonconsensual sex is morally permissible has colored countless discussions of the topic of *ignorantia juris*,"[38] he notes. Moreover, the politically motivated terrorist who truly believes in the cause would seem similarly to escape punishment under Husak's theory.[39] Husak offers some ideas on how to escape these apparent instances of *reductio*. It is understandable, given the myriad other issues he explores in detail, that he does not devote much attention to the question of when moral imperatives should yield in the face of these unacceptable consequences.

A second worry derives from Husak's views on the role of law in establishing wrongdoing. Because he rejects the view that violating a democratically adopted law is always morally wrong, he acknowledges a disconnect between his theory of responsibility and his project on mistake of law. If knowing you are violating a law does not establish you're wrong, then how can ignorance of law be exculpatory? Here, Husak responds by accepting the importance of legality in translating moral norms into criminal law acceptable in a liberal society. But his legality arguments focus on the reasons that a state should not punish an actor for immoral conduct that does not violate preexisting law. One might distinguish punishing for immoral but legal conduct from the related but different question – whether an actor who knows he is violating the law should still be able to defend on the grounds that he did not think his conduct was immoral.

On Husak's first worry, the problem extends beyond the terrorist and the serial rapist unconcerned with a partner's consent. As mentioned previously, criminals will appreciate the wrongfulness of their conduct with varying degrees of precision – some muggers no doubt understand that their victims suffer not just a loss of property but also a lost sense of security. Husak's preferred theory implies that this fact is relevant to just punishment, an implication that rings true. But the law does not generally make inquiries of this type – at least, not formally.

38 Ibid.

39 Model Penal Code § 210.6(4)(d) (the attractiveness of Husak's theory of responsibility gains support from the Model Penal Code, which recognized the actor's belief in the justifiability of conduct as a reason against imposing the death penalty).

Does that fact reveal that Husak's brand of retributivism is repudiated by everyday experience?

A threshold deontologist might well recognize that facts like these matter to an offender's moral desert but nevertheless support immoral law that does not consider them, at least so long as the offender knew that the conduct in question was illegal. Efforts at concealment, flight, and the like will often convince us that an actor at least suspected that his or her conduct might be criminal. While a person's awareness of illegality implies awareness of at least the risk of immorality, the ability to rationalize one's own bad behavior would make the inference at least somewhat doubtful in many cases. How do we fathom whether a thief is being truthful when claiming that the unjust distribution of goods in society morally justified the thief's property crimes? Adjudicating *mens rea* questions the law currently asks can be difficult, but adjudicating *mens rea* regarding morality would be far more difficult. And making the question legally relevant might itself promote a failure to internalize sound moral norms.

23.4 THE MISSING CHEER

To this point, I have tried to rebut challenges to threshold deontology and show how the concept could reconcile current law with a robust retributive norm against punishing the innocent. Doing so might enhance clarity about ideal moral theory by reducing pressures to adjust the theory to fit the world. A variable N drives this approach. If the N to enact criminal law departing from moral blame were the same as the N to kill or torture an innocent, it would not be met. If we litigated whether defendants perceived the immorality of their own conduct, neither New York nor Newark nor even Ottumwa would fall.

If threshold deontology is deployed in this way, then, it will be deployed more often than in cases conjured up by the phrase "moral catastrophe." Treating a robust norm against punishing the innocent as an "absolute," overridden only when N is satisfied, means that N is often satisfied – when many, if not most, criminal laws are enacted, and perhaps even whenever a person is punished in the presence of some doubt. Such an approach might have bad consequences in the areas in which threshold deontology was first introduced. We expect decisions to kill known innocents to be rare. We once expected decisions to torture to be rare, and may still so expect even in an era of terror. Saying that N may often be satisfied regarding the norm against punishing the innocent may mislead people into thinking that N is too easy to satisfy as regards more serious transgressions.

Whether these concerns should limit threshold deontology turns in part on the alternatives available to reach morally sound outcomes. One could give up on viewing the norm against punishing the innocent as an "absolute." Or one could limit the "absolute" norm to the legally (but not morally) innocent, viewing the norm against punishing the morally innocent to be amenable to being traded off to achieve other goods.[40] Either strategy might be thought to dilute the moral force of retributivism's arguments against utilitarianism. And distinguishing legal guilt from moral guilt is in tension with typical retributive objections to strict liability and seems to treat the core retributive objection to utilitarianism as focused on lying rather than on justice.

If these objections are dismissed, then one could generate the same results by viewing the duty not to punish the innocent as either an "absolute" norm or as an intrinsic good. The consequentialist move would not collapse into utilitarianism, as the evil of punishing the innocent would not depend solely on welfare effects. The value assigned to the inherent evil of punishing the innocent could outweigh predicted welfare benefits of punishing the innocent in exactly the same cases as would an "absolute" norm, subject to a threshold. It's just that the value assigned to the inherent evil of punishing the innocent would be the focus, rather than N.

However, some object to consequentialist retributivism itself. David Dolinko has argued that "'consequentialist retributivism' is not, in fact, a coherent form of retributivism at all, given a quite standard view … as to what retributivism is"; that "to be both a consequentialist and a retributivist is not, after all, a tenable position; it is well-nigh impossible, given a standard account of retributivism"; and "that a consequentialist version of retributivism actually encounters grave difficulties, and that these difficulties reflect the problematic nature of retributivism itself."[41] Those convinced by Dolinko's arguments will not view consequentialist retributivism as a costless haven.

I leave the reader to decide whether the problems with a generally applied threshold deontology are preferable to the alternatives. Thinking about the impacts of various versions of threshold deontology might seem at odds with deontological commitments. But the tension is more apparent than real. How the deontologist would resolve concrete cases does not change – only how they are explained. Labels are not the stuff of morality.

[40] See Moore, *Placing Blame*, 172.

[41] The quotations are identified in Cahill, "Retributive Justice in the Real World," 864–65nn155–56 (quoting David Dolinko, "Retributivism, Consequentialism, and the Intrinsic Goodness of Punishment," *Law and Philosophy* 16, no. 5 (1997): 507, 510, 513, 508); see also Christopher, "The Prosecutor's Dilemma," 146–69 (canvassing Dolinko's arguments without explicitly embracing them). Cahill himself is unconvinced by Dolinko's arguments. See Cahill, "Retributive Justice," 865–66.

23.5 CONCLUSION

I hope to have shown the potential significance of threshold deontology for real-world criminal law – and some difficulties. I also hope to have rebutted Larry Alexander's "moral ballast" critique. As always, though, his critique is careful, thoughtful, challenging, and important.

24

Conclusion

Appreciation and Responses

Larry Alexander

Before responding to the authors in this volume, I want to express my immense gratitude for their serious attention to my work, even if it is work with which they disagree. We scholars obviously believe that what we write is correct, at least at the time we write it. And if we have not recanted our previous views, then naturally, believing those views to be correct, we hope to convert everyone to our point of view. But of course, being realists, we know how unlikely that result will be. Moreover, we also, being realists, know that many, if not all, the views of which we are currently convinced will ultimately be shown to be erroneous. Our more realistic hope is that those views will be treated seriously, and, if incorrect, their errors will prove instructive for other scholars as they seek the truth.

So it is a fulfillment of my scholarly ambition that such an esteemed group of scholars has responded to my work in this volume and at the conference that preceded it. I want to thank each and every one of them for doing so. As you will see in what follows, I was generally not convinced by their criticisms. At most, they administered "only flesh wounds." But perhaps I am just being obstinate, with my ego preventing me from confessing error. You, the reader, will decide.

Finally, I want to thank those who made this Festschrift volume possible: the University of Illinois Program in Law and Philosophy and the dean of that law school, Vikram Amar; Yale Law School and its then dean, Robert Post; and above all, Heidi Hurd. Heidi conceived of this volume and its preceding conference, organized it, got Cambridge University Press to publish it, wrote the introduction and edited the contributions, and in general worked tirelessly to make it all happen. I am eternally indebted to her for her heroic efforts on my behalf, and I thank her from the bottom of my heart.

24.1 RESPONSES TO PART I

The authors in this part are Douglas Husak, Antony Duff, David Brink, Peter Westen, and Gideon Yaffe. I will respond to them in that order.

Douglas Husak argues that we retributivists have paid precious little attention to the modes of retributive punishments. When we argue that in virtue of Sue's culpable conduct she deserves punishment, we tend to then shut up and move on to something else. Not only do we not dwell on how much punishment Sue deserves – our neglect of how to equilibrate desert with cardinal levels of punishment is an embarrassing lacuna, one that our critics have noted – but we have also neglected, though not entirely, the relation between deserved punishment and deserved suffering. What suffering does and does not count as the suffering deserved for purposes of punishment?

Husak's concern with modes of punishment encompasses the latter question, if not the former. But it also addresses questions that are different from those. Incarceration, for example, produces deserved suffering through its duration. One advantage it has is that it keeps open the possibility that we will discover that the prisoner was innocent of the crime for which he is doing time, and that we will do so in time to release him and make some kind of compensation. Another advantage is that incarceration incapacitates as well as punishes. On the other hand, incarceration surely has its drawbacks: It is expensive, often criminogenic, and quite uneven in the amount of suffering it inflicts.

Consider, by contrast, this ancient but now unused mode of punishment, corporal punishment. Corporal punishment is cheap. It takes little time out of the offender's life. It is not known to be criminogenic. And it can probably be tailored to deliver equivalent amounts of suffering to offenders who are similarly deserving but who have different pain tolerances. On the other hand, errors in determining offenders' deserts will often be revealed too late to stop the punishment, leaving only compensation as the available remedy for the injustice. And corporal punishment provides little incapacitation of those offenders likely to reoffend.

Husak himself, although making the point that retributivists have been unconcerned with the mode by which deserved punishment is delivered, endorses what he calls the deferential view that justifies retributivists' lack of concern qua retributivists. He concedes that if dignity rules out some or all corporal punishments, and dignity is viewed as internal to retributivism, then retributivism might have a position on the modes of punishment. And he notes that Kant, an arch retributivist, endorsed the *lex talionis*, which is all about such modes. But Husak is not sure whether the principles against undignified or barbaric modes of punishment are internal to retributivism or are instead external constraints on the delivery of retributivist punishments.

Near the end of his comment, Husak takes up an issue that should be central to retributivism, namely, how to distinguish punishment from other causes of offenders' suffering. Must that suffering be intended as a response to desert, and if so, by whom – the legislature, the judge, the warden? (If an offender is "punished" by vigilantes, has she already been "punished" enough when she is brought to trial by the state?) Or does some unintended (as punishment) suffering also count? (If an offender suffers a painful injury on the way to being flogged for an offense, has she then already been "punished" enough? Or if she was mistakenly punished in the past for a crime she didn't commit, and commits that very crime, has she already been punished enough? Or how does other undeserved suffering in her life count when we ask what punishment she deserves for an offense?)

I think, as does Husak, that these are enormously important questions for retributivists. And they have been relatively neglected by them. I thank Husak for making sure they are on our agenda.

Antony Duff takes on one of Kim Ferzan's and my most controversial positions, namely, that results do not affect culpability and desert. A completed attempt to kill, steal, or rape is, for us, as deserving of punishment as killing, a theft, or a rape. And reckless endangerment is as deserving of punishment as reckless killing, injuring, or destroying – assuming that the degree of recklessness is the same.

Duff, on the other hand, is in the "results matter" camp. He begins his criticism of our view by looking at a hypothetical I used in an article before I teamed up with Ferzan. In that hypothetical, a gang has the following initiation rite: Each would-be member is given a rifle and told that it contains either a blank or a live shell, with blanks being far more likely than a live shell. The would-be member is then told that to be admitted to the gang, he must put the barrel of the rifle through a hole in an opaque screen, behind which a hapless individual has been shackled. The hole through which the barrel of the rifle is inserted is positioned so that the barrel points at the shackled person's heart. Having been told this, the would-be member must then pull the trigger. If he refuses, he will not be admitted to the gang.

Suppose, in addition, that there are several candidates for admission to the gang, and each is given the same instructions. And suppose most or all of them pull the trigger of their rifles.

If they believed what the gang told them and still pulled the trigger, I would deem all who did so culpable for recklessly risking homicide. It would not matter to me whether there really was someone shackled behind the screen, and if there was, whether some initiate who pulled a trigger had a live round that killed the shackled person. Based solely on what those who pulled their triggers believed, they would be equally culpable, whether or not there was a death, and if not, whether there was ever a potential victim or a live round. On the other hand, their culpability is individual, not collective, for they are not collaborators. They have no guarantee that others will pull their triggers, and their admittance into the gang does not depend on what others do. The bottom line: If they pull their trigger, they are culpable for recklessly endangering a life, whether or not they have a live round, whether or not there really is someone behind the screen, and whether or not, if there is, that person is killed by their bullet, by someone else's, or not at all.

Duff, because he is a "results matter" theorist, obviously disagrees with my conclusions. Presumably, in the absence of collaboration – agreement among the would-be members that they will all pull their triggers – he would convict the one who pulled the trigger of the gun with a live bullet, which kills the person behind the screen, of reckless homicide, and he would convict all the others who pulled their triggers of the lesser crime of reckless endangerment. As I said, I would convict the "killer" of reckless endangerment along with the others, which crime I might punish more severely than Duff perhaps would. That's the basic difference between us "results don't matter" folks and the "results matter" folks like Duff.

Duff defends the significance of results by noting the possible psychological reaction to the attempted killing that fails. If the unsuccessful attempter is sincerely repentant, he might say, "Thank God I failed."

Is the unsuccessful attempter letting himself off the hook he would have been impaled on had he succeeded? Duff does not think so. And Duff is surely correct that, psychologically, we do think "results matter." If we drive recklessly and narrowly miss hitting a pedestrian, we breathe a sigh of relief and after a short time tend to forget about it, whereas if we injure or kill a pedestrian, we are often wracked with guilt even if we did not drive recklessly.

Duff relies on such psychological facts. But there are psychological facts on my side. If we have told our young sons not to hit baseballs in the backyard because the balls could go over the fence and onto the neighbor's property, but they ignore our command and both hit balls over the fence – one ball landing harmlessly in the neighbor's yard, the other breaking a window – we do not conduct a forensic test to determine which kid hit which ball. We punish them equally.

Or if a friend has lost a valuable ring somewhere on a field, and Joe says he'll search the north half of the field, and Barb says she'll search the south half, do we really want to say that the one who finds the ring deserves more praise and thanks than the one who didn't, at least if they searched equally diligently? I do not think Duff would praise the finder more than the other. But if "results matter," shouldn't he dole out unequal praise in that situation, and unequal punishment of the disobedient young batters?

Duff mentions, somewhat in passing, the debate among theorists over the unknowingly justified offender. The "deeds" theorists believe that because the offender's act turned out to be justifiable – for example, the person he killed was, unknown to him, a terrorist about to detonate a bomb – the offender is guilty only of an attempt. The "reason" theorists believe that he is guilty of a homicide because he did not believe the killing was justified.

We "results don't matter" folks do not see this as a consequential debate. For we do not distinguish, in terms of culpability and desert, between attempts and successes. The outcome of the unknowingly justified offender debate only matters for the "results matter" side.

David Brink's comment advocates a more fine-grained, scalar approach to criminal responsibility. The current approach of the criminal law is to treat criminal responsibility as essentially a binary choice between full and none. But criminal responsibility is not an all-or-nothing affair, argues Brink, and I agree.

Indeed, not only do I agree with Brink, but, in our book on criminal law theory, Ferzan and I argue for a very fine-grained approach to culpability, which for us is the sole determinant of retributive desert. The factors that Brink believes determine the degree of criminal responsibility we also accept. We also consider, in addition to these excusing or mitigating factors, such culpability-determining factors as the legally protected interests the defendant believed his act was placing at risk and his beliefs about the degree to which each interest was placed at risk; any potentially aggravating or mitigating facts the defendant believed were or might be present; and, if the defendant is culpable, what his reasons were for acting as he did. Because the risks the defendant believes he is imposing are scalar, because aggravating and mitigating facts are scalar in their effect on culpability, and because the defendant's degree of confidence that those factors exist is also scalar, culpability on our account will perforce be scalar.

In our final chapter on implementing our theory, we suggest, in a concession to practicalities, that sentences be meted out in a somewhat less fine-grained manner than culpability itself. Nonetheless, we advocate a more fine-grained approach to guilt and punishment than even Brink does in his comments. Both Brink and we understand the difficulty any human institution will have in accurately capturing degrees of culpability. But we think we can do better than not only bivalent, but also trivalent and tetravalent determinations. Brink may conclude that we are cockeyed optimists about this; but he should be happy that not only are we on his side but have outflanked him.

Peter Westen argues that I am ambivalent about the defense of duress and that I am right to be ambivalent – though not for the reasons I give. So let me set forth how I view duress, how it differs from the lesser evils defense, and whether it should be understood to be an excuse or a justification.

The lesser evils defense applies when the defendant believes the consequences of abiding by the criminal law will be worse than the consequences of violating it. If the consequences were as he believes them to be, not only would he be justified in violating the criminal law, but others would be justified in assisting his violation, and the victims of his violation would not be justified in resisting. Take the famous Trolley hypothetical. The person who turns the trolley to save the five trapped workers but thereby kills the worker on the sidetrack has committed homicide, but he has done so justifiably by choosing the lesser evil. He may be assisted in turning the trolley by third parties. And the trapped worker may not *justifiably* resist, although he may be *excused* for doing so (more on this latter point in a moment).

Of course, the lesser evils justification is not, at least for me, solely a consequentialist matter. That is why pushing someone into the path of the trolley to save the five differs from turning the trolley onto the occupied sidetrack. The pursuit of good consequences is constrained by the means principle, the prohibition on using another's body, labor, and talents without that person's consent to produce those good consequences.

So much for lesser evils. Duress comes to the fore when the lesser evils justification is unavailable, either because the consequentialist balance doesn't support the violation, or, if it does, because the violation produces the good consequences by using the victim as a means.

So take the case where Al is driving on a narrow road, with a cliff on one side and a sheer drop on the other. He sees two toddlers in each lane of the road. As he begins to stop, Bob, his passenger, pulls a gun and orders him to continue driving and thereby run over at least two of the toddlers. If Al does so, he cannot claim the lesser evils defense. The killing of two toddlers is not a better consequence, from an agent-neutral perspective, than the loss of his life.

On the other hand, because Al was faced with death were he to avoid the toddlers, we can sympathize with his choice to save his life. If Al acted no differently from how a "person of reasonable firmness" would have acted, we should afford him the excuse of duress.

Indeed, Al should get the excuse in some cases even when the balance of consequences favors the violation. If Al were told by Bob, "Run over those two toddlers or else I'll call Sally and tell her to execute your wife and three children," Al would still not have a lesser evils defense to killing the toddlers, even though two deaths are a lesser evil than four deaths. That is because Al would be using the toddlers' deaths as the means of saving his family.

For me, the defense of duress as defined by the Model Penal Code is far too limited. It should apply not just to cases in which one commits a crime in response to an illegal threat, but to all cases that present the defendant with an equivalent hard choice. If, in the original hypothetical involving Al, Bob, and the two toddlers, we take Bob out of the passenger seat and have him start a boulder rolling down the cliff towards Al's car, forcing Al either to accelerate and kill the toddlers, go over the side to his death, or get crushed to death by the boulder, Al should still get the defense of duress if he accelerates. That is so even though Bob was no longer *threatening* an illegal act but had acted. Indeed, Al should get the defense if we take Bob completely out of the picture and have the plunging boulder be the result of natural forces. Finally, I see no reason in the logic of duress as an excuse why the threat facing the defendant need be an illegal one. If Bob is Al's lawful executioner, and thus is legally threatening Al with death, and Al commits the crime of escaping prison to avoid execution, the defense of duress should be available. In other words, the logic of duress as a "hard choice" excuse cannot distinguish between illegal human threats, legal human threats, and natural threats. All of them can give rise to hard choices.

The "ambivalence" I have about duress is whether it should be deemed an excuse – which would make it akin to such true excuses as insanity and infancy – or whether it should be deemed an agent-relative justification, a permission to give one's person, one's family, and perhaps one's projects more weight than they possess from an agent-neutral perspective. Either way, however, the consequences for criminal liability are identical. The defendant who acts under duress is not culpable, but he cannot be assisted by third parties (other than his family), and his victim may resist him.

Those are my views on duress. With which of them does Westen cavil? In the first third of his comment, Westen quite accurately describes my views. The next section of his comment reveals that Westen is squarely in the camp of duress as an agent-relative justification or permission. For the question the law of duress asks – Would the person of reasonable firmness in the actor's situation have acted as the defendant did? – is clearly seeking to determine if the defendant did or did not fall below a normative standard. And if the defendant did not, then he did not act impermissibly. Westen does not deny that such an agent-relative justification does not permit unrelated third parties to assist or forbid the victim from resisting. But he thinks that even if the defendant committed an agent-neutral wrong, if he acted as would the person of reasonable firmness in his situation, then he acted permissibly.

Westen could be correct that duress in standard cases is better conceptualized as an agent-relative permission than as an excuse. So, thus far, I do not have any fundamental disagreement with him. Where I part ways with Westen is over his contention that the Model Penal Code's restriction of duress to human threats of illegal acts is warranted. Westen's view is that the "evil" Al faces from Bob's threat to shoot him – death at the hands of a human actor who intended it – differs qualitatively from the evil he faces from the avalanche. (I am not sure how he would regard the evil Al faces from an avalanche intentionally caused by Bob.) I just don't agree. I realize that my view of the proper scope of duress – whether as an excuse or an agent-relative permission – goes beyond its scope in the law as it stands today. For as I said, I believe it applies to both natural threats and lawful human threats, not just unlawful human threats. For I do not believe, when Al or his family is threatened with death from an avalanche, Al needs to ask whether the avalanche was caused by a human, and, if so, whether the human did so lawfully. Westen and I will just have to agree to disagree.

Gideon Yaffe's comment focuses on an issue I raised about the lesser evils justification. I asked whether, to be granted that justification as a defense to the commission of a crime, the crime the defendant committed must have been believed by him to be the *least* evil available, not just a *lesser* evil than abiding by the criminal law. And my answer was – and still is – that choice of the lesser evil should suffice for the defense.

My reasoning is as follows: Complying with the criminal law is a safe harbor. A defendant who does not commit a crime cannot be charged with the noncrime of failure to avert the greater evil. Therefore, if we want defendants to commit crimes when doing so averts the greater or greatest evil, we cannot use the threat of criminal sanctions as the motivation.

So consider the following variation on the familiar runaway trolley hypothetical. There are the five trapped workers on the main track. There is the one trapped worker on the sidetrack. And in this hypothetical, there is a second sidetrack on which no one is trapped. Failure to switch the trolley from the main track is the greatest evil but is not a crime. Switching it to the sidetrack with the one worker – the crime of knowing or reckless homicide – is a lesser evil. And switching it to the unoccupied sidetrack – not a crime – is the least evil.

So suppose our defendant, aware of these three options, chooses the second, the crime of homicide. Should he get the lesser evils defense? I say he should.

Consider the consequence if we deny him the defense. The next defendant in his situation, lacking any motivation to choose the least evil, and wishing to avoid punishment for choosing the lesser evil, will just let the trolley proceed on its course and kill the five. So unless he has an obligation to save the five – his job with the trolley company, or the fact that one of the five is his child – punishing those who choose the lesser evil may result in the greatest evil, not the least evil.

Put somewhat differently, the defendant who says, "I didn't do the best that I could, but I did better than I was obligated to do," may not be admirable. In my hypothetical, he saved four lives net, though he could have saved five. But I deny that he is culpable.

Yaffe appears to agree that choice of the lesser rather than the least evil should get the defense. Or, as he puts it, the defendant who chooses better but not best should get it. He believes that my argument for that result is defective, however, because it appears to assume consequentialism.

Yaffe argues for the same result through a different route, one that he labels "procedural estoppel." His is, he says, a political rather than a moral defense. In short, he argues that the government would be acting inconsistently were it to punish one who chooses the lesser rather than the least evil. It would be committed to preventing the greater evil but also committed to preventing the greater evil's prevention.

I prefer my moral route to my conclusion over Yaffe's political route. I deny that I am assuming consequentialism. In the original trolley hypothetical, if, instead of switching the trolley to the sidetrack with the one worker, the defendant pushes Al and Betty onto the main track so that their combined bodies stop the trolley and save the five, the lesser evils defense will be unavailable for the crime of killing Al and Betty. The defendant cannot claim that he chose a lesser over the least evil in that case, because there is a deontological constraint on using others' bodies (without consent) as the means of averting the greatest evil. So consequentialism does not lie behind my defense of my position, although consequences surely do.

24.2 RESPONSES TO PART II

The authors in this part are Connie Rosati, Jeffrey Goldsworthy, Larry Solum, Frederick Schauer, Lawrence Claus, Alon Harel, and Brian Leiter. I will respond to them in that order.

Several of my commentators critique various aspects of my views regarding legal interpretation. Before discussing those critiques, however, I think it would be useful to give a summary of my views point by point, so that I can identify the precise point or points with which each commentator is quarreling.[1]

On the Nature of Texts

1. A text, as I shall be using the term, is a set of symbols – of any kind – that is meant by its producer – the author(s) – to communicate a message to the intended audience. The symbols used can be marks, sounds, dots and dashes, smoke, flags, pictures – indeed, anything can be used as symbols capable of conveying messages. And although we are usually interested in the actual authors of a text, texts produced by one author can be appropriated by another author to convey the same or a different message. And one can meaningfully ask what message a text would convey if it had been produced not by its actual author, but by some different author.
2. If there is no author – no person who produced the marks, sounds, etc. in order to convey a message – then we do not have a text. The marks, sounds,

[1] I just recently came across a forthcoming book chapter by the German legal philosopher Rolf Poscher, who quite elegantly makes the precise points that I adumbrate in what follows. See Rolf Poscher, "The Hermeneutics of Law," in *The Cambridge Companion to Hermeneutics*, ed. Michael Forster and Kristin Gjesdal (Cambridge: Cambridge University Press, forthcoming).

etc. may be a sign of something, much as smoke is a sign of fire, or geese flying south is a sign that winter is coming. Marks that might look like symbols, when we understand they are not – think of cloud formations that resemble the letters C-A-T – render certain questions nonsensical that would make sense were there an author. (Consider: Are the clouds speaking English or French? Are they referring to all felines or only to tabby cats?) Even when there is an author and a text, the text may be a sign of something other than the message conveyed. For example, the text may be a sign that the author has poor handwriting or can use word processing. Or its message may be a sign that the author was angry, or agitated, or in love.

3. Texts are individuated by the messages their authors are intending to convey thereby. That is why the text of the US Constitution in Spanish can be the same as its text in English, or why its text in one font can be the same as its text in a different font. Even though those tokens of the text differ from one another, they are tokens of the same text if the message they convey is the same.
4. When our interest is in the actual authors of a text and the message they intended to convey thereby, we are acting as "originalists." If we are unsure of the meaning some word in the text, then, given that our interest is in the message the actual authors intended to convey, we will consult dictionaries contemporaneous with their authoring, not later dictionaries. And when their words produce an ambiguity, to resolve it we will ask about the context in which they were authoring, not about contexts that post- or pre-date their authoring.
5. The "conventional meanings" of words – what meaning dictionaries would assign them – are merely the meanings most people at a particular time and in a particular locale would intend to convey by those words. These meanings are therefore time and place bound, and can and do change over time and from place to place. But authors may, and often do, employ unconventional meanings. They may use codes or idiolects or malapropisms. If their intended audience understands the code or the idiolect they're employing, or recognizes the malapropism and its actual intended referent, then the authors can be successful in conveying their message to their intended audience. If one is interested in knowing what message the authors are intending to convey, one will want to know what code, idiolect, etc. the author is employing.[2]

[2] Rosati's quarrels with my assertion that texts do not by themselves declare the language in which they are written. She points out that a long sequence of symbols that look like a well-formed English sentence are quite unlikely to be in a language other than English, or to be markings made by natural forces. That is true; but what Rosati neglects is that when one infers that it is in English, one is inferring the existence of an English-speaking author who intentionally produced those symbols

6. Authors rely on implicatures and implicitures in conveying their intended messages. They often mean more, and sometimes less, than they actually say. "John and Mary are married," uttered when they're observed walking together, usually conveys the message that they are married to each other. "It is an aggravating circumstance to use a gun in the commission of a crime" usually conveys the message that it is aggravating when the gun is used as a weapon but not as an item of barter for illegal drugs.

On Interpreting Legal Texts

7. In whomever the authority to enact legal norms resides – in constitutional ratifiers, in legislatures, in administrators, in judges – then, when they decide which norms to enact and attempt to communicate those norms through a written or oral text, the job of the intended audience is to figure out what norms the authors enacted and intended to communicate. If the audience chooses legal norms that differ from those the authors chose to enact and communicate, the authority of the authors is undermined. Only originalism is authority-preserving.
8. Any departure from originalism either transfers authority from the authors to someone else – for example, to judges – or to some mindless process, such as the process by which the meanings of words change over time, as would occur if contemporary dictionary meanings rather than the meanings contemporaneous with authorship were relied on in "interpreting" legal texts.
9. Originalism is implicit in jurisprudential theories such as Scott Shapiro's planning theory of law. When those with authority to make the plans communicate the plans they have decided upon, others must then follow the plans the planners intended – their originally intended plans. Shapiro denies that his theory implies originalism but, with respect, he is plainly mistaken. He thinks that if the planners trust others with a delegation of planning authority, that undermines originalism. But that's a confusion. If the plan is to delegate, that *is* its original meaning. Shapiro is worried that if his theory is to be generally applicable, it must account for nonoriginalist interpretation, as that

to convey a message. And even in such a case, without knowing more about the author and his circumstances, one cannot tell whether the language is American English circa 2017 or American English circa 1789, or whether it's American English, South African English, Australian English, some other English-related idiolect, or even a Russian language code masquerading as English. We only can resolve these questions by reference to what we know about the author and his intended audience. We employ, as we always do in interpreting messages, circumstantial evidence: Was the text found in Australia or in America? Does it use words that are commonplace now but were not in 1789? And so on.

is common. But nonoriginalist interpretation really represents a transfer of authority – in Shapiro's case, planning authority – from one body or person to another or to some mindless (nonplanning) process. For Shapiro's theory, these transfers should be seen as problematic.

Another way of seeing this issue of trust is by reference to the distinction between norms that are rules and norms that are standards. When those with authority to enact legal norms enact standards, they are entrusting other actors – citizens, administrators, judges – with the authority to engage in first-order practical reasoning within the interstices of existing rules. That reasoning is not interpretation. Interpretation is at an end when the interpreters conclude that the authorities enacted a standard. That is the original intended meaning of the norm. Giving substance to that standard is not itself interpretation, however.

10. Interpretation of legal texts is an empirical, not a normative, endeavor. The interpreter wants to know what norm the authorities intended to communicate through their text. It is often quite difficult to answer the interpreter's question. The authorities may have expressed their intended norm poorly. Or the text may be old or ambiguous, and the context of its promulgation unclear or unknown. But, however difficult interpretation may be, it is unavoidable if the norms we are to be governed by are the norms those with authority to govern us intended.
11. Finally, interpretation of legal texts must deal with the fact that some legal authorities are multimember bodies, and sometimes bicameral multimember bodies, and can enact legal norms only with the concurrence of majorities or supermajorities. What is *the* intended meaning of a legal text when the members who voted to enact it did not intend to convey the same meanings and, hence, the same norms by it? This is the aggregation problem. In my view, it cannot be avoided. And when there is no shared meaning that the requisite number of norm enactors endorse, then the text they enact is legal gibberish. It is a composite of different intended norms that cannot be combined into a single norm. Perhaps that unfortunate result is rare. Perhaps it can be avoided by having those who vote for the text accept the meaning intended by some person or committee without having that meaning in mind themselves. I see no way, however, to make the aggregation problem disappear without at the same time undermining the authority of those who are supposed to possess it.

The above eleven points are a succinct account of positions I have taken in numerous articles and books going back at least to 1995. I now turn to my commentators and their worries.

Connie Rosati hits me with a farrago of worries. She says that the "principal considerations in support of his form of originalism fail to support it." Her overall verdict is not "wrong," but – the more charitable Scottish verdict – "not proven."

After briefly describing the difference between original public meaning originalists, whom she calls textualists, and original intended meaning originalists (like me), Rosati then asks whether originalism is a semantic thesis, a thesis about the nature of interpretation, or a normative thesis. She says that I seem to waiver among these three positions. Actually, as one can see from the points above, I embrace all three theses. Legal interpretation includes theses about how language is used (semantics and pragmatics) and a normative thesis about why in interpreting we should defer to the intended meanings of the authors of legal texts.

Rosati argues that I beg the question against textualists when I say that interpreting texts necessarily involves seeking the author's intended meaning. But textualists – that is, public meaning originalists – do not deny what I assert. If the reasonable member of the public with publicly available evidence – the interpretive touchstone of public meaning originalists – would believe, on the basis of that evidence, that the author's intended meaning in the text was X, then X is the meaning they would assign to the text. They are seeking the author's intended meaning on the basis of publicly available evidence at the time of the text's promulgation, *just as I would do*. (Rosati seems to think that the reasonable person at the time of promulgation is seeking the meaning of the words, but not the author's intended meaning of those words. I think she is mistaken to assume these are different, or that public meaning originalists think they are different.) The only difference between the public meaning originalists and me pertains to what to do when evidence of authorial intended meaning becomes publicly available at some time subsequent to the time of promulgation. I would consult it, whereas they would not. More on this when I turn to Jeffrey Goldsworthy's comments.

I can be brief with respect to Rosati's other quarrels. First, I have no quarrel with the existence of sentence meaning. It is merely what most speakers (authors) at a particular time and place would mean had they uttered (written) the text in question. I've said that we can always ask what a text would mean had it been authored by someone other than its actual author. We could also ask what it would mean in various codes. And so on. So yes, there can be different meanings given to a set of symbols. True, but irrelevant to the enterprise of legal interpretation.

Rosati homes in on the aggregation problem. It is one not avoided by public meaning originalists. I'll have more to say about it when I take up Steve Smith's comments. But any "solution" should avoid the frying pan of law enacted by those who lack authority or the fire of law produced by a mindless process.

Finally, Rosati suggests that the enacting legal authorities might be subject to normative constraints with respect to how their legal texts are to be understood. But those constraints would have to be legal constraints and would themselves have to have superior legal authority to that of the text's enactors.

Having responded to Rosati's various objections, I want to conclude my discussion of her comments by thanking her for the seriousness and comprehensiveness with which she took my views on legal interpretation and for the (usual) intelligence of her critique. She has attempted to put as many potholes in the road to my position as she can think of, and I quite appreciate that attempt. For if I can manage to avoid those potholes, I can reach my destination intact.

Jeffrey Goldsworthy, unlike Rosati, is a fellow traveler in the originalism camp. Any disagreements we might have would be tantamount to an intrafamily quarrel – although quarrel is really too fractious a term to capture the rather minimal degree of our disagreement.

Goldsworthy belongs to the majority wing of originalists, the original public meaning wing, whereas I belong to the author's intended meaning wing. Or, as he puts, Goldsworthy subscribes to "objective intentionalism" (OI), and I, by contrast, subscribe to "subjective intentionalism" (SI).

Now although I characterized Goldsworthy's position as one that places him in the original public meaning camp – the OPM camp, according to Goldsworthy's acronym for it – Goldsworthy himself wants to distinguish his OI from OPM as well as from SI. Indeed, Goldsworthy places himself in the intentionalist camp, so that any disagreement we have is even smaller and friendlier than I implied. Here is how Goldsworthy characterizes the difference between his position and mine:

> SI maintains that judges should seek the lawmaker's actual subjective intentions, whereas OI holds that those intentions are relevant only insofar as they were publicly manifested, in that sufficient evidence of them was made readily available to the public or at least to legal advisers.

Goldsworthy distinguishes general OI as an account of the meaning of any linguistic communication from legal OI, which he describes as "a distinctively legal thesis about actual and/or desirable restrictions on what evidence of legislative intentions legal interpreters should take into account." Goldsworthy is a proponent of both general OI and legal OI, though he recognizes that some, including our mutual friend Richard Ekins, can reject general OI in favor of general SI but nonetheless accept legal OI.

Goldsworthy's argument in favor of general OI seems to me to trade on a confusion between what is said and what is meant. Or, to put it in terms that I think are more apt, Goldsworthy's distinction is between what your audience is likely to take you to have meant by your statement and what you intended them to take you to have meant by it. You may fail to convey your intended meaning for any number of reasons, many of which will be your fault. But I think it is a mistake to say that the meaning of what you said is what the audience is likely to think is its meaning. Or at least it trades on an ambiguity about meaning.

For example, suppose I am using code to convey a message to my audience, a secret cell of insurgents. If I utter "the red fish swims at dawn," and this is the code for "blow up the dam," then my intended audience will likely understand me perfectly. The audience I am not intending to communicate with will not understand me. They will think I meant to convey my thoughts about a colorful aquatic creature. That is precisely the point of my using a code. But if the security forces have broken my code, then they, too, will understand my meaning.

Or consider malapropisms. If those with whom I'm conversing know that I mean "raises the question" when I say "begs the question," then they will understand me perfectly. The fact that I do not use words in the way they are conventionally used may cause others who are unaware of my particular idiolect to misunderstand me, but I may nevertheless convey my intended meaning to those who do understand my idiolect. And it will be quite accurate to say that what my statements mean is what the latter group, not the former, will take me to have meant.

I doubt that Goldsworthy disagrees with what I have said regarding codes, malapropisms, idiosyncratic idiolects, and so forth. Indeed, there are several passages that indicate his agreement. What causes him to dissent from SI appears to be that he equates the meaning of a statement with the uptake the speaker's intended audience is likely to have, so that if one misuses a term, and one's audience does not have sufficient evidence that one is misusing it, then what it *means* is what the intended audience is likely to take it to mean and not what the speaker intends to mean by it.

Goldsworthy concludes his defense of general OI with a concession that I think shows that OI and SI are not opposed positions but are actually two different ways of characterizing the same thing.

> But Alexander is right that "objective" legislative intentions are conceptually dependent on subjective intentions. An "objective" intention is what a reasonable audience would conclude was the author's "subjective" intention, given all the publicly available evidence of it. Indeed, the existence of a subjective intention is a crucial presupposition of an attribution of an objective intention to the author of a text. If we knew that the creators of a text had no relevant subjective intention (for example, they were monkeys pounding randomly on keyboards), we would have no rational basis for attributing any objective intention to the text either.

In other words, an audience is always seeking the intended meaning of the author even if, quite possibly due to the fault of the author, the audience's reasonable uptake is not what the author intended it to be.

Goldsworthy, after defending general OI, turns to legal OI. For even if one accepts general SI, as does Richard Ekins, one can still advocate legal OI, as Ekins himself does. According to legal OI, legislative intended meaning may be inferred only from publicly available evidence.

At this point I want to advert to my statement, at the outset of my reply to Goldsworthy, that Goldsworthy is a member of the OPM wing of originalism, even though Goldsworthy himself distinguishes between his legal OI position and OPM. For, as he later says, OPM is a version of OI, and his quote of Larry Solum reveals that OPM – and Solum is perhaps its leading proponent – is pretty much identical to OI as Goldsworthy elaborates it.

Let me also put aside the possibility that a legal system might have rules limiting legal interpreters to only certain types of evidence. As I said, such rules, if they existed, would have to be legally superior to the authority of the legislators, as the rules would legally constrain how they could communicate their intended norms.

With that possibility put aside, is there more than a dime's worth of difference between (legal) OI and (legal) SI? Hardly. Rational lawmakers take cognizance of the evidence of their intended meaning that their target audience is likely to possess. The aforementioned Richard Ekins, quoted approvingly by Goldsworthy, asserts that "the secret diary or private correspondence of the … lawmaker is irrelevant (even if discovered and published) to the legal meaning and effect of his enactments." But why would a rational lawmaker expect that his *secret* intended meaning would be the uptake of an audience not in on the secret? Remember that the author's intended meaning just is the uptake that he wants to produce in his audience. So if he intends his audience to think "cat," then "cat" is his intended meaning, even if he claims in his secret diary to mean "dog." Secret intended meanings are incoherent. At most, one can speak in a code understandable by an audience of one with whose uptake the speaker is solely concerned.

The real nub of the disagreement between the legal OI and legal SI camps has to do with what happens when the publicly available evidence points to meaning A but the lawmaker intended the meaning B and mistakenly believed meaning B would be the uptake of their target audience. It is on this point that legal OI and legal SI might diverge.

So suppose the lawmakers intended meaning B but, given what their audience could be expected to know, expressed meaning B sufficiently inaptly to warrant the reasonable member of the target audience to believe the lawmakers meant A. And suppose that at some time subsequent to when the lawmakers promulgated their text, publicly available evidence comes into our possession and shows that the lawmakers intended meaning B. Legal SI – my view – would dictate that we now say that the legal norm the text communicates is B, not A. That is so even though it is perfectly understandable why, before the evidence we now possess had become publicly available, interpreters would conclude that the text communicated A. And that "misinterpretation" may be laid at the feet of the lawmakers, who mistakenly believed that the evidence we now possess was publicly available at the time of promulgation. The point is, we (faultlessly) misunderstood them then, but we do understand them now.

That is the position legal SI takes. Does legal OI differ? Does it take the position that the promulgated norm is A, despite the existence of publicly available evidence that B was intended? It bears emphasis that both positions rely only on evidence that is publicly available. For no rational communicator can be said to have intended an uptake while aware that his target audience lacked the evidence necessary to infer that intended uptake. Nor could we ever discover that the intended uptake was B rather than A without evidence that the lawmakers could have assumed, albeit erroneously, its audience possessed. Without such evidence, the mistake about what was intended would remain unknown.

My conclusion, on the basis of the analysis above, is that Goldsworthy is wrong to think there is a dime's worth of difference between legal SI and legal OI. Legal OI and its equivalent, OPM, will produce the same interpretations as legal SI. (In the example above, the interpretation of the legal norm will be B, not A.) Nor will or should legal SI and legal OI differ on what to do about any period during which the texts are misinterpreted: No one should suffer because of reasonable reliance on an interpretation later shown to have been mistaken. And neither legal OI nor legal SI can avoid the aggregation problem, as that problem can be revealed by publicly available evidence. If my legal SI is in a stew, Goldsworthy's legal OI is in it with me.

Larry Solum, with his characteristic sophistication regarding all things linguistic, argues that my simple-minded originalism – my approach to the interpretation of legally authoritative texts applied to the Constitution – is "simply wrong." He quite accurately states the two propositions that underlie my simple-minded originalism: (1) meaning is essentially intentional; and (2) constitutional legitimacy requires a legitimate author. He then proceeds to attack each one.

As I understand Solum's attack on the first proposition, he quarrels with my contention that the *only* meaning of a text is the intended meaning of its author. Solum asserts, rather, that a text's conventional meaning is also its meaning. Indeed, he proclaims, it is its actual meaning, as opposed to its hypothetical meaning (the meaning it would have had if its author had intended the conventional meaning).

Solum recognizes that conventional meanings are the meanings most people at a particular time and place intend when they employ certain symbols. So conventional meanings derive from intended meanings. Moreover, symbols can be employed nonstandardly, and employed successfully if the intended audience knows it is dealing with a nonstandard use. Thus, to use an example from my reply to Goldsworthy, when the leader of the cell sends the message to the cell's members, "the red fish swims at dawn," and the members know this is the code for "blow up the dam at midnight," its meaning is just that. To say that its meaning describes the habits of colorful aquatic creatures is to posit a hypothetical meaning, the meaning it would have had if its author were not the cell leader but a biologist employing conventional English.

What about linguistic mistakes? They occur when the author's audience reasonably believes the author intends a meaning that the author does not intend. They happen all the time. We sometimes use a word that conventionally means X but we think means Y. If our audience knows that we are confused, then the word will, for them, mean Y, even if for those who don't know of our confusion it will mean X. I think that's all that can be said on this point, except this: If we later discover the author's error but fail to follow the meaning we now know she actually intended, we will, in the case of a normative statement, be following a norm no one intended us to follow.

Let me turn to Solum's critique of my second proposition. First, let me make clear that I view the Constitution's ratifiers, not its authors, as those who had the authority to create constitutional norms. So it is their intended meanings that are constitutionally authoritative, not the intended meanings of the Philadelphia authors to the extent they were different.

So far, I see no problem. But what if the ratifiers intended "whatever meaning the authors intended"? For isn't it a commonplace occurrence in legislative bodies for those with legislative authority to vote on bills drafted by committees or lobbyists without understanding what is in them or even reading them? And if so, then isn't my second proposition problematic? For does it not condemn seemingly meaningful laws to gibberish by virtue of the absence of an intended meaning by those with legitimate authority (the legislative majority)?

I think it is quite possible to intend another's intended meaning. "I intend to convey whatever she intends to convey by that text" is the stance I sometimes take when voting in a faculty meeting on a proposal drafted by a committee that I am too lazy or uninterested to read, much less understand. I don't know if the Constitution's ratifiers intended their own meanings or intended the meanings of the drafters or of prominent spokesmen. But if they intended to delegate to the intended meanings of others, then the latter *are* the ratifiers' intended meanings.

My occasional coauthor, Frederick Schauer, rejects any quest for the lawmaker's intended meaning. He is happy to concur with my argument that free speech law should turn on the question of whether the lawmakers are seeking to interdict messages based on their content. I am happy to have Schauer on my side, for free speech theory is another topic on which I hold a minority position.

When it comes to legal interpretation, however, Schauer and I part ways. Schauer disagrees with me on point 2 above, where I deny that marks or signs have any meanings, conventional or otherwise, in the absence of the assumption of some author who means something by them. (Schauer says my C-A-T cloud formation means cat, not dog, because of existing conventions. But how do we know the clouds are speaking conventional English rather than in some cloud code in which C-A-T refers to a canine?)

Despite his disagreement with my view, which Schauer deems it charitable to deny that I might actually believe, he trains his primary critical guns on my linking an author's intended meaning with the need to preserve legal authority in legal interpretation. Although both of us are proponents of law's settlement function, we part ways when it comes to the desirability of "mindless" settlements. Schauer believes that if monkeys on typewriters produce symbols that would have a conventional meaning in, say, English were they produced by an author, that conventional meaning might be a superior mode of settlement to one that seeks the intended meaning of actual authors who produce symbols to communicate the settlement they intend.

I demur. First, for reasons I have already given, I deny that conventional meanings of symbols exist in the absence of authors intending messages thereby. If the monkeys' "text" has ambiguities or polysemes, or produces absurdities, how should those be handled? I regard asking such questions of a text produced by monkeys the equivalent of asking whether the C-A-T cloud formation is in English or French, or whether it refers to all felines or only tabbies. Second, I think mindless law should be an anathema. The vision it conjures is of lawmakers choosing symbols but then some mindless process determining what they shall mean. This seems to me little different from being governed by consulting the entrails of an ox or the oracle of Delphi. For all the many imperfections of human lawmakers and of those seeking to glean the lawmakers' intended meanings, I think we should prefer them to the mindlessness of nonexistent conventional meanings.

My colleague Laurence Claus is concerned with the role of the Supreme Court vis-à-vis the Constitution. His focus is on my endorsement, in articles coauthored with Schauer and with Solum, of the kind of judicial supremacy associated with the Court's decision in *Cooper v. Aaron*.[3]

Claus focuses specifically on the constitutional framers' enumeration of Congress's legislative powers. His bottom line, one that I agree with, is that the enumeration by itself would not settle the extent of congressional powers, and the Supreme Court's assistance in specifying and policing those powers was both necessary and recognized to be so by the framers.

I believe a moment's reflection will show that Claus – and the framers – are correct. Grants of powers are not amenable to rule-like determinacy. Does the power "to establish post offices" include the power to hire world-class architects to make them not only functional but also aesthetic masterpieces? Does that power include

[3] 358 U.S. 1 (1958).

the power to purchase art for the lobbies of those post offices? Are these powers "necessary and proper" means of implementing the power to establish post offices?

This kind of uncertainty plagues all of the enumerated powers, as the history of litigation over the scope of the power "to regulate Commerce … among the several States …" illustrates.

The enumerated powers function as standards, not rules. They thus must be given determinacy by further lawmaking. And because Congress cannot be relied on to determine the extent of its own powers, that job must inevitably fall to the courts, with the Supreme Court having the final word. That is Claus's position and one with which I surely concur.

Neither Claus nor I would claim that the Court's performance of that function has been stellar. The history of Supreme Court decision making under the Commerce Clause has been a particularly unpretty one of doctrinal shifts, inconsistencies, retreats (from 1937 to 1995), and then attacks (from 1995 to Obamacare). The Court's various "tests" have failed to give rule-like guidance, which should be the *raison d'être* of judicial lawmaking. Whether or not the Court has done a good job as lawmaker, that is its job when it comes to the enumerated powers.

Alon Harel endorses my settlement role for the Supreme Court. He also endorses my more general view that the basic function of law is settlement. So Harel and I have no disagreement over these positions.

Do we have any disagreement over what Harel argues in his chapter? I think so. For Harel's basic point is that constitutional legal settlements differ from nonconstitutional ones in a fundamental way: The former have an intrinsic value as well as furthering the settlement goals that all law does.

Although Harel seems to be suggesting that constitutions generally or always have the value of recognizing preexisting rights, I demur that this is a necessary feature of constitutions or that this feature is a clearly desirable one. As I argued in an article Harel does not cite, constitutional law can be distinguished from all other law based on its supremacy, based on its degree of entrenchment, or based on its importance. Almost always, a norm that is hierarchically superior to norms enacted after its enactment is somewhat entrenched; otherwise, its superiority in the legal hierarchy cannot be maintained. So the hierarchal superiority of constitutions usually goes hand in hand with their entrenchment.

The relative importance of constitutional norms is a contingent matter: Many, if not all, constitutions deal with matters that are less important than some matters that are dealt with by statutes, by treaties, by common law judicial decisions, by executive orders, and so forth. Still, constitutional entrenchment usually reflects the judgment that matters that are entrenched are so because of their relative importance.

The recognition of preexisting rights, which for Harel is perhaps the most important feature of constitutions, is an aspect of constitutions about which I am less enthusiastic. I believe in an objective morality that specifies the duties moral agents have to other creatures and maintains that those creatures possess moral rights corresponding to such moral duties. But is it a good idea for constitutions to incorporate such moral rights and duties? As Schauer and I wrote in a different article from the ones Harel cites, when constitutions attempt to incorporate moral rights by specifying them, they may fail to carve moral reality at the joints that actually exist. Take the rights recognized in the US Constitution, for example. There may be no freedom of expression right in the ontological cupboard of morality. There may be no free exercise right. And so on. Moreover, true incorporation of moral rights threatens the settlement function, for it licenses courts to rely on their own moral views rather than on determinate rules laid down by the constitutions. And morality, knowing no limits other than its own, may be inconsistent with virtually all aspects of the constitutions in which they are recognized. Incorporation potentially warrants judges declaring the nonrights portions of constitutions (other than those portions dealing with their own appointments) to be inconsistent with moral rights and thus unconstitutional. Incorporating moral rights is a powerful elixir for a judiciary. Harel wants to give them that elixir; I am quite wary of doing so.

Brian Leiter's comment intersects with my views of freedom of expression and academic freedom. Leiter and I are basically in agreement about these things. With respect to freedom of expression, both of us recognize that the content of expression can cause serious harms. It can incite or solicit violence. It can threaten. It can mislead, deceive, and defraud. It can defame. It can insult, offend, and emotionally disturb. It can reveal private, embarrassing facts, confidential communications, and military secrets. It can breach contracts and take others' intellectual property. And so on.

If expression can cause so many types of serious harms, what then is the case for its protection? Leiter and I agree that it is based on distrust of the government's ability to regulate expression wisely. It is really a case of mutual disarmament. You may not trust me when I'm in power, and I may not trust you when you're in power. So we arrive at a modus vivendi in which there will be a heavy judicial thumb on the scale against the validity of certain types of regulations of the content of expression.

Leiter and I also agree that academic freedom is not the same thing as freedom of expression. It is not some special additional realm of freedom of expression that academics possess but ordinary citizens do not. Rather, it is the immunity to adverse job consequences for things that one writes or teaches so long as one complies with the standards of his discipline. In other words, academic freedom is the freedom to research, publish, and teach in accordance with disciplinary standards, and within the constraints that apply to expression outside the academy. (Scholars may not defame, incite violence, and so forth with any greater latitude than nonscholars possess.) Nor does freedom of expression exempt them from adverse job consequences if what they teach or write is deficient by the standards of their discipline.

Universities, whether public or private, do not have to grant academic freedom – although if they do not, they will be discredited as universities. And private universities need not accord full freedom of expression to their employees.

I believe Leiter agrees with all this. I do find it somewhat off-putting that all his examples of free speech horrors are on the Right, although I could find many, if not more, on the Left. Perhaps it is because Leiter dwells in that proletarian redoubt of Hyde Park. Be that as it may, on the theoretical points Leiter and I are in complete agreement.

24.3 RESPONSES TO PART III

The authors in this part are Steven Smith, Emily Sherwin, Leo Katz and Alvaro Sandroni, William Baude, and Mitchell Berman. I will respond to them in that order.

The first group of commentators I will respond to all in one way or another deal with my views on the role of authority in legal and constitutional theory.

I first take up my colleague Steve Smith's very charitable and clever paper, as I regard it as a bridge between the interpretation critiques and the authority critiques. Smith says a lot of intelligent and, in my view, correct things about various accounts of authority, including those of John Finnis and Joseph Raz. (He also mentions, in passing, the current anti-authority views of Abner Greene and our mutual colleague Laurence Claus.)

In the second half of his paper, Smith connects his ruminations on authority with my "authority-preserving" account of legal interpretation. And he trains his sights on the aggregation problem that arises when the legal authorities are multimember bodies, such as legislatures and constitutional ratifiers.

Suppose norms, to become legally binding, must be adopted by a majority of legislators or, in the case of constitutional norms, a supermajority of ratifiers. And suppose the text that is supposed to communicate a norm has been duly voted on by the requisite number of such lawmakers. Yet, suppose that there is no majority (or supermajority) who intended to communicate the same norm through the text they approved. One group in the majority intended to communicate norm A through the text, while another intended to communicate norm B. And perhaps many who voted "aye" had little or no idea of what norm they were approving. If a legal interpreter realizes this, what norm, if any, should she declare has been duly enacted?

I said earlier that sometimes the correct answer is that the text is legal gibberish. No legal norm was enacted even though a text was enacted. Smith seems to agree that on my analysis of interpretation – one that he hints, but does not directly declare, he accepts – that is the proper result.

What about the, I suspect, more common situation where the majority, rather than intending different norms, is not aware of the norm they are supposedly enacting? Suppose, for example, most who vote "aye" are essentially adopting "whatever norm the committee chair, or the committee staff, is intending." In other words, they are delegating norm-enacting authority to somebody other than a majority of themselves.

Smith thinks such a delegation would be improper according to my account of authority and interpretation. Perhaps it would even be unconstitutional for the US Congress to do so per *INS v. Chadha*.[4] Perhaps it would be tantamount to my bugaboo of "mindless lawmaking," sort of like having lawmakers pick the letters and then having a machine turn those letters into a "text."

I am not so sure, however. Is it an improper delegation of my legislative authority as a voting faculty member for me to declare, with respect to a faculty committee's proposed modification of the faculty rules, one that I have been too busy or too lazy to read, "I vote to approve whatever it is they recommend"? After all, unlike truly mindless lawmaking, the new faculty rule will be the product of the committee members' minds. The fact that I am delegating norm-selecting authority to this subgroup of the faculty seems kosher, at least to me. And if it is, why would it not be kosher for the many minds of Congress to delegate to the fewer minds of the committee or its staff, *Chadha* notwithstanding?

I leave this as a question for which I have no rock-solid answer. Smith has surely noted a problem that my authority-preserving view of legal interpretation raises. And it is, no doubt, a serious one. Smith himself offers no solution. But I thank him for quite fairly and insightfully taking my thoughts to where they lead.

Another of my frequent coauthors, Emily Sherwin, pursues a different line on the topic of legal authority. It is one about which she and I have written at length: "the gap." "The gap" refers to the following phenomenon: In a large and complex society, even the most well-intentioned members will have moral disagreements and domains of moral uncertainty. Such disagreements and uncertainties will lead to conflict, error, and lack of coordination, all of which will produce, from everyone's moral perspectives, huge moral costs. To avert those moral costs, all will endorse the creation of authorities who can promulgate binding norms that will settle what must be done despite those disagreements and uncertainties. But those norms cannot require that those subject to them engage in first-order moral reasoning in order to comply with them, for to do so would lead to the same disagreements and uncertainties that those norms were supposed to avert. Rather, the norms must be capable of being applied in the same way by people of differing moral beliefs. In short, they must be rather blunt, determinate rules.

4 462 U.S. 919 (1983).

The problem of "the gap" arises because when what those rules require diverges from what the first-order moral reasoning of those subject to the rules dictates, the subjects will be faced with the choice: follow the rules, which our first-order moral reasoning tells us we must have, or follow what our first-order moral reasoning dictates that we do in the particular circumstances we face. That is the dilemma of "the gap." (Schauer calls the same phenomenon the "asymmetry of authority": Authorities have reason to issue rules that their subjects have no reason to comply with.)

Sherwin and I believe that "the gap" dilemma is insoluble. We also believe it is the most important prism through which to view legal phenomena. It frequently explains the disagreement between the majority and the dissent: One prefers rule-based decision making; the other, first-order-reasoning decision making (i.e., standards). It frequently explains changes in legal doctrines over time: When rules prevail, there's a yearning for the first-order-reasoning standards; when the latter prevails, there's a yearning for rules. The same goes for our ambivalence regarding bureaucrats: They either seem to have too much, or not enough, discretion.

I also agree with Sherwin's linking "the gap" to the more general issue of the rationality of following plans and sticking with one's decisions. Someone who keeps reconsidering his plans and decisions is irrational. But so is one who never reconsiders them. And the Goldilocks degree of reconsideration seems impossible to locate theoretically.

Because I agree with Sherwin with respect to "the gap," I can do no more than to encourage her to keep harping on its theoretical importance. And I thank her for bringing it to the attention of the readers of this volume.

Leo Katz and his coauthor Alvaro Sandroni also focus on "the gap." A good deal of their comment is spent on elaborating how "the gap" arises and then going through the various methods of overcoming "the gap" that Sherwin and I argued were unsuccessful.

Katz and Sandroni agree that the phenomenon of "the gap" exists and that none of the methods for overcoming it succeed. They then helpfully analogize that dilemma to Greg Kavka's famous toxin puzzle and paradox of deterrence. I have also compared the dilemma to the toxin puzzle. In the puzzle, it would be really profitable to intend at midnight to drink the noxious liquid sometime thereafter, as that would guarantee us irrevocably a million dollars. And we would gladly drink the liquid to obtain that amount. The problem, of course, is that we cannot intend to do something we know we'll have no reason to do. Similarly, it would be morally good for us to have rules to settle our moral disagreements and uncertainties. But because even the best rules will conflict in many cases with what our moral reasoning prescribes, we will have no reason to comply with those rules in those cases – which are the only cases in which the rules matter. And rules that fail to give people reasons to comply will thereby fail to settle what we needed settled. The structure of the dilemma of "the gap" is parallel to the structure of the toxin puzzle, just as Katz and Sandroni aver. (And likewise, it is parallel to Kavka's paradox of deterrence: It would be good for deterrence to intend to launch a retaliatory nuclear strike, but it would be irrational to do so, deterrence having failed. So nuclear deterrence requires an intention to do what will be irrational to do.)

Katz and Sandroni reject David Gauthier's "package deal" solution to these puzzles and paradoxes. I agree with that rejection. However, they speculate at the end of their comment that some package deal solution might work to solve the dilemma of "the gap." The examples they give – the possible intransitivity of situations of duress, or contrived creations of justifiable self-defense – whatever they illustrate, do not show a way to avoid "the gap." They understand that and suggest only that a method of avoidance might be found.

William Baude argues that my view that the originalist's Constitution is our supreme law conflicts with my view in support of judicial supremacy à la *Cooper v. Aaron*. Baude, who supports the *res judicata* but not the *stare decisis* position regarding judicial interpretations of the Constitution – *Marbury v. Madison*,[5] but not *Cooper* – thinks that I cannot have it both ways. Either I must side with the Constitution or with the Court.

As I see it, the conflict, or at least the potential for it, stems not from *Cooper* itself, but from an overly strong view of precedent. In any norm-governed activity, such as a legal system, in which the norms are not so clear and transparent that they can be applied faithfully and correctly by all the participants, it will be necessary to have an umpire to resolve uncertainties and disagreements. Chess and golf can generally proceed successfully without umpiring officials – though in golf, officials are occasionally consulted. But a complex legal system, and a constitutional system such as ours, requires officials, not just for fact finding, but for interpreting less than fully transparent legal and constitutional norms.

When the legal officials – the courts – interpret legal norms, they can, of course, err. Their interpretations may not be correct interpretations of the norms those with lawmaking authority intended to enact. And thus, when the Supreme Court interprets the Constitution, it is always open for anyone to disagree with its interpretation. Nevertheless, insofar as the legal system is concerned, a Supreme Court's interpretation of the Constitution, not the Constitution as others interpret it, is the "supreme law of the land." It is the supreme law of the land, that is, until the Supreme Court decides that its interpretation is erroneous and overturns its own precedent. And that is, in my opinion, how it not only is but should be.

[5] 5 U.S. (1 Cranch) 137 (1803).

The real action is located in the Court's attitude toward its precedents. How strong should *stare decisis* be when it comes to constitutional decisions by the Court? Some believe that the doctrine of *stare decisis*, including in constitutional cases, is provided for in the Constitution itself, perhaps in the notion of "the judicial power" in Article III. Others believe it is to be found in the general law that was the legal context in which the Constitution was adopted.

I think both of those positions are difficult to maintain. The latter assumes a general law that operates to entrench erroneous interpretations of a Constitution that, unlike the general law, is supposed to be "the supreme law of the land." And the former view imagines that those who put into the Constitution very specific and difficult procedures for its amendment also put in place the possibility of judicial amendment through erroneous interpretations.

I think the correct solution to the conflict between the Court and the Constitution is that the latter prevails. That is not to say *Cooper* was wrong. Rather, it is to say that the Court should not regard its constitutional decisions as sacrosanct. When it comes to believe those decisions were wrong, it should be prepared to reverse them, while making sure to avert catastrophic or highly unfair consequences.

Mitchell Berman's comment attempts to make the case for legal principles, a case I have rejected in several articles spanning a generation. Because Berman begins his comment with such generous remarks, and because he is painstakingly accurate and charitable in his characterizations of my principles skepticism, it almost seems churlish of me to refuse to budge. But alas, I do refuse.

Berman and I have argued about this for several years. His case for legal principles in this volume is a much telescoped version of the case he makes in the law review article he cites. By the same token, my response to him will perforce be much shorter than the longer response I gave him when he sent me a draft of his article.

What are the significant characteristics of legal principles as Berman understands them? The first is that they have no canonical linguistic form. Berman is correct that a single rule can be formulated in different ways. "It is forbidden to park here after 6 am" is the same rule as "Parking here after 6 am is not permitted." But legal principles cannot be captured by any verbal formulation. Words may be used to refer to them. But, unlike rules, no verbal formulation provides an algorithm for their application.

Their second significant feature is that of weight. Rules either do or do not apply, but if they do, they fully determine outcomes. Principles are forces that incline towards some result but do not necessarily dictate that result. There can be countervailing principles that outweigh them, at least in the context at issue. And it is because principles have weight that they cannot be captured in algorithmic verbal formulae.

Now I do not deny the possible existence in morality's ontological cupboard of moral principles – really, moral reasons that have the dimension of weight. But law, being a human artifact, is different. For there to be legal principles, as both Berman and I understand them, human beings have to have the ability to create norms with weight. They can surely create complex rules, and complexity might give the appearance that the rules have weight. But the reality is that rules, however complex, are weightless. They either apply and determine a result or they do not.

My argument, reduced to its nub, is that humans cannot create norms with weight. They cannot directly posit weight. (Weight cannot be enacted.) They cannot do so in the manner Dworkin describes (by having their rules and decisions combined with moral principles). Nor can they be created through the sort of amorphous process Berman describes, which involves various mental states of various actors making various decisions and invoking various verbal formulae.

Take just one of Berman's examples of a legal principle, one that would seem to be as plausible as any, "federalism." If the scope and weight of that principle arise from a complex set of attitudes and decisions, whose attitudes and decisions count, and how are they to be combined to produce *the* principle of federalism? Do only the attitudes of judges count, or do lawyers, legal scholars, and members of the public in general get in on the action of constructing *the* principle of federalism? Suppose Al believes federalism has wide scope but little weight, whereas Betty believes it is narrow but strong. And suppose Larry Alexander believes there is no such principle, only a constitutionally specified division of powers between the federal government and the states. Do my views count, and if so, how do they factor into the metes and bounds and weight of the federalism principle? I could go on and on with such questions.

Here is another problem. Berman assumes that whoever belongs to the relevant group of actors, their attitudes and beliefs are the building blocks of legal principles. But it is fair to ask why they believe in the existence of these principles. A regress looms if they reason "I believe this principle (and its scope and weight) exists because I believe this principle (and its scope and weight) exists because … ad infinitum." To avoid this regress, they must believe the principles and their scopes and weights exist because others so believe. And the others must so believe because *they* believe, and they believe because the others believe, etc., etc. A vicious circle? Even if not, the problem is magnified if, as I indicated, some believe principle P has scope S and weight W, others believe P has scope S– or S+ and weight W– or W+, and still others, like me, deny P exists at all. What is the truthmaker in such a (realistic) case about P and its scope and weight?

I am deeply skeptical about whether Berman can come up with such a truthmaker and vindicate his case for the existence of legal principles. But in the charitable spirit that he displayed towards my view, I shall respond, as Rosati did with respect to my case for originalism, with the Scottish verdict: not proven.

24.4 RESPONSES TO PART IV

The authors in this part are Kimberly Ferzan, Richard Arneson, Kevin Cole, Michael Moore, and Kasper Lippert-Rasmussen. I will respond to them in that order.

My response to Kimberly Ferzan's comment will be very brief. That is because I endorse fully what she says in it. Indeed, the substance of that comment will find its way into chapter seven of the forthcoming book she and I are coauthoring.

As her comment reveals, in contrast to Arneson, Ferzan is a proponent of the means principle (MP). Her comment is an excellent explication of it and some of its implications. It both reveals Ferzan's analytical rigor and the reason I deem myself extremely fortunate to have her as my coauthor.

Richard Arneson is a consequentialist and thus is no fan of deontological constraints. He attacks my version of those constraints, the MP. He denies its plausibility both as an account of deontological constraints and as an absolute bar to the production of good consequences or the prevention of bad ones. Finally, he quarrels with my application of it to rights over natural resources.

Let me state briefly how I came to endorse the MP. The MP is an attempt to ground the widely shared intuition that turning a runaway trolley from a track on which there are five trapped workers to a sidetrack on which there is one trapped worker is permissible, whereas knocking a fat man onto the track to stop the trolley from killing the five is impermissible. In that sense, the MP is a cousin of the more famous deontological constraint, the doctrine of double effect (DDE). The difference is that the DDE is focused on the mental state of the actor who is attempting to produce the best consequences, whereas the MP is focused on the claims of those, like the one trapped worker and the fat man, who are harmed by the actor, not on the actor's mental state. Under the MP, the actor's mental state is relevant to the actor's culpability but not to the permissibility of his act.

Arneson's recital of the MP and my defense of it is generally accurate, but it is perhaps misleading in two respects. First, one could get the impression from Arneson's comment that I believe the MP is the only moral constraint there is. But that would be a serious misreading of my account. For I pointed out that actors are generally constrained not to act in ways that produce bad consequences. They cannot drive recklessly, shoot guns for pleasure on crowded streets, or act in myriad other harmful ways. What the MP denies is that they can be compelled to produce good consequences through the use of their bodies, labor, or talents, unless, that is, they consent. (The major exception is when, because of culpable acts, they deserve a punitive response, which can take the form of using them as a means to produce good consequences.)

The second possible misleading part of Arneson's comment is the implication that, for me, the MP is absolute and applies no matter how horrendous the consequences of abiding by it. In other words, Arneson implies that I reject the existence of a deontological threshold.

Now it is true that I wrote an article that made some skeptical points about so-called threshold deontology. Those points consisted in pointing out some weird effects that could obtain at such a threshold and the more general concern that there was no theory that could justify the location of that threshold. (To be precise, there are two possible deontological thresholds that need to be justified: a quantitative one and a qualitative one. The former deals with how many persons must face harm H before someone can be used as a means and suffer harm H in order to avert H for those at risk. The latter asks how much harm H+ must threaten one person before another may be used as a means and suffer harm H– to avert H+.)

Arneson correctly notes that some of my weirdness examples fall short. Others that he does not mention involve taking persons who will suffer a little harm and tossing them into the crowd facing major harm in order to get the size of the crowd up to the threshold number (N) and thus saving them by overcoming the deontological constraint. But my main skeptical point in that article was over the absence of any theory to justify the location of the threshold. Consequentialism has a theoretical basis. So, too, does deontology. Neither rests solely on intuitions. But is there, and can there be, a theoretical basis for the location of the deontological threshold? If Al intuits that the fat man can only be permissibly shoved in front of the trolley to save five lives, Sally intuits that shoving him is permissible only if ten lives are at risk, and Dana thinks the threshold is twenty, is there any theory that can establish whose intuition is correct?

I remain skeptical. But I share the intuition that, Taurek notwithstanding,[6] there must be thresholds, both quantitative and qualitative. I am not a deontological absolutist, despite my skepticism regarding deontological thresholds.

That brings me to Arneson's criticism of my view of how the MP applies to natural resources. I denied that equal division of such resources is consistent with the MP. Arneson says that my example of Tall, who cannot reach the apples on the lower branches, and Short, who cannot reach the ones on the upper branches, fails to show that giving each the right to half the apples only the other can reach violates the MP.

I agree that giving each a veto over the other's use of the apples only he can reach does not itself violate the MP. So if Short tells Tall, "you may not pick any apples

[6] See John M. Taurek, "Should the Numbers Count?," *Philosophy and Public Affairs* 6, no. 4 (1977), 293.

unless I get half of them," the MP has not been violated. But why should Short have a veto power over apples that, in the absence of Tall, he could never enjoy? Suppose there are great resources on Mars that we cannot access. Do we have a moral claim that the Martians not use those resources unless they send us a pro rata share of them? If not, then the only way we can enjoy the Martian resources – and Short can enjoy the apples on the high branches – is by compelling the Martians and Tall to labor and gather and then convey those resources.

Finally, I believe Arneson misunderstands my view on the relation of the MP to property rights. I believe the MP applies to property that has been created by one's labor and talents (or that has been conveyed by another who created it through her labor and talents). It does not extend to other kinds of property, nor does it extend to occupied spaces, however permissible one's occupation. That is why turning the trolley toward the one trapped worker does not violate the worker's MP-protected "property" in the space he's occupying, even if he is there permissibly.

My colleague Kevin Cole, like Arneson, focuses on my discussion of threshold deontology. Much of his critique of my "weirdness at the threshold" examples parallels Arneson's, so I will not repeat what I said in my response to Arneson. (Both Arneson and Cole deal with the problems caused by the threats to the threshold number of victims (N) being diachronic rather than synchronic. Neither deals with the oddity that where N–1 victims are threatened with synchronic harm H, and another with harm H–, the latter might be shoved into the path of harm H, thus satisfying N, and thereby being saved from all harm by the violation of the deontological constraint.)

Cole asks whether threshold deontology might justify proxy crimes – crimes that do not require proof beyond a reasonable doubt that the defendants are culpable with respect to the harms that the proxy crimes are meant to avert. Retributivists typically are opposed to proxy crimes because such crimes authorize the punishment of the nonculpable. I join that opposition.

Suppose, however, that a very high percentage of those proved beyond a reasonable doubt to have violated the proxy crime are also culpable with respect to the ultimate harms. Would that not justify proxy crimes?

The answer, in short, is no. Retributivists will permit some level of risk that the nonculpable will be punished. For any human institution such as that of convicting and punishing criminals, mistakes are inevitable. The burden of proof is supposed to reflect the permissible level of risk that the nonculpable will be deemed culpable.

So assume that the appropriate level of risk is reflected by the requirement of proof beyond a reasonable doubt. (It could be a lower standard, but the analysis that follows applies whatever the standard is.) Suppose that proof beyond a reasonable doubt translates into proof that is 90 percent likely to be correct. And suppose, finally, that those who violate the proxy crime are 90 percent likely to be culpable.

On those assumptions, proof beyond a reasonable doubt that the defendant violated the proxy crime would not prove beyond a reasonable doubt that he was culpable. (He would be only 81 percent likely to be culpable.) Only if the correlation between the proxy crime and culpability were 100 percent would proof beyond a reasonable doubt of violating the proxy crime satisfy the retributivist's burden of proof of culpability. But in such a case, there would be no need for a proxy crime, for culpability could be proved directly by whatever evidence would otherwise have proved the proxy crime.

Cole's interesting speculation is whether there might be a threshold deontology justification for lowering the burden of proving culpability in some cases. In other words, if the negative consequences without proxy crimes surpass N, proxy crimes might be justified even though they do not establish culpability at the deontologically required level. I think that is surely a theoretical possibility, and Cole deserves credit for pointing it out.

Michael Moore's contribution, like Arneson's and Cole's, deals with the topic of threshold deontology. Moore's approach is, characteristically, a view of the topic from the summit ofMount Everest. He gives us an eight-point theory of the relation among deontological obligations and between deontological obligations and consequentialist ones. The medium of exchange is, for him, stringency: The more stringent obligation, of whatever flavor, overrides the less stringent one. A deontological threshold is, thus, a situation in which one's more stringent consequentialist obligation overrides one's less stringent deontological obligation.

Moore does not view what he says about threshold deontology as contradicting any position I hold, nor does it. I can endorse the basic points of Moore's position and the existence of deontological thresholds. Nonetheless, Moore's position does not allay my basic worry about such thresholds, even as I grant their necessity.

As I said before, there are really two deontological thresholds, a quantitative one and a qualitative one. The quantitative one is the more familiar of the two. If violating a deontological constraint will cause harm of magnitude H, what number of people who will be saved from suffering harm of magnitude H were the constraint violated will justify violating that constraint?[7] Take the case of Fat Man, for example. If tossing Fat Man onto the trolley track will cause his death but will save trapped workers from death, what number of trapped workers will justify and override the deontological constraint that will be violated by tossing Fat Man? Is it two? Five? A hundred?

7 The existence of a quantitative threshold obviously assumes that harms to different people can be aggregated with the result that the harm to several is a greater harm than the harm to any individual. In other words, the existence of a quantitative threshold assumes the Taurek challenge can be met. See Taurek, "Should the Numbers Count?" 293.

Let us call the number that is our quarry here N. N is the quantitative deontological threshold. And the question I raised in the article to which Moore, Arneson, and Cole advert is whether it is possible to justify the choice of N. If Bill says N is five and Sue says it's ten, is there any way of getting beyond their conflicting intuitions? Can there be a theory of N?

I expressed doubts in that article, and nothing Moore (or Arneson or Cole) writes in these pages allays those doubts. Nor am I asking for something that ethics generally cannot deliver. Consequentialists have theories to support their intuitions about cases. So, too, do we deontologists. We start with intuitions – about, say, Trolley and Fat Man, or Strategic Bomber and Terrorist Bomber – and then develop theories to account for them. My theory is patient centered. Moore's is agent centered. And there are others on offer.

But I have seen no theory to support anyone's intuition about N. And my worry is that no theory of N is possible, a worry that I fully explain in my article on threshold deontology.

The other deontological threshold is a qualitative one. If violating a deontological constraint will cause Able harm H but prevent Baker from suffering harm H+, how much greater than H must H+ be to justify the harm to Able? 2H? 3H? 10H?

Again, and for the same reason, I doubt that a theory of the qualitative deontological threshold will be forthcoming. I hope I'm wrong. And I encourage Moore to try his hand at such a theory. If anyone can pull this rabbit out of the hat, it is Moore. So, Michael, prove my doubts to be baseless. But merely repackaging talk of N or of H+ as talk about relative stringency merely restates, but does not solve, the problem.

Kasper Lippert-Rasmussen's comment rejects certain discriminator-focused views of the wrongfulness of wrongful discrimination, including the view I put forward in my 1992 article on that topic. As he points out, I have since rejected that view. (I have a certain ambivalence about the frequent reference in the discrimination literature to that 1992 piece. On the one hand, the piece puts forward a view that I now reject. On the other hand, it does vindicate my view that until I published that piece, the wrongfulness of wrongful discrimination was woefully undertheorized, making my piece something of a starting point for other theorists.)

Lippert-Rasmussen gives his own reason for rejecting my discriminator-focused view. And he notes that in a 2015 book review, I expressed sympathy with a view that would locate the wrongfulness of discrimination in its consequences. That view is one Lippert-Rasmussen finds congenial. Indeed, he has devoted an entire monograph to the defense of such a view, a monograph I cited favorably in the 2015 piece.

That piece does not represent my latest thoughts on the topic, however. In an unpublished piece that I presented at a conference at Hebrew University in 2016 – a conference Lippert-Rasmussen also attended and at which he presented a version of his present comment – I raised doubts about the social-consequences approach

I had endorsed only a year before. For, as I pointed out, that approach seems to leave the victim of the wrongful discrimination out of the picture – the prince out of Hamlet. Many acts of discrimination that are generally considered wrongful may not be socially harmful even if they are harmful to their victims. Of course, it is likewise true that sometimes acts of wrongful discrimination may end up benefitting their victims. Indeed, it may even be the case that sometimes both the victims and society are benefitted by acts of discrimination that are nonetheless considered wrongful.

Skepticism about the consequentialist account does not lead me to reconsider my rejection of the discriminator-focused view. Instead, it only makes me more skeptical about whether any account of discrimination's wrongfulness can succeed, as the title of that unpublished paper attests.

Let me conclude by reiterating what I said earlier: I am very grateful to those who wrote in this volume. (I did, of course, provide them with a target-rich environment.) And I am very grateful to the University of Illinois and Yale University law schools for providing the resources that produced the conference at which some of these chapters were aired. Finally, most of all, I am extremely grateful to Heidi Hurd for making the conference and this book a reality.

Bibliography of Works by Larry Alexander

BOOKS

Reflections on Crime and Culpability: Problems and Puzzles. Cambridge: Cambridge University Press, forthcoming. (With Kimberly Kessler Ferzan)

Crime and Culpability: A Theory of Criminal Law. Cambridge: Cambridge University Press, 2009. (With Kimberly Ferzan and Stephen Morse)

Demystifying Legal Reasoning. Cambridge: Cambridge University Press, 2008. (With Emily Sherwin)

Is There a Right of Freedom of Expression? Cambridge: Cambridge University Press, 2005.

The Rule of Rules: Rules, Principles, and the Dilemmas of Law. Durham, NC: Duke University Press, 2001. (With Emily Sherwin)

Freedom of Speech. Farnham: Ashgate, 2000.

Legal Rules and Legal Reasoning. Farnham: Ashgate, 2000.

Constitutionalism: Philosophical Foundations. Cambridge: Cambridge University Press, 1998.

Contract Law. London: Dartmouth, 1991.

Whom Does the Constitution Command? Westport: Greenwood Press, 1988. (With Paul Horton)

ARTICLES AND REVIEW ESSAYS

"Retributive Justice." In *Oxford Handbook of Distributive Justice*, edited by Serena Olsaretti. Oxford: Oxford University Press, 2018, pp. 177–194.

"Goldsworthy on Interpretation of Statutes and Constitutions: Public Meaning, Intended Meaning, and the Bogey of Aggregation" (forthcoming, 2018).

"Is There a Case for Strict Liability?" *Criminal Law and Philosophy* (forthcoming).

"Brexit and the Future of Liberal Democracy." *Cardozo Law Review* (forthcoming). http://ssrn.com/abstract=2909229.

"The Need to Attend to Probabilities (for Purposes of Self-Defense and Other Preemptive Actions)." *San Diego Law Review* (forthcoming). http://ssrn.com/abstract=2909273.

"Law and Politics: What Is Their Relation?" *Harvard Journal of Law & Public Policy* 41, no. 1 (2018): 355–64.

"Hard Incompatibilism, and the Rejection of Moral Responsibility: A Skeptical Look at an Optimistic Account." San Diego Legal Studies Paper No. 17-259 (2017). http://ssrn.com/abstract=2921469.

"Aggregating States of Mind: A Response to Fallon." San Diego Legal Studies Paper No. 17-258 (2017). http://ssrn.com/abstract=2916864.

"Alexander on Koppelman on Alexander." *San Diego Law Review* 54, no. 2 (2017): 339–44.

"Brettschneider and 'Democratic Persuasion.'" *Jurisprudence* 8, no. 2 (2017): 370–79.

"Robert Nagel and the Emptiness of the Supreme Court's Standards of Review." *University of Colorado Law Review* 88, no. 2 (2017): 325–32.

"Duties to Act Triggered by Creation of the Peril: Easy Cases, Puzzling Cases, and Complex Culpability." In *The Ethics and Law of Omissions*, edited by Dana Kay Nelkin and Samuel C. Rickless. Oxford: Oxford University Press, 2017.

"Is Wrongful Discrimination Really Wrong?" San Diego Legal Studies Paper No. 17-257 (2016). http://ssrn.com/abstract=2909277.

"Against Equality." San Diego Legal Studies Paper No. 17-255 (2016). http://ssrn.com/abstract=2909237.

"Freedom of Religion and Expression." In *A Companion to Applied Philosophy*, edited by Kasper Lippert-Rasmussen, Kimberley Brownlee, and David Coady. Hoboken: Wiley-Blackwell, 2016.

"Recipe for a Theory of Self-Defense: The Ingredients and Some Cooking Suggestions." In *The Ethics of Self-Defense*, edited by Christian Coons and Michael Weber. Oxford: Oxford University Press, 2016.

"Consent Does Not Require Communication: A Reply to Dougherty." *Law and Philosophy* 35, no. 6 (2016): 655–60. (With Heidi Hurd and Peter Westen)

"Ignorance as a Legal Excuse." In *Perspectives on Ignorance from Moral and Social Philosophy*, edited by Rik Peels. Abingdon: Routledge, 2016.

"The Means Principle." In *Legal, Moral, and Metaphysical Truths: The Philosophy of Michael S. Moore*, edited by Kimberly Kessler Ferzan and Stephen J. Morse. Oxford: Oxford University Press, 2016. The unabridged version is available on SSRN at http://ssrn.com/abstract=2378608.

"Legal Positivism and Originalist Interpretation." *Revista Argentina de Teoría Jurídica* 16 (2015): 1–10.

"The Misconceived Search for the Meaning of 'Speech' in Freedom of Speech." *Open Journal of Philosophy* 5, no. 1 (2015): 39–42.

"Free Speech and Speaker's Intent: A Reply to Kendrick." *Columbia Law Review Sidebar* 115, no. 1 (2015): 1–3.

"Free Speech and 'Democratic Persuasion': A Response to Brettschneider." In *Philosophical Foundations of Human Rights*, edited by Rowan Cruft, S. Matthew Liao, and Massimo Renzo. Oxford: Oxford University Press, 2015.

"Judicial Activism: Clearing the Air and the Head." In *Judicial Activism*, edited by Luís Pereira Coutinho, Massimo La Torre, and Steven D. Smith. Berlin: Springer, 2015.

"Galston on Religion, Conscience, and the Case for Accommodation." *San Diego Law Review* 51, no. 4 (2014): 1065–68.

"The Search for Legislative Intent." *University of Queensland Law Journal* 33, no. 2 (2014): 397–402.

"Hart and Punishment for Negligence." In *Hart on Responsibility*, edited by Christopher Pulman. London: Palgrave Macmillan, 2014.

"Constitutional Theories: A Taxonomy and (Implicit) Critique." *San Diego Law Review* 51, no. 3 (2014): 623–44.
"Confused Culpability, Contrived Causation, and the Collapse of Tort Theory." In *Philosophical Foundations of the Law of Torts*, edited by John Oberdiek. Oxford: Oxford University Press, 2014. (With Kimberly Kessler Ferzan)
"The Most Persuasive Frankfurt Example, and What It Shows: Or Why Determinism is Not the Greatest Threat to Moral Responsibility." *Open Journal of Philosophy* 4 (2014): 141–43.
"The Ontology of Consent." *Analytic Philosophy* 55, no. 1 (2014): 102–13.
"Fish on Academic Freedom: A Merited Assault on Nonsense, But Perhaps a Bridge Too Far." *Florida International Law Review* 9, no. 1 (2013): 1–8.
"What Are Principles, and Do They Exist?" San Diego Legal Studies Paper No. 13-119 (2013). https://papers.ssrn.com/sol3/papers.cfm?abstract_id=2277787.
"Did *Casey* Strike Out? Following and Overruling Constitutional Precedents in the Supreme Court." In *Precedent in the United States Supreme Court*, edited by Christopher J. Peters. Berlin: Springer, 2013.
"Is Freedom of Expression a Universal Right?" *San Diego Law Review* 50, no. 3 (2013): 707–20.
"The Objectivity of Morality, Rules, and Law: A Conceptual Map." *Alabama Law Review* 65, no. 2 (2013): 501–18.
"Originalism, the Why and the What." *Fordham Law Review* 82, no. 2 (2013): 539–44.
"Freedom of Expression." In Vol. 1 of *Encyclopedia of Modern Political Thought*, edited by Gregory Claeys, Michael S. Cummings, and Lyman Tower Sargent, 304–6. Washington, DC: CQ Press, 2013.
"Yaffe on Attempts." *Legal Theory* 19, no. 2 (2013): 124–35.
"Other People's Errors." *Ethical Theory and Moral Practice* 16, no. 5 (2013): 1049–59.
"Race Matters." *Constitutional Commentary* 29, no. 1 (2013): 31–57. (With Maimon Schwarzschild)
"Causing the Conditions of One's Defense: A Theoretical Non-Problem." *Criminal Law and Philosophy* 7, no. 3 (2013): 623–28.
"Disparate Impact: Fairness or Efficiency?" *San Diego Law Review* 50, no. 1 (2013): 191–96.
"Can Self-Defense Justify Punishment?" *Law and Philosophy* 32, no. 2/3 (2013): 159–75.
"You Got What You Deserved." *Criminal Law and Philosophy* 7, no. 2 (2013): 309–19.
"Redish on Freedom of Speech." *Northwestern University Law Review* 107, no. 2 (2013): 593–602.
"Voluntary Enslavement." In *Paternalism: Theory and Practice*, edited by Christian Coons and Michael Weber. Cambridge: Cambridge University Press, 2013.
"Fletcher on the Fault of Not Knowing." In *Fletcher's Essays on Criminal Law*, edited by Russell L. Christopher. Oxford: Oxford University Press, 2013. (With Kimberly Kessler Ferzan)
"Reply to Berman, Brison, and Schauer." *APA Newsletter on Philosophy and Law* 12, no. 1 (2012): 13–14.
"Ferzander's Surrebuttal." *Criminal Law and Philosophy* 6, no. 3 (2012): 445–62. (With Kimberly Kessler Ferzan)
"Self-Defense." In *The Routledge Companion to Philosophy of Law*, edited by Andrei Marmor. Abingdon: Routledge, 2012.
"Danger: The Ethics of Preemptive Action." *Ohio State Journal of Criminal Law* 9, no. 2 (2012): 637–67. (With Kimberly Kessler Ferzan)
"The Method of Text and ?: Jack Balkin's Originalism with No Regrets." *Illinois Law Review* 2012, no. 3 (2012): 611–21.

"Risk and Inchoate Crimes: Retribution or Prevention?" In *Seeking Security: Pre-Empting the Commission of Criminal Harms*, edited by G.R. Sullivan and Ian Dennis. Oxford: Hart, 2012. (With Kimberly Kessler Ferzan)

"Reply to Dolinko." *Criminal Law and Philosophy* 6, no. 2 (2012): 281–87 (With Kimberly Kessler Ferzan)

"Precedential Constraint, Its Scope and Strength: A Brief Survey of the Possibilities and Their Merits." In Vol. 3 of *On the Philosophy of Precedent: Proceedings of the 24th World Congress of the International Association for Philosophy of Law and Social Philosophy, Beijing, 2009*, edited by Thomas Bustamante and Carlos Bernal-Pulido. Stuttgart: Steiner, 2012.

"Legal Objectivity and the Illusion of Legal Principles." In *Institutionalized Reason: The Jurisprudence of Robert Alexy*, edited by Matthias Klatt. Oxford: Oxford University Press, 2012, pp. 75–82.

"What's Inside and Outside the Law." *Law and Philosophy* 31, no. 2 (2012): 213–41.

"'Moore or Less' Causation and Responsibility." *Criminal Law and Philosophy* 6, no. 1 (2012): 81–92. (With Kimberly Kessler Ferzan)

"Freedom of Expression." In *Encyclopedia of Applied Ethics*, 2nd ed., edited by Ruth Chadwick, 339–44. Cambridge: Academic Press, 2012.

"Michael Moore and the Mysteries of Causation in the Law." *Rutgers Law Journal* 42, no. 2 (2011): 301–14.

"There Is No First Amendment Overbreadth (But There Are Vague First Amendment Doctrines); Prior Restraints Aren't 'Prior'; and 'As Applied' Challenges Seek Judicial Statutory Amendments." *Constitutional Commentary* 27, no. 2 (2011): 439–54.

"Simple-Minded Originalism." In *The Challenge of Originalism: Essays in Constitutional Theory*, edited by Grant Huscroft and Bradley W. Miller. Cambridge: Cambridge University Press, 2011.

"Deontological Constraints in a Consequentialist World: A Comment on Law, Economics, and Morality." *Jerusalem Review of Legal Studies* 3, no. 1 (2011): 75–90.

"Duff on Attempts." In *Crime, Punishment, and Responsibility: The Jurisprudence of Antony Duff*, edited by Rowan Cruft, Mathew H. Kramer, and Mark R. Reiff. Oxford: Oxford University Press, 2011.

"Culpability." In *The Oxford Handbook of Philosophy of Criminal Law*, edited by John Deigh and David Dolinko. New York: Oxford University Press, 2011.

"Beyond the Special Part." In *Philosophical Foundations of Criminal Law*, edited by R.A. Duff and Stuart Green. Oxford: Oxford University Press, 2011. (With Kimberly Kessler Ferzan)

"Criminal and Moral Responsibility and the Libet Experiments." In *Conscious Will and Responsibility: A Tribute to Benjamin Libet*, edited by Walter Sinnott-Armstrong and Lynn Nadel. Oxford: Oxford University Press, 2010.

"Response to Professor Kent Greenawalt's Lecture." *San Diego Law Review* 47, no. 4 (2010): 1153–56.

"Plastic Trees and Gladiators: Liberalism and Aesthetic Regulation." *Legal Theory* 16, no. 2 (2010): 77–90.

"Response to Critics." *Law and Philosophy* 29, no. 4 (2010): 483–504. (With Kimberly Kessler Ferzan)

"Telepathic Law." *Constitutional Commentary* 27, no. 1 (2010): 139–50.

"What Are Constitutions, and What Should (and Can) They Do?" *Social Philosophy and Policy* 28, no. 1 (2010): 1–24.

"Waluchows – Living Tree Constitutionalism." *Law and Philosophy* 29, no. 1 (2010): 93–99.

"Constitutions, International Law, and the Settlement Function of Law: A Schema for Further Reflection." *San Diego International Law Review* 11, no. 1 (2009): 43–57.

"Facts, Law, Exculpation, and Inculpation: Comments on Simons." *Criminal Law and Philosophy* 3, no. 3 (2009): 241–45.

"Law and Philosophy at Odds." In *On Philosophy in American Law*, edited by Francis J. Mootz III. Cambridge: Cambridge University Press, 2009. (With Emily Sherwin)

"Constitutionalism and Democracy: Understanding the Relation." In *The Supreme Court and the Idea of Constitutionalism*, edited by Steven Kautz, Arthur Melzer, Jerry Weinberg, and M. Richard Zinman. Philadelphia: University of Pennsylvania Press, 2009.

"Constitutionalism." In *Contemporary Debates in Political Philosophy*, edited by Thomas Christiano and John Christman. Hoboken: Wiley-Blackwell, 2009.

"Of Living Trees and Dead Hands: The Interpretation of Constitutions and Constitutional Rights." *Canadian Journal of Law and Jurisprudence* 22, no. 2 (2009): 227–36.

"Kent Greenawalt and the Difficulty (Impossibility?) of Religion Clause Theory." *Constitutional Commentary* 25, no. 2 (2009): 243–47.

"Rules of Recognition, Constitutional Controversies, and the Dizzying Dependence of Law on Acceptance." In *The Rule of Recognition and the U.S. Constitution*, edited by Matthew Adler and Kenneth Himma. Oxford: Oxford University Press, 2009. (With Frederick Schauer)

"Against Negligence Liability." In *Criminal Law Conversations*, edited by Paul H. Robinson, Kimberly Kessler Ferzan, and Steven P. Garvey. Oxford: Oxford University Press, 2009. (With Kimberly Kessler Ferzan)

"Results Don't Matter." In *Criminal Law Conversations*, edited by Paul H. Robinson, Kimberly Kessler Ferzan, and Steven P. Garvey. Oxford: Oxford University Press, 2009. (With Kimberly Kessler Ferzan)

"Tempest in an Empty Teapot: Why the Constitution Does Not Regulate Gerrymandering." *William & Mary Law Review* 50, no. 1 (2008): 1–62. (With Saikrishana Prakash)

"What is Freedom of Association, and What Is Its Denial?" *Social Philosophy and Policy* 25, no. 2 (2008): 1–21. Reprinted in *Freedom of Association*, edited by Ellen Frankel Paul, Fred D. Miller, Jr., and Jeffrey Paul. Cambridge: Cambridge University Press, 2009.

"Constitutions, Judicial Review, Moral Rights, and Democracy: Disentangling the Issues." In *Expounding the Constitution: Essays in Constitutional Theory*, edited by Grant Huscroft. Cambridge: Cambridge University Press, 2008.

"Culpable Acts of Risk Creation." *Ohio State Journal of Criminal Law* 5, no. 2 (2008): 375–405. (With Kimberly Kessler Ferzan)

"Scalar Properties, Binary Judgments." *Journal of Applied Philosophy* 25, no. 2 (2008): 85–104.

"Is There Logical Space on the Moral Map for Toleration? A Brief Comment on Smith, Morgan, and Forst." In *Toleration and Its Limits*, edited by Melissa S. Williams and Jeremy Waldron. New York: New York University Press, 2008.

"Is Policy within Law's Limited Domain?" *University of Queensland Law Journal* 26, no. 2 (2007): 221–35. (With Frederick Schauer)

"How to Understand Legislatures: A Comment on Boudreau, Lupia, McCubbins, and Rodriguez." *San Diego Law Review* 44, no. 4 (2007): 993–1000.

"Judicial Review and Moral Rights." *University of Queensland Law Journal* 33, no. 1 (2007): 1–18.

"Deontological Ethics." In *The Stanford Encyclopedia of Philosophy*, edited by Edward N. Zalta (first published November 21, 2007, substantive revision October 17, 2016). https://plato.stanford.edu/archives/win2016/entries/ethics-deontological/. (With Michael Moore)

"Judges as Rulemakers." In *Common Law Theory*, edited by Douglas E. Edlin. Cambridge: Cambridge University Press, 2007). (With Emily Sherwin)

"Expression, Freedom of." In *Encyclopedia of Law and Society: American and Global Perspectives*, edited by David S. Clark. Thousand Oaks: Sage, 2007.

"Delegations Really Running Riot." *Virginia Law* Review 93, no. 4 (2007): 1035–80. (With Saikrishna Prakash)

"Law's Limited Domain Confronts Morality's Universal Empire." *William & Mary Law Review* 48, no. 5 (2007): 1579–1603. (With Frederick Schauer)

"Compelled Speech." *Constitutional Commentary* 23, no. 2 (2006): 147–62.

"Academic Freedom." *University of Colorado Law Review* 77, no. 4 (2006): 883–900.

"What Is the Problem of Judicial Review?" *Australian Journal of Legal Philosophy* 31, no. 1 (2006): 1–13.

"When Are We Rightfully Aggrieved?: A Comment on Postema." *Legal Theory* 11, no. 3 (2005): 325–32.

"Lesser Evils: A Closer Look at the Paradigmatic Justification." *Law and Philosophy* 24, no. 6 (2005): 611–43.

"Popular? Constitutionalism?" *Harvard Law Review* 118, no. 5 (2005): 1594–640. (With Lawrence B. Solum)

"Unknowingly Justified Actors and the Attempt/Success Distinction." *Tulsa Law Review* 39, no. 4 (2004): 851–60.

"*Grutter* or Otherwise: Racial Preferences and Higher Education." *Constitutional Commentary* 21, no. 1 (2004): 3–14. (With Maimon Schwarzschild)

"The Jurisdiction of Justice: Two Conceptions of Political Morality." *San Diego Law Review* 41, no. 3 (2004): 949–66.

"'Is That English You're Speaking?' Some Arguments for the Primacy of Intent in Interpretation." *San Diego Law Review* 41, no. 3 (2004): 967–96. (With Saikrishna Prakash)

"Constitutionalism." In *The Blackwell Guide to the Philosophy of Law and Legal Theory*, edited by Martin P. Golding and William A. Edmundson. Malden, MA: Blackwell, 2004.

"Constitutional Rules, Constitutional Standards, and Constitutional Settlement: *Marbury v. Madison* and the Case for Judicial Supremacy." *Constitutional Commentary* 20, no. 2 (2003): 369–76.

"Mother May I? Imposing Mandatory Prospective Rules of Statutory Interpretation." *Constitutional Commentary* 20, no. 1 (2003): 97–110. (With Saikrishna Prakash)

"Reports of the Delegation Doctrine's Death Are Greatly Exaggerated." *University of Chicago Law Review* 70, no. 4 (2003): 1297–330. (With Saikrishna Prakash)

"Introduction to the Conference on Legal Transitions." *Journal of Contemporary Legal Issues* 13, no. 1 (2003): 1–4.

"Freedom of Expression as a Human Right." In *Protecting Human Rights: Instruments and Institutions*, edited by Tom Campbell, Jeffery Goldsworthy, and Adrienne Stone. Oxford: Oxford University Press, 2003.

"Deception in Morality and Law." *Law and Philosophy* 22, no. 5 (2003): 393–450. (With Emily Sherwin)

"Is Judicial Review Democratic? A Comment on Harel." *Law and Philosophy* 22, no. 3/4 (2003): 277–83.
"Rule-Guidance, Rationality, and Constraint." In *Legal and Political Philosophy*, edited by Enrique Villanueva. Leiden: Brill, 2002.
"Equal Protection and the Prosecution and Conviction of Crime." *The University of Chicago Legal Forum* (2002): 155–62.
"The Legal Enforcement of Morality." In *A Companion to Applied Ethics*, edited by R.G. Frey and Christopher Heath Wellman. Hoboken: Blackwell, 2003.
"Equal Protection and the Irrelevance of Groups." *Issues in Legal Scholarship* 2, no. 1 (2002): 1–12.
"Illiberalism All the Way Down: Illiberal Groups and Two Conceptions of Liberalism." *Journal of Contemporary Legal Issues* 12, no. 2 (2002): 625–36.
"Criminal Liability for Omissions: An Inventory of Issues." In *Criminal Law Theory: Doctrines of the General Part*, edited by Stephen Shute and A.P. Simester. Oxford: Oxford University Press, 2002.
"Interpreting Rules: The Nature and Limits of Inchoate Intentions." In *Legal Interpretation in Democratic States*, edited by Jeffery Goldsworthy and Tom Campbell. Farnham: Ashgate, 2002. (With Emily Sherwin)
"The Philosophy of Criminal Law." In *The Oxford Handbook of Jurisprudence and Legal Philosophy*, edited by Jules Coleman and Scott Shapiro. Oxford: Oxford University Press, 2001.
"Mistake." In *Encyclopedia of Crime and Justice*, edited by Joshua Dressler. New York: Macmillan, 2001.
"The Supreme Court, the Florida Vote, and Equal Protection." *San Diego Law Review* 38, no. 4 (2001): 1077–80.
"Ripstein, Reasonableness, and Objectivity." *Law and Philosophy* 20, no. 6 (2001): 617–35.
"Defending Judicial Supremacy: A Reply." *Constitutional Commentary* 17, no. 3 (2000): 455–82. (With Frederick Schauer)
"Deontology at the Threshold." *San Diego Law Review* 37, no. 4 (2000): 893–912.
"Rules, Rights, Options, and Time." *Legal Theory* 6, no. 4 (2000): 391–404.
"Theory's A What Comes Natcherly." *San Diego Law Review* 37, no. 3 (2000): 777–82.
"The Uncertain Relationship Between Libertarianism and Utilitarianism." *Quinnipiac Law Review* 19, no. 4 (2000): 657–64. (With Maimon Schwarzschild)
"Insufficient Concern: A Unified Conception of Criminal Culpability." *California Law Review* 88, no. 3 (2000): 931–54.
"Stare Decisis." In *Encyclopedia of the American Constitution, Supplement II*, edited by Leonard W. Levy, Kenneth L. Karst, and Adam Winkler. New York: Macmillan Reference, 2000.
"Nonjudicial Interpretation of the Constitution." In *Encyclopedia of the American Constitution, Supplement II*, edited by Leonard W. Levy, Kenneth L. Karst, and Adam Winkler. New York: Macmillan Reference, 2000.
"Incitement and Freedom of Speech." In *Freedom of Speech and Incitement Against Democracy*, edited by David Kretzmer and Francine Kershman Hazan. Leiden: Brill, 2000.
"State Action." In *The Philosophy of Law: An Encyclopedia*, edited by Christopher Berry Gray. Abingdon: Routledge, 1999.
"Subversive Thoughts on Freedom and the Common Good." *Michigan Law Review* 97, no. 6 (1999): 1813–27. (With Maimon Schwarzschild)

"With Me, It's All er Nuthin: Formalism in Law and Morality." *University of Chicago Law Review* 66, no. 3 (1999): 530–65.
"A Unified Defense of Preemptive Self-Protection." *Notre Dame Law Review* 74, no. 5 (1999): 1475–506.
"Can the Law Survive the Asymmetry of Authority?" In *Rules and Reasoning: Essays in Honour of Fred Schauer*, edited by Linda Meyer. Oxford: Hart, 1999. Reprinted in *Quinnipiac Law Review* 19, no. 3 (2000): 463–82.
"Hate Speech." In *The Constitution and Its Amendments*, edited by Roger K. Newman. New York: Macmillan Reference, 1998.
"Good God, Garvey: The Inevitability and Impossibility of a Religious Justification of Free Exercise Exemptions." *Drake Law Review* 47, no. 1 (1998): 35–44.
"Affirmative Action and Legislative Purpose." *Yale Law Journal* 107, no. 8 (1998): 2679–84.
"Constitutional Tragedies and Giving Refuge to the Devil." In *Constitutional Stupidities, Constitutional Tragedies*, edited by William N. Eskridge and Stanford Levinson. New York: New York University Press, 1998.
"The Banality of Legal Reasoning." *Notre Dame Law Review* 73, no. 3 (1998): 517–34.
"Banishing the Bogey of Incommensurability." *University of Pennsylvania Law Review* 146, no. 5 (1998): 1641–50.
"Are Procedural Rights Derivative Substantive Rights?" *Law and Philosophy* 17, no. 1 (1998): 19–42.
"Discrimination by Proxy." *Constitutional Commentary* 14, no. 3 (1997): 453–64. (With Kevin Cole)
"Replies to Our Critics." *Iowa Law Review* 82, no. 3 (1997): 923–42. (With Kenneth Kress)
"Mens Rea and Inchoate Crimes." *Journal of Criminal Law and Criminology* 87, no. 4 (1997): 1138–93. (With Kimberly Kessler Ferzan)
"Freedom of Speech." In *Encyclopedia of Applied Ethics*, edited by Ruth Chadwick. Cambridge: Elsevier, 1997.
"Is Morality Like the Tax Code?" *Michigan Law Review* 95, no. 6 (1997): 1839–50.
"On Extrajudicial Constitutional Interpretation." *Harvard Law Review* 110, no. 7 (1997): 1359–87. (With Fred Schauer)
"Sometimes Better Boring and Correct: *Romer* as an Exercise of Ordinary Equal Protection Analysis." *University of Colorado Law Review* 68, no. 2 (1997): 335–49.
"Still Lost in the Political Thicket (or Why I Don't Understand the Concept of Vote Dilution)." *Vanderbilt Law Review* 50, no. 2 (1997): 327–38.
"Bad Beginnings." *University of Pennsylvania Law Review* 145, no. 1 (1997): 57–88.
"Incomplete Theorizing." *Notre Dame Law Review* 72, no. 2 (1997): 531–44.
"Is It Really Racist Not To Be Racist? A Reply to Professor Spann." *Duke Law Journal* (1997). (With Maimon Schwarzschild)
"The Supreme Court, Dr. Jekyll, and the Due Process of Proof." *The Supreme Court Review* (1996): 191–218.
"Are *Smith* and *Hialeah* Reconcilable?" *Constitutional Commentary* 13, no. 3 (1996): 285–90.
"The Moral Magic of Consent (II)." *Legal Theory* 2, no. 3 (1996): 165–74.
"Precedent." In *A Companion to the Philosophy of Law and Legal Theory*, edited by Dennis Patterson. Malden: Blackwell, 1996.
"Affirmative Duties and the Limits of Self-Sacrifice." *Law and Philosophy* 15, no. 1 (1996): 65–74.

"Negligence, Crime, and Tort: Comments on Hurd and Simons." *Boston University Law Review* 76, no. 1/2 (1996): 301–6.
"Impossible." *Denver University Law Review* 72, no. 4 (1995): 1007–10.
"Originalism, or Who Is Fred?" *Harvard Journal of Law & Public Policy* 19, no. 2 (1995): 321–26.
"Banning Hate Speech and the Sticks and Stones Defense." *Constitutional Commentary* 13, no. 1 (1996): 71–100.
"Is There Such a Thing as Extraconstitutionality?: The Puzzling Case of *Dalton v. Specter*." *Arizona State Law Journal* 27, no. 3 (1995): 845–74. (With Evan Lee)
"Free Speech and Speaker's Intent." *Constitutional Commentary* 12, no. 1 (1995): 21–28.
"Fancy Theories of Interpretation Aren't." *Washington University Law Quarterly* 73, no. 3 (1995): 1081–84.
"Against Legal Principles." In *Law and Interpretation*, edited by Andrei Marmor. Oxford: Oxford University Press, 1995. Reprinted in *Iowa Law Review* 82, no. 3 (1997): 739–86. (With Kenneth Kress)
"All or Nothing at All? The Intentions of Authorities and the Authority of Intentions." In *Law and Interpretation*, edited by Andrei Marmor. Oxford: Oxford University Press, 1995.
"Crime and Culpability." *Journal Contemporary Legal Issues* 5, no. 1 (1994): 1–30.
"Constitutional Theory and Constitutionally Optional Benefits and Burdens." *Constitutional Commentary* 11, no. 2 (1994): 287–314.
"The Deceptive Nature of Rules." *University of Pennsylvania Law Review* 142, no. 4 (1994): 1191–228. (With Emily Sherwin)
"Harm, Offense, and Morality." *Canadian Journal of Law and Jurisprudence* 7, no. 2 (1994): 199–216.
"Liberalism, Religion, and the Unity of Epistemology." *San Diego Law Review* 30, no. 4 (1993): 763–98.
"What We Do and Why We Do It." *Stanford Law Review* 45, no. 6 (1993): 1885–904.
"The Public/Private Distinction(s)." *Constitutional Commentary* 10, no. 2 (1993): 361–78.
"Trouble on Track Two: Incidental Regulations of Speech and Free Speech Theory." *Hastings Law Journal* 44, no. 4 (1993): 921–62.
"Practical Reason and Statutory Interpretation." *Law and Philosophy* 12, no. 3 (1993): 319–28.
"Constitutional Torts, the Supreme Court, and the Law of Noncontradition: An Essay on *Zinermon v. Burch*." *Northwestern University Law Review* 87, no. 2 (1993): 576–96.
"Inculpatory and Exculpatory Mistakes and the Fact/Law Distinction: An Essay in Memory of Myke Bayles." *Law and Philosophy* 12, no. 1 (1993): 33–70.
"Self-Defense, Justification, and Excuse." *Philosophy and Public Affairs* 22, no. 1 (1993): 53–66.
"The ADL Hate Crime Statute and the First Amendment." *Criminal Justice Ethics* 11, no. 2 (1993): 49–51.
"Voluntary Acts: The Child/Davidson Trilemma." *Criminal Justice Ethics* 11, no. 2 (1993): 98–99.
"What Makes Wrongful Discrimination Wrong? Biases, Preferences, Stereotypes, and Proxies." *University of Pennsylvania Law Review* 141, no. 1 (1992): 149–220.
"Proving the Law: Not Proven." *Northwestern University Law Review* 86, no. 4 (1992): 905–15.
"Foreword: Coleman and Corrective Justice." *Harvard Journal of Law & Public Policy* 15, no. 3 (1992): 621–36.
"A Comment on Cass Sunstein's Equality." *Constitutional Commentary* 9, no. 2 (1992): 189–90. (With Emily Sherwin)
"Self-Defense, Punishment, and Proportionality." *Law and Philosophy* 10, no. 3 (1991): 323–28.

"The Gap." *Harvard Journal of Law & Public Policy* 14, no. 3 (1991): 695–802.
"Law and Exclusionary Reasons." *Philosophy Topics* 18, no. 1 (1990): 5–22.
"Of Two Minds About Law and Minds." *Michigan Law Review* 88, no. 8 (1990): 2444–49.
"Reconsidering the Relationship Among Voluntary Acts, Strict Liability, and Negligence in Criminal Law." *Social Philosophy and Policy* 7, no. 2 (1990): 84–104. Reprinted in *Controversies in Criminal Law: Philosophical Essays on Responsibility and Procedure*, edited by Michael Gorr and Sterling Voss Harwood. San Francisco: Westview Press, 1992.
"Lost in the Political Thicket." *University of Florida Law Review* 41, no. 3 (1990): 563–80.
"Understanding Constitutional Rights in a World of Optional Baselines." *San Diego Law Review* 26, no. 2 (1989): 175–88.
"Constrained by Precedent." *Southern California Law Review* 63, no. 1 (1989): 1–64.
"Comment: Personal Projects and Impersonal Rights." *Harvard Journal of Law & Public Policy* 12, no. 3 (1989): 813–26.
"Low Value Speech." *Northwestern University Law Review* 83, no. 3 (1989): 547–54.
"The Constitution as Law." *Constitutional Commentary* 6, no. 1 (1989): 103–14.
"Legal Theory and Judicial Accountability: A Comment on Seidman." *Southern California Law Review* 61, no. 6 (1988): 1601–6.
"Striking Back at the Empire: A Brief Survey of Problems in Dworkin's Theory of Law." *Law and Philosophy* 6, no. 3 (1987): 419–38.
"The Relationship Between Procedural Due Process and Substantive Constitutional Rights." *University of Florida Law Review* 39, no. 2 (1987): 323–44.
"Justification and Innocent Aggressors." *Wayne Law Review* 33, no. 4 (1987): 1177–90.
"Causation and Corrective Justice: Does Tort Law Make Sense?" *Law and Philosophy* 6, no. 1 (1987): 1–23.
"Scheffler on the Independence of Agent-Centred Prerogatives from Agent-Centered Restrictions." *Journal of Philosophy* 84, no. 5 (1987): 277–83.
"Takings of Property and Constitutional Serendipity." *University of Miami Law Review* 41, no. 1 (1986): 223–34.
"Liberalism, Neutrality, and Equality of Welfare versus Equality of Resources." *Philosophy and Public Affairs* 16, no. 1 (1986): 85–110. (With Maimon Schwarzschild)
"Freedom of Contract and the Family: A Skeptical Appraisal." In *The American Family and the State: Pacific Studies in Public Policy*, edited by Joseph R. Peden and Fred R. Glahe. Cambridge: Cambridge University Press, 1986). (With Paul Horton)
"Consent, Punishment, and Proportionality." *Philosophy and Public Affairs* 15, no. 2 (1986): 178–82.
"Fair Equality of Opportunity: Rawls' (Best?) Forgotten Principle." *Philosophy Research Archives* 11 (1985): 197–208.
"Electronic Monitoring of Felons by Computer: Threat or Boon to Civil Liberties." *Social Theory and Practice* 11, no. 1 (1985): 89–95. (With Elaine Alexander)
"Is There an Overbreadth Doctrine?" *San Diego Law Review* 22, no. 2/3 (1985): 541–54.
"Pursuing the Good – Indirectly." *Ethics* 95, no. 2 (1985): 315–32.
"Consumer Boycotts and Freedom of Association: A Comment on a Recently Proposed Theory." *San Diego Law Review* 22, no. 2/3 (1985): 555–64. (With Maimon Schwarzschild)
"Reiman's Libertarian Interpretation of Rawls' Difference Principle." *Philosophy Research Archives* 10 (1984): 13–18.

"Kidney Pooling." *Cogito* 2, no. 1 (1984): 15.
"Another Look at Moral Blackmail." *Philosophy Research Archives* 10 (1984): 189–96.
"Natural Advantages and Contractual Justice." *Law and Philosophy* 3, no. 2 (1984): 281–97. (With William Wang)
"The Impossibility of a Free Speech Principle." *Northwestern University Law Review* 78, no. 5 (1983): 1319–58. (With Paul Horton)
"Retributivism and the Inadvertent Killing of the Innocent." *Law and Philosophy* 2, no. 2 (1983): 223–46.
"Painting Without the Numbers: Noninterpretivist Judicial Review." *University of Dayton Law Review* 8, no. 3 (1983): 447–64.
"Zimmerman on Coercive Wage Offers." *Philosophy and Public Affairs* 12, no. 2 (1983): 160–64.
"Liberalism as Neutral Dialogue: Man and Manna in the Liberal State." *UCLA Law Review* 28, no. 4 (1981): 816–58.
"Modern Equal Protection Theories: A Metatheoretical Taxonomy and Critique." *Ohio State Law Journal* 42, no. 1 (1981): 3–68.
"Commercial Speech and First Amendment Theory: A Critical Exchange." *Northwestern University Law Review* 75, no. 2 (1980): 307–15. (With Daniel Farber)
"The Doomsday Machine: Proportionality, Prevention and Punishment." *The Monist* 63, no. 2 (1980): 199–227.
"Stork Markets: An Analysis of 'Baby Selling.'" *Journal of Libertarian Studies* 4, no. 2 (1980): 173–96. (With Lyla O'Driscoll)
"Hercules or Proteus? The Many Theses of Ronald Dworkin." *Social Theory and Practice* 5, no. 3/4 (1980): 267–303. (With Michael D. Bayles)
"*Ingraham v. Wright:* A Primer for Cruel and Unusual Jurisprudence." *Southern California Law Review* 52, no. 5 (1979): 1305–404. (With Paul Horton)
"Motivation and Constitutionality: A Postscript." *San Diego Law Review* 16, no. 5 (1979): 885–90.
"Introduction: Motivation and Constitutionality." *San Diego Law Review* 15, no. 5 (1978): 925–52.
"The Province of Constitutional Law Casebook Jurisprudence Redetermined." *Stanford Law Review* 29, no. 6 (1977): 1299–310.
"Speech in the Local Marketplace: Implications of *Virginia State Board of Pharmacy v. Virginia Citizens Consumer Council, Inc.* for Local Regulatory Power." *San Diego Law Review* 14, no. 2 (1977): 357–77.
"Self-Defense and the Killing of Noncombatants: A Reply to Fullinwider." *Philosophy and Public Affairs* 5, no. 4 (1976): 408–15. Reprinted in *International Ethics*, edited by Charles R. Beitz. Princeton: Princeton University Press, 1985.
"Cutting the Gordian Knot: State Action and Self-Help Repossession." *Hastings Constitutional Law Quarterly* 2, no. 4 (1976): 893–934.
"The Authentication of Documents Requirement: Barrier to Falsehood or to Truth?" *San Diego Law Review* 10, no. 2 (1973): 266–79. (With Elaine Alexander)
"The New Racism: An Analysis of the Use of Racial and Ethnic Criteria in Decision-Making." *San Diego Law Review* 9, no. 2 (1972): 190–263. (With Elaine Alexander)

UNTITLED BOOK REVIEWS

Review of *The New Philosophy of Criminal Law*, edited by Chad Flanders and Zachary Hoskins. *Notre Dame Philosophical Review* (2016). https://ndpr.nd.edu/news/the-new-philosophy-of-criminal-law/.

Review of *Philosophical Foundations of Discrimination Law*, edited by Deborah Hellman and Sophia Moreau. *Ethics* 125, no. (2015): 872–79.

Review of *The Hateful and the Obscene: Studies in the Limits of Free Expression*, by L.W. Sumner. *Ethics* 116, no. 4 (2006): 809–13.

Review of *The Autonomy of Law*, by Robert P. George. *Ethics* 108, no. 3 (1998): 600–2.

Review of *Words That Bind: Judicial Review and the Grounds of Modern Constitutional* Theory, by John Arthur. *Philosophical Review* 106, no. 3 (1997): 461–64.

Review of *Automatism, Insanity, and the Psychology of Criminal Responsibility*, by Robert F. Schopp. *Ethics* 103, no. 3 (1993): 594–96.

Review of *Interpreting the Constitution*, by Harry H. Wellington and *On Reading the Constitution*, by Laurence H. Tribe and Michael C. Dorf. *Constitutional Commentary* 8, no. 2 (1991): 463–69.

Review of *Liberal Neutrality*, edited by Robert E. Goodin and Andrew Reeve. *Constitutional Commentary* 8, no. 1 (1991): 255–59.

Book Note, *Ethics* 101, no. 3 (1991): 676.

Review of *The Rights Retained by the People*, edited by Randy E. Barnett. *Constitutional Commentary* 7, no. 2 (1990): 396–403.

OTHER WRITINGS

"Paying the Price for Breakdown of the Country's Bourgeois." *The Philadelphia Inquirer*, August 9, 2017. www.philly.com/philly/opinion/commentary/paying-the-price-for-breakdown-of-the-countrys-bourgeois-culture-20170809.html/. (With Amy Wax)

"Fighting for Words." *National Review*, November 29, 2012. www.nationalreview.com/magazine/2012/11/29/fighting-words/.

"Publicly Subsidized Boarding Schools." *San Diego Union-Tribune*, May 22, 1996.

"Balance of Trade and Protectionism." *San Diego Union-Tribune*, April 9, 1996. (With Chris Wonnell)

"Flag-burning Amendment." *San Diego Union-Tribune*, October 9, 1989.

Index

academic freedom
  contract law and, 115
  definition of, 113, 117
  as distinctive right, 116, 119
  extramural expression, 113
  freedom of expression, distinction from, 427
  harm and, 129, 133
  knowledge and, 130
  LA's responses to contributors, 427
  LA's theory, 11
  legal status of, 114
  and Marcuse, Herbert, 129
  other countries compared with USA, 118
  positivism and, 117
  private employees, 117
  reasons for protecting speech, 119
  scientific inquiry, nature of, 130
  tenure and, 115
  truth and, 130
action
  intention and, 206
Alexander, Candy (sister), 3
Alexander, David (son), 20
Alexander, Elaine (wife), 3, 4
Alexander, Helen Rosenwasser (mother), 2
Alexander, Jenny (daughter), 20
Alexander, Jonathan (son), 20
Alexander, Lawrence (Larry) (indicated elsewhere in the index as LA)
  and Alexander, Elaine, 3, 4
  early life, 2
  family, 20
  present volume as 'readers guide', 2
  responses to contributors, 407
  scholarly method, 5
  scholarship on constitutional law, overview, 9
  scholarship on criminal law, overview, 6
  scholarship on jurisprudence, overview, 14
  scholarship on moral philosophy, overview, 16
Alexander, Simon Ray (father), 2
anarchism
  authority and, 273, 283
  definition of, 272
animals
  moral status, 321
Arendt, Hannah, 276, 277
Arneson, Richard, 18, 350, 372, 434
attempts. *See* criminal attempts
Austin, J.L., 82
authority
  anarchism and, 273, 283
  "asymmetry" of, 303, 430
  definition of legal authority, 272
  dissolution of, 276
  epistemic authority, 275
  intentionalism and, 279
  interpretation and, 15, 279, 428
  LA's responses to contributors, 428
  LA's theory of, 15, 277
  lawmaking authority, seat of, 281
  modern theories of, 273
  obligation and, 274, 275
  and original public meaning originalism (textualism), 280
  premodern origins of, 273
  reasons for obeying, 275
  See also rules

Barnett, Randy, 161
Baude, William, 15, 260, 431
benevolent despotism
  denial of freedom of expression, 121
Berger, Raoul, 165
Berman, Mitchell, 14, 92, 241, 432
Blackstone, William, 49
blame. *See* criminal responsibility
Bratman, Michael, 293, 300
Brest, Paul, 160
Brink, David, 7, 39, 411
Brudner, Alan, 89

Canada
  judicial supremacy, 146
capital punishment
  constitutionality of, 165
capitalism
  and freedom of expression, 124, 128
causation
  and criminal attempts, 65
choice
  rationality and, 292
Chomsky, Noam, 132
Christopher, Russell, 391, 392, 394
Cicero, 81
Claus, Laurence, 13, 134, 277, 425
coercion. *See* duress
Cole, Kevin, 19, 372, 388, 436
colonialism
  denial of freedom of expression, 121
competence. *See* criminal responsibility
conditional relevance, 5
consent
  authority and, 273
  and moral obligation, 16
consequentialism
  deontological ethics, 17, 350
  means principle, 355
  punishment. *See* punishment
constitutional law
  constitutionalism, concept of, 238
  death penalty, constitutionality of, 165
  entrenched laws, 10
  enumeration of powers, 143
  free speech. *See* freedom of expression
  gerrymanders, 10
  interpretation, 12
  LA's responses to contributors, 415
  LA's theories, 9
  lawmaking authority, seat of, 281
  legal status of Constitution, 264
  legislative delegations of power, 10
  originalism and constitutional authority, 265
  overview of present volume contributions, 9
  preconstitutional rule of constitutional authority, 264
  and rule of recognition, 265
  "self-validating" constitutions, 230
  separation of powers, 147
  settlement as primary function of, 262
  state action defense, 9
  supremacy of Constitution, 226, 231, 260, 269, 431
  unconstitutional conditions theory, 10
  See also academic freedom; democracy; intentionalism; interpretation; judicial supremacy; originalism; settlement
constraint principle
  originalism, 190
  threshold deontology, 355
construction. *See* interpretation
contract law
  academic freedom and, 115
control. *See* criminal responsibility
Converse, Philip, 124
crimes, criminal acts. *See* offenses
criminal attempts
  causation and, 65
  collective responsibility, 62, 64, 75
  culpable mental states, 67
  example scenarios
    failed murder attempt, 64
    firing squad, 62
    use of, 61
  individual responsibility, 62, 64, 75
  justifications, 67
  LA's responses to contributors, 409
  LA's theory, 7
  "moral ledger" concept, 68
  outcome of, effect on offender's liability ("results matter" argument), 60
  and reckless actions, 60, 68
  relief over failed attempts ("Thank God you failed" response), 74
  remorse, effect on offender's liability ("Thank God I failed!" response), 64, 74
  retributivist approach, 69
  unexpected (but welcome) consequences, 65
criminal law
  bivalent character of, 39
  LA's responses to contributors, 408
  LA's theories, 6
  overview of present volume contributions, 6

retributivist character of, 40
See also criminal attempts; criminal responsibility; defenses; duress; lesser evils defense; punishment
criminal responsibility
for attempts. *See* criminal attempts
bivalent approach, 39, 46
collective responsibility, 62, 64, 75
conditions of, 9
culpability and, 40, 43
culpable mental states, 67
defenses. *See* defenses
determinations of degrees of, 52
diminished responsibility, 53
excuse in inverse relation to, 42
individual responsibility, 62, 64, 75
LA's responses to contributors, 411
M'Naghten rule, 43
negligence, 9
normative competence, condition of, 43, 46, 49
partial responsibility
examples of, 40
ideal theory of, 46
nonideal theory of, 51
summary overview of options, 58
proportionality, 39, 46
recklessness, 9
scale of, 39, 46
situational control, condition of, 43, 44, 45
tetravalent approach, 56
thresholds, 50
trivalent approach, 53
wrongdoing and, 40
culpability. *See* criminal responsibility
Curtin, Hoyt, 155

Darwall, Stephen, 324
death penalty
constitutionality of, 165
defenses
availability of, 99
contrived defenses
intransitivity and, 313
morality and rationality in relation to, 311
diminished responsibility, 53
duress. *See* duress
excuse
justification and. *See* duress
responsibility and, 42, 46
incompetence, 42
insanity, 54
justification
excuse and. *See* duress
usages of term, 109
lesser evils defense, 8
provocation, 46
self-defense, 8
self-defense, contrived, 313
state action defense, 9
democracy
and constitutional authoritative settlement, 234
and freedom of expression, 123
See also constitutional law
deontological ethics
consequentialism and, 17, 350, 373
consequentialist obligations, strength (stringency) of, 378, 384
deontological obligations, strength (stringency) of, 379, 384
LA's responses to contributors, 434
LA's theories, 17, 351
means principle. *See* means principle
morality of, 373
as nonconsequentialism, 350
obligations
conflict of, 375, 381, 383, 384
strength (stringency) of, 377, 378, 379, 381, 383, 384
problems with, 350
purpose of, 350
and retributive punishment, 19
threshold deontology
and constraint principle, 355
justification for, 386
LA's "moral ballast" critique of, 395, 398
LA's responses to contributors, 436
LA's theory, 18, 354, 371
limitations of, 404
nature of thresholds, 373
punishment and, 388
rationality of, 371
deprivation. *See* punishment
desert. *See* punishment
despotism. *See* benevolent despotism
dignity. *See* human dignity
diminished responsibility
defense of, 53
discrimination, 320
contempt and, 326
disrespectful discrimination, 318, 323, 326, 329, 332
egalitarian and inegalitarian beliefs, 321
intrinsically wrongful discrimination, 320

discrimination (*cont.*)
  LA's responses to contributors, 438
  LA's theory, 16, 317
  moral status of animals, 321
  moral status of persons, 318, 321
  positive discrimination, wrongfulness of, 320
  wrongfulness of, 16, 317, 438
distributive justice
  equality and, 16
double effect
  doctrine of, 336, 347, 352, 388, 392, 434
Dressler, Joshua, 87
Driver, Justin, 268
Duff, Antony, 60, 90, 93, 409
duress
  applicability to any crime, 77
  "average person" standard, 87
  broader defense, 78
  coercion, 77, 83
  coercive and noncoercive threats contrasted, 93
  defense of, 42
  and defense of others, 78
  distinction between justification and excuse, 81
  elements of, 77
  example scenarios
    alternative trial outcomes, 85
    comparison between, 85
    fleeing felon, 80, 95
    housekeeper, 84, 90
    novelist's laptop, 88
    phobic manager, 84, 85
  as excuse, 76, 78, 80, 83, 90, 94, 95, 96
  as exoneration, 76, 94
  intransitivity and, 312
  as justification, 76, 80, 83, 90, 94, 95, 96
  LA's ambivalent approach, 76, 80
  LA's responses to contributors, 411
  LA's theory, 78
  and lesser evils defense, 79, 411
  and mistakes of law, 89
  and moral weakness, 87
  and nature of harm, 93
  offenses committed under, 8
  paradoxical theories of, 90
  "person of reasonable firmness in the actor's situation" standard, 83
  as residual defense, 79
  and self-defense, 78
  and situational control, 44
  threats, contrast between coercive and noncoercive, 93
Dworkin, Ronald, 14, 165, 242, 243, 248, 250, 256

egalitarianism
  discrimination and, 321
Eidelson, Benjamin, 323, 326, 329, 332
Eisenhower, Dwight, 268
Ekins, Richard, 176, 177, 180, 181, 422
Ellsworth, Oliver, 141
employment contracts. *See* academic freedom
enforcement. *See* punishment
England and Wales
  academic freedom, 118
  diminished responsibility defense, 54
  freedom of expression, 121
  interpretation, 176
  judicial supremacy, 135
  Montesquieu and English Constitution, 147
  use of force, mistaken belief in legality of, 89
enlightenment
  and freedom of expression, 122
enumeration of powers
  judicial supremacy and, 143
equality
  as discrete moral value, 14
  and distributive justice, 16
  See also discrimination
Eser, Albin, 91
estoppel
  and lesser evils defense, 107, 414
ethics. *See* consequentialism; deontological ethics
evidence
  conditional relevance, 5
excuses. *See* defenses; duress
expression. *See* freedom of expression

failed attempts. *See* criminal attempts
Feldman, Richard, 297
Ferzan, Kimberly Kessler, 18, 333, 409, 411, 434
finality. *See* settlement
Finnis, John, 274
Fish, Stanley, 178
force
  mistaken belief in legality of use, 89
Founding Fathers
  and judicial supremacy, 138, 262, 425
freedom of expression
  argument for, 127
  "bad speech" and "good speech," 127
  capitalism and, 124, 128
  democracy and, 123
  denial by benevolent colonial despotism, 121
  enlightenment and, 122
  free speech, 10
  government speech, 11

government's regulatory intention
importance of, 208
inquiry into, 207
language in relation, 220
LA's theory, 208
reason for enterprise as context for, 219
harm and, 127
ignorance and, 123
knowledge and, 123
LA's responses to contributors, 427
and Marcuse, Herbert, 12, 120, 122, 124, 126, 128
and Mill, John Stuart, 12, 119, 121, 125, 126
reasons for protecting speech, 119
regulation and suppression by private interests, 125, 128
truth and, 122
value of, 121
See also academic freedom
Freud, Sigmund, 375
Fuller, Lon, 159
function of law
judicial supremacy and, 134
settlement as primary function, 15, 221, 223, 262

Gardner, John, 90
Garvey, Stephen, 91
Gauthier, David, 292, 308
Germany
academic freedom, 118
criminal responsibility, 54
freedom of expression, 128
judicial supremacy, 140
gerrymanders
LA's theories, 10
Goldsworthy, Jeffrey, 13, 170, 420
Green, Leslie, 274
Greenberg, Mark, 176
Greene, Abner, 277
guilt. *See* punishment

Habermas, Jürgen, 134
Harel, Alon, 13, 221, 426
Harlan, John Marshall, 259
harm
and academic freedom, 129, 133
duress and, 93
and freedom of expression, 127
Harm Principle (J.S. Mill), 121
means of preventing. *See* means principle
Hart, H.L.A., 264, 265, 274, 277
Hegel, Georg Wilhelm Friedrich, 126, 127
Henry, Patrick, 142
Holmes, Oliver Wendell, 206
Horder, Jeremy, 89
Horkheimer, Max, 126
human dignity
punishment and, 30
Huq, Aziz, 115
Hurd, Heidi, 1, 284, 407
Husak, Douglas, 23, 87, 408

ignorance
and freedom of expression, 123
immorality. *See* morality and law
incarceration. *See* punishment
incompetence
defense of, 42
inegalitarianism
discrimination and, 321
innocent persons, punishment of. *See* punishment
insanity
defense of, 54
intention
action and, 206
consequence and, 206
freedom of expression. *See* freedom of expression
legislative intention. *See* interpretation
and means principle, 347
reason for enterprise as context for, 219
and rule following, 292, 300
intentionalism
author and adopter intentions in relation, 164
authority and, 279
constitutionality of death penalty as example, 165
general objective intentionalism, 175, 177
group-produced texts, intended meaning of, 161, 280, 418
intended meaning and interpretive intentions in relation, 162
interpretation rules and norms, 170
legal objective intentionalism, 175, 179
meaning and message in relation, 158
nonintentionalism
arguments against, 172
definition of, 170
objective intentionalism
arguments against, 182
arguments for, 176

intentionalism (*cont.*)
and authority of rules, 183
basic premises, 170
and confusion over different meanings, 184
LA's responses to contributors, 420
and mistaken meanings, 186
practical effects of, 188
and subjective intentionalism, 175, 182
original intended meaning originalism (intentionalism), 154, 191
and principles/rules distinction, 245, 254
problems with, 160, 166
sentences
completion to avoid absurdity, 174
context of, 173
elliptical sentences, 174
implied meanings, 173
subjective intentionalism, 170, 175, 184, 420
as underdeveloped theory, 168
interpretation
authority and, 15, 279, 428
constitutional law, 12
construction distinguished, 192
conventional meanings of words, definition of, 416
group-produced texts, intended meaning of, 161, 280, 418
intention
importance of, 208
language in relation, 220
LA's theory, 213, 415
LA's responses to contributors, 428
of legal texts, 417
rules and norms of, 170
texts, definition of, 415
See also intentionalism; judicial supremacy; originalism
intervention to prevent harm
permissibility of, 336
third-party intervention, 340
intransitivity
rationality and, 312

Jackson, Andrew, 261
Jefferson, Thomas, 145, 261, 273
Johnson, William Samuel, 139
judgments
choices and values in, 16
judicial review
LA's theory, 15
judicial supremacy
argument for, 134
constitutional convention foundations of, 137, 142, 149, 152
and enumeration of powers, 143
and Federal/State division of powers, 138
Founding Fathers and, 142, 262, 425
and function of law, 134
and judicial lawmaking, 149
LA's defence of, 260
LA's responses to contributors, 425, 431
and legal status of Constitution, 264
originalism and, 265, 267
over constitutional authoritative settlement, 222, 223, 227, 231
positivism and, 264
power apportionment strategies, 142
and preconstitutional rule of constitutional authority, 264
respect for, 261
and separation of powers, 147
settlement as primary function of, 134, 262
and supremacy of Constitution, 260, 261, 269, 431
juries
and punishment, 51
jurisprudence
authority of law, 15
criminal. *See* criminal law
distributive justice, 16
equality, 14
judicial review, 15
LA's responses to contributors, 428
LA's theories, 14
law and morality in relation, 16
overview of present volume c ontributions, 14
precedent, 14
reasoning, 14
rule following, rationality of. *See* rules
See also authority; judicial supremacy; morality and law; principles/rules distinction; rules
justifications. *See* defenses; duress

Kahan, Dan, 37
Kant, Immanuel, 17, 122, 318, 371, 375, 376
Katz, Leo, 16, 303, 430
Kavka, Gregory, 306, 308
Kay, Richard, 182, 183, 185, 187, 188
Kelsen, Hans, 264
Kierkegaard, Søren, 276
Knapp, Steven, 184

knowledge
and freedom of expression, 123, 130
of legal principles, 256
Kramer, Larry, 142, 268
Kress, Ken, 241, 243, 245, 248, 249, 257

language and linguistics. *See* intentionalism; interpretation; originalism; principles/rules distinction
Lawson, Gary, 249
legal moralism. *See* morality and law
legal principles and rules. *See* principles/rules distinction
legal reasoning. *See* reasoning
legal texts, interpretation of. *See* intentionalism; interpretation; judicial supremacy; originalism
Leiter, Brian, 11, 113, 427
lesser evils defense
applicability of, 100
availability of, 99
"better" choice of criminal action
non-permissibility of, 101
permissibility of, 103
duress and, 79, 411
as excuse, 109
as justification, 109
LA's theory, 8
operation of, 98
procedural estoppel defense, 107, 414
rationale for, 99, 101
states of world (Worst, Better, Best), 100
three or more options available to defendant, 98
use of, 98
lex talionis (law of retaliation). *See* punishment
liability. *See* criminal responsibility
liberalism
punishment and, 73
libertarianism
means principle and, 355, 367
liberty of expression. *See* freedom of expression
Lincoln, Abraham, 261
Lippert-Rasmussen, Kasper, 17, 317, 438
Lukács, Georg, 126
Lyon, David, 17

Madison, James, 139, 141, 145
Marcuse, Herbert, 12, 120, 122, 124, 126, 128, 129
Marshall, John, 141, 142
Marx, Karl, 126
McMahan, Jeff, 336
meaning
law and, 281
means principle
absolutism of, 354
choice of actions for harm preventer, 345
complicating factors, 342
consequentialism, 355
and constraint principle, 356
deontological ethics, 17
double effect, doctrine of, 336, 347, 352, 388, 392, 434
double preventions of harm, 339
ducking cases, 339, 340
exceptions to, lack of, 354
impermissible prevention of harm preventer, 342
intention and, 347
intervention to prevent harm, permissibility of, 336
LA's endorsement of, 434
LA's responses to contributors, 434
LA's theory, 17, 351, 370
libertarianism, 355, 367
permissions to intervene, distinction between, 346
persons used as means, 363
prevention of use, as means, 334
third-party intervention to prevent harm, 340
usefulness of, 348
mental state. *See* criminal responsibility
Michaels, Walter Benn, 184
Mill, John Stuart, 12, 119, 121, 125, 126, 129
mistakes of fact
mistakes of law in relation, 7
mistakes of law
duress and, 89
mistakes of fact in relation, 7
use of force, mistaken belief in legality of, 89
mitigation. *See* punishment
M'Naghten rule
criminal responsibility, 43
Mogensen, Andreas, 334
Montesquieu, 147
Moore, Michael, 14, 17, 18, 71, 371, 392, 437
morality and law
consent and moral obligation, 16
defensibility of legal moralism, 16
equality as discrete moral value, 14
judgments, choices and values in, 16
LA's responses to contributors, 434
LA's theories, 16

morality and law (*cont.*)
  "moral ledger" concept, 68
  moral limitations on choice of punishment, 29
  moral responsibility for others' immoral actions, 16
  moral rights, settlement and, 229, 230, 231, 426
  moral weakness, duress and, 87
  overview of present volume contributions, 17
  paternalism, legitimacy of, 16
  rationality of rule following, 15, 310
  See also deontological ethics; discrimination; lesser evils defense; means principle

negligence
  criminal responsibility, 9
Nelson, Caleb, 269
nonconsequentialism
  deontological ethics, 350
nonintentionalism. *See* intentionalism
norms. *See* principles/rules distinction
Nozick, Robert, 351, 390
nuclear deterrence paradox
  and rationality of rule following, 306, 308

obligation
  authority and, 274
offenders
  punishment as communicative engagement with, 73
  recidivism, risk of, 28
offenses
  crimes and criminal acts, definition of, 100
omissions
  liability for, 7
originalism
  author's meaning, 198
  constraint principle, 190
  convergence of different versions, 191
  definition of, 154
  determinacy of text, 193
  distinction between construction and interpretation, 192
  ecumenical originalism, 192
  fixation thesis, 190
  framers' understandings originalism, 191
  and judicial supremacy, 265, 267
  LA's responses to contributors, 417
  as normative thesis, 157, 159, 166
  original intended meaning originalism (intentionalism), 154, 191
  original law originalism, 191
  original methods originalism, 191
  original public meaning originalism (textualism)
    and authority of rules, 183
    arguments against, 182
    arguments for, 182
    authority and, 280
    author's meaning and, 198
    and mistaken meanings, 187
    practical effects of, 188
    sentence meaning and, 198
    theory of, 154, 191
  sectarian originalism, 192
  as semantic thesis, 156
  sentence meaning (conventional meaning), 154, 198, 419
  simple-minded originalism
    authority and authorship in relation, 200
    incompleteness of, 193
    LA as simple-minded originalist, 153, 189, 258
    LA's responses to contributors, 423
    and principles/rules distinction, 242, 257
    propositions for, 189
    role of author's intentions in production of meaning, 194
    second-order intentions, 203
    type of originalism, 191, 193
    within constitutional theory, 190
    wrongness of, arguments for, 190, 205, 423
  speaker's meaning (authorial or intended meaning), 154
  strengths of, 154
  text interpreted as rule or as standard, 167
  as thesis about nature of interpretation, 156, 158
  See also intentionalism

Parfit, Derek, 309
partial responsibility. *See* criminal responsibility
paternalism
  legitimacy of, 16
Pinckney, Charles, 139
Plato, 126, 127
political authority. *See* authority
Popper, Karl, 126
positivism
  and academic freedom, 117
  and judicial supremacy, 264
  in LA's legal thought, 15
  and principles/rules distinction, 245, 250
  and simple-minded originalism, 257
Posner, Eric, 10
Pound, Roscoe, 249, 258
Prakash, Saikrishna, 10

precedent
  LA's theories, 14
principles/rules distinction
  agreement as to existence of principles, 252
  agreement as to weight of principles, 253
  examples of principles, 246
  general acceptance of, 241
  general overview of, 243
  importance of, 242
  intentionalism and, 245, 254
  knowledge of principles, 256
  language and linguistics in relation, 432
  LA's arguments against, 251, 432
  LA's rejection of, 241, 243
  LA's responses to contributors, 432
  legality of principles, 249
  metaphysical status of principles, 251
  moral (Dworkinian) conception of, 242, 243, 248, 250, 256
  positivist conception, 245, 250, 257
  principles as supplementary to rules, 248
  productions of rules by principles/facts interactions, 248, 255
  and simple-minded originalism, 242, 257
  social ground of, 242, 253
  weight of principles, 242, 248, 253, 432
promises
  and rule following, 289, 300
proportionality
  criminal responsibility, 39, 46
  punishment, 26, 38, 41, 46
provocation
  defense of, 46
proxy crimes
  and threshold deontology, 389
punishment
  alternatives to, 36
  as appropriate (fitting) response, 31, 41
  collateral consequences of, 35
  as communicative engagement with offender, 73
  consequentialist approach, 8, 24, 25, 28, 31, 33, 38, 41
  deferential view about kinds of punishment, 24, 27, 408
  and deontological ethics, 19
  deprivation element, 34, 37
  desert-based theory of, 25, 26, 28, 32, 40
  elements of theory of, 41
  guilt and, 47
  and human dignity, 30
  incarceration, alternatives to, 37
  incarceration, policy of, 26, 37
  incommensurability of, 37
  of innocent persons
    double effect, doctrine of, 388, 392
    means principle, 388, 392
    retributive norm against punishing, 391, 400
    threshold deontology, 388
  introduction to, 23
  juries, role of, 51
  lack of scholarship on, 23
  LA's responses to contributors, 408
  LA's retributive theory of, 6
  law of retaliation (*lex talionis*), 31
  least-cost option, 31
  in liberal states, 73
  mitigation, 48
  moral limitations on, 29
  nature of, 33
  nature of punishment, 33
  non-desert-based factors, 41
  overpunishment, 49, 56
  philosophical concerns with, 25
  proportionality, 26, 38, 41, 46
  proxy crimes, 389
  punitive effect of, 34
  and rationality of rule-following, 308
  recidivism, risk of, 28
  retributive norm against punishment of innocent
    factual-error problem, 391
    immoral-law problem, 392
    plea bargaining and, 395
    and threshold deontology, 400
  retributivist approach, 25, 26, 27, 28, 29, 31, 32, 37, 38, 39, 40, 69, 408
  sentencing, 24, 41, 48
  stigmatizing effect of, 35, 37
  success of, 36
  success of punishment, prospect of, 36
  suffering and, 70, 72, 409
  and threshold deontology
    deontological retributivism, 388
    double effect, doctrine of, 388
    "moral ballast" critique of, 395, 398
    proxy crimes, 389
    retributive norm against punishment of innocent, 400
  underpunishment, 49, 56
  See also offenders

Quine, Willard van Orman, 256
Quinn, Warren, 306

Randolph, Edmund, 138
Raz, Joseph, 223, 230, 274, 275, 291, 307
reasoning
  LA's theories, 14
recidivism
  risk of, 28
recklessness
  and criminal attempts, 60, 68
  criminal responsibility, 9
respect
  discrimination and, 317
responsibility
  criminal. *See* criminal responsibility
  epistemic, 296
retaliation. *See* punishment
retribution. *See* punishment
rights
  settlement and, 228, 230
Rosati, Connie, 13, 153, 419
rule of recognition
  constitutional authority and, 265
rules
  benefits of, 287
  definition of rule, 286
  divergence of rule and purpose of rule ("doing law" or "doing justice"), 303
  exceptions to, proper exercise of, 287
  exclusionary effect of, 288, 307
  principles distinguished. *See* principles/rules distinction
  rationality of rule-following
    application of rules, 288
    avoidance of punishment, 308
    and contrived defenses, 311
    deceptive undermining of, 308
    divided perspectives of rule makers and rule followers ("the gap"), 15, 286, 288, 301, 303, 429
    epistemic rationality, 295, 300, 302
    epistemic responsibility, 296
    exclusionary reasons for, 307
    inability to close "the gap," 302, 307, 430
    intention and, 292, 300
    intransitivity and, 312
    irrationality and, 308
    LA's responses to contributors, 429
    mistakes over, 287
    morality and, 310
    and nuclear deterrence paradox, 306, 308
    practical rationality, 16, 292, 295, 300, 302
    presumptive rule following, 289
    priority to which rationality? (practical or epistemic?), 300
    promises and, 289, 300
    rationality and choice, problem of, 292
    "rule-sensitive particularism," 307
    and self-torturer paradox, 306
    and toxin puzzle, 309, 430
  standards distinguished, 167, 418
Rutledge, John, 138

Sachs, Stephen, 266
sanctions. *See* punishment
Sandroni, Alvaro, 16, 303, 430
Sartre, Jean-Paul, 376
Scalia, Antonin, 165, 180
Scanlon, Thomas, 212
Schauer, Frederick, 13, 14, 134, 136, 206, 221, 260, 265, 268, 303, 424, 427, 430
scientific inquiry. *See* academic freedom
Searle, John, 172–73
Segev, Re'em, 336
self-defense
  LA's theory, 8
self-torturer paradox
  and rationality of rule following, 306
sentences (utterances of)
  completion to avoid absurdity, 174
  context of, 173
  elliptical sentences, 174
  implied meanings, 173
sentencing. *See* punishment
separation of powers
  judicial supremacy and, 147
settlement
  authoritative settlement, concept of, 221
  constitutional authoritative settlement
    democracy and, 234
    greater importance of, 228
    judicial supremacy over, 222, 223, 227, 231
    legal authoritative settlement distinguished, 237, 426
    as to moral rights, 229, 230, 231, 426
    purpose of, 222
    and supremacy of Constitution, 226, 231
    value of, 221, 222, 226, 228
  and created rights, 228, 230
  importance of, 134
  and judicial supremacy, 262
  legal authoritative settlement
    arguments against, 237
    constitutional authoritative settlement distinguished, 237, 426

as to created rights, 230
determinateness of, 226
justness and rightness of, 225
purpose of, 222
reasons for superiority of, 224
stability of, 225
success of, 225
value of, 221, 222, 224
and moral rights, 229, 230, 231
need for, 223
as primary function of law, 15, 221, 223, 262
Shapiro, Scott, 292, 417
Sherman, Roger, 143
Sherwin, Emily, 12, 16, 168, 277, 286, 303, 304, 310, 429
Shiffrin, Seana Valentine, 290
simple-minded originalism. *See* originalism
Smith, Steven, 15, 260, 428
Smith, William French, 38
Solum, Lawrence, 13, 134, 137, 182, 189, 423
speech. *See* freedom of expression
standards
rules distinguished, 167, 418
state action defense
LA's theory, 9
stigmatization. *See* punishment
suffering
punishment and, 70, 72, 409
Supremacy Clause (Article VI of the Constitution)
judicial supremacy and, 261
Supreme Court. *See* judicial supremacy

Tadros, Victor, 337
Taurek, John, 435
texts
definition of, 415
third-party intervention
prevention of harm, 340
threats
duress and, 93
threshold deontology. *See* deontological ethics
Thucydides, 125
Toh, Kevin, 255
toxin puzzle
and rationality of rule following, 309
trials, criminal. *See* punishment
Tribe, Laurence, 10, 209
truth
and freedom of expression, 122, 130

unconstitutionality. *See* constitutional law
United Kingdom. *See* England and Wales
use of force. *See* force

Van Alstyne, William, 114, 116, 117
Vermeule, Adrian, 10
von Humboldt, Wilhelm, 119, 131

Westen, Peter, 8, 76, 411
White, Michael, 276
Williams, Bernard, 168
Wilson, James, 138, 141, 145, 150
Wittgenstein, Ludwig, 264
Wolff, Robert Paul, 273
words
conventional meanings, definition of, 416
wrongdoing. *See* criminal responsibility
wrongful discrimination. *See* discrimination

Yaffe, Gideon, 8, 98, 414
Yeats, W.B., 277